Witches of the Atlantic World

Witches
of the Atlantic World

A Historical Reader & Primary Sourcebook

Edited by Elaine G. Breslaw

NEW YORK UNIVERSITY PRESS
New York and London

NEW YORK UNIVERSITY PRESS
New York and London
© 2000 by New York University
All rights reserved

Library of Congress Cataloging-in-Publication Data

Witches of the Atlantic world : a historical reader and primary sourcebook / edited by
Elaine G. Breslaw.
    p. cm.
  Includes bibliographical references and index.
  ISBN 0-8147-9850-0 (cloth : alk. paper)—ISBN 0-8147-9851-9 (pbk. : alk. paper)
    1. Witchcraft—History—Sources. I. Breslaw, Elaine G., 1932–
BF1566.W755 2000
133.4'3'09—dc21

00-040216

Manufactured in the United States of America

10 9 8 7 6 5 4 3 2 1

IN MEMORY OF MY PARENTS
MARY BELENKE GELLIS (1909–1964)
AND MAX GELLIS (1907–1998)

Contents

Preface and Acknowledgments

The idea for this book was a matter of serendipity. New York Univerisity Press was considering an anthology on witchcraft as an addition to its list and I was creating a new course on American witchcraft in world perspective. My usual course on witchcraft in the American colonies had left me uneasy because it did not fit those episodes into the broader historical and geographic contexts. I was going to add more on the European background and introduce information on African beliefs and the American Indian spiritual world. The syllabus for my new course, including the primary source documents that were not easily available and that I thought essential for understanding the past, became the basis for a proposal to the press. The result is *Witches of the Atlantic World*.

Although this work is not a collaborative effort, it does reflect input from others. Many of the selections were collated from my courses on witchcraft and colonial America. Those reading lists included works suggested by colleagues and friends, who invariably told me about their favorite work on witchcraft somewhere in the world. The selections that have been printed here were the ones that students found interesting and that were most likely to stimulate discussion. I have omitted material that just didn't seem to work in the classroom or that students described as dull and unrewarding. Special thanks go to all my students at Johns Hopkins School of Continuing Studies and the University of Tennessee for their comments and unintended contribution to the creation of this reader.

Niko Pfund of New York University Press has been a major force in prodding me to put the material together in record time. His infectious enthusiasm for the project has been my major inspiration. I have also benefited from the advice and criticism of my colleagues in the history department at the University of Tennessee, several of whom looked at and commented on parts of the introduction. Of particular help were Robert Bast, Paul Pinckney, John B. Finger, and Catherine Higgs. Ellen Macek not only made some very perceptive comments, but also has been instrumental in suggesting reading material on the European setting and women's history over the last few years. I am especially appreciative of the keen eye, attention to detail, and tactful suggestions of my copy editor, Rosalie Morales Kearns. Whatever errors remain, after all this advice was considered, are my responsibility alone.

The University of Tennessee history department office staff has provided a great deal of assistance. I owe a special debt of gratitude to Penny Hamilton for all her support and to Brady Majury for his help in the office. Even though I hold only adjunct status, the head of the department, John B. Finger, generously allowed me free use of office equipment and supplies. The assistance of a graduate student, Arris Oakley, in proofreading and collating material has been invaluabe. I certainly appreciated his comment about the primary source documents: "this is good stuff."

This work could not have been completed without the services of the University of Tennessee Library. Anne Bridges, in particular, was always cheerful in response to my many requests and invariably found the information needed. The Special Collections Department very generously permitted me to reproduce pages from their rare book collection. The material reprinted from Matthew Hopkins, *The Discovery of Witches;* Michael Dalton, *The Country Justice;* and Samuel Willard, *A Compleat Body of Divinity* all came from that collection of rare books.

I am grateful to all the publishers and authors of material who responded so quickly and graciously to my requests for permission to reprint their material. Several authors made suggestions about editing their work; others accepted the cuts as submitted. I will cherish a note from Jon Butler, who said he was pleased to have me use his 1979 article because "At 20 years of age, it's happy to be alive." It has been my pleasure to be able to reprint not just his article but some other older works and bring them to the attention of new readers.

Every effort has been made to locate current copyright holders and to note their permissions to reprint material, but the vicissitudes and perambulations of publishing houses have frustrated some of my inquiries. I apologize to anyone who has not been properly acknowledged. We will be pleased to make proper attribution in future printings if notified by those claiming control of a copyright that has not been acknowledged in the text.

And finally I wish to thank my husband, John Muldowny, who patiently tolerated my mental absence as I worked on this project while consistently providing the emotional support so necessary during periods of stress.

Note on editorial procedures: For ease of reading, I have modernized the spelling and puncutation in the primary sources, although I have not tried to Americanize standard English spelling. When abbreviations have been spelled out, American spelling has been adopted. Words in square brackets mark additions to the text or clarification of word use. Words in parentheses are part of the original work and do not indicate editorial clarifications. For the secondary works, all note citations have been omitted, but some of the works cited by those authors are described in my bibliographic essay and some have been included among the primary sources and other selections in this reader.

Introduction

No one will learn how to be a witch from this collection of readings. Those currently involved in the newer cults will, however, become better acquainted with the heritage of witchcraft beliefs of the past. Some of what they learn will be disappointing—I offer little support for many of the myths surrounding modern-day witchcraft. On the other hand they might be pleased to learn that magical rituals have a long and often distinguished past, that witches have not always been despised, and that some scholars recognize occult practices as legitimate religious behavior.

My focus in this collection is on the significance of witchcraft and witch hunts in a variety of cultures that rim the Atlantic Ocean. The readings examine what witchcraft means and has meant in the context of a particular society, both as the people involved defined it for themselves and as scholars have interpreted their actions. Thus the primary sources allow us to glimpse what those in the past said about witches and magic in their own communities. The secondary commentary analyzes those statements and the behavior of the historical figures, looking for clues that can explain how and why witchcraft beliefs and fears functioned in that society. In some cases witchcraft has been a threat to group solidarity; in other places or times it served an important social function, often as a respected and useful ritual.

A witch hunt that is, an attempt to eliminate what was feared as an evil presence—might be a bonding experience bringing the community together against a common internal (and in unusual circumstances, external) foe. Such has been the point of view of historians who follow the functionalist anthropological approach spearheaded by Keith Thomas and Alan Macfarlane. At other times a witch hunt might benefit the leadership as a distraction for the population—to attack a scapegoat and thus reinforce the status quo. Witch hunts could also be decidedly disruptive of social cohesion and could, as in Salem, seriously undermine the sense of community. As Norman Cohn notes, witch hunts were attempts to purify the world by eliminating some category of people identified as evil agents of corruption. The result of such a moral crusade could be disastrous.

But does witchcraft really exist? That is, is it possible for a person to change the course of events using some magical ritual—a charm, a curse, a spell—or an emanation from the eye? Probably not in the sense that such behaviors have a direct, immediate connection to the effect. The causal relationship is psychological and depends on the power of suggestion. Only believers will respond to magical rituals. Nature, of course, is immune. But if an earthquake follows a magical incantation, it

I

can be reassuring to be able to blame it on a human agent. Coincidence had no place in the thinking of sixteenth- and seventeenth-century people; witchcraft, therefore, was a reasonable explanation for calamities.

Witches, in turn, are people who think they can influence spiritual forces directly in order to affect material existence. Through the performance of some occult action they attempt to bring about death, disease, droughts, stillbirths, or infertility; or they can employ a variety of helpful techniques to locate lost objects, provide love potions, divine future events, assure victory in battle, or promise good crops. Such has been a consistent thread that runs through the beliefs of all the societies examined in this reader.

Not all the people studied in these readings agreed on whether this power to manipulate occult forces was a natural or acquired ability. Nor is there agreement as to the nature of the spiritual forces or how to appeal to them. The magical rituals mentioned here differed radically. What is essential to note is that the effectiveness of any ritual or belief depended largely on cultural conditioning. What seemed to work in one culture did not necessarily have any effect among those who were unfamiliar with that practice. By the same token, witchcraft can still kill if the belief in its power to do so is strong enough.

Anthropologists make a distinction between witches and sorcerers. Witches are those whose power is inborn, part of their very nature, and possibly due to some physiological abnormality. Sorcerers differ in that their skill requires the use of artifacts, is learned rather than inherited, and is a deliberately directed magic usually for harmful purposes. Historians generally have ignored these distinctions and either lump both groups in one category of occult practitioners called witches or use the two terms interchangeably. Both scholarly approaches are used in the readings.

Before the eighteenth century, people everywhere lived in a world populated by invisible supernatural forces, their presence sensed in even the most mundane aspects of life. Those forces, feared because of their potential power, had to be pacified, venerated, appeased. Magical rituals working in the visible realm became a means of communication with the spirits in the invisible. As long as people believed, first, that spiritual forces existed, second, that such forces could influence material existence, and, third, that human beings could manipulate those forces by using some esoteric occult ritual to bring about a desired result, witchcraft could be a real power.

The scholars who examine these beliefs and rituals generally do not believe that witchcraft has any concrete reality beyond the psychological. They are interested in the social, emotional, and religious context of occurrences attributed to witchcraft and the role of witches in these communities. They are also concerned about witch hunts and want to know why they occur. What sets them off, and what effects do they have on their social environments? Who are the accused? Why are some people more likely to be persecuted than others? All these questions and more are addressed in these various selections. The how of witchcraft, the magical rituals associated with witchcraft, may be mentioned in passing or as an illustration to support an argument. But such references are not usually the major concern here.

I have limited the geographic and thus cultural scope of this anthology to the

Atlantic world—those areas that participated, either passively or actively, in the European westward expansion and the exchange of ideas from the fifteenth to the eighteenth century that helped to shape American society. Because witchcraft beliefs cannot be understood apart from the religious sentiments and creeds of their time and place, I begin with the religious background. I have compiled here commentaries on the European religious heritage forged in the ancient folk traditions of the Continent, the Roman Catholic Church, and the newer Reformation churches. The readings explore English Protestantism and its many variations in North America and the Caribbean, the multiplicity of West African societies on the Atlantic coast that interacted with European traders and contributed bodies and spiritual concerns to a New World, and the diverse American Indian spiritual traditions as they were transformed under the impact of European invasions and as they, in turn, reshaped the thinking of the invaders.

During the period under study in these readings, the meaning of witchcraft was in flux and many of the selections reflect the changes under way at a particular moment. The Atlantic world between the end of the fifteenth century (beginning with the Portuguese explorations of Africa and Columbus's voyages to the west) and the end of the seventeenth century participated in an expanding trading venture and massive incursions of European powers into relatively isolated communities adjacent to the Atlantic Ocean. With trade and new settlement came the intrusion of novel ideas and traditions that in turn sometimes subtly and sometimes dramatically altered old patterns and facilitated a usually unconscious cultural exchange. No one was immune to this transformation, neither aggressor nor victim. A study of witchcraft traditions and the religions of which they were a part reveals one aspect of this process. These readings offer some insight into the way people adapt to each other, borrowing ideas and restructuring their mental worlds to make sense of the unfamiliar.

The practice of witchcraft was one way for many peoples to explain the presence of evil, to establish a cause for misfortune and disease, to justify natural occurrences like storms and earthquakes, to give meaning to mysterious events, to provide answers to problems that seemingly defied reasonable explanations. Without the benefit of later scientific discoveries and lacking the concepts of chance and accident that support modern notions of causation, people in this Atlantic world understood such inexplicable occurrences as having some divine or magical purpose. In some cases they assumed there was a human agent, identified as a witch or sorcerer. What was universal among these societies is the belief that misfortune—whether disease, death, a loss of crops, an earthquake—came from the deliberate actions of a spiritual force. Harmful events and human adversity were never accidents. Somehow, they felt, there was purpose and direction to every event.

The nature and extent of the power of evil forces varied from culture to culture. Harm could come from a variety of gods or spiritual entities capable of doing both good and evil deeds. When the gods inflicted harm it was sometimes in retaliation for human behavior that violated a sacred practice. Or misfortune could be due to inherently evil individuals who manipulated a spiritual power through magic to cause harm. In the first case, people had to appease the gods through some socially acceptable magical rituals; in the second case, they had to control, banish, or even destroy those individuals who demonstrated malicious intent. Calamities, if not due to a divine providence, could be traced to an evil human agent working through that invisible spiritual realm.

In Europe and elsewhere there were some whose odd and usually antisocial behavior left them open to accusations of conjuring, or "black" magic, a harmful use of the occult. Such people were feared everywhere, avoided by the larger society, shunned, often banished or sometimes killed. In general, outside the Christian tradition, folk in the Atlantic world shared the view that evil witches were deviant people who threatened to disrupt the harmony of the community. They were often people who could not get along with their neighbors. They were known to argue, complain, and demand more than their due. Labeled a witch or sorcerer, such a person became a visible, physical presence that could be blamed for the workings of an invisible malignancy.

Medieval Christian traditions, on the other hand, rejected the notion of a deity capable of both good and evil and the idea that people could independently utilize magical powers. By the fifteenth century all magical rituals came to be associated totally with evil in the minds of the European theologians. Their reasoning (presented here in greatly simplified form) postulated God as a benevolent and omniscient being ready to provide divine help to his believers. Such a God could do no evil, although he might test his followers by putting adversity in their paths. Evil itself was promoted by a lesser force called Satan, a devil, a ruler of darkness who was determined to overthrow the true deity by subverting his kingdom on earth. Although the notion of an evil force was transcultural, the idea of a devil as a separate, malevolent spiritual entity is a unique part of the Judeo-Christian (and Islamic) tradition that distinguishes European witchcraft beliefs and witch hunts from all other societies studied in this collection of readings.

There is a long tradition of magical practices throughout the world that is foreign to the Christian notion of Satan or a diabolical pact. Astrologers in Europe consulted the stars to foretell the future, cunning folk on the continent and England carried on an oral tradition of healing with herbs invested with magical powers. In Africa the obeah and the oracle, and among the American Indians the shaman, acted much as the cunning folk in Europe—curing illness, divining the future, resolving interpersonal conflicts.

There is a witchcraft lore in Europe, a lore of cunning people or wise men and women, that is much older than Christianity and has little connection to official religious dogma. What is patently obvious everywhere is that ordinary people in Europe were not concerned about Satan's involvement with witchcraft unless provoked to think along those lines by church officials. Occult practices of the cunning folk were more often welcomed to comfort and cure. They could provide a sense of security in a very insecure world of periodic crop failures, fires, epidemics, and other dangers, especially when the civil or religious authorities failed to protect them, as they obviously had no power to do. Among the laypeople in Europe witches were not always a menace to society. They had much to offer. Only after contact with

Christianity was there a blurring of the distinction between those witches who were evil and those who were socially useful.

This difference between Christians and other groups in defining evil witchcraft is crucial to understanding why early Protestant and Catholic theologians tended to view all magical techniques performed by laypeople outside the established church as inherently evil. In the early Christian churches, mystical rituals such as prayer, the Eucharist, baptism, bell ringing, or the use of crosses were considered part of the worship of God and therefore by definition a valid exercise of religious expression to a benevolent deity. Outside the church similar rituals, said the theologians, appealed to the devil, the Antichrist. Such practices were satanic in origin. Thus all magic of the folk or of other religious traditions, by their very nature non-Christian, were associated with devil worship.

The clash of these two notions—the Christian and the non-Christian—regarding the source of the witch's power partially explains the ferocious and sporadic witch hunts of the sixteenth and seventeenth centuries in the European world. These events have no counterpart among other peoples who allowed for a variety of acceptable occult practices. Witch hunts became a way to assure a conformity of religious practices in Europe and America, in moral terms to institute a communal spiritual cleansing. Destruction of other belief systems was supported by a mandate to wipe out the forces opposing the true God, thus justifying large-scale witch hunts.

Witch hunters became even more zealous as the Reformation heated up on the Continent. The leaders of newly created non-Catholic churches (Protestants) were anxious to impose their ideas on the uninitiated and the partially Christianized folk who continued to practice older occult rituals. The Catholic Counter Reformation retaliated with its own attempts to wipe out dissident Protestant ideas easily associated with Satan's supporters. Political leaders may have found the Inquisition and witch trials in local courts useful means of getting rid of their secular opposition, but the religious justification, the urge to combat the devil, provided the moral force. To destroy evil, the moral ends justified the cruelty of the means. Continental Protestants—both Lutherans and Calvinists—further elaborated demonological belief by giving it a firmer scriptural basis.

Courts in Protestant countries on the Continent also followed the inquisitional procedures that had been used in Catholic countries to stamp out witchcraft. Lay (rather than clerical) officials, acting in secret, initiated action, investigated the heresy, and handed down judgments on guilt or innocence without requiring public input. Torture remained the most effective means of eliciting confessions of diabolical collusion. Once found guilty, the accused, usually after confessing, were executed by being burned at the stake (more likely garroted first). Such admissions of guilt and the public executions that followed, in turn, confirmed the morality and legitimacy of the new Protestant regimes.

Witch hunters, regardless of locale, faced the difficult task of proving the existence of a satanic pact. In theory the work of the witch and his/her diabolical master was invisible to ordinary eyes. Heretics carried on their nefarious deeds in a secret world and only the results—storms, diseases, dead infants, and found items—were evident.

The Inquisition had solved the problem of identifying the witch by the use of torture to extract confessions. Such forced stories also enriched the inquisitor's arsenal of information about what witches did and how they did it.

In England, although confessions to witchcraft were desired, the procedures and definition of the crime differed. Witchcraft, when it was brought under the jurisdiction of civil authorities for the first time in 1542, became a crime against society. Even though witchcraft continued to be interpreted as a heresy in the eyes of the church, the accused were subject to secular and not ecclesiastical law. They were entitled to the same legal procedures and protections as any other violator of criminal law, including the provision that required two witnesses to the deed. The civil authorities were prohibited from using torture as a method of eliciting confessions.

English jurisprudence relied not on the Continental inquisitional system but rather on an adversarial procedure that by the sixteenth century had become a public verbal combat between the accused and the prosecution. Judgments were rendered by lay juries and trials became public exhibitions. If the accused were found guilty of this or any other capital offense, death would be by hanging. Burning was reserved for cases in which a wife murdered her husband or a servant his or her master. Most witchcraft, however, unlike theft or outright homicide that left behind visible evidence, continued to be a very difficult crime to prove and prosecute, especially when torture could not be used by the courts and lay juries sat in judgment of an act that took place in the spiritual realm.

England, generally, lagged behind the Continental countries in the wholesale legal punishment of witches. The first English statute regarding a magic act did not appear until 1542. Before that witchcraft as on the Continent was treated as an ecclesiastical offense, a heresy, and left to the church—at first Catholic and then Anglican—to handle. Because witchcraft was not then a secular crime, punishment was left to the church alone, which could not deprive a person of life, limb, or property. The law of 1542 defined witchcraft as the doing of harm—*maleficium*—through the use of invocation, conjuration, or sorcery to find money, or to waste, consume, or destroy any person, or to provoke anyone to unlawful love. Witchcraft was now made punishable by death. Unlike Continental notions, however, the idea of a satanic pact did not enter into that early legal definition. The emphasis was on *maleficium*—a folk notion of evil works through magical means.

This law was repealed five years later. Official actions against witchcraft were left to the church courts again until 1563, when new legislation broadened the legal definition to focus on intent rather than consequences. It criminalized consultation with or invocation of evil spirits with or without the purpose of doing harm. But only harm through occult manipulation carried the death penalty. A lesser penalty of one year's imprisonment was imposed for the mere use of magic that did not result in death.

Finally in 1604 another law, passed during the reign of King James I, brought English statutes closer to the Continental model. Christian theology on the Continent had dictated that all witchcraft resulted from a conscious agreement between a person and the devil. The English law, which was the one in effect when the American colonies were founded and continued until repealed in 1736, now required that such a pact be proven as a matter of fact before conviction. It prohibited acts to "consult, covenant with, entertain, employ, feed, or reward any evil and wicked spirit to or for any intent or purpose," adding that the death penalty for all occult practices was to be imposed without "benefit of clergy."

This latter expression requires an explanation. All clergy in the English world traditionally were exempt from the death penalty except in cases of heresy. In an age when a small percentage outside the church were literate, proof of theological training was the ability to read. In time, English law permitted literate laypeople, a growing proportion of the population, to claim the same privilege ("benefit of clergy") for all felonies except treason. That privilege, however, could be used only once. The English law of 1604 denied that lifesaving privilege to those found guilty of witchcraft. Once convicted, they were to be hanged alongside the illiterate.

In England and in the American colonies getting a conviction to a secret act continued to present several dilemmas to the jurists. Ancient popular fears of witchcraft were traditionally focused on any evil intent. Magical rituals that had approved social values—curing sickness, finding lost items, resolving interpersonal conflicts—seldom resulted in complaints or trials, much less punishment. On the other hand, people suspected of causing harm were feared and liable to be found guilty. Intent and consequence were thus uppermost in the minds of juries. The law may have ignored what was important to most people and made any magical act a crime, but English juries continued to act in accordance with lay fears and prejudices. They looked for evidence of harm rather than diabolical action. Judges, on the other hand, were increasingly skeptical of the whole business and tried to restrain overzealous juries.

Traditionally Protestants (especially historians) have accused Catholics of inspiring magical rituals, fomenting witch hunts, and being more superstitious. In actual fact recent research indicates that the witch craze of the sixteenth and seventeenth centuries in the newly Protestant countries was just as severe in number of people persecuted as in Catholic countries. It is possible that the Reformation inadvertently led to an increase in witch activity, which, in turn, incited more witch hunts.

Witchcraft among Protestants, for instance, may have been encouraged by changes in the religious climate brought on by the reform of the church liturgy and the greater emphasis on biblical authority. Protestants, by denying the efficacy of traditional sacred practices in the church such as rites of exorcism, and rejecting the intercessionary power of the saints, while playing up the reality of the devil, actually encouraged dependence on sorcerers and charmers to do what was forbidden. The new clergy had put their flock into the intolerable position of asserting the reality of witchcraft while denying any effective and legitimate cure of its evil effects. It is no accident that cases of religious possession, sometimes interpreted as bewitchment, usually occurred in situations of intense religious experience. Witch hunts followed.

When it comes to counting heads and incidents there is substantial support for the connection between the Reformation and the greater zeal to destroy witch practices. Places that experienced some of the most traumatic witch hunts, where accusations were made against large proportions of the populations, were areas in Germany where Lutherans and Catholics vied for control; Scotland, where Calvinist Presbyterians were dominant; Switzerland, the source of Calvinism; and Salem, the home of Calvinist Puritans. As a new intellectual force, a revolutionary set of beliefs whose proponents were determined to reform church polity, Protestantism had to secure its place by requiring conformity. Where the Catholic Church already had hegemony and faced few threats, as in Spain and Italy, it could be more relaxed and permit minor deviances. But when threatened, as in Germany and France, it too became aggressive in its hunt for heretics.

In Protestant countries the situation was complicated by the absence of a central or controlling authority like the Inquisition under the mantle of a pope, which could and did keep control over the more zealous witch hunters, as it did in Italy. Local authorities, particularly in Scotland and Puritan New England, sometimes caught up in panics about supposed witchcraft, took matters into their own hands unrestrained by more distant authorities. In Lutheran Germany the witch hunt became a way of disposing of political opposition and consolidating the powers of the new local authorities. The Catholics may have created the modern stereotype of the witch, but the Protestants made more zealous use of it.

Witchcraft, in the European experience, had also come to be a peculiarly female act. In cases of witchcraft, unlike most other crimes in the Anglo-American world, the husband was not held accountable for his wife's illegal actions. Christian theologians, both Catholic and Protestant, set out extensive evidence to explain why women were more vulnerable to Satan's appeal than men were, justifying the greater persecution of women during witch hunts. In most places the stereotype of the witch was of an old woman, widowed or never married, poor and dependent on others for sustenance, with an unpleasant and abrasive personality, who was often at odds with others. Such disagreeable people became useful scapegoats in times of adversity.

The story of witchcraft is, therefore, also the story of the oppression of women and the violence visited on them. The analyses of witchcraft and witch hunts reveal much about the role of women in these various societies, about gendered fears and conflicts, about lines of authority, about sexual relations and marital concerns of the time and place. Such woman bashing, however, is not universal and the witch as woman stereotype, as some of the readings note, does not apply to all societies.

As these Christian traditions moved out into the African and American Indian world—whether motivated by gold, glory, or the gospel—Europeans considered the "others" they met followers of the devil. The Spanish way of handling the problem was to forcibly convert Indians and Africans to Catholicism; the English, after a very short attempt at proselytizing, preferred to drive the devil away by removing the Indian presence, as they did their own religious dissenters. They generally chose to ignore African beliefs unless the practices interfered with work activities or directly threatened the lives of the whites. There was more toleration of African magic than of Indian rituals in English-controlled settlements.

Conversion of the Spanish kind meant a more dramatic exchange of ideas, with Indians and Africans integrating Christian notions into their preexisting concepts of the spirit world and gradually creating a new branch of Catholicism that paralleled the syncretic development process that followed early church efforts in Europe. The English attempt at extirpation of the Native peoples, their disdain for and possibly secret admiration for Native peoples, had a more subtle influence on Indian notions of magic than can be found among the Spanish-dominated people.

American Indians, although fearing evil witchcraft and practicing magical rituals akin to both African and European techniques, may have held somewhat different notions about the effect and source of supernatural powers. Less is known about their ideas because of a dearth of written records. The task is complicated by the historical reluctance on the part of Indian groups during the sixteenth and seventeenth centuries to include Europeans in or inform them of their spiritual traditions. Indians were not evangelists for their way of life and when possible preferred to maintain the integrity of their identity separate from Europeans, whom they generally held in contempt.

Only a handful of Europeans, mostly fur traders and captured women, willingly lived among Indians and came close to understanding their worldview. They have, unfortunately, left pitifully few written accounts of their observations. Most of the available information about American Indian spiritual life and the magical practices associated with it has to be filtered through the biases of Europeans who, except in very few instances, misunderstood what they observed, distorting the meaning of Indian traditions to fit their own religious or political agenda. By the eighteenth century, when more sympathetic firsthand observers recorded their impressions, Indian ways had already been influenced by Christian and probably African beliefs, and radically changed by the demands of a European commercial culture.

For Africans in the English colonies the experience of cultural exchange was very different from that of the Native American peoples. The weak physical position of the African as slave cultivated more contempt than fear and thus the African worldview was ignored, left to forge its own path in the American wilderness with little interference from the English except possibly in Puritan New England. The result was the retention of many shared African ideas about the spiritual realm and the imaginative merging of magical practices taken from a variety of cultures.

Information about African American spiritual life can also be gleaned from modern West Africa, which, for anthropologists, has become a living laboratory for understanding past beliefs. Specific aspects of seventeenth- and eighteenth-century African American practices have been traced to rituals found in parts of Africa two centuries later. We know that Africans came from societies in which spirits of dead ancestors were believed to act regularly on the destiny of living human beings. A variation of that notion along with traditional herbal remedies infused with magical properties persisted in the American environment.

In all cases new centers of ideas about magic, witchcraft, and evil were created in the New World in which all sides participated and contributed to a greater or lesser degree. This collection of readings and primary source documents is intended to illustrate the wide variety of beliefs about witchcraft and magic in existence in this early modern world and how they were reformulated under the pressure of contact with other groups.

I have chosen the selections to highlight the distinctive qualities of African, European, and American Indian concepts of evil, sorcery, and witchcraft between the fifteenth and the eighteenth centuries, and then to consider how each group's ideas influenced, reinforced, or altered the others. The Salem, Massachusetts, incident of 1692, coming at the end of two centuries of vigorous witch persecutions, is in many ways a culmination of this process of cultural convergence. It is best understood in the context of witch hunts that preceded it, the rigor and paradoxes of Puritan religious beliefs, and the peculiar American setting of the late seventeenth century that gave it impetus.

In a world that routinely executed witches, there was something about the Salem experience that takes it beyond the ordinary. The events of 1692 continue to both repel and fascinate the public after more than three hundred years. The drama of the persecutions has captured the literary imagination worldwide as it has intrigued American scholars over the years. The events have led not only to a continuing controversy over the causes of such a horror, but also to the question of whether Salem was somehow outside the tradition of European witch hunting. This collection will show that it was both. Salem followed the general pattern of earlier witch hunts in its attempt to maintain an orthodoxy that was perceived to be weakening, but at the same time it incorporated ideas borrowed from the folklore of other cultural groups and was influenced by the stress of Indian-English relations. It is best understood as a reaction of traditional European witchcraft fears in a multicultural setting. This anthology will suggest the peculiar nature of that setting by highlighting the various strains of witchcraft beliefs that may have influenced the thinking of those Puritans of late-seventeenth-century Massachusetts and to contrast those evolving ideas with more distant cultural transformations. Salem, then, represents a culmination and useful ending for a study of witchcraft and witch hunts at the end of the seventeenth century in the Atlantic world.

The readings in this anthology are to some extent an idiosyncratic collection. In most cases I have included selections because the writing is of such exceptional quality and the interpretation so well-thought-out that they are a real pleasure to read. Some excerpts were chosen because they offer contrasting views of a particular development, as in the nature of American Indian beliefs; or they express an interpretation that has become commonplace; or they explore a variety of aspects of a particular topic, for instance, the role of gender in the witch hunts. Occasionally, especially in the choice of primary sources, particular writings were used because they are not easily available or accessible in readable form.

The field of writings on witchcraft is now so extensive that it is not possible to sample all that has been written on the subject for all parts of the Atlantic world. A great deal had to be left out. I have neglected parts of Europe in order to give more space to England and its colonies. Much more can be said about American Indians and the African experience. I am well aware that selections dealing with the French empire in America or the Dutch influences have not been included. Nothing is said about the Germans, Swedes, or other ethnic minorities in the English colonies. Moreover, no attempt has been made here to deal with current notions about witchcraft or present-day theological arguments regarding magic and evil. That would be the task of another collection.

Limitations had to be imposed or this collection would have been terribly un-wieldy. I do hope that readers will find the material suggestive enough to pursue aspects of the subject by looking at the full work from which I have chosen these excerpts or some of the suggested readings given in the bibliographic note at the end. Ultimately, the choice of which works to include and which topics to emphasize must represent my own personal inclinations and professional interests.

I

Christian Perspectives on Witchcraft in Europe and North America

RELIGIOUS CREEDS AND WITCHCRAFT practices are both aspects of supernatural belief—their focus is the spiritual realm. From the Christian perspective, however, witchcraft is in opposition to religion and is linked to demonic practices. The four primary sources excerpted in part 1, written between 1486 and 1689, illustrate the variety of notions prevalent among the educated Christian population about the working of witches and the devil in Europe, England, and England's Puritan colonies.

The first selection, from the *Malleus Maleficarum* (also known as the "Hammer of Witches"), was compiled by two Dominican priests and inquisitors in Germany in the fifteenth century, the Inquisitor General Father Jacob Sprenger and Father Heinrich Krämer, called by his Latinized name, Institoris, who was the main author. The work became the most important source of information on witches and witchcraft for both Protestants and Catholics and was consulted by theologians as late as the eighteenth century. Their compilation of witch stories provides both a theoretical support for the idea of an evil witch and a practical manual for identifying diabolical supporters. Much of what they report in this excerpt was part of the occult folklore of medieval and pre-Christian Europe. But a great deal of the elaboration, extracted under torture, came from the fantasies, both sexual and diabolical, suggested by the inquisitors themselves.

Krämer, who was the major instigator of witch persecutions in Germany, was particularly anxious to prove the guilt of those he tortured and to place their crimes within the theological context of a devil's pact and conspiracy. Sprenger later regretted his approval of Krämer's excessive methods.

The stereotype of the witch, according to the *Malleus*, was one who, through an agreement with the devil, acquired special powers to both do harm and solve problems or cure sickness. Unlike European folk beliefs regarding occult practices, the Catholic inquisitors and later the Protestant witch finders made no distinction between helpful witchcraft and the intent to do harm. All witchcraft, they assumed, derived from the devil and was therefore inherently evil or at least anti-Christian. The Catholic inquisitors inspired a new conspiratorial mythology about witches as people who made a solemn agreement to serve the devil by participating in a variety of antisocial acts (such as sexual orgies among themselves and with Satan), promoting the murder of infants, committing acts of cannibalism, and seducing more follow-ers. All this, they argued, was with the intention of subverting Christianity. Their theories about the demonic focus of magical practices lingers on in the mythology of witchcraft today.

Matthew Hopkins, a Protestant, was England's most active witch hater in the seventeenth century. Under the influence of the *Malleus*, he set out to prove that witches in league with the devil were rampant in parts of eastern England in the 1640s. Hopkins established himself as a "witch finder," testified against those of questionable reputation, forced confessions using forms of torture slightly more subtle than the Continental rack, and inflicted countermagic on his victims such as the water test, which had been rejected by English theologians and most jurists. In his 1647 pamphlet excerpted here, Hopkins defended himself against charges of personally benefiting from these actions. He also claimed that his methods had ferreted out and brought on the death of two hundred people. At the same time Hopkins had added new elements to the lore surrounding witches by giving the devil's helpers a variety of ludicrous new names and bodily shapes.

Not all English thinkers took the folklore about witches seriously. Reginald Scot, a learned Protestant layman and country gentleman with scientific interests, was moved by what he thought was an unwarranted persecution of old women to write his *Discoverie of Witchcraft* (1584). He thought that many of those confessing to witchcraft suffered from some psychic disorder. In arguing against the witch trials he was highly critical of the demonologists such as the authors of the *Malleus*.

In dissecting demonological lore as an illusion and witchcraft stories as delusions, Scot also suggests what has been affirmed by modern scholars about the origin of the accusations. A quarrel between a poor old woman and her potential benefactor could result in harsh words that, when followed by some accident or illness in the benefac-tor's family, led him or her to blame the old woman for causing the problem through her witchcraft. Charges made against such helpless and possibly senile old women often led to confessions that were partly the result of the power of suggestion. Scot acknowledges that a confession could give such women a feeling of control. They reasoned, he thought, that if they were accused of such power over others, maybe it was true. He also observes that some of the confessions were due to the effects of "melancholy," an old term for depression, leading to delusions.

In a typically Protestant mode, Scot attributes the witchcraft lore to the work of learned Catholic writers and absolves the Protestant thinkers. His refutation of witch-craft beliefs is in part an attack on Catholic sacraments. He was offended by the continued acceptance of older magical religious rites even by those professing to be Protestants. Scot's arguments became a model for later writers who continued to link witchcraft only with Catholicism and attempted to disassociate their own belief system from the demonized magic of witchcraft.

In America, where few people were persecuted for witchcraft before the 1660s, belief in magical powers was still part of the mental baggage the Puritans brought from old England. Those English folk beliefs regarding witchcraft were reinforced by zealous Puritan reformers concerned about the decline in religious fervor after the early years of settlement. The excerpt from Cotton Mather's 1689 *Memorable Providences"* details what he thought was evidence of the devil's work in the covenanted Puritan community. He associates religious backsliders with diabolical acts. He does not call for any mass executions of suspected witches; rather, he calls for a spiritual renewal to prevent the spread of their activities. In the process he provides a concise outline of his beliefs about witches, their powers, and why they appeared in Massachusetts.

Mather accepts the notion of a diabolical pact and the idea that God permits evil spirits to roam as a warning. Satan's presence was to test the faith of men. The appearance of witches and their use of witchcraft in the Puritan community, therefore, implied a decline in religious conviction—a loss of faith among God's chosen. By publishing this evidence of a diabolical presence, Mather hoped to reform the less zealous and offer them the possibility of redemption through prayer and confession. His stories, though, may well have contributed to popular fears by confirming folktales of such miraculous happenings and paving the way for the more vigorous prosecution of witches in New England.

Faced with these examples from the learned community and a host of other commentaries both lay and clerical on the witchcraft infection, twentieth-century scholars have concluded that most of the theological arguments were based on myth and fantasy and an understandable misconstruction of the causes of natural disasters. The following selections from five scholars on Continental, English, Scottish, and American theological beliefs about witchcraft explore the mental world that predisposed people to accept such ideas as fact. The authors all point out the close connections between the religious environment and witchcraft beliefs. The selections analyze the origins of the stereotype of the witch and the theological notions that prevailed at the time.

Norman Cohn dismantles the notion, propounded by Margaret Murray and others, that the European witch hunt from the fifteenth to the seventeenth centuries was aimed at a society of witches that actually existed, adherents of a highly organized pre-Christian religion that was practiced throughout Europe and had descended from ancient fertility cults. Cohn does not dispute the persistence of pre-Christian beliefs or practices; rather, his point is that there is simply no historical evidence for the existence of an organized body of witches as posited by the witch hunters. Claims that witches practiced infanticide, kissed the behind of a toad or a goat, or participated in a secret conspiratorial society of witches were pure fiction, Cohn maintains. These stereotypes belong in the realm of literary creations or possibly drug-induced hallucinations.

Keith Thomas, less concerned with the truth or falsehood of particular witchcraft lore, explores the intersection of religion with ideas about evil and magic in both popular and elite thinking. In England, where the idea of devil worship seems to have been peripheral to most accusations of witchcraft, the crucial factor in any witch scare was the preoccupation with *maleficium*, the doing of harm. But not all harmful events or natural disasters were attributed to witchcraft. Drawing on anthropological theory, Thomas argues that witchcraft is chosen as a satisfactory explanation when it is possible to take action against some likely scapegoat. The identification of such a witch happens as a result of interpersonal tension or grudges motivating an act of vengeance. In England, witch and accuser, he discovered, always knew each other and had a history of prior conflict.

Moreover, witch beliefs served a variety of social functions. They may have provided some sense of control over the gravest misfortune while also helping to maintain communal harmony. Thomas suggests that accusations of witchcraft were a means of restraining deviant people, usually the poor with unacceptable social characteristics. On the other hand, the threat by these dependent members of the society to use evil magic gave the poor themselves some control over their own lives—a means of retaliation against those who would deny them some benefit. Their curses offered the same protective effect against oppression as the courts gave to the wealthy. Accusations of witchcraft had as much to do with social problems and social structure as they did with supernatural concerns and theological justifications.

Building on the work of both Cohn and Thomas, Christina Larner takes as a given that most of the early modern witchcraft beliefs were amalgamations of more ancient lore elaborated by the elite for their own political or theological purposes. She compares the witch hunts in Scotland, which reached the ferocious intensity of those in Germany, with the milder events in England in the seventeenth century. Although Scotland's witch hunters added little to theories about witchcraft, she notes that because of the unusual political structure in that country, the pattern of accusations and beliefs differed from those in England and on the Continent while borrowing from both. As on the Continent, Larner points out, the competitive spirit of the local clergy in league with civil authorities often fueled witch panics. As in England, the fantasies of the witches' coven had few horrific details, and charges of sexual orgies or acts of cannibalism were rare.

In Scotland as everywhere else there was no single continuous witch hunt but rather sporadic occurrences between 1590 and 1662 and thereafter a decline. King James VI of Scotland (soon to become James I of England), convinced that demons were infesting the land, certainly encouraged the earliest outbreaks. Then a second wave coincided with the peak of Continental trials during the 1620s. But the most sustained period occurred between 1649 and 1661, an era of reforming Presbyterianism in Scotland and Puritan ascendancy in England, finally ending soon after the restoration of the Anglican monarchy in the 1660s. These were times of acute tension between church and state, reflecting a determination on the part of the reforming ministry to secure legitimacy and maintain control.

What is even more significant, Larner notes, the Protestant stress on the personal relationship with the devil and the idea of a covenant, a people's pact with God, so central to the Calvinist idea, gave the concept of a diabolical pact a peculiar intensity. That Calvinist emphasis would be echoed across the Atlantic in the Puritan villages of New England.

The American version of radical Protestantism in New England certainly encouraged fantasies of diabolical action. Richard Weisman focuses on the specific relationship between Puritan doctrines and witchcraft beliefs in New England. The intellectual dilemma faced by the theologians was to reconcile a variety of paradoxical beliefs—God was sovereign, yet there existed a powerful devil; the God-given social order was immutable, yet arbitrary events could occur; God had a divine, providential plan for humans, yet occult practices violated God's law. The concept of a diabolical pact resolved these dilemmas, giving Puritans both a scapegoat for their own religious decline and a temporarily satisfying way out of their theological paradoxes. Thus the strengthened belief in witchcraft may have been an essential element of the peculiar Puritanism developing in America.

In the broader intellectual context, Europeans of the time, whether Puritans or not, like their Indian and African counterparts discussed in part 2, lived in a world of supernatural forces that could trip them up and cause calamities for unknown reasons. David Hall evokes the mentality of that seventeenth-century world, both folk and elite, that saw all natural events as the work of invisible forces. Theological language and the printing industry might have helped shape the thinking about those wonders, but it did not stop the tendency to see prodigies and evil omens in everyday events or a general belief in the efficacy of magical rituals to resolve problems. While the printing industry inspired even greater interest in supernatural lore among the folk, the clergy tried to shift attention to the wonder workings of God rather than demons and witches. The failure of the ministry to overcome the attraction of both folklore and zealous publishers suggests another reason for the continuing focus on witches and witchcraft among the lay population. The English, of course, were not unique in these beliefs.

The source of those wonders and portents in the sixteenth- and seventeenth-century world may have differed among different classes and cultures, but ordinary people assumed that the world was a mysterious place full of miraculous occurrences. Almost everyone everywhere in the Atlantic world of the time, the literate and the illiterate, the highly placed elite and the common people, imagined that remote and unseen forces guided their destinies and caused their misfortunes. How satisfying it must have been to give a face and name to the cause of such unhappiness, to find a witch.

PRIMARY SOURCES

[1]

The Methods of the Devil

Heinrich Krämer and Jacob Sprenger

The Malleus Maleficarum *(1486), authored by the inquisitors Heinrich Krämer (1430–1505) and Jacob Sprenger (ca. 1436–1495) and called familiarly the "Hammer of Witches," was a compilation of witch beliefs that had been extracted under torture. The ideas expressed in the* Malleus *were so widespread that many of the details appear in later confessions and learned treaties even in England. In this excerpt describing how people are subverted into witchcraft and make a pact with the devil, the authors give lurid details of infanticide, cannibalism, and copulation with demons.*

•

Chapter 1. Of the Several Methods, by Which Devils through Witches Entice and Allure the Innocent to the Increase of That Horrid Craft and Company

There are three methods above all by which devils, through the agency of witches, subvert the innocent, and by which that perfidy is continually being increased. And the first is through weariness, through inflicting grievous losses in their temporal possessions. For, as St. Gregory says: "The devil often tempts us to give way from very weariness." And it is to be understood that it is within the power of a man to resist such temptation but that God permits it as a warning to us not to give way to sloth. . . . Devils, therefore, by means of witches, so afflict their innocent neighbours with temporal losses, that they are as it were compelled, first to beg the suffrages of witches, and at length to submit themselves to their counsels as many experiences have taught us.

We know a stranger in the diocese of Augsburg, who before he was forty-four years old lost all his horses in succession through witchcraft. His wife, being afflicted with weariness by reason of this, consulted with witches and, after following their

From Heinrich Krämer and Jacob Sprenger, *The Malleus Maleficarum*, transalted with an introduction, bibliography, and notes by Montague Summers (1486; London: Pushkin Press, 1948), 96–100, 104, 107–12.

counsels, unwholesome as they were, all the horses which he bought after that (for he was a carrier) were preserved from witchcraft.

And how many women have complained to us in our capacity of inquisitors, that when their cows have been injured by being deprived of their milk, or in any other way, they have consulted with suspected witches, and even been given remedies by them on condition that they would promise something to some spirit. And when they asked what they would have to promise, the witches answered that it was only a small thing, that they should agree to execute the instructions of that master with regard to certain observances during the Holy Offices of the Church, or to observe some silent reservations in their confessions to priests. . . .

Here it is to be noted that the devil is more eager and keen to tempt the good than the wicked, although in actual practice he tempts the wicked more than the good, because more aptitude for being tempted is found in the wicked than in the good. Therefore the devil tries all the harder to seduce all the more saintly virgins and girls; and there is reason in this, besides many examples of it.

For since he already possesses the wicked, but not the good, he tries the harder to seduce into his power the good whom he does not, than the wicked whom he does, possess. Similarly any earthly prince takes up arms against those who do not acknowledge his rule rather than against those who do not oppose him . . . And here is an example. Two witches were burned in Ratisbon. One of them, who was a bath-woman, had confessed among other things the following: that she had suffered much injury from the devil for this reason. There was a certain devout virgin, the daughter of a very rich man whom there is no need to name, since the girl is now dead in the disposition of Divine mercy and we would not that his thoughts should be perverted by evil. And the witch was ordered to seduce her by inviting her to her house on some Feast Day, in order that the devil himself, in the form of a young man, might speak with her. And although she had tried very often to accomplish this, yet whenever she had spoken to the young girl, she had protected herself with the sign of the Holy Cross. And no one can doubt that she did this at the instigation of a holy Angel to repel the works of the devil.

Another virgin living in the diocese of Strasburg confessed to one of us that she was alone on a certain Sunday in her father's house, when an old woman of that town came to visit her and, among other scurrilous words, made the following proposition; that, if she liked, she would take her to a place where there were some young men unknown to all the townsmen. "And when," said the virgin, "I consented and followed her to her house, the old woman said, 'See, we go upstairs to an upper room where the young men are; but take care not to make the sign of the cross.' I gave my promise not to do so, and as she was going before me and I was going up the stairs, I secretly crossed myself. At the top of the stairs, when we were both standing outside the room, the hag turned angrily upon me with a horrible countenance, and looking at me said, 'Curse you! Why did you cross yourself? Go away from here. Depart in the name of the devil.' And so I returned unharmed to my home."

It can be seen from this how craftily that old enemy labours in the seduction of souls. For it was in this way that the bath-woman whom we have mentioned, and who was burned, confessed that she had been seduced by some old woman. A different method, however, was used in the case of her companion witch, who had met the devil in human form on the road while she herself was going to visit her lover for the purpose of fornication. And when the Incubus devil had seen her, and had asked her whether she recognized him, and she had said that she did not, he had answered, "I am the devil; and if you wish, I will always be ready at your pleasure, and will not fail you in any necessity." And when she had consented, she continued for eighteen years, up to the end of her life, to practice diabolical filthiness with him together with a total abnegation of the Faith as a necessary condition.

There is also a third method of temptation through the way of sadness and poverty. For when girls have been corrupted, and have been scorned by their lovers after they have immodestly copulated with them in the hope and promise of marriage with them, and have found themselves disappointed in all their hopes and everywhere despised, they turn to the help and protection of devils, either for the sake of vengeance by bewitching those lovers or the wives they have married, or for the sake of giving themselves up to every sort of lechery. Alas! experience tells us that there is no number to such girls, and, consequently, the witches that spring from this class are innumerable. Let us give us a few out of many examples.

There is a place in the diocese of Brixen where a young man deposed the following facts concerning the bewitchment of his wife. "In the time of my youth I loved a girl who importuned me to marry her; but I refused her and married another girl from another country. But wishing for friendship's sake to please her, I invited her to the wedding. She came, and while the other honest women were wishing us luck and offering gifts, she raised her hand and, in the hearing of the other women who were standing round, said, 'You will have few days of health after to-day.' My bride was frightened, since she did not know her (for, as I have said, I had married her from another country), and asked the bystanders who she was who had threatened her in that way and they said that she was a loose and vagrant woman. None the less, it happened just as she had said. For after a few days my wife was so bewitched that she lost the use of all her limbs, and even now, after ten years, the effects of witchcraft can be seen on her body."

If we were to collect all the similar instances which have occurred in one town of that diocese, it would take a whole book; but they are written and preserved at the house of the Bishop of Brixen, who still lives to testify to their truth, astounding and unheard-of though they are . . .

Chapter 2. Of the Way whereby a Formal Pact with Evil Is Made

The method by which they profess their sacrilege through an open pact of fidelity to devils varies according to the several practices to which different witches are addicted. . . . There are . . . three kinds of witches; namely those who injure but cannot cure; those who cure but, through some strange pact with the devil, cannot injure; and those who both injure and cure. And among those who injure, one class in particular stands out. . . . those who, against every instinct of human or animal nature, are in the habit of eating and devouring the children of their own species.

And this is the most powerful class of witches, who practice innumerable other harms also. For they raise hailstorms and hurtful tempests and lightnings; cause sterility in men and animals; offer to devils, or otherwise kill, the children whom they do not devour. But these are only the children who have not been re-born by baptism at the font, for they cannot devour those who have been baptized, nor any without God's permission. They can also, before the eyes of their parents and when no one is in sight, throw into the water children walking by the water side; they make horses go mad under their riders; they can transport themselves from place to place through the air, either in body or in imagination; they can affect judges and magistrates so that they cannot hurt them; they can cause themselves and others to keep silence under torture; they can bring about a great trembling in the hands and horror in the minds of those who would arrest them; they can show to others occult things and certain future events, by the information of devils, though this may sometimes have a natural cause; they can see absent things as if they were present; they can turn the minds of men to inordinate love or hatred; they can at times strike whom they will with lightning, and even kill some men and animals; they can make of no effect the generative desires, and even the power of copulation, cause abortion, kill infants in the mother's womb by a mere exterior touch; they can at times bewitch men and animals with a mere look, without touching them, and cause death; they dedicate their own children to devils. . . . But it is common to all of them to practice carnal copulation with the devils. . . .

Now the method of profession is twofold. One is a solemn ceremony, like a solemn vow. The other is private and can be made to the devil at any hour alone. The first method is when witches meet together in conclave on a set day, and the devil appears to them in the assumed body of a man, and urges them to keep faith with him, promising them worldly prosperity and length of life; and they recommend a novice to his acceptance. And the devil asks whether she will abjure the Faith and forsake the holy Christian religion and the worship of the Anomalous Woman (for so they call the Most Blessed Virgin MARY), and never venerate the Sacraments; and if he finds the novice or disciple willing, then the devil stretches out his hand, and so does the novice, and she swears with upraised hand to keep that covenant. And when this is done, the devil at once adds that this is not enough and when the disciple asks what more must be done, the devil demands the following oath of homage to himself; that she give herself to him, body and soul, forever, and do her utmost to bring others of both sexes into his power. He adds, finally, that she is to make certain unguents from the bones and limbs of children, especially those who have [not] been baptized; by all which means she will be able to fulfill all her wishes with his help.

We Inquisitors had credible experience of this method in the town of Breisach in the diocese of Basel, receiving full information from a young girl witch who had been converted, whose aunt also had been burned in the diocese of Strasburg. And she added that she had become a witch by the method in which her aunt had first tried to seduce her.

For one day her aunt ordered her to go upstairs with her, and at her command to go into a room where she found fifteen young men clothed in green garments after the manner of German knights. And her aunt said to her, "Choose whom you wish from these young men, and I will give him to you, and he will take you for his wife." And when she said she did not wish for any of them, she was sorely beaten and at last consented, and was initiated according to the aforesaid ceremony. She said also that she was often transported by night with her aunt over vast distances. . . .

When she was asked whether it was only in imagination and phantastically that they so rode, through an illusion of devils, she answered that they did so in both ways. She said also that the greatest injuries were inflicted by midwives, because they were under an obligation to kill or offer to devils as many children as possible; and that she had been severely beaten by her aunt because she had opened a secret pot and found the heads of a great many children. . . .

There was lately a general report brought to the notice of Peter the Judge in Boltingen, that thirteen infants had been devoured in the State of Berne and public justice exacted full vengeance on the murderers. And when Peter asked one of the captive witches in which manner they ate children, she replied: "This is the manner of it. We set our snare chiefly for unbaptized children . . . and with our spells we kill them in their cradles or even when they are sleeping by their parents' side in such a way that they afterwards are thought to have been overlain or to have died some other natural death. Then we secretly take them from their graves, and cook them in a cauldron, until the whole flesh comes away from the bones to make a soup which may easily be drunk. Of the more solid matter we make an unguent which is of virtue to help us in our arts and pleasures and our transportations. . . ."

Chapter 3. How They Are Transported from Place to Place

And now we must consider their ceremonies and in what manner they proceed in their operations, first in respect of their actions towards themselves and in their own persons. Among their chief operations are being bodily transported from place to place, and to practice carnal connexion with Incubus devils. . . .

Now the following is their method of being transported. They take the unguent which, as we have said, they make at the devil's instruction from the limbs of children, particularly of those whom they have killed before baptism, and anoint with it a chair or a broomstick whereupon they are immediately carried up into the air, either by day or by night, and either visibly or, if they wish, invisibly; for the devil can conceal a body by the interposition of some other substance. . . . At times [the devil] transports the witches on animals which are not true animals but devils in that form; and sometimes even without any exterior help they are visibly carried solely by the operation of the devil's power . . .

Chapter 4. Here Follows the Way whereby Witches Copulate with Those Devils Known as Incubi

As to the method in which witches copulate with Incubus devils, six points are to be noted. First, as to the devil and the body which he assumes [and] of what element it is formed. Second, as to the act, whether it is always accompanied with the injection of semen received from some other man. Third, as to the time and place, whether one time is more favourable than another for this practice; fourth, whether the act is visible to the women, and whether only those who were begotten in this way are so visited by devils; fifth, whether it applies only to those who were offered to the devil at birth by midwives; sixth, whether the actual venereal pleasure is greater or less in this act. And we will speak first of the matter and quality of the body which the devil assumes.

It must be said that he assumes an aerial body, and that it is in some respects terrestrial, in so far as it has an earthly property through condensation. . . .

So when it is asked of what sort is the body assumed by the devil, it is to be said that with regard to its material, it is one thing to speak of the beginning of its assumption, and another thing to speak of its end. For in the beginning it is just air; but in the end it is inspissated [i.e., thickened] air, partaking of some of the properties of earth. And all this the devils, with God's permission, can do of their own nature; for the spiritual nature is superior to the bodily. . . .

How in Modern Times Witches Perform the Carnal Act with Incubus Devils, and How They Are Multiplied by This Means

But no difficulty arises out of what has been said with regard to our principal subject, which is the carnal act which Incubi in an assumed body perform with witches unless perhaps anyone doubts whether modern witches practice such abominable coitus and whether witches had their origin in this abomination.

In answering these two doubts we shall say, as to the former of them, something of the activities of the witches who lived in olden times, about 1400 years before the Incarnation of Our Lord. It is, for example, unknown whether they were addicted to these filthy practices as modern witches have been since that time, for so far as we know history tells us nothing on this subject. But no one who reads the histories can doubt that there have always been witches, and that by their evil works much harm has been done to men, animals, and the fruits of the earth, and that Incubus and Succubus devils have always existed, for the traditions of the canons and the holy doctors have left and handed down to posterity many things concerning them through many hundreds of years. Yet there is this difference, that in times long past the Incubus devils used to infest women against their wills. . . .

But the theory that modern witches are tainted with this sort of diabolic filthiness is not substantiated only in our opinion, since the expert testimony of the witches themselves has made all these things credible; and that they do not now, as in times past, subject themselves unwillingly, but willingly embrace this most foul and miserable servitude. For how many women have we left to be punished by secular law in various dioceses, especially in Constance and the town of Ratisbon, who have been for many years addicted to these abominations, some from their twentieth and some from their twelfth or thirteenth year, and always with a total or partial abnegation of the Faith? All the inhabitants of those places are witnesses of it. For without reckoning those who secretly repented and those who returned to the Faith, no less than forty-eight have been burned in five years. And there was no question of credulity in accepting their stories because they turned to free repentance; for they all agreed in this, namely, that they were bound to indulge in these lewd practices in order that the ranks of their perfidy might be increased. But we shall treat of these individually in the Second Part of this work, where their particular deeds are described, omitting those which came under the notice of our colleague the Inquisitor of Como in the County of Burbia, who in the space of one year, which was the year of grace 1485, caused forty-one witches to be burned, who all publicly affirmed, as it is said, that they had practiced these abominations with devils. Therefore this matter is fully substantiated by eye-witnesses, by hearsay, and the testimony of credible witnesses. . . .

Notice also St. Thomas, the *Second Book of Sentences* (dist. 4, art. 4), in the solution of an argument, where he asks whether those begotten in this way by devils are more powerful than other men. He answers that this is the truth, basing his belief not only on the text of Scripture in *Genesis* vi: And the same became the mighty men which were of old; but also on the following reason. Devils know how to ascertain the virtue in semen: first, by the temperament of him from whom the semen is obtained; secondly, by knowing what woman is most fitted for the reception of that semen; thirdly, by knowing what constellation is favourable to that corporeal effect; and we may add, fourthly, from their own words we learn that those whom they beget have the best sort of disposition for devils' work. When all these causes so concur, it is concluded that men born in this way are powerful and big in body.

Therefore, to return to the question whether witches had their origin in these abominations, we shall say that they originated from some pestilent mutual association with devils, as is clear from our first knowledge of them. But no one can affirm with certainty that they did not increase and multiply by means of these foul practices, although devils commit this deed for the sake not of pleasure but of corruption. And this appears to be the order of the process. A Succubus devil draws the semen from a wicked man and, if he is that man's own particular devil and does not wish to make himself an Incubus to a witch, he passes that semen on to the devil deputed to a woman or witch; and this last, under some constellation that favours his purpose, that the man or woman so born should be strong in the practice of witchcraft, becomes the Incubus to the witch.

And it is no objection that those of whom the text speaks were not witches but only giants and famous and powerful men. For, as was said before, witchcraft was not perpetrated in the time of the law of nature because of the recent memory of the creation of the world, which left no room for idolatry. But when the wickedness of man began to increase, the devil found more opportunity to disseminate this kind of perfidy. Nevertheless, it is not to be understood that those who were said to be famous men were necessarily so called by reason of their good virtues.

[2]

On Witchcraft

REGINALD SCOT

In 1584 Reginald Scot (1538–1599), an English Protestant layman, published an articulate refutation of witchcraft lore. Although King James I called for the burning of the book in 1603, it was reprinted several times during the century and appeared in a Dutch translation in 1609 with a second edition in English in 1637. New editions were available in 1651 and 1665. In this excerpt from The Discoverie of Witchcraft *Scot asserts that to attribute supernatural power to witches is to ignore the will of God and the workings of the natural world that God created. Even voluntary confessions of witchcraft, he maintains, are the result of delusion, and he states flatly that there has never been any credible evidence for the witch's supposed pact with Satan. Scot also refutes the fanciful proofs of diabolical acts postulated by the Frenchman Jean Bodin in his treatise on witchcraft,* De la Démonomanie des Sorciers *(1580).*

•

Book 1, Chapter 1. An Impeachment of Witches' Power in Meteors and Elementary Bodies Tending to the Rebuke of Such as Attribute Too Much unto Them

The fables of witchcraft have taken so fast hold and deep root in the heart of man that few or none can (nowadays) with patience endure the hand and correction of God. For if any adversity, grief, sickness, loss of children, corn, cattle, or liberty happen unto them, by and by they exclaim upon witches. [It is] as though there were no God in Israel that ordereth all things according to His will, punishing both just and unjust with griefs, plagues, and afflictions in manner and form as he thinketh good, but that certain old women here on earth, called witches, must needs be the contrivers of all men's calamities. . . .

Such faithless people (I say) are also persuaded that neither hail nor snow, thunder nor lightning, rain nor tempestuous winds come from the heavens at the command-

From Reginald Scot, *The Discoverie of Witchcraft*, ed. Hugh Ross Williamson (1584); Carbondale: Southern Illinois University and Centaur Press, 1964), 25, 29–31, 64–68, 92, 98–100. © 1964 by Centaur Press. Reprinted by permission of Open Gate Press incorporating Centaur Press (1954).

ments of God, but are raised by the cunning and power of witches and conjurers. Insomuch as a clap of thunder, or a gale of wind is no sooner heard, but either they run to ring bells, or cry out to burn witches, or else burn consecrated things hoping by the smoke thereof to drive the devil out of the air as though spirits could be fraid [frightened] away with such external toys. . . .

But certainly, it is neither a witch, nor devil, but a glorious God that maketh the thunder. . . . But little think our witchmongers that the Lord commandeth the clouds above or opens the doors of heaven . . . but rather that witches and conjurers are then about their business. . . .

But if all the devils in hell were dead and all the witches in England burned or hanged, I warrant you we should not fail to have rain, hail, and tempests, as now we have according to the appointment and will of God and according to the constitution of the elements and the course of the planets, wherein God hath set a perfect and perpetual order.

I am also well assured that if all the old women in the world were witches and all the priests, conjurers, we should not have a drop of rain nor a blast of wind the more or the less for them, for the Lord hath bound the waters in the clouds and hath set bounds about the waters until the day and night come to an end. Yea it is God that raiseth the winds and stilleth them, and he saith to the rain and snow, "be upon the earth" and it falleth. . . .

Chapter 3. Who They Be That Are Called Witches, with a Manifest Declaration of the Cause That Moveth Men So Commonly to Think, and Witches Themselves to Believe That They Can Hurt Children, Cattle, etc., with Words and Imaginations; and of Cozening Witches

One sort of such as are said to be witches are women which be commonly old, lame, bleary-eyed, pale, foul, and full of wrinkles; poor, sullen, superstitious, and papists; or such as know no religion; [those] in whose drowsy minds the devil hath gotten a fine seat. So as, [what] mischief, mischance, calamity, or slaughter is brought to pass, they are easily persuaded the same is done by themselves, imprinting in their minds an earnest and constant imagination hereof. They are lean and deformed, showing melancholy in their faces to the horror of all that see them. They are doting, scolds, mad, devilish, and not much differing from them that are thought to be possessed with spirits, so firm and steadfast in their opinions as whosoever shall only have respect to the constancy of their words uttered, would easily believe they were true indeed.

These miserable wretches are so odious unto all their neighbors and so feared as few dare offend them or deny them anything they ask. Whereby they take upon them, yea and sometimes think, that they can do such things as are beyond the ability of human nature. These go from house to house and from door to door for a pot full of milk, yeast, drink, potage, or some such relief, without the which they could hardly live, neither obtaining for their service and pains, nor by their art, nor yet at the devil's hands (with whom they are said to make a perfect and visible bargain) neither beauty, money, promotion, wealth, worship, pleasure, honor, knowledge, learning, or any other benefit whatsoever.

It falleth out many times that neither their necessities nor their expectation is answered or served in those places where they beg or borrow; but rather their lewdness is by their neighbors reproved. And further, in tract [i.e., the passage] of time the witch waxeth odious and tedious to her neighbors and they again are despised and despited of her. So as sometimes she curseth one and sometimes another and that from the master of the house, his wife, children, cattle, etc. to the little pig that lieth in the sty. Thus in process of time they have all displeased her and she hath wished evil luck unto them all perhaps with curses and imprecations made in form. Doubtless, at length, some of her neighbors die, or fall sick, or some of their children are visited with diseases that vex them strangely—as apoplexies, epilepsies, convulsions, hot fevers, worms, etc., which by ignorant parents are supposed to be the vengeance of witches. Yea, and their opinions and conceits are confirmed and maintained by unskillful physicians. According to the common saying, witchcraft and enchantment is the cloak of ignorance, whereas indeed evil humors and not strange words, witches, or spirits are the causes of such diseases. Also some of their cattle perish, either by disease or mischance. Then they, upon whom such adversities fall, weighing the fame that goeth upon this woman (her words, displeasure, and curses meeting so justly with their misfortune) do not only conceive but also are resolved that all their mishaps are brought to pass by her only means.

The witch, on the other side, expecting her neighbors' mischances and seeing things sometimes come to pass according to her wishes, curses, and incantations (for Bodin himself confesses that not above two in a hundred of their witchings or wishings take effect) being called before a Justice, by due examination of the circumstances, is driven to see her imprecations and desires and her neighbor's harms and losses to concur and as it were to take effect, and so confesseth that she (as a goddess) hath brought such things to pass. Wherein, not only she, but the accuser and also the Justice are foully deceived and abused as being through her confession and other circumstances persuaded (to the injury of God's glory) that she hath done or can do that which is proper only to God himself.

Another sort of witches there are, which be absolutely cozeners [i.e., deliberate frauds]. These take upon them, either for glory, fame, or gain, to do anything, which God or the devil can do, either foretelling of things to come, betraying of secrets, curing of maladies, or working of miracles.

Book 3, Chapter 9. How Melancholy Abuseth Old Women, and of the Effects Thereof by Sundry Examples

If any man advisedly mark their words, actions, cogitations, and gestures, he shall perceive that melancholy abounding in their head and occupying their brain hath deprived or rather depraved their judgments and all their senses. I mean not of cozening witches, but of poor melancholic women, which are themselves deceived. For you shall understand that the force which melancholy hath and the effects that it worketh in the body of a man, or rather of a woman, are almost incredible. For as some of these melancholic persons imagine, they are witches and by witchcraft can work wonders and do what they list [i.e., wish]. So do others troubled with this disease imagine many strange, incredible, and impossible things. Some [say] that they are monarchs and princes, and that all other men are their subjects; some that they are brute beasts; some that they be urinals or earthen pots greatly fearing to be broken; some that every one that meeteth them will convey them to the gallows and yet in the end hang themselves. One thought that Atlas, whom the poets feign to hold up heaven with his shoulders, would be weary and let the sky fall upon him. . . . One Theophilus a physician, otherwise sound enough of mind (as it is said) imagined that he heard and saw musicians continually playing on instruments in a certain place of his house. . . .

Now, if the fancy of a melancholic person may be occupied in causes which are both false and impossible, why should an old witch be thought free from such fantasies, who (as the learned philosophers and physicians say), upon the stopping of their monthly melancholic flux or issue of blood in their age must needs increase therein, as (through their weakness both of body and brain) the aptest persons to meet with such melancholic imaginations [so that] their imaginations remain even when their senses are gone. [This] *Bodin* laboreth to disprove, therein showing himself as good a physician as elsewhere a divine.

But if they may imagine that they can transform their own bodies, which nevertheless remaineth in the former shape, how much more credible is it that they may falsely suppose they can hurt and enfeeble other men's bodies, or which is less, hinder the coming of butter, etc.? But what is it that they will not imagine and consequently confess that they can do, especially being so earnestly persuaded thereunto, so sorely tormented, so craftily examined, with such promises of favor as whereby they imagine that they shall ever after live in great credit and wealth?

If you read the executions done upon witches either in times past in other countries or lately in this land, you shall see such impossibilities confessed, as none having his right wits will believe. Among other like false confessions we read that there was a witch confessed at the time of her death or execution that she had raised all the tempests and procured all the frosts and hard weather that happened in the winter 1565, and that many grave and wise men believed her.

Chapter 10. That Voluntary Confessions May Be Untruly Made, to the Undoing of the Confessors, and of the Strange Operation of Melancholy, Proved by a Familiar and Late Example

But that it may appear that even voluntary confession (in this case) may be untruly made though it tend to the destruction of the confessor and that melancholy may move imaginations to that effect, I will cite a notable instance concerning this matter, the parties themselves being yet alive and dwelling in the parish of Sellenge in Kent and the matter not long sithence [i.e., since] in this sort performed.

One Ade Davie, the wife of Simon Davie, husbandman, being reputed a right honest body and being of good parentage, grew suddenly (as her husband informed me and as it is well known in these parts) to be somewhat pensive and more sad than in times past. Which thing, though it grieved him, yet he was loath to make it so appear as either his wife might be troubled or discontented therewith or his neighbors informed thereof least ill husbandry should be laid to his charge (which, in these quarters, is much abhorred). But when she grew from pensiveness to some perturbation of mind so as her accustomed rest began in the night season to be withdrawn from her through sighing and secret lamentation, and that, not without tears, he could not but demand the cause of her conceit and extraordinary mourning. But, although at that time she covered the same acknowledging nothing to be amiss with her, soon after notwithstanding she fell down before him on her knees, desiring him to forgive her for she had grievously offended (as she said) both God and him. Her poor husband being abashed at this her behavior, comforted her as he could, asking her the cause of her trouble and grief. [She] told him that she had (contrary to God's law) and to the offense of all good Christians, to the injury of Him, and, especially, to the loss of her own soul, bargained and given her soul to the devil to be delivered unto him within short space. Whereunto her husband answered saying, "wife, be of good cheer, this thy bargain is void and of no effect, for thou hast sold that which is none of thine to sell. It belongeth to Christ who hath bought it and dearly paid for it even with his blood which he shed upon the cross so as the devil hath no interest in ye." After this, with like submission, tears, and penitence, she said unto him, "Oh, husband, I have yet committed another fault and done you more injury. For I have bewitched you and your children." "Be content," quoted he, "by the grace of God, Jesus Christ shall unwitch us, for no evil can happen to them that fear God."

And (as truly as the Lord lives) this was the tenor of his words unto me which I know is true as proceeding from unfeigned lips, and from one that fears God. Now when the time approached that the devil should come and take possession of the woman according to his bargain, he watched and prayed earnestly and caused his wife to read psalms and prayers for mercy at God's hands. And, suddenly, about midnight, there was a great rumbling below under his chamber window, which amazed them exceedingly. For they conceived that the devil was below, though he had no power to come up because of their fervent prayers.

He that noteth this woman's first and second confession, freely and voluntarily made, how everything concurred that might serve to add credit thereunto and yield matter for her condemnation, would not think but that if Bodin were foreman of her inquest, he would cry, "Guilty," and would hasten execution upon her. . . . But God knoweth she was innocent of any [of] these crimes, howbeit she was brought low and pressed down with the weight of this humor. . . . And yet, I believe, if any mishap had ensued to her husband or his children, few witchmongers would have judged otherwise but that she had bewitched them. And she (for her part) so constantly persuaded herself to be a witch, that she judged herself worthy of death. [When] retained in her chamber, [if] she saw anyone carrying a faggot to the fire, but she would say it was to make a fire to burn her for witchery. But God knoweth she had bewitched none, neither ensued there any hurt unto any by her imagination, but onto herself.

And as for the rumbling, it was by occasion of a sheep which was flayed and hung by the walls so [that] a dog came and devoured it, whereby grew the noise which I before mentioned. And she being now recovered, remaineth a right honest woman, far from such impiety and shamed of her imaginations, which she perceiveth to have grown through melancholy. . . .

Book 5, Chapter 1. Of Transformations, Ridiculous Examples Brought by the Adversaries for the Confirmation of Their Foolish Doctrine

Now that I may with the very absurdities contained in their own authors and even in their principal doctors and last writers confound them that maintain the transubstantiations of witches, I will show you certain proper stuff which Bodin (their chief champion of this age) hath gathered out of *Malleus Maleficarum* and others, whereby he laboreth to establish this impossible, incredible, and supernatural, or rather unnatural doctrine of transubstantiation.

First, as touching the devil (Bodin saith) that he doth most properly and commonly transform himself into a goat. . . . Howbeit, he sometimes alloweth the devil the shape of a black Moor. . . . As for witches, he saith they especially transubstantiate themselves into wolves and then whom they bewitch into asses. . . .

Chapter 3. Of a Man Turned into an Ass, and Returned Again into a Man by One of Bodin's Witches

It happened in the city of Salamin in the kingdom of Cyprus (wherein is a good haven) that a ship laden with merchandise stayed there for a short space. In the meantime many of the soldiers and mariners went to shore to provide fresh victuals, among which number a certain Englishman, being a sturdy young fellow, went to a woman's house a little way out of the city and not far from the sea side, to see whether she had any eggs to sell. [She] perceiving him to be a lusty young fellow, a stranger, and far from his country, so as upon the loss of him there would be the less miss or inquiry, she considered with herself how to destroy him and willed him to stay there a while, while she went to fetch a few eggs for him. But she tarried long, so as the young man called unto her desiring her to make haste. For he told her that the tide would be spent and by that means his ship would be gone and leave him behind. Howbeit, after some detracting of time, she brought him a few eggs, willing him to return to her if his ship were gone when he came. The young fellow returned towards his ship but, before he went aboard, he would need eat an egg or two to satisfy his hunger and within a short space he became dumb and out of his wits (as he afterwards said). When he would have entered into the ship, the mariners beat him back with a cudgel saying: "What a murren [i.e., helmet] lacks the ass? Whither the devil will this ass?" The ass or young man (I cannot tell by which name I should term him) being many times repelled and understanding their words that called him ass, considering that he could speak never a word and yet could understand everybody, he thought that he was bewitched by the woman at whose house he was. And therefore, when by no means he could get into the boat, but was driven to tarry and see her departure, being also beaten from place to place as an ass, he remembered the witch's words and the words of his own fellows that called him ass and returned to the witch's house, in whose service he remained by the space of three years, doing nothing with his hands, all that while but carried such burdens as she laid on his back, having only this comfort, that although he were reputed an ass among strangers and beasts, yet that both this witch and all other witches knew him to be a man.

After three years were passed over, in a morning betimes, he went to town before his dame, who, upon some occasion (of like to make water) stayed a little behind. In the meantime, being near to a church, he heard a little saccarine bell ring to the elevation of a morrow [i.e., morning] mass and not daring to go into the church lest he should have been beaten and driven out with cudgels, in great devotion he fell down in the churchyard upon the knees of his hinder legs and did lift his forefeet over his head as the priest doth hold the sacrament at the elevation. [This] prodigious sight when certain merchants of Genoa espied and with wonder beheld, anon cameth the witch with a cudgel in her hand beating forth the ass. And because (as it hath been said) such kinds of witchcrafts are very usual in those parts, the merchants aforesaid made such means as both the ass and the witch were attached by [i.e., brought before] the judge. And she, being examined and set upon the rack, confessed the whole matter and promised that if she might have liberty to go home, she would restore him to his old shape. And being dismissed, she did accordingly. Notwithstanding they apprehended her again and burned her and the young man returned to his country with a joyful heart . . .

Chapter 4. A Summary of the Former Fable, with a Refutation Thereof, after Due Examination of the Same

Concerning the verity or probability of this interlude between Bodin, *Malleus Maleficarum*, the witch, the ass, the mass, the merchants, the inquisitors, the tormentors, etc., first I wonder at the miracle of transubstantiation; secondly at the impudence of Bodin and James [i.e., Jacob] Sprenger for affirming so gross a lie, devised belike by the knight of the Rhodes to make a fool of Sprenger and an ass of Bodin; thirdly that the ass had no more wit than to kneel down and hold up his forefeet to a piece of starch or flour, which neither would, nor could, nor did help him; fourthly that the mass could not reform that which the witch transformed; fifthly, that the merchants, the inquisitors, and the tormentors could not either severally or jointly do it but refer the matter to the witch's courtesy and good pleasure. . . .

But to proceed into the probability of this story. . . . you hear that at the inquisi-tors' commandment and through the tormentors' correction, she promised to restore him to his own shape and so she did as being thereunto compelled. I answer that as the whole story is an impious fable, so this assertion is false and disagreeable to their own doctrine which maintaineth that the witch does nothing but by the permission and leave of God. For if she could do or undo such a thing at her own pleasure or at the commandment of the inquisitors, or for fear of the tormentors, or for the love of the party, or for remorse of conscience, then is it not either by the extraordinary leave nor yet by the like direction of God except you will make him a confederate with old witches. . . .

Chapter 5. That the Body of a Man Cannot Be Turned into the Body of a Beast by a Witch, Proved by Strong Reasons, Scriptures, and Authorities

But was this man an ass all this while? Or was this ass a man? Bodin saith (his reason only reserved) he was truly transubstantiated into an ass so as there must be no part of a man but reason remaining in this ass. And yet . . . an human soul cannot receive any other than an human body, nor yet can light into a body that wanteth reason of mind. . . .

God hath enbued every man and every thing with his proper nature, substance, form, qualities, and gifts, and directeth their ways. As for the ways of an ass, he taketh no such care, howbeit they have also their properties and substance several to themselves. For there is one flesh (saith Paul) of men, another flesh of beasts, another of fishes, another of birds. And, therefore, it is absolutely against the ordinance of God (who hath made me a man) that I should fly like a bird, or swim like a fish, or creep like a worm, or become an ass in shape. Insomuch as if God would give me leave, I cannot do it for it were contrary to his own order and decree and to the constitution of any body which he hath made. . . .

What a beastly assertion is it, that a man, whom GOD hath made according to his own similitude and likeness, should be by a witch turned into a beast? What an impiety is it to affirm that an ass's body is the temple of the Holy Ghost? Or an ass to be the child of God and God to be his father, as it is said of man? . . .

Now if a witch or devil can so alter the shape of a man as contrarily to make him look down to hell like a beast, God's works should not only be defaced and degraced, but his ordinance should be wonderfully altered and thereby confounded. . . .

Book 16, Chapter 2. By What Means the Common People Have Been Made Believe in the Miraculous Works of Witches, a Definition of Witchcraft, and a Description Thereof

The common people have been so besotted and bewitched with whatsoever poets have feigned of witchcraft, either in earnest, in jest, or else in derision, and with whatsoever loud liars and cozeners for their pleasures herein have invented, and with whatsoever tales they have heard from old doting women, or from their mother's maids, and with whatsoever the grand fool their ghostly father, or any other morrow mass priest had informed them, and finally with whatsoever they have swallowed up through tract of time or through their own timorous nature or ignorant conceit, concerning these matters of hags and witches. As they have so settled their opinion and credit thereupon that they think it heresy to doubt in any part of the matter, especially because they find this word witchcraft expressed in the scriptures. . . .

And now to come to the definition of witchcraft, which hitherto I did defer and put off purposely that you might perceive the true nature thereof by the circumstances. . . . Witchcraft is in truth a cozening art, wherein the name of God is abused, profaned, and blasphemed, and his power attributed to a vile creature. In [the] estimation of the vulgar people, it is a supernatural work contrived between a corporeal old woman and a spiritual devil. The manner thereof is so secret, mystical, and strange, that to this day there hath never been any credible witness thereof. It is incomprehensible to the wise, learned, or faithful, a probable matter to children, fools, melancholic persons, and papists. The trade is thought to be impious; the effect and end thereof to be sometimes evil, as when thereby man or beast, grass, trees, or corn, etc. is hurt; sometimes good, as whereby sick folks are healed, thieves betrayed, and true men come to their goods, etc. The matter and instruments wherewith it is accomplished, are words, charms, signs, images, characters, etc., which words, although any other creature do pronounce in manner and form as they do, leaving out no circumstance requisite or usual for that action, yet none is said to have the grace or gift to perform the matter except she be a witch and so taken either by her own consent or by others' imputation.

The Discovery of Witches

In Answer to Several Queries

MATTHEW HOPKINS

Matthew Hopkins (d. 1647) and his associate, John Stearne, were professional witch finders operating in England in the 1640s. Hopkins defended his actions in this 1647 pamphlet, The Discovery of Witches. *He writes in a question-and-answer format, referring to himself in the third person as the Discoverer.*

•

Query 3. From whence then proceeded this his skill [i.e., witch finding]? Was it from his profound learning, or from much reading of learned authors concerning that subject?

Answer [Hopkins]. From neither of both, but from experience, which though it be meanly esteemed of, yet the surest and safest way to judge.

Query 4. I pray where was this experience gained? And why gained by him and not by others?

Answer. The Discoverer [Hopkins] never traveled far for it, but in March, 1644, he had some seven or eight of that horrible sect of witches living in the town where he lived, a town in *Essex* called *Maningtree*, with divers other adjacent witches of other towns, who every six weeks in the night (being always on the Friday night) had their meeting close by his house, and had their several solemn sacrifices there offered to the Devil, one of which this discoverer heard speaking to her *Imps* one night, and bid them go to another witch, who was thereupon apprehended, and searched by women who had for many years known the devil's marks, and found to have three teats about her, which honest women have not. So upon command from the *Justice* they were to keep her from sleep two or three nights, expecting in that time to see her *familiars*, which the fourth night she called in by their several names, and told them what shapes, a quarter of an hour before they came in, there being ten of us in the room. The first she called was,

From Matthew Hopkins, *The Discovery of Witches, A Study of Master Matthew Hopkins Commonly Call'd Witch Finder Generall*, ed. Montague Summers (London: At the Cayme Press, 1928), 50–57, 59–62.

1. *Holt*, who came in like a white kitten.

2. *Jarmara*, who came in like a fat spaniel without any legs at all, she said she kept him fat, for she clapped her hand on her belly, and said he sucked good blood from her body.

3. *Vinegar Tom*, who was like a long-legged greyhound, with an head like an ox, with a long tail and broad eyes, who when this Discoverer spoke to, and bade him go to the place provided for him and his angels, immediately transformed himself into the shape of a child of four years old without a head, and gave half a dozen turns about the house, and vanished at the door.

4. *Sack and Sugar*, like a black Rabbit.

5. *Newes*, like a polecat. All these vanished away in a little time. Immediately after this witch confessed, several other witches, from whom she had her *Imps*, and named to divers women where their marks were, the number of their *Marks*, and *Imps*, and *Imps*' names as *Elemanzer, Pyewacket, Peckin* the *Crown, Grizzel, Greedigut*, etc. which no mortal could invent. Upon their searches the same marks were found, the same number, and in the same place, and the like confessions from them of the same Imps (though they knew not that we were told before) and so peached [i.e., informed on] one another thereabouts that joined together in the like damnable practice, that in our hundred in *Essex*, 29 were condemned at once, 4 brought 25 miles to be hanged where this Discoverer lives, for sending the Devil like a bear to kill him in his garden. So by seeing diverse of the men's paps, and trying ways with hundreds of them, he gained this experience, and for ought he knows any man else may find them as well as he and his company, if they had the same skill and experience.

Query 5. Many poor people are condemned for having a pap, or teat about them, whereas many people (especially ancient people) are, and have been a long time, troubled with natural wrets [wrens or warts] on several parts of their bodies, and other natural excrescencies as hemorrhoids, piles, childbearing, etc. And these shall be judged only by one man alone, and a woman, and so accused or acquitted.

Answer. The parties so judging can justify their skill to any and show good reasons why such marks are not merely natural, neither that they can happen by any such natural cause as is before expressed and for further answer for their private judgments alone, it is most false and untrue, for never was any man tried by search of his body. But commonly a dozen of the ablest men in the parish or elsewhere were present and most commonly as many ancient skillful matrons and midwives present when the women are tried, which marks not only he and his company attest to be very suspicious, but all beholders, the skillfullest of them, do not approve of them, but likewise assent that such tokens cannot in their judgments proceed from any [of] the above mentioned causes.

Query 6. It is a thing impossible for any man or woman to judge rightly on such marks, they are so near to natural excrescences, and they that find them durst not presently give oath they were drawn by evil spirits till they have used unlawful courses of torture to make them say anything for ease and quiet, as who would not do? But I would know the reasons he speaks of, how, and whereby to discover the one from the other and so be satisfied in that.

Answer. The reasons in brief are three, which for the present he judgeth to differ from natural marks; which are:

1. He judgeth by the unusualness of the place where he finds the teats in or on their bodies, being far distant from any usual place, from whence such natural marks proceed.

2. They are most commonly insensible, and feel neither pin, needle, awl, etc. thrust through them.

3. The often variations and mutations of these marks into several forms, confirms the matter, [so] as if a witch hear a month or two before that the *Witch-finder* (as they call him) is coming, they will have put out their imps to others to suckle them, even to their own young and tender children. These upon search are found to have dry skins and films only, and be close to the flesh. Keep her 24 hours with a diligent eye that none of her spirits come in any visible shape to suck her. The women have seen the next day after her teats extended out to their former filling length, full of corruption ready to burst. And leaving her alone then one quarter of an hour, and let the women go up again, and she will have them drawn by her Imps close again. . . .

Query 7. How can it possibly be that the Devil being a spirit, and wants no nutriment or sustenance, should desire to suck any blood? And indeed, as he is a spirit, he cannot draw any such excrescences, having neither flesh nor bone, nor can be felt.

Answer. He seeks not their blood, as if he could not subsist without that nourishment, but he often repairs to them and gets it, the more to aggravate the witches' damnation and to put her in mind of her *Covenant*. And as he is a spirit and prince of the air, he appears to them in any shape whatsoever, which shape is occasioned by him through joining of condensed thickened air together, and many times doth assume shapes of many creatures. But to create any thing he cannot do it, it is only proper to God. But in this case of drawing out of these teats, he doth really enter into the body, real, corporeal, substantial creature, and forceth that creature (he working in it) to his desired ends, and useth the organs of that body to speak withal to make his compact up with the witches, be the creature cat, rat, mouse, etc. . . .

Query 9. Beside that unreasonable watching, they were extraordinarily walked, till their feet were blistered, and so forced through that cruelty to confess, etc.

Answer. It was in the same beginning of this discovery, and the meaning of walking of them at the highest extent of cruelty, was only they to walk about themselves the night they were watched, only to keep them waking. And the reason was [that] when they did lie or sit in a chair, if they did offer to couch down, then the watchers were only to desire them to sit up and walk about, for indeed when they be suffered so to couch, immediately comes their familiars into the room and scareth the watchers, and hearteneth the witch. Though contrary to the true meaning of the same instructions, diverse have been by rustical people (they hearing them confess to be witches) misused, spoiled, and abused, diverse whereof have suffered for the same. But [it] could never be proved against this Discoverer to have a hand in it, or consent to it; and hath likewise been unused by him and others, ever since the time they were kept from sleep.

Query 10. But there hath been an abominable, inhumane, and unmerciful trial of these poor creatures, by tying them, and heaving them into the water; a trial not allowable by law or conscience, and I would fain know the reasons for that.

Answer. It is not denied but many were so served as had paps, and floated, others that had none were tried with them and sunk, but mark the reasons.

1. For first the Devil's policy is great, in persuading many to come of their own accord to be tried, persuading them their marks are so close they shall not be found out, so as diverse have come 10 or 12 miles to be searched of their own accord, and hanged for their labor (as one Meggs, a Baker did, who lived within 7 miles of Norwich and was hanged at Norwich Assizes for witchcraft), then when they find that the devil tells them false they reflect on him, and he (as 40 have confessed) adviseth them to be sworn, and tells them they shall sink and be cleared that way, then when they be tried that way and float, they see the Devil deceives them again, and have so laid open his treacheries.

2. It was never brought in against any of them at their trials as any evidence.

3. King *James* in his *Demonology* saith, it is a certain rule, [that] (saith he) witches deny their baptism when they covenant with the devil, water being the sole element thereof, and therefore saith he, when they be heaved into the water, the water refuseth to receive them into her bosom (they being such miscreants to deny their baptism), and suffers them to float, as the froth on the sea, which the water will not receive, but casts it up and down, till it comes to the earthy element the shore, and there leaves it to consume. . . .

Query 13. How can any possibly believe that the devil and the witch joining together should have such power as the witches confess to kill such and such a man, child, horse, cow, or the like. If we believe they can do what they will, then we derogate from God's power, who for certain limits the devil and the witch. I cannot believe they have any power at all.

Answer. God suffers the devil many times to do much hurt, and the devil doth play many times the deluder and impostor with these witches, in persuading them that they are the cause of such and such a murder wrought by him with their consents, when and indeed neither he nor they had any hand in it. . . .

Query 14. All that the witch-finder doth is to fleece the country of their money, and therefore rides and goes to towns to have employment and promiseth them fair promises, and it may be doth nothing for it and possesseth [i.e., convinces] many men that they have so many wizards and so many witches in their town and so heartens them on to entertain him.

Answer. You do him a great deal of wrong in every of these particulars. For, first,

1. He never went to any town or place, but they rode, writ, or sent often for him and were (for ought he knew) glad of him.

2. He is a man that doth disclaim that ever he deter a witch, or said, "Thou art a witch;" only after her trial by search, and their own confessions, he as others may judge.

3. Lastly, judge how he fleeceth the country and enriches himself by considering the vast sum he takes of every town. He demands but 20 shillings a town, and doth

sometimes ride 20 miles for that, and hath no more for all his charges thither and back again (and it may be stays a week there) and find there 3 or 4 witches, or if it be but one, cheap enough, and this is the great sum he takes to maintain his company with 3 horses.

[4]

On Witches and Witchcraft

COTTON MATHER

The Reverend Cotton Mather (1663–1728) of Massachusetts was a prominent and widely published Puritan minister. He served as pastor of North Church in Boston for over forty years. He wrote several pieces about witchcraft; in the work excerpted here, Memorable Providences Relating to Witchcraft *and* Possessions *(1689), Mather is eager to assert against skeptics that devils and witches do exist. He relates various incidents of witchcraft activity and expresses the hope that fear of demons will turn people to a renewed faith and trust in God. The preface was addressed to the physician Wait Winthrop, grandson of the first governor of Massachusetts (John Winthrop) and soon to be appointed a judge on the 1692 Court of Oyer and Terminer. Four of Mather's fellow ministers endorsed his essay.*

•

To the Honourable Wait Winthrop Esq;
Sir

By the special disposal and Providence of the Almighty God, there now comes abroad into the world a little history of several very astonishing witchcrafts and Possessions, which, partly my own ocular observation and partly my undoubted information, hath enabled me to offer unto the public notice of my neighbours. . . . Had I on this occasion before me handled the doctrine of demons or launched forth into speculations about magical mysteries, I might have made some ostentation [i.e., pretense] that I have read something and thought a little in my time; but it would neither have been convenient for me nor profitable for those plain folks whose edification I have all along aimed at. I have therefore here but briefly touched every thing with an American pen. . . .

C. Mather

To the Reader

The old heresy of the sensual Sadducees, denying the being of angels either good or evil, died not with them; nor will it, while men (abandoning both faith and reason) count it their wisdom to credit nothing but what they see and feel. How much this

From Cotton Mather, *Memorable Providences Relating to Witchcrafts and Possessions* (1689), in *Narratives of the Witchcraft Cases, 1648–1706*, ed. George Lincoln Burr (New York: Charles Scribner's Sons, 1914), 93–99, 135–36, 141–43. The identification of names is from Burr's notes.

fond opinion has gotten ground in this debauched age is awfully observable; and what a dangerous stroke it gives to settle men in atheism is not hard to discern. God is therefore pleased (besides the witness born to this truth in Sacred Writ) to suffer devils sometimes to do such things in the world as shall stop the mouth of gainsayers and extort a confession from them.

It has also been made a doubt by some, whether there are any such things as witches, i.e. such as by contract or explicit covenant with the devil, improve [i.e., empower] or rather are improved [empowered] by him to the doing of things strange in themselves and besides their natural course. But (besides that the Word of God assures us that there have been such and gives order about them) no age passes without some apparent demonstration of it. For, though it be folly to impute every dubious accident or unwonted effect of providence to witchcraft, yet there are some things which cannot be excepted against but must be ascribed hither.

Angels and men not being made for civil converse together in this world, and all communion with devils being interdicted us, their nature also being spiritual, and the Word of God having said so little in that particular concerning their way of acting, hence it is that we can disclose but a little of those mysteries of darkness, all reports that are from themselves or their instruments being to be esteemed as illusions, or at least covered with deceit, filled with the impostures of the father of lies. . . .

The following account will afford to him that shall read with observation a further clear confirmation that there is both a God and a devil and witchcraft; that there is no outward affliction but what God may (and sometimes doth) permit Satan to trouble His people withal; that the malice of Satan and his Instruments is very great against the children of God; that the clearest Gospel-light shining in a place will not keep some from entering hellish contracts with infernal spirits; that prayer is a powerful and effectual remedy against the malicious practises of devils and those in covenant with them; that they who will obtain such mercies of God, must pray unto perseverance; that God often gives to His people some apparent encouragements to their faith in prayer though He does not presently perfect the deliverance sought for; that God's grace is able to support His children and preserve their grace firm under sorest and continuing troubles; that those who refuse the temptation to use doubtful or diabolical courses to get the assaults of the devil and his agents removed, choosing to recommend all to God, and rather to endure affliction, than to have it removed to His dishonour and the wounding of their own consciences, never had cause to repent of it in the end. . . .

Charles Morton
James Allen
Joshua Moodey
Samuel Willard

The Introduction

It was once the mistake of one gone to the congregation of the dead, concerning the survivors, *If one went unto them from the dead, they will repent.* The blessed God hath made some to come from the damned for the conviction (may it also be for the conversion) of us that are yet alive. The devils themselves are by compulsion come to confute the atheism and sadducism, and to reprove the madness of ungodly men. Those condemned prisoners of our atmosphere have not really sent letters of thanks from hell to those that are on earth promoting of their interest. Yet they have been forced, as of old, to confess that Jesus was the holy one of God, so of late to declare that sin and vice are the things which they are delighted in. But should one of those hideous wights [i.e., demons] appear visibly with fiery chains upon him and utter audibly his roarings and his warnings in one of our congregations, it would not produce new hearts in those whom the Scriptures handled in our ministry do not affect. However, it becomes the ambassadors of the Lord Jesus to leave no stroke untouched that may conduce to bring men from the power of Satan unto God, and for this cause it is that I have permitted the ensuing histories to be published. They contain things of undoubted certainty, and they suggest things of importance inconceivable. Indeed they are only one head of collections which in my little time of observation I have made of memorable providences, with reflections thereupon to be reserved among other effects of my diversion from my more stated and more weary studies. . . .

Go then my little book, as a lackey to the more elaborate essays of those learned men. Go tell mankind that there are devils and witches, and that though those night-birds least appear where the day-light of the Gospel comes, yet New England has had examples of their existence and operation; and that not only the wigwams of Indians, where the pagan Powaws [i.e., powwows or Indian shamans] often raise their masters in the shapes of bears and snakes and fires, but the houses of Christians, where our God has had His constant worship, have undergone the annoyance of evil spirits. Go tell the world what prayers can do beyond all devils and witches, and what it is that these monsters love to do, and, though the demons in the audience of several standers-by threatened much disgrace to thy author if he let thee come abroad, yet venture that, and in this way seek a just revenge on them for the disturbance they have given to such as have called on the name of God.

Witchcrafts and Possessions

Example 4

So horrid and hellish is the crime of witchcraft, that were God's thoughts as our thoughts, or God's ways as our ways, it could be no other but unpardonable. But that the Grace of God may be admired and that the worst of sinners may be encouraged, behold, witchcraft also has found a pardon. Let no man despair of his own forgiveness but let no man also delay about his own repentance how aggravated soever his transgressions are. From the hell of witchcraft our merciful Jesus can fetch a guilty creature to the glory of heaven. Our Lord hath sometimes recovered those who have in the most horrid manner given themselves away to the destroyer of their souls.

There was one Mary Johnson tried at Hartford, in this country, upon an indictment of familiarity with the devil. She was found guilty of the same chiefly upon her own confession and condemned. [A Mary Johnson was indicted for witchcraft at Hartford in 1648 but the other details in Mather's story can no longer be corroborated in the records.]

Many years are past since her execution and the records of the Court are but short, yet there are several memorables that are found credibly related and attested concerning her.

She said, that a devil was wont to do her many services. Her master once blamed her for not carrying out the ashes, and a devil did clear the hearth for her afterwards. Her master sending her into the field to drive out the hogs that used to break into it, a devil would scowre [i.e., scare] them out, and make her laugh to see how he feaz'd [i.e., tossed] them about.

Her first familiarity with the devils came by discontent, and wishing the devil to take that and the other thing, and the devil to do this and that, whereupon a devil appeared unto her tendering her the best service he could do for her.

She confessed that she was guilty of the murder of a child, and that she had been guilty of uncleanness with men and devils.

In the time of her imprisonment, the famous Mr. Samuel Stone was at great pains to promote her conversion unto God and represent unto her both her misery and remedy, the success of which was very desirable and considerable. [Samuel Stone (1602–1663), another Puritan minister, came to Massachusetts in 1633.]

She was by most observers judged very penitent, both before and at her execution, and she went out of the world with many hopes of mercy through the merit of Jesus Christ. Being asked what she built her hopes upon, she answered on those words, "Come to me all ye that labour and are heavy laden, and I will give you rest," and those, "There is a fountain open for sin and for uncleanness." And she died in a frame extremely to the satisfaction of them that were spectators of it.

Our God is a great Forgiver. . . .

Examples 6 and 7

Had there been diligence enough used by them that have heard and seen amazing instances of witchcraft, our number of memorable providences under this head, had reached beyond the perfect. However, before I have done writing, I will insert an example or two communicated unto me by a gentleman [probably the Reverend Nicholas Noyes of Salem Town] of sufficient fidelity to make a story of his relating credible. The things were such as happened in the town whereof himself is minister, and they are but some of more which he favoured me with the communication of. But, it seems I must be obliged to conceal the names of the parties concerned lest some should be offended, though none could be injured by the mention of them.

In a town, which is none of the youngest in this country, there dwelt a very godly and honest man who, upon some provocation, received very angry and threatening expressions from two women in the neighbourhood. Soon upon this, diverse [i.e., various] of his cattle in a strange manner died and the man himself sometimes was haunted with sights of the women, as he thought, encountering of him. He grew indisposed in his body very unaccountably and one day repaired unto a church meeting, then held in the place, with a resolution there to declare what he had met withal. The man was one of such figure and respect among them that the Pastor singled out him for to pray in the assembly before their breaking up. He prayed with a more than usual measure of both devotion and discretion, but just as he was coming to that part of his prayer wherein he intended to petition heaven for the discovery of witchcrafts which had been among them, he sank down speechless and senseless and was by his friends carried away to a bed where he lay for two or three hours in horrible distress, fearfully starting and staring and crying out, "Lord, I am stabbed!" And now looking whistly [i.e., quietly] to and fro, he said, "O here are wicked persons among us, even among *us*," and he complained, "I came hither with a full purpose to tell what I knew, but now," said he, "I lye like a fool!" Thus he continued until the meeting was over, and then his fits left him, only he remained very sore. One or two more such fits he had after that, but afterwards a more private sort of torture was employed upon him. He was advised by a worthy man to apply himself unto a magistrate and warned that he would shortly be murdered if he did not. He took not the counsel but languished for some weeks, yet able to walk and work, but then he had his breath and life suddenly taken away from him in a manner of which no full account could be given.

The man had a son invaded with the like fits, but God gave deliverance to him in answer to the prayers of His people for him.

In the same town there yet lives a very pious woman that from another woman of ill fame received a small gift, which was eaten by her. Upon the eating of it, she became strangely altered and afflicted and hindered from sleeping at night by the pulls of some invisible hand for a long while together. A shape or two of, I know not who, likewise haunted her and gave her no little trouble. At last, a fit extraordinary violent came upon her wherein she pointed her hand and fixed her eye much upon the chimney and spoke at a rate that astonished all about her. Anon, she broke forth into prayer and yet could bring out scarce more than a syllable at a time. In her short prayer she grew up to an high act of faith and said (by syllables, and with stammerings), "Lord, Thou has been my hope, and in Thee will I put my trusts; Thou has been my salvation here, and wilt be so forever and ever!" Upon which her fit left her and she afterwards grew very well, still remaining so.

There were diverse [i.e., various] other strange things, which from the same hand, I can both relate and believe as of a child bewitched into lameness and recovered immediately by a terrour given to the vile authoress of the mischief; but the exact print, image and colour of an orange made on the child's leg, presently upon the sending of an orange to the witch by the mother of the child, who yet had no evil design in making of the present. And of other children, which a palpable witchcraft made its impressions on; but *Manum de Tabula* [hands off the slate, i.e., stop writing].

I entreat every reader to make such a use of these things as may promote his own welfare and advance the Glory of God; and so answer the intent of the writer.

COMMENTARIES

[5]

The Non-Existent Society of Witches

Norman Cohn

In this excerpt from his 1975 book Europe's Inner Demons, *the historian Norman Cohn reviews the stereotypes of witches and their sabbats. Cohn is also well known for his book* The Pursuit of the Millennium: Revolutionary Millenarians and Mystical Anarchists of the Middle Ages *(1957). His interest in European witch hunts has also led to research on the dynamics of persecution in the modern world. He is the editor of the Columbus Centre's "Studies in the Dynamics of Persecution and Extermination" and won the 1967 Anisfield-Wolf Award for* Warrant for Genocide: The Myth of the Jewish World-Conspiracy and the Protocols of the Elders of Zion.

•

Hundreds of books and articles have been written about the great European witch-hunt of the fifteenth, sixteenth and seventeenth centuries, and during the last few years the subject has received more attention from historians than ever before. But that does not mean that nothing remains to be said. On the contrary, the more is written, the more glaring the disagreements. Were there people who regarded themselves as witches? If so, what did they do, or believe themselves to do? Were they organized, did they hold meetings? What are we to make of covens and sabbats? Again, when and where did the great witch-hunt begin? Who launched it, who perpetuated it, and for what motives? And just how "great" was it—did the numbers of those executed run into thousands, or into tens of thousands, or into hundreds of thousands? On most of these questions there is still no consensus amongst historians— and even where consensus exists, it is not necessarily correct. . . .

We may start with the stereotype of the witch as it existed at the times when, and the places where, witch-hunting was at its most intense. The profile of that stereotype at least is established beyond all dispute. We possess not only the records of innumerable witch-trials, but also memoirs and manuals by half a dozen witch-hunting

From Norman Cohn, *Europe's Inner Demons: An Enquiry Inspired by the Great Witch-Hunt* (New York: Basic Books, 1975), 99–103, 107–11, 113–18, 124–25. © 1975 by Basic Books. Reprinted by permission of the Peters Fraser and Dunlop Group Limited on behalf of Norman Cohn.

magistrates; and the figure of the witch that emerges could not be clearer or more detailed.

A witch was a human being—usually a woman but sometimes a man or even a child—who was bound to the Devil by a pact or contract, as his servant and assistant.

When the Devil first appeared to a future witch he was clad in flesh and blood; sometimes his shape was that of an animal but usually it was that of a man, fully and even smartly dressed. Almost always he appeared at a moment of acute distress—of bereavement, or of utter loneliness, or of total destitution. A typical pattern was that an elderly widow, rejected by her neighbours and with nobody to turn to, would be approached by a man who would alternatively console her, promise her money, scare her, extract a promise of obedience from her, in the end mate with her. The money seldom materialized, the copulation was downright painful, but the promise of obedience remained binding. Formally and irrevocably the new witch had to renounce God, Christ, the Christian religion, and pledge herself instead to the service of Satan; whereupon the Devil set his mark on her—often with the nails or claws of his left hand, and on the left side of the body.

If becoming a witch rarely brought either wealth or erotic pleasure, it had other rewards to offer. A witch was able to perform *maleficium*, i.e. to harm her neighbours by occult means. The pact meant that the Devil would demand this from his servant, but it also meant that he would supply her with supernatural power for the purpose. With the Devil's aid a witch could ruin the life of anyone she chose. She could bring sudden illness, or mental disorder, or maiming accidents, or death, on man, woman or child. She could bedevil a marriage by producing sterility or miscarriages in the woman, or impotence in the man. She could make cattle sicken or die, or cause hailstorms or unseasonable rain to ruin the crops. This was her reward; for a witch's will, like her master's, was wholly malignant, wholly set on destruction.

Witches were believed to specialize in the killing of babies and small children. More than mere malice was at work here—witches needed the corpses for all sorts of reasons. They were cannibals, with an insatiable craving for very young flesh; according to some writers of the time, to kill, cook and eat a baby which had not yet been baptized was a witch's greatest pleasure. But the flesh of infants was also full of supernatural power. As an element in magical concoctions it could be used to kill other human beings, or else to enable a captured witch to keep silent under torture. It could also be blended in a salve which, applied to a witch's body, enabled her to fly.

At regular intervals witches were required to betake themselves to the sacrilegious and orgiastic gatherings known first as "synagogues", later as "sabbats". There were ordinary sabbats, which were usually held on Fridays and were small affairs, involving only the witches of a given neighbourhood; and there were œcumenical sabbats, held with great ceremony three or four times a year, and attended by witches from all quarters. A sabbat was always a nocturnal happening, ending either at midnight or, at the very latest, at cockcrow. As for the locality, it might be a churchyard, a crossroads, the foot of a gallows; though the larger sabbats were commonly held at the summit of some famous mountain in a faraway region.

To attend the sabbat, and in particular to attend the œcumenical sabbat, witches had to cover great distances in very little time. They did so by flying. Having anointed themselves with the magic salve they would fly straight out of their bedrooms, borne aloft on demonic rams, goats, pigs, oxen, black horses; or else on sticks, shovels, spits, broomsticks. And meanwhile the husband or wife would sleep on peacefully, quite unaware of these strange happenings; sometimes a stick laid in the bed would take not only the place but also the appearance of the absent spouse. Thanks to this arrangement, some witches were able to deceive their mates for years on end.

The very numerous accounts of the sabbat differ from one another only in minor details, so it is easy to construct a representative picture. The sabbat was presided over by the Devil, who now took on the shape not of a mere man but of a monstrous being, half man and half goat: a hideous black man with enormous horns, a goat's beard and goat's legs, sometimes also with bird's claws instead of hands and feet. He sat on a high ebony throne; light streamed from his horns, flames spouted from his huge eyes. The expression of his face was one of immense gloom, his voice was harsh and terrible to hear.

The term "sabbat", like the term "synagogue", was of course taken from the Jewish religion, which was traditionally regarded as the quintessence of anti-Christianity, indeed as a form of Devil-worship. For the sabbat was above all an assertion of the Devil's mastery over his servants, the witches. First the witches knelt down and prayed to the Devil, calling him Lord and God, and repeating their renunciation of the Christian faith; after which each in turn kissed him, often on his left foot, his genitals or his anus. Next delinquent witches reported for punishment, which usually consisted of whippings. In Roman Catholic countries witches would confess their sins—for instance, attending church—and the Devil would impose whippings as a penance; but everywhere witches who had missed a sabbat, or who had performed insufficient *maleficia*, were soundly whipped. Then came the parody of divine service. Dressed in black vestments, with mitre and surplice, the Devil would preach a sermon, warning his followers against reverting to Christianity and promising them a far more blissful paradise than the Christian heaven. Seated again on his black chair, with the king and queen of the witches on either side of him, he would receive the offerings of the faithful—cakes and flour, poultry and corn, sometimes money.

The proceedings ended in a climax of profanity. Once more the witches adored the Devil and kissed his anus, while he acknowledged their attentions in a peculiarly noxious manner. A parody of the Eucharist was given, in both kinds—but what was received was an object like the sole of a shoe, black, bitter and hard to chew, and a jug full of nauseous black liquid. After this a meal would be served; and often this too would consist of revolting substances—fish and meat tasting like rotten wood, wine tasting like manure drainings, the flesh of babies. Finally, an orgiastic dance, to the sound of trumpets, drums and fifes. The witches would form a circle, facing outwards, and dance around a witch standing bent over, her head touching the ground, with a candle stuck in her anus to serve as illumination. The dance would become a frantic and erotic orgy, in which all things, including sodomy and incest, were permitted. At the height of the orgy the Devil would copulate with every man, woman and child present. Finally he would bring the sabbat to a close by sending the participants off to their homes, with instructions to perform every conceivable *maleficium* against their Christian neighbours.

That is how witches were imagined when and where witch-hunting was at its height. It will be observed that they were thought of as a collectivity: though they perform *maleficium* individually, they are a society, assembling at regular intervals, bound together by communal rites, subject to a rigid, centralized discipline. In every respect they represent a collective inversion of Christianity—and an inversion of a kind that could only be achieved by former Christians. That is why non-Christians, such as Jews and Gypsies, though they might be accused of *maleficium*, were never accused of being witches in the full sense of the term. Witchcraft was regarded as apostasy—and apostasy in its most extreme, most systematic, most highly organized form. Witches were regarded as above all a sect of Devil-worshippers.

*   *   *

How did this strange stereotype come into being? Ever since historical research into these matters began, in the second quarter of the nineteenth century, two principal explanations have been offered. Some scholars have argued that a sect of witches really existed, and that the authorities who pursued and tried witches were in effect breaking the local organizations of that sect. Others have argued that the notion of a sect of witches first developed as a by-product of the campaign of the Inquisition against Catharism, and that the stereotype was first used in a massive inquisitorial witch-hunt that claimed hundreds of victims in southern France during the fourteenth century.

When it was first propounded, the first of these two theories represented a radical innovation. In the eighteenth and early nineteenth centuries practically no educated person believed that there had ever been a sect of witches; it is only since around 1830 that this has gradually ceased to be taken for granted. Not, of course, that those scholars who have maintained that there really was a sect of witches have claimed that the sect did all those things it was originally believed to do. They have not argued that witches flew through the air to the sabbat, or that the Devil presided over it in corporeal form. But they have argued, and very forcibly, that witches were organized in groups under recognized leaders; that they adhered to a religious cult that was not only non-Christian but anti-Christian; and that they assembled, under cover of night, at remote spots, to perform the rituals of that cult. On this view, what we find in the witch-trials and the writings of witch-hunters represents a distorted perception of groups that really existed, of meetings that physically took place. Propounded by academics at leading universities in Europe and North America, often in works published by university presses, this interpretation has been taken on trust by multitudes of educated people. It still is: when conversation turns to the great witch-hunt, it is assumed more often than not that the hunt must have been directed against a real secret society. . . .

In his notes to *The Waste Land*, T. S. Eliot lists, as one of the works to which he was most indebted, *The Golden Bough* by Sir James Frazer—"a work of anthropology . . . which has influenced our generation profoundly". Unlike some of Eliot's other notes, this one was perfectly serious: first published in 1890, reissued with enlargements in twelve volumes between 1907 and 1915, *The Golden Bough* had indeed launched a cult of fertility cults. At least in the English-speaking world it became fashionable to interpret all kinds of rituals as derivatives of a magic originally performed to encourage the breeding of animals and the growth of plants, and to see in the most diverse gods and heroes so many disguises for the spirit of vegetation. It was to be expected that this kind of interpretation would be applied also to the history of European witchcraft; and so it was, in *The Witch-Cult in Western Europe*, by Margaret Murray. The year was 1921, and the influence of *The Golden Bough* was at its height. (*The Waste Land*, with Eliot's comment, appeared the following year.)

The impact of *The Witch-Cult in Western Europe* has been extraordinary. For some forty years (1929–68) the article on "Witchcraft" in successive editions of the *Encyclopædia Britannica* was by Margaret Murray and simply summarized the book's argument, as though it were a matter of established fact. By 1962 a scholar was moved to comment with dismay: "The Murrayites seem to hold . . . an almost undisputed sway at the higher intellectual levels. There is, amongst educated people, a very widespread impression that Professor Margaret Murray has discovered the true answer to the problem of the history of European witchcraft and has proved her theory." Since that was written the Murrayite cause has received formidable reinforcements. The Oxford University Press, the original publishers of the *Witch-Cult*, re-issued it in 1962 as a paperback, which has been frequently reprinted since and is still selling well. In a foreword to this new edition the eminent medievalist Sir Steven Runciman praises the thoroughness of the author's scholarship and makes it plain that he fully accepts her basic theory. Some leading historians of seventeenth-century England have shown themselves equally trusting. Even amongst scholars specializing in the history of witchcraft the book has exercised and—as we shall see—continues to exercise considerable influence. It has also inspired a whole library of new works, which have disseminated the doctrine amongst more or less serious readers. It is significant that in Britain even that respectable series, Pelican Books, having published an anti-Murrayite work on witchcraft by Professor Geoffrey Parrinder in 1958, replaced it in 1965 by the Murrayite work of the late Pennethorne Hughes. More dramatically, the *Witch-Cult* and its progeny have stimulated the extraordinary proliferation of "witches' covens" in Western Europe and the United States during the past decade, culminating in the foundation of the Witches International Craft Association, with headquarters in New York. In 1970 the association, under the leadership of Dr Leo Martello and his "high priestess" Witch Hazel, held "the world's first public Witch-In for Halloween" in Central Park. Even Margaret Murray, one imagines, would have been surprised by the development of the Witches' Liberation Movement, with its plans for a Witches' Day Parade, a Witches News Service, a Witches' Lecture Bureau and a Witches' Anti-Defamation League.

The argument presented in the *Witch-Cult* and elaborated in its successor *The God of the Witches* (1933) can be summarized as follows:

Down to the seventeenth century a religion which was far older than Christianity persisted throughout Western Europe, with followers in every social stratum from kings to peasants. It centred on the worship of a two-faced, horned god, known to the Romans as Dianus or Janus. This "Dianic cult" was a religion of the type so abundantly described in *The Golden Bough*. The horned god represented the cycle of the crops and the seasons, and was thought of as periodically dying and returning to life. In society he was represented by selected human beings. At national level these included such celebrated personages as William Rufus, Thomas à Becket, Joan of Arc and Gilles de Rais, whose dramatic deaths were really ritual sacrifices carried out to ensure the resurrection of the god and the renewal of the earth. At village level the god was represented by the horned personage who presided over the witches' assemblies. Hostile observers, such as inquisitors, naturally took this personage to be, or at least to represent, the Devil; so that to them witchcraft seemed a form of Satan-worship. In reality, the witches were simply worshipping the pre-Christian deity Dianus; and if they appeared to kiss their master's behind, that was because he wore a mask which, like the god himself, had two faces.

The preservation of the Dianic cult was largely the work of an aboriginal race, which had been driven into hiding by successive waves of invaders. These refugees were of small stature—which was the reality behind stories of "the little people", or fairies. Shy and elusive, they nevertheless had sufficient contact with the ordinary population to transmit the essentials of their religion. The witches were their disciples and intellectual heirs.

The organization of the Dianic cult was based on the local coven, which always consisted of thirteen members—twelve ordinary members, male and female, and one officer. The members of a coven were obliged to attend the weekly meetings, which Dr Murray calls "esbats", as well as the larger assemblies, or sabbats proper. Discipline was strict: failure to attend a meeting, or to carry out the instructions given there, was punished with such a beating that sometimes the culprit died. The resulting structure was remarkably tough: throughout the Middle Ages the Dianic cult was the dominant religion, Christianity little more than a veneer. It was only with the coming of the Reformation that Christianity achieved enough hold over the population to launch an open attack on its rival—the result being the great witch-hunt.

Margaret Murray was not by profession a historian but an Egyptologist, archaeologist and folklorist. Her knowledge of European history, even of English history, was superficial and her grasp of historical method was non-existent. In the special field of witchcraft studies, she seems never to have read any of the modern histories of the persecution; and even if she had, she would not have assimilated them. By the time she turned her attention to these matters she was nearly sixty, and her ideas were firmly set in an exaggerated and distorted version of the Frazerian mould. For the rest of her days (and she lived to 100) she clung to those ideas with a tenacity which no criticism, however well informed or well argued, could ever shake.

There has been no lack of such criticism. George Lincoln Burr, Cecil L'Estrange Ewen, Professor Rossell Hope Robbins, Mr Elliot Rose, Professor Hugh Trevor-Roper, Mr Keith Thomas are amongst those who, from the 1920s to the 1970s, have either weighed the theory and found it wanting, or else have dismissed it as unworthy of consideration. But other scholars have taken a different view and have maintained that beneath its manifest exaggerations, the theory contains a core of truth. The reason is given by Arno Runeberg in his book *Witches, demons and fertility magic* (1947). He points out that some of the accounts of witches' assemblies quoted by Murray have no fantastic features but are perfectly plausible. The witches go to and from the sabbat not by flying but on foot or on horseback; the "Devil" has nothing supernatural about him but sits at the head of the table like an ordinary man; the meal is quite unremarkable; the participants even specify who supplied the food and drink. . . . According to this view these commonplace happenings, themselves perhaps neither very frequent nor very widespread, represent the reality around which fantasies clustered, gradually building up the whole phantasmagoria of the witches' sabbat as we find it in other and better known accounts. It would be a powerful argument if the accounts quoted by Murray were really as sober as they appear to be—but are they? The only way to find out is to examine her sources in their original contexts—a tiresome task, but one which is long overdue.

The relevant passages in the *Witch-Cult* carry references to some fifteen primary sources, mostly English or Scottish pamphlets describing notorious trials. Now, of all these sources only one is free from manifestly fantastic and impossible features—and even in that one the Devil, though "a bonny young lad with a blue bonnet", has the conventional requirements of a cold body and cold semen, and gladly mates with a witch aged eighty. To appreciate the true import of the other sources one has only to compare, in half a dozen instances, what Murray quotes with what she passes over in silence. . . .

The Somerset trials of 1664 are regarded by Murray as particularly illuminating. She quotes from the evidence of Elizabeth Styles:

"At their meeting they have usually wine and good beer, cakes, meat or the like. They eat and drink really when they meet in their bodies, dance also and have music. The man in black sits at the higher end, and Anne Bishop usually next him. He uses some words before meat, and none after, his voice is audible, and very low."

She does not quote the sentence immediately preceding: "At every meeting the Spirit vanishes away, he appoints the next meeting place and time, and at his departure there is a foul smell." Nor is there any mention of certain other details supplied by the same witness. For Elizabeth Styles said that, while the Devil sometimes appeared to her as a man, he usually did so in the form of a dog, a cat or a fly; he was apt to suck at the back of her head. He also provided his followers with oil with which to anoint their foreheads and wrists—which enabled them to be carried in a moment to and from the meetings. On the other hand, Elizabeth added that sometimes the meetings were attended by the witches' spirits only, their bodies remaining at home. . . .

Similar use is made of Isobel Gowdie's confession (or rather confessions, for under increasing pressure she made four) at Auldearn, in Nairn, in 1662:

We would go to several houses in the night time. We were at Candlemas last in Grangehill, where we got meat and drink enough. The Devil sat at the head of the table, and all the Coven about. That night he desired Alexander Elder in Earlseat to say the grace before meat, which he did; and is this: "We eat this meat in the Devil's name" (etc.) And then we began to eat. And when we had ended eating, we looked steadfastly to the Devil, and bowing ourselves to him, we said to the Devil, We thank thee, our Lord, for this.—We killed an ox, in Burgie, about the dawning of the day, and we brought the ox with us home to Aulderne, and feasted on it.

The simple dash between the two stories conceals much, including the following items:

All the coven did fly like cats, jackdaws, hares and rooks, etc., but Barbara Ronald, in Brightmanney, and I always rode on a horse, which we would make of a straw or a bean-stalk. Bessie Wilson was always in the likeness of a rook. . . . (The Devil) would be like a heifer, a bull, a deer, a roe, or a dog, etc., and have dealings with us; and he would hold up his tail while we kissed his arse.

Isobel Gowdie had much more to say. When she and her associates went to the sabbat they would place in the bed, beside their husbands, a broom or a three-legged stool, which promptly took on the appearance of a woman. At the sabbat they made a plough of a ram's horn and yoked frogs to it, using grass for the traces. As the plough went round the fields, driven by the Devil with the help of the male officer of the coven, the women followed it, praying to the Devil that the soil might yield only thistles and briars.

Murray cites Isobel Gowdie as an example of a witch who rode to and from meetings on horseback; the proof being Isobel's own words, "I had a little horse, and would say, 'Horse and Hattock, in the Devil's name!' " This, however, is the very phrase that fairies were believed to use as they flew from place to place; and the rest of Isobel's account shows that, in a desperate effort to find enough material to satisfy her interrogators and torturers, she did indeed draw on the local fairy lore:

I had a little horse, and would say, "Horse and Hattock, in the Devil's name!" And then we would fly away, where we would, even as straws fly upon a highway. We would fly like straws when we please; wild-straws and corn-straws will be horses to us, if we put them between our feet and say, "Horse and Hattock, in the Devil's name!" If anyone sees these straws in a whirlwind, and do not bless themselves, we may shoot them dead at our pleasure. Any that are shot by us, their souls will go to Heaven, but their bodies remain with us, and will fly as our horses, as small as straws. I was in the Downie-hills, and got meat from the Queen of Fairie, more than I could eat. The Queen of Fairie is bravely clothed in white linen.

At this point Isobel's interrogators cut her short: she was straying too far from the demonological material they required. After a further three weeks in gaol she produced a version in which the fairies were duly integrated into the Devil's kingdom. The Devil himself, she asserted, shaped "elf-arrow-heads" and handed them over to small hunch-backed elves, who sharpened them and in turn passed them to the witches for shooting. As the witches had no bows, they flicked the arrows from their thumb-nails as they sailed overhead on their straws and bean-stalks; and the arrows killed those they hit, even through a coat of armour. This is the passage that led Murray to her theory about the fugitive aboriginal race; others will interpret it in a different sense. Certainly we are a long, long way from those commonplace feastings at Grangehill and Auldearn. . . .

Murray is of course aware of these fantastic features—but she nevertheless contrives, by the way she arranges her quotations, to give the impression that a number of perfectly sober, realistic accounts of the sabbat exist. They do not; and the implications of that fact are, or should be, self-evident. Stories which have manifestly impossible features are not to be trusted in any particular, as evidence of what physically happened. Since the stories of witches' sabbats adduced by Murray abound in such features, they are to be strongly distrusted. As soon as the methods of historical criticism are applied to her argument that women really met to worship a fertility god, under the supervision of the god's human representatives, it is seen to be just as fanciful as the argument which Michelet had propounded, with far greater poetic power, some sixty years earlier.

If Arno Runeberg had troubled to trace Murray's quotations back to their origins, he would perhaps never have produced *Witches, demons and fertility magic* at all. But once published—by the Finnish Academy of Sciences in 1947—the book lent new credibility to Murray's central thesis. For it [Runeberg's book] is by no means an unsophisticated work. It contains a mass of valuable information about European folk-beliefs, much of it directly relevant to the age-old popular image of the witch. It has no use at all for such fancies as the aboriginal race of dwarfs, or even for the Dianic cult in the sense of a homogeneous religion. Precisely because it avoids such eccentricities it has persuaded some serious historians, right down to the present day, that the witchcraft we hear of at the close of the Middle Ages was indeed derived from a fertility cult.

Runeberg starts from pre-historic times. In a world still dominated by the wilderness, primitive hunters and farmers developed a form of magic which was intended to influence the spirits of forests and rivers and mountains. Popular fertility rites, such as have survived in many peasant communities almost to the present day, are derived from that magic. But apart from these rites, which were celebrated publicly, with the whole village participating, there existed a secret art, known only to specialists, i.e. to professional magicians. These magicians were men and women who had learned how to penetrate into the world of nature-spirits, how to become like those spirits, how to influence them and to partake of their powers. In the primitive worldview, nature-spirits and magicians alike "bestow fertility, wealth and strength on whomever they wish, at the same time that they smite their enemies with sickness and death". The notion of the maleficent magician, or witch, arose from that of the "magical transfer": witches used magic to procure fertility and abundance in their own crops and herds, which implied inflicting a corresponding deprivation on one's neighbours.

The magicians formed associations, which met secretly, at night, to perform communal rites; and by the close of the Middle Ages these associations were being severely persecuted by the Church, for practising a pagan cult. The Cathars were also being persecuted; and it was only natural that the two harassed and outlawed breeds should form an alliance, should indeed amalgamate. Effected in the first instance in the inaccessible valleys of southern France and of the Alps, this alliance or amalgamation gave rise to a new heretical sect, which spread gradually over vast areas of western Europe. This is the sect that we meet in the protocols of the witch-trials and the books of the witch-hunting magistrates. For Cathars and magicians alike, under the pressure of persecution, turned to Devil-worship. Traditional magic was transformed: "The participants in the 'sabbath' were no longer made up of primitive people who tried to influence fertility for their own benefit and according to their own conception of nature, but of sensation-mad, degenerated individuals who actually were convinced that they worshipped Satan himself. The incarnated deity of the witches was enacted by adventures and rogues. . . ."

Runeberg points out, too, that the witches' Devil has some very unexpected features: he is often called by a name which is far more appropriate to a wood spirit than to the Devil of Christian demonology. Moreover at the end of the sabbat the Devil sometimes burns himself up—and this also happens to various puppets representing the corn-spirit or the wood-spirit. All this leads Runeberg to the truly Frazerian conclusion: popular fertility rites and the secret fertility rites of the witches have one and the same object—to kill the "old" spirit of nature and then to resurrect the same spirit in a new, youthful guise. Through all the deformations resulting from contact with Catharism and from the pressures of ecclesiastical persecution, this original sub-structure can still be discerned.

On the face of it, a plausible argument. Nevertheless, it does not prove the existence of an organized body of witches. There is simply no evidence that there ever was a secret society of magicians, devoted to fostering or exploiting the fertility of crops or herds; no theological treatise or confessor's guide even hints at such a thing. In his efforts to trace such a society Runeberg turns not to the Middle Ages, when he claims it existed, but to the sixteenth and seventeenth centuries; and not to primary sources but to Margaret Murray. In the end the only evidence he can produce turns out to consist of those very same accounts of witches' sabbats that we have just shown to be spurious. And the parallels between fertility rites and sabbats can all be explained without assuming that sabbats ever took place. A full century before Runeberg, Jacob Grimm established that certain folk beliefs, including beliefs about fertility, entered into the picture of the sabbat; but that proves nothing about the reality of the sabbat. Moreover, some of the features listed by Runeberg have a far more obvious explanation. It is not really surprising that when the Lord of Hell has to vanish, he should do so in flames. And if the times of the year when the large sabbats were supposed to be held were the times for fertility rites, they also coincide with major feasts and saints' days in the calendar of the Church. As witchcraft was imagined as a blasphemous parody of Christianity, it was only to be expected that witches would foregather at times which Christians regarded as particularly sacred. On the other hand, most forms of *maleficium* cannot possibly be explained as Runeberg tries to explain them, in terms of "magical transfer". Witches were supposed to harm their neighbours for the sake of revenge, or out of pure malice, or on the Devil's orders, and only occasionally and incidentally for the purpose of augmenting their own stocks of food. . . .

My grounds for not accepting even in part the tales of witches' sabbats, as they were retailed from the fifteenth century onwards, have been made abundantly clear. . . . In my view, stories which contain manifestly impossible elements ought not to be accepted as evidence for physical events.

There is a further reason why the notion of a secret society of witches cannot be satisfactorily explained by postulating the real existence of such a society. . . . Present-day anthropologists have found very similar notions firmly embedded in the world-views of "primitive" societies in various parts of the world. Bands of destructive witches who kill human beings, especially children; who travel at night by supernatural means; and who foregather in remote spots to devour their victims— these crop up again and again in anthropological literature. But anthropologists are agreed that these bands exist in imagination only; nobody has ever come across a real society of witches. And that indeed is the nub: . . . the tradition we have been considering has suffered from the same defect, of grossly underestimating the capacities of human imagination.

Taken as a whole, that tradition itself forms a curious chapter in the history of ideas. Over a period of a century and a half, the non-existent society of witches has been repeatedly re-interpreted in the light of the intellectual preoccupations of the moment. The theories of Jarcke and Mone were clearly inspired by the current dread of secret societies; that of Michelet, by his enthusiasm for the emancipation of the working classes and of women; those of Murray and Runeberg, by the Frazerian belief that religion originally consisted of fertility cults; those of Rose and Russell, maybe, by the spectacle of the psychedelic and orgiastic experiments of the 1960s.

The Relevance of Social Anthropology to the Historical Study of English Witchcraft

Keith Thomas

The historian Keith Thomas has been most interested in folk beliefs current in sixteenth-and seventeenth-century England and especially the parallels with African witchcraft. In this excerpt from a 1970 essay, Thomas draws on anthropological theory to look for the "practical utility" of witchcraft beliefs.

•

Definitions

The term "witchcraft" was used loosely in Tudor and Stuart England, and was at one time or another applied to virtually every kind of magical activity or ritual operation that worked by occult methods. Village diviners who foretold the future or who tracked down lost property were often called "witches"; so were the "wise women" who healed the sick by charms or prayers. Contemporary scientists whose operations baffled the ignorant were sometimes suspected of witchcraft, while the label was readily attached by Protestant polemicists to the ritual operations of the Catholic Church. Theologians invariably distrusted any claims to supernatural activity which their own religion did not authorize; a conjuror who invoked spirits to gain occult knowledge was a "witch" so far as they were concerned, however innocent his own intentions.

The historian has, therefore, to impose his own classification upon the bewildering variety of semantic usage presented by the literature of the period. . . . I propose to restrict the term "witchcraft" to mean the employment (or presumed employment) of some supernatural means of doing harm to other people in a way that was generally disapproved of by the mass of society. (A Protestant who prayed successfully that God might blast the Catholic enemies of the English Church would not be a witch in

From Keith Thomas, "The Relevance of Social Anthropology to the Historical Study of English Witchcraft," in *Witchcraft Confessions and Accusations*, ed. Mary Douglas (London: Tavistock, 1970), 48–50, 54–68. © 1970 by the Association of Social Anthropologists of the Commonwealth. Reprinted by permission of Taylor and Francis Books Ltd.

the eyes of most of his fellow-citizens. But a Catholic who did the same in reverse might conceivably be so regarded.) A witch was thus a person of either sex (but in belief and practice more often female) who could mysteriously injure or kill other people. She could also molest farm animals and frustrate such domestic operations as making butter, cheese, and beer. In England her acts of damage—*maleficium*, as it was technically called—usually came under one of these heads. It was very rare for her to be accused of interfering with the weather or of frustrating sexual relations between man and wife, as was said to happen on the European Continent.

Many contemporary theologians, however, would not have agreed that the essence of witchcraft lay in the damage it did to other persons. For them witchcraft was not malevolent magic as such, but a heretical belief—Devil-worship. The witch owed any power she might possess to the pact she had made with Satan; and her primary offence was not injuring other people, but heresy. Indeed, whether or not she injured others, she deserved to die for her disloyalty to God. The lawyer, Sir Edward Coke, accordingly defined a witch as "a person that hath conference with the Devil, to consult with him or to do some act". Around this notion was built up the extensive concept of ritual Devil-worship, involving the nocturnal sabbath at which the witches gathered to do homage to their master and to copulate with him.

From the sociological point of view, the problem presented by the concept of ritual Devil-worship is not the same as that raised by the popular belief in the existence of persons capable of doing harm by occult means. Much recent historical writing has concentrated exclusively on the origins of the idea of Devil-worship and attempted to establish the circumstances which led to its fabrication by the medieval Church and its adoption by many contemporary clergy and intellectuals. Most of the relevant material was collected by Lea and dazzlingly summarized by Trevor-Roper. But I intend to ignore this concept of witchcraft here because I think it was never as important in England as it is said to have been on the Continent. This is not to deny that many educated Englishmen imbibed the notion during the sixteenth and seventeenth centuries, or that it was reflected in many contemporary treatises and in the actual working of the criminal law: when an accusation of *maleficium* reached the courts it could easily turn into one of Devil-worship, if it happened to fall into the hands of interested lawyers or clergy. But, so far as the beliefs of the uneducated populace and the mass of actual witch accusations are concerned, there is every reason to think that the idea of Devil-worship was essentially peripheral. Contemporary intellectuals may have assimilated the idea, but it made much less impact at the village level, where most of these accusations originated. Even the Acts of Parliament which made witchcraft a statutory offence reflected the popular emphasis on damage (*maleficium*) rather than Devil-worship. There were three Acts—1542 (repealed 1547), 1563 (repealed 1604), and 1604 (repealed 1736). Neither of the first two contained any reference to the diabolical compact, although the second forbade the invocation of evil spirits for any purpose. The 1604 Act made it a capital offence to covenant with, or to entertain, evil spirits, but it still displayed the earlier preoccupation with *maleficium* by making it a felony to kill anyone by witchcraft, while imposing a lesser penalty for less serious types of injury.

Most of the actual prosecutions under these Acts, moreover, related to alleged acts of damage and seldom involved allegations of Devil-worship. Thus, of the approximately 200 persons who are known to have been convicted under the Acts on the Home Circuit (Essex, Hertfordshire, Kent, Surrey, Sussex) between 1558 and 1736, there were (if we except the highly untypical prosecutions initiated in 1645 by the witch-finder Matthew Hopkins) only seven, or possibly eight, who were not found guilty of having inflicted mysterious acts of damage upon their neighbours or their goods. Even half of those convicted, under Hopkins's influence, of keeping evil spirits were also found guilty of killing other people or their animals. For most men, therefore, "witchcraft" remained essentially the power to do supernatural harm to others. As one contemporary observed, "In common account none are reputed to be witches, but only such who are thought to have both will and skill to hurt man and beast." English witch beliefs are thus more suitable for comparison with African ones than is sometimes appreciated. The essential preoccupation with *maleficium* makes the differences arising from the English religious tradition less important. . . .

The Explanatory Role of Witch Beliefs

After several generations of anthropological writing it is hardly necessary to stress that English witch beliefs, like those elsewhere, helped to account for the misfortunes of daily life. The sudden death of a child, the loss of a cow, the failure of some routine operation to achieve its result—such unexpected disasters could all, in default of any more obvious explanation, be attributed to the influence of some malevolent neighbour. Particularly in the field of medicine, where professional advice was scarce, expensive, and largely worthless, there was a standing disposition to attribute to witchcraft many diseases which would cause us no intellectual problem today. Indeed, Justices of the Peace were instructed in a contemporary handbook that the first likely sign of witchcraft was "when a healthful body shall be suddenly taken . . . without probable reason or natural cause appearing".

Any otherwise inexplicable event was therefore susceptible of explanation in such terms. Charges of diabolical aid were freely thrown around by politicians baffled by the success of their rivals, whether Cardinal Wolsey, who (like Anne Boleyn) was believed to have bewitched Henry VIII, or Oliver Cromwell, who was well known to have made a contract with the Devil on the eve of the Battle of Worcester. This "face-saving function" of witchcraft, as it has been called, was not, I think, typical of the average accusation. Witch beliefs were occasionally invoked to account for a commercial rival's success or to explain some particularly blatant example of that social mobility to which Tudor Englishmen could never adjust themselves. But witchcraft beliefs did not usually have an egalitarian function or provide a check upon individual effort in the way they have been known to do elsewhere. "Face-saving" allegations of this kind were rare in England; and disingenuous charges made by those seeking to excuse their own incompetence or to discredit some enemy were essentially parasitic to the main corpus of witch accusations. Even so, many accusations emanated from servants or children seeking to excuse their own negligence, sometimes by deliberate lying, sometimes by an unconscious desire to exculpate themselves. The Elizabethan Vicar of Brenchley, Kent, who kept losing his voice when conducting the service in Church, chose to blame this upon the sorceries of one of his parishioners, but the wiser members of the congregation were unconvinced, for they knew he had the French pox.

It is thus important to recognize that many accusations were dishonest. It must also be remembered that there were many different levels of belief and intellectual sophistication coexisting in England at this period. This means that generalizations of the kind made by anthropologists about small homogeneous societies are extremely difficult to handle when applied to fit a country of five million inhabitants, with a developing economy, and an intellectual life capable of throwing up giants of the stature of Shakespeare, Wren, or Newton. Scepticism about the existence of witchcraft is, I understand, not unknown in African societies, but it is clearly marginal or unimportant in most of the work of most leading anthropological studies. The meaning and function of witchcraft are bound to be different in a society like seventeenth-century England, where scepticism of varying degrees was widespread. They are also different when a printed literature in several different languages brings accounts of witchcraft in other societies to the knowledge of the better-educated inhabitants. Continental accounts of witch trials influenced English thought in this period, just as today the Bible and Shakespeare help to sustain the belief in spirits among modern Africans. Social anthropologists are primarily concerned to study witchcraft in relationship to social structure, but the student of English witchcraft has also to consider the impact of a great number of different cultural traditions at a variety of different levels, social, intellectual, and regional.

A further difference between England and Africa is that Tudor Englishmen did not find it necessary to explain all misfortunes in terms of some supernatural belief, whether witchcraft or anything else. There seem to be many primitive societies where virtually all deaths are attributed to witchcraft or to ancestral spirits or to some similar phenomenon. In England, by contrast, it seems that the possibility of "accident" and "misadventure" was fully recognized, as was that of death by purely natural causes. It is true that academic theologians resolutely denied the existence of chance and insisted that all otherwise unexplained natural events were the direct work of divine Providence, but the role which this idea played in the lives of the population at large is problematical.

Nevertheless, witchcraft in England, as elsewhere, had to compete with other supernatural explanations of misfortune. Explanations in terms of unlucky days, unlucky stars, or the neglect of some elementary ritual precaution were also prevalent. So was the disposition to attribute disasters of certain kinds to the activities of secret enemies of society, notably the Papists. But most important was the theological idea that the disaster had been caused by God, either to punish sin or to try the believer, or for some other unknown but undoubtedly just purpose. This theological explanation of misfortune was not, however, strictly speaking, an alternative to an explanation in terms of witchcraft, but an additional gloss upon it. Theologians upheld the reality of the Devil and the existence of witches. They usually agreed that

God might try or punish his servants through the activities of witches no less than by any other means.

Why was it, therefore, that a man sometimes turned to the occult malevolence of his neighbour rather than to some other supernatural or natural explanation of his misfortune? The answer to this question obviously depends in part upon the education and intellectual equipment of the individual concerned. But it also depends, as the anthropologists have shown, upon the social context in which the suspicion originated.

One prior attraction of witch beliefs, however, is obvious. A man who decided that God was responsible for his illness could do little about it. He could pray that it might be cured, but with no very certain prospect of success, for God's ways were mysterious, and, though he could be supplicated, he could not be coerced. Protestant theologians taught that Christians should suffer stoically like Job, but this doctrine was not a comfortable one. The attraction of witch beliefs, by contrast, was that they held out precisely that certainty of redress which the theologians denied. A man who feared that a witch might attack him could invoke a number of magical preservatives in order to ensure his self-protection. If the witch had already struck, it was still open for him to practise counter-magic against his supposed persecutor. By burning a piece of thatch off the witch's roof, or by burying a bottle of urine, he could force the witch to come hurrying to the scene of her crime. Once she appeared, the victim could put an end to his illness by scratching her and drawing blood; this was "the most infallible cure", said the witnesses in a Leicester witch trial in 1717. Best of all, the victim could have the witch prosecuted and executed. For the point of such witch trials was not merely that they afforded the gratification of revenge, but that, according to contemporary belief, they positively relieved the victim. "The malefice", wrote one authority, "is prevented or cured in the execution of the witch." Or, as James I put it, the destruction of the witch was "a salutary sacrifice for the patient."

Witch beliefs thus seemed preferable to a theological explanation of misfortune; for although the divines recognized the possibility of *maleficium* they strenuously denied that the Christian could lawfully employ counter-magic to rid himself of it; even scratching the witch was a diabolical action, as they saw it. Before the Reformation the Catholic Church had provided an elaborate repertoire of ritual precautions designed to ward off evil spirits and malevolent magic. This, I think, is why so few cases of misfortune in England are known to have been blamed upon witches before the mid-sixteenth century, even though legal machinery, both ecclesiastical and secular, undoubtedly existed for their prosecution. A man who fell victim to witchcraft did not need to take his case to the courts since there was a variety of alternative procedures available. Indeed, a good Christian who used holy water, the sign of the cross, and the aid of the priest ought not to be so afflicted at all. After the Reformation, by contrast, Protestant preachers strenuously denied that such aids could have any effect. They reaffirmed the power of evil, but left believers disarmed before the old enemy. The only way out in these circumstances was recourse to counter-magic (and this had to be clandestine) or, better still, to the now approved method of legal prosecution. Hence the multiplication of witch trials during the following century. On the Continent, by contrast, theologians seem to have lost faith in the curative power of religious symbols long before the Reformation; and trials were accordingly initiated much earlier.

In England most trials can be shown to have originated at a local level and to have reflected local animosities rather than to have been initiated from above. The only parallel to the African witch-finding campaigns of modern times was the crusade conducted by Matthew Hopkins in the Eastern Counties between 1645 and 1647. This drive unearthed several hundred witches and led to many executions. It may have had its millenarian aspects, but the evidence suggests that Hopkins merely exploited local tensions in such a way as to bring accusations into the courts at an unprecedented rate. . . .

The Identification of the Witch

So far, the English evidence has confirmed the anthropological truism that the most satisfactory interpretation of misfortune is that which allows effective action to be taken against it. But why were witch beliefs invoked at one moment rather than another, and what were the circumstances that brought them into play? The answer to these questions can be discovered only by studying the relationships between the witch, her victim, and her accuser. This is an approach which has been successfully pioneered by the social anthropologists, and it is worth applying to the English data.

The first feature that emerges from a scrutiny of surviving witchcraft accusations is an obvious one, but is nevertheless important. This is that it was excessively rare for men to decide that they had been the victims of witchcraft without also having a particular suspect in mind. Once they had diagnosed witchcraft as the cause of their sufferings, it seldom took them long to identify the probable source. Usually they knew at once who it must have been. Sometimes they even had the suspect in mind before the witchcraft had been committed. "I have a suspicion in thee," said Mary Dingley to Margery Singleton in 1573, "and if any in my house should miscarry thou shalt answer for it."

This feature is admittedly difficult to establish in all cases, since the first extant evidence is usually the formal indictment, in which the offence and the accused are named simultaneously, and it is impossible to reconstruct the thought-processes which had previously gone on in the victim's mind. But even these bald statements show us that the accused did not operate from a distance against strangers, but lived in the same neighbourhood, usually the same village, and was already in some sort of social relationship with her victim before she had begun to practise her malice.

The depositions show that the witch's dentity was established in one of various standard ways. The victim might recall the person with whom he had quarrelled before the misfortune had occurred, sometimes denouncing him on his death-bed. Alternatively, he might have nocturnal visions of the witch, or cry out in his fits against her. Very often he would invoke the assistance of a diviner—a "white witch", "cunning man", or "wise woman", as such people were called. The client would go to the wizard, describe his symptoms, and invite a diagnosis. The action he subsequently took might be considerably determined by the advice he received.

This is the point at which the historian can only envy the anthropologist's ability to be present at some of these critical moments. But the surviving accounts of the process of Tudor and Stuart divination can be suggestively interpreted in the light of what has been found out about the cunning man's modern African counterparts. We know that most forms of divination are capable of manipulation, that diviners are sensitive to the reactions of their audience, that they often proceed on a trial-and-error basis, and that in many cases they merely confirm the suspicions in the client's own mind by serving them back to him as the supposed product of their magical skill. The English evidence suggests that diviners sometimes created suspicions which would not otherwise have arisen; they may have been less statesmanlike than those of their African counterparts who act as a brake on public opinion. It was in their interest to diagnose witchcraft, after all, because they had a near-monopoly of the techniques necessary for dealing with it. In England, as among the Azande, the belief in malevolent witches could not have existed without the parallel existence of witch-doctors ready to confirm their presence.

But my overall impression, and it can, alas, never be more than an impression, is that usually the client suspected witchcraft before he ever went to the diviner, and that it was he who did the actual identification, by recognizing a face in a mirror or polished stone, or by supplying a list of suspects to be narrowed down by divination. As a contemporary summarized the procedure:

> "A man is taken lame; he suspecteth that he is bewitched; he sendeth to the cunning man; (who) demandeth whom they suspect, and then sheweth the image of the party in a glass."

. . . In another case a worried mother consulted a wizard as to who was the cause of her child's illness. Back came the answer, via a servant: "Your mistress knows as well who hath wronged her child as I." In these and many similar cases, we can see how it was the function of the cunning man to make the victim face up to the suspicions he had already formed, to strengthen them by the addition of a magical *imprimatur*, and thus to create the circumstances necessary for converting a mere suspicion into a positive accusation. Yet the diviner's role has been virtually ignored in most historical writing about witchcraft, and without some acquaintance with anthropological studies of African divination I doubt whether I should ever have thought about it.

So far, I have suggested that the witch was always a person known to her accuser. A further fact emerges from the depositions and pamphlet accounts and that is that she was almost always believed to bear a grudge against him. This may be obvious, but it does at least rule out the possibility of motiveless malignity. Contemporaries were horrified by the witch's activities, but they seldom denied that she had some genuine reason for wishing ill upon her victim. Here the English situation is neater than that in some African societies, where witches are sometimes believed to be largely capricious in their motivation.

The crucial question, therefore, is that of the prior animosity believed to exist between the English witch and her victim. Did it usually conform to a pattern or was every type of grudge liable to be involved? The answer can be extracted only from those cases where the depositions or pamphlet accounts are sufficiently detailed, and is therefore difficult to represent statistically. But one fact seems to be clear. The charge of witchcraft was normally levelled, not just when the accuser felt that the witch bore a grudge against the victim (or his family), but when he felt that the grudge was a *justifiable* one. The witch, in other words, was not merely being vindictive. She was thought to be avenging a definite injury. . . .

The most common situation of all was when the victim (or his parents) had turned away empty-handed an old neighbour who had come to the door to beg or borrow some food or drink, or the loan of some household utensil. The overwhelming majority of English witch cases fell into this simple pattern. The witch was sent away, perhaps mumbling a malediction, and in due course something went wrong with the household or one of its members, for which she was immediately held responsible. The requests made by the witch varied, but they were usually for food or drink— butter, cheese, yeast, milk, or beer. Sometimes she asked for money or a piece of equipment. In all cases denial was followed by retribution, and the punishment often fitted the crime. Thus at Castle Cary around 1530, Isabel Turner denied Christian Shirston a quart of ale, whereupon "a stand of ale of twelve gallons began to boil as fast as a crock on the fire". Joan Vicars would give her no milk, and thereafter her cow yielded nothing but blood and water. Henry Russe also refused her milk, only to find himself unable to make cheese until Michaelmas.

These depressing peregrinations from door to door were the background to most witchcraft accusations. They are not to be confused with simple begging. Rather, they illustrate the breakdown of the tradition of mutual help upon which many Protestants English village communities were based. The loan of equipment or the giving of food and drink were normal neighbourly activities. What was notable in these cases was that they should have been refused. The fact that Christian Shirston was accused of witchcraft by the very people who had failed to fulfil their accepted social obligations to her illustrates the essential conflict between neighbourliness and individualism which generated the tensions from which the accusations of witchcraft were most likely to arise. When shutting the door in Christian Shirston's face, her neighbours were only too well aware of having departed from the accepted ethical code. They knew they had put their selfish interests before their social duty. When some minor accident overtook them or their children it was their guilty conscience that told them where to look to find the source of their misfortunes.

Two essential features thus made up the background to most of the allegations of witchcraft levied in sixteenth-and seventeenth-century England. The first was the occurrence of a personal misfortune for which no natural explanation was forthcom- ing. The second was an awareness on the victim's part of having given offence to a neighbour, usually by having failed to discharge some customary social obligation. As often as not the link between the misfortune incurred and the obligation neglected was furnished by the frank expression of malignity on the part of the suspected witch. Old women (most accused witches were women, and it is likely, but unprovable, that they tended to be elderly) did not like being turned away from the door, and made no bones about their malevolence. The court books of the Anglican Church abound in reports of men and women who prayed or cursed in a highly ritual way that God would shorten the lives of their enemies, burn their homes, kill their children, destroy their goods, and blast them and their descendants.

But in many cases it was not necessary for the suspected witch to have given evidence of her malevolence. The victim's guilty conscience was sufficient to provoke an accusation, since, when a misfortune occurred, his first reaction, like that of most primitives, was to ask what he had done to deserve it. When, in 1589, a Southampton tanner's pigs expired, after having "danced and leaped in a most strange sort, as if they had been bewitched", he recalled how on the previous day Widow Wells had come to his door on two occasions, "there sitting (and) asking nothing; at length, having not anything given unto her [we may underline his assumption that something should have been], she departed". On the basis of the next day's occurrences, he warned her that "if he took any hurt by her afterwards he would have her burned for a witch". Yet there is no evidence of any expressed malevolence on her part at all.

The Witch's Point of View

A few words ought to be said about the position of the accused witch. We have seen that she was usually a relatively dependent member of society and this explains, I think, why witches were so often women and especially widows, whose means of subsistence were often inadequate without neighbourly support. The position of such people had been weakened by the decline of customary manorial arrangements for the support of the elderly; and it is this, rather than any sexual tensions, that accounts for the frequency with which old women were cast by society for the role of witch. Many were dependent upon their neighbours, while lacking the institutional recognition afforded to those in receipt of poor relief. It was the ambiguity in their situation that was their downfall.

Something about the feelings of these unfortunates can be inferred from the confessions extracted at the trials, and from their other *obiter dicta*. The veracity of such confessions has been the subject of much historical controversy, and anthropologists have often found them equally embarrassing, choosing to put them down to "malnutrition", or "depression", just as seventeenth-century intellectuals attributed them to "melancholy". But some anthropological insight on this subject is extremely illuminating; for example, Dr Douglas's observation that, among the Lele, suspects sometimes welcome the chance to submit themselves voluntarily to tests for witchcraft in order to clear their name in the community. This makes good sense when applied to the unsolicited examinees who came forward during the Hopkins crusade.

Confessions of relations with the Devil are more difficult to interpret, and I doubt if social anthropologists can help the historian much here. But in principle there seems no reason why alienated individuals, filled with genuine malice for their neigh-bours, may not have personified their evil desires in this way. Contemporary religious teaching portrayed the Devil as the symbol of everything evil and antisocial; indeed, it was common for Devil-worship to be one of the temptations experienced by those undergoing the depressive state that usually preceded a Puritan religious conversion. If many felt the temptation, there is no reason to doubt that some may have suc-cumbed.

It is also certain that malevolent magic was often practised, just like sorcery in Africa—extant magical formulae and the observation of witnesses both confirm this. But witches' sabbaths were almost certainly non-existent, and their alleged devotees present problems similar to those raised by the African "night-witches", of whose existence anthropologists remain in doubt, even after long residence in a community. The most important point about the witch's resort to curses, black magic, or even Devil-worship, seems to be that it sprang from frustration. She was too weak to avenge herself against the community by physical force; and she could not take her persecutors to law. Magic was a substitute for impotence. The only alternative was arson, and this secret and indiscriminate means of wreaking vengeance on a com-munity was occasionally practised, and even more often threatened, by persons in positions similar to those of accused witches. I do not wish to suggest that all those accused of witchcraft had malicious thoughts about their neighbours. But some certainly did, though we shall never know what proportion. This was why some of the most powerful intellects of the day believed in punishing witches, though totally sceptical about their powers. Thomas Hobbes wrote:

> "As for witches, I think not that their witchcraft is any real power; but yet that they are justly punished, for the false belief they have that they can do such mischief, joined with their purpose to do it if they can."

To have a reputation for witchcraft, indeed, could be an old woman's last form of defence. "These miserable wretches are so odious unto all their neighbours," wrote Reginald Scot, "and so feared, as few dare offend them, or deny them any thing they ask." The belief in witchcraft helped to ensure that neighbourly obligations were not neglected, and that an old woman's requests were not automatically denied. As the Chartist, William Lovett, recalled from his Cornish childhood, a reputed witch was treated with respect: "Anything that Aunt Tammy took a fancy to, few who feared her dared to refuse."

The Function of Witch Beliefs

The essentially village context of witchcraft accusations determined their main char-acter in England. They were seldom made between members of the same family or between close relations. The preoccupation with different types of kinship system, which has dominated so much anthropological writing about witch beliefs, is thus largely irrelevant in the English context; though no doubt the absence of many witchcraft accusations within the English family is itself a subject calling for comment. It may be that, as in African towns today, the family was more tightly integrated, so that members who suffered misfortune would look outside for the source of mystical evil-doing. But other signs of hostility within the family, like homicide and violence, were not unknown, so the explanation may be more complicated than this.

Most English witch accusations can, therefore, be understood only within the structure of the English village community, and here there is much historical research waiting to be done. At first glance, however, it seems that the primary function of witch beliefs was a conservative one. They reinforced accepted moral standards by postulating that a breach in the norms of neighbourly behaviour would be followed by material repercussions. As Professor Evans-Pritchard wrote of the Azande, "belief in witchcraft is a valuable corrective to uncharitable impulses, because a show of spleen or meanness or hostility may bring serious consequences in its train". Witch beliefs, like the parallel belief in divine Providence, were a manifestation of the primitive assumption that a likely cause of material misfortune is to be found in some breach of moral behaviour—that the natural order and the moral order are related to each other. They made men hesitate before departing from the traditional norms of neighbourly conduct. "I am loath to displease my neighbour, Allridge," said an Elizabethan husbandman, "for I can never displease him, but I have one mischance or another amongst my cattle." Conversely, the fear of being accused of witchcraft made old women think twice before giving vent to curses and other expressions of malignity. From this point of view, witch beliefs may be fairly described as "conservative social forces" upholding the norms of village life, and worthy to be studied alongside such other props to traditional behaviour as gossip, the lack of privacy, and the risk of denunciation as a scold or troublemaker to the ecclesiastical courts.

But there is another side to the picture. Witch beliefs also had a function which may be described as radical. They arose at a time when the old tradition of mutual charity was being sapped by the introduction of a national Poor Law. This made the model householder's role essentially ambiguous. The clergy still insisted on the duty of local charity, whereas local authorities were beginning to forbid householders to give indiscriminate alms at the door. It is this unhappy conjunction of private and public charity that accounts for the uncertain light in which contemporaries viewed the poor. On the one hand, they hated them as a burden to the community and a threat to public order. On the other, they still recognized that it was their Christian duty to give them help. The conflict between resentment and a sense of obligation produced the ambivalence which made it possible for men to turn begging women brusquely from the door and yet to suffer torments of conscience after having done so. This ensuing guilt was fertile ground for witchcraft accusations, since subsequent misfortune could be seen as retaliation on the part of the witch. The tensions that produced witchcraft allegations were thus those generated by a society which no longer held a clear view as to how its dependent members should be treated; they reflected the ethical conflict between the twin and opposing doctrines that those who did not work should not eat, and that it was blessed for the rich to support the poor. . . .

Witch beliefs are thus of interest to the social historian, no less than the social anthropologist, for the light they throw upon weak points in the social structure. The witch and her victim existed in a state of concealed hostility for which society provided no legitimate outlet. They could not take each other to law, neither could they have recourse to open violence. It was the particular social context that explained why witchcraft was invoked to explain some misfortunes but not others. Witches were not interchangeable with such other bogeys as Jews or Catholics. Paranoia about Popery might suggest an explanation for a disaster like the Fire of London, which affected a whole community; but it was seldom employed to explain why a mysterious fire should have burned down the barn of one individual but not that of his neighbour. Papists were the enemies of society as a whole; witches were the enemies of individuals. Only those who thought of witches as an organized sect of Devil-worshippers could plausibly blame them for misfortunes common to everyone. Nor was the belief in witchcraft interchangeable with that in divine Providence, though theologians tried to make it so. Providence was most likely to be invoked when the victim felt he had sinned against God; witchcraft when he was more conscious of having sinned against his neighbour.

[7]

Scottish Witchcraft in Its Comparative Setting

CHRISTINA LARNER

In this excerpt from her 1981 book Enemies of God: The Witch-Hunt in Scotland, *Christina Larner compares the witch hunts in Scotland to those in England and Europe. Larner taught history, sociology, and politics at the University of Glasgow. Her later work,* Witchcraft and Religion: The Politics of Popular Belief, *was published posthumously in 1984.*

•

The Scottish witch-hunt was arguably one of the major witch-hunts of Europe. During its peaks it was matched only by those of the German principalities and Lorraine. As in Germany its effects were local and highly concentrated. There were periods in 1649 and 1661 when no mature woman in Fife or East Lothian can have felt free from the fear of accusation. The Scottish hunt, however, had its own distinct characteristics.

Scotland played no part at all in the development of the educated witch theory, although echoes of incubi and succubi and references to the higher occult are to be found in early Scottish humanist writings of the sixteenth century. The educated witch theory was imported from the continent in 1591. It is clear from literary sources, however, that a lively popular belief in sorcery, in the Devil, and in a variety of fairies and demons had existed for some time prior to that. The Witchcraft Act of 1563, like other similar European acts, was part of the secularizing of the law by a new nation state.

So far as political ideology goes the Scottish witch-hunt coincided exactly with the period spanned by the doctrines of the divine right of kings and the godly state. Post-Reformation Scotland was in the hands of a new regime whose ideology primarily distinguished them from their old dominant allies and quasi-rulers, the French, and allied them with the English. By the time that James was mature and throughout the seventeenth century it was necessary to make ideological distinctions from that new

From Christina Larner, *Enemies of God: The Witch-Hunt in Scotland* (Baltimore: Johns Hopkins University Press, 1981), 197–202. © 1981 by Christina Larner. Reprinted by permission of Johns Hopkins University Press.

friend in maintaining a Presbyterian form of Protestantism. The peculiarly Presbyterian machinery for social control, developed for a city state, was also admirably adaptable for control in rural areas. The immediate impetus to the witch-hunt after the machinery was established was given by the king whose person had been directly attacked by a conspiracy of witches. This attack on his divine person amounted to an attack on God. It demonstrated, as the contemporary pamphlet *Newes from Scotland* urged, that James was the greatest enemy that Satan had in this world. The entire process vindicated his virtue, his relationship to God, and his concern for his people. Once established witch-hunting never needed quite so specific a reason again.

With the departure of the king for England the godly state took over the position vacated by the divine king. It was less personal, but equally vulnerable and was the ideological focus of loyalty. Yet the next major hunt, that of the late 1620s, cannot be explained purely in terms of legitimizing the Scottish state. It coincided with the climax of the European hunt and was preceded by a gradual build up of cases and by a general injunction on the need for tightening up of law and order. The 1649 outbreak had no connection with events on the continent. It had a clearly ideological source in that this was a period when the Covenanting party had a stronger hold on central government than at any other time. There was much unrest and distress caused by war; the importance of demonstrating control both in terms of belief and behaviour was paramount. The last great hunt at the Restoration was under way in the closing years of the Protectorate and cannot be said to have been generated entirely by the setting up of a new regime and the need to cleanse the stables though this was partly the case. The absence of a machinery for law and order during the months before the restoration of the Privy Council seems to have engendered an anxiety among the ruling classes amounting to a "moral panic." This was the last national purge of God's enemies. After 1662 it was only at a local level that such cleansings were attempted. By the eighteenth century the prospect of the Union of the Parliaments had made the concept of the godly state redundant. Whatever godliness was to be retained by such of the Scottish polity as was to remain autonomous, no-one assumed that the Act of Union involved embracing anything other than Mammon.

The pattern in Scotland, then, relates as exactly as for any part of Europe to the life-time of Christianity as ideology. The peasantry were Christianized for the first time. The regime was new, keeping itself distinct first from France and then from England. It demanded a new conformity of both formal adherence and inner acceptance expressed in appropriately ordered behaviour. In other ways it reflects patterns found in some European hunts and not in others. The Scottish hunt was mainly rural. A large number of the cases said to come from Aberdeen, Dumfries, Stirling or Edinburgh were in fact merely tried there. The accused mostly came from settlements outside. There was no equivalent in Scotland to the German urban hunts in which burgomasters and substantial tradesmen and craftsmen were accused. Nor was there any trace of peasant or class unrest. It was not to distract peasants from revolt but to bind them to the aristocratic and gentry supporters of, variously, bishop, covenant, presbytery, or king, that the peat bales were heaped against the stake. Foreign war was noticeable by its absence. Only once during the century did the Scottish armies move south. There were no Turks, Jews, or Moors for the people to combine against. There were only the English, and in 1652 the English came as conquerors. They took over the administration of justice, and fearing no consequences, needing no other loyalty than respect for their swords, they let the witches free. Occupying forces do not require ideological conformity.

Recent writers on European witch-hunting have stressed the significance of border areas. That was where legitimacy was most at peril. It is a marked feature of the Scottish border that witchcraft cases occur right along its line. The Scottish cases run in a line from Berwick through Kelso, Jedburgh, Hawick, and Canonbie to Gretna. Across that border there are none. The English border was not very important to England. It was a long way to the vulnerable places. James VI had policed and pacified the Scottish border, previously an area of marauding tribes and bandits, in the last year of his Scottish residence and the first of his English reign. First the central government tamed the border men, it might be argued, and then it tamed their women; but the witch-hunting pattern is the same as in Lorraine, in the Basque country, in the Franche-Comté, on the borders of France, where the call of the centre was weakest.

This pattern was partially modified for Scotland. While the border outbreaks were marked, so was the attraction of the centre. Ease of access to Edinburgh was important, and on all sides of that well-trodden path from the Scottish capital to the English border there were cases; likewise on the road from Stirling to Edinburgh and from Glasgow to Edinburgh.

The parallelism with parts of the continent are strong. The special nature of the Scottish hunt, however, can perhaps best be seen when placed alongside that of her English neighbour. The relative mildness of the English hunt can partly be explained by a lower level of religious intensity. The English do not seem to have had the same sharp break with tradition that the Scots had at the Reformation. Except for certain strongly Puritan areas changes were gradual and the intense evangelical zeal that characterized the Scottish church was largely absent in England. The struggle for legitimacy had been won earlier in England by Henry VII and the break from Rome was a mere completion of effective Tudor control. The most important differences, however, were probably in the nature of the judicial machinery. England's Witchcraft Acts of 1542 and 1563 contained detailed instructions in relation to different types of sorcery. Minor offences warranted minor penalties. The Acts knew nothing of the notion common to Roman Law countries such as Scotland that the crime was that of being a witch, that the primary act of witchcraft was the Demonic Pact, and that all witches were part of a Satanic conspiracy. Admittedly these ideas were current in Puritan writers such as Perkins and Gifford, but they did not penetrate to the law courts, which were separate and secular. The organization, too, of English law was not conducive to the creation of mass hunts or national panics. Because there was no notion of conspiracy there was no need of torture to extract the names of accomplices. Further, the crime of witchcraft was not centrally managed. The circuit judges dealt with witchcraft on site, and there was no machinery for one witch-finding judge to transmit his enthusiasm elsewhere.

In Scotland the central organization, combined with the competitive spirit of local clergy and landlords, helped to stimulate panics. Yet in one aspect Scottish witch-beliefs had more in common with English than with continental beliefs. The witches' communal occasions were relatively non-horrific. There was very little actual Devil worship or other forms of inverted Christian ceremony. Reported sexual orgies, other than private copulations with the Devil, were relatively rare, and baby-eating almost unknown. Even when a baby was believed to be eaten it was not specially murdered for the purpose. It was dug up and made into a pie to improve the consumers' powers of sorcery. On the whole Scottish witches' meetings were similar to the very few English ones which were reported. They were jollifications for eating, drinking, and dancing of which in Scotland at least peasants were in real life deprived.

The feature which Monter has shown is especially typical of Protestant Europe is the witch's mark. He has demonstrated that it was a common feature of trials in Protestant Jura and much less common in trials in Catholic Jura. Protestants laid stress on the personal relationship with the Devil; Catholics on the potency of communal worship. The dominance of the witch's mark, which provided an intellectual bridge between popular and educated belief, and the consequent role of the pricker, also appear strongly in Scotland.

There are two theological factors which seem particularly significant in Scotland. The first is that Calvinists believed that a just God rewarded sin with earthly afflictions. Misfortune was therefore not to be seen as the afflictions of Job: as a test of virtue and fidelity. They were to be seen as an indication of sin and of God's just punishment for this sin. Witchcraft was an alternative and under these circumstances particularly attractive explanation for disease, bereavement, or economic misfortune. This is a psychological factor which one would expect to be present in all Protestant, and particularly Calvinist, cultures although its actual operation is difficult to demonstrate. The second factor which is even more characteristic of Scotland is the potency and political significance of the idea of covenant. The legal records in Scotland normally referred to a pact or paction with the Devil, but they did sometimes use the actual term covenant. The central position of the Old Testament concept of the covenanted people in Scottish political thought gave the inversion of a covenant with Satan a power and an intensity which it may not have had under other regimes.

It would in some respects be true to say that Scotland offers a middle position between the witchcraft of England and that of the continent. There are similarities with England in the local functioning of witch-beliefs and in the details of the Demonic Pact, though in Scotland the Demonic Pact is more prominent. There are similarities with the continent in the operation of the law, in the inquisitorial system, and in the belief in conspiracy and witches' meetings, though in Scotland the concept of meetings was weaker and less ritualistic than on the continent. The idea of a middle position is perhaps most convincing in the practice of the Court of Justiciary where the continental inquisitorial system was uneasily juxtaposed with an emerging adversary system in which the outcome depended on a duel between prosecution and defence. It is nevertheless misleading to think of witch-beliefs and witchcraft control operating on a range from severe continental to gentle English, with Scotland in the middle. There were parts of the continent such as Denmark and Russia where witchcraft control was similar in its operation to England, and other parts where governments did not hunt witches at all. There were regions, especially in France and Switzerland, where witchcraft control was similar to, or slightly milder than in Scotland. In particular, Protestant areas of continental Europe resembled Scotland in their beliefs and practices. In the European context then, witchcraft control in Scotland should be seen as fairly severe.

[8]

Witchcraft and Puritan Beliefs

Richard Weisman

Richard Weisman is a sociologist who draws heavily on historical materials as well as the literature of sociology and anthropology. In this excerpt from Witchcraft, Magic, and Religion in Seventeenth-Century Massachusetts *(1984), Weisman discusses the function of witchcraft beliefs in the larger context of Puritan theology.*

•

The role of the New England clergy in the formation of attitudes and policy toward witchcraft has been much discussed in early American historiography, although most frequently in the context of partisan debate. Thus writers unsympathetic to the body of ideas developed within Puritan theology or suspicious of the political power wielded by the Puritan ministers have found in the sermon literature on witchcraft a useful vehicle with which to express their condemnation. Conversely, there has been a tendency among historians who find Puritan thought at least in part congenial either to minimize the importance of theological contributions to witchcraft belief in New England or to portray the clergy as a moderating rather than an aggravating influence upon witchcraft prosecutions. Such discussions, whether in behalf or in criticism of the clergy, have invariably focused upon ecclesiastical participation in the Salem trials.

Yet the historical observer who seeks to situate the theology of witchcraft within the larger body of Puritan beliefs enters a surprisingly unexplored domain of inquiry—and perhaps for ample reason. For, apart from several treatises produced during the latter part of the seventeenth century, the New England clergy are more notable for their absence than their prominence in the contemporary literature on witchcraft. Indeed, their output on this subject was meager even in comparison with that of fellow Puritan divines in England.

Given this literary void, the several sermons and narratives that did in fact deal directly with witchcraft appear all the more conspicuous, and it is easy to exaggerate

From Richard Weisman, *Witchcraft, Magic, and Religion in Seventeenth-Century Massachusetts* (Amherst: University of Massachusetts Press, 1984), 23–38. © 1984 by the University of Massachusetts Press. Reprinted by permission of the publisher.

their importance both with respect to Puritan theology and with respect to the life histories of their authors. The contributions of Increase Mather (1639–1723) and, more particularly, his son Cotton Mather (1663–1728) have thus frequently been credited with defining the ecclesiastical response to witchcraft in New England, and the Mathers themselves have been portrayed as excessively preoccupied with the subject. If the names of these ministers have become closely associated with their works on witchcraft, it is not because of the emphasis they gave to this subject in their own lifetimes. Although Increase maintained a genuine interest in supernatural occurrences throughout his life, witchcraft received little consideration in his writings on these events. Similarly, Cotton's involvement with witchcraft constituted but one episode in a remarkably eventful public career, and his two extended treatises on the subject comprised only a negligible proportion of his total published works.

Accordingly, despite the frequent discussion of witchcraft by succeeding generations of American historians, one might well agree with Perry Miller's assessment of the bearing of the Salem trials and of witchcraft belief in general on the major social events of colonial New England: "the intellectual history of New England up to 1720 can be written as though no such thing ever happened. It had no effect on the ecclesiastical or political situation, it does not figure in the institutional or ideological development." And, in the histories produced by the Puritan leaders themselves, from John Winthrop's *Journal* covering the period from 1630 to 1649 through William Hubbard's *General History of New England* published in 1680, the occurrences of witchcraft are given only passing reference. It is a fact with which the researcher must come to terms that the clergy and other intellectuals of seventeenth-century New England were more apt to disattend than to emphasize witchcraft as a part of their ecclesiastical history.

If Puritan theology can be adequately interpreted without reference to witchcraft, it remains the case that witchcraft in Massachusetts cannot be understood outside the context of Puritan theology. It is necessary to appreciate, however, that witchcraft was not of pivotal importance to Puritan dogma but was rather itself a derivative from more crucial assumptions about God, nature, and humanity. Thus it is with these core assumptions rather than with witchcraft that the student must begin if he is to locate his subject matter within Puritan thought.

In the following sections, an attempt is made to show how and in what terms the category of witchcraft was incorporated within the mainstream of Puritan ideas. One of the tasks of such an examination is to demonstrate that the ministers who wrote on the subject, however idiosyncratic their personal style, sought to interpret witchcraft within the confines of established Puritan doctrine and that they were for the most part successful in this undertaking. Another equally important task is to show that, even in the hands of skillful interlocutors, witchcraft fit but uncomfortably within this body of thought.

Witchcraft and Divinity

For Puritan ministers, as for contemporary Christian theologians in general, belief in witchcraft was anchored upon belief in Satan. It is by examining their writings on the relationship between God and Satan that the theological doctrine of witchcraft and its implications for Puritan piety may be most clearly explicated.

As realized in the numerous sermons on the subject, Satan was the formidable and ubiquitous opponent of God. The Reverend Deodat Lawson well summarizes the orthodox formulation of his manifold roles: "Satan is the Adversary and Enemy. He is the Original, the Fountain of Malice, the Instigator of all Contrariety, Malignity, and Enmity." Indeed, as conceived by the clergy, the range of Satan's destructive powers was enormous. He was at least a party to if not the prime mover in all sins of commission and omission against God; he was capable of leading men to despair and suicide and of causing violent pain and sickness. Not the least of his extraordinary powers was his ability to produce natural wonders such as thunder and lightning. In sevententh-century Massachusetts, it was no mere stylistic mannerism to mention the devil as codefendant in virtually all criminal indictments and not just in crimes of witchcraft.

In all his varied activities, whether as tempter or destroyer, Satan enjoyed considerable advantage over his victims. It was not unusual for Puritan ministers to expound at length on the vulnerability of individuals when faced with such an adversary. As Increase Mather explained, any angel, whether of God or fallen from God, as the devil, could "destroy all the men upon the face of the Whole Earth, in a very little time." But, even without this power over nature, Satan had a hold on all humanity by virtue of its fall from grace. According to Samuel Willard, all persons were in their spiritual estate the children of Satan, although in their natural estate they were the children of God. And even though an individual might come to accept God as a regenerate Christian, Satan never fully relinquished his control over the inner workings of human nature. Thus the ministers described the desperate battle Christians must wage in order to defend their souls against a superior foe.

However formidable the worldly activities of Satan, the New England clergy nevertheless firmly adhered to the doctrine that his movements were effectively limited and contained by the infinite and unlimited power of God. As Willard asserted after recounting the awesome powers of the devil, "God is the Supream Governour over the whole World; and though the Devils are risen up in rebellion against him, yet he holds them in his hands, curbs in their rage, and lets it out as and when he pleaseth." More briefly, Lawson wrote of Satan's dependence: "he is absolutely Bounded and Limited by the Power and Pleasure of the Great and Everlasting God." Accordingly, Satan acted not as an independent being in his assaults on humanity but rather by the liberty granted to him by God.

That God should permit such evil in the world was an obvious paradox that by no means escaped the attention of the New England clergy. It is in the curiously ambivalent resolution to this paradox that a fundamental tension arose between Puritan doctrine and Puritan piety, and it is this tension that permeated the theological response to witchcraft. Within the framework of Puritan doctrine, the resolution was really quite simple. Lawson's sermon may again be quoted for the orthodox formulation: "The Sovereign Power of the Great God to rebuke Satan, appears, In that he doth Manage, all his Motions and Operations, to serve his own most Holy Ends, and to advance his own Glory in the winding up." Thus, if God gave leave to Satan to tempt the believing Christian, it was in order that his faith be tested and thereby strengthened. Similarly, God might use Satan as one of his many instruments to punish the disbeliever or to warn the believer to further exert himself. But whether Satan appeared in his characteristic role of tempter or, more directly from God, in the role of destroyer, God's purpose in permitting these worldly manifestations was in some manner to promote the spiritual welfare of humanity.

The more complete and unambiguous the doctrinal resolution to the paradox, however, the less adequate were its implications for Puritan piety, for if God's triumph over his adversary were an absolute certainty and the terms of his victory easily understood, then the believing Christian might have grounds for complacency in aligning himself with the forces of righteousness. If God intended greater piety from his people by granting Satan his freedom, then it might be assumed that the believer could exact protection from God by means of his spiritual exertions.

Nothing could be more antithetical to the form of piety that the Puritan ministers sought to engender among their followers. Far from taking comfort in the triumph of good over evil, the believer was enjoined never to relax in his own struggle to defeat Satan within himself. That God had a design in permitting this struggle must be accepted on doctrinal grounds, but the minister preferred to remain as vague as doctrine would allow in divulging the specific purpose of this design. Granted that God intended greater piety from the believer; it did not thereby follow that his spiritual improvement would once and for all defeat Satan. Nor did it follow that God's ultimate goals were realized. The minister would demand of the believer that, if through fear of Satan he might reach out to God, he must continue to reach out even if his peril were unabated.

Thus one notes a tendency in the Puritan literature on Satan toward a perfunctory acknowledgment of his specific part in the divine plan. Hence Willard could remark cryptically of Satan's activities in the world, "God hath some glorious design in it, else it should not be," whereas elsewhere he would write, "Let us expect that Satan will fall upon us again, and therefore take heed of growing secure." And Cotton Mather, who embodied this tension between doctrine and piety as fully as any Puritan minister, would eventually be charged with having conceived of Satan as an independent being. If, for the sake of doctrine, it were necessary to reject the idea of Satan's autonomy, as in fact Mather and other ministers were able to do in good faith, yet, for the sake of piety, it was important that the limits of this autonomy remain obscure and that the believer, even while accepting the fact of God's supremacy, never underestimate the power of Satan both in himself and in the world.

Now the doctrine of witchcraft and the implication of this doctrine for piety were almost a precise derivation from the theological rendering of Satan. As the most conspicuous manifestation of Satan's presence, witchcraft was both a proof of Satan's existence and a demonstration of his substantial powers. At the same time, witchcraft was possible only through God's allowance. The highly articulate Englishman William Perkins met these doctrinal requirements with perhaps the most adequate definition offered by a Puritan divine: "Witchcraft is a wicked Arte, serving for the working of wonders, by the assistance of the Devil, so farre forth as God shall in justice permit." And although Cotton Mather omitted reference to divine intervention in one of his own formulations—"Witchcraft is the doing of strange (and for the most part ill) things by the helpe of evil Spirits, covenanting with (and usually representing of) the woeful Children of Men"—he too later conceded in the course of a heated debate with his Boston critic, the merchant Robert Calef, "If any man will ask mee too Grant, that the Divels are in all the Efforts of their Power and Malice, limited to the God of Heaven, I do most readily grant it, and give thanks to God for it."

When, however, the ministers moved from doctrine to piety, as in their writings on Satan, the emphasis shifted from the ultimate accountability of the witch to God to human vulnerability to witchcraft even though one might seek comfort from God. Indeed, Mather observed that the ravages of witchcraft spared no one, not even the most pious individual. . . .

This is not to suggest, however, that the New England clergy offered their followers a despairing faith. The defense against witchcraft, as against all instruments of Satan, was spiritual reformation, both individual and collective. Thus Lawson recommended prayer as a solution to the problem of witchcraft:

> Let us use this Weapon [prayer]; It hath a kind of Omnipotency, because it interests us, in the help of the Omnipotent: Satan, the worst of all our Enemies called in Scripture a DRAGON, to note his Malice; a SERPENT, to note his Subtlety, a LYON, to note his Strength. But none of all these can stand before prayer.

Characteristically, Mather's counsel was more impassioned: "Let us pray much, and we need fear nothing. Particularly, Let Ejaculatory Prayers be almost continually in our minds, and so we shall never lie open to the fiery darts of the wicked one." With these efforts at greater piety, the believer would have the promise, if not the certainty, of divine protection against witchcraft.

But if it were not a despairing faith, it was nonetheless demanding. The minister would offer the victim of witchcraft no easy solution to his distress and no guarantee of remedial action. God might listen to the prayers of his people, and a saving reply could be cautiously anticipated. But that he might not listen was always a possibility, and that he need not listen was to be accepted as a divine prerogative.

Thus the Puritan ministers in their sermons on witchcraft and on Satan sought to achieve a delicate balance of piety that moved the believer beyond complacency to a point close to but short of despair, a balance that was barely contained within their doctrinal framework. That this balance would prove too difficult to maintain for a people suffering the immediate effects of witchcraft will become clear in later discussion.

Witchcraft and Nature

That witchcraft and witches existed as real occurrences was as thoroughly uncontroversial an assertion to the colonial of New England as it was to his contemporaries in western Europe. The proof consisted merely of pointing to the relevant biblical texts. How witchcraft occurred—whether in conformity with or in contravention of the laws of nature—was another matter altogether. Although the Bible, particularly the Old Testament, contained frequent and explicit reference to witchcraft, nowhere did it specify the manner of its operation. The problem of filling this void would challenge the skills of some of the ablest minds of post-Reformation Europe and America. Only in the framework of their general conception of the relationship between God and nature is it possible to appreciate the Puritans' concern with this problem, for it was in behalf of this conception that the reconciliation of witchcraft with nature would be undertaken.

In Puritan cosmology, all events in nature were believed to result from the intervention of a ubiquitous divine presence. The regularities and patterns revealed in nature arose not from any inner necessity but rather from the ever-present enactment of God. Each instant of nature represented an act of divine will, and it lay within the power of God to alter or to bring to a halt the course of natural events at his pleasure.

Such a view of providence imbued the natural order with an ethical rather than a mechanical imperative. By means of nature, God communicated to humanity the purpose of his cosmic design. Sometimes, when he punished misdeeds or rewarded exemplary piety, his purpose was unmistakable. The eventual violent demise of Anne Hutchinson at the hands of Indians was an obvious judgment against her apostasy in the explosive Antinomian Controversy; and that one of her followers, Mary Dyer, should bear a hideously deformed child was simply an extension of that judgment. At other times, God's intentions were less apparent as, for example, when he chose to take the life of a young child or visit suffering upon a devout believer. Thus, on the occasion of the impending death of his daughter, the Reverend Michael Wigglesworth could resolve in his diary to trust these intentions, however obscure: "And shall he not do with his own as he will, either to afflict it or take it to himself. His glory is better than the eas of the creature, and yet his glory shall be coincident with our good." Whether in misfortune or deliverance, the natural order was perceived as the vehicle through which transcendent ethical realities were given tangible form.

Yet the Puritans united to this conception of a personal and arbitrary deity an unshakable belief that nature constituted a rational order. The reconciliation between these ideas required the utmost ingenuity in Scholastic reasoning. The central premise in the reconciliation consisted of positing that God voluntarily confined himself to work within the boundaries of the very same laws of nature that he had created. Thus, while God ruled the universe according to an arbitrary cosmic design, he nonetheless conveyed his design through the orderly and predictable sequences of nature.

The paradoxes latent in this position are ably expressed by Perry Miller: "Puritan thought . . . presupposed a natural framework in which arbitrary power was confined within inviolable order, yet in which the order was so marvelously contrived that all divinely avowed ends were swiftly accomplished." The Puritans would endow the universe with the moral stamp of a willful and arbitrary ruler, and yet they would observe the consequences of this governance in the orderly and predictable arrangement of natural processes. Although they would attribute to this rule a direct personal involvement in human affairs, they would discover this involvement not in the working of divine miracles but in the ordinary laws of cause and effect.

This thesis, which maintained so careful a balance between God's control over nature and God's willing confinement within the limits of nature, formed one of the central lines of continuity in orthodox Puritan thought throughout the seventeenth century. In the shift in Puritan writings from emphasis upon one of these premises in the early decades to emphasis upon the other in the later decades, it is possible to discern the profound changes in intellectual climate that characterized the period.

To the earlier Puritan divines who wrote in England just prior to the New England migration, the primary danger to the scheme lay in a prevailing tendency to overestimate the violability of nature. The tradition of esoteric magic had gained a measure of intellectual respectability largely through the efforts of such hermeticists as Paracelsus and Ficino. Accompanying this resurgent interest in speculative magic was the growing responsiveness of contemporaries to astrological prophecy, healing remedies derived from magical beliefs, and other occult practices. Under these conditions, the response of the Puritan clergy was to stress the reasonableness of God and the immutability of the natural order. Thus John Preston, among the most influential of the Puritan ministers, flatly observed in 1629 that "God alters no Law of nature." And William Ames, one of the leading Puritan theoreticians, argued that the power of God is better demonstrated in his control of natural processes than in his interruption of these processes.

In the latter part of the seventeenth century, the strategy of disputation underwent a major shift to meet the now more pressing challenge of mechanical philosophy. As exemplified by such luminaries as Thomas Hobbes, the implications for Puritan cosmology were obvious. Nature was likened to a self-regulating mechanism that proceeded without reference to a first cause. That God created the universe was of course easily conceded by the proponents of this viewpoint, but the additional conclusion that God was now a passive spectator to his own creation clashed directly with the Puritan concept of a concerned and active deity.

It was partly in response to this challenge that the New England clergy came to give greater attention to events in which it was believed that God had revealed his presence directly before humanity. Although the recording of such events had been carried on informally since the inception of the colony, the first attempt at systematization can be traced to a general meeting of prominent ministers on May 12, 1681. On this occasion, several proposals "concerning the Recording of Illustrious Providences" were submitted for general approval. Included among these proposals was this recommendation: "In order to the promoving of a design of this nature, so as shall be indeed for Gods glory, it is necessary that utmost care shall be taken that all and only Remarkable Providence be recorded and published." Increase Mather's *Essay for the Recording of Illustrious Providences* of 1684 was one of the outcomes of this joint venture.

The specific types of events classified as special providences were given in another of the recommendations:

> Such Divine judgments, tempests, floods, earthquakes, thunders, as are unusual, strange apparitions, or whatever else shall happen that is prodigious, witchcrafts, diabolical possessions, remarkable judgments upon noted sinners, eminent deliverances, and answers of prayer, are to be reckoned among illustrious providences.

The unifying feature of such occurrences was that in each case God had manifested himself more directly than he did in the ordinary course of nature. Moreover, they were distinguishable from miracles in that they were effected not in contravention of the existing laws of nature but rather by the substitution of God for the usual agent in nature. In effect, then, these events constituted a residual category of anomalous occurrences that could not be explained within the contemporary framework of scientific knowledge. Their importance as justifications for Puritan cosmology was that they demonstrated the existence of a proximate God, but not in violation of his rational order. . . .

Yet, with the exception of Cotton Mather, the ministers were in general reluctant to effect the epistemological changes that would have been necessary to accommodate their cosmology to a plausible contemporary scientific explanation of witchcraft. Among the clergy, Mather alone permitted himself to grapple with some of the far-reaching implications of such a reconciliation of witchcraft with nature. To account for the invisible powers of the witch without violating the laws of nature required the positing of a form of nonmaterial causation. The most concerted intellectual effort in this direction had been initiated by a group of English philosophers and scientists referred to by historians as the Cambridge Platonists. One of these men, Joseph Glanvill, had produced a powerful treatise in defense of belief in witchcraft entitled *Saducismus Triumphatus,* and the New England ministers almost uniformly cited this work in their own discussions of the subject. For the most part, however, they borrowed Glanvill's illustrations while neglecting the intellectual system that underlay them.

Among their other concerns, the Platonists endeavored to provide theology with a firm empirical foundation by eliminating from scientific thought the materialist view of the universe that later became identified with it. Against the assertion that natural processes were merely the result of matter in motion, the men of this school argued for the primacy of spiritual agency in nature. One of the Cambridge men, Ralph Cudworth, had referred to this spiritual agency immanent in the universe as the plastic nature. It is this concept that Mather introduced in his major work on witchcraft, *Wonders of the Invisible World*, when he wrote: "Witchcraft seems to be the skill of Applying the Plastic Spirit of the World, unto some unlawful purposes, by means of a Confederacy with Evil Spirits." . . .

The efforts of the other clergy to confront the mechanical philosophies with the evidence of the preternatural were far less ambitious in scope. Both Increase Mather and Deodat Lawson accepted the fact of worldly intercessions by Satan on scriptural authority alone. From this apriorist position, Increase cleverly used the growing respectability of science to bolster his arguments in behalf of the invisible world. If humanity could produce wonders by means of its scientific knowledge, then could not the devil easily surpass these accomplishments with his greater understanding of natural laws? Thus Mather argued in defense of Satan's power to cause thunder:

> an orthodox and rational man may be of the opinion, that when the devil has before him the vapors and materials out of which thunder and lightning are generated, his act is such that he can bring them into form. If chymists can make their Aurum fulminens, what strange things may this infernal chymist effect?

Likewise, with respect to Satan's ability to create special illusions, he argued that the devil "has perfect skill in Opticks, and can therefore cause that to be invisible to one, which is not so to another, and things also to appear far otherwise than they are." It followed then that the supernatural powers of the witch were made possible by the transfer of these diabolic skills at the time of the satanic pact or covenant.

The attempt to rescue Puritan cosmology from mechanistic philosophy and, eventually, from Newtonian physics continued well into the eighteenth century, and among the evidences to be offered in defense of theology, witchcraft would prove to be among the least reliable. Indeed, the sudden prominence of witchcraft in the writings of the New England ministers reflected less its actual importance to Puritan thought than the precariousness of the intellectual edifice within which it was rather indifferently maintained. Ultimately, the ministers would find in earthquakes and other cataclysmic events a more durable demonstration of the divine presence.

For one brief moment, however, the Puritan clergy came perilously close to anchoring the credibility of their grand vision of divine supremacy on the manifest operations of the witch. It was this moment of intellectual legitimation—however unfinished—that coincided with the Salem trials.

Witchcraft and Humanity

It was in the language of spiritual conversion that the clergy formulated the subtle dynamics of human complicity in witchcraft. The morphology of transformation from person to witch was conceived in terms that roughly corresponded to the stages of an individual's progress toward true faith in God. If, for the Puritans, the distance that a person must ascend to relate to God required the utmost of human effort, the spiritual access of humanity to Satan was that of moral proximity. Indeed, the real threat posed by witchcraft was not the damage it wrought upon its victims but the temptation it offered to an easily corruptible human nature.

From this vantage point, witchcraft was merely the endpoint of a continuum of iniquity along which all men and women could be situated; or, as Cotton Mather expressed it, witchcraft was "the furthest Effort of our Original Sin." Likewise, the witches themselves were only the extreme embodiments of a fundamentally human impulse toward evil. As the English Puritan, Richard Bernard, attested, almost in identification with the witch, "By nature are we the children of wrath, and bemired with the filth of sin, as well as they [the witches]." Within such a framework, it was but a small and inevitable logical progression from the assumption that witchcraft lay well within the scope of human possibility to its corollary that much of human predisposition lay within the periphery of witchcraft.

In the actual making of the witch, the clergy posited two sequences: one from the standpoint of humanity and the other from the standpoint of Satan. In the first of these sequences, the volitional element of witchcraft received primary emphasis. Here the initial step in establishing contact with Satan consisted of moral preparation. Bernard described this stage in the following terms: "Before the Divell can come to solicitte for witchcraft, hee findeth some preparedness in such parties, to give him hope to prevaile."

The form that this preparation might take included a wide variety of sins of commission and omission. Usually, the clergy cited the basic repertory of human vices such as greed, anger, malice, or lust as the most frequent predisposition to witchcraft. Though it was recognized that these iniquities might be rooted in poverty or misfortune, the Puritans refused to excuse such impiety on grounds of extenuating circumstances. Thus, during the Salem trials, Lawson counseled even the person who might be falsely accused of witchcraft by his neighbors not to surrender himself to malice or envy lest "the Great Accuser (who loves to fish in troubled waters) should take advantage upon you." Similarly, Mather's remarks on discontent reveal an equal disinclination to mitigate personal responsibility for witchcraft:

> When persons through discontent at their poverty, or at their misery, shall be always murmuring, and repining at the Providence of God, the Devils do then invite them to an Agreement with, and a Reliance on them for help. Downright Witchcraft is the upshot of it.

The fact that preparatory vices could be extended to include sins of omission as well as acts of unwitting complicity left the category potentially unbounded. Virtually any believer who failed to fully exert himself in reaching toward God could be viewed as a candidate for witchcraft. Such a premise may well have been overextended in the admonition of the Reverend Samuel Parris to his votaries in the first month of the Salem proceedings: "examine we ourselves well, what we are—what we Church-members are; We are either Saints or Devils—The Scripture gives us no medium." But the advice, however incendiary, forcefully conveys the sense of spiritual precariousness that informed the Puritan lecture on witchcraft.

Following the stage of preparation, the prospective witch received a promise of general assistance from Satan. This promise might be delivered in the form of either an explicit or an implicit contract. In the explicit contract, Satan or a lesser demon made an appearance before the prepared party to give a more permanent seal to their alliance. The extreme simplicity of this ritual, as conceived by the ministers, well reflected the general absence of ecclesiastical ceremony in Puritan liturgy. There is no mention either of ritual profanation such as the drinking of murdered infant's blood or of any of the elaborate staging devices so frequently found in Continental versions of the pact. . . .

As a result of this covenant, however conceived, the full-fledged witch at last received the benefits of Satan's promise, which, according to Bernard, could consist variously of an offer "to help the poore to foode, the sicke to health, the irefull to be revenged . . . or the satisfying of lust to the lecherous." In addition, the witch now enjoyed the ability to perform supernatural works with the devil's assistance. While the clergy tended not to be specific about the scope of these acquired powers, it was understood that they could never exceed those of Satan himself.

This human declension from original sin to preparation for further iniquity to the solemn pledge with the devil yielded a different sequence when charted from the standpoint of Satan. From this perspective, the initial phase of participation consisted of Satan's temptation of the prospective witch. Because of his subtle understanding of the weaknesses in human nature, he was frequently able to realize his goals. As Lawson observed, "indeed his [Satan's] Angelical Activity is such as doth render him capable to Operate far beyond Human Power of Resistance."

After he had successfully tempted the candidate, Satan then exacted a pledge of loyalty in return for his favors. In this pledge, the future witch fully renounced his faith in God and offered his soul to the devil. The effect of this renunciation was to place the witch at the service of Satan in his unremitting war against God and true piety.

Now it was in the relationship between these two sequences rather than in the specific morphology of each sequence that the Puritan approach to witchcraft most distinguished itself from that of other Christian theologies. The crucial question consisted not in how a person became a witch but in whether the human categories for willing witchcraft corresponded to Satan's categories for imposing witchcraft. Human understanding was regarded at best as a fallible guide to the operations of the invisible world. Moreover, as the instrument of God, Satan partook of the character of divine inscrutability.

Thus, on the one hand, the believer could be provided only with the more noticeable signs of incipient witchcraft. The problem of evil in humanity and, by implication, human susceptibility to witchcraft was not so simple or obvious that it could be uncovered by superficial detection. The affinity between reprobate humanity and Satan might be sketched in rough outline, but its fine details were discernible only through a most rigorous self-examination. As Cotton Mather warned his congregation in 1689, no person could afford to dispense with such introspection: "They that are witches now, once little dreamed of ever becoming so. Let him that stands, take heed lest he fall."

On the other hand, neither was the design of Satan so obvious that the identity of the witch could be easily detected by others. Unlike the Continental theologians, the Puritans provided no social or demographic profile of the likely witch. In the sermon literature on witchcraft, only William Perkins mentioned the preference of Satan for women over men and then more as an aside than as a point of emphasis. Satan was far too canny to reveal himself in familiar social stereotypes or to guarantee visible social coordinates for his invisible operations.

Such lack of equivalence between human understanding and satanic design made the problem of identification an extremely complex theological issue. If human perceptions were unreliable in ascertaining one's own spiritual condition and if the clues offered by Satan to expose the witch were apt to be obscure or misleading, then a most frightful predicament resulted. Anyone—even the most pious of believers—could suspect himself and be suspected by others of witchcraft. Yet no one—no matter how obviously malevolent—could be demonstrated to be a witch.

Ultimately, the ministers were willing to allow for the possibility of visible signs of witchcraft that derived from the act of making a covenant with the devil. . . . Throughout the history of the crime in Massachusetts the clergy remained hesitant, if not unwilling, to issue the stamp of infallibility to any testimony short of the actual confession of the witch. Even this evidence, however, would be doubted in the aftermath of the Salem trials.

[9]

A World of Wonders

DAVID HALL

In this excerpt from his 1989 book Worlds of Wonder, Days of Judgment, *the historian David Hall describes the impact of the seventeenth-century "wonder tales" published in London and circulated widely in New England. Among his other publications are* The Faithful Shepherd: A History of the New England Ministry in the Seventeenth Century *(1972) and a collection of material in* Lived Religion in America: Toward a History of Practice *(1997). He is also known for his essays on reading interests, a number of which are in his* Cultures of Print: Essays in the History of the Book *(1996).*

•

The people of seventeenth-century New England lived in an enchanted universe. Theirs was a world of wonders. Ghosts came to people in the night, and trumpets blared, though no one saw the trumpeters. Nor could people see the lines of force that made a "long staff dance up and down in the chimney" of William Morse's house in Newbury. In this enchanted world, the sky on a "clear day" could fill with "many companies of armed men in the air, clothed in light-colored garments, and the commander in sad [somber]." The townsfolk of New Haven saw a phantom ship sail regally into the harbor. An old man in Lynn espied

> a strange black cloud in which after some space he saw a man in arms complete standing with his legs straddling and having a pike in his hands which he held across his breast . . . After a while the man vanished in whose room appeared a spacious ship seeming under sail though she kept the same station.

Voices spoke from heaven and children from their cradles.

All of these events were "wonders" to the colonists, events betokening the presence of the supernatural. Some wonders were like miracles in being demonstrations of God's power to suspend or interrupt the laws of nature. The providence of God was

From David Hall, *Worlds of Wonder, Days of Judgment: Popular Religious Belief in Early New England* (New York: Knopf, 1989), 71–72, 81, 93–94, 100–102, 114–16. © 1989 by David D. Hall. Reprinted by permission of Alfred A. Knopf.

"wonder-working" in making manifest the reach of his sovereignty; such acts of "special providence" represented God's clearer and more explicit than usual intervention into the affairs of man. But he was not alone in having supernatural power. The events that Cotton Mather described in *Wonders of the Invisible World* were the handiwork of Satan and his minions. A wonder was also any event people perceived as disrupting the normal order of things—a deformity of nature such as a "monster" birth, a storm or devastating fire. Always, wonders evidenced the will of God.

Many of the colonists experienced such wonders. Many also read about or were told stories of them. There was nothing odd about this practice. Everywhere in Europe people were observing the same kinds of portents and telling the same kinds of stories. Everywhere these stories drew upon a lore of wonders rooted in the Bible and antiquity. Chaucer used this lore in *The Canterbury Tales*, as did the fourteenth-century author of *The Golden Legend*, a collection of saints' lives. Whenever the colonists spoke or wrote of wonders, they relied on an old tradition; theirs was a borrowed language.

The transmitters of this language were the London printers and booksellers, who churned out tales of wonders in abundance. Portents and prodigies were the stuff of scores of English printed broadsides. "Strange news from Brotherton," announced a broadside ballad of 1648 that told of wheat that rained down from the sky. "A wonder of wonders" of 1663 concerned an invisible drummer boy who banged his drum about the streets of Tidworth. In "Strange and true news from Westmoreland," a tale of murder ended with the Devil pointing out the guilty person. Newssheets, which began appearing with some regularity in the 1620s, carried tales of other marvels. Pamphlets contained reports of children speaking preternaturally and offered *Strange and wonderful News . . . of certain dreadfull Apparitions*. The yearly almanacs weighed in with their accounts of mystic forces emanating from the stars and planets. . . .

* * *

The same wonder tales that circulated in seventeenth-century England turn up in the colonies, often via books imported from the London book trade. As a student at Harvard in the 1670s, Edward Taylor had access to a copy of Samuel Clarke's *Examples*, out of which he copied "An account of ante-mortem visions of Mr. John Holland." In sermons of the 1670s, Increase Mather quoted frequently from Clarke and Beard. Imported or reprinted broadsides made some of Beard's stories familiar to New England readers; John Foster, the founder of the Boston press, published in 1679 his version of a London broadside, *Divine Examples of Gods Severe Judgments against Sabbath-Breakers*, a set of illustrated warning tales drawn mostly from *The Theatre of Gods Judgments*. Booksellers were importing copies of English wonder books in the 1680s. Many more such books and broadsides reached New England in the seventeenth century, though leaving no specific trace of their existence. . . .

These public texts taught the importance of the Protestant community. So did the record-keeping in such churches as Dorchester and Roxbury. John Eliot, the minister in Roxbury, noted the drowning of two "ungodly" servants who went out at night to gather oysters: "a dreadful example of God's displeasure against obstinate servants." But God protected those in covenant, as in the providential healing of the deacon's daughter from a head wound that exposed her brains, and another of a man so badly hurt blood gushed from his ear; yet "thro' Gods mercy he recovered his senses . . . to the wonder of all men." Similarly, private diaries detailed portents that signified protection of a family or a household. People told the story of their lives in this same fashion, as when John Dane of Ipswich composed "A Declaration of Remarkabell Proudenses in the Corse of My Lyfe," to which he added a long poem that celebrated his prosperity as one of the godly. Always in such texts the private and the public—self, household, church, community—were not differentiated, but conjoined. And always they provided reassurance. Even after learning of a new defeat in King Philip's War, a layman voiced the wisdom that "It is a day of the wicked's tryumph, but the sure word of God tells us his tryumphing is *brief*." The lore of wonders held the lesson that the godly, should they live up to their values, would pass safely through all trial and tribulation.

At a still deeper level, the wonder story embodied confusing lessons about danger and security. The people of New England viewed the world about them as demonstrating pattern. This was the order of God's providence, the order of a theocentric universe. It was also teleological, its structure the grand scheme laid out in the Apocalypse, the war of Antichrist against the godly. Evil was a force of great strength and cunning, so much so, indeed, that the providential order could seem to be "overthrowne and turned upside downe, men speak[ing] evil of good, and good of evil, accounting darknesse light, and light darknesse." Disorder was profound in other ways, as Winthrop half perceived in struggling to make sense of the array of portents. The world was rife with violence—of neighbors angered by stray animals or slander, of death that came to children without apparent cause, of Indians on the rampage, of great storms and terrifying earthquakes.

The people of New England acted out their fear of what such wonders revealed at moments like the earthquake of 1638, which "shook the earth . . . in a very violent manner to our great amazement and wonder" (as the residents of Newbury recorded in the town records) and caused

> divers men (that had never knowne an Earthquake before) being at worke in the Fields, to cast downe their working tooles, and run with gastly terrified lookes, to the next company they could meet withall.

On Cape Ann in 1692, phantoms roused men into frenzied firing of their guns. A servant girl in Boston, awakened by a fire near the water, saw its "Light . . . reflecting from a Black Cloud, and came crying to [her master] under Consternation; supposing the last Conflagration had begun." People felt uneasy when the sun passed into the darkness of an eclipse, and the officers of Harvard College postponed commencement in 1684 because it fell too close to one of these events. Witches too were terrifying in their power to disrupt community.

Each kind of violence was attuned to every other, as were the forms of order. Certainly the order of the universe often seemed to be hidden or difficult to decipher.

If there was purpose and plan, there was also mystery at the heart of things. . . . Death could strike at any moment, the Devil could mislead, the earth begin to tremble. In dramatizing all these possibilities, the wonder tale evoked the radical contingency of a world so thoroughly infused with invisible forces. It came down to this, that nothing was secure, that no appearance of security could hide the mystery beneath. . . .

*   *   *

Prophecy and magic were alike in helping people to become empowered, prophecy because it overturned the authority of mediating clergy and magic because it gave access to the realm of occult force. It may be that some of those who practiced magic and/or witchcraft were explicitly rebellious. One or two at times articulated a world-view that was clearly blasphemous—William Barker at Salem in 1692, and a woman in Connecticut in 1663 who a witness testified had come to her and said that "god was naught, god was naught, it was very good to be a witch," while adding that "she should not ned far going to hell, for she should not burne in the fire." Perhaps this taint of blasphemy is why many of the colonists confused prophecy and fortune-telling with witchcraft, as though prophets could cause death or sickness. When William Graves of Stamford came to his daughter's house not long before she went into labor, he "suddenly began to counsail" her, "sayeing Abigall fitt theyselfe to meet the Lord." Were his words a curse that caused her death? Was he acting out of love or malice, as witch or caring father? Dozens of such questions arose in the flow of everyday experience, questions springing from the doubleness of prophecy and healing.

Such acts were open to interpretation as white magic—or as black. It was in the interests of the clergy to resolve this situation by declaring *all* magic unlawful. Yet the hostility of elite magistrates and ministers was shared by many of the colonists, who came to see the cunning folk as threatening. In denouncing them at Salem or in other trials for witchcraft, lay men and women resolved their suspicion that the witch who healed was not far removed from the witch who harmed their children. Nor was it clear that prophets and fortune-tellers were depending on the Holy Spirit rather than the Devil.

Hence the fascination in 1637 and 1638 with two medical disasters that were open to interpretation as judgmental portents. In October 1637, Anne Hutchinson's close friend and supporter, Mary Dyer, gave birth to a stillborn and premature fetus, "so monstrous and misshapen, as the like hath scarce been heard of." Winthrop, who promptly ordered the fetus exhumed once he learned of its existence, worked telling clues into his description of the object—a midwife who was "notorious for familiarity with the devil," a sudden illness that struck most of the women who were helping with the birth, a violent rocking of the mother's bed at the moment when the fetus died, the coincidence of hearing of the monster "that very day Mistris Hutchinson was cast out of the Church for her monstrous errours, and notorious falsehood." Not long thereafter, Anne Hutchinson herself gave birth to a deformed fetus that, gruesomely described in Winthrop's journal, was summed up in Thomas Weld's report of the whole controversy as "30. monstrous births" corresponding to the "about 30 [misshapen] opinions" she had expressed. Weld, who was then in England, estimated that these were "such monstrous births as no Chronicle (I thinke) hardly ever recorded the like."

Here was one form of response to the "fearful uproar" of prophesying: describe would-be prophets as deluded liars, and link them with Satan. So the ministers in 1638 informed Anne Hutchinson herself that her revelations were from "Satan." Anyone in later years who prophesied against the orthodox ran the greater risk of being accused of witchcraft. So did those who practiced fortune-telling. Included in the nineteen persons executed in 1692 were Parker, Hoar, and Wardwell. Mary Hawkins, the midwife who assisted Mary Dyer in 1637, had previously been executed as a witch. Though not executed on this charge, Quaker women were stripped and their bodies searched for certain growths that, according to the lore of witchcraft, were unique to witches.

Hundreds of the colonists participated in witch-hunting—and did so with such a vengeance as, from time to time, dismayed the magistrates and ministers. The special contribution of the ministers was twofold. First, it was they who made much of the Devil, portraying him as the grand conspirator ever plotting to subvert the godly and install the "Kingdom of Darkness." Their second contribution was to proscribe certain beliefs as *too* magical, and not suited to a godly people. In *An Essay for the Recording of Illustrious Providences*, Increase Mather denounced several practices and artifacts—"herbs and plants to preserve from witchcrafts," "characters, words, or spells, to charm away witches, devils, or diseases," drawing "blood from those whom they suspect for witches," putting "urine into a bottle," nailing horseshoes "at their door, or the like, in the hope of recovering health thereby"—as "unlawful" customs that drew their force (and Mather said they sometimes worked) from the Devil. He went on to criticize the water trial for witches, "divination by sieves," and the "foolish sorcery of those women that put the white of an egg into a glass of water, that so they may be able to divine of what occupation their future husbands shall be." He labeled all such matters "superstitious," and denounced the people involved in them as "implicitly" in compact with the Devil. John Hale resumed this critique in *A Modest Enquiry*, his effort to make sense of Salem witchcraft. As though to illustrate his own confusion, he told tales of fortune-telling that had been exposed as falsehoods while also citing episodes in which it seemed to work. One basic point, like Mather's, was that visions, charms, astrology, conjuring, and prophecy depended on the Devil. Yet Hale was less rhetorical than Mather, perhaps because he seemed to think that no one in New England really practiced the "foreseeing art" or because he "excuse[d] . . . those that ignorantly" used such means of answering their "vain curiosity."

Hale and Mather each drew on the reasoning of learned men in Europe in decrying certain beliefs as mere superstitions. There was much else in the learned tradition to deploy against practices like prophecy. For one, the ministers insisted on the point that revelations ceased with Christ and the apostles. For another, they evoked the natural world of medicine with its descriptions of the diseases of melancholy and lunacy. For a third, they drew on a critique of dreams that originated with the Greeks. These lines of criticism converged in a book that Marmaduke Johnson, the Cambridge printer, published in 1668, an English translation of a sixteenth-century attack on the Anabaptists. Its main theme was the unreliability of visions, dreams, prophecy, and portents as manifested in the troubled-history of Thomas Muntzer and his fellow Anabaptists. Equating dreams with "Satanical illusions," the French author described Muntzer as an opportunist who "preached dreams" in order to "cheat and deceive the poor ignorant people." Deception, not truth, "madness," not sanity, "rage," not peace—such were the qualities or consequences of this way of acting. Nor had Muntzer told the truth in citing portents like a rainbow to encourage his troops. As narrated by this critic, in another city Anabaptists went out into public "quite naked . . . crying after a horrible manner, Wo, wo, wo, Divine vengeance, Divine vengeance." Madmen all in their behavior, the Anabaptists were an object lesson in the danger of uncontrolled interpretation. The New England clergy pointed out this danger time and time again in justifying their repression of "enthusiasm" like Anne Hutchinson's.

But the best defense of all was to take the offense and match prophecy for prophecy, portent for portent. The politicizing of Mary Dyer's "monster" was part of such a campaign, one in which a London printer happily cooperated by issuing *Newes from New England of A most strange and prodigious Birth* in 1642. Down through the years the story lived on—cited in the almanac of 1648, remembered by Nathaniel Mather, remarked on by English writers, retold by Nathaniel Morton in *New-Englands Memoriall*, disputed by Quakers anxious to defend a woman who became an early convert. . . .

*   *   *

Even though the wonder became fictive in the hands of printers, and though partisans of different causes shamelessly politicized the process of interpretation, people never stopped believing that God signaled his intentions through extraordinary events like a fire or an earthquake. The colonists who kept diaries or wrote letters repeatedly referred to prodigies and portents as having real significance; in these private statements, as in public, they perceived the wonder as betokening God's judgments.

When Michael Wigglesworth, a Harvard tutor, learned of a "great fire" that destroyed part of Boston, he wrote in his diary that

> my heart was much affected and dejected within me upon deep thoughts of these things and what I have heard god speak to me in his word, (for he met with sundry of my sins and gave dreadful examples of gods judgments that should have warned me from them). . . .

Writing of the battles they were fighting in King Philip's War, other men consistently referred to victories and defeats as providential. Still others manifested a mentality of fearfulness by the way they behaved when they thought the Day of Judgment had arrived—the maid who fled to her master when she saw reflected in the clouds another Boston fire, Samuel Sewall's children when an earthquake shook their home.

The same kinds of people demonstrated time and time again their belief that dreams, strange sounds, and accidents had occult or prophetic meaning. Not always, but often, people traced misfortune to the powers of a witch. Those who became Quakers believed that they could prophesy. So did others who were orthodox; the sense of having special knowledge of the future—or of serving as the voice of God—was endemic in this culture.

A world so full of wonders, of supernatural forces that seeped into daily life, was a world that many different kinds of people essayed to interpret. The process of interpretation remained open-ended. In part this happened because stories circulated in bewildering confusion, and by routes that no one could control—conversations, rumor, letters, and public demonstrations, and in such forms of print as broadsides and cheap pamphlets. Printers played a crucial role in keeping older lore afloat, and in adding to the stock of stories. Surprisingly, the same role suited learned men like Beard and Clarke. Never, in New England, did the learned culture impose systematic order on the meaning of the wonder. Nor could the clergy silence or suppress the prophesying that lay people or outsiders like the Quakers practiced. It was in the very nature of the wonder that it be "surprising," that it run against the grain of routine expectations. In a culture that empowered every layman to interpret Scripture, the wonder was as meaningful to ordinary men and women—and as open to quotation or retelling—as the Book of Psalms. Bewildered though they often were by prodigies and portents, lay people in New England were free to accept or reject the meanings for these events that the clergy might propose.

Yet the clergy also taught them to prefer a certain set of meanings. One of these concerned God's providential guidance of New England and, more generally, of Protestants. Here the clergy more or less reiterated attitudes that lay writers also voiced, and that had their great original in Foxe's *Book of Martyrs*. A more distinctive meaning, though not solely voiced by clergy, had to do with morals and the good society. A long line of clergy, from Thomas Beard to Cotton Mather, insisted that the lesson of the wonder was that people must give up "Sabbath-breaking" and behave in keeping with a moral code. John Winthrop voiced a broader vision of what portents signified for daily life, an ethic of community or fellowship.

Out of all these uses emerged the most common meaning that the clergy offered for the wonder, that it signified impending judgment. In one sense there was nothing new in this interpretation; the motif of judgment (or disaster) was prefigured in the Bible, the lore descended from antiquity, and the message of exempla in the Middle Ages. The story line of judgment was in every sense a cliché of the times, a convention that hack writers used as freely as the preachers. Yet what made this theme distinctive as employed by the clergy was its kinship to their message about sin. For them a world of wonders was a world of fallen sinners who must learn to plead for forgiveness from a sovereign, judging God. The wonder served this end by instructing people in the doctrine of God's providence and its corollary, the message of man's weakness in God's presence.

II

Non-Christian Beliefs

WHILE ELITES AND NONELITES shared some common theories and fears about the power of witches, folk notions about occult techniques and their relative values varied throughout the Atlantic world. The excerpts in this part deal with the magical practices and mystical beliefs that either preceded or stood apart from Christian traditions. To the extent possible in a limited anthology, they are here examined in their own isolated cultural and historical contexts. In time, as these selections indicate, non-Christian beliefs were eventually influenced by European theological concepts.

Carlo Ginzburg and Norman Cohn examine the rich set of folk beliefs and ritual magical practices in Europe that had nothing to do with demons or Satan. Such beliefs were related to the calamities of early death and repeated epidemics, droughts and floods, and hopes for good harvests and many offspring. Both Ginzburg and Cohn see a world of beliefs that existed parallel to religion, that satisfied areas of life that religion did not touch, and that sometimes substituted for religion. Even when told by church authorities that such practices were heresy, people continued with what Cotton Mather in America had called their "little sorceries."

Such practices may have been part of earlier religious traditions now branded by church leaders as witchcraft in much the same way that Protestants attacked the Roman Catholic rite of exorcism as superstition. Carlo Ginzburg examines the sixteenth-century fantasy of the ancient benandanti (literally "well-farers"), whose nocturnal battles the Catholic Church condemned as witches' sabbats. Instead of a malevolent ritual, he finds a connection with benign ancient fertility rites that had nothing to do with satanic practices. The Ember Seasons celebrated by the benandanti reflected the Roman agricultural cycle of planting, harvesting, and wine making that occurred in June, September, and December of each year.

Norman Cohn traces the legend of the night-flying witch to various traditions, including the Romans' mythical strix and the Germanic notion of a cannibalistic female who flies at night. Such popular beliefs, he argues, merged with the fantasies of the witch hunters to enhance the mythology of witchcraft. The result was a confirmation of the *Malleus Maleficarum* and the new stereotype of the witch. The lay population of Europe drew on a long tradition of myths and legends to confirm their beliefs in the efficacy of magic and the existence of beings with supernatural power.

Although Cohn and Ginzburg agree on the ancient origins of these legends and traditions, they differ on whether the rituals were actually practiced. Stressing the imaginary nature of these images, Cohn, for instance, denies that the benandanti in actual fact fought battles against witches.

Other half-transformations occurred in old England and its colonies. An ancient folklore continued in spite of clerical admonitions and the threat of judicial punishment. George Lyman Kittredge details some of the ancient folklore that persisted into sixteenth-century England and probably continues in parts of the English-speaking world to the present. Kittredge focuses mainly on the widespread use of image magic, a practice based on the theory that like things produced like results and that the appearance of something, that is, its image, captured the spirit of the person or thing it resembled. Manipulating the image—sticking a pin in a doll or waxed image— would, therefore, have the same effect on that targeted person. It should be noted that this theory was not limited to folk magic. Even university-educated physicians were not immune to image magic. It was acceptable to use snakeroot to cure snake bite because the root resembled the snake, or maidenhair fern to overcome infertility in women.

Delving into New England sources, Richard Godbeer finds some of this lore described by Kittredge carried over to colonial America. Many of these occult practices were generally known by the lay population. But cunning folk, those wise in the ways of herbal remedies and the more esoteric magical rituals, were also present in New England and practiced their Old World craft when called on.

He notes too that the ubiquitous image magic was related to a similar belief in sympathetic magic, an idea reinforced by the Neoplatonist theory popular among the elite that there was no clear line dividing matter and spirit. Thus a material object retained its spiritual connection to its original source even though physically separated, that is, it kept a sympathetic relationship. The nail parings of an individual or a hair from his or her head then put on the doll image could be manipulated to cause something to happen to that person regardless of the distance from the object. Puritans, with their high rate of literacy in the seventeenth century, may well have read some of the more esoteric magic books that drew on this neoplatonism to supplement the oral traditions. But as in old England, Godbeer states, charms and spells were well known even by ordinary people.

In the sixteenth and seventeenth centuries, sub-Saharan Africans and Europeans shared many assumptions about the nature of witches. These beliefs, like the diseases found on both continents, probably derived from continuous contact over the previous centuries or, as Geoffrey Parrinder suggests, from a common origin. But unlike Europeans, who are less likely to take these beliefs seriously today, many Africans display a remarkable continuity in their fears and practices regarding witchcraft and the power of sorcery. Thus modern researchers find Africa an excellent laboratory in which to study ideas regarding witches and the function of magical practices as they were understood at an earlier time in Europe. Unfortunately this selective living laboratory methodology can convey the impression that African beliefs about evil and witchcraft have remained static over the last few centuries when they have in fact responded to new influences. The result of assuming an unchanging religious climate may be that non-Africans have a distorted perception of current African worldviews. On the other hand, these anthropological studies, even though flawed, help to link Africans in the European colonies of America to their African ancestors.

Parrinder stresses the similarity between the cultures anthropologists have studied in nineteenth- and twentieth-century sub-Saharan Africa and those groups historians have investigated in Europe during the earlier period. He assumes that the African witch, as in the European tradition, is often female. Whether transforming herself into an animal, participating in night-riding activities, taking part in blood sucking and cannibalistic rituals, or causing wasting diseases, the witch in Africa was not much different from her or his European counterpart. Such people were thought to attack only members of the village and not strangers, although Africans, unlike Europeans, believed that the family of the witch was especially vulnerable to her evil ways. The witch in both areas was never a stranger to her victims. Thus in both African and European societies, the use of witchcraft was closely related to interpersonal conflicts. On the other hand, in some tribes all death could be attributed to witchcraft, whereas in Europe, he notes, it was the unusual death that was blamed on evil magic. There were, however, few documented incidents of witch hunts in Africa even though there were occasions when individual witches were murdered.

While Parrinder looked for the similarity of beliefs on the two continents, E. E. Evans-Pritchard, in a now classic study of witchcraft among the Azande, examined the major distinguishing characteristics of African witchcraft beliefs. He concentrated his studies on one particular tribe in the west central part of the continent, a large area that came under the control and therefore subject to the influence of several European nations and Egypt at one time or another. The Azande, according to Evans-Pritchard, traditionally make a distinction between two types of evildoers—witches and sorcerers—a distinction that has influenced the categories of evil magic used by anthropologists since he began his work. Witches, according to this scheme, are born with occult powers, their evil doings the result of their very presence; sorcerers learn a craft using magical objects.

Thus the Azande believe that witches are people who have an inherited physical quality that gives them special magical powers that they may or may not know about or use. The effect requires no artifacts, merely a look or emanation. When misfortune occurs a person respected for his or her ability to identify and locate those with evil power must then determine whether they have used it. Sorcerers, on the other hand, with no inherited evil tendency, learn to use spells and charms and have knowledge of poisons and other harmful magical rites. Witches and sorcerers in this African culture can be either men or women and all are feared equally. Africans rely on other magical rituals to protect themselves against the evil that causes suffering or turn to oracles, divination tools, to identify the evildoers, who can then be punished. The Azande, rather than fomenting witch hunts, have devised cleansing rites that reconcile the witch with his or her victim.

Africans, like their other sixteenth- and seventeenth-century Atlantic counterparts, lived in a world inhabited by spirits that continually acted on the destiny of human beings. Basic to the cosmos of many Africans was the twin belief that the spirits of the dead continue to reside in the village among the living and that all human suffering and adversity have a spiritual cause. The harmful effects of these spirits, sometimes due to ancestors who have been offended, could be relieved only by appropriate rituals performed by the witch doctor as a healer. Thus the witch doctor's skill in magical healing was especially respected and needed in Africa as much as witches and sorcerers were and are feared and avoided.

A strong belief in the spiritual basis of disease and death along with the sensitivity to witchcraft and sorcery was carried over to America by Africans brought as slaves. Philip D. Morgan emphasizes the selective nature of these carryovers and the regular adoption by Africans of both American Indian and English ideas when they seemed to be appropriate. In the area of magical practices, he finds little evidence for the presence of a natural-born witch of the West African kind. Rather, various types of sorcery, called conjuring or witchcraft by the English, predominated in the southern English colonies. The sorcerers, known as obia (or obeah), were familiar with charms that caused sickness and death as well as the cures. They were knowledgeable in the use of poisons assumed to have magical properties, in reality deadly herbal compounds or hallucinogenic drugs.

William D. Piersen believes that much more important as an African carryover of magic in New England was the practice of divining, that is, foretelling the future or finding lost or stolen items. This was the traditional function of the oracle in Africa. The belief in magical divining was especially effective as a psychological device used by Africans in America to identify criminals and thus a method of reducing conflict within their own black communities, both slave and free.

There is no doubt, however, that, as Pierson indicates, traditional African religions contributed to the continuing belief in witchcraft and the fear of ghosts, those spirits of the dead who might return to haunt the living who had offended them in life. Because of this idea that the spirits of the dead continue to reside among the living and can cause harm (or protect the family if adequately venerated), it was essential to show respect toward those who had died. Morgan points out too that treatment of the dead body was one way to demonstrate that respect, or could be intended as a way to control the future activities of the spirit.

Funerals are an important source of information on attitudes toward witchcraft and sorcery among Africans and African Americans. Jerome Handler links mortuary practices in Barbados, an English colony in the Caribbean, to the existence of witchcraft beliefs among Africans living on the island in the seventeenth century. Using archaeological evidence, he supports the literary evidence, used by many scholars of the African American experience, of a profound fear of witchcraft and spirits who could cause harm. Africans living in the New World not only retained Old World practices under the most adverse conditions of enslavement, but also found ways to express fears and hopes that were hidden from European eyes. Archaeology can bring to light some of those traditions.

In sharp contrast to the European view of evil, either folk or clerical, is that of American Indians, for whom the very concept of a wholly evil spiritual force was contrary to common sense and their basic religious beliefs. Fernando Cervantes points out how alien the notion of a devil appeared to the Indians of Mexico, who conceived of evil and benevolence as an essential duality within the same spiritual forces. Directly under the control of the Spanish and forced to convert to the Roman Catholic Church, these Indians of Mexico learned to filter the unfamiliar concepts through their own mental imagery. As the Spanish churchmen tried to demonize Indian practices and as Catholic rites were adopted by the local population, there was an assimilation of the Christian devil concept into the Indian cosmology that did not completely eradicate the older notion of a God who was both creator and destroyer. What appears to be a haphazard process in the eyes of Western observers is in fact a logical progression from the Indian point of view. Thus Cervantes sees a persistence of Indian beliefs regarding supernatural evil in Mexican Catholicism that parallels the experience of Europeans in earlier centuries as a raw Christianity was transformed in its contact with the folk magic of Europe.

The potency of evil witchcraft lore is not as evident or clear-cut in the American Indian experience as it is in either African or European cultures. It is very likely that North American Indians before the intrusion of Europeans lived in a world populated by invisible but morally neutral spirits. The notion of a totally good God was an absurdity, since their experience taught that all gods were capable of doing good or causing harm. Preventing evil doings was more a matter of avoidance—not to offend the spirits because that would disrupt a cosmic balance. Misfortune was not so much the result of evil acts as of broken taboos and human failings. Ritual magic was essential to restore the balance in the cosmic order by appealing to the good will of the spirits.

As Alfred Cave notes in his study of Indian shamans in New England, Englishmen saw these Indian rituals, which resembled their own kind of sympathetic magic, as a pacification of the devil through sacrifice. In the English mind, there was a close association of Indian rites with devil worship. Strangely enough, in spite of the assumption of a diabolical connection, such Indian magic was never associated even by the English with harm.

There is a curious absence of any fear of magical malevolence among the Indians studied by Cave. Indians, unlike the English, gave no indication that they feared magic from within the group, and this reaction is reflected in English commentary. As a result, Cave is skeptical of reports by the English of witch murders. The shaman, the magical practitioner, was a respected person in those Indian communities. It is possible that the belief in evil witchcraft and the occurrence of witch hunts among New England Indians were the result of contact with European ideas and European cruelty and not part of an indigenous belief system. North American Indians may have had no concept of a separate evil power among their own gods, but they did associate the acts of their adversaries, especially the Europeans and the diseases they brought, with malevolent forces.

By contrast, Marc Simmons argues that witchcraft treachery and the witch mania among Indians in the southwestern part of the United States antedate contact with Europeans. But it should be noted, and Simmons does comment on the fact, that there is a strong resemblance between the lore of such evildoings among the Pueblo Indians and both European and African notions of evil magic, tricksters, and witches' meetings. Given Cervantes's description of how Mexican Indians rapidly fused Christian ideas onto their own cosmology, it is possible that what Simmons has examined is part of this process of transformation and the demonization of Indian religious rituals and curing ceremonies by the Spanish rather than a set of autochthonous practices and beliefs.

This is not to say that Indians lacked a sense of an evil presence. As these readings indicate, American Indian lives were infused with strong spiritual forces acting on their everyday activities. They held elaborate mystical beliefs, especially regarding illness and death. But witch persecution as found after the Spanish conquest and English intrusion onto Indian soil may well be a result of that European contact. Once the concept of the Christian devil took hold, American Indians then came to endow magical rituals with even more extraordinary potency and to fear the practitioners. Thus Simmons's study shows us the development of that syncretic process among a people already intensely involved with ceremonial cures and other elaborate rituals.

Such rituals often included elements of image magic, but whether necessarily for evil purposes is not always evident. The assumption that images were used to cause harm is not borne out by the early work of Walter E. Roth among South American Indians. He suggests another explanation for the presence of dolls or "manikins" found among the artifacts used by medicine men in South America in his 1908 report to the Smithsonian Institution. It was, he surmises, a divining instrument in a curing ceremony and not, as others have suggested, a means of causing harm. Such apparent contradictions regarding American Indian notions of occult practice as evil magic suggest that much more research is necessary. It may well be that the range of beliefs among American Indians is so extraordinarily wide that no generalizations are possible.

Roth also found groups in those areas of the Orinoco River valley with a tendency to blame strangers—other tribes—for suspected cases of evil charms causing disease rather than members of their own group. The evil spirit could just as well be a vengeful outlaw and former member of the tribe but now considered an outsider. Accusations of evil witchcraft among these Indians, he finds, was not a function of interpersonal conflict as was true in the European or African worlds. They served other purposes more closely related to intertribal enmity than social problems within the group.

More recent anthropological studies of South American Indians may provide additional clues to how Native Americans before contact with Europeans viewed the source of evil and its connection to witchcraft. Peter Rivière looks at two groups in north and central eastern South America living in territory between the Orinoco River and Brazil. The fear of evil magic is very real in that area, but among the Trio, living in the northern part of Brazil, the culprit is invariably a stranger or one who has separated himself from the community. The victims of such magic do not necessarily know who has caused the problem. Thus an accusation of sorcery (not witchcraft in anthropological terms because it is not an inherent quality) separates the villager from the outsiders. The conflict is between the villagers and strangers. The Trio believe that those within the community would not cause harm to neighbors, and malevolent witchcraft, therefore, comes from outside the group. As among the tribes that Roth studied, witchcraft is not associated with the face-to-face contact that characterizes Europe and African accusations of evil magic but a means of establishing boundaries between themselves and others.

Rivière's contrasting group, the Shavante, fear evil magic practiced by members of the same village. Like Europeans, the Shavante associate sorcery with the weaker members of the society, reflecting a conflict among different classes within the group. The concept of evil magic, therefore, according to Rivière, serves different social purposes depending on the structure of the society. In neither case, of course, was there anything resembling a satanic influence.

Thus although there are some similarities to be found in all these non-Christian cultures regarding the workings of magic in general and witchcraft in particular, significant differences remain to be explored and explained. This is especially so among American Indians before contact with Europeans. The dynamic demographic circumstances, the result of that contact, have brought on such extensive borrowing from and assimilation of foreign notions that it is extremely difficult to sort out the separate strands of magical beliefs. Perhaps archaeology coupled with a more careful reading of the existing written sources will answer those questions in the future.

A. EUROPEANS AND NORTH AMERICAN COLONISTS

[10]

The Night Battles

Carlo Ginzburg

The historian Carlo Ginzburg is primarily concerned with the nucleus of popular beliefs found in religious attitudes. In the work excerpted here, The Night Battles *(originally published in Italian in 1966), he describes the testimony of sixteenth-century Italian villagers who claimed to belong to a secret society called the benandanti. His better-known book in English,* The Cheese and the Worms: The Cosmos of a Sixteenth-Century Miller *(1980), was a pioneering study in popular culture that also drew on Inquisition records to reconstruct the mentality of the Italian peasantry.*

•

On 21 March 1575, in the monastery of San Francesco di Cividale in the Friuli, there appeared before the vicar general, Monsignor Jacopo Maracco, and Fra Giulio d'Assisi of the Order of the Minor Conventuals, inquisitor in the dioceses of Aquileia and Concordia, a witness, Don Bartolomeo Sgabarizza, who was a priest in the neighbouring village of Brazzano. He reported a strange occurrence of the week before. He had heard from a miller of Brazzano, a certain Pietro Rotaro, whose son was dying from a mysterious ailment, that in an adjacent village, Iassico, there lived a man named Paolo Gasparutto who cured bewitched people and said that "he roamed about at night with witches and goblins." His curiosity aroused, the priest, Sgabarizza, had summoned the fellow. Gasparutto admitted that he had told the father of the sick child that "this little boy had been possessed by witches, but at the time of the witchery, the vagabonds were about and they snatched him from the witches' hands, and if they had not done so he would have died." And afterwards he had given the parent a secret charm which could cure the boy. Pressed by Sgabarizza's questioning, Gasparutto said that "on Thursdays during the Ember Days of the year they were forced to go with these witches to many places, such as Cormons, in front of the church at Iassico, and even into the countryside about Verona," where "they fought, played, leaped about, and rode various animals, and did different things

From Carlo Ginzburg, *The Night Battles: Witchcraft and Agrarian Cults in the Sixteenth and Seventeenth Centuries* (Baltimore: Johns Hopkins University Press), 1–12, 24–26. © 1983 by Routledge and Kegan Paul. Reprinted by permission of Johns Hopkins University Press.

among themselves; and . . . the women beat the men who were with them with sorghum stalks, while the men had only bunches of fennel."

Disconcerted by these strange tales, the good priest immediately went to Cividale to consult with the inquisitor and the patriarch's vicar; and chancing upon Gasparutto again, conducted him to the monastery of San Francesco. In the presence of the father inquisitor, Gasparutto readily confirmed his account and furnished new details about the mysterious nocturnal meetings: "when the witches, warlocks, and vagabonds return from these games all hot and tired, as they pass in front of houses, when they find clear, clean water in pails they drink it, if not they also go into the cellars and overturn all the wine"; therefore, warned Gasparutto, addressing Sgabarizza, one must always have clean water on hand in the house. And since the priest did not believe him, Gasparutto offered to include him, along with the father inquisitor, in the mysterious gatherings: there were to be two before Easter, and "having promised, one was then obliged to go." And he declared that there were others who attended these reunions at Brazzano, Iassico, Cormons, Gorizia, and Cividale, but their names could not be revealed, because "he had been badly beaten by the witches for having spoken about these things." Trying confusedly to make some sense out of Gasparutto's tales, Sgabarizza concluded that there existed, or so it appeared, witches like Gasparutto himself, "who are good, called vagabonds and in their own words benandanti . . . who prevent evil" while other witches "commit it."

A few days went by. On 7 April, the priest of Brazzano reappeared before the Holy Office and reported that he had gone to Iassico to say Mass the Monday after Easter, and that he had run into Gasparutto there. After the Mass, as was customary, the priest had gone to a feast prepared in his honour. "During the meal," said Sgabarizza, "I spoke about matters appropriate to the season, that is, guarding against sin and pursuing good and holy works." But Gasparutto, who was present in his capacity as *commissairo* (he must have been well-off: elsewhere there is a possible reference to his servants), interrupted him to describe exploits of the usual company the night before: "They crossed several great bodies of water in a boat, and . . . at the river Iudri one of his companions became afraid because a fierce wind had come up, and the waters were rough, and he remained behind the others . . . ; and . . . they were in the countryside not far away, and they jousted and busied themselves with their usual pastimes." The priest, his curiosity greatly aroused, had not been able to contain himself. "I brought him home with me, and treated him kindly so as to draw other details out of him, if I could." But this was to no avail.

The substance of Sgabarizza's depositions was confirmed by Pietro Rotaro, father of the child treated, though in vain, by Paolo Gasparutto. When Rotaro suspected that his son had been bewitched, he had appealed to Paolo, since the latter "is known to go about with these witches and to be one of the benandanti". Also Gasparutto had talked at length with him about the nocturnal gatherings:

> "Sometimes they go out to one country region and sometimes to another, perhaps to Gradisca or even as far away as Verona, and they appear together jousting and playing games; and . . . the men and women who are the evil-doers carry and use

the sorghum stalks which grow in the fields, and the men and women who are benandanti use fennel stalks; and they go now one day and now another, but always on Thursdays, and . . . when they make their great displays they go to the biggest farms, and they have days fixed for this; and when the warlocks and witches set out it is to do evil, and they must be pursued by the benandanti to thwart them, and also to stop them from entering the houses, because if they do not find clear water in the pails they go into the cellars and spoil the wine with certain things, throwing filth in the bungholes."

At the judges' request, Rotaro added details about the way Gasparutto had said he went to these gatherings, namely, . . . "in spirit", and astride such animals as hares, cats, and so on. Rotaro also had heard it said that even at Cividale there was one of these "witches", a public crier named Battista Moduco, who, talking to friends in the square, had declared that he was a benandante and that he went forth at night, "especially Thursdays". At this point Troiano de'Attimis, a noble of Cividale, was called to testify. He confirmed that he had learned from his brother-in-law, chatting in the piazza, that "some of these witches were in Brazzano, and that there was one even in Cividale, not far from us." Then Troiano had noticed Battista Moduco nearby and had asked him:

"And you, are you one of those witches?" He told me that he is a benandante, and that at night, especially on Thursdays, he goes with the others, and they congregate in certain places to perform marriages, to dance and eat and drink; and on their way home the evil-doers go into the cellars to drink, and then urinate in the casks. If the benandanti did not go along the wine would be spoilt. And he told other tall tales like these which I did not believe, and so I did not question him further."

The vicar general, Maracco, and the inquisitor, Giulio d'Assisi, must have agreed with the scornful conclusion of the nobleman of Cividale; tall tales and nothing more. After this deposition, in fact, the interrogations set in motion by Gasparutto's revelations were halted. They were to begin again five years later, at the initiative . . . of another inquisitor.

*　　*　　*

Vague and indirect as this evidence may be, it does none the less allow us to state with assurance that there did in fact exist in the area around Cividale, in the second half of the sixteenth century, a complex of beliefs (not limited to an individual, private sphere), that were otherwise unrecorded, and were strangely blended with well-known traditions. The witches and warlocks who congregated on Thursday nights to give themselves over to "dancing", "games", "marriages", and banquets, instantly evoke the image of the sabbat—the sabbat which demonologists had minutely described and codified, and that inquisitors had condemned at least from the mid-fifteenth century. And yet there are obvious differences between the gatherings described by the benandanti and the traditional popular image of the diabolical sabbat. It appears that in the former, homage was not paid to the devil (in fact, there was no reference at all to his presence), there was no abjuration of the faith, trampling of crucifixes, or defilement of sacraments. The essence of these gatherings was an obscure rite: witches and warlocks armed with sorghum stalks jousting and battling with benandanti armed with fennel stalks.

Who were these benandanti? On the one hand they declared that they were opposed to witches and warlocks, and their evil designs, and that they healed the victims of injurious deeds by witches; on the other, like their presumed adversaries, they attended mysterious nocturnal reunions (about which they could not utter a word under pain of being beaten) riding hares, cats, and other animals. This ambiguity was reflected even in the language. The notion of the profound difference, even real antagonism, between witches and warlocks (that is "men and women who commit evil") and "men and women benandanti", seems in fact to have been difficult to grasp even at the popular level. Thus, a country priest like Sgabarizza (who at first, significantly, used a rough translation for what he considered a strange word, "vagabonds and in their language benandanti") and the miller Pietro Rotaro spoke of "benandanti witches"—where the adjective gained meaning only when linked to a noun already firmly established. The benandanti were witches: but "good" witches, Sgabarizza asserted, who tried to protect children or provisions in homes from the perfidy of the evil witches. Right from the start, therefore, the benandanti appear to us in the form of a contradiction which subsequently influences profoundly the course of their existence.

*   *   *

Five years later, on 27 June 1580, a new inquisitor, Fra Felice da Montefalco, revived the case left unfinished by his predecessor and ordered one of the two benandanti, Paolo Gasparutto, to appear before him. Gasparutto declared that he did not know why he had been summoned. He had been going to confession and receiving communion from his parish priest annually; he had never heard it said that at Iassico "there is anyone who is a Lutheran and leads an evil life." When Fra Felice asked if he knew anyone who was a witch or a benandante, Gasparutto replied in the negative. And then he suddenly exploded with laughter: "Father, no, I really do not know . . . I am not a benandante, that is not my calling." Then the inquisitor bombarded him with questions: had he ever tried to cure the son of Pietro Rotaro? Rotaro called me, Gasparutto replied, but I told him I knew nothing about such things and I could not help him. Had he ever spoken about benandanti with the previous inquisitor and with the priest of Iassico? At first Gasparutto denied this: later he admitted, with great mirth, that he had said he dreamed of fighting witches. But in the face of incessant questioning by the inquisitor, who reminded him of details from conversations held five years before, he repeated his denials, between peals of laughter. The friar finally asked: "Why do you laugh so much?" Unexpectedly Gasparutto replied: "Because these are not things to inquire about, because they are against the will of God." The inquisitor, more and more baffled, persisted: "Why is it against God's will to ask about these things?" The benandante now realized that he had gone too far: "Because you are asking about things that I know nothing about," he replied, and resumed his denials. The questions continued: had he ever spoken of nocturnal battles with witches, had he ever invited Sgabarizza and the inquisitor to these gatherings? His eyes shut, Gasparutto obstinately insisted that he remembered none of this. After Fra Felice recalled for him his descriptions of witches and benandanti returning exhausted from their games, and how, when they did not find water in the houses, they went into cellars, "urinating and spoiling the wine", Gasparutto exclaimed with mocking laughter, "Oh, what a world." But nothing could budge him from his silence and in vain did Fra Felice promise him pardon and mercy if he would only tell the truth. At this point the interrogation ceased and Gasparutto was imprisoned.

*   *   *

The same day the other benandante, the public crier Battista Moduco, nicknamed *Gamba Secura* was also interrogated. Born at Trivignano, he had lived in Cividale for the previous thirty years. He too declared that he had gone to confession and taken communion regularly, and that he did not know any heretics. But when he was asked about witches and benandanti, he quietly replied: "Of witches I do not know if there are any; and of benandanti I do not know of any others besides myself." Fra Felice immediately inquired, "what does this word 'benandante' mean?" But Moduco seemed to have regretted his hasty reply and tried to turn the matter into a joke: "Benandanti I call those who pay me well, I go willingly." Nevertheless, he ended up admitting that he had told several people he was a benandante, and added: "I cannot speak about the others because I do not want to go against divine will." (We should note at this point that there is no evidence that Moduco and Gasparutto knew each other, or had even met.) Moduco did not hesitate to say of himself:

> "I am a benandante because I go with the others to fight four times a year, that is during the Ember Days, at night; I go invisibly in spirit and the body remains behind; we go forth in the service of Christ, and the witches of the devil; we fight each other, we with bundles of fennel and they with sorghum stalks."

It is not difficult to imagine the inquisitor's bewilderment over these benandanti who in so many ways themselves resembled the very witches against whom they acted as defenders of Christ's faith. But Moduco had not yet finished: "And if we are the victors, that year there is abundance, but if we lose there is famine." Later he clarified this:

> "In the fighting that we do, one time we fight over the wheat and all the other grains, another time over the livestock, and at other times over the vineyards. And so, on four occasions we fight over all the fruits of the earth and for those things won by the benandanti that year there is abundance."

Thus, at the core of the nocturnal gatherings of the benandanti we see a fertility rite emerging that is precisely patterned on the principal events of the agricultural year.

Moduco added that he had not belonged to the company of the benandanti for more than eight years: "One enters at the age of twenty, and is freed at forty, if he so wishes." Members of this "company" are all those who "are born with the caul . . . and when they reach the age of twenty they are summoned by means of a drum the same as soldiers, and they are obliged to respond." Fra Felice interrupted, trying to put difficulties in the way of the benandante: "How can it be that we know so many gentlemen who are born with the caul, and nevertheless are not vagabonds?" (We can see that the friar, almost as if to keep his distance, was trying not to use the popular term which was foreign to him.) But Moduco stood his ground: "I am saying everybody born with the caul must go." All this seemed incredible to the inquisitor, who insisted on knowing the truth about entry into this "profession"; and Moduco replied simply, "nothing else happens, except that the spirit leaves the body and goes wandering.". . . .

But the inquisitor demanded still more information, and above all, the names of the other benandanti. Moduco refused: "I would be beaten by the entire company," and he even declined to reveal the names of the witches. "If you say that you fight for God, I want you to tell me the names of these witches," Fra Felice insisted. But Moduco was stubborn. He declared that he could not accuse anyone "whether he be friend or foe . . . because we have a life-long edict not to reveal secrets about one side or the other. . . . This commandment was made by the captains of each side, whom we are obliged to obey." Only after another of the friar's objections ("This is just an excuse; since you assert that you are no longer one of them, you cannot be obliged to obey them: so tell me who these witches are") did Moduco finally yield and furnish two names, one of which was that of a woman who had supposedly deprived livestock of their milk. Moduco's interrogation ended here; evidently his replies had not put him in such a bad light in the eyes of the Inquisition, since Fra Felice let him go.

*   *   *

On 28 June, Paolo Gasparutto was interrogated a second time. One day's imprisonment had convinced him of the futility of persisting in his denials. He admitted entering the company of the benandanti at the age of twenty-eight, summoned by the captain of the benandanti of Verona, of having remained in it for ten years, and of having abandoned it four years previously. "Why," the inquisitor asked, "did you not tell me this yesterday?" Gasparutto replied: "Because I was afraid of the witches, who would have attacked me in bed and killed me." But to the friar's next question, "The first time that you went did you know that you were going with benandanti?" he responded at length: "Yes, father, because I had been warned first by a benandante of Vicenza, Battista Vicentino by name . . . thirty-five years of age, tall in stature, with a round black beard, well built, a peasant." Battista had presented himself in "the month of December, during the Ember season of Christmas, on Thursday about the fourth hour of the night, at first sleep." And here the motif underlying the rites of the benandanti, which we saw in Moduco's interrogation, re-emerges especially clearly: "He told me that the captain of the benandanti was summoning me to come out and fight for the crops. And I answered him: 'I do want to come, for the sake of the crops.'" . . .

Gasparutto's story, like Moduco's, ended with the accusation of two witches—one from Gorizia, the other from the village of Chiana, near Capodistria. The inquisitor seemed satisfied and freed Gasparutto, ordering him to reappear within twenty days, this time not in Cividale but in Udine, at the monastery of San Francesco.

* * *

The proceedings described above took place on 28 June. On 24 September the inquisitor ordered that Gasparutto, who had not kept the appointment at Udine, (he later tried to excuse himself, claiming that he had been ill) be brought there, and had him incarcerated. Two days later the questioning of the benandante resumed.

Thus far Moduco's and Gasparutto's accounts match almost entirely. But now a difference appeared. Gasparutto modified his confession on one key point by introducing a new element: "I have come to think that I should tell the truth," he declared at the beginning of the interrogation. The inquisitor restated a question which was intended to undermine the most important theological point in his confession: "Who led you to enter the company of these benandanti?" To this Gasparutto replied unexpectedly: "The angel of God . . . at night, in my house, perhaps during the fourth hour of the night, at first sleep . . . an angel appeared before me, all made of gold, like those on altars, and he called me, and my spirit went out. . . . He called me by name, saying: 'Paolo, I will send you forth as a benandante and you will have to fight for the crops.' I answered him: 'I will go, I am obedient.' "

How are we to explain this change? At first glance it would seem reasonable to suppose that, faced by the prolongation of the interrogations and the renewed imprisonment, Gasparutto might try to extricate himself from the clutches of the Inquisition by placing greater weight on the Christian motivation of his "profession". Perhaps he thought he could do this by introducing the theme of an angel, not realizing that he was thereby aggravating his own situation. But two points should be kept in mind: the detail of the angel who participated in the meetings of the benandanti (to whom Gasparutto referred) and who will reappear, if only briefly, in two later trials of 1618–19, and 1621; and the fact that after he was led back to prison, Gasparutto mentioned the angel to Moduco. This undercuts the hypothesis that it was a spontaneous invention he concocted for his defence. All in all, it makes sense to suppose that in his first confession Gasparutto had kept silent about the appearance of the angel precisely because he discerned its intrinsic danger.

Gasparutto had barely finished speaking about the apparition of the angel "all made of gold" when the inquisitor broke in with an abrupt insinuation: "What did he promise you, women, food, dancing, and what else?" Gasparutto's allusion to the angel was all that was needed to convince Fra Felice of the basically diabolical character of the benandanti's "games" and of their identity with the sabbat. Gasparutto vehemently denied this, and defended himself by shifting the accusation to the enemy, the witches: "He did not promise me anything, but those others do dance and leap about, and I saw them because we fought them." Now the inquisitor turned to another key point in Gasparutto's story: "Where did your spirit go when the angel summoned you?" "It came out because in the body it cannot speak," Gasparutto replied. The exchanges now came in rapid succession: "Who told you that your spirit had to come out if it was to speak with the angel?" "The angel himself told me." "How many times did you see this angel?" "Every time that I went, because he always came with me," and a little later he added: "He stays in person by our banner."

Thus far we have had what amounts to a monologue on Gasparutto's part, interrupted only by the inquisitor's requests for clarification. As long as the benandanti's tales of their nocturnal "games" were merely startling facts, even though silently suspect, but at least not out of line with traditional demonological schemes, Fra Felice had maintained a passive attitude of mild astonishment and detached curiosity. But with the opening that Gasparutto had suddenly provided, the technique of the interrogation changed, becoming openly suggestive. The inquisitor now began in earnest to try and make the benandante's confessions conform to the existing model—the sabbat.

First of all he subtly endowed the figure of the angel with demonic attributes: "When he appears before you or takes his leave, does this angel frighten you?" "He never frightens us, but when the company breaks up, he gives a benediction," Gasparutto stubbornly answered. "Does not this angel ask to be adored?" "Yes, we adore him just as we adore our Lord Jesus Christ in church." At this point Fra Felice changed the subject: "Does this angel conduct you where that other one is seated on that beautiful throne?" In Gasparutto's tale, needless to say, there had been no mention of devils or thrones. This time too the reply was prompt and tinged with exasperation: "But he is not of our company, God forbid that we should get involved with that false enemy! . . . It is the witches that have the beautiful thrones." The inquisitor persisted: "Did you ever see witches by that beautiful throne?" And Gasparutto, gesturing with his arms, sensing that he had been caught in the inquisitor's trap: "No sir, we did nothing but fight!" Fra Felice was implacable. "Which is the more beautiful angel, yours or the one on the beautiful throne?" And Gasparutto, contradicting himself in his desperation: "Didn't I tell you that I have not seen those thrones? . . . Our angel is beautiful and white; theirs is black and is the devil."

*   *   *

By now the trial was nearing its conclusion. On the whole, the inquisitor had managed to adapt Gasparutto's testimony to his own notions and theological preconceptions: the meetings of the benandanti and of the witches were nothing but the sabbat, and the "company" of the benandanti which falsely proclaimed that it enjoyed divine protection and fought under the guidance and aegis of an angel was diabolical. Under the pressure of the inquisitor's questioning Gasparutto's self-assurance seemed to weaken, as if the reality of his beliefs had suddenly changed and was slipping out of his grasp. A day or two later, once more before Fra Felice, he declared: "I believe that the apparition of that angel was really the devil tempting me, since you have told me that he can transform himself into an angel." The same thing happened to Moduco in his interrogation of 2 October: "Ever since I heard from that friend of mine who is in prison that an angel appeared to him, I have come to think that this is a diabolical thing, because our Lord God does not send angels to lead spirits out of bodies, but only to provide them with good inspiration." Were these retractions sincere? It is impossible to reply with certainty. What counts is that the events in this trial—the crisis of beliefs evidenced by the two benandanti, their incorporation, at the inquisitor's insistence, into the latter's mental and theological world—epitomised and anticipated the general evolution of the cult that was to define itself, little by little, over more than half a century. . . .

So the benandanti with fennel stalks battled witches armed with stalks of sorghum. It is not clear why sorghum was the weapon of the witches—unless it could be identified with the broom, their traditional symbol (the so-called "broom sorghum", one of the most common varieties of sorghum, is a type of millet). It is a compelling theory, especially in light of . . . the nocturnal gatherings of the witches and benandanti as the antecedents of the diabolical sabbat—but obviously this is a theory which should be advanced with caution. In any case, for the benandanti the sorghum seemed to symbolize the evil power of the witches. The parish priest of Brazzano, Bartolomeo Sgabarizza, reported having had this conversation with Gasparutto: "He begged me not to sow sorghum in my field, and whenever he finds any growing he pulls it up, and he curses whoever plants it; and when I said that I wanted to sow it, he began to swear." To fennel, instead, whose healing qualities were recognized in popular medicine, was attributed the power of keeping witches away: Moduco affirmed that the benandanti ate garlic and fennel "because they are a defence against witches".

It may be supposed that this combat re-enacted, and to a certain extent rationalized, an older fertility rite in which two groups of youths, respectively impersonating demons favourable to fertility and the maleficent ones of destruction, symbolically flayed their loins with stalks of fennel and sorghum to stimulate their own reproductive capacity, and by analogy, the fertility of the fields of the community. Gradually the rite may have come to be represented as an actual combat, and from the uncertain outcome of the struggle between the two opposed bands would magically depend the fertility of the land and the fate of the harvests. At a later stage these rites would cease to be practised openly and would exist precariously, between the dream-like and the hallucinatory, in any case on a purely internal emotional plane—and yet without quite sliding into mere individual fantasizing.

But these are pure conjectures that can be confirmed only on the basis of solid evidence, unavailable at present, about preceding phases of the cult. There is absolutely nothing in the statements of the benandanti that can be interpreted as a relic of this hypothetical original rite. More plausible perhaps is the analogy between the battles of benandanti against witches and ritual contests between Winter and Summer (or Winter and Spring) which used to be acted out, and still are today, in some areas of north-central Europe . . .

*   *   *

In the confessions of these benandanti, religious elements of very different origin were superimposed on this agrarian rite, seemingly self-sufficient in its internal motivations. Moduco and Gasparutto both asserted that they could not discuss the nocturnal conventicles in which they participated because by doing so they would be flouting the will of God; and Moduco clarified this point: "We go forth in the service of Christ and the witches in the service of the devil." The company of the benandanti was a divine entity, virtually a peasant army of the faith established by God ("we believe that it is given by God, because we fight for the faith of Christ"): at its head, according to Gasparutto, was an angel of God; within the group, Moduco related, God and the saints were piously invoked, and its members were certain to go to paradise after death.

The contrast between fighting "for love of the crops" and fighting "for the faith of Christ" is indeed glaring. To be sure, in this popular religiosity, so composite, interlaced with the most varied elements, such syncretism is not surprising. But we should ask ourselves the reason for this Christianization of agrarian rites performed by the benandanti—which undoubtedly was "spontaneous" in this period and widespread throughout the Friuli. Perhaps it was a method adopted in a distant past to shield from the eyes of the church a rite that was not quite orthodox (just as the groups of young people celebrating ancient fertility rites placed themselves under the protection of a patron saint); or it may be that the ancient agrarian rite gradually received a Christian motif from those who ingenuously joined the good cause of the fertility of the fields with the holy cause of the faith of Christ. Finally, we may even suppose that, in the face of the progressive assimilation . . . of diabolical elements on the part of their enemies, the witches, the benandanti instinctively and correspondingly identified their cause with that of the faith.

There may be some truth in each of these assumptions. At any rate, it is clear that this attempt at Christianization did not (and could not) succeed, and indeed was not favourably received by the Inquisition. It faded away within a few decades. Two primary elements coexisted within the medley of beliefs of which the benandanti were the bearers: an agrarian cult (probably the more ancient of the two) and a Christian cult, and in addition a number of other elements capable of being assimilated by witchcraft. When inquisitors failed to understand the first and decisively rejected the second, this composite of myths and beliefs, for lack of other outlets, inevitably had to debouch in the last direction.

The Night-Witch in Popular Imagination

Norman Cohn

Norman Cohn's 1975 book Europe's Inner Demons *was also excerpted in part 1. Here he explores the folk origins of the image of the night-flying witch and the literal interpretation of those beliefs by witch hunters later on. For this reason, he also questions Carlo Ginzburg's interpretation of the benandanti's battles.*

•

The ancient Romans already knew of a creature which flew about at night, screeching, and lived on the flesh and blood of human beings. Their literature in the first two centuries after Christ abounds in references to it. They called it a *strix*, from a Greek word meaning "to screech"; usually they thought of it as an owl, and granted it feathers and even eggs, but they were also clear that it was no mere bird. Pliny the Elder admitted that he could not fit the *strix* into any recognized species of bird; and he added that according to popular belief it offered its breasts to babies to suck. Its purpose in so doing was sinister: Serenus Sammonicus, who wrote about medical science, considered that its milk was poison. . . .

It is plain that *striges* were indeed thought of not as ordinary birds but as beings into which certain women could transform themselves. There is a relevant comment in Ovid's description, in the *Amores*, of the procuress and witch Dipsas. She is an old hag, who specializes in destroying the chastity of the young, but she also possesses vast magical powers. Dipsas not only understands the occult use of herbs, she can conjure up the dead, cleave the solid ground, make a river flow back to its source. Moreover, says Ovid, "if I may be believed, I have seen the stars drip blood, and blood darken the moon. I believe that then (Dipsas), transformed, was flying through the darkness of the night, her hag's carcase clad in feathers. This I suspect, and such is the report." . . .

In other words, the *strix* is a witch who is a woman by day but at night flies through the air on amorous, murderous or cannibalistic errands. Thus the grammar-

From Norman Cohn, *Europe's Inner Demons: An Enquiry Inspired by the Great Witch-Hunt* (New York: Basic Books, 1975), 206–14, 216–21, 223–24. © 1975 by Basic Books. Reprinted by permission of the Peters Fraser and Dunlop Group Limited on behalf of Norman Cohn.

ian Festus, in his work on the meanings of words, defines the late Latin word *strigae* as "the name given to women who practise sorcery, and who are also called flying women".

Most of these writers knew perfectly well that there were no such things as *striges* or *strigae*; they were simply using the idea to ornament their fiction. And certainly the law took no cognizance of these mysterious creatures. It did recognize maleficent sorcery, and people were frequently tried and sentenced as sorcerers. But nobody was taken into custody for being a *strix*.

Yet the literary references are clearly to a belief which was taken seriously in some quarters, and it may well be that amongst the common people belief in *striges* was real and widespread. Certainly this was the case amongst the Germanic peoples before they came under first Roman and then Christian influence. The notion of a witch as an uncanny, cannibalistic woman had developed amongst them too—it seems, independently of outside influence. And the earliest body of Germanic law, the *Lex Salica*, which was written in the sixth century but which reflects the beliefs and attitudes of a still earlier age, treats the *striga* or *striga* as a reality, and her cannibalism as something that really occurred. It hints at assemblies of witches with cauldrons; it fixes the fine to be paid "if a *stria* shall devour a man and it shall be proved against her"; and it also fixes the fine in the event that "anyone shall call a free woman a *stria* and shall not be able to prove it". . . .

The notion of of cannibalistic witches, then, was familiar to many of the Germanic peoples in the early Middle Ages. Moreover the linguistic evidence suggests that, like their Roman precursors, these creatures were imagined as flying at night. The Latin of the early medieval laws is, admittedly, fairly debased—and nevertheless the clerics who wrote it must certainly have known that *striga* was derived from *strix*, and that a *strix* was something that flew about, screeching, in the dark. If they had not wished to convey this idea they could very well have used the term *malefica*, which also meant "witch" but had no bird-like associations.

In any case, by the beginning of the eleventh century there is firm evidence that in parts of Germany the image of the cannibalistic woman often, if not invariably, included the ability to fly about at night. . . .

Because the night-witch was known to the Romans also, it has often been assumed that the Germanic peoples must have taken the idea from them; or more precisely, that wherever the night-witch appears in a medieval text, it is due to the influence of Latin literature. Yet the balance of evidence is heavily against this view. The earliest written Germanic law, the *Lex Salica*, treats the night-witch as a reality—and no Roman law ever did that. And later laws, which deny the reality of the night-witch, are clearly directed not against the sophisticated fancies of *literati* raised on Ovid, but against beliefs which were so deep and widespread amongst the common people that they were liable to express themselves in insults and violence. Down to the thirteenth century, it was the educated elite who, in the name of Christian doctrine, rejected the night-witch; while the common people continued to believe in her. And one can go a little further. Burchard's penitential shows that some women assimilated the belief so completely that they imagined themselves to be night-witches. It condemns such women—not for doing harm to others but for indulging in a pagan superstition. What they were really doing was living out, in their dreams, a collective fantasy or folk-belief that was traditional amongst the Germanic peoples.

*　*　*

There was another popular belief, of a very different kind, concerning women who travelled at night in a supernatural manner. Around 906 Regino, formerly abbot of Prüm, was asked by the archbishop of Trier to write a guide to ecclesiastical discipline for the use of bishops when carrying out visitations of their dioceses. He included in his book a canon which probably originated in a lost capitulary of the ninth century and which later received the title *Canon Episcopi* from its opening phrase, "Episcopi episcoporumque ministri". The key passage reads as follows:

> . . . there are wicked women who, turning back to Satan and seduced by the illusions and phantoms of the demons, believe and openly avow that in the hours of the night they ride on certain animals, together with Diana, the goddess of the pagans, with a numberless multitude of women; and in the silence of the dead of night cross many great lands; and obey (Diana's) orders as though she were their mistress, and on particular nights are summoned to her service. Would that they alone perished in their perfidy, without dragging so many others with them into the ruin of infidelity! For a numberless multitude of people, deceived by this false view, believe these things to be true and, turning away from the true faith and returning to the errors of the pagans, think that there exists some divine power other than the one God.

And the canon reminds priests of their duty: they must, from the pulpit, warn their congregations that this is all illusion, inspired not by the spirit of God but by that of Satan. For Satan knows how to deceive foolish women by showing them, while they sleep, all kind of things and of people. But who has not, in dreams, gone out of himself, so that he believed he was seeing things which he never saw when awake? And who would be so foolish as to think that things that happened only in the mind have also happened in the flesh? Everyone must be made to realise that to believe such things is a sign that one has lost the true faith, and that one belongs not to God, but to the Devil. . . .

[Regino's canon] bulks large in most modern histories of European witchcraft; yet if one studies it carefully, it has no obvious bearing on witchcraft at all. The women it criticizes do not imagine themselves as night-witches, addicted to murderous and cannibalistic enterprises, but as devotees of a supernatural queen who leads and commands them on their nocturnal flights.

This supernatural queen deserves closer attention. Like Regino, Burchard calls her "Diana, goddess of the pagans", but he adds the phrase "or Herodias"; and in another paragraph of the *Corrector* he refers to her as "Holda". Between them, these names lead straight to one particular body of folk-belief.

The Roman goddess Diana continued to enjoy a certain cult in the early Middle Ages. A life of St Caesarius, who was bishop of Arles early in the sixth century, mentions "a demon whom the simple people call Diana". Gregory of Tours describes how, in the same century, a Christian hermit in the neighbourhood of Trier destroyed a statue of Diana which, though no doubt of Roman origin, was worshipped by the native peasantry. Further east, in what is now Franconia, the cult was still vigorous late in the seventh century; the British missionary bishop St Kilian was martyred when he tried to convert the east Franks from their worship of Diana. Goddess of the moon and lover of the night, Diana was also, in one of her aspects, identified with Hecate, goddess of magic. And it was characteristic of Hecate that she rode at night, followed by a train of women, or rather of souls disguised as women—restless souls of the prematurely dead, of those who had died by violence, of those who had never been buried.

With Diana, Burchard equates Herodias, the wife of Herod the tetrarch and the instigator of the murder of John the Baptist. Legends clustered around this figure. Already in the tenth century we hear of her from Ratherius, who was a Frank by origin but who became bishop of Verona. He complains that many people, to the perdition of their souls, were claiming Herodias as a queen, even as a goddess, and were affirming that a third part of the world was subject to her; as though, he remarks, that were the reward for killing the prophet. In the twelfth century a Latin poem on Reynard the Fox, called *Reinardus*, provides further details. It describes how Herod's daughter, here also called Herodias instead of Salome, falls in love with the Baptist, who repulses her. When his head is brought to her on a platter she still tries to cover it with tears and kisses, but it shrinks away. Its lips begin to blow violently, until Herodias is blown into outer space, where she must hover for ever-more, a sorrowful queen. Yet she has some consolations. She has her cult, and a third part of mankind serves her. And from midnight until cockcrow she can sit on oaktrees and hazelbushes, resting from her eternal travelling through the empty air.

But it is the queen's other name, Holda, that shows most clearly how her followers regarded her. When Burchard gives this as an alternative to Diana and Herodias, he is evoking a figure who was to remain prominent in German folklore right down to the nineteenth century—and nowhere more so than in Hesse, where Burchard was born. Holda (Hulda, Holle, Hulle, Frau Holl, etc.) is a supernatural, motherly being who normally lives in the upper air, and circles the earth. She is particularly active in the depths of winter; snowflakes are the feathers that fall when she makes her bed. She travels in the twelve days between Christmas and Epiphany, and this brings fruitfulness to the land during the coming year—from which one may conclude that originally she was a pagan goddess associated with the winter solstice and the rebirth of the year. She can sometimes be terrifying—she can lead the "furious army" which rides through the sky on the storm, she can also turn into an ugly old hag with great teeth and a long nose, the terror of children. Yet in the main she becomes terrifying only when angered—and what angers her is above all slackness about the house or the farm.

For Holda is not always in the sky; she visits the earth, and then she functions as patroness of husbandry. The plough is sacred to her, she assists the crops. She is particularly interested in the women's work of spinning and weaving; and if she punishes laziness she rewards diligence, often by pushing gifts through the window. She is also concerned with childbirth—babies come from her secret places, her tree, her pond. Fruitfulness and productivity of every kind are her special preoccupations. . . .

Such beliefs, or fantasies, where by no means confined to Germany. Guillaume d'Auvergne, bishop of Paris, who died in 1249, has similar tales to tell from France. He has heard of spirits who on certain nights take on the likeness of girls and women in shining robes, and in that guise frequent woods and groves. They even appears in stables, bearing wax candles, and plait the horses' manes. Above all these "ladies of the night" visit private homes, under the leadership of their mistress Lady Abundia (from *abundantia*), who is also called Satia (from *satietas*, meaning the same). If they find food and drink ready for them, they partake of them, but without diminishing the quantity of either; and they reward the hospitable household with an abundance of material goods. If on the other hand they find that all food and drink have been locked away, they leave the place in contempt. Inspired by this belief, foolish old women, and some equally foolish men, open up their pantries and uncover their barrels on the nights when they expect a visitation. The bishop, of course, knows just what to think of such practices. Demons trick old women into dreaming these things; and it is a grievous sin to think that abundance of material goods can come from any other source than God. . . .

Even today, many Sicilian peasants believe in mysterious beings whom they usually call "ladies from outsides", but also sometimes "ladies of the night", "ladies of the home", "mistresses of the home", "beautiful ladies" or simply "the ladies". According to the few who have ever seen them, these are tall and beautiful damsels with long, shining hair. They never appear by day, but on certain nights, especially Thursdays, they roam abroad under the leadership of a chief "lady". When they find a well-ordered house they will enter through cracks in the door or through the keyhole. Families who treat them well and offer them food and drink, music and dancing, can expect every kind of blessing in return. On the other hand any sign of disrespect or any resistance to their commands will bring poverty and sickness on the house—though even then they are quick to forgive, if they find themselves properly treated at their next visit. Though they are feared, as supernatural and uncanny beings, they are not confused with witches. Whereas witches are human beings, and essentially evil, the "ladies from outside" are spirits, and essentially good. In fact they are guardians, not destroyers.

From all this there emerges a coherent picture of a traditional folk-belief. Its origins seem to lie in a pre-Christian, pagan world-view. It is certainly very ancient; and despite certain variations of details, it has remained constant in its main features over a period of at least a thousand years and over a great part of western Europe. It is concerned with beneficent, protective spirits, who are thought of above all as female, and who are sometimes associated with the souls of the dead. In the past, it has been taken seriously in peasant communities: people tidied up their houses and left food and drink to win the favour of these spirits. Moreover some people—notably old women—used to dream or fantasy that they could attach themselves to these spirits and take part in their nocturnal journeyings. And here this age-old folk-belief can be brought into relation with equally ancient beliefs about witches. In both cases, we find that women are believed—and sometimes even believe themselves—to travel at night in a supernatural manner, endowed with supernatural powers by supernatural patrons. One belief is indeed the opposite of the other; with the canni-balistic witch, symbol of destruction, disorder and death, one can contrast the woman who joins the radiant "ladies" on their benign missions for the encourage-ment of hospitality and good housekeeping.

Inevitably, the official attitude of the Church to the "ladies of the night" was very different from that of the half-pagan peasantry. Just as, down to the thirteenth century, the Church denied the existence of night-witches, so it denied that these more welcome visitors were what they seemed to be. Belief in either kind of nocturnal voyager was condemned as pagan superstition. From the *Canon Episcopi* in the ninth century to Guillaume d'Auvergne in the thirteenth, there is unanimity amongst the orthodox: the "ladies of the night" belong to the world of dreams. The demons are indeed involved, but only in so far as they try, by means of these dreams, to seduce the dreamers from the true faith. To take such dreams for reality, above all to believe that one has oneself taken part in a nocturnal journey—this is to turn away from Christianity, it is to fall into the errors of the pagans and the snares of the Devil. Even so, it is not a horrific sin; and the penance imposed is much lighter than the penance for praying or lighting candles at a former pagan shrine.

But in the thirteenth century the attitude begins to change. Already Jacobus de Voragine takes a different view of the matter, and this is still truer of Jacopo Passa-vanti in the fourteenth century. The traditional picture of the nocturnal visitors changes; no longer tall, beautiful ladies, they have all the appearance of known individuals of both sexes, in fact they look just like one's neighbours. And the traditional interpretation also changes. These are no mere apparitions in a dream, they are demons visiting this earth in the guise of human beings; and they can also be seen and heard by human beings who are fully awake and in full possession of their senses. Something that hitherto has happened only in the minds of silly old women has taken on an objective, material existence. The implication is clear: a human being who takes part in such a gathering is no longer merely relapsing into pagan superstition, but is actually consorting with demons. The old fantasy of the supernatural queen and her train is beginning to blend with the new fantasy of the witches' Sabbat. . . .

Folk-beliefs about the "ladies of the night" would never, by themselves, have given rise to the great witch-hunt of the fifteenth, sixteenth and seventeenth centuries; but they did provide materials which could be exploited by the witch-hunters. The "ladies of the night" were, after all, imagined as a highly organized body, under a supernat-ural leader—and this meant that, in the eyes of the orthodox, the women who dreamed that they joined this throng were dreaming of submitting themselves to the absolute rule of a demon. Cannibalistic night-witches, on the other hand, had not traditionally been imagined in this way. Though there are hints—in the *Pactus legis Salicae* and again in Burchard's *Corrector*—that they operate collectively, the early medieval sources never suggest that they associate with demons, let alone that they are organized under demonic leadership. Night-witches and "ladies of the night" alike belonged to the world of popular imagination, particularly peasant imagination; and there they were kept quite separate from one another. But to the educated, looking at these fantasies from outside and from above, the distinction was not necessarily so absolute. . . .

*   *   *

It is clear that already in the Middle Ages some women believed themselves to wander about at night on cannibalistic errands, while others believed themselves to wander about, on more benign errands, under the leadership of a supernatural queen. Later, after the great witch-hunt had begun, some women genuinely believed that they attended the sabbat and took part in its demonic orgies: not all the confessions, even at that time, are to be attributed to torture or the fear of torture. In an age such as ours, with its interest in psychedelic experiments, one is bound to ask whether these delusions could have been the result of drugs.

Writing in 1435–7, the German Johann Nider tells the story of a peasant woman who imagined herself to fly at night with Diana. When a visiting Dominican tried to disabuse her, she offered to show him how she did it. One night, in the presence of the Dominican and another witness, she placed herself in a basket, rubbed herself with an ointment, and fell into such a stupor that not even falling to the floor could wake her. When finally she awoke she assured the observers that she had been with Diana, and could hardly be persuaded that she had never left the spot at all. At the same date the Spaniard Alfonso Tostato also tells of such women, and adds that while in their stupor they are insensible to blows and even to fire. A century later the Italian Bartolommeo Spina knew of women who anointed themselves and, in a deep stupor, imagined themselves to fly through the air with their mistress and a host of dancers. And by 1569 the Dutch physician Johannes Weyer was even able to supply recipes of solutions and ointments that were supposed to be favoured by witches.

How seriously should all this be taken? The fact that some of the recipes include real narcotics, such as belladonna, has roused curiosity. Some bold spirits, notably in Germany, recently tried them out on themselves—and promptly experienced—very much what the witches are supposed to have experienced. Yet there are grounds for doubt. Not one of those tales about women anointing themselves even pretends to come from an eyewitness—even Nider, who goes into most detail, merely repeats what his teacher had once told him about an unnamed Dominican. Moreover the earliest recipes, from the fifteenth century, consist not of narcotics but of such disagreeable but non-toxic substances as the flesh of snakes, lizards, toads, spiders and (of course) children; and the ointments are less commonly applied to the witch's body than to the chairs and broomsticks on which she rides. All in all, there is hardly more reason to take these stories seriously than to believe that the witch Pamphile, in Apuleius, was really able, with the help of a concoction of laurel and dill, to grow an owl's feathers, beak and claws and fly off hooting. The true explanation lies in quite a different direction—not in pharmacology but in anthropology; for the night-witch is known in many non-European societies today.

The anthropological literature on witchcraft is vast and continues to grow at a prodigious rate, but to clarify this particular problem one need only turn to J. R. Crawford's *Witchcraft and sorcery in Rhodesia*. Mr Crawford's book, which is based on judicial records of witchcraft and sorcery allegations between 1956 and 1962, shows very clearly what the Shona peoples of Rhodesia believe about night-witches. They believe that certain women strip themselves naked and fly through the air at night, usually on a hyena, ant-bear, owl or crocodile. The purpose of the flight is cannibalism or, rather, necrophagy—something which the Shona regard with even greater horror, if possible, than does our own society. The witch is supposed to exhume newly buried corpses and eat the flesh—but also to kill people, especially children, in order to devour them. That is the general belief amongst the Shona, and it has many counterparts in other areas of Africa, and, indeed, in Asia and Central and Southern America also. . . .

Set against this background the discoveries of the Italian scholar Dr Carlo Ginzburg, which he has described in his fascinating book *I Benandanti*, take on a fresh significance. By archival research Ginzburg unearthed the existence, in the late sixteenth century, of a curious group of anti-witches at Friuli, near Udine in northeastern Italy. These peasants saw themselves as entrusted with the task of going out, during the Ember days, to fight witches who were trying to destroy the fertility of the crops and also to kill children. Their steeds could be goats or cats as well as horses, their weapons consisted of sticks of fennel; the outcome of the battle decided whether the coming year would be one of plenty or of famine. Because of this, Ginzburg decided that he had stumbled upon a survival of an age-old fertility cult; and other writers have adopted and developed the idea. Yet there is nothing whatsoever in Ginzburg's material to justify such a conclusion.

The experiences of the Benandanti—the rides, the battles with the witches, the rescuing of the crops and the children—were all trance experiences. The Benandanti—as they themselves repeatedly stated—underwent these experiences in a state of catalepsy: throughout the relevant period they lay motionless in bed, in a stupor. It was, they said, their spirits that went out to do battle; indeed, if a spirit failed to return promptly, the body died. Moreover, the summons to enlist in the Benandanti came to a person in his sleep; it was brought by an angel—described as golden, like the angels on altars—and the same angel stood by the banner of the Benandanti during the battle.

The Benandanti believed absolutely that their experiences were real, and that they were collective; but they never for a moment suggested that they were bodily—the witches too were said to fight only in spirit. As with the Shona women, "it only came to them as if they were dreaming". Indeed, to be a Benandante at all it was necessary to have been born with a caul, which was regarded as a bridge by which the soul could pass from the everyday world into the world of spirits.

What Ginzburg found in his sixteenth-century archives was in fact a local variant of what, for centuries before, had been the stock experience of the followers of Diana, Herodias or Holda. It has nothing to do with the "old religion" of fertility postulated by Margaret Murray and her followers. What it illustrates is—once more—the fact that not only the waking thoughts but the trance experiences of individuals can be deeply conditioned by the generally accepted beliefs of the society in which they live.

This is merely to re-state, in modern terms, what was taken for granted by educated people almost to the close of the Middle Ages. As we have seen, until the late fourteenth century the educated in general, and the higher clergy in particular, were quite clear that these nocturnal journeyings of women, whether for benign or for maleficent purposes, were purely imaginary happenings. But in the sixteenth and still more in the seventeenth centuries, this was no longer the case. And that is what made the great witch-hunt possible: witch-hunting reached massive proportions only where and when the authorities themselves accepted the reality of the nocturnal journeyings. For without such journeyings, no witches' sabbats.

Image Magic and the Like

GEORGE LYMAN KITTREDGE

In this excerpt from his 1929 book Witchcraft in Old and New England, *George Lyman Kittredge (1860-1941) describes a variety of forms of image magic used in England. Kittredge, a scholar of early English literature, was the author of* Chaucer and His Poetry *(1915) and* The Old Farmer and His Almanack *(1904) and the editor of several Shakespearean dramas.*

•

On January 22, 1470, Jacquette de Luxembourg, Duchess of Bedford, was cleared of a slanderous accusation of witchcraft brought against her by Thomas Wake. He had exhibited an image of lead, "made lyke a Man of Armes, conteynyng the lengthe of a mans fynger, and broken in the myddes, and made fast with a Wyre," which he asserted she had fashioned; and he had also urged John Daunger, a parish clerk of Northamptonshire, to testify that the duchess had manufactured two other images, one representing Edward IV and another Elizabeth Grey, whom the king married. On the day mentioned, both Wake and Daunger were examined before the Bishop of Carlisle, and the accusation broke down, for Daunger refused to give any such evidence. The old scandal was revived by Richard III in 1483 in his attempt to show that there had never been a valid marriage between King Edward and Queen Elizabeth. It was then asserted that "the pretensed Mariage" was brought about "by Sorcerie and Wichecraft" committed by Elizabeth and her mother, according to "the common opinion of the people and the publique voice and fame thorough all this Land." Obviously the notion was that two of the figures were used in love magic.

In 1490 Johanna Benet was called before the Commissary of London for sorcery with a candle of wax: "as the candle consumes, the man must waste away." A similar story was told at Norwich as late as 1843 in the course of a prosecution for assault, and candle witchcraft is still practised in England, it seems, to torment and recall a truant lover. About 1500 Alice, wife of John Huntley of Southwark, was charged

From George Lyman Kittredge, *Witchcraft in Old and New England* (New York: Russell and Russell, 1956), 84–87, 92–94, 97–99, 102–3. © 1929, 1956 by H. C. Kittredge. Reprinted by permission of Harvard University Press.

with image magic. She had, it was said, long "used and exercised the feetes of Wychecraft and Sorsery ayenst the lawe of the Chirche and of the kyng." There were found in her house, according to the petition in Chancery filed by John Knyght, chaplain, one of the searchers, "dyverses mamettes [images] for wychecraftes and enchauntementez, with other stuffe beryed and depely hydd under the erthe." What the outcome was we cannot tell. Our sole information is derived from Knyght's petition, from which it appears that he had been arrested, probably at Mistress Alice's suit, and was then in the Marshalsea. It was likewise about the year 1500 that the Bishop of St. David's undertook to discipline Thomas Wyriott, Gentleman, and a woman named Tanglost for adultery. This was the beginning of troubles. Wyriott's wife died soon after, and it was common fame that she was killed by witchcraft worked or procured by Tanglost. The bishop banished Tanglost from the diocese. Thereupon she hired a witch at Bristol, one Margaret Hackett, and brought her to Wyriott's house, where, in a room inappropriately styled Paradise Chamber, the two women made a pair of waxen images in order to destroy the prelate. Margaret was arrested, and she confessed; but another witch was hired and a third figure of wax was fashioned. Tanglost was then examined for heresy by four doctors of divinity, who referred her to the bishop for "correction." . . .

In 1538 there was great excitement about a wax baby with two pins stuck in it, discovered when about to be buried in a London churchyard. A scrivener named Poole, skilled in sorcery, was consulted. He declared that the maker of the puppet, whoever he was, "was not his craft's master, for he should have put it either in horse dung or in a dunghill." The authorities looked into the affair. The talk at Oxford was that the image represented Prince Edward, that there was a knife through the head or heart, and that as the image "did consume, so likewise should the Prince." The preamble to the Witchcraft Statute of Henry VIII (1542) expressly notes the prevalent manufacture of "dyvers Images and pictures of men women childrene Angelles or develles beastes or fowles. . . ."

That image witchcraft went on through the reigns of Elizabeth and James I, was a matter of course. Indeed, it has continued to the present time in uninterrupted succession from remote antiquity. . . .

A recent lawsuit in the Upper Congo grew out of image magic. Two men quarrelled. *A* had heard that *B* paid a witch-doctor to call up *A*'s image, which was then repeatedly stabbed by *B*. But *B* insisted that it was another person's image, not *A*'s, that the sorcerer had evoked. Among the Northern Bantu and elsewhere you may kill your enemy by spearing his shadow. So, in an ancient Irish saga, Find "saw before him Cuirrech's shadow, and throughout the shadow he hurled a spear, chanting a spell over its head, and it strikes into Cuirrech, who fell thereby." A wizard of Lincoln once revealed a thief by making his shadow appear on a wall. In Africa you may stab your enemy's outline drawn in sand; in North Carolina, if you mark out his figure on a board and shoot it, he feels pain in the corresponding part of his body. In 1903 a mountaineer in that state, finding that butter would not come when his wife churned, declared that a woman of the neighborhood had bewitched the milk, pinned up a portrait of her on the wall, and shot a silver bullet through it. In Nova Scotia, "if bewitched, draw a figure of the witch on a board and fire a charge of shot into it. This, done before sunrise, will break the spell." . . .

To use an animal instead of a figurine as representative of the person to be injured was common enough in ancient *defixiones*. Thus along with the cursing tablet there might be buried a cat or a cock that had been tortured or mutilated. The object was, of course, to cause one's enemy to be afflicted or disabled in like manner. So in the county of Durham in 1861, when a woman was thought to be suffering from witchcraft, pins were run into a live pigeon by each member of her family, and the bird was roasted. The witch, it was hoped, would feel these torments and thus would be forced to come and remove the curse. About 1920 in Devon a cockerel was tortured to death with pins; then the feathers were singed off and the carcass was thrown away. A spell was recited, beginning:

> With this pin I thee prick,
> My enemy's heart I hope to stick.

Here we have a performance and a spell precisely like those of the ancients. Compare a Latin tablet from the proconsular Province of Carthage: "This cock's tongue I have torn out while he was alive. . . . So may the tongues of my enemies be made dumb against me!" and a Greek tablet from the same region: "As this cock is fast bound in feet and hands and head, so bind the legs and the hands and the head and the heart of Victoricus the charioteer."

Sometimes the animal thus maltreated was regarded as an offering to the infernal gods; and this idea has descended to our own times, for the sacrifice of a cock is a recognized feature of ancient, mediæval, and modern sorcery. In the proceedings against Dame Alice Kyteler in 1324 it was alleged that she had offered cocks at the crossroads to a demon, tearing them limb from limb, and had used the entrails in the preparation of magical powders and unguents. In 1879 in Ireland a black cock was cut into quarters and offered at the four corners of a field to bring ill fortune upon the owners of the land. To baptize a dog or a cat was a powerful rite to command demons, and sometimes, in such cases, the creature was slaughtered as if it were a human sacrifice. This comes out unmistakably in the trial of two treasure-digging sorcerers in 1465: they had promised their demon "the body of a Christian man," but they cheated him by offering up a cock which they had baptized by a Christian name. "A redd cock beinge dead" was seized among the miscellaneous paraphernalia of two men caught in the act of "witchcrafte or conjuringe" in a field near London in 1590; presumably it had been sacrificed to a demon, for they also left behind in their flight "a fayre cristall stone" with *Sathan* written on it. . . .

It is even now a common practice to torment an enemy by sticking pins, needles, or thorns in an animal's heart and (often) roasting it or parching it in the chimney. Here the beast's heart serves your malefic sorcery as well as an image of wax or the whole animal would do. The custom is manifestly of immemorial antiquity and differs in no essential from the burial of a mutilated cat or cock in the ancient *defixiones*: indeed, the heart may be cut out of a living animal. About 1842, by a white wizard's directions, six bullocks' hearts—two stuck with pins, the others with new nails—were slowly melted, and thus the witch's heart was to be melted too; then nails were driven into a butt and it was rolled downhill, to torture the witch further; she was killed by this treatment and showed the marks. In Yorkshire, in the eighteenth century, a cow's heart was boiled and stuck with pins to check the cattle plague. In the South Downs, rather recently, when pigs had been "overlooked" (made sick by the evil eye), a heart was pierced with nails and pins and then roasted. A similar case occurred in Somerset in 1875. In Devonshire, some years ago, when a pony went lame, an animal's heart was burned; the witch came and tried to buy apples, which were refused; the pony got well. The classic cock reappears in the county of Durham: about 1855, to cure a sick horse, a black fowl's heart stuck with pins was roasted. In Somerset, in 1882, as a counter-charm when a woman had gone mad, an animal's heart with pins in it was to be roasted and then put in the chimney to waste away and thus rot the witch's heart. In South Devon, also as a counter-charm to avenge the black witchcraft that had killed cows or sheep, a sheep's heart was pierced with pins and nails. Against bad luck in fishing, caused by witchcraft, a pigeon's heart was filled with pins and roasted in Yorkshire. To keep out Dorset witches a piece of bacon stuck with pins used to be hung up in the chimney. An elaborate piece of sorcery to stop death of cattle is reported by the Rev. J. C. Atkinson from Cleveland: an ox-heart was pierced with nine new pins, nine new needles, and nine new nails and burned at midnight to the accompaniment of two verses of a [cursing] psalm. About 1897 a Devonshire woman, tormented by witch-craft, laid a sheep's heart stuck with pins on the bar that holds up the pothooks in the fireplace and repeated the following spell:

> May each pin
> Thus stuck in
>   This poor heart
> In hers go
> Who hurts me so
>   Till she departs.

The patient recovered and the witch died, so they say. Sometimes the heart, instead of being burned, is buried in the ground or concealed in the fabric of a house or under the foundation. The process may be purely malefic or may be resorted to as a counter-spell. The heart may be extracted from a living animal: in Yorkshire, for example, to ward off witchcraft, take a black hen's heart out of the living bird, stick it full of pins, and bury the hen.

We must remember that these performances are not fictitious. A calf's heart, thus pierced, was exhumed in 1827 opposite the threshold of an old Dalkeith tenement (apparently under the flagstones of the floor) and was sent to Sir Walter Scott as a curiosity. Scott sent it to the Society of Antiquaries, in whose museum it may still be seen. The Taunton Museum shows two dried pigs' hearts, thick set with pins, both found in an old chimney in Somerset. . . .

In 1610 Joan Bayly of Rye, an octogenarian, deposed that, thinking Thomas Hart's child bewitched, she told Mistress Hart to get a piece of red cloth, sixty needles, and a half-pennyworth of pins. Then, to force the witch to come, Joan stuck the pins and needles in the cloth, put it in the fire, and pierced it with a dagger. After a long time the cloth was consumed, and, says Joan, "at length it did seem to be like unto a toad, but no party came in," and she declares that she does not know who bewitched the child. Probably the cloth was cut to the shape of a heart. A corked greybeard jug containing clippings of hair and of fingernails along with such a cloth heart stuck full of bent pins, was dug up at Westminster in 1904. In Yorkshire "when a child was born, and it proved either unhealthy or deformed, it was generally supposed some evil-disposed person must have pricked its name with pins on a pin-cushion. When such a discovery was made by an expectant wife, nothing was said to the person working the evil, but the cushion was stolen, the pins withdrawn one by one, and stuck into the heart of a calf. This had to be buried in the churchyard." . . .

To drive a nail (preferably redhot), or pins or a knife, into a person's footmark makes him lame, and this means of detection or vengeance is often utilized against a witch. In the Scottish Highlands a square of turf is pierced with pins and put in the fire to punish the hag who has afflicted a child. Burning a handful of thatch from a witch's cottage forces her to reveal herself, according to a theory long accepted by country people in England; so, in Joan Cason's case (1586), a tile from the witch's house, put in the fire, compelled her to come in person.

A bottle buried, or put by the fire, with pins or spikes from a thornbush in it—or pins, needles or nails (sometimes also hair, bits of fingernails, etc.)—will work malefically, and is a good remedy, therefore, against witchcraft. In Lincolnshire, jugs called greybeards and other vessels are found now and then beneath the foundation or threshold or hearthstone of old buildings; they may contain horseshoe nails, scraps of iron, needles, pins, etc. In West Sussex about fifty years ago, if you filled a quart bottle with pins and heated them redhot, they would prick the heart of the witch that had given you epilepsy and make her take off the spell. Boiling pins in urine will force a Sussex wizard to come to your house (1919). To bury a bottle containing the urine of a bewitched person or animal will afflict the witch with strangury: this (as well as to draw the witch's blood or hang up a horseshoe) Increase Mather regards as an illicit measure of protection. His son Cotton also disapproves "the Urinary experiment" by which "the Urine must be bottled with Nails and Pins, and such Instruments in it as carry a shew of Torture with them, if it attain its end." . . .

Charm bottles have often come to light. One found in a Wharfedale garden in 1845 was filled with pins, needles, human hair, fragments of fingernails, brimstone, etc. Another, buried upside down, filled with dark water and containing nine bent pins, was under the clay floor of a cottage in Staffordshire. A jar containing spikes from a thornbush as well as pins was exhumed in a Devon churchyard in 1895, and a bottle with pins in the cork was turned up in 1900 in digging a grave in the same county. A similar discovery was made some sixty or seventy years ago in a grave at Bodmin. Tombs, we remember, were the favorite places of deposit for cursing tablets in antiquity. Two large coils of human hair, recently deposited, were uncovered about 1900 in a kistvaen near Postbridge. The following elaborate recipe comes from the same county (Devon): "To destroy the power of a witch. Take three small-necked stone jars: place in each the liver of a frog stuck full of new pins, and the heart of a toad stuck full of thorns from the holy thorn bush. Cork and seal each jar. Bury in three different churchyard paths seven inches from the surface and seven feet from the porch. While in the act of burying each repeat the Lord's prayer backwards. As the hearts and livers decay, so will the witch's power vanish. After performing this ceremony no witch can have any power over the operator."

[13]

Divining, Healing, and Destroying

RICHARD GODBEER

In this excerpt from his 1992 book The Devil's Dominion, *the historian Richard Godbeer discusses the reasons for the popularity of divination and other practices of folk magic.* The Devil's Dominion *won the American Historical Association Pacific Coast Branch Book Award in 1993. Godbeer has also written several articles on sexual behavior in early America, including "Chaste and Unchaste Covenants: Witchcraft and Sex in Early Modern Culture," in* Wonders of the Invisible World, 1600–1900, *ed. Peter Beres (1994); his book* Sex and Sensibility in Early America *is forthcoming.*

•

Ecclesiastical magic had no place in the religious life of seventeenth-century New England. But folk magic survived the journey across the Atlantic and flourished in the northern colonies. Cunning folk lived and provided magical services in every kind of New England town: in farming communities, seaports, and on the frontier. In Andover, Massachusetts, an agricultural community twenty miles northwest of Boston, townsfolk came to Samuel Wardwell to have their fortunes told. In Easthampton, Connecticut, a small farming town on the eastern tip of Long Island, Elizabeth Garlick practiced as a healer. Wethersfield, Connecticut, over thirty miles inland, was a chiefly agricultural community, but had a good harbor and developed a healthy trade in hemp, furs, and cattle. The people of Wethersfield could call on Katherine Harrison, a healer and fortune-teller. Beverly, Massachusetts, a coastal town just north of Salem, had a fortune-teller named Dorcas Hoar. Lynn, Massachusetts, site of a thriving shoemaking industry and the famous ironworks, had two healers, Anna Edmunds and Ann Burt. In Boston itself, Jane Hawkins and Mary Hale were also known as healers. Not all cunning folk were settled members of a community: Caleb Powell, a sailor who drifted into Newbury, Massachusetts, in the late 1670s, claimed to possess occult knowledge and offered his services to the townsfolk there.

From Richard Godbeer, *The Devil's Dominion: Magic and Religion in Early New England* (Cambridge: Cambridge University Press, 1992), 30–46, 52–53. © 1992 by Cambridge University Press. Reprinted by permission of Cambridge University Press.

When New Englanders wanted to use magic in order to resolve problems and crises, they did not always turn to experts. Some magical techniques required no particular expertise; people could and did use such techniques independently of cunning folk. New Englanders used magic to surmount the barriers of time and space, to look into the future and across vast distances. Magic also enabled them to harness the world and adapt it to their own ends: to heal the sick, to protect against harm, and also to inflict harm. Through magic, men and women overcame their natural limitations: it made the world a more immediate and accessible place, giving new powers of perception and action to those who mastered its possibilities.

Unfortunately, there is no way to gauge the number of magical practitioners in seventeenth-century New England, or how many people actually consulted them. Nor is it possible to estimate how many New Englanders experimented with magic on their own. But it is clear that resort to magic was not uncommon. New England court records contain many references to magical activity. Legal testimony was often recorded in summarized form and so some of these entries are maddeningly compact, but others provide detailed descriptions of magical techniques and the contexts in which they were used. Puritan sermons, treatises, diaries, and correspondence also testify to the persistence of magical practices: in these writings, the godly reported and condemned popular recourse to magic. None of those describing magical experiments, whether in court testimony or elsewhere, ever suggested that such activities were in any way unusual. The ministers themselves were evidently convinced that magical practice was widespread. This is not to suggest that magic was ubiquitous in early New England, but those who did turn to magical techniques were clearly members of a sizeable constituency.

The extant sources reveal nothing about magical practice during the initial period of settlement. As noted above, most evidence relating to magic originates in clerical sources or legal depositions in which witnesses described the activities of cunning folk whom they suspected of witchcraft: few clerical writings survive from this early period and there were no witch trials before 1647. The absence of witch trials during the early years of settlement is not surprising: a formal accusation was unlikely to take place until there had been time for a gradual build-up of public hostility toward a suspect individual within the new community; townsfolk rarely brought charges until they had accumulated a substantial body of evidence against the suspect witch. Accounts of the first witch trials contain hints of magical activity. When Margaret Jones of Charlestown, Massachusetts, was tried for witchcraft in 1648, her neighbors admitted that they had used countermagic to identify Jones as the person responsible for "mischief" that had "befel" their livestock. But even in this instance, the only surviving record of the townsfolk having used countermagic is a brief mention of the incident in John Hale's treatise about witchcraft, written some fifty years after Margaret Jones's execution. This experiment did not necessarily take place as late as 1648; witnesses in witchcraft cases often mentioned incriminating incidents that had occurred many years prior to the trial. Margaret Jones herself had a reputation for making predictions that "came to pass accordingly" and may well have been a fortune-teller. If colonists were using countermagic in or before 1648, so too could they have experimented with other kinds of magic, although we will never know for sure.

*   *   *

Magic enabled people to see through obstacles, across space and over time: they could locate lost or stolen possessions; they predicted future events. They became seers. Divining magic served different purposes in Old and New England. In early modern England, divination was used not only to predict the future, but also to locate stolen goods and to identify thieves. Theft was a major problem throughout the country, and there was no reliable official mechanism for the recovery of goods. John Selden, a legal scholar and prominent parliamentarian during the first half of the seventeenth century, wrote that the presence of conjurors "kept thieves in awe, and did as much good in a country as a justice of peace." In New England, on the other hand, people used divination principally to predict the future. Cotton Mather, minister of Boston's First Church, knew "a Person who missing anything, would use to sitt down and mutter a certain Charm, and then immediately, by an Invisible Hand be directly led unto the place where the Thing was to be found." But there is little evidence to suggest that other cunning folk engaged in similar activities. The use of divination to recover stolen property may have been rendered unnecessary by the informal but effective system of surveillance that New Englanders exercised over each other and that facilitated the detection of criminal activity.

New England diviners operated primarily as fortune-tellers. Katherine Harrison of Wethersfield, Connecticut, was "one that tould fortunes." Before coming to Wethersfield, Harrison had lived and worked in Hartford as servant to John Cullick, a merchant. One of her fellow servants, Elizabeth Bateman, was being courted by a young man called William Chapman, but her master disapproved of the match. Harrison predicted that Elizabeth would never marry a man named William and that her husband would be called Simon. Sure enough, Elizabeth eventually married a man named Simon Smith. There could be any number of explanations for Harrison's accuracy: she may have realized that their master's opposition to the marriage was unshakeable; she may have been using the medium of fortune-telling to lobby on Simon Smith's behalf. What matters for our purpose here is that townsfolk not privy to such explanations automatically assumed that Harrison had occult powers. . . .

Unquestioning faith in the accuracy of fortune-tellers' predictions sometimes resulted in tragedy. When William Adams, a Harvard graduate soon to be ordained as minister of Dedham, visited the town of Wenham in August 1672, he heard about the recent "strange death" of Thomas Whitteridge's wife. A fortune-teller had told Goody Whitteridge "that she should meet with great trouble, if she escaped with her life." This aroused "great horror" in Goody Whitteridge, who told her son that night "that it would be as the fortune teller had said." The boy tried to calm his mother, but she panicked and left the house "with great violence." The next morning, she was found nearby, dead from unknown causes. Twenty years later, during the winter of 1691–92, a girl who belonged to a fortune-telling group in Salem Village, Massachusetts, fashioned a primitive crystal ball by suspending the white of an egg in a glass. She hoped to identify "her future Husbands Calling." To the girl's horror, there appeared in the glass "a Spectre in likeness of a Coffin." Soon afterward, several of those who belonged to the fortune-telling group fell ill and began to suffer strange fits. We will never know exactly what occurred in the girls' minds, but it is clear that they took their experiment in divination all too seriously.

Fortune-tellers used a number of different techniques. John Hale, the minister at Beverly, Massachusetts, had met diviners who claimed "to tell persons their Fortunes (as they call it) or future Condition by looking into their hands." One of Hale's parishioners, Dorcas Hoar, "did pretend sum thing of fort[une] telling." She admitted to Hale that she "had borrowed a book of Palmistry" in which "their were rules to knoe what should come to pass." Samuel Wardwell of Andover, Massachusetts, also used palmistry: Ephraim Foster had seen Wardwell telling fortunes and testified in court that "said Wardwell would look in their hand and then would Cast his Eyes down upon the ground allways before he told Eny thing." In addition to reading palms, Dorcas Hoar could calculate a person's life expectancy by observing "veins abought [the] ey[e]s." John Winthrop, the governor of Massachusetts, mentioned in a journal entry for 1644 a man recently arrived from Virginia "who professed himself to have skill in necromancy," the use of magical ritual to communicate with demons, spirits, or the dead in order to discover future events or locate stolen goods.

The mastery of magical techniques such as palmistry and necromancy demanded training, and some practitioners learned their art from experts. Caleb Powell, a sailor who was staying in Newbury toward the end of 1679, claimed to have been instructed in the occult by Francis Norwood, a Quaker farmer from neighboring Gloucester. Other cunning folk learned about divination from instruction manuals; these were the products of contemporary intellectual enquiry. There was a clear parallel between the fashionable doctrines of Neoplatonic philosophy and the assumptions underlying popular magic, although it was only through the occasional use of treatises and manuals by magical practitioners that intellectuals exercised any direct influence over folk magic. Indeed, it was intellectual curiosity about folk traditions that stimulated the codification of magical formulas and techniques. Scholars such as Agrippa and Paracelsus published treatises describing the philosophical principles that, they believed, underlay the ritual techniques of the village conjuror. These learned tomes and their less esoteric derivatives usually contained detailed descriptions of folk rituals, which conjurors could then use as a practical guide. In other words, these manuals acted as a conduit for the transmission of popular culture.

People consulted instruction manuals in both Old and New England. Bearing in mind the unusually high rate of literacy in the northern colonies, there may have been a substantial constituency for such literature there. Unfortunately, no manuals have survived from colonial New England, but it is clear that at least some were in circulation. Cotton Mather complained that such "books had stole into the land, wherein fools were instructed how to become able fortune-tellers." John Bradstreet of Rowley, Massachusetts, told his neighbors that he had "read in a book of magic." According to John Hale, Dorcas Hoar was in possession of "a book of fortune telling

... w[i]th streaks and pictures in it and that it was about the bigness of such a book poynting to a gramer, or book of like magnitude." Hoar had borrowed the book from a neighbor, John Samson, which suggests the existence of an informal network for the circulation of such material. When Katherine Harrison was a maidservant in Hartford, Connecticut, she "would oft speake and boast, of her great familiaritie with mr Lilley," a famed English astrologer. Harrison claimed that she had read an astrological treatise by William Lilly while she was living in England. Perhaps she believed that this would enhance her credibility as a diviner in the eyes of her friends and neighbors. Certainly, she was eager to publicize her "skill," of which she "boast[ed]" to her neighbours: Harrison was "a common and professed fortune-teller . . ."

Cunning folk did not have a monopoly on magical practice. There were ritual techniques that called for no expert knowledge, and some New Englanders experimented with these procedures on their own. One such technique involved balancing a sieve on opened scissors or shears and then asking a question; if the sieve trembled or turned, the answer to the question was affirmative. In a similar procedure, a key was placed inside a book, usually a bible or psalter, which was then held loosely while the diviner asked a question; if the book turned or fell, the answer was positive. Sometimes, the name of an individual mentioned in the question was written on a piece of paper, which was then placed in the hollow end of the key. Neither of these techniques required particular expertise; anybody could master them. In 1692, Rebecca Johnson of Andover "acknowledged the turneing of the sieve, in her house by hir daughter." Sarah Hawkes, daughter-in-law to fortune-teller Samuel Wardwell, also lived in Andover and also "turned the Sive and [Scissors]." Henry Salter, yet another Andover citizen, apparently told a servant called Mary Warren that he had used both "the seive and scissors" and "the Key and bible." Did these three Andover sieve-turners know of each other's experiments? Did they share information about the techniques they were using? Did one teach the others? Was Samuel Wardwell mixed up in any of their activities? There are, unfortunately, no answers to these questions in the surviving records, but it is clear that magic was not necessarily esoteric, and that amateurs as well as experts could use it to divine the future.

*　　*　　*

Magic enabled New Englanders to change their world as well as to see it more clearly. Transformative magic was a double-edged weapon: people used it both to heal the sick and to hurt their enemies. This kind of magic operated by treating chosen objects as the images of other objects or people. Such images were not merely symbolic: each participated in the substantive reality of what it represented, so that changes wrought in an image could be reproduced in its counterpart. Thus, when an individual stuck pins or thorns in the representation of an enemy, the image served as much more than a symbol: it was an actual extension of a person; harm inflicted upon the image would also be undergone by the enemy. Charms operated in a similar way to image magic. Specific formulas and ceremonies could produce physical change in an object or person: a spell or ritual was taken to represent a given effect, so that its performance brought about the effect. Just as an effigy was mutilated to harm the individual represented, so the recitation of a spell brought about the effect that it was understood to symbolize.

Through the use of image magic, people could reach and transform anything or anybody. Goodwife Glover, a Catholic Irish-woman who lived in Boston and who used image magic to attack her enemies, was brought to trial in 1688 for afflicting the children of her neighbor John Goodwin. According to Cotton Mather's account, "Order was given to search the old womans house, from whence there were brought into the court, several small Images, or Puppets, or Babies, made of Raggs, and stuff't with Goat's hair, and other such Ingredients." Glover "acknowledged, that her way to torment the Objects of her malice, was by wetting of her Finger with her Spittle, and stroaking of those little Images." Mather knew another, unnamed woman "whose Brother was tortured with a cruel, pricking, Incurable Pain in the Crown of his Head: which continued until there was found with her a Poppet in Wax, resembling him, with a pin stuck into the Head of it; which being taken out, he Recovered Immediately." . . .

Whereas image magic was used only to afflict, charms could serve both good and evil purposes. Healers sometimes used charms as part of their treatment. Cotton Mather knew a woman "who upon uttering some Words over very painful Hurts and Sores, did . . . presently cure them." Mather had heard that in some towns it was "a usual thing for People to cure Hurts with Spells." The boundary between magical and non-magical medicine was often blurred in the early modern period. Traditional folk medicine combined three elements: commonsensical remedies, the application of medicinal plants and minerals, and the use of ritual charms. According to Protestant theologians, the inclusion or not of a charm indicated whether magic was involved, but many layfolk tended to confuse physicians in general with magical practitioners; such men and women did not make a clear distinction between medical and occult responses to illness. Not all New England healers were magicians, but at least some did use magical charms. In his *Essay for the Recording of Illustrious Providences*, Increase Mather gave two examples of charms prescribed by healers in Boston.

> A man in Boston gave to one a Sealed Paper, as an effectual remedy against the tooth-ache[e], wherein were drawn several confused characters, and these words written, In Nomine Patris, Filii, et Spiritus Sancti, Preserve thy Servant, such an one.

> Not long since a Man left with another in this Town, as a rare secret a cure for the Ague, which was this: five letters, viz, x, a, etc, were to be written successively on pieces of Bread and given to the Patient, on one piece he must write the word Kalendant, and so on another the next day, and in five days (if he did believe) he should not fail of cure.

The phrase "In Nomine Patris, Filii, et Spiritus Sancti" was derived from Catholic ritual, as was the formula recited by Rebecca Johnson's daughter when she used the sieve and scissors to find out whether her brother Moses Haggat was alive: "By Saint Peter and Saint Paul, if Haggat be dead, let this sieve turn around." The recitation of Catholic prayers as an ingredient in magical ritual was a survival from belief in the supernatural powers of the medieval church.

Other New Englanders were believed to use charms or spells for less benevolent purposes. In the late 1680s, Wilmott Reed of Marblehead quarreled with Mistress Simms of Salem Town, who had accused Reed's maid, Martha Laurence, of stealing her linen. When Simms threatened to take legal action, Reed cursed her, wishing that "she might never mingere [urinate] or carcare [defecate], if she did not goe." Soon afterward, Simms "was taken with the distemper of the dry Belly-ake, and so continued many months during her stay in the Towne, and was not cured whilst she tarryed in the Countrey." When Mercy Short visited the Boston gaol during the witch crisis of 1692, Sarah Good, one of the accused, asked her for some tobacco. Mercy refused, "throwing a Handful of Shavings at her and saying, That's Tobacco good enough for you." Sarah Good, enraged by this insult, "bestowed some ill words upon her," whereupon Mercy "was taken with . . . Fits" that lasted for several weeks. A few years prior to this, Mercy Disborough of Fairfield, Connecticut, told Thomas Benit "that she would make him as bare as a birds taile." Thereafter, he lost several of his livestock. Thomas Benit believed that there was a direct link between Disborough's curse and his subsequent misfortune: by speaking of the evil she willed upon him, Disborough had caused the evil to occur.

*   *   *

New Englanders were not defenseless against occult attack. They could use magic to undo as well as to cause harm. Countermagic, a technique that reversed image magic, demanded no special training and was often used by people who did not regard themselves as cunning folk. When someone used image magic to injure a person or damage an object, a two-way channel of communication was believed to open between practitioner and victim. The mischief could be undone, and the malefactor identified, by inflicting harm upon the damaged object or something closely associated with the injured person; this harm would then be translated back to the individual responsible. The purpose of countermagic was as much to identify and punish the malefactor as it was to heal the victim: it exacted revenge. Since the occult channel between afflicter and afflicted was already open, countermagic did not require any particular skill.

One of the commonest countermagical techniques involved burning the affected object in a fire: the person responsible would be drawn to the fire, or be found to have burns if examined afterwards. As minister John Hale pointed out, this method assumed a "sympathy in nature" between the damaged object and the malefactor's body. In or prior to 1665, Margaret Garrett of Hartford, Connecticut, found one side of a cheese she had made full of maggots. She suspected foul play and flung the cheese into the fire, whereupon Elizabeth Seager, who was in the barn, "Cryed out exceedingly." Seager came into the house and "cryed out she was full of Paine, and sat wringeing of her body and crying out, what do I aile? what do I aile?" Garrett concluded that Seager had used occult means to damage the cheese.

New Englanders used countermagic to cure both livestock and human beings suffering from inexplicable ailments. When an animal fell ill for no apparent reason, the owner might suspect that his livestock had been "bewitched." If so, he might decide to injure the animal in the hope of undoing the "bewitchment" and identifying the individual responsible. In 1658, Goody Hand testified in court that Elizabeth Garlick of Easthampton, Connecticut, had bewitched a sow: Hand told the court that her neighbors "Did burne the sowes tale [tail] and presently Goody Garlicke Did come in." When Henry Grey's heifer fell ill in 1692, he decided to experiment with countermagic. First, he cut off a piece of the heifer's ear. When this did no good, "he sent for his Cart whip and gave the Cow a stroak with it." Within an hour, the animal was well. Next morning, neighbor Mercy Disborough "Lay on the bed and stretht [stretched] out her arme and said. . . . I am allmost kild." This confirmed Grey's prior suspicion that Disborough had caused the heifer's illness.

Physical mistreatment of the sort meted out to bewitched animals was unacceptable when dealing with human victims. Instead, the hair or urine of the afflicted would be heated over a fire. In 1685, one of the children of Samuel Shattock, a Quaker who lived in Salem Village, fell ill. The Shattocks called in a doctor, who concluded that the boy was "under an ill hand." A few days later, neighbors cut off some of the boy's hair and boiled it in a skillet. If the experiment worked, the person who had caused the child's illness would be burned or drawn to the fire. After the hair had boiled for some time, Mary Parker "Came in and asked if [Shattock] would buye Soom Chickens." The neighbors were sure that Parker had no chickens to sell at that time and so concluded that she had been drawn by the boiling hair. . . .

Another popular form of countermagic entailed heating the victim's urine in a bottle, sometimes with nails and pins. This may have derived from the use of pins to stab images and was clearly intended to injure the malefactor. As Cotton Mather put it, "the Urine must be bottled with Nails and Pinns, and such Instruments in it as carry a Shew of Torture with them, if it attain its End." Over twenty seventeenth-century witch-bottles have been found in England. All have urine-traces; some contain pins, nails, and representations of the human heart, cut out of cloth or felt and then pierced. Most of these English specimens are stoneware vessels with bearded human masks, known to contemporaries as *greybeards* or *bellarmines*. The malevolent faces on these vessels served to symbolize the malefactor against whom the bottle was directed: this was image magic at its most grimly anthropomorphic.

No witch-bottles have been discovered in New England, but, as the following incident shows, colonists were familiar with the technique. In 1682, the household of Quaker George Walton in Portsmouth, New Hampshire, was disturbed by the "throwing about" of stones, bricks, hammers, spits, and other domestic utensils. This disruption was blamed on neighbor Hannah Jones, with whom Walton was involved in a land dispute. Richard Chamberlain, Secretary of the Province of New Hampshire, was living with the Waltons at the time and recorded their unsuccessful response. They "set on the Fire a Pot with Urine and crooked Pins in it, with design to have it boil." The Waltons had been "advised" that boiling the urine would end their ordeal and "give Punishment to . . . the wicked Procurer or Contriver of this Stone Affliction." Unfortunately for the Waltons, the malefactor was one step ahead of them. Just as the urine began to change temperature, a stone appeared, broke the top of the pot and knocked it off its stand, spilling the urine. The Waltons refilled the pot and put it back over the fire, but another stone broke the handle off and again knocked the pot over so that the urine escaped. Once the pot was refilled and repositioned a second time, a third stone appeared and broke the pot into several pieces, "and so the Operation became frustrate and fruitless."

Seven years later, Cotton Mather published an account of another "Urinary Experiment," which took place in Northampton, Massachusetts. One of the townsmen there had been "taken with many Ails and pains that increased on him to great Extremity." The sick man had recently quarreled with a neighbor whose wife was "under Suspicion for Witchcraft." His friends suspected that she was responsible for the illness and so decided to try countermagic as a remedy. They "went to the Traditional Experiment of Botteling Urine; but they could get no Urine from him, a strange Hole through the Urinary Passage shedding the water before they could receive it into the vessel." The thwarted friends were convinced that this "strange Hole" was a subterfuge by whoever had caused the illness. Meanwhile, the victim "languish[ed], decay[ed], and die[d]." After his death, a jury of inquest confirmed that there was "an Hole . . . quite thro[ugh] his Yard," which had "hindered their Saving of any Urine, and gave a Terrible Torture to him." According to Mather, "all concluded with good Reason, the Occasion of his Death to be something preternatural."

Not all countermagical experiments were unsuccessful. When fifteen-month-old Moses Godfrey of Hampton, New Hampshire, fell ill in 1680, Goodwife Godfrey and her daughter Sarah decided to experiment with the child's urine. Sarah "took some embers out of the fire and threw them upon the child's water; and by and by Rachel Fuller [a suspected neighbor] came in and looked very strangely." In 1681, Michael Smith came "very sick" to Hannah Weacome's house in Boston; Smith claimed that healer Mary Hale "had bewitched him." Weacome "advised the people that watched with him, to take the water of said Michaell and close it in A Bottell." This having been done, Weacome then locked the bottled urine in a cupboard. As long as the bottle remained there, Goody Hale "did not seace [cease] walking to and fro, about the House of the said Weacome." After about an hour, some of those inside the house "Desired the Bottell to be unstoped." Immediately this was done, Goody Hale left.

*   *   *

At first sight, it might seem odd that magic was widespread in Puritan New England, the one place where it should have been utterly discarded. Magic was surely a vital part of the corrupt world Puritans sought to leave behind them in England. Indeed, the close correspondence between folk magic and Catholic ritual made the former doubly abhorrent to the Puritan sensibility. Yet magical traditions persisted even in the New-English Israel. There are three reasons for this apparent anomaly. First, not all New Englanders were Puritans. Second, some members of the godly community were driven to magic by fears and uncertainties arising from predestinarian theology. And third, godly colonists who used magical techniques, for whatever reason, were generally disinclined to problematize their behavior: these layfolk were much less rigorous in their beliefs and practices than their ministers would have liked. Their attitude toward the supernatural world was essentially pragmatic and inclusive. . . .

There was a close symmetry between New England's theological and magical orientations: divination provided a release for precisely those tensions engendered by religious doctrine. The anxieties induced by predestinarian theology turned upon an individual's future; this may help to explain why most magical divination in New England served to predict the future. In England, many people had access to at least a few preachers who did not necessarily hold identical theological positions. The spiritual environment in England was far from closed, and those unable to endure the rigors of one ministry might seek at least occasional relief in other quarters. New Englanders, by contrast, did not have ready access to alternative theological viewpoints. The range of positions held by preachers was relatively narrow: New England pastors were, with few exceptions, unrelentingly predestinarian. It is, then, hardly surprising that magical divination in the northern colonies was more oriented toward fortune-telling than in England. Some of those New Englanders who turned to divination were devout people who needed a sense of future certainty, however limited or short-term. Knowing one's "future Husbands Calling," for example, was certainly insignificant when compared with the issue of salvation, but such knowledge did offer some certitude about the future, a kind of certitude that Puritanism was unlikely to offer. Some New Englanders went further and used divining techniques in an attempt to penetrate the mystery of election itself. According to Cotton Mather, such people let their bibles fall open and then determined "the state of their souls" from the first word they focused on. Clearly, these colonists turned to magic not in defiance but in default of Puritanism.

That willingness to use magic in the service of religion testifies to an open-ended pragmatism that constitutes the third and perhaps most significant reason for recourse to magic in early New England. By no means all those "that ma[d]e a profession of Christianity" discriminated between the supernatural strategies sanctioned by Puritan doctrine and those it condemned. Instead of eschewing all magical traditions and techniques, some layfolk included magic and astrology as well as organized religion in an eclectic worldview. This is not to suggest that all, or even most, godly layfolk used magic: each congregation contained a core of individuals whose faith was quintessentially Puritan in its exclusivity. But others were less rigorous, and thus willing to employ magical techniques if and when they seemed useful. Ignorance of official opposition to magic may explain in part godly recourse to magical techniques: even in towns and villages as thoroughly ministered as those of New England, by no means was everybody well informed. . . . Some of those who used magic were surprised and horrified when ministers confronted them and explained that their actions were illicit. Increase Mather was convinced that some "practise[d] such things in their simplicity." But although some layfolk did not realize that magic was offensive to Puritan theology, others may have heard but chose to ignore official strictures on the subject; at the very least, those strictures conveniently slipped their minds from time to time. Theological rigor may have meant less to some people than did the practical and emotional advantages to be gained by using magic.

Such colonists did not necessarily make a self-conscious decision to disregard official teaching: they merely set it aside when convenient. Their commitment to orthodoxy was selective and intermittent, but nonetheless sincere. In order to fulfill all their needs, they turned sometimes to religion, sometimes to magic.

B. AFRICANS

[14]

Activities of African Witches

GEOFFREY PARRINDER

The theologian Geoffrey Parrinder's scholarly works have focused on mysticism and African religions. He is the author of numerous works on world religions, including Religion in Africa *(1969),* African Mythology *(1968), and* Mysticism in the World's Religions *(1976). In this excerpt from his 1963 book* Witchcraft: European and African, *Parrinder surveys the anthropological literature on witchcraft beliefs of various African peoples.*

•

Becoming a Witch

Witchcraft is supposed to be either inherited or to be caught. The Ibo of southern Nigeria believe that witches can infect innocent people by putting a spiritual substance into their food. Having partaken of it this person is susceptible to the influence of the witch who then administers a drug to "make his mouth blunt". This medicine induces a craving for human flesh and so the neophyte seeks admission to the guild of witches and is told to meet them at night.

Rather similarly the Nupe of northern Nigeria, many of whom are now Mohammedans, suppose that witchcraft is acquired by rubbing a medicine into the eyes or on to the body, and packets of the medicine are supposed to be hidden in the witch's hair or belt. Witchcraft is not hereditary, except in the sense that like a craft it may continue in one family. If anyone wishes to become a witch she is said to go to the female head of the market, who is also supposed to be head of the witches, and is told to meet the other witches under a tree at night. It is believed that both men and women can become witches, but the power of the males is much weaker than that of the females. The men do not eat souls, but play tricks on the unsuspecting and may even be used to give protection against robbers.

The Gã of Ghana think that witchcraft can either be inherited, or else may be imposed upon the witch against her will. It may come to the witch at birth, or as a

From Geoffrey Parrinder, *Witchcraft: European and African* (London: Faber and Faber, 1963), 141–49, 168–69.

heritage from a dying relative. Or it may be bought at a very low price. The Gã people are said to think that the witch possession comes from a spirit or a demon, an idea that is rare elsewhere in Africa. The possessing spirit may master its hostess so that she suffers from what a psychologist would call a "compulsion-neurosis," feeling forced to do things against her better self. Hence the witch may confess to having harmed some person but can find no reason for hating the victim. Many people suffer agonies from fear of becoming a witch, and they dread that some unnatural power is trying to get hold of them for its own purposes.

The Azande of the eastern Sudan have a belief in a witchcraft-substance, which is somewhat comparable to the Gã idea of a witch's demons. They are rather vague as to what sort of substance this is. Some say it is an oval blackish swelling in which small objects may be found, others say that it is red and contains seeds which the witch has eaten in his neighbours' plantations. This substance is said to be discover-able by autopsy, and to be found near the liver or gall-bladder; it may be the bladder or part of the small intestine. A post-mortem examination may be held at the grave of a man who had been accused of witchcraft, the relatives attending as witnesses and the operation being performed by a blood-brother. Gashes are made in the belly, and the intestines are then taken out for examination to see if witch-substance is there. If it is not, the relatives rejoice and put the intestines back. If the substance is there the accusers hang the intestines on a tree.

Azande believe witchcraft to be inherited from parents, the father only transmit-ting witchcraft to his sons and mothers to their daughters. A man who is proved to be a witch, but whose father was not one, is called a bastard. But the witchcraft may remain in abeyance throughout a man's life; if he does not use his powers then he is not dangerous to his friends. Hence men do not ask the oracles who are the witches in the village, but only when bewitching power is felt do they inquire who is now exercising his faculties.

The Lovedu of Transvaal believe that the "night-witch" is born a witch, and that he is taught the craft in childhood by his mother. But a witch may keep his powers in reserve and only use them to protect his own crops. The great majority of such witches are female; they drink in the witchcraft with their mother's milk. The mother is said to begin the training, teaching the child to cling to the wall like a bat long before it can walk. Night-witchcraft cannot be bought, nor can it be learnt from someone outside the family. There is no belief in a witchcraft-substance.

Basuto witches are mostly women and inherit their state and their familiars from their parents, usually the mother. They are not as dangerous as are the sor-cerers, but they are rather mischievous and immoral. They harm men with their perverted sense of humour. They make horses shy by turning into fireballs, or give children convulsions in their sleep, or give men sexual dreams like the succubi of the Middle Ages. Witches are held responsible for the accidents and fears of the night.

The Witches' Assemblies

Of great interest, in view of the comparison with Europe, are the meetings and organization of witches, as they are supposed to exist in Africa.

Most Gã witches confess that they belong to companies which meet at night to hold discussions and eat human flesh. The societies are said to be about ten in membership. The company is like a court and has a chief, a messenger, and an executioner. Dr. Field quotes confessions in which witches said they belonged to companies of seven, that they were chief of the company or could name the chief and fellow-witches. Some of the companies are mixed, men and women. At the meetings the witches rival each other in performing marvels. The witch with the most demons, or marvels, is made chief. Since witches are thought thus to meet together, they are believed to be able to recognize one another in the daytime and to be able to tell who are other witches. At the same time, these meetings are spiritual, for it is thought that the witch's body remains on her bed while her soul goes off to the assembly.

The Nupe witches are thought to send out their "shadow-soul" at night, while their bodies are still asleep in their houses. The witches meet under a tree outside the village, and there they eat souls and work out their plans. There is an order of members and they cooperate in providing a victim in turn. But it is said that rivalry and quarrels are common among witches. Their recognized head (*lelu*) is the woman who supervises the women of the town and the market.

Ibo witches are said to be formed into guilds, so that they can work together to procure victims. Hence they are known to each other and meet at night at an hour indicated by the cry of birds, when they all get up from their beds and go to the place of assembly. An accused witch may be forced to march round the village calling on members of her guild to surrender the parts of their victim that they have taken.

Azande witches are believed to meet together, with elders who are chosen from the older and more experienced members. They have small drums, the membranes of which are made of human skin, and as the drums are beaten to call members to the meeting they give out the call, "human flesh, human flesh." The leaders instruct the younger witches and consider their proposals, for a witch is not allowed to kill a man on his own, but his suggestions have to be discussed and accepted by the whole assembly. Then the witches go off to the victim's house, dance around it, and the witch who hates him enters and throws him outside the door where the assembled ghouls worry him and seize parts of his flesh which they take off to cook at their meeting-place. Yet Azande opinion is quite clear that the witch's body remains asleep on his bed, and that it is only the victim's soul, or "the soul of his flesh," which is taken away. So this cannibalism is not so horrible as it sounds.

The night-witches of the Lovedu are believed to go out at night with their whole being, and not just their souls. Companions remaining in the hut are thrown into a profound sleep, or a hyena may be left in the image of a witch. So witches may be caught, with certain medicines, and remain immobile till found when they flee away naked. The witches meet in an assembly and know each other. Sometimes they fight witches of other villages and receive wounds which they hide in the daytime and which may prove fatal.

Basuto witches gather together and sing and dance naked. Sometimes they visit a village and send all its inhabitants into a deep slumber while they kill an ox for a feast. But when the dawn comes they remove the spell from the sleepers, resurrect the ox with medicine, and return home. They leave no traces behind, unless it happens that one has gnawed an ox bone too harshly, when the animal will limp the next day. These nocturnal revels are invisible, and yet travellers tell of hearing the witches singing in the distance, and they run away as quickly as possible lest they be captured by the witches. Hence people will not travel alone and unprotected at night.

Flying and Familiars

The universal fantasy of flying is found in Africa. Gā witches are believed to fly to their meetings like balls of fire which are said to appear over land and sea. It is possible that the phosphorescence of the waves may have suggested this idea to this coastal people. Many people who see lights in front of their eyes, the sparks and spots of the liverish, may be led to suspect that witches are about or that they themselves are becoming witches. Many others feel worms, snakes, and toads crawling about inside their bodies. As nearly everybody suffers from worms, it is not surprising that they should attribute these uncomfortable feelings to witchcraft.

Those who do not fly as fire are believed to ride on animals, especially on owls, antelopes, and leopards, all nocturnal creatures. Snakes are regarded as witches' steeds, familiars, and doubles, so that a witch may turn into a snake. Some witches say that they wear snakes round their heads or carry them in their private parts. These are fantasies, though there are non-poisonous pythons which are kept tame by some people and are found in some religious cults. Some of the worst witches are thought to have hooks or spurs growing on their heels, a sign of their animal nature.

Ibo witches are believed to appear as balls of fire in the treetops which men can extinguish by the use of the appropriate medicine. They can turn into the smallest insect and so enter tightly closed houses and bite men as flies do at night. They can turn into owls, lizards, vultures, and night-birds. If a night-bird rests on a house men will do all they can to drive it away. Strange bird cries indicate that witches have begun their meeting. The Nupe witches, too, are said to breathe fire from their mouths, and to suck their victims' blood like vampires. It is significant that witches are said to meet in baobab and iroko trees. These trees are pollinated by bats which make a twittering noise like people talking.

The Azande believe that bats can be vehicles of the souls of witches. Particularly is this so when crops are attacked by bats. If a man catches one of these bats he burns it, and places the ashes in beer which people are invited to taste, when the man who sent the bat tastes the beer he vomits and is accused of bewitching the crops. The soul of an Azande witch goes out at night giving off a bright light, like firefly beetles but much brighter. They rub a special ointment into their skin to make themselves invisible. Witchcraft may also be found in animals and birds, if so proved by the poison oracle. Bats, owls, jackals, dogs, and cats may all be witches. The wild animals of the bush may be credited with witchcraft if they are particularly cunning. Especially do wild cats have witchcraft attributed to them, and the males are said to be like incubi to women who give birth to kittens and suckle them like children.

The snake familiars appear again in Zulu and Lovedu belief. Witches send a snake which penetrates the body and kills unborn children. Some say that everybody has a snake in his stomach. The psychologist will easily explain the phallic symbolism of the snake, especially in a tropical country. Other familiars are hyenas, skunks, and owls. The familiars are sent to cause damage to a neighbour's property or to milk his cows. A snake that seems to attack one person only in a crowd must be a witch's snake. The worst of all familiars is a human being who has been killed by the witch and has become his slave. He is kept in a pot or a cave, and he hoes or works evil for his master by night.

The Basuto believe that witches have powerful medicines to make them fly, or they have magic wands on which they ride after the manner of European witches on their broomsticks. One wand is red and the other black. The black one can send men into a deep sleep or raise the dead; the red one can reverse these spells before dawn. Witches can turn themselves into animals: monkeys, snakes, owls, or cows. They frighten men in these shapes and if a man sees a crow on his hut he knows the witches are after him. Witches' familiars may also be little men, two or three feet high, with long hair and organs like monkeys. These familiars are inherited or bought, and are sent out by their owners to annoy and harm men, children, and animals. They may destroy crops, drive out cattle, and set huts on fire. The little man attracts women and causes various perversions, like an incubus. These familiars may become semi-independent of their owners, and they are difficult to get rid of and may have to be exorcized.

Cannibalism and Souls

The unnatural cannibalism of which European witches were accused is also admitted by African witches. Some have confessed to have killed many people, including their own children, and eaten them in the witches' assemblies. They describe in detail how that each witch takes a part of the body, the feet or the hands, and that when they arrive at the heart the victim dies.

Yet all this is not meant to indicate eating the real flesh; it is all symbolical. It is the victim's soul which is eaten, and the victim's body is not harmed, except by disease. Nor is there evidence that corpses are dug up and devoured by witches, though sorcerers are known to have done this. The Gā believe that just as the witches' assembly is spiritual, attended by the souls of the witches only, so is the eating of their victims. Their witches are said to have a pot which contains the "blood" of their victims, but to normal people this blood would appear as mere water. Similarly when a witch confesses she sometimes makes a pretence of vomiting the blood of her victims, but this blood is invisible to mortal sight. One is met by the statement, here as elsewhere, that only those with the right kind of eyes can see the witches at their work.

Similarly the Ibo witches are said to have to contribute the soul-substance of their victims on initiation into the guild. The victim is often a close relative, a child, husband, brother, or cousin. This may appear unnatural, but there are social and psychological reasons why relatives should be thought to be killed by witches. The witch may place a magical preparation in her victim's house to assist in his capture. She then divulges the name to the chief witch who wounds the victim with a spiritual arrow. The witches divide the body between them, and when the heart is eaten the man dies. Impotence and barrenness are also caused by witchcraft.

The chief work of Nupe witches is "the eating of souls". Every member of the guild has to contribute a human victim in turn. If she cannot get an outsider, because of his protective magic, she brings one of her own family, a child or a brother, for she has more power over them. She brings the body (soul) and the witches divide it among them, and keep on eating till the victim dies. If the witch cannot find a victim she is liable to be killed herself, and divided and eaten in the same manner.

The Azande also insist that the meeting and eating by witches is spiritual. They remove the psychic part of the victim and devour it spiritually. Their assembly drum calls out for human flesh, metaphorically. When they have danced around the victim's hut, they seize and divide him, cooking lumps of flesh in a small witchcraft-pot.

Lovedu witches are supposed to cause mysterious deaths to come upon their victims. No death is regarded as natural. The witches may pour blood over their victims and make them die. Or they may cut off parts of their bodies and put the pieces in sand or corn, which causes great pain to the rest of the body. If a man feels tired and full of aches, it is because a witch has beaten him, or made him hoe his garden, or forced him to ride a bicycle all night, without his conscious knowledge. Witches are supposed to kill men to enslave them. When the shadow is buried the witch retains the real person in a cave or pot and sends it out on nefarious errands.

Basuto witches have a taste for human flesh, and they are held to violate graves to satisfy their craving, particularly new graves which are not sufficiently protected with charms. They can raise the dead and seize the spirit before it reaches the abode of the departed. This is easily done if the full funeral rites have been delayed. With this ghost they frighten people and the relatives of the deceased. With their black wands they can raise the dead, and with their red wands they can reverse the process.

*   *   *

Some of the above seems remarkably like real cannibalism. It is true that this has taken place in some parts of Africa, though not in most of the areas we have referred to. The societies of leopard-men who indeed and in truth preyed on their fellows are notorious in the forests of the Congo and adjacent areas, but not in most parts of East and West Africa. In Basutoland there are horrible ritual murders, which take place from time to time. But these evil practices are daylight and conscious activities, and are distinguished by the Basuto from the witchcraft which we have described among them above.

It is possible that the notion of witches eating human flesh may be derived from racial memories of what took place ages ago. This is speculative but not impossible. Whatever the case, it is certain that the tribes mentioned insist that the eating done by witches today is as incorporeal as their assemblies.

A further point is that in many parts of Africa there are societies which believe that men can take on animal form, and in which some men dress up in animal skins. The strong belief in reincarnation not infrequently takes the form of metamorphosis, that is, that men change into animals: leopards, monkeys, deer, snakes, and the like. Some think this change only takes place after death. Others think that there are particular people, witches and wizards, who possess the special faculty of changing form. Others again belong to secret societies in which they dress in animal skins to impersonate the dead or totemic ancestors. But these are daylight and conscious activities, and always distinguished from witchcraft.

Some of these beliefs may throw light on European witchcraft. Others are strange to Europe, where the idea of reincarnation has never taken much root.

It has been emphasized that Africans generally believe the witchcraft activities to take place in spirit. However, it must be made fully clear that this does not imply that Africans consider witchcraft to be illusory. Quite the contrary. They are convinced that witches do meet, and actually devour their prey, albeit spiritually. The spirit world is so real that there is never a shadow of doubt in the African's mind that the witches really do all that they are accused of doing. . . .

The Sufferers from Witchcraft

When a man suffers from misfortune or sickness he asks himself why this has happened. He knows that there are many potential witches, and that to harm him they must be actuated by hatred or jealousy towards himself in particular. So he begins to think of those who might have a grudge against him, either for some offence or through envy at his success, and who are now trying to weaken him.

From this it follows that witchcraft is often suspected among a man's closest acquaintances. "A man's foes shall be those of his own household." As those we know best are the ones with whom there may be the greatest friction, so it proves that accusations of witchcraft are often levelled against close relatives, and rarely against those who live at a distance. The latter have not sufficient social contacts to make them feel hatred. . . .

When a man believes that he is suffering from witchcraft his feelings may range from anger to terror. If the witch is thought to be destroying the crops or causing the game to go away, the sufferer will have recourse to a witch-doctor or an oracle, to find out who is responsible for the damage.

It is usually thought that it is sufficient to unveil the witch's secret for the harm to be checked. Witches love to work in secret and darkness, and when brought to light they lose their power. This is almost like the modern psychological treatment of bringing complexes to the surface so as to dissolve them.

If a witch is thought responsible for someone's death then more serious action will be taken, and the witch will at least be obliged to flee from the village. The witch may be arraigned before the chief's court and, in olden days, death was often the penalty for a witch accused of killing someone by eating his soul. . . .

Since witchcraft is such a common phenomenon, it may be taken for granted to the extent of no proceedings being taken against its perpetrators, if no useful purpose can be served by concerted action against suspected witches. If the harm done cannot be righted then there is no point in taking any action about it. Witchcraft is one of the facts of life, so one bows to the inevitable. One does not go to the unnecessary trouble and expense of consulting oracles and imposing ordeals if nothing can come of it.

Belief in witchcraft serves as a check upon the hostile words and deeds which men might use in society. For, on the one hand, men are careful not to offend others since they might be witches; one can never tell who is a witch. On the other hand, enmity is an expression of witchcraft, and in expressing hatred so openly one might render oneself liable to an accusation of witchcraft. One arrives at a negative morality— that it is better not to make enemies since hatred is the constant motive of witchcraft.

[15]

Witchcraft among the Azande

E. E. EVANS-PRITCHARD

The anthropologist E. E. Evans-Pritchard was the author of numerous works on African cultures, including several on the Azande. In this excerpt from Witchcraft, Oracles and Magic among the Azande *(1937), Evans-Pritchard interprets Azande beliefs about witchcraft. Among his other publications are* Kinship and Marriage among the Nuer *(1951),* The Azande: History and Political Institutions *(1971) and* Man and Woman among the Azande *(1974).*

•

Azande believe that some people are witches and can injure them in virtue of an inherent quality. A witch performs no rite, utters no spell, and possesses no medicines. An act of witchcraft is a psychic act. They believe also that sorcerers may do them ill by performing magic rites with bad medicines. Azande distinguish clearly between witches and sorcerers. Against both they employ diviners, oracles, and medicines. . . .

When Azande consult oracles they consult them mainly about witches. When they employ diviners it is for the same purpose. Their leechcraft and closed associations are directed against the same foe.

I had no difficulty in discovering what Azande think about witchcraft, nor in observing what they do to combat it. These ideas and actions are on the surface of their life and are accessible to any one who lives for a few weeks in their homesteads. Every Zande is an authority on witchcraft. There is no need to consult specialists. There is not even need to question Azande about it, for information flows freely from recurrent situations in their social life, and one has only to watch and listen. *Mangu,* witchcraft, was one of the first words I heard in Zandeland, and I heard it uttered day by day throughout the months.

Azande believe that witchcraft is a substance in the bodies of witches, a belief which is found among many peoples in Central and West Africa. Zandeland is the

From E. E. Evans-Pritchard, *Witchcraft, Oracles and Magic among the Azande* (Oxford: Clarendon, 1937), 21–27, 29–37, 63–65, 387–89, 391. © 1937 Clarendon Press. Reprinted by permission of Oxford University Press.

north-eastern limit of its distribution. It is difficult to say with what organ Azande associate witchcraft. I have never seen human witchcraft-substance, but it has been described to me as an oval blackish swelling or bag in which various small objects are sometimes found. When Azande describe its shape they often point to the elbow of their bent arm, and when they describe its location they point to just beneath the xiphoid cartilage which is said to "cover witchcraft-substance". They say:

> "It is attached to the edge of the liver. When people cut open the belly they have only to pierce it and witchcraft-substance bursts through with a pop."

I have heard people say that it is of a reddish colour and contains seeds of pumpkins and sesame and other food-plants which have been devoured by a witch in the cultivations of his neighbours. Azande know the position of witchcraft-substance because in the past it was sometimes extracted by autopsy. I believe it to be the small intestine in certain digestive periods. This organ is suggested by Zande descriptions of autopsies and was that shown to me as containing witchcraft-substance in the belly of one of my goats. In an autopsy two lateral gashes were made on either side of the xiphoid cartilage and witchcraft-substance either popped out immediately or was afterwards discovered in the intestines.

This account does not support the contention of my friend Dr. Gayer-Anderson that "the possession of a vermiform appendix is said to be diagnostic". On the other hand, it agrees with Mgr. Lagae's statement that witchcraft-substance is several centimetres long and is found near the liver or gall-bladder. De Calonne-Beaufaict suggests that it may be an enlarged viscus, perhaps the gall-bladder, and Hutereau says that it is found near the stomach at the beginning of the intestine, though he adds that Azande describe as *Mangu* any deformation of an organ, deformation of the stomach being especially considered as such. Major Larken writes: "If a person is a witch, there is to be found in the belly a round hairy ball, which may have teeth, and which is very dreadful to look at." Major Brock writes that witchcraft is described by Azande "as being like a mouth with large sharp teeth" and thinks that a witch may be "a person suffering from appendicitis, perhaps accompanied by an internal abscess".

A witch shows no certain external symptoms of his condition though people say:

> "One knows a witch by his red eyes. When one sees such a man one says he is a witch and this is true also of a woman with red eyes. But at present what happens is this: if they consult the poison oracle about a man and the oracle says that he is a witch the kinsmen of the sick man give him a fowl's wing that he may blow water on it. That man is a witch."

It is also said that if maggots come out of the apertures of a dead man's body before burial it is a sign that he was a witch.

* * *

Witchcraft is not only a physical trait but is also inherited. It is transmitted by unilinear descent from parent to child. The sons of a male witch are all witches but his daughters are not, while the daughters of a female witch are all witches but her sons are not. Mgr. Lagae quotes a Zande text:

> "If a man has witchcraft-substance in his belly and begets a male child, this child also has witchcraft-substance because his father was a witch. It is the same with women. If a woman has witchcraft-substance in her belly and gives birth to a female child, the child also has witchcraft-substance because her mother was a witch. Thus witchcraft does not trouble a person born free from it by entering into him."

Biological transmission of witchcraft from one parent to all children of the same sex is complementary to Zande opinions about procreation and to their eschatological beliefs. Conception is thought to be due to a unison of psychical properties in man and woman. When the soul of the man is stronger a boy will be born; when the soul of the woman is stronger a girl will be born. Thus a child partakes of the psychical qualities of both parents, though a girl is thought to partake more of the soul of her mother and a boy of the soul of his father. Nevertheless in certain respects a child takes after one or other parent according to its sex, namely, in the inheritance of sexual characters, of a body-soul, and of witchcraft-substance. There is a vague belief, hardly precise enough to be described as a doctrine, that man possesses two souls, a body-soul and a spirit-soul. At death the body-soul becomes a totem animal of the clan while its fellow soul becomes a ghost and leads a shadowy existence at the heads of streams. Many people say that the body-soul of a man becomes the totem animal of his father's clan while the body-soul of a woman becomes the totem animal of her mother's clan.

At first sight it seems strange to find a mode of matrilineal transmission in a society which is characterized by its strong patrilineal bias, but witchcraft like the body-soul is part of the body and might be expected to accompany inheritance of male or female characters from father or mother.

To our minds it appears evident that if a man is proven a witch the whole of his clan are *ipso facto* witches, since the Zande clan is a group of persons related biologically to one another through the male line. Azande see the sense of this argument but they do not accept its conclusions, and it would involve the whole notion of witchcraft in contradiction were they to do so. In practice they regard only close paternal kinsmen of a known witch as witches. It is only in theory that they extend the imputation to all a witch's clansmen. If in the eyes of the world payment for homicide by witchcraft stamps the kin of a guilty man as witches, a post-mortem in which no witchcraft-substance is discovered in a man clears his paternal kin of suspicion. Here again we might reason that if a man be found by post-mortem immune from witchcraft-substance all his clan must also be immune, but Azande do not act as though they were of this opinion.

Further elaborations of belief free Azande from having to admit what appear to us to be the logical consequences of belief in biological transmission of witchcraft. If a man is proven a witch beyond all doubt his kin, to establish their innocence, may use the very biological principle which would seem to involve them in disrepute. They admit that the man is a witch but deny that he is a member of their clan. They say he was a bastard, for among Azande a man is always of the clan of his *genitor* and not of his *pater*, and I was told that they may compel his mother if she is still alive to say who was her lover, beating her and asking her, "What do you mean by going to the bush to get witchcraft in adultery?" More often they simply make the declaration that the witch must have been a bastard since they have no witchcraft in their bodies and that he could not therefore be one of their kinsmen, and they may support this contention by quoting cases where members of their kin have been shown by autopsy to have been free from witchcraft. It is unlikely that other people will accept this plea, but they are not asked either to accept it or reject it.

Also Zande doctrine includes the notion that even if a man is the son of a witch and has witchcraft-substance in his body he may not use it. It may remain inoperative, "cool" as the Azande say, throughout his lifetime, and a man can hardly be classed as a witch if his witchcraft never functions. In point of fact, therefore, Azande generally regard witchcraft as an individual trait and it is treated as such in spite of its association with kinship. At the same time certain clans, especially the Abakunde and the Avundua clans, had a reputation for witchcraft in the reign of King Gbudwe. In Gangura's province this reputation clung to the Aböka and Abanzuma clans. No one thinks any worse of a man if he is a member of one of these clans.

Azande do not perceive the contradiction as we perceive it because they have no theoretical interest in the subject, and those situations in which they express their beliefs in witchcraft do not force the problem upon them. A man never asks the oracles, which alone are capable of disclosing the location of witchcraft-substance in the living, whether a certain man is a witch. He asks whether at the moment this man is bewitching him. One attempts to discover whether a man is bewitching some one in particular circumstances and not whether he is born a witch. If the oracles say that a certain man is injuring you at the moment you then know that he is a witch, whereas if they say that at the moment he is not injuring you you do not know whether he is a witch or not and have no interest to inquire into the matter. If he is a witch it is of no significance to you so long as you are not his victim. A Zande is interested in witchcraft only as an agent on definite occasions and in relation to his own interests, and not as a permanent condition of individuals. When he is sick he does not normally say: "Now let us consider who are well-known witches of the neighbourhood and place their names before the poison oracle." He does not consider the question in this light but asks himself who among his neighbours have grudges against him and then seeks to know from the poison oracle whether one of them is on this particular occasion bewitching him. Azande are interested solely in the dynamics of witchcraft in particular situations.

Lesser misfortunes are soon forgotten and those who caused them are looked upon by the sufferer and his kin as having bewitched some one on this occasion rather than as confirmed witches, for only persons who are constantly exposed by the oracles as responsible for sickness or loss are regarded as confirmed witches, and in the old days it was only when a witch had killed some one that he became a marked man in the community.

* * *

Death is due to witchcraft and must be avenged. All other practices connected with witchcraft are epitomized in the action of vengeance. In our present context it will be sufficient to point out that in pre-European days vengeance was either executed directly, sometimes by the slaughter of a witch, and sometimes by acceptance of compensation, or by means of lethal magic. Witches were very seldom slain, for it was only when a man committed a second or third murder, or murdered an important person, that a prince permitted his execution. Under British rule the magical method alone is employed.

Vengeance seems to have been less a result of anger and hatred than the fulfilment of a pious duty and a source of profit. I have never heard that to-day the kin of a dead man, once they have exacted vengeance, show any rancour towards the family of the man whom their magic has struck down, nor that in the past there was any prolonged hostility between the kin of the dead and the kin of the witch who had paid compensation for his murder. To-day if a man kills a person by witchcraft the crime is his sole responsibility and his kin are not associated with his guilt. In the past they assisted him to pay compensation, not in virtue of collective responsibility, but in virtue of social obligations to a kinsman. His relatives-in-law and his blood-brothers also contributed towards the payment. As soon as a witch is to-day slain by magic, or in the past had been speared to death or had paid compensation, the affair is closed. Moreover, it is an issue between the kin of the dead and the kin of the witch and other people are not concerned with it. They have the same social links with both parties.

It is extremely difficult to-day to obtain information about victims of vengeance-magic. Azande themselves do not know about them unless they are members of a murdered man's closest kin. One notices that his kinsmen are no longer observing taboos of mourning and one knows by this that their magic has performed its task, but it is useless to inquire from them who was its victim because they will not tell you. It is their private affair and is a secret between them and their prince who must be informed of the action of their magic since it is necessary for his poison oracle to confirm their poison oracle before they are permitted to end their mourning. Besides, it is a verdict of the poison oracle and one must not disclose its revelations about such matters. . . .

* * *

Azande often speak of *aboro kikpa* (men of the gall-bladder), and though this is an organic trait analogous to witchcraft we must distinguish between them. It is believed that the gall-bladder in some persons is exceptional in size, giving rise to marked psychological traits. Spiteful and resentful and ill-tempered persons come into this category. "They brood over things" and are loath to make up a quarrel, being little ready to forgive those who have offended them. For instance, when you join a gathering and those present salute you one man may just look at you and say nothing, and you attribute his rudeness to his gall-bladder and seek in your mind the occasion of the grudge he bears you. Some people say that minor injuries may be caused by a gall-bladder man, such as knocking your toe against a stump of wood or treading on a thorn or incurring temporary unpopularity at court: "People are angry with you at court for the prince is not gracious to you. You speak to the prince but what you say does not find favour in his eyes." If a man shows spite towards you the test whether he is a gall-bladder man or a witch lies in subsequent events. If you suffer a serious misfortune you will immediately suspect witchcraft, but if no serious misfortune befalls you you suspect only gall-bladder.

Azande have mostly told me that everybody is a gall-bladder man in the sense that everybody possesses a gall-bladder, but in some men it is more pronounced than in others. When they tell you of such men they advise you to steer clear of them. The behaviour of gall-bladder men towards their neighbours may be compared to the behaviour we indicate when we say that a man has a "liver".

Gall-bladder men are quite different from witches. Nobody minds greatly the ill nature of a gall-bladder man. They may keep out of his way but they are not afraid that he will injure them unless he is also a witch. If he is a witch his ill nature may lead to any misfortune, even death. Spitefulness does not matter so long as there is no witchcraft to back it up, and if you suspect that witchcraft may be present in a man who has made his dislike of you very apparent you may consult the oracles to establish whether he is trying to injure you with witchcraft. Sometimes the poison oracle in telling you that a man is not bewitching you will expressly add that he is a gall-bladder man. It does this by seeming to kill a fowl in affirmation of witchcraft and then reviving it. A gall-bladder man and a witch both display the same dispositions, but only a witch can translate these dispositions into serious injuries.

*   *   *

Being part of the body, witchcraft-substance grows as the body grows. The older a witch the more potent his witchcraft and the more unscrupulous its use. This is one of the reasons why Azande often express apprehension of old persons. The witchcraft-substance of a child is so small that it can do little injury to others. Therefore a child is never accused of murder, and even grown boys and girls are not suspected of serious witchcraft though they may cause minor misfortunes to persons of their own age. . . . Witchcraft operates when there is ill feeling between witch and victim, and ill feeling is unlikely to arise frequently between children and adults. Only adults can consult the poison oracle and they do not normally put the names of children before it when asking it about witchcraft. Children cannot express their enmities and minor misfortunes in terms of oracular revelations about witchcraft because they cannot consult the poison oracle.

Nevertheless, rare cases have been known in which, after asking the oracle in vain about all suspected adults, a child's name has been put before it and he has been declared a witch. But I was told that if this happens an old man will point out that there must be an error. He will say: "A witch has taken the child and placed him in front of himself as a screen to protect himself."

Children soon know about witchcraft, and I have found in talking to little boys and girls, even as young as six years of age, that they apprehend what is meant when their elders speak of it. I was told that in a quarrel one child may bring up the bad reputation of the father of another and say to him:

> "Kid ha! as you argue with me like this your eyes are just like the eyes of your father and since you are bad witches do not pick a quarrel with me lest you bewitch me and die for sure."

However, people do not comprehend the nature of witchcraft till they are used to operating oracles, to acting in situations of misfortune in accordance with oracular revelations, and to making magic. The concept grows with the social experience of each individual.

Men and women are equally witches. Men may be bewitched by other men or by women, but women are generally bewitched only by members of their own sex. A sick man usually asks the oracles about his male neighbours, while if he is consulting them about a sick wife or kinswoman he normally asks about other women. This is because ill feeling is more likely to arise between man and man and between woman and woman than between man and woman. A man comes in contact only with his wives and female kinsmen and has therefore little opportunity to incur the hatred of other women. It would, in fact, be suspicious if he consulted the oracles about another man's wife on his own behalf, and her husband might surmise adultery. He would wonder what contact his wife had had with her accuser that had led to disagreement between them. Nevertheless, a man frequently consults the oracles about his own wives, because he is sure to displease them from time to time, and often they hate him. I have never heard of cases in which a man has been accused of bewitching his wife. Azande say that no man would do such a thing as no one wishes to kill his wife or cause her sickness since he would himself be the chief loser. Kuagbiaru told me that he had never known a man to pay compensation for the death of his wife. Another reason why one does not hear of fowls' wings being presented to husbands in accusation of witchcraft on account of the illnesses of their wives is that a woman cannot herself consult the poison oracle and usually entrusts this task to her husband. She may ask her brother to consult the oracle on her behalf, but he is not likely to place his brother-in-law's name before it because a husband does not desire the death of his wife.

I have never known a case in which a man has been bewitched by a kinswoman or in which a woman has been bewitched by a kinsman. Moreover, I have heard of only one case in which a man was bewitched by a kinsman. A kinsman may do a man wrong in other ways but he would not bewitch him. It is evident that a sick man would not care to ask the oracles about his brothers and paternal cousins, because if the poison oracle declared them to have bewitched him, by the same declaration he would himself be a witch, since witchcraft is inherited in the male line.

Members of the princely class, the Avongara, are not accused of witchcraft, for if a man were to say that the oracles had declared the son of a prince to have bewitched him he would be asserting that the king and princes were also witches. However much a prince may detest members of his lineage he never allows them to be brought in disrepute by a commoner. Hence, although Azande will tell one privately that they believe some members of the noble class may be witches, they seldom consult the oracles about them, so that they are not accused of witchcraft. In the past they never consulted the oracles about them. There is an established fiction that Avongara are not witches, and it is maintained by the overwhelming power and prestige of the ruling princes.

Governors of provinces, deputies of districts, men of the court, leaders of military companies, and other commoners of position and wealth are not likely to be accused of witchcraft unless by a prince himself on account of his own hunting or on account of the death of some equally influential commoner. Generally lesser people do not dare to consult the oracles about influential persons because their lives would be a misery if they insulted the most important men in their neighbourhood. Therefore Bage, the chief's deputy in the settlement where I resided, could tell me that never in his life had he been accused of witchcraft and could challenge a crowd of listeners to instance a single occasion when this had happened to him. The rich and powerful are immune as a rule from accusations of witchcraft because no one consults the oracles to their names and therefore the oracles cannot give a verdict against them. It is only when the poison oracle has a name placed before it frequently that sooner or later it is sure to kill a fowl to the name. So we may say that the incidence of witchcraft in a Zande community falls equally upon both sexes in the commoner class while nobles are entirely, and powerful commoners largely, immune from accusations. All children are normally free from suspicion.

The relations of ruling princes to witchcraft are peculiar. Though immune from accusations they believe in witches as firmly as other people, and they constantly consult the poison oracle to find out who is bewitching them. They especially consult it about their wives. A prince's oracle is also the final authority which decides on all witchcraft cases involving homicide, and in the past it was also used to protect his subjects from witchcraft during warfare. When a lesser noble dies his death is attributed to a witch and is avenged in the same way as deaths of commoners, but the death of a king or ruling prince is not so avenged and is generally attributed to sorcery or cats.

* * *

While witchcraft itself is part of the human organism its action is psychic. What Azande call *mbisimo mangu*, the soul of witchcraft, is a concept that bridges over the distance between the person of the witch and the person of his victim. Some such explanation is necessary to account for the fact that a witch was in his hut at the time when he is supposed to have injured some one. The soul of witchcraft may leave its corporeal home at any time during the day or night, but Azande generally think of a witch sending his soul on errands by night when his victim is asleep. It sails through the air emitting a bright light. During the daytime this light can only be seen by witches, and by witch-doctors when they are primed with medicines, but any one may have the rare misfortune to observe it at night. Azande say that the light of witchcraft is like the gleam of fire-fly beetles, only it is ever so much larger and brighter than they. These beetles are in no way associated with witchcraft on account of their phosphorescence. Mgr. Lagae records a Zande text which runs:

"Those who see witchcraft on its way to injure some one at night say that when witchcraft moves along it shines just like flame. It shines a little and then goes out again."

Azande say that a man may see witchcraft as it goes to rest on branches for "Witchcraft is like fire, it lights a light". If a man sees the light of witchcraft he picks up a piece of charcoal and throws it under his bed so that he may not suffer misfortune from the sight.

I have only once seen witchcraft on its path. I had been sitting late in my hut writing notes. About midnight, before retiring, I took a spear and went for my usual nocturnal stroll. I was walking in the garden at the back of my hut, amongst banana trees, when I noticed a bright light passing at the back of my servants' huts towards the homestead of a man called Tupoi. As this seemed worth investigation I followed its passage until a grass screen obscured the view. I ran quickly through my hut to the other side in order to see where the light was going to, but did not regain sight of it. I knew that only one man, a member of my household, had a lamp that might have given off so bright a light, but next morning he told me that he had neither been out late at night nor had he used his lamp. There did not lack ready informants to tell me that what I had seen was witchcraft. Shortly afterwards, on the same morning, an old relative of Tupoi and an inmate of his homestead died. This event fully explained the light I had seen. I never discovered its real origin, which was possibly a handful of grass lit by some one on his way to defecate, but the coincidence of the direction along which the light moved and the subsequent death accorded well with Zande ideas.

This light is not the witch in person stalking his prey but is an emanation from his body. On this point Zande opinion is quite decided. The witch is on his bed, but he has dispatched the soul of his witchcraft to remove the psychical part of his victim's organs, his *mbisimo pasio*, the soul of his flesh, which he and his fellow witches will devour. The whole act of vampirism is an incorporeal one: the soul of witchcraft removes the soul of the organ. I have not been able to obtain a precise explanation of what is meant by the soul of witchcraft and the soul of an organ. Azande know that people are killed in this way, but only a witch himself could give an exact account of what happens in the process. One man described an attack by witches as follows:

"Witches arise and beat their drum of witchcraft. The membrane of this drum is human skin. They stretch human skin across it so that they can sound their call on it to summon the members of their order. Their drum call is 'human flesh, human flesh, human flesh'.

"They go to bewitch that man whose 'condition' is bad. That witch who hates him goes with a company of witches to his dwelling-place. They dance around his hut. That witch who hates him opens his door and in a witchcraft-struggle carries him off his bed and throws him outside. All the witches collect around him and worry him almost to death. When each witch has seized part of his flesh they rise and return to their meeting-place.

"They take a small witchcraft-pot and begin to cook the flesh of this man in it. They place the lumps of flesh around the edge of the pot. They tell one of their company to push his lump so that it will fall into the pot. All of them act in this manner, each pushing his portion so that it falls into the pot. But that witch who was responsible for calling the assembly cheats with his portion of flesh and hides it. The other witches will die on account of the death of the man whose flesh they have taken, for they all eat of his flesh. But that witch who summoned the assembly hides his portion.

"The man falls sick and is sick nigh unto death and his relatives consult the oracles about his welfare. The oracles disclose to them the name of the man who called the assembly. They consult the poison oracle and it kills a fowl to his name. They take the wing of the fowl and give it to this witch and say to him, 'So-and-so, you are killing that man.' He replies: 'Well, if it is I who am killing that man he will recover from my witchcraft.' He takes a draught of water and blows it out and speaks thus: 'I have blown water on the fowl's wing.'

"When darkness falls he rises again as a witch and as a witch (i.e. incorporeally) takes the flesh of this man and as a witch returns it and places it on his body. He refrained from eating human flesh in the company of witches and cheated the other witches lest he should be slain in vengeance for the man's death. He did this in order to take the flesh back again so that when the man died and his relatives made magic the medicine would come and merely look at him without striking him. It would see that he had not eaten human flesh and would pass him by to kill those other witches who ate the flesh of the man.

"Therefore Azande speak thus about the matter: A man who is a great witch is not likely to die on account of the deaths of men because he does not bewitch people to eat their flesh but bewitches a man to hide his flesh. It is for this reason that he continues to live because if he ate human flesh it would not be long before he died from magic of vengeance made on account of the deaths of men."

Azande use the same word in describing the psychical parts of witchcraft-substance and other organs as they use for what we call the soul of a man. Anything the action of which is not subject to the senses may likewise be explained by the existence of a soul. Medicines act by means of their soul, an explanation which covers the void between a magical rite and the achievement of its purpose. The poison oracle also has a soul, which accounts for its power to see what a man cannot see.

The action of witchcraft is therefore not subject to the ordinary conditions which limit most objects of daily use, but its activity is thought to be limited to some extent by conditions of space. Witchcraft does not strike a man at a great distance, but only injures people in the vicinity. If a man leaves the district in which he is living when attacked by witchcraft it will not follow him far. Witchcraft needs, moreover, conscious direction. The witch cannot send out his witchcraft and leave it to find its victim for itself, but he must define its objective and determine its route. Hence a sick man can often elude its further ravages by withdrawing to the shelter of a grass hut in the bush unknown to all but his wife and children. The witch will dispatch his witchcraft after his victim and it will search his homestead in vain and return to its owner.

Likewise, a man will leave a homestead before dawn in order to escape witchcraft, because then witches are asleep and will not observe his departure. When they become aware that he has left he will already be out of range of their witchcraft. If, on the other hand, they see him starting they may bewitch him and some misfortune will befall him on his journey or after his return home. It is because witchcraft is believed to act only at a short range that if a wife falls sick on a visit to her parents' home they search for the responsible witch there and not at her husband's home, and if she dies in her parents' home her husband may hold them responsible because they have not protected her by consulting the oracles about her welfare.

The farther removed a man's homestead from his neighbours the safer he is from witchcraft. The wide extent of bush and cultivations that intervene between one Zande homestead and the next was remarked by the earliest travellers and has often puzzled visitors to Zandeland. When Azande of the Anglo-Egyptian Sudan were compelled to live in roadside settlements they did so with profound misgivings, and many fled to the Belgian Congo rather than face close contact with their neighbours. Azande say that their dislike of living in close proximity to others is partly due to a desire to place a stretch of country between their wives and possible lovers and partly to their belief that a witch can injure the more severely the nearer he is to his victim.

The Zande verb "to bewitch" is *no*, and in its only other uses we translate this word "to shoot". It is used for shooting with bow and arrow or with a gun. By a jerk of a leg witch-doctors will shoot (*no*) pieces of bone into one another at a distance. We may notice the analogy between these different shootings and their common factor, the act of causing injury at a distance. . . .

* * *

Witchcraft beliefs also embrace a system of values which regulate human conduct.

Witchcraft is ubiquitous. It plays its part in every activity of Zande life; in agricultural, fishing, and hunting pursuits; in domestic life of homesteads as well as in communal life of district and court; it is an important theme of mental life in which it forms the background of a vast panorama of oracles and magic; its influence is plainly stamped on law and morals, etiquette and religion; it is prominent in technology and language; there is no niche or corner of Zande culture into which it does not twist itself. If blight seizes the ground-nut crop it is witchcraft; if the bush is vainly scoured for game it is witchcraft; if women laboriously bale water out of a pool and are rewarded by but a few small fish it is witchcraft; if termites do not rise when their swarming is due and a cold useless night is spent in waiting for their flight it is witchcraft; if a wife is sulky and unresponsive to her husband it is witchcraft; if a prince is cold and distant with his subject it is witchcraft; if a magical rite fails to achieve its purpose it is witchcraft; if, in fact, any failure or misfortune falls upon any one at any time and in relation to any of the manifold activities of his life it may be due to witchcraft. Those acquainted either at first hand or through reading with the life of an African people will realize that there is no end to possible misfortunes, in routine tasks and leisure hours alike, arising not only from miscalculation, incompetence, and laziness, but also from causes over which the African, with his meagre scientific knowledge, has no control. The Zande attributes all these misfortunes to witchcraft unless there is strong evidence, and subsequent oracular confirmation, that sorcery or [other], evil agents . . . [have] been at work, or unless they are clearly to be attributed to incompetence, breach of a taboo, or failure to observe a moral rule.

When a Zande speaks of witchcraft he does not speak of it as we speak of the weird witchcraft of our own history. Witchcraft is to him a commonplace happening and he seldom passes a day without mentioning it. Where we talk about the crops hunting, and our neighbours' ailments the Zande introduces into these topics of conversation the subject of witchcraft. To say that witchcraft has blighted the ground-nut crop, that witchcraft has scared away game, and that witchcraft has made so-and-so ill is equivalent to saying in terms of our own culture that the ground-nut crop has failed owing to blight, that game is scarce this season, and that so-and-so has caught influenza. Witchcraft participates in all misfortunes and is the idiom in which Azande speak about them and in which they explain them. Witchcraft is a classification of misfortunes which while differing from each other in other respects have this single common character, their harmfulness to man.

Unless the reader appreciates that witchcraft is quite a normal factor in the life of Azande, one to which almost any and every happening may be referred, he will entirely misunderstand their behaviour towards it. To us witchcraft is something which haunted and disgusted our credulous forefathers. But the Zande expects to come across witchcraft at any time of the day or night. He would be just as surprised if he were not brought into daily contact with it as we would be if confronted by its appearance. To him there is nothing miraculous about it. It is expected that a man's hunting will be injured by witches, and he has at his disposal means of dealing with them. When misfortunes occur he does not become awestruck at the play of supernatural forces. He is not terrified at the presence of an occult enemy. He is, on the other hand, extremely annoyed. Some one, out of spite, has ruined his ground-nuts or spoilt his hunting or given his wife a chill, and surely this is cause for anger! He has done no one harm, so what right has any one to interfere in his affairs? It is an impertinence, an insult, a dirty, offensive trick! It is the aggressiveness and not the eeriness of these actions which Azande emphasize when speaking of them, and it is anger and not awe which we observe in their response to them.

Witchcraft is not less anticipated than adultery. It is so intertwined with everyday happenings that it is part of a Zande's ordinary world. There is nothing remarkable about a witch—you may be one yourself, and certainly many of your closest neighbours are witches. Nor is there anything awe-inspiring about witchcraft. We do not become psychologically transformed when we hear that some one is ill—we expect people to be ill—and it is the same with Azande. They expect people to be ill, i.e. to be bewitched, and it is not a matter for surprise or wonderment. . . .

* * *

Magic is the chief foe of witchcraft, and it would be useless to describe Zande magical rites and notions had their beliefs in witches not previously been recorded. Having grasped the ideas Azande have of witchcraft, we shall have no difficulty in understanding the main purpose of their magic. But I do not wish to define the attributes of magic in this chapter for the reason that in Zande opinion some magic is to be classed, from the legal and moral standpoint, with witchcraft.

As we look at their culture there is a great difference, in theory at any rate, between an act of witchcraft and an act of magic, because a witch obviously cannot perform the action attributed to him, whereas there is no reason why a magical rite should not be performed. To Azande themselves the difference between a sorcerer and a witch is that the former uses the technique of magic and derives his power from medicines, while the latter acts without rites and spells and uses hereditary psycho-psychical powers to attain his ends. Both alike are enemies of men, and Azande class them together. Witchcraft and sorcery are opposed to, and opposed by, good magic. . . .

Azande do not stigmatize magic as bad because it destroys the health and property of others, but because it flouts moral and legal rules. Good magic may be destructive, even lethal, but it strikes only at persons who have committed a crime, whereas bad magic is used out of spite against men who have not broken any law or moral convention. Good medicines cannot be used for evil purposes. Certain medicines are classified as good, certain medicines as bad, while about yet others there is no strong moral opinion or Azande are uncertain whether to place them in the category of good or bad. . . .

Here I will mention at random a few examples [of good magic]: hunting magic, agricultural magic, magic to protect the person, magic of song and dance, magic of sickness. Any of these types of magic may be performed privately. Privacy is a characteristic of all Zande magic, for Azande object to others witnessing their actions and are always afraid lest sorcerers and witches get to know that they are making magic and interfere with it. A man's friends and neighbours know, or think they know, what magic he possesses. He does not try to conceal his ownership. But sorcery is a secret rite in a very different sense. It is performed at dead of night, for if the act is witnessed the sorcerer will probably be slain. No one, except the fellow sorcerer who has sold him the medicines, knows that he possesses them.

Neither by virtue of privacy in performance nor of destructive qualities is good magic distinguished from sorcery. Indeed, *bagbuduma*, magic of vengeance, is the most destructive and at the same time the most honourable of all Zande medicines. Its purpose is typical of the purposes of good magic in general. When a man dies Azande consider that he is a victim of witchcraft or sorcery and they make vengeance-magic to slay the slayer of the dead man. It is regarded as a judge which seeks out the person who is responsible for the death, and as an executioner which slays him. Azande say of it that "it decides cases" and that it "settles cases as judiciously as princes". Like all good magic, it acts impartially and according to the merits of the case. Hence Azande say of a medicine either that "it judges equitably" (*si nape zunga*) or that "it is evil medicine".

Were a man to use a medicine like vengeance-medicine to kill out of spite a man innocent of crime it would not only prove ineffectual but would turn against the magician who employed it and destroy him. Azande speak of the medicine as searching for the criminal and eventually, being unable to find him, for he does not exist, returning to slay the man who sent it forth. At the first stroke of sickness he will try to end its activity by throwing it into cold water. Therefore before making vengeance-magic Azande are supposed to seek from the poison oracle assurance that their kinsman died at the hands of witch or sorcerer and not as a result of his own misdeeds through the action of good magic. For vengeance-magic may seek in vain for a witch or sorcerer responsible for the death and return pregnant with undelivered judgement to destroy the magician who sent it forth and who wears the girdle of mourning. . . .

I wish to emphasize that to a Zande the whole idea of *pe zunga* is equivalent to the carrying out of justice in the sense in which we use the expression in our own society. Magic used against persons can only receive the moral and legal sanction of the community if it acts regularly and impartially.

Sorcery, on the other hand, does not give judgements (*si na penga zunga te*). It is not only bad medicine but also stupid medicine, for it does not judge an issue between persons but slays one of the parties to a dispute without regard to the merits of the case. It is a personal weapon aimed at some individual whom the sorcerer dislikes.

Good magic is moral because it is used against unknown persons. For if a man knows who has committed adultery with his wife or stolen his spears or killed his kinsman he takes the matter to court. There is no need to make magic. It is only when he does not know who has committed a crime that he uses good magic against unknown persons. Bad magic, on the other hand, is made against definite persons, and for this reason it is evidently bad, because if the person against whom it is used had injured the magician in any way recognized by law the matter would have been taken to court and damages claimed. It is only because the sorcerer has no legal case against a man that he uses magic to destroy him.

C. AFRICAN AMERICANS

[16]

Magical Practices and Beliefs

Philip D. Morgan

In this excerpt from his 1998 book Slave Counterpoint, *the historian Philip D. Morgan discusses conjuring practices among slaves in the colonial South, as well as their beliefs about death and the afterlife.* Slave Counterpoint *has won awards from many professional organizations, including the American Historical Association's Albert J. Beveridge Award.*

•

The Black World

A major development that took place in the metaphysics of the slave community, in response to the enforced coexistence with other African groups and to the grave, everyday problems of dealing with harsh taskmasters, was an expanded role for the realm of lesser spirits, particularly those deemed useful in injuring others. Melville Herskovits, who pioneered so many of the most fruitful avenues of African American research, wondered whether in the New World "African religion goes underground, and manifests itself in an increase of magic (especially black magic)." This development occurred in the slave cultures of both Virginia and South Carolina to a degree. Not all resort to magic was to injure people—for a spectrum of activities, from outright sorcery to folk healing, from witchcraft to divination, certainly existed— but the dominant trend may be labeled a shift from "saints" (the benevolent lesser spirits so prominent in traditional cosmologies) to "sorcery" (the harming of others by secretive means).

Anglo-Americans described slaves' attempts to harm others by secretive means as either "poisoning" or "conjuring." Even granting the white predilection to see malevolence behind what might have been innocent black actions, many slaves clearly believed in conjuring, often resorted to it, and on occasion sought to harm others by it. The slaves' alleged use of poisons against the white community gained most

From Philip D. Morgan, *Slave Counterpoint: Black Culture in the Eighteenth-Century Chesapeake and Lowcountry* (Chapel Hill: University of North Carolina Press, 1998), 612–16, 619–25, 640–42, 657–58. © 1998 by the University of North Carolina Press. Reprinted by permission of the publisher.

notoriety. In eighteenth-century Virginia, at least 175 slaves were brought before the county courts on charges of poisoning, and a large proportion had white masters or overseers as their ostensible targets. The revulsion felt by whites is captured in some of the sentences. In Orange County, a slave woman named Eve, found guilty of poisoning her master, was drawn on a hurdle to the place of execution and there burnt at the stake. . . .

In South Carolina, white fears of black poisonings appear to have been even more intense than in Virginia. In 1741, a newspaper report claimed that a sinister drug had been used by a "Negro Doctor" to poison a white infant. The black was burned at the stake. Three years later, a black man was hanged in chains on a gibbet near Dorchester for allegedly poisoning his master. In 1749, the "horrid practice of poisoning White People," another editorial expostulated, led to several executions "by burning, gibbeting, [and] hanging." That same year, the *South-Carolina Gazette* printed a letter from Dr. Milward to the president of the Royal Society on "Indian or Negro poison" in the West Indies, indicating the extent of the interest in the matter. . . . Suspected poisoning scares recurred throughout the century—in 1761, for example, slaves reportedly had "begun again the hellish practice of poisoning"—and whites retaliated savagely, gibbeting and burning alive the suspects.

Poisonings, however, were as much, if not more, directed inwardly at blacks as targeted outwardly against whites. Indeed, some observers thought that poisonings of whites were infrequent. A French visitor to Virginia during the Revolutionary war was poorly informed when he reported, "We never hear in this country of masters poisoned by their Negroes," but he was undoubtedly correct when he claimed that the practice was much more extensive in the French West Indies. Peter Kalm observed that the "dangerous art of poisoning" was well known among North American blacks and that they used it primarily against one another. . . .

Intrablack conflict, stemming perhaps from frictions among African ethnic groups or between Africans and creoles or perhaps from the natural stresses to which all slave communities were subject, lay at the heart of many poisonings. Tangled webs of claims and counterclaims, all pointing to serious divisions among blacks, characterize a number of poisonings. Thus, many whites in Louisa County believed that a slave named Peter had prepared substances as an "Ostentatious charade to increase his Credit with Those Negroes who had pressed him to Destroy . . . their Enemies," when in fact his supposed clients hoped to betray him "as a person Guilty of poisoning and conjuring." . . .

Blacks and whites alike testified to the important role of the dispenser of poisons (or medicines or charms) within the slave community. In the Chesapeake, at least one conjurer was brought to trial. Tom, a Caroline County slave, was accused of causing the death of another slave, Joe, by administering "several poisonous powders, roots, herbs and simples." Acquitted of this offense, Tom was transported for giving "powder to other Negroes." More often, however, the role of the conjurer became apparent only when his or her clients came before the courts. Thus, seventy-six Spotsylvania County residents sought a pardon for two slave blacksmiths accused of poisoning their master on the grounds that these "orderly well behaved" men had been duped by "a Negro wench, or Conjurer" belonging to a neighboring planter.

Similarly, a Fauquier County slave accused of arson elicited the support of neighboring whites because his chief accuser was "a notorious Villan," a slave named Ben, who "pretend[ed] to be a conjourer or fortune teller." Three slave men accused of murdering a white overseer in Powhatan County revealed the crucial role of Pompey, a neighbor's slave, who was "reputed among the Negroes as a Conjurer." The plotters had frequently consulted Pompey, "relied much on [his] art . . . to prevent detection," and had even paid him a fee. Henry Knight's observation that Virginia slaves were "very superstitious" and relied on "their poison-doctors, and their conjurers" was well founded. . . .

Slaves fitted unfamiliar substances and techniques into familiar ways of thinking. The blue color that outlined windows and doors of Lowcountry slave cabins and acted as a protection against evil spirits derived from the scrapings of indigo vats. Blacks acquired knowledge from whites and from Indians. In the late seventeenth century, the Reverend John Clayton heard of "a very strange and extraordinary cure" performed by an Indian on a black slave in Virginia. Perhaps this folk remedy passed into black lore. In South Carolina, Boston King recalled that his mother took care of the sick, "having some knowledge of the virtue of herbs, which she learned from the Indians." Richard Parkinson told of a white conjurer who apparently produced charms that blacks found powerful. Some superstitions held by blacks comported well with those found in the white community and were thereby reinforced. Others might have been derived from whites entirely. When a Virginia master noted that his "travelling servant," a slave named George, was "much afraid of Spirits and being alone in the night," there is no reason to think that this belief was African in origin. In the realm of supernatural beliefs, blacks absorbed so much because the additions complemented, or acted in place of, traditional convictions.

Although slave magical practices and beliefs drew on many sources, the African dimension seems most evident in the prevalence of sorcery. In E. E. Evans-Pritchard's classic distinction, both witches and sorcerers seek to injure people, but sorcery is the deliberate attempt by an individual to harm others by secretive means (whether by magic or poison), whereas witchcraft is the unconscious harming of others by magical means. Witchcraft is an inherent quality; sorcery is a deliberate, conscious action. Rarely were eighteenth-century Southern slaves linked to witchcraft, but sorcery was widespread. The most common term for sorcery was *obi* or *obia* (with many other variant spellings), which had multiple African origins, including Efik *ubio* (a charm to cause sickness or death) and Twi *o-bayifo* (sorcerer). The term was current among North American slaves. A Virginia slave accused of poisoning a white was known as Obee. A South Carolina slave, Hector, said to possess magical powers, claimed, "Let the fire kindle as fast as it will, he will Engage by his obias to stiffle and put it out." In Johnston County, North Carolina, Quash, otherwise known as an "Ober Negro," sold "a small mater of truck" or "Ober" to other slaves. In the nineteenth century, W. B. Hodgson, a Georgian who was knowledgeable about African slaves still living in his vicinity, spoke of "the Obi practices and fetish worship, of the Pagan negroes early imported into this country, and of which traditional traces may still be discovered."

More important than etymological parallels were the similarities in the practice of *obeah* between mainland and West Indian islands. First, North American conjuring was clearly an individual practice, with "professionals" often receiving payment from clients. Second, the ingredients of fetishes and charms on the mainland—"Scorpions heads, Sarsparilla, spiders, and glass bottles powdered" in one case, "snake and scorpion heads . . . and great quantity of Roots" in another—resemble those employed by obeah-men in Jamaica. Finally, canes or wands embellished with entwined serpents and frogs, important to the ritual practices of both conjurers and obeah-men, have been found on the mainland as well as in the West Indies.

A variety of charms and magical symbols has been found among the debris of slave quarters. At a site in Baltimore County, Maryland, three polygonal objects shaped from glass, earthenware, and wood appear to have been ritual objects. A raccoon *baculum*, or penis bone, recovered from George Washington's Mount Vernon slave quarter, might well have been a fertility symbol; the incision of a line encircling one end suggests that it was hung around the neck by a cord. Blue glass beads, made in Europe but perhaps conceived by Africans and African Americans as having magical properties, have been excavated at various slave sites. On Parris Island, South Carolina, four thousand glass beads were found in a small pit; they might well have played a role in an African American religious ritual. An African cowrie shell has been found along Mulberry Row at Monticello. These items were probably used to ward off the "evil eye." Similarly, three brass amulets shaped like human fists uncovered at the Hermitage plantation in Tennessee and a hand-shaped hook-and-eye discovered at the Charles Calvert home in Annapolis, Maryland, have all been attributed to an African-American interest in hand images, which were thought to confer spiritual power.

In South Carolina, a number of African words associated with magic, particularly magic aimed at causing harm, were in use well into the twentieth century. The Hausa word *huduba*, meaning "to arouse resentment," was simplified to *hudu*, meaning "to cause bad luck"; the Mende word *ndzoso*, meaning "spirit or magic," was simplified to *joso*, meaning "charm, witchcraft." Other words with essentially similar meanings were also employed, such as *juju* for "evil spirit," *kafa* for "charm," *moco* for "witchcraft or magic," *wanga* for "charm, witchcraft," and, most famous of all, *wudu* for "sorcery." Perhaps most significantly, some African words that seem to have had benign meanings became associated with sorcery in Gullah. Thus the Ewe word *fufu*, which simply means "dust," became in Gullah "a fine dust used with the intention of bewitching one or causing harm to one." Likewise, the Mende word *gafa*, meaning "spirit, soul, or idol," became for Gullah speakers "evil spirit, or devil." Transferred from the Chesapeake to the Lowcountry, Charles Ball noted the difference when he described cotton slaves as "exceedingly superstitious . . . beyond all other people that I have ever known." They "uniformly believe," Ball continued, "in witchcraft, conjuration, and the agency of evil spirits in the affairs of human life."

Important as the association of sorcery with an African influence clearly was, the practice had to appeal to creoles or it would soon have fossilized. The South Carolina Assembly recognized this danger in 1751 when it made it a capital offense for "any slave [to] teach or instruct another slave in the knowledge of any poisonous root, plant, herb, or other sort of poison whatever." But apparently whites were powerless to halt the dissemination of knowledge. As early as 1724, the minister of Saint James Goose Creek lamented that the "secret poisonings" in his parish stemmed, not from unassimilated Africans, but from those slaves converted to Christianity. A generation later, the minister of Saint George Dorchester was surprised to find a baptized slave accused of poisoning. She told the startled minister "that notwithstanding what was alledged against her, she still hoped to be saved because she believed in Christ." He attributed her optimism to the influence of "our sectaries." Perhaps South Carolina officials showed great wisdom in reimbursing Culcheth Golightly's estate for a whole family of slaves, transported to Jamaica on suspicion of poisoning their master. Diffusion would surely take place within a family, they might have decided.

In piedmont Virginia, one case of poisoning involved the apparent transmission of magical knowledge from African father to African American son. Joe, the son, was found guilty of poisoning. A number of the county's white residents petitioned for a pardon on the grounds that it was Joe's father, a slave with the African name Mazar, who "compounded and administered medicines." Indeed, Joe had once "informed his father who was very Deaf that physic was wanted stronger than some he had given before," but also "cautioned his Father to beware and take care not to take life." Furthermore, Joe's "crime" appeared less heinous to many of his white neighbors because part of the evidence against him lay merely in his prediction that sick people would die on the return of warm weather. At worst, this was little more than harmless fortune-telling. . . .

The boundary between conjuring and folk medicine was porous. In an age where diseases struck often and mysteriously, a lingering illness could easily be attributed to magic. Particularly was this true when blacks revealed a strong interest in herbs and pharmacopoeia as panaceas for everyday problems. In the early eighteenth century, John Brickell observed that North Carolina slaves gathered snakeroot on Sundays; at midcentury, Dr. Alexander Garden pointedly noted that, were it not for what had been learned from "Negroe Strollers and Old Women," South Carolinians would not "know a Common Dock from a Cabbage Stock"; and, at the end of the century, Benjamin Henry Latrobe learned that "Negro woodmen" in Virginia rubbed swamp plantain onto snakebites. Slaves were undoubtedly well versed in the medicinal powers of various plants. . . .

Funerals

One area where African ideas merged with the new environment in complicated ways was that of attitudes toward the dead. For West Africans, as Herskovits has observed, "the funeral is the true climax of life, and no belief drives deeper into their thought." The dead played an active role in the lives of the living. In fact, African kin groups are often described as communities of both the living and the dead. As Equiano described his native Igbo, the spirits of "their dear friends or relations, they believe always attend them, and guard them from the bad spirits of their foes." When a Catholic priest told a "Grandee" at Whydah on the African coast that he and his people would burn in hell if they continued in their traditional ways, he received a sharp riposte: "Our Fathers, Grandfathers, to an endless Number, Liv'd as we do, and Worship'd the same Gods as we do; and if they must burn therefore, Patience, we are not better than our Ancestors, and shall comfort our selves with them." No direct evidence exists that elaborate beliefs about dead ancestors or friends survived the Middle Passage—at least among North American slaves. However, the importance of funerals to slaves and their distinctive practices on such occasions suggest some continuity with traditional beliefs. . . .

[The] belief in a return to Africa was one way for slaves to retain a link to ancestors and friends. In midcentury Delaware, a missionary observed that African slaves had "a notion, that when they die, they are translated to their own countrey, there to live in their former free condition." Some Africans, particularly "Keromantees," he continued, committed suicide calmly and deliberately as a result of their faith. Johann Bolzius saw the same behavior among Lowcountry Africans who "frequently take their own lives out of desperation, with the hope of resurrection in their homeland, and of rejoining their people." The Africans that Charles Ball encountered in the Lowcountry "universally" believed in a return to Africa after death. With this expectation, an African former priest buried his son with a small bow and arrows, a little bag of food, a stick seemingly in the form of an agricultural tool, a piece of cloth "with several curious and strange figures painted on it in blue and red, by which, he said, his relations and countrymen would know the infant to be his son," and a miniature canoe and paddle "with which he said it would cross the ocean to his own country." After casting a lock of his own hair into the grave, the father "then told us the God of his country was looking at him, and was pleased with what he had done."

Mortuary practices also demonstrate the close relation slaves saw between the living and the dead. Ten eighteenth-century blacks buried in a group near Stratford Hall in Virginia were interred in traditional European fashion in coffin and shroud, but three black men wore African-style clothing to the grave. At other sites in the Chesapeake, a string of beads interred with an infant and concentrations of seeds on coffin surfaces suggest African-style burial offerings. At Utopia quarter on the James River in Virginia, a burial ground containing twenty-five individuals has been dated to the first half of the eighteenth century. The burials appear to have been arranged in family groups. Three adults had English clay tobacco pipes placed under their arms, and one was interred with a glass bead necklace around the neck. In the Lowcountry, the African influence in burial goods was more notable. In Liberty County, Georgia, the remains of a plate directly above the head of an early-nineteenth-century slave skeleton accords with the testimony of "a Gullah Negro on the Santee River," who explained "that it was their custom to place the last plate, the last glass and spoon used before death on the grave." A depiction of a black burial, attributed to early-nineteenth-century northern Florida, showing a scaffold, dead animal skin, and a variety of personal possessions, has been linked to a number of precise African traditions. More generally, the broken crockery, upturned bottles, seashells, and particular plants that mark black graves in cemeteries particularly throughout the Lowcountry have African analogues. All of these practices were ways of propitiating the dead, of easing their journey to the spirit world, and of ensuring that they did not return to haunt the living. . . .

*   *   *

Two broad developments characterized the religious life of slaves in the Chesapeake and Lowcountry. The first and perhaps most important, at least in the eighteenth century, was the enhanced role of magic. Before Christianity penetrated the world of slaves, magical beliefs and practices, particularly those associated with harming individuals, had assumed a prominent place that they would retain even after widespread Christianization. Second, even when African slaves came into contact with Christianity, they did not accept it wholesale. Rather than adding a high god to their pantheon of lesser spirits, they seem to have elaborated on a traditional concept of a supreme being. If this development encouraged Africans and their descendants to adapt Christianity to their needs rather than having it thrust upon them, such discrimination was certainly evident in their distinctive funeral practices, their particularly expressive religious behavior, their apocalyptic visions, and the charisma of some of their preachers.

The religion of slaves in eighteenth-century British America highlights how blacks, laboring under extreme hardships and in radically different settings, managed to preserve some deep-level principles drawn from their African heritage. Much was lost: few priests and almost no collective rituals survived the passage to British North America. One exception seems to have occurred in the household of Jacob Stewart (Jacobo Estuart), a free black from the Lowcountry who lived in Spanish Florida in 1784 and then migrated to New Providence in the Bahamas. He celebrated "Negro rites in the style of Guinea" in his Florida home. Thus, contrary to one interpretation, North American plantation slaves generally could not practice "African religion," nor did they appropriate only those values that could be absorbed into their "Africanity." This is to make excessive claims for the autonomy of slaves and the primacy of their African background. Ultimately, such an argument belittles the slaves' achievements by minimizing the staggering obstacles they faced in forging a culture. "The glory of Afro-Americana," Mintz states, "depended—had to depend—on creativity and innovation far more than on the indelibility of particular culture contents."

Opting for the opposite extreme, however, and arguing that North American slaves experienced an "African spiritual holocaust" is no more persuasive. Rather, at the fundamental level of epistemological beliefs, interpersonal relations, and expressive behavior, slaves kept alive a measure of their African "character." They engaged in a process of selective appropriation or structured improvisation in which values and practices were reinterpreted as they were incorporated. At bottom, blacks shared a similar outlook on how the world worked as well as common means of cultural expression, but they borrowed widely, melding older cultural traits with new ones, the mix always varying from place to place, but overall creating a distinctive pattern of their own.

[17]

Archaeological Evidence for a Possible Witch in Barbados, West Indies

Jerome Handler

In this essay the anthropologist Jerome Handler describes slave burial practices and witchcraft beliefs in Barbados. Among his other works are The Unappropriated People: Freedmen in the Slave Society of Barbados *(1974) and with Frederick W. Lange,* Plantation Slavery in Barbados: An Archeological and Historical Investigation *(1978). He has also compiled a major* Guide to Source Materials for the Study of Barbados History, 1637–1834, 2 vols. *(1971 and 1991). The data for this essay can be found in "A Prone Burial from a Plantation Slave Cemetery in Barbados, West Indies,"* Historical Archaeology 30 *(1996): 76–86.*

•

The Caribbean island of Barbados was England's first American territory to depend on sugar plantations and African slave labor. From around the 1630s until emancipation in the 1830s, many thousands of people, slave and free, were buried on this small island, about twenty-one miles long by fourteen miles wide. Free people were usually interred in church cemeteries, but the vast majority of the several hundred thousand slaves who perished were not baptized (slave baptism was not common in any of England's early New World colonies) and thus were not buried in consecrated grounds, particularly those of the Anglican Church, the established church of Barbados. The great majority of these slaves were buried in unmarked plantation cemeteries that were scattered throughout the island. Although excavated in the early 1970s, the cemetery at Newton Plantation, in southern Barbados, is still the only plantation cemetery discovered on the island as well as the earliest undisturbed plantation slave cemetery yet reported for the British colonies in America.

Although only a small portion of the cemetery was excavated, the remains of 104 individuals were found; they were interred from about 1660 to 1820. This essay focuses on one of the more distinctive burials, unique not only to Newton but also to early African cemetery sites in the Americas.

Newton's slave cemetery is close to the site of the former slave village, in an

This is an original essay written for this reader.

uncultivated field surrounded by sugarcane. The field contained several low, formless mounds arranged in no particular pattern: before excavation these mounds appeared as slight undulations in the dense grass surface that covered the entire site. Some of the mounds turned out to be natural features of the terrain, while others were humanly created and contained burials.

Mound 1, the largest and most clearly defined of the Newton mounds, was roughly circular in shape and contained only one interment. Reflecting the anonymity of so many early slaves, the individual remains nameless. Designated Burial 9 after the order in which it was excavated, the individual had been placed in a prepared subsurface pit, a shallow excavation into the underlying bedrock.

Burial 9 was a young adult female, around twenty years of age, who probably had been born in the New World. A chemical method for measuring skeletal lead content yielded a very high amount of lead, more than twice the average for all of the skeletons as well as for those in her own age group. Grave goods or associated artifacts were absent from Burial 9, and she lacked a coffin. Her skeleton was fully articulated on an east-west axis with the head facing west. Mound 1 contained only this solitary burial, but what is especially significant is that Burial 9 was the only interment in the cemetery buried on its stomach, that is, in a prone position. Aside from one or two flexed burials, all others were extended on their backs in a supine position.

Physical evidence from the excavated mound and the surrounding area suggests that Burial 9 was interred during the late 1600s or early 1700s, an early period in the cemetery's history and at a time when many Barbados slaves had been born in Africa or were the first generation of New World birth.

If Mound 1 was, indeed, constructed early, why it was not used again in later years becomes a relevant question in interpreting Burial 9 because a smaller mound, Mound 2, immediately west of Mound 1, was repeatedly used over a relatively long period, apparently from the late 1600s through the early 1800s, and grew as new burials were added over the years. The people burying their dead in Mound 2 surely were aware of the neighboring and much larger Mound 1. Yet they avoided using it. A tradition seems to have developed among Newton's slaves concerning this large mound and the individual it contained.

The identity of Burial 9 will never be known, but questions can be raised about her status in the slave community. Burial 9's unique features as the cemetery's only prone burial and the only one interred in the cemetery's largest mound suggest that she possessed unusual characteristics or died under special circumstances. The extremely high lead level in her bones suggests that at death she would have been suffering from the effects of serious lead poisoning, and might have displayed symptoms that could have been interpreted as bizarre behavior. For example, people around her would have noticed such behavior as sudden, abrupt episodes of clutching her abdomen, moaning or crying out in pain; these episodes could occur abruptly and unpredictably. Whatever the case, her skeleton displayed no physical evidence of an unusual cause of death, and Burial 9 was probably viewed as having special social characteristics.

The relatively abundant documentary sources on Newton lack any specific infor-

mation for an interpretation of Burial 9, and there are no contemporary data from
Barbados that would help interpret the burial. For suggestive ideas one must turn to
more general data on Barbadian slave culture and the literature on mortuary practices
in West Africa, the vast region from which the majority of slaves transported to
Barbados came during the period of Burial 9's interment.

Although data on earthen mounds in West Africa are very sparse and sometimes
vague, the few references to mounds seem to link them to high-status people whose
communities viewed them positively or in a favorable light. There is one exception,
however, and this exception is suggestive of an interpretation for Burial 9.

The LoDagaa of northwestern Ghana, according to the anthropologist Jack
Goody, have three main methods of "disposing of the dead." The "ordinary" burial
involves digging a new grave in the form of a "bell-shaped chamber," while the other
two methods are reserved for community members "who are considered dangerous."
In one method a "trench grave" is dug in an area removed from where normal people
have been buried and without the usual funeral ceremonies. Trench grave burials can
include victims of epidemics, suicides, those convicted of various crimes, and witches;
the body of a witch, in fact, "is simply disposed of as quickly as possible in an old
grave, which is never again reopened." Another burial for "dangerous" persons
involves the "building of a mound above the corpse." Although this method is mainly
used for infants who are not yet considered fully human, Goody implies that it can
also be used for suicides and witches. Goody explains that the principle governing
the mound burial "appears to be the avoidance of burial within the earth itself" and
"one way of minimizing contact with the earth is to build the grave above ground."
Thus, an "evil-doer" is "buried under a pile of earth," but even persons buried in
trench graves are considered to have "sinned against the Earth shrine"; witches fall
well within this category as witchcraft is considered "an offense against the earth."

I am not suggesting that the Burial 9 mound can be literally interpreted as the
LoDagaa explain their mound burials, but their practices raise the possibility that
mounds could be associated with persons who possessed unusual characteristics or
negatively viewed traits. Such an interpretation is strongly reinforced by West African
data on prone burials. As indicated above, virtually every Newton burial was in an
extended supine position, a common position in West Africa, as were flexed and
extended lateral burials; all three positions could occur within the same geographic
and cultural areas and are regularly reported in the literature. Information on prone
positions, however, is much more limited and has been far more difficult to obtain.

I was able to find only a few specific references to prone burials. In each case the
person was considered to have socially negative traits or had been convicted of
witchcraft, a criminal offense in all West African societies. Among several cultural
groups in the western Cameroons, people convicted of a "special form of witchcraft"
were, according to the anthropologist Edwin Ardener, "buried face downward so
that if they attempt to come out of their graves they will move in the wrong direction." Not far to the west, in southern Nigeria, A. P. Talbot reported that the Ibibio
normally buried their dead in extended supine or flexed positions, but the bodies of
"undesirables whose return is not wished are placed in the grave face downward";

and the anthropologist Daryll Forde recorded that among the Efik Ibibio of Old Calabar "corpses of witches were sometimes buried with the face to the ground" so that the "witch ghost" would be prevented from returning to "wreak havoc among the living."

Finally, John Matthews, an Englishman residing in Sierra Leone during the late 1780s, described the execution of a convicted witch among the closely related Temne (or Timne) and Bulum. He was forced to dig his own grave and stand at "the edge of the foot of it, with his face towards it"; he was then struck from behind with "a violent blow upon the nape of the neck, which causes him to fall upon his face into the grave; a little loose earth is then thrown upon him, and a sharp stake of hard wood is drove [*sic*] through the expiring delinquent, which pins him to the earth; the grave is then filled up, and his or her name is never after mentioned."

When specific West African evidence on prone burials is combined with broader mortuary evidence from West Africa that burial practices usually differed for people who had died in special or unusual ways, for example, suicide, in pregnancy or childbirth, from lightning; who possessed unusual physical characteristics, for example, albinos or twins; or who possessed negatively viewed social traits, for example, sorcerers or witches, the case is strengthened for interpreting Burial 9 as a probable witch or some other negatively viewed person with supernatural powers. African witches were often executed for their crimes and received no interment rites. Practices regarding the disposition of their corpses varied from culture to culture, and their bodies, clothed or naked, could be burned, sometimes after being hacked to pieces, merely thrown into the bush, left on the surface to decompose, or simply placed in a grave without any ceremony. In brief, whatever the culture, the bodies of witches were treated differently than those of other people.

Only at great personal risk from their masters could Barbadian slaves execute or murder one of their own, but, it has to be emphasized, they were relatively free to bury their dead according to their own customs; relative freedom in mortuary practices was widespread in the Americas, especially during the early colonial periods. An interpretation of Burial 9 as a negatively viewed member of the slave community is further reinforced by evidence from Mound 2, the smaller mound that contained many burials interred over a relatively long period. People continued to bury their dead in Mound 2, as well as in non-mound areas of the cemetery, within plain view of Mound 1. Newton's slaves possibly avoided putting new burials in Mound 1 because a tradition was perpetuated that some person associated with evil supernatural powers was buried there.

Barbadian slaves, like West Africans in general, did not consider major illness and death accidental; rather, such misfortunes were caused primarily by supernatural forces that acted through human agents. Thus, evil magic was a major factor in their lives, and witchcraft, in particular, was frequently invoked to explain major personal calamities. In considering evil magic I follow a common anthropological distinction between sorcery and witchcraft. In sorcery, magic is consciously performed to injure, even destroy, others. Sorcerers acquire their knowledge through learning, and theoretically their techniques can be carried out by anyone with the requisite knowledge and skill. Although the witch's power might be acquired through special ritual procedures, it is usually inborn or inherited. However acquired, this power cannot be learned; it resides within the individual and is directed against others for evil purposes. Witchcraft, then, is a psychic or mental act whose believers affirm that the harmful power of the witch is unleashed merely through the activation of certain negative thoughts. Barbadian slaves, at least during the seventeenth century and early eighteenth, when slave life was more directly influenced by the African-born and first-generation creoles, may have made distinctions between witchcraft and sorcery in a broadly similar manner to many West Africans. These distinctions, however, went unrecognized by the whites who reported on Barbadian slave life, and thus are difficult to isolate in the historical record. In any event, beliefs in witchcraft and sorcery were pervasive features of the world in which slaves lived—as they were in the West African homelands, and slaves clearly subscribed to an essentially African view of witches: a witch is everything a good person should not be; witches are universally feared and despised.

A final point should be made concerning Burial 9. It was certainly not unique at Newton in its absence of grave goods, and that absence alone would not make it a very special case. In West Africa, grave goods were common and included materials ranging from food and drink to personal articles or possessions of one kind or another. West Africans explained grave goods in a variety of ways, but whatever the explanations, there is no evidence that grave goods were interred with persons who their communities viewed negatively. In brief, the evidence is very clear that grave goods were placed only with persons who were positively regarded in their communities or who were considered ordinary people.

Thus, mortuary evidence on Burial 9 includes data like the burial's solitary location in Mound 1, prone position, absence of grave goods, body forced into a grave pit that was too small, possibly suggesting a disdain or lack of care for the corpse, and the possible behavior associated with severe lead poisoning. This evidence, combined with West African mortuary data on the treatment of witches or other despised/feared persons and slave beliefs concerning evil magic, leads to an interpretation of Burial 9 as a witch or sorceress—in any case someone who, following African custom, was feared or socially ostracized because she was a vehicle for supernatural contagion.

[18]

An Afro-American Folk Religion

William D. Piersen

The historian William D. Piersen devoted his scholarly life to emphasizing the key role of African culture in the formation of American culture. His studies drew on folk sources as much as written and material records. In this excerpt from his 1988 book Black Yankees, *Piersen describes how African Americans in New England drew on their ancestral cultures and Euro-American traditions in the development of their own folk religion. Among his other publications are* Black Legacy: America's Hidden Heritage *(1993) and* From Africa to America: African-American History from the Colonial Era to the Early Republic, 1526–1790 *(1996).*

•

Habit, an old African proverb tells us, is "a full-grown mountain, hard to get over or pull down." So it was for Africans in the New World. As a Barbados master complained in 1750, slaves were "very tenaciously addicted to the rites, ceremonies, and superstitions of their own countries, particularly in their plays, dances, music, marriages, and burials. And even such as are born here, cannot be entirely weaned from these customs." Yankee slaves, like other New World blacks, fused their ancestral beliefs in the afterworld, in witchcraft, protective charms, divination, herbal medicine, evil spirits, devils and ghosts to surrounding Euro-American traditions; in doing so, they created their own Yankee version of the Afro-American folk religions found throughout the Americas. . . .

Beliefs in the power of amulets and talismans to protect wearers from illness or misfortune were widespread in Africa, and such traditions crossed the ocean almost intact. Many a Yankee slave felt there were evil spirits all about, and so wore charms for protection. If a slave was sick, the devil was believed the cause and had to be driven out by some sort of incantation or ritual. The typical slave, it was said, had "many gods, mostly unkind," which had to be propitiated. "In one form or another," a Yankee observer reported, "fetish worship . . . was almost inherent." Even when

From William D. Piersen, *Black Yankees: The Development of an Afro-American Subculture in Eighteenth-Century New England* (Amherst: University of Massachusetts Press, 1988), 74, 80–86. © 1988 by the University of Massachusetts Press. Reprinted by permission of the publisher.

Afro-Americans adapted to the idea of a supreme Christian god and devil, the spirits
of good and evil remained African in essence with "as many moods as all the gods
and goddesses in Valhalla to be appeased every one, by some self-prescribed inflic-
tion." This is visible in the attitudes of Titus Kent, the Christian slave of the Reverend
Ebenezer Gay of Suffield, Connecticut, regarding his charms:

> In a mild sort of way he became a fetish worshiper. . . . He always carried a frog's
> foot in his pocket to keep off the colic demon, for he thought there was a special
> imp for each disease. Around his neck he carried four rattle-snake's buttons, so
> suspended as to hang over his lungs. These he considered a sovereign remedy for
> consumption, and of course valued them highly, as most of his best friends had died
> of that dreaded disease. On one occasion he lost them and it is a mild statement to
> say that he made things lively in the neighborhood. He bored every one he met
> about "dose buttons," until at last one of the boys found them for him, or at least
> killed another snake; and so gave him a new set which he wore to the end of his
> days.

Given such beliefs, it is not surprising that in the seventeenth century African
slaves joined other New Englanders in their fear of witches; indeed, the flying witches
of Africa who rode victims during the night seemed to be visiting Massachusetts as
well. Because of the similarity of beliefs, New England's black population added little
new to the white witchcraft traditions. While they were occasionally accused of
witchcraft, blacks were not singled out for alien beliefs or heathen practices. As early
as 1656, Old Ham was called one of three male witches at Strawberry Bank, New
Hampshire, by Elizabeth Rowe. During the infamous Salem trials of 1692, four local
blacks were suspected of witchcraft. Old Pharaoh, the slave of Zaccheus Collins of
Lynn, was accused of being one of those who came to torment and entice Mercy
Lewis during the trials. Mercy Lewis also was among the girls naming Mary Black,
the Negro slave of Nathaniel Putnam, as a witch. Of course, the most famous of the
accused was the much romanticized Tituba, an Afro-Carib slave from Barbados, who
may have taught several local girls some West Indian conjuring tricks.

A more likely candidate as a real conjurer was Candy, a slave and fellow islander
of Tituba's, who was accused of witchcraft by Ann Putnam. At her trial, Candy
denied any such heritage, explaining that in Barbados neither she nor her mother had
been witches; she said that she had become a witch in Salem only under the instruction of her white mistress. But since Candy did show the court a conjuring aid with
clear African and Afro-American parallels—"a handkerchief wherein several knots
were tied, rags of cloth, a piece of cheese and a piece of grass"—it is possible she
may have known about, and practiced, conjuring techniques. Nonetheless, despite
Candy and the others, the evidence is much too slim to find significant Afro-American
origins or impetus behind New England's witchcraft hysteria. For the most part it
was local white citizens, rather than the exotic black newcomers, who were chosen
the scapegoats of the witchcraft madness.

Blacks, like the other citizens of Massachusetts, found themselves the victims of
witchcraft. In December 1679, Wonn, a black slave belonging to John Ingerson,

helped indict Bridget Oliver for witchcraft by testifying in the Salem quarterly court that the month before, she had bewitched the horses of his sled so that they "ran down the swamp up to their bellies." When he returned to the barn, he said, he saw her sitting "upon the beam with an egg in her hand"; and later at dinner, after seeing two strange black cats, he was mysteriously pinched. During the Salem troubles a little over a decade later, Peter Tuft of Charlestown complained that his black woman was being persecuted by acts of witchcraft committed by Elizabeth Fosdick and Elizabeth Paine. According to a letter left by Rhode Island's Willet Carpenter, his maternal great-grandfather Powell "protected" his slave, Peter, in a very different manner:

> [Powell] was a Newport merchant, and made frequent journeys to Boston and Salem, attended by his Negro servant, Peter, who, whilst at one of these places, went into the Court-house, where some of the witches were on trial. On his return to the house where his master lodged, he was taken apparently with convulsive fits, falling down in great agony, and the people of the house called him bewitched, but Mr. Powell, who had expressed much indignation at the scenes he had lately witnessed, declared with much energy that nobody would be hanged for Peter, for he would himself undertake his cure. Accordingly, he applied his horsewhip to Peter (but for the first and only time), with such effect that he gladly returned to his duty.

Unfortunately, such a cure was not used on the girls of Salem.

The most interesting reference to Afro-American conjuring practices in New England comes from the local traditions of late eighteenth-century Narragansett, traditions which have been romantically embellished in Alice Morse Earle's *In Old Narragansett*. Tuggie Bannock, the conjurer of Earle's tale, was a slave of Rowland Robinson and the daughter of an African woman given the name Abigail. Abigail was well known in local tradition as a woman of royal status, who with the support of her owner returned to Africa to find the son from whom she had been separated. Mother and son returned to Rhode Island, where the boy subsequently became a governor of the black community. Like other Afro-Americans of her day, Tuggie respected and feared the supernatural power of conjuring; in Earle's words she was "far more afraid of being bewitched than she was confident of bewitching." To protect herself from evil spirits, Tuggie wore her petticoats inside out and hung a bag of eggshells around her neck. To work revenge on an enemy she would place a dough heart or dough baby on the victim's fence or doorstep. She might also "burn a project," as she once did, to give Bosum Sidet "the misery," using incantations handed down to her by her mother, Queen Abigail.

According to Earle, "Everyone in Narragansett knew that when a project began to boil, the conjured one would begin to suffer some mental or bodily ill." One of Tuggie's projects was once broken up when the door of her cabin crashed open and she was knocked to the floor by a heavy object that she at first believed to be a terrifying "moonack" or devil. In actuality it was the bobsled of some local boys. The literal truth of such anecdotes cannot be established, but the fact that such conjuring practices were well enough known to be part of the local folklore is important; indeed, we can only wonder how much of the true Afro-American folk culture of New England has been censored from the white records.

Afro-American conjuring practices were often confused by white observers with poisoning, as can be seen in the 1748 description by Peter Kalm of the witchcraft "poisoning" of black collaborationists by their fellow slaves in New York:

> Only a few of them know the secret, and they likewise know the remedy for it; therefore when a negro feels himself poisoned and can recollect the enemy who might possibly have given him the poison, he goes to him, and endeavors by money and entreaties to move him to deliver him from its effects. But if the negro is malicious, he not only denies that he ever poisoned him, but likewise that he knows an antidote for it. This poison does not kill immediately, as I have noted, for sometimes the sick person dies several years afterward. But from the moment he has the poison he falls into a sort of consumption state and enjoys but few days of good health. Such a poor wretch often knows that he is poisoned the moment he gets it. The negroes commonly employ it on such of their brethren as behave well toward whites, are beloved by their masters, and separate, as it were, from their countrymen, or do not like to converse with them. They have likewise often other reasons for their emnity; but there are few examples of their having poisoned their masters. Perhaps the mild treatment they receive, keeps them from doing it, or perhaps they fear that they may be discovered, and that in such a case, the severest punishment would be inflicted on them.

Such "poisoning" is an almost perfect description of "voodoo death" (the psychosomatic effect of the fear of being bewitched), a syndrome common throughout the culture areas of Africa and Afro-America. As Griffith Hughes explained from eighteenth-century Barbados, "If once a Negro believes, that he is bewitched, the Notion is so strongly riveted in his Mind, that, Medicine seldom availing, he usually lingers till death puts an End to his Fears."

Whether the three blacks arrested in Newport in 1772 for allegedly poisoning a fellow slave woman were conjuring or using real poison is unclear, but frightened by the fiendish reputation of Africans as master poisoners, white Americans kept a wary eye against possible revenge by disgruntled house servants. Sometimes the vigilance may have paid off, as in 1735 when Yaw, a Negro man, and a black boy named Caesar were apprehended for attempting to poison the Humphrey Scarlett family by putting arsenic in their breakfast chocolate. Twenty years later the slaves of John Codman of Charlestown, Massachusetts, conspired to poison him in order to gain new masters and be free of his harsh rule. Mark, the leader of the conspiracy, had been trained as a Christian; but this was not sufficient protection for his master. Mark read the Bible through in order to discover how Codman could be killed with impunity and concluded that according to scripture it could be done if the act was accomplished without bloodshed.

An African retention much more important to the folk beliefs of New England than conjuring or witchcraft was the use of divination. Here there could be an easy syncretism since fortune-telling was a popular pastime with white colonials, and the exotic nature of Afro-American seers made them especially believable. At first, black diviners followed traditional African patterns, with little emphasis on fortune-telling per se, but whites tended to frown upon such practices as quackery. Indeed, as early as 1709, authorities took a complaint to the Bristol county court about "Negro-Mancy," arguing that certain black seers were "pretending to discover lost or stolen goods and to find out the persons that have them."

Despite court action other black diviners continued to find employment for their occult skills in New England. A black man in Newfane, Vermont, was remembered to have "told fortunes, discovered lost property, and performed strange feats." Similarly, in 1795, the Reverend Paul Coffin reported that a Negro in Gilmanton, New Hampshire, consulted about missing property, divined that there was a theft, and successfully put a spell upon the white culprit. As Coffin explained, "A man in Gilmanton lost a bar of iron and suspecting such a neighbor, a negro quack gave him directions to find it. These followed, tormented the suspected man, and his brother paid for the iron."

Well into the nineteenth century, Jude, an African woman of Salem, Massachusetts, and Silvia Tory, an African-born slave of Narragansett, Rhode Island, continued to profitably dispense charms and fortunes. It was said that the "obscure rites and ceremonies" Silvia had brought with her out of Africa gave her tea readings an especially exotic allure. Silvia also received certain older applicants who understood the value of the more African aspects of her hidden powers. "Did a cow stray beyond boundaries, or was a horse stolen, the bereaved owner hastened to inquire to Silvia, who would obligingly furnish him with various occult directions, by a strict adherence to which, the lost might be found." Many of the black women of New England who told fortunes also gathered and sold herbs, a calling facilitated by traditional African, Afro-American, and Indian expertise in herbal medicine.

In an interesting reversal of roles, folk tradition recalls one perceptive master who used his servant's belief in divination for his own purposes. Phineas Sprague of Melrose, Massachusetts, convinced his slaves that by using arithmetic as a kind of white man's magic, he could divine any mischief they had been up to.

> When a neighbor made a complaint that he had reason to believe a certain negro had stolen a cart chain, Sprague called the negro up and told him he suspected he had been doing wrong, and unless he owned up, he (Phineas) should figure it out. There being no confession, he would then take his chalk and board and sit down to cipher. In a few moments he would musingly say, "Links three inches long; links three inches long, what does that mean?" Then turning to his "boy" he would say, "Pomp," or whatever his name might be, "Pomp, you have been stealing sausages," Pomp astonished at such arithmetic, would say, "No, Massa, me no steal sausage, me steal cart chain."

While this story was remembered as a kind of black "Polish joke," the anecdote also reveals a Euro-American adaptation of an African method for discovering criminal behavior.

Another African religious retention that helped shape Yankee traditions was a strong belief in ghosts. Fear of ghosts was common to Afro-Americans through the

New World; as Francis Varnod reported from South Carolina in 1724, "Some of our negro pagans have . . . dismal apprehensions of apparitions." Such beliefs had been carried from Africa and seemed even more frightening in a land filled with strange new spirits, where the benevolent protection of sympathetic ancestors could be of no avail. Thus both Rhode Island and South Carolina blacks wore their clothes inside out as a protective device during night journeys, when they felt especially vulnerable to ghosts. Since the dread of ghosts was reinforced by parallel ideas common among the Euro-American population, it is not surprising that the "African imagination" was given credit for several Yankee traditions that certain houses or sections of the New England countryside were haunted.

It is at first perplexing that so many folk beliefs of New England's Afro-Americans contained strong African survivals in a culture which had a puritanical devotion to the ideal of a Christian commonwealth. The explanation lies to a great extent in the similarities of folk religions in Europe and Africa. Black folk beliefs were close enough to white traditions to make them seem relatively harmless superstitions in the eyes of the white authorities. In addition, the Narragansett region, where the retention of African ideas was strongest, was an island of concentrated black population safely ensconced in the religiously tolerant colony of Rhode Island. Many African religious ideas also survived because they remained functional; indeed, white New Englanders as well as blacks visited black mediums and diviners, both feared the power of ghosts, witches, and conjurers, and both believed in the efficacy of herbal medicine and carried protective fetish charms for good luck. Thus, while it might seem surprising given the general perception of Yankee folklife, the folk traditions of white New England met and blended with those of Africa to reinforce one another in a new Yankee folklore—a folklore that may have looked Euro-American, but was instead a complex, intercontinental alloy.

D. AMERICAN INDIANS

[19]

The Indian Response

FERNANDO CERVANTES

In this excerpt from his 1994 book The Devil in the New World, *Fernando Cervantes discusses the interaction between Native spirituality in Mexico and the Catholicism of the Spanish conquerors, especially in regard to the concept of evil. Cervantes, who teaches Hispanic and Latin American studies at the University of Bristol in England, is also the author of* The Idea of the Devil and the Problem of the Indian: The Case of Mexico in the Sixteenth Century *(1991) and coeditor with Nicholas Griffiths of* Spiritual Encounters: Interactions between Christianity and Native Religions in Colonial America *(1999).*

•

When we turn to the specific concepts of evil and the devil, we are faced with the . . . difficulty that such concepts were alien to the Mesoamerican mind. In contrast with the typically western conception of evil as mere absence of being or privation of good (which implied that in strict ontological terms evil did not exist), the Mesoamerican notions of evil and the demonic were inextricably intertwined with their notions of good and the divine. Evil and the demonic were in fact intrinsic to the divinity itself. In the same way as in Hinduism Brahma represented both creation and destruction, or in the works of Homer there was no clear distinction between the concepts *theos* and *daimon*, so, too, Mesoamerican deities represented both benevolence and malevolence, creativity and destructiveness. The Nahua word *teotl*, for instance, is ambivalent, and its common translation as "god" is misleading. Its glyph is the figure of a sun, which conveys a sense of vastness and awesomeness, but also one of difficulty and danger. There is thus an equal dose of the divine and of the demonic in the word. . . . Quetzalcoatl, the benign deity associated with the sun and believed to have a special sympathy for the fate of humanity, had at the same time an evil reputation through his association with the morning star, and his twin brother, Xolotl, was depicted as a monstrous demon who operated in the underworld.

From Fernando Cervantes, *The Devil in the New World: The Impact of Diabolism in New Spain* (New Haven: Yale University Press, 1994), 40–42, 56–64, 67–68. © 1994 by Fernando Cervantes. Reprinted by permission of Yale University Press London.

189

These dualistic properties should not obscure the strictly monistic nature of Mesoamerican religion. Negative and destructive forces were not the enemies of positive and constructive ones. Both were essential components of the cosmos. Life came from death, creation from destruction. Disharmony was as necessary as harmony. The goddess Tlaleuctli (earth lady), for instance, was the palpable rock, soil and slime on which men lived, but she was also the earth into which they were lowered at death. Revered on the one hand as a benign source of food and life, in art she was depicted as a gargantuan toad slavering blood and displaying clashing jaws at every joint in a dramatic representation of chaos. So too, Ilamateuctli (leading old woman) wore a Janus mask as a symbol of her dual role as the giver of life and the cause of death, and Tlazolteotl, the goddess of sex and fertility, was also the goddess of filth and corruption. It is true that entropy eroded order, but at the same time it was fertile and it provided the energy and the substance for the reestablishment of order. Thus, opposite forces did not engage in a cosmic battle of good against evil or even of order against chaos. Although order had to be wrested from chaos through sacrifice, this did not entail any severance from chaos. Indeed, chaos was itself the source of life.

Consequently, the European notions of good and evil, personified in the concepts of god and devil, implied a degree of benevolence and malevolence that was totally alien to the Mesoamerican deities. The notion of a totally good god was an absurdity in Mesoamerican thought. Such a being would have lacked the essential power to disrupt in order to create. Likewise, an evil devil would have lacked the power to create that would enable it to disrupt. Moreover, a god who threatened to take his place not just as a further god in the native pantheon but as the *only* god, to the exclusion of all others, was an explosive liability which put the whole cosmic order in extreme peril. . . .

*   *   *

The scattered pieces of information that are at present available from central Mexico seem to fit into a pattern of gradual assimilation and incorporation of the Christian notion of the devil into the Indian mental world. Just as it was hoped that the identification of the Virgin with a native goddess would lead eventually to the veneration of the Virgin, so too it was hoped that the identification of the devil with the more malevolent representations of the native deities would gradually lead the Indians to repudiate the devil and his works. . . .

Although in the early stages such methods seem to have reinforced rather than contradicted Nahua understandings, a clearer differentiation between morally positive and morally negative supernatural beings had begun to sink in by the end of the sixteenth century. In 1598, for example, a mestizo called Juan Luis defended himself against an inquisitorial accusation by blaming Gabriel Sánchez Mateo, an Indian from Xochimilco, for having advised him to pray to the devil. When called for questioning, the Indian willingly confirmed Juan Luis's testimony and stated that nobody had taught him to pray to the devil and to ask for his help, but that the desire to do so had been "born in his heart" after remembering how the Indians, in their antiquity, used to invoke the devil seeking his help and how the devil used to help them; and that, in order that the devil would come to help him, he had forsaken God and his saints, because the devil flees from them, and thus he had turned away from them so that the devil would come.

There is a clear interplay in this testimony between an emerging Christian concept and a receding pre-Hispanic memory. Gabriel Sánchez Mateo had assimilated the concept of the devil as the enemy of God and his saints. Yet this did not prevent him from seeing the devil as a friend whose help could be invoked just as the Indians used to do "in their antiquity". It was precisely this identification of the devil with the pre-Hispanic rites that the friars hoped would eventually persuade the Indians to reject the devil and their ancient practices. But at this stage the development was still very much in that "middle ground" that the Dominican Diego Durán had described so aptly only a few decades earlier when he had come across an Indian who persevered in his "idolatry." 'Being reproached for the evil that he had done", writes Durán,

> he replied: "Father, you should not be alarmed that we are still *nepantla*." And wanting a better understanding of what he meant by that word and metaphor which means "to be in the middle," I again asked him to explain in which "middle" they were. To this he said that, since they were not yet firmly rooted in the faith, I should not be alarmed, for they were still neutral and held on to neither to one law nor to the other; or, in other words, that they believed in God but at the same time they reverted to their old customs and rites of the devil.

The same opinion is found in more coherent form in the remarkable set of *Coloquios* composed in Nahuatl in the 1560s under the direction of Bernardino de Sahagún. After the Franciscans have proclaimed the existence of the Christian god and the consequent falseness and perversity of the native deities, whom they equate with demons, the indigenous priests openly acknowledge the Christian god, but at the same time argue for the preservation of their own divinities, who from time immemorial have provided the Indians with spiritual and material sustenance. . . .

The view of the extirpators and of too many subsequent thinkers that Christianity sat, in its purity, like a layer of oil over Mesoamerican magic is a highly misleading one. For the Christian religion was itself intermingled with a great deal of magic. Necromancers, enpsalmers and conjurers of clouds often competed directly with parish priests in early modern Castile. Inquisition records show that many of them were themselves clergy or religious, sometimes involved in such practices as dealing with locusts by holding them up for trial and excommunicating them, or holding matches with wizards to see who was best at chasing clouds. It is true that they were widely regarded with suspicion and often accused of having sided with the cause of Satan; but even so, it could not be denied that the Church itself had its own arsenal of orthodox and legal prayers and exorcisms to be used on similar occasions.

It is a mistake, therefore, to regard all magical practices as standing outside official teaching and worship. In the context of a world-view where humanity was permanently assailed by hostile armies of demons, against which the appropriate official remedy was the incantatory (a manual invocation of the cross or names of Christ),

magical practices can hardly be regarded as mere constructs of the folk imagination.
. . . There thus existed a symbiotic relationship between the official orthodox remedies and the apparently superstitious practices that became the most common objects
of concern and criticism among the educated. The *Malleus Maleficarum*, for instance,
specifically recognized that many popular practices, though fallen into the hands of
"indiscreet and superstitious persons", were entirely sacred in origin and legitimate
when applied by pious people, whether lay or religious. And even when such remedies
as holy water, the sign of the cross, holy candles, church bells, or consecrated herbs
had failed, the *Malleus* recommended the use of popular magic provided it did not
involve demonic invocation or transfer of diseases. Sacred words worn round the
neck, or placed by the sick or given them to kiss, constituted an entirely lawful
practice, even if the user could not understand the words, for "it is enough if such a
man fixes his thoughts upon the divine virtue and leaves it to the divine will to do
what seems good to his mercy".

If by the middle of the sixteenth century such practices had come under deep
suspicion, the line between "magical" and "orthodox" remedies remained thin. In
seventeenth-century Mexico it is interesting to observe that those very people who
were especially suspicious of Indian magical practices often found themselves working almost on identical assumptions to those they were so keen to condemn. Jacinto
de la Serna, for instance, had no qualms about attributing the healing powers of an
Indian to a demonic compact; yet, in the very same passage, he describes how he
himself performed a similar healing practice on his Indian servant Agustina:

> Seeing that there was no remedy . . . nor any adequate knowledge of the ailment
> that would point to the suitability of a homely cure, it so happened that I had in
> my possession a piece of bone from the saintly and venerable body of Gregorio
> López. . . . With the utmost devotion known to me . . . I gave her a tiny piece of the
> bone to drink in a spoonful of water.

Agustina's subsequent recovery was, to Serna's mind, evident proof that "the saintly
Gregory had performed two miracles: the one, to return that convalescent woman to
health . . . and the other, to help spread the rumour that she had been bewitched".

Not only is there no essential difference between Serna's healing rite and those
practised by Indians, there is even open competition between them in a way very
similar to that described by William Christian between conjurers and parish priests
in Castile. What was under attack, therefore, was not the belief in the magical utility
of certain objects. Such belief was scientifically accepted: it stemmed from current
systems of classification that assumed the existence of correspondences and analogies
between different parts of creation which, as late as 1702, still allowed a group of
physicians in Puebla to ask permission from the Inquisition to attempt a cure for
epilepsy with the use of the skulls of hanged men. In such a context, attacks on
magic, and especially Indian magic, did not stem from the fear that it was superstitious or irrational or even "wrong" but, on the contrary, that it was powerful and
efficacious and, therefore, dangerous. Recourse to magic was a practice accepted by
both cultures and understood and put into effect in very much the same way.

If this was true of the likes of Jacinto de la Serna, it was even more so of the average Europeans and Africans who had steadily begun to populate the new continent. The clear differences that the immigrants necessarily encountered between the New World and the world they had left behind led them increasingly to rely on the Indians not only for the physical knowledge of the environment but, more often, for the local spiritual forces that they understood so much better. The recurrent involvement of Indians in inquisitorial cases dealing with diabolism suggests that a large number of people opted to defer to the Indians' superior knowledge of their world and its spiritual forces. But, likewise, the meticulous care that the inquisitors took to deal with such cases is a clear indication that even those who chose not to defer to Indian magic were far from denying its reality and efficacy.

. . . The process did not flow only in one direction. From the beginning Christian "magic" was believed by the Indians to be efficient, and its association with the dominant sectors of society gave it a charisma that native magic, for all its local efficacy, lacked. Indian healing rites soon came to be accompanied by Christian prayers and invocations, and hallucinogens like peyote and ololiuhqui are known to have been associated with Christ, the angels, Mary, the Child Jesus, the Trinity, St Nicholas and St Peter. In an illustrative example recorded by Serna, an Indian healer called Catalina claimed that she had not been taught the art of healing by any human person but directly by God. An angel, she claimed, had appeared to her saying:

> "Do not be sad, Cata, God has sent you this gift to relieve you from your poverty and great misery, that you may get chilli and salt with it; with it also you will have the power to heal wounds by the mere touch of your tongue. . . ." And after saying this . . . he crucified her, nailing her hands to a cross; and it was while she was nailed to the cross that she was taught the art of healing.

. . . . The vacuum left by the native shamans was adequately filled by the many hermits, ascetics and "venerables" that began to populate New Spain's hagiographic literature from the late sixteenth century onwards. That the prestige of such men should have depended upon their power as wonder-workers, or that men and women should have sought them in the same way as they had formerly resorted to pagan shrines or healers, is often seen as evidence of the limitations of the missionary enterprise or even of the non-Christian character of Spanish American Catholicism. Yet the climate of these years is no less genuinely Christian than that of the early centuries of the middle ages, which saw the rise of the cult of the saints, to which Gregory of Tours contributed so much. Behind its syncretic mixtures, it was in this twilight world that the Indians came face to face with a transcendent power in which the harsh realities of existence no longer dominated their lives and where human suffering and misfortune could find a remedy. Indeed, it was precisely in this world of mythology—of the cult of the saints and their relics and their miracles—that the vital transfusion of Christianity with Mesoamerican tradition was most successfully achieved. For it would have been very difficult for a people without a tradition of written literature or philosophy to assimilate the metaphysical distinctions of Christian doctrine or the subtleties of medieval scholasticism. When, however, the new religion was manifested to the Indians visibly in the lives and example of men seemingly endowed with supernatural powers, it became incomparably more accessible to them. . . .

Consequently, the intense asceticism of Indian Christianity in Mesoamerica is not to be explained as a mere imposition of the Franciscan way of life, for at a much deeper level it responded to an urgent and essential psychological need. Its marked otherworldliness, moreover, differed emphatically from much that we have come to associate with the word in its modern pietist form, with its individualist, subjective and idealist connotations. Nothing could be further from the otherworldliness of Mesoamerican Christianity, which was collective, objective and realist. Although the world to which it aspired was outside history and beyond time, it was nonetheless the ultimate end towards which time and history were moving. Furthermore, the Church could claim to possess a corporate experience and communion with the eternal world in the sacred mysteries. Just as the Mesoamerican world had found its centre in the ritual order of sacrifice around which the whole life of the community revolved, so now the Christian liturgy came to hold a similar position. . . .

It is in this climate of ascetic otherworldliness and corporate liturgical expression that the best sense can be made of what has misleadingly come to be known as the "spiritual conquest." What we see at work is not so much an imposition of a new way of life but a manifestation of a new spiritual power that the Indians came to find virtually inescapable. No matter how many similarities there might have been between the cult of the saints and the sacrificial propitiation of the old tutelary deities, in practice the cult of the saints became inseparable from the Christian liturgy and the commemoration of the feasts of the saints provided an element of corporate identity and social continuity by which every community and every town found its liturgical representative and patron. Moreover, the Indians came to view this liturgical participation in the mysteries of salvation with an overwhelming sense of realism. It is hardly an exaggeration to suggest that the Christian liturgy had become for them the only context in which the passing of the old ritual order could be explained and raised on to a plane where eternity had invaded the world of time and where creation had been brought back to the spiritual source that kept it in being.

In the midst of this process of transfusion, the growing distrust of indigenous cultures and the tendency to demonize the Indian past that we detected from the middle of the sixteenth century onwards were doubly tragic. It was, to a great extent, the feeling of frustration derived from this tendency (and especially from the ensuing prohibitions to ordain a native clergy) that led to the many Indian efforts to appropriate the Christian ritual and to incorporate it into their autochthonous liturgical practices. Such initiatives were especially in evidence in those areas where Christian priests were scarce or indolent. It is known that often, when a priest failed to turn up on a feast day, an Indian would readily step in and celebrate a "dry mass", as the variant of the Mass which omitted consecration was known. The increasing discouragement of such practices as "abusive" and "dangerous" from the time of the first Mexican provincial council in 1555, led to their association with idolatry and diabolism. Yet, despite the initial misunderstandings, . . . which led to the somewhat ironical collaboration by many Indians in the process of their demonization, the devil that came to dominate Indian mythology by the middle of the seventeenth century had very little in common with the devil that theologians and inquisitors had increasingly come to see at the centre of idolatry. The numerous testimonies in the Inquisition linking the practice of demonic pacts with clandestine Indian rituals do not find parallels in the bulk of Indian testimonies known to us. Indeed, the apparent inconsistency of Indians who accused themselves of idolatry and then denied ever having made a pact with the devil, or possessing a written compact, was so recurrent that it had to be specifically considered as a serious theological problem at the end of the seventeenth century. In those rare cases when Indians were summoned for questioning at inquisitorial courts, they invariably expressed a bewildered consternation at the common assumption that their seemingly extraordinary powers were derived from a demonic pact.

Such was the case of the Indian Antonio de la Cruz who, when questioned in 1691 about the alleged demonic possession of a group of women, declared that he knew the cause of the possessions and assured the inquisitors that he could "cure" the victims. Yet he furiously denied that his knowledge was derived from a pact with the devil. On the contrary, it had come to him directly from God, through "infused science". It was the witch responsible for the *maleficium* who had made a pact with Satan, whom she worshipped in the shape of a goat. All remedies would thus be inefficacious until the pact was dissolved, and this would come about if the demoniacs made three acts of contrition and then said the *Salve Regina* three times with devotion to the Blessed Virgin.

There is no trace of any syncretic mixture or of any pre-Hispanic remnant in Antonio de la Cruz's diagnosis. Not only did he see the devil as an enemy, he also knew him to be inferior and subordinate to God, since divinely infused science would be sufficient to bring about his defeat. So, too, his suggested "cure" for dissolving the pact was in tune with the traditional Christian view that an essential weapon against the devil was repentance, a conscious turning away from sin, which necessarily involved the acts of contrition that Antonio had recommended. Moreover, since the Virgin Mary had increasingly come to be seen as the Christian's most powerful ally against Satan, Antonio's recommendation to say the *Salve Regina*, much more than a mere disguise to gain the favour of the inquisitors, was a pious practice in tune with traditional Catholic orthodoxy. . . .

If anything of the old pre-Hispanic order was remembered by the Indians at this stage, it was largely in the form of disjointed residues which lacked a unified pattern and which no longer formed part of the mainstream of the religious system. In contrast to the views of the scattered priests and extirpators who saw in these remnants proof of a ubiquitous Satanic mimetism, the Indians, and indeed the bulk of the population, seem to have regarded them as cultural expressions that were perfectly at home in a Christian culture.

[20]

Indian Shamans and English Witches

ALFRED CAVE

The historian Alfred Cave's main scholarly interest is in the history and culture of the early Indians in Massachusetts, rather than in witchcraft as such. His 1996 book The Pequot War *concerns the 1636–37 war between English colonists and Pequot Indians. In this excerpt from his 1992 article, Cave describes early English colonists' attitudes toward Native American shamanism and their tendency to equate it with devil worship and witchcraft.*

•

Outbreaks of witchcraft hysteria in New England villages in the late seventeenth century, as James Kences has noted, often coincided with war scares or Indian hostilities. After four years of fighting the French and their Indian allies, Puritan New England in 1692 was war weary. "Public morale was poor . . . in the wake of periodic massacres in isolated communities and as a result of the rampant inflation" generated by war expenditures. Fatigued and edgy, New England villagers facing possible Indian attack sometimes mistook illusions for real enemies. In July, soldiers guarding the approaches to the town of Gloucester fired their muskets at what they believed to be blue-coated Frenchmen accompanied by a hoard of Indians with "black bushy hair." But their bullets passed right through the wavering images of the attackers. In panic, the soldiers called for reinforcements, crying that the town was besieged by spectral Indians.

While wartime anxieties clearly helped shape the diabolical images that troubled Puritan New England in 1692, the linkage of witches and the Devil with native Americans cannot be explained entirely or even primarily as an outgrowth of Indian hostilities. Belief that Indians were devil worshipers and their religious leaders witches long antedated the founding of English colonies in North America. The reports of sailors and explorers published in England by Richard Hakluyt in three massive compendia between 1598 and 1600 included numerous references to Indian sorcery.

From Alfred Cave, "Indian Shamans and English Witches," *Essex Institute Historical Collections* 128 (October 1992): 241–54. © 1992 by the Essex Institute. Reprinted by permission of the Peabody Essex Museum, Salem, Massachusetts.

To cite a few examples, Sir Francis Drake claimed that Indians cavorting around a fire on a South American beach in 1577 were endeavoring to summon the Devil to sink his ship. He gave thanks to God for thwarting their satanic efforts. The chronicler of Martin Frobisher's third voyage in 1578 reported that the natives of Newfoundland "made us to understand, lying groveling with their faces upon the ground, and making a noise downward, that they worship the devill under them." The report of John Davis's second voyage in search of the Northwest Passage in 1586 related an encounter with a race of "witches" who employed "many kinds of inchantments." The narrator declared that their spells failed to do harm only because of God's special protection of Christians. A chronicler of Raleigh's ill-fated Roanoke venture (1584–87) claimed that after some of the Indians tried to use sorcery against the English, God punished "their witches" by infesting the offending villages with a plague.

Closer contact with native Americans did little to correct such misconceptions. From Jamestown, Captain John Smith reported that the Powhatan Indians were devil worshipers who slaughtered their own children in satanic rituals, while one of his colleagues claimed that they had immolated a captive Englishman in a human sacrifice. *A priori* assumptions based upon such reports of Indian satanism shaped English perceptions of native American behavior during Puritan New England's formative years. Governor William Bradford, in his history of the Plymouth colony, asserted that soon after sighting the Pilgrims, the Indians of Cape Cod "got all the Powachs of the country, for three days together in a horrid and devilish manner, to curse and execrate them with their conjurations, which assembly they held in a dark and dismal swamp." Bradford believed that it was only after their discovery that their sorcery was impotent against Christians that the Indians decided to go "to the English to make friendship." Bradford's fellow Pilgrim Edward Winslow reported to London in 1624 that the Indians' "many plots and treacheries" would have destroyed the colony had God "not filled the hearts of the savages with astonishment of us." Winslow claimed that Indian "priests" had abandoned the worship of the Creator, whom they called "Kietan" and were now in league with an evil spirit named Hobbomoch. Repeating John Smith's error, he misinterpreted descriptions of Algonquian puberty rites and concluded that the Indians sometimes sacrificed their own children to the Devil.

Other early English colonists agreed with Winslow that a satanic presence permeated native American life. Roger Williams, who was generally sympathetic to the Indians, declared that their "priests" were "no other than our English witches . . . the Devill . . . drives their worships." Williams refused to look too closely, for "after once being in their houses and beholding what their worship was, I durst never bee an eye witness, spectator, or looker on, lest I should have been a partaker of Satan's inventions and worships, contrary to Ephesians 5:14."

Some English observers were less reticent than Williams and did provide eyewitness descriptions of those presumably satanic practices. But there is a curious and significant anomaly in their accounts. Williams's facile equation of Indian shamanism with English witchcraft, though echoed by Puritan writers throughout the seventeenth century, was not supported by their own descriptions of Algonquian sorcery.

Fundamental to the English conception of the danger witchcraft presumably posed to the community was *maleficium*, the use of diabolical powers to injure or kill. English witches were said to inflict horrendous physical and mental torments on their victims. They were often accused of killing infants or livestock. At the least, they engaged in petty acts of malice, such as causing milk cows to go dry or cheese to rot. But no such specific allegations of the inflicting of personal injury through sorcery are to be found in early Puritan descriptions of Indian "witchcraft." While Puritan theologians taught that the practice of folk magic and the use of love charms and healing potions were to be regarded as the work of the Devil, and thus as a form of witchcraft, no one in New England was prosecuted for such benign practices. In the popular mind, witches were malevolent. Witch-hunts always involved allegations of *maleficium*. But that essential characteristic is virtually absent in early Puritan accounts of Indian customs.

In 1624 Edward Winslow reported that the main "Office and duty of the Powah" was "curing diseases of the sick or wounded." To accomplish this, Winslow claimed that the Powah "promiseth to sacrifice many skins of beasts, kettles, hatchets, beads, knives, and other the best things they have, to the Fiend, if he will come to the party diseased." To establish the diabolical nature of the Indian medicine man's practice, Winslow employed vivid language that declared him "fierce in countenance . . . antic [grotesque] and laborious" in "gestures" and finally, "hellish" in determination to see the Devil, who, significantly, most commonly manifested himself to the powwow as a "snake." It is striking that, despite his use of sinister terminology evocative of English fears of satanism, Winslow's account offers no concrete evidence of *maleficium*. He suggested that shamans had power over the weather and sometimes summoned up a storm "when they intend[ed] the death or destruction of other people." But he offered no details or examples. Winslow's account of what he presumed to be Indian witchcraft makes no mention of charms, hexes, intrusive or sympathetic magic, or any of the other practices English witches were said to employ against their enemies. He did relate that some Algonquian warriors believed that through diabolical means they had gained invulnerability from their enemies' arrows. But they did not claim the power to maim or kill through witchcraft. *Maleficium* is thus virtually absent in Winslow's account. His Indian witches were deficient in the black arts.

In a somewhat more detailed report published in London in 1634, William Wood accepted uncritically Winslow's claim that the Indians were devil worshipers. To underscore their presumed abandonment of the worship of the Creator and their alliance with the Devil, Wood quoted a verse from the *Aeneid*: "*flectere si nequeo, acharonta movebo*" ("If I cannot sway the gods above, I'll stir up hell"). But Wood's examples of presumed satanic practices were, like Winslow's, devoid of real malevolence. His principal case, that of the sachem/shaman Passaconaway, clearly involves a benign sort of magic rather than *maleficium*. Passaconaway, Wood wrote, "can make the water burn, the rocks move, the trees dance, metamorphise himself into a flaming man . . . in winter, when there is [*sic*] no green leaves to be had, he will burn an old one to ashes, and putting those into the water produce a new green leaf which you shall not only see but substantially handle and carry away." Passaconaway could also, according to Wood's Indian informants, "make of a dead snake skin a living snake, both to be seen, felt and heard."

The only application of Indian "exorcisms and necromantic charms" to human beings that Wood recorded related to healing. "Through the Devil's help," he wrote, a powwow was able to heal "a patient with the stump of some small tree run through his foot." The wound was "past the care of his ordinary surgery." But the powwow wrapped a beaver skin over the punctured foot and then, by sucking on the pelt, miraculously extracted "the stump which he spat out into a tray of water, returning the foot as whole as its fellow in short time." To establish the presumed diabolical nature of the powwows' capacity as healers, Wood, like Winslow, relied upon verbal characterizations of their practices as bizarre, grotesque, and irrational. In public healing rituals, the medicine man, Wood wrote, gives "violent expression" to "many a hideous bellowing and groaning . . . sometimes roaring like a bear, other times groaning like a dying horse, foaming at the mouth like a chased boar, smiting his naked breast and thighs with such violence as if he were mad. Thus will he continue sometimes half the day, spending his lungs, sweating out his fat, and tormenting his body in this diabolical worship." Though granting that the purpose of the ritual was the healing of the sick, Wood ended his description with a vague and rather illogical assertion that the Devil, "in former time" occasionally kidnapped Indian women and children in order to force their husbands and fathers to persist in "their devilish religion." Thus Wood diverted the readers' attention from the essentially benevolent purpose of the ritual he had described.

Roger Williams's testimony also, on balance, provides grounds for skepticism regarding his claim that Indian shamans were "no other than our English witches." While Williams, unlike Winslow and Wood, provided no eyewitness account of an Indian "conjuration," he did have a command of Algonquian dialects that they lacked. From his Indian informants, Williams gained some insights into their understanding of the powwows' healing process. Contrary to the claims of Winslow and Wood, that process, as Williams described it, was not based upon the intervention of an evil spirit comparable to, or identical with, the Devil of Christian mythology. Instead, the powwow utilized forces or spirits within the sufferer's body as he "conjures out the sickness. . . . They conceive that there are many gods or divine powers within the body of a man: In his pulse, his heart, his lungs, etc." Given our present understanding of shamanism, it is clear that Williams's description and other early Puritan accounts fit, not the patterns of English witchcraft, but rather the characteristics of shamanic practice. While the shaman "receives his healing and vitalizing powers from the spirits," those spirits are not conceived of as essentially malevolent or diabolical. The powers they confer are properly used in various ways for the benefit of the community. The native American shaman healed the sick and placated or manipulated those spirits or forces whose goodwill was essential to the well-being of the group. Shamans were often called upon to use their occult knowledge to ward off evil spirits, a process often misunderstood as devil worship by early European observers. The shaman played a useful and honorable role in the life of his village. He cannot properly be equated with the marginalized and presumably malicious individuals whom the English and other Europeans in the sixteenth century commonly stigmatized as witches.

Shamanic power could be abused by the vicious and the mercenary. Ethnologists and ethnohistorians have found evidence of malevolent sorcery in a number of native American societies, including the Iroquois. James Axtell notes that "bewitchment was the most feared calamity in Indian life because the assailant and the cause were unknown unless discovered by a shaman whose personal power was greater than that of the witch." Since there is evidence from outside New England that shamans suspected of using witchcraft against other members of the group were sometimes killed, it has generally been assumed that southern New England Algonquian shamans also occasionally misused their gifts and were therefore objects of fear. The leading authority on this subject has concluded somewhat cautiously that "although the *powwow* was not responsible for all the misdeeds Indians and Englishmen attributed to him, some did bewitch others deliberately." A recent study of Indian converts to Puritan Christianity asserts more boldly that shamans were "greatly feared by those less well connected to the spirit world." Christian missionaries thus presumably "offered freedom from sorcery with no loss of communication with the spirit world."

We need to be rather skeptical of such claims. While it is probably not possible to prove categorically that the Algonquians of southern New England never tried to employ shamanic power to inflict personal injury on rivals or enemies, we must recognize that the evidence that they did so is both sketchy and suspect. As we have seen, English sources from the first decade of Puritan settlement contain little evidence that so-called Indian witches were malevolent. A review of later source materials also suggests that *maleficium* was not a characteristic of local shamanic practice. The Puritan chronicles, war narratives, and correspondence relating to the conflict with the Pequot Indians in 1636–37 offer extensive commentary on the Pequots' alleged depravity and degradation. But they contain no claims that Pequot shamans tried to bewitch their enemies, many of whom were "pagan" Indians such as the Narragansetts who enjoyed no presumed immunity from Indian witchcraft. There are only two references to Pequot sorcery in the primary source materials on the war. Shortly before the outbreak of hostilities, Roger Williams informed John Winthrop that "the Pequts heare of your preparations etc. and Comfort them selves in this that a witch amongst them will sinck the pinnaces by diving under water and making holes." After the Pequot defeat, the Bay Colony historian Edward Johnson in describing the massacre at Ft. Mystic reported that some of the Puritan soldiers found it difficult to pierce Pequot bodies with their swords and therefore believed that "the devil was in them." Without elaborating or even explaining, Johnson added that the Pequots "could work strange things with the help of Satan." While those reports shed light on Puritan attitudes towards their adversary, they offer little support for later Puritan allegations regarding Indian witchcraft. It is noteworthy that neither Johnson nor any other contemporary writer on the Pequot war made any claim that the Pequots had endeavored to use as weapons against the English or their Indian allies the charms and incantations commonly associated with witchcraft in the English popular mind.

During King Philip's War forty years later, there were some vague allegations that the Indians had used witchcraft to foment storms or to silence barking dogs. But the image of the Indian shaman as a malevolent witch using the black arts to torment and kill had its origins in the testimony of some of the Puritan missionaries who organized the praying villages in the mid-seventeenth century. Invoking that testimony, the Reverend Increase Mather claimed, in a sermon delivered shortly after the last of the Salem witchcraft trials, that a number of Indian shamans, upon embracing the Christian faith, confessed that "they had, whilst in their Heathenism, by the hands of Evil Angels murdered their neighbors." But a careful reading of the reports of Indian conversions and confessions contained in the Eliot Tracts raises some serious doubts about that assertion. None of the specific Indian confessions recorded in those sources indicates that the shamans who converted to Christianity made any admission of *maleficium*. Instead, some insisted that although they had erred grievously in seeking the aid of the Devil, their "witchcraft" had harmed no one but had been intended to heal. Some also explained that since the coming of the English, they had lost their powers, had seen numerous friends and loved ones sicken and die, were often ill themselves, and therefore sought in Christ the protection of a stronger power. The missionaries made a special effort to tell shamans that they bore a particularly heavy burden of guilt because of their relationship to the Devil. The Reverend John Eliot acknowledged that in exhorting a powwow he had made use of "a sterne countenance and unaccustomed terror." As Eliot related the content of their confessions, Indian converts freely admitted committing a variety of sins, including "powwowing," but the use of shamanic power to torment or to kill was not among them.

While some missionaries did claim that Indian witches were sometimes murderous, they did not stress that theme and offered very little evidence to support it. That evidence, such as it is, can be summarized very quickly. In one of the Eliot Tracts, we read that a group of Indians meeting with missionaries in 1649 "fell to a great discourse about the Pawwawes power to kill men," but no concrete details are given, and the account lacks both substance and credibility. In the same tract, we encounter a somewhat more believable story about an abusive and boastful shaman who tried unsuccessfully to use his powers against Indian converts. Less plausibly, a letter from Thomas Mayhew, a missionary on Martha's Vineyard, published in a later Eliot Tract, claimed that powwows carried "Imps" of Satan in their bodies and used them "to hurt their enemies, and heal their friends." Mayhew also asserted that through witchcraft the Devil would sometimes be prompted to enter the body of a snake, slither toward the victim, and "shoot a bone . . . into the Indians Body, which sometimes killeth him."

There are some indications that those stories were not taken very seriously. In explaining the meaning of the term "powwow," Eliot's associate Thomas Shepard made no mention of *maleficium*, but rather defined them as simply "Witches or Sorcerors that cure by help of the devill." Daniel Gookin, superintendent of Indian Affairs for the Massachusetts Bay Colony, some twenty years later offered the same definition, writing that Indian powwows were "partly wizards and witches, holding familiarity with Satan . . . and partly . . . physicians . . . sent for by the sick and wounded . . . by their diabolical spells, mutterings, exorcisms, they seem to do wonders [in healing]." John Josselyn, an English visitor to New England in 1674, also defined powwows as witches who had gained through their association with the Devil "power . . . in the curing of disease." Given Puritan New England's aversion to all aspects of native American culture, one is struck by the omission of any reference to shamanic malevolence in those definitions. It is reasonable to conclude that in stressing the role of Indian shamans as healers, Shepard, Gookin, and Josselyn were not trying to portray them in a favorable light. These chroniclers simply lacked any real basis for portraying them in any other way, given the vague and insubstantial nature of rumors of their malevolence.

Although Indians were often indicted and tried in English courts for violating colonial laws, there is no record of any Puritan magistrate, missionary, or Indian commissioner ever bringing specific legal charges of malevolent witchcraft against any New England Indian. While Puritans believed that the evil spirits to which shamans had recourse had no power to harm Christians, Indians not in a state of grace were presumably not immune. But the Puritan missionaries who organized the praying villages apparently did not regard witchcraft as much of a threat to their unconverted charges. Under the ordinances adopted for the villages, powwowing was punished by fine, while moral offenses such as adultery and buggery carried the death penalty. But under the legal codes of both old and New England, witchcraft was also a capital offense. Given the missionaries' recurrent complaints that Indians in the praying villages continued to seek the help of powwows, it is likely that the lesser penalty prescribed for Indian witchcraft indicates that the missionaries recognized that shamanic practices were harmful only in the sense that they were not Christian but rather pagan and hence by definition "diabolical" in nature. The Mathers' association of English witches and Indian devil worshipers obscures a very important distinction. Seventeenth-century Puritan accounts of Algonquian customs seldom accused Indian witches of acting malevolently. The shamans' crime in Puritan eyes was not that they did evil, but rather that they used their presumed alliance with the Devil to do good. Puritan observers generally portrayed powwows as equivalent, not to the sinister witches of the popular imagination, but to the English "cunning people" who practiced a benign form of folk magic.

The Puritans' identification of Indian shamanism with devil worship and witchcraft reflected in part the clergy's belief that all magical practices were of diabolical origin. But it was also an outgrowth of the Puritans' conception of unregenerate Indians as "the antagonists of the new chosen people . . . villains in a sacred drama" wherein God and the Devil struggled for control of the American wilderness. In the Puritan worldview, native American culture was of diabolical origin. The question of the precise nature of shamanic practice was thus not of vital importance. Benign or malignant, its elimination was one of the objectives of Puritan missionary endeavors, just as Puritan divines in the English settlements looked forward to the disappearance of the last vestiges of superstition and magic among God's people.

As Indian converts to Christianity became acculturated, some came to accept conceptions of shamanism that belatedly included *maleficium*. In 1692, Matthew Mayhew wrote from Martha's Vineyard to report that his Christian Indians had threatened, with lynching, a shaman suspected of bewitching a sick man. In 1761, the celebrated Indian preacher Samson Occom told a story about Indian shamans who inflicted "great pain" on their rivals through an obscure practice Occom did not quite understand but that apparently involved the use of poison. (Simmons believes he was referring to intrusive magic.) Admitting that he had no actual firsthand knowledge of their activities, Occom declared of the rumor that powwows tormented and killed: "I don't see for my part, why it is not as true, as the English or other nation's witchcraft." As a Christian, Reverend Occom assumed that Indian witches must have been as wicked as their English counterparts.

Later Indian converts to Christianity also espoused the same view of native American shamanism. In 1904, Mohegan and Niantic informants told the anthropologist Frank Speck that "since the Indians have taken up Christianity, the witches have gone off to the heathen where they still flourish and cause evil." In his subsequent fieldwork among the Penobscots of northern New England, Speck discovered that they were in the habit of blaming witches "for every mishap" that afflicted the community but paradoxically had no recollection of ever punishing anyone for witchcraft. The New England Indian folklore compiled by Speck, Tantaquidgeon, Simmons, and others contains stories that hold Indian witches responsible for a variety of bizarre occurrences and malicious actions. But most of those stories show clear evidence of European influence. Others are of African origin. The traditional native American elements in those stories are often hard to perceive. In many instances, they are totally absent. While linguistic evidence in Speck's analysis of Penobscot accounts of shamanism suggests that fragmentary references to older authentic shamanic beliefs and practices are present in some of their recollections, New England Indian folklore on balance offers no clear-cut evidence of a pre-contact tradition of malevolent witchcraft. Since English sources during the early years of contact also fail to provide such evidence, it may well be that the indigenous inhabitants of New England first learned about *maleficium* from the English.

[21]

Pueblo Witchcraft

Marc Simmons

Marc Simmons's scholarly works focus on southwestern U.S. history, particularly Native American history. In this excerpt from his 1974 book Witchcraft in the Southwest, *he discusses the elaborate witchcraft beliefs of the Pueblo Indians. His other books include* Massacre on the Lordburg Road: A Tragedy of the Apache Wars *(1997),* Treasure Trails of the Southwest *(1994), and* The Last Conquistador: Juan de Oñate and the Settling of the Far Southwest *(1991).*

•

Belief in witchcraft and in manipulation of supernatural powers for evil purposes was practically universal among American Indians. Many of the rites and customs of black magic indulged in by inhabitants of the New World bore striking resemblance to practices found in Europe, Africa, the South Seas, and elsewhere, for in whatever tribe or environment the craft appeared, there could be found the common belief that blame for human suffering often rested upon deliberate misuse of otherworldly powers by persons versed in the black arts.

Many Indian modes of bewitching paralleled those reported in Europe and New England. Native witches sought locks of hair, nail parings, saliva, urine, or fragments of perspiration-stained clothing from their prey so that these might be employed in occult treatments to produce disease or misfortune. Among tribes of the Northwest Coast, witches made images of enemies, then tortured those parts of the body in which they desired to instill pain. The Chippewa of the Great Lakes followed similar practice, except their images were not dolls or effigies, but figures drawn in the sand or the ashes of a campfire. Among the ancient Aztecs of Mexico, doll-like representations of *amatl* paper were fashioned to serve the needs of witches. The Tarahumara of the Sierra Madre of Chihuahua dispensed with images and relied upon a rasping stick and song to cause injury or death, to adversely control the weather, or to provoke other misfortune.

From Marc Simmons, *Witchcraft in the Southwest: Spanish and Indian Supernaturalism on the Rio Grande* (1974; Lincoln: University of Nebraska Press, 1980), 69–80, 82–86, 88–89, 93–95. © 1974 by Marc Simmons. Reprinted by permission of the University of Nebraska Press.

A technique for bewitching encountered among most Indian groups involved the injection of some foreign object into a victim, such as an arrowhead, spearpoint, or piece of bone. Witches accomplished this, not through direct physical means, but by symbolic propulsion or by exerting mental energy. The Haida believed witches introduced mice inside a person's body and that if these could be expelled health returned. The Cheyenne of the Great Plains used the "intrusion theory" to explain serious illness, and their medicine men, employing supernatural rites, were called upon to locate and extract the disturbing element. Most tribes attributed to an evil medicine man the power to draw out a person's soul and fill the vacuum with the spirit of an animal or snake.

For native peoples of the New World no crime loomed more heinous nor brought swifter retribution than that of witchcraft. Often, mere suspicion resulted in condemnation and execution. Had a victim many relatives or friends, further bloodshed might follow if they sought revenge. Yet more frequently, execution of a witch served a useful therapeutic function for the society as a whole: with removal of the scapegoat upon whom all blame had been heaped for things gone wrong, anxieties were relieved and the community or tribe felt purged of evil.

For the Pueblo Indians of the Southwest, the nature and extent of witchcraft belief is fairly well known since these people have been studied meticulously by anthropologists for almost eighty years. Moreover, as we have seen, Spanish-colonial records beginning in the seventeenth century contain many references to witches and their activities. These documents, including trial records, reports of the missionaries, and statements by civil officials, clearly reveal the long and intense involvement of the Pueblos with witchcraft and allied matters of an occult character.

Evidently the Pueblo Indians' concern with magical systems extends well back into prehistoric times, but of this, precise details are lacking since information supplied by archeology is generally restricted to aspects of material culture. Nevertheless, rock art (incised or painted pictures left on cliff faces or cave walls), fetishes, and other ceremonial objects that have been discovered and studied by scholars strongly suggest that witchcraft was a tangible and threatening reality to the earliest inhabitants of the Rio Grande Valley. Furthermore, Pueblo mythology and folk history are rich in descriptive detail concerning the misdeeds of witches, adding more weight to the suggestion that such belief is grounded in ancient tradition.

A tale of witch treachery current among the people of Jemez Pueblo is always related as having taken place "in the beginning." Then, the Jemez dwelled in several villages along a stream at the foot of the Nacimiento Mountains and were prey to a band of witches (referred to as *sawish* in the Towa language of Jemez) who plotted to destroy them. Once when these evil persons met late in the night at a secret rendezvous their conversation was overheard by a young Pueblo boy. Hastening to his father, who was a native priest possessed of supernatural powers, the boy reported that the witches intended to burn the Jemez villages by wrapping pine gum in cedar bark, igniting these bundles, and casting them upon roof tops while the people slept. At once the father prepared sacred prayer sticks, and taking these, together with some clay canteens, he proceeded to a place not far from the village called Black

Rocks. Here he set up the sticks in the canteens to serve as a defensive line against the inroads of witchcraft. Looking up from his work he saw one of the neighboring pueblos ablaze and the fire sweeping out of control directly toward him. But when the flames reached Black Rocks the prayer sticks went into action, spewing out streams of water and quenching the fire. The other pueblos, lacking this protection, were all destroyed, and only those Indians who escaped to the river were saved. For that reason, according to popular Jemez belief, only one of their pueblos exists today, and it continues to be bedeviled by witches in its midst who seek to complete the ruin of their predecessors.

A figure common in Pueblo folk tales is Coyote, the arch trickster, who receives blame for introducing witchcraft among the Indians. According to a Tewa story, Coyote married Yellow Corn Girl and taught her how to change herself into an animal by leaping through a ring. Following this transformation she and Coyote slew her mother and brother by witchcraft, and from that point on witches have plied their iniquitous trade along the Rio Grande. Several elements of this tale—metamorphosis into an animal, passing through a ring, and the Coyote figure—are features that recur again and again in southwestern witchcraft lore, both Indian and Spanish.

Before discussing the theory and practice of Pueblo witchcraft, some mention must be made of religion and the Indian's view of the natural and spiritual worlds. Although each of the thirty or more pueblos existing today possesses its own set of beliefs and ceremonial patterns, enough uniformity may be found to justify describing in generalities the principal features of religious custom and activity.

Unlike some Indian groups elsewhere in North America, the Pueblos adhere to no belief in a single anthropomorphic, supreme being or great spirit. For them a universal spirit permeates the world, even inanimate objects. By the use of carefully ordered prayers and rituals, this cosmic spirit may be influenced for man's benefit; but, conversely, evil forces may also be activated by persons familiar with proper procedures and secret formulas. In thus assigning spiritual qualities to objects and forces in nature, the religion might best be describes as formal animism.

Traditionally a hierarchy of native priests, led by a *cacique* or "head priest," directs all phases of village life, acting through clans or medicine societies. In the Pueblos' own view of their society, the priest maintains a special relationship with a pantheon of personalized gods, who bring blessings upon the people. At the other pole stands the witch who personifies evil and whose dark machinations continuously tilt individuals or the tribe toward disaster. In actual fact, the concept of evil in Pueblo religion is poorly defined—certainly it lacks the precise delineation found in Christianity—and as a result witchcraft provides a convenient vehicle for explaining situations and human activities that run counter to the normal course of events.

Both native priest and witch are powerful figures cast in antithetical roles, each favored by possession of extraordinary knowledge. The motives of witches are directed toward benefiting themselves, whereas Pueblo ethics affirm that the highest good comes from mutual cooperation and sharing and that supernatural knowledge should be directed toward improvement of the world at large. . . . Persons who excel in any endeavor or become conspicuously rich may come under suspicion as witches since to all appearances their energies are directed toward personal aggrandizement rather than the common good.

The struggle to overcome the injurious effects of witchcraft has been institutionalized among the Pueblos in their highly specialized curing societies, although the village cacique because of his esoteric knowledge may at times act alone to exorcise witches. Belief prevails that representatives of good inevitably triumph, but their victory comes neither easily nor swiftly. Thus practitioners of a curing society must expend considerable effort and time and demonstrate exceptional courage when they agree to treat a person suffering from bewitchment. Since witches may cause illness in two ways, either stealing the heart (soul) of the victim or shooting objects into his body, the societies, to produce a cure, must suck the objects from the body or retrieve the heart by engaging the evil thieves in combat.

In the Keresan Pueblos, medicine men of the healing society paint their faces red and black and, dressed only in a breechcloth, appear at the patient's bedside to smoke, sing, pray, mix sacred matter in a bowl, and massage the body after rubbing their hands with ashes. When they discover some foreign object, they suck it out and spit it into a clay bowl. If the doctors conclude the heart has been stolen by witches, they announce their intention to find and retrieve it. To accomplish this they leave the sick chamber armed with flint knives and bear amulets for protection and disappear in the darkness. If forced to travel far, the medicine men may leave the ground and fly through the air. Once the witches are discovered a momentous battle ensues and occasionally the evil ones temporarily get the upper hand. In such cases, they overpower their opponents by blowing a foul breath in their faces and then tying them up with baling wire. If the doctors are having a bad time of it in the fight, they are allowed to seek refuge in the nearest church to renew their strength. Usually, though, they emerge victorious, capture a witch, and take him home where he is shot full of arrows by the war chief. As evidence of their fierce struggle their bodies may be smeared with blood or soot. With the witch, the medicine men bring back the lost heart, often in the form of a ball of rags containing a grain of corn in the center. The patient is given this grain to swallow and forthwith recovers his health. At the conclusion of the ceremony, the exhausted practitioners are given food (chile stew, bread, and coffee) and baskets of cornmeal by the patient's relatives as payment for their services.

The elaborate rituals as well as mock battles engaged in by the curing societies serve quite effectively to allay anxiety and promote a "cure" among persons suffering mental distress, particularly when they firmly believe their condition is caused by a witch. The elaborate shock treatment, so artfully contrived, attacks the root of bewitchment, eliminates it, and, at least briefly, restores the patient. Unfortunately within Pueblo cosmology there is no provision for final defeat of witches, so that a person cured by ceremony gains no immunity.

An elaborate pattern of beliefs associated with witches' deeds is shared by all southwestern village Indians, although significant variations may be discerned among the several language groups or even within individual pueblos. In broad terms, all are concerned with witchcraft as the cause of sickness, weather adversity, or any calamity that threatens tribal welfare, and with the identification and extermination of witches. It would be no exaggeration to declare that the Pueblos are obsessively preoccupied with the threat posed by adherents to the black craft and that this fear is endemic, occasionally breaking forth even today, as in the past, in witch scares or crazes that may convulse an entire village.

Two widely separate pueblos, those of Nambé and Zuñi, have been particularly susceptible to witch mania. . . . But other villages have experienced serious internal dislocations no less severe nor less damaging to the psychic and physical well-being of their inhabitants. According to early sources, the Pueblo of Zia declined sharply in population toward the end of the seventeenth century because excessive witch phobia resulted in an inordinate number of executions. For similar reason, the Tewa community of Santa Clara dwindled in size during the last years of the Spanish colonial period. And at least one scholar has stated that the Hopi pueblo of Awatobi was destroyed in 1700 and its male inhabitants massacred by the other Hopi because of the village's dedication to witchcraft.

The malevolent actions of Pueblo witches are manifested in a variety of ways, but to the Indians the most common activity of such persons is that relating to sickness and death. When people become ill, if the real cause is not immediately apparent, witchcraft ordinarily receives full blame. The ailing victim has deliberately or inadvertently offended a witch and the illness has been meted out as his punishment. In some cases the malady may be diagnosed as "loss of the heart or soul," and, as described above, members of the curing society will be summoned to perform ritually a recovery of the stolen part. Far more commonly, the disease is thought to follow magical injection of some foreign object into the body such as a thorn, stick, splinter of bone, piece of sharp glass, or even an insect or snake. Often the witch achieves this injection through use of a doll or image. A clay figure made from earth upon which the victim has urinated is especially potent. Using prickly pear spines or any other pointed article, the witch pierces those parts of the image in which he wishes to cause pain in the person.

Dolls of deer hide, cloth, or wool are also made. They are given the name of the party to be injured, and are then punctured with a thorn or other object. In this sinister work, the image may sometimes be smeared with the blood of a coyote or snake. A lingering illness, one that does not yield to the usual herbal remedies known by the people of the Rio Grande, will sooner or later be classed as a case of bewitchment, and a plea for aid brings the medicine man. The doctors among some pueblos waved eagle wing feathers over the body of the patient to purify it and locate the sharp particle that had penetrated the vital organs. The eagle is considered good medicine because he soars high over the earth and has eyes strong enough to see small things far below. Parts of the bear also figured prominently in many curing ceremonies. For example, the skin of a bear's leg with the claws attached was slipped over the arm of a practitioner who struck forceful blows on his patient's back and chest chasing out pockets of evil and imparting strength and long life. Some medicine men implored the assistance of badgers since by burrowing underground they could locate buried witch bundles.

As indicated, sucking out a foreign object is a standard procedure in the medicine kit of all native healers. At Acoma Pueblo a number of years ago, according to an Indian witness, a priest had sucked and swallowed several things from a patient's body, but for some reason was unable to vomit them up again and was seized with terrible pain. A fellow medicine man came to his aid and laid the sick doctor on his back. With a large flint knife he cut him open, the incision running in a line down his thorax and abdomen. Those standing around could see the heart, stomach, and other internal parts. The doctor probed inside and found a big ball of cactus thorns, which he threw into the refuse bowl. Then he closed the grisly incision, rubbed the flint over it, clapped his hands and blew on it, and all was as before. The spectators could not discern where the cut had been made. Then the fellow who had swallowed the thorns got up and went about his work. . . .

Not only individual sickness but epidemic disease is imputed to witchcraft. Plague or mass illness is always looked upon with particular horror since it threatens the existence of the entire tribe; and, as a consequence, during such times of stress a frenetic search for witches may end in considerable bloodletting. Although colonial records are not conclusive on this point, it is plausible to suggest that the numerous and virulent epidemics that swept across the Southwest during the Spanish period were inevitably followed by witchcraft trials and executions among the Pueblos and perhaps among the superstition-ridden European settlers as well. The same might have ensued after destruction of crops by plagues of caterpillars or grasshoppers, since these insects were regarded as agents of witches. . . .

What exactly motivates Pueblo witches to go about their nefarious trade? With them there is no pact with the Devil nor any conscious self-dedication as handmaidens of evil such as appears common among notions of European witchery. Pueblo witchcraft is strongly individualistic in tone and its application generally follows upon some personal grievance, since a witch who feels an injury will retaliate. Revenge, envy, or simple spite are motives that move witches to commit harm. Jealousy, too, may cause them to persecute some innocent person. Once a good man was appointed governor of his pueblo by the council of elders and given the customary black cane as his symbol of office. The same night his family was awakened by a great commotion on the roof and realized with horror that witches were dancing over the spot where the new governor was sleeping. Apparently they frolicked with such intensity that the cane hanging on the wall shook and joined in the dance. The members of the family knew without question that this was a death ritual, and notwithstanding that the man was a tubercular, his passing that night was charged to the witches. They had been jealous of his honor.

Witches, it is true, habitually wreak vengence on men, but they may also be called upon to provide love potions or charms for persons needing supernatural help in winning the attention of another. Hispano villagers residing near the pueblos and recognizing the magical power of Indian witchcraft often sought out native philters to engage the affection of someone they loved. In all probability traffic in amorous charms among Pueblo witches derived from European practice borrowed from early Spanish colonists. In the Old World, as early as the fifth century B.C., Greek poets speak of resorting to magic to bring lovers to the same bed, and witches throughout the continent traditionally supplied potions to those who requested their services. Occasionally Indian witches exercised their powers of seduction on their own behalf. . . .

A serious aspect of the witchcraft phenomenon was the identification of practitioners. A great deal of fear was bred in the Pueblos by the fact that no one could ever be sure who might turn out to be a witch. Many Indians, prone to flights of imagination, lived in constant terror of being conjured, a state that not only affected their psychic equilibrium, but proved dangerous to all persons with whom they came in contact since they recklessly fastened their suspicions upon relatives, friends, and strangers alike. Many young mothers were particularly careful to cover their infants' faces when anyone approached, because children were believed to be the special targets of witches. A man of Isleta Pueblo refused to allow visitors to enter his house, so timorous was he that one might prove to be a witch in disguise.

Witches, in the Pueblo view, are most apt to be persons living in your own village or even in your own household. Apprehension over suspicious conduct of relatives abounds at Zuñi and other places. Even medicine men may come under a cloud if their conduct deviates the slightest degree from the accepted norm. It is freely acknowledged that disciples of the black arts are as common among Hispano neighbors as among the Indians themselves, but there is no general agreement on the incidence of witchcraft among Anglos. Except for anthropologists, whose probing into village affairs makes them suspect, the White community is thought to contain few if any witches, primarily because it places no faith in the craft.

Given all the uncertainty, most Pueblos are exceedingly careful to be courteous to everyone they meet, whatever their origin, lest they unwittingly offend a witch and provoke trouble. Father Noel Dumarest, writing in the early part of this century, suggested that the social timidity of these Indians was closely connected to their witchcraft theories. He wrote, "Why are the Pueblos so pacific? Why do they not try even to defend themselves in quarrels? Because from their youth their elders have taught them that nobody can know the hearts of men. There are witches everywhere."

The non-Pueblo Pima of southern Arizona established a way to ferret out witches: they buried feathered wands in the desert and whoever accidentally found them was immediately branded a witch. However, among the Rio Grande villagers there was no single well-defined method for exposing evildoers. Certain categories of individuals were acutely vulnerable to accusations of witchcraft. These included old women and even men, particularly if they happened to be senile or otherwise ravaged by age; anyone with a physical deformity; persons careless in their speech, dishonest, or possessed of wealth from unknown sources; anyone who had made an enemy of a prominent member of the tribe; and people who went prowling about the village late at night peering into windows. Lurking about a house where someone is ill invites suspicion, and homes of invalids as a matter of course are kept under surveillance in order to trap witches responsible for causing the sickness.

It is not unusual for persons to gain reputations for being witches and yet live for long periods unmolested. Their neighbors, nevertheless, regard them with circum-spection and take pains to stay on their good side. For many years a couple resided at Isleta, the man from San Felipe and his wife a Laguna, who were generally conceded to be witches, but though much whispering was done no serious charge was ever filed against them. While decisive action may never be taken against such suspected parties they are shunned as discreetly as possible without being offered overt offense.

If some untoward event occurs and blame needs to be fixed, medicine men may have recourse to obsidian (black volcanic glass) or rock crystal, gazing into these for purposes of divination. Normally, though, an accusation of witchcraft by a victim is quite enough in itself to establish the identity of a witch and, if a crime has been committed, to bring him to trial. In a few pueblos charges may be constantly and incautiously bandied about, but only should a bewitchment result in serious illness or death does a trial and punishment of a witch ensue. . . .

In a few places the Indians believe witches have organized themselves in a society under their own officers. This feature is vaguely reminiscent of the European covens or underground cells of witches composed of twelve members and a leader. According to information from Laguna Pueblo, witch society members are bound to the orders of their officers, and, when bidden, they must go out and make people sick. To be initiated a candidate is obliged to sacrifice or bewitch someone to death. At Isleta whenever the medicine societies initiate a new member, the local lodge of witches feels compelled to follow suit so that their special enemies will not get an edge upon them. If they cannot find anyone willing to join, they may exhume from the graveyard someone whose death they recently caused and initiate him. . . .

Lycanthropy, or the ability to change oneself into a wolf and back again, is a conspicuous feature of European witchery. From this derived the popular supersti-tion, strongest in Germany, of werewolves who killed people and feasted on their flesh. Among the Pueblos, belief in animal metamorphosis was firmly rooted. In assuming the shape of beasts, Indian witches could more easily go about their wicked pursuits and escape detection. Yet there was danger too, for if the animal was killed, the evil turned back on the witch and she died. Elsie C. Parsons, who was well-versed in Pueblo customs, says that the belief that wounding or killing the witch animal produces the same effect in the witch person is of European derivation.

The forms that a witch may assume tend to vary from one village to another. At Santo Domingo Pueblo it may be a dog, coyote, or owl; at San Felipe, an owl; at Cochití, a crow, coyote, bear, or wolf; at Zia, a donkey or rat; and at Santa Ana, an owl, dog, coyote, or a tiny figure of a man with feathers in his hair. Among the Zuñi there is a story current that a witchwoman turned herself into a deer using as an aid ear wax from that animal. The domestic cat, on account of its stealthy habits and fondness for roaming at night, is a form often taken by witches. Indeed, the associa-tion of witches and cats is almost worldwide and its presence even among the Pueblos is not surprising. . . .

Transformation by passing through a ring is a pervasive element in southwestern witchcraft lore. Many Indians are convinced that by going through a magic hoop or artificial rainbow, witches change themselves into various animals and birds, and it is in this state that they may be most easily captured and destroyed. The Laguna people maintain that placing a loop of twisted yucca fibers on the head allows a person to assume any form he desires. A professed Zuñi witch declared that by jumping through a hoop of yucca, he could make himself into a dog, cat, coyote, hawk, crow, or owl for the purpose of passing quickly and in disguise about the country.

Almost without exception the several Pueblo groups associate owls and crows with witchery and spellbinding. Members of the Keresan villages carefully avoid contact with the feathers of either bird for this reason. At Cochití a man heard two owls calling and recognized the voices of persons he knew. His son chased the birds away by firing a bullet marked with a cross in the air. At the same pueblo some crows once threw rocks at a house where five men were sick. When two of the men died, it was known witches were masquerading as the crows.

Another conviction shared by the Pueblos is that witches may manifest their presence at night by appearing as flashes of light. Taos and Laguna people credit witches with being able to travel as balls of fire. The Cochití describe such enchanted fireballs as measuring six to twelve inches in diameter and consisting of a black center with a surrounding surface of fiery, red flames. Indians of San Juan speak of witches "walking as fire." The Southern Tewa explain that strange lights perceived in the night are likely to be flying witches on some noxious errand. As a result of this belief, when the Isletas saw their first train locomotive with its flashing lights they identified it as an agent of witchcraft. A light which is seen and vanishes suddenly is interpreted by both the Laguna and Zuñi as an omen of death for some loved one. . . .

Since witches shun the company of virtuous men, they love the night and lurk in shadows and darkness where their activities may go undetected. For this reason their favorite rendezvous is a cave. Other tribes, including the Navajo and the Opata of Sonora, also believe witches haunt the black void of caverns. According to Pueblo tradition, Indians of Sandía once had a settlement at a place called *Shimtua* which was located adjacent to a cave where witches assembled. Sandía today, situated just north of Albuquerque, is still considered a haven for witches by some persons who refuse to visit the village.

In spite of what has just been said, information on Pueblo witchcraft is more uncertain and in smaller supply than is the case for most other aspects of the culture. This is easily understood when it is realized that the Indians are loath to discuss the subject in any detail for fear that supernatural powers may somehow retaliate. Many Pueblos deny that witchcraft is still practiced today, or that people continue to believe in it. Others will admit that it existed in the past and that some people died, and a few will tell what they claim to have heard secondhand about witchcraft in another village. In rare instances, this writer, as well as other investigators, has been told of incidents which the informant claimed to have experienced himself. But in the end, our knowledge of the nature and practice of witchcraft among the Pueblos must remain sketchy and incomplete.

22

The Medicine Man and the Kanaima

WALTER E. ROTH

The anthropologist Walter E. Roth was a commissioner for the Pomeroon district of British Guiana. The study excerpted here appeared as a paper accompanying the thirtieth annual report for the U.S. Bureau of American Ethnology of the Smithsonian Institution for 1908–9. In it Roth describes the activities of medicine men and beliefs concerning evil spirits among the indigenous peoples of Guiana.

•

The Medicine-Man

285. There is abundant evidence that the medicine-men practised what they preached, and had every confidence in the powers with which they had been intrusted. . . . The real causes of the existing prejudice against the medicine-men are not far to seek, and have often been clearly expressed. "As doctors, augurs, rainmakers, spell-binders, leaders of secret societies, and depositaries of the tribal traditions and wisdom, their influence was generally powerful. Of course it was adverse to the Europeans, especially the missionaries, and also of course it was generally directed to their own interest or that of their class; but this is equally true of priestly power wherever it gains the ascendency, and the injurious effect of the Indian shamans on their nations was not greater than has been in many instances that of the Christian priesthood on European communities." On the other hand, there is not a single recorded instance of the Guianese Indian priesthood ever having submitted those of their people holding religious views different from their own to either torture or the block. The Creole term for the priest-doctor is *piai*-man, a hybrid that seems to have been first recorded by Waterton in the form of *pee-ay*-man, who is an enchanter; he finds out things lost. In its simple form, the word of course came into use much earlier, and is seemingly derived from the Carib *piache*, which

From Walter E. Roth, *An Inquiry into the Animism and Folk-Lore of the Guiana Indians* (Washington, D.C.: Smithsonian Institution, 1915; reprint, New York: Johnson Reprint Company, 1970), 327–33, 346–47, 354–57.

Gumilla employs, and is still met with among the Pomeroon group of these Indians as *piésan*. . . .

286. Both alive and dead, the medicine-men had the respect and fear of the community. They were the teachers, preachers, counsellors, and guides, of the Indians; "regarded as the arbiters of life and death, everything was permitted, and nothing refused them; the people would suffer anything at their hands without being able to obtain redress, and with never a thought of complaining". . . . They were said to renew their *piai* power from time to time by drinking tobacco juice, but in doses not so strong as at the time of installation. As stated above, even dead the medicine men were still respected. . . .

Bates gives a curious example of such veneration and sanctity, met with at a spot on the Jaburu channel, Marajo Island, at the mouth of the Amazon, "which is the object of a strange superstitious observance on the part of the canoe-men. It is said to be haunted by a Pajé, or Indian wizard, whom it is necessary to propitiate, by depositing some article on the spot, if the voyager wishes to secure a safe return from the *sertaô*, as the interior of the country is called. The trees were all hung with rags, shirts, straw hats, bunches of fruits, and so forth. Although the superstition doubtless originated with the aborigines, yet I observed, in both my voyages, that it was only the Portuguese and uneducated Brazilians who deposited anything. The pure Indians gave nothing; but they were all civilized Tapuyos.". . . .

288. The insignia and "stock-in-trade" of the medicine-man, in his highest stage of development, comprise a particular kind of bench, a rattle, a doll or manikin, certain crystals, and other kickshaws, generally something out of the common, all except the first mentioned being packed away when not in use, in a basket, or pegall, which is usually of a shape different from that employed by the lay fraternity. The peculiarity of the basket among Arawaks and Warraus lies in both top and bottom being concave. St. Clair reports that on the Corentyn, among Arawaks, he came across the "magical shell" (rattle) supported by three pieces of stick, the ends of which were stuck into the ground, in the middle of the floor; it is not clear, however, whether in this situation the implement was being used or not. At any rate, all the insignia were taboo to the common folk and were kept out of harm's way in a special shed, the piai's consulting-room, so to speak. Were they to be profaned, they would lose their intrinsic virtues, while the delinquents would suffer misfortunes of various descriptions. . . .

289. The rattle, *maráka* (an Arawak word), the *shakshak* of the Creoles, differs somewhat in shape, size, and ornamentation throughout the various tribes. It consists essentially of a large cleaned-out "calabash," containing stones and other objects, through which a closely fitting tapering stick is run from end to end by means of two apertures cut for the purpose. This gourd shell (*Crescentia cujete* Linn.), which may or may not be painted in various colors, is provided with certain small circular holes as well as with a few long narrow slits, both kinds of openings being too small to allow of the contents (either quartz-crystals or a species of agate) dropping out. Seeds may be employed with or without the stones—small pea-like seeds variegated with black and yellow spots which, it is commonly believed, will occasion the teeth to fall

out if they are chewed, or hard red ones. But whether seeds or stones, they usually have some out-of-the-way origin; the former, for instance, may have been extracted from the piai teacher's stomach; the latter may be the gift of the Water Spirits. According to a Kaliña, the power of the *maráka* lies in the stones contained therein. The thicker, projecting part of the stick constitutes the handle, to prevent its slipping; it may be wrapped with cotton thread. The exposed thinner end is ornamented with feathers, as those of the parrot, inserted in a cotton band, which is then wound spirally on it. An Arawak medicine-man assured me that the feathers must not only be those of a special kind of parrot (*Psittacus oestivus*), but that they must be plucked from the bird while alive. A string of beetles' wings may be superadded. Gumilla states his belief that the Aruacas [Arawaks], the cleverest of the Indians, were the inventors of the *maráka*, which even in his day, some two centuries ago, had "also been introduced into other nations." From the fact that, according to Indian tradition, the original rattle was a gift from the Spirits, Dance accounts for the great veneration in which it is held even by Christian converts who have ceased to use it. Brett confirms this, saying that there are Indians who fear to touch it or even to approach the place where it is kept. I have had personal experience that the same holds true today in the Pomeroon. . . .

290. Gumilla says that the medico makes the Indians believe that the maráka speaks with the Spirit (*demonio*), and that by its means he knows whether the sick person will live or not. This statement does not exactly agree with the evidence handed down to us by other reliable authors, nor does it quite agree with what I have been taught and have seen put into practice. The object of the rattle is to invoke the Spirits only; it is rather the business of the manikin, or doll, to give the prognosis, to lend assistance, etc. Mention is made of such an object in *Timehri* (June, 1892, p. 183): "Some few months ago, a gold expert and prospector while traveling along the Barima River, came upon the burial-place of an Indian Peaiman or Medicine-man. The house under which the burial had been made was hung round with five of the typical peaiman's rattle or shak-shak, and over the grave itself was placed the box of the dead man, containing the various objects which had been the instruments, or credentials, of his calling. The contents of this box . . . were a carved wooden doll or baby." The doll, or manikin, which I saw used for the purpose on the Moruca River, was a little black one about 2 ½ inches long, balanced "gingerly" on its feet, which bore traces of having been touched with some gummy substance: if during the course of the special incantation it remained in the erect position, the patient would recover, but if it fell over, this would be a sure sign of his approaching death. In parts of Cayenne the doll is replaced by the Anaan-tanha, or Devil-figure, which is unmercifully thrashed with a view to compelling the Evil Spirit to leave the invalid. The identity of this mainland doll, or manikin, with the idol, or *cemi*, of the Antilleans has already been indicated.

291. The crystals are employed for charming, bewitching, or cursing others, though the references in the literature to their application in this manner are exceedingly scarce. Indeed, I can call to mind only the following from Crévaux: "I notice on the neck of one of them [Guahibos of the Orinoco] a bit of crystal set in the

cavity of an alligator's tooth. The whole has the name of guanare. . . . It is with this guanare that the Guahibos throw spells (*jettent des sortilèges*) on their hated neighbors, the Piaroas. . . . Every mineral that presents in its lines and shape a certain regularity is to them the work of a devil or a sorcerer." Cursing and similar procedure are not, however, the sole prerogative of the medicine-man, at least not in the Pomeroon District of the present day; the procedure is known as *hó-a* to both Warraus and Arawaks, and is practised, I am told, by very old people. As a remedy for over-fatigue, Schomburgk describes "Macusis and Wapisianas cutting each other's legs with a piece of rock crystal, an instrument to which they ascribed particular virtue, refusing instead of it my offer of a lancet." . . .

293. The office of the medicine-man appears to have been hereditary and to have passed to the eldest son. If he has no son the piai picks a friend as his successor, although the same authority (Schomburgk) elsewhere states that, under these circumstances, he chooses the craftiest among the boys. It is likely that the secrets and mysteries of the profession may also have been imparted to outsiders for a consideration. I happen to have known one of the fraternity who taught another his profession for the sum down of eleven dollars together with the gift of his daughter. Im Thurn says: "If there was no son to succeed the father, the latter chose and trained some boy from the tribe—one with an epileptic tendency being preferred. . . . It has been said that epileptic subjects are by preference chosen as piaimen, and are trained to throw themselves at will into convulsions." Perhaps this idea had its origin in the fact that through the use of a narcotic powder, the piais can throw themselves into a condition of wild ecstasy: several such powders were known to some of the Guiana Indians, as the *Yupa*, etc. On the other hand I can find no references in the literature to the choice of epileptic subjects; furthermore, the unlikelihood is turned into impossibility, when it is borne in mind that the victim of such a convulsion would be unconscious during its progress. . . .

307. Disease or death is not a "natural" phenomenon, so to speak, but is usually due to one of two agencies. It may be the work of some Spirit, perpetrated either judicially or of mere malice, as some affirm, or through the importunity of a votary. An evil Spirit, one who causes an evil, might send an animal to bite or sting a person, or cause a tree to fall upon him, his ax to cut him, water to drown him, or some other calamity. Now, except through the agency of the piai, the influence of this Spirit causing the evil can not usually be counteracted. Berman alone for the Mainland makes the statement, which I must regard as confirmed by the practice of a similar custom on the Islands, that "when sickness assails them, they [laymen,] present a propitiation to the Evil Spirit, consisting of a piece of the flesh of any quadruped. If recovery follows, they suppose the Evil Spirit to have regarded and accepted the offering," but if no recovery, the conjurer is called in, etc. The piais are undoubtedly believed to have the power of influencing the Spirits not only in removing the causes of the disease which they (the Spirits) have inflicted, but also in sending sickness elsewhere. In the spring of 1907 the Ojanas (Cayenne) suffered from an epidemic of bronchitis, or "galloping consumption," from which many died; . . . It is possible, however, that the medicine-men, independently of Spirits, and certain old

people, can inflict sickness on folks at a distance; for instance, the Apaläi Indians of the upper Parou, Cayenne, when they can not subdue their sicknesses revenge themselves by sending an evil charm to a woman of the neighboring tribe. It is not at all uncommon for one tribe to put the blame of some real or imagined ill on the shoulders of another. For example, the Wapisianas consider the Makusis the most dangerous poisoners and Kanaimas—every illness is ascribed by them to the wickedness of the Makusis. Similarly, on the Tiquie River (Rio Negro) the Makus are blamed for everything. There is a certain skin disease, believed to be a *vitiligo*, which the Piapocos of the lower Guaviar (Orinoco River) call *sero*: it is always contracted by drinking the *yocuto* (*couac* mixed with water) of an enemy affected with this trouble, who has mixed in the brew a few drops of his blood. Death and other evils may be due also to some human enemy more or less disguised, modified, or influenced by a peculiarly terrible Spirit known as Kanaima, against whose machinations the power of the piai avails nothing. To this belief in Kanaima I propose devoting a separate chapter. . . .

Kanaima; The Invisible or Broken Arrow

320. An individual becomes exceedingly ill. All the ordinary everyday remedies have been resorted to, the piai has invoked his Familiar Spirit, yet the patient dies; or he may sometimes expire without warning. The very fact of the medicine-man's inability to effect a cure serves only to confirm the belief held in certain tribes—Akawaios, Makusis, Arekunas, for example—that the victim's condition is the work of some human agency more or less disguised, modified, or influenced by a peculiarly terrible Spirit known as Kanaima. The word itself is said to be Akawaio; the Arawak term is Mahui, which thus comes to be applied by this people to all Akawaios in general. According to inquiry made of the Arawaks, who, like the Caribs and Warraus, do not appear to know very much about the subject, and that only at second-hand, Kanaima is said to be the name of a certain tree growing in the savannahs, of which the sap has remarkable properties. After rubbing himself with it a man will go mad and become changed into some animal, as a tiger or a snake, and do people harm. The sap can also be thrown over other folk with similar results. But the word mentioned has really a very extended meaning; it is the expression of the law of retaliation, which is sacredly observed among the Indians of Guiana, at least, certainly among the Makusis, Akawais, Wapisianas, and Arekunas. Though applied to the man who has devoted himself to perform a deed of blood, it seems more properly to belong to the murderous Spirit under the influence of which he acts, and which is supposed to possess him; it indicates also the person whose rights have been injured as well as the whole mode of procedure, including the means, poison, etc., employed. Thus, the audacity of the Akawais "in these predatory excursions is astonishing. If a party can muster eight or ten stand of fire-arms it will fight its way through all the mountain tribes, though at open war with them; and by the rapidity of their marches and nightly enterprises, which they call Kanaima, they conceal the weakness of their

numbers, and carry terror before them." Schomburgk says it was impossible to learn clearly how Kanaima is regarded, because he appears not only as an evil invisible Being (*dämonisches Wesen*) and, in many cases, as a particular personality (*individuelle persönlichkeit*), but always as the avenger of a known or an unknown injury. Who and what Kanaima was, they could not tell us, but they reckoned that every casualty (*Todesfall*) was due to him. I had already observed the thirst for vengeance among the Warraus which often overcomes and tortures an Indian to the point of madness, as soon as he considers himself injured in his reputation or in his wife; a thirst which is but quenched with the death of the offender, or in the annihilation of his whole family.

The same author gives an account of a certain waterfall on the upper Cotinga which his terrified Indians tried to get past as quickly and as quietly as possible. Kanaima, the hereditary enemy of the human race, was being followed by a powerful Spirit: the pursuer was close at hand, escape seemed impossible, the steep bank preventing further flight over level ground, but in this opening it was possible: he burrowed in here, and came out again on the opposite shore of the river bank about ten or twelve miles farther on, whence he emerged to continue afresh his torments upon mankind.

320A. And yet again it is quite possible that the term Kanaima may have an easily intelligible origin based on the bloody exploits of certain of the Rio Branco tribes, whose reputation, through the avenues of exchange and barter, could easily have reached the Indians of British Guiana. As a matter of fact, I can not recall at present a single instance of Kanaima culled from the literature dealing with Cayenne, Surinam, or the Orinoco region. At the head of the River Jauapiry and River Taruman-Assu (streams flowing into the Rio Negro to the eastward of the Rio Branco) are a series of wild tribes. These tribes are not wild in the sense of making war on civilized and quiet peoples (*mansos*), but are Kanaima tribes (*tribus canaémés*), as the Indians of the upper Rio Branco call them, that is, they are tribes of cut-throats by profession, educated from generation to generation in murder and theft, killing for the pleasure of killing, not even eating their victims but utilizing their tibias for flutes and their teeth for necklaces. Indians of a dozen tribes have assured me, says Coudreau, that there exists among the *canaémés* an association of piais who exert great influence. What makes the thing appear very probable is that it is known that these various Kanaima tribes are allied and more or less united (*solidaires*).

321. As already hinted, the Kanaima may just as often be in the form of an animal. "Many of the Indians believe that these 'Kanaima' animals are possessed by the spirits of men who have devoted themselves to deeds of blood and cannibalism. To enjoy the savage delight of killing and devouring human beings, such a person will assume the form, or his soul animate the body, of a jaguar, approach the sleeping-places of men, or waylay the solitary Indian in his path." One can tell, by the effects, the particular animal whose characteristics Kanaima has assumed. Does he give a blow that stretches his victim on the ground? Then he is a "tiger." Does he in wrestling find his arms encircling the neck of him devoted to destruction? Then he imbibes the spirit of the camudi, and like the constrictor, strangles. He may appear

also in the form of a bird, and may even enter a person's body in the form of an insect, a worm, or even an inanimate object.

322. When a person dies it is only the piai who knows whether the death is due to an evil Spirit, or to the "poison" [blood-revenge] of another Indian. If to the former, he is buried with the usual ceremonial, but if the verdict is that he was sacrificed for some offence, the corpse is carefully examined, and should only a blue spot or something unusual be found on it, the piai will show that here the victim was wounded with the invisible poisoned arrow.

323. Once the handiwork of Kanaima has been recognized, the piai's powers, as such, are not brought into further requisition, in the way of retaliation or revenge on the particular individual with whose connivance this terrible Spirit has wrought the mischief. It is not the Kanaima but his human agent who is sought for punishment. The retaliation and revenge are matters for the victim's relatives and friends to deal with, and various measures are adopted by them to discover the particular individual specially concerned. [Among the Arawaks] in order to ascertain this a pot is filled with certain leaves [and water] and placed over a fire: when it begins to boil over they consider that on whichever side the scum first falls, it points out the quarter from whence the murderer came. Among the Makusis, above the Waraputa Falls, Essequibo River, Schomburgk relates the following striking instance: "A Makusi boy had died of dropsy, and his relatives endeavored to discover the quarter to which the Kanaima, who was supposed to have slain him, belonged . . . the father, cutting from the corpse both the thumbs and little fingers, both the great and the little toes, and a piece of each heel, threw these pieces into a new pot which had been filled with water. A fire was kindled, and on this the pot was placed. When the water began to boil, according to the side on which one of the pieces was first thrown out from the pot by the bubbling of the water, in that direction would the Kanaima be." A consultation is thereupon held, the place is pointed out, and the individual whose death is to atone for that of the deceased. If any one—man, woman, or child—has incurred the hatred of the all-powerful piai, or should the latter be desirous of the wife of some Indian, this or the other would be the cause of the death.

324. A near relative is charged with the work of vengeance: he becomes a Kanaima, is supposed to be possessed by the destroying Spirit so-called, and has to live apart according to strict rule, and submit to many privations until the deed of blood be accomplished. If the individual can not be found, or rather if the favorable opportunity for committing the deed does not present itself, although it will be sought for years, any other member of his family will suffice. Sometimes the near relative will charge himself with the duty: a little Warrau boy of about 12 years of age avenges his father's and mother's death by smashing in the piai's skull with a club when the latter lies drunk in his hammock. Formerly, the Indians at the Great Falls of the Demerara were employed by the Arawaks of the lower district to work their vengeance as Kanaima mercenaries. . . . These Arekunas, chosen for the deed of blood on account of the remoteness of their habitation as likely to baffle all trace of the originators, came over from a great distance. Some Indians, who are adepts in the art of making subtle poisons, hire themselves out to rid their employers of any

obnoxious individuals, and these are called Kanaimas. These examples serve to show how the work of vengeance could be deputed to strangers and mercenaries.

325. But whoever it may be that is charged with the duty of avenging the death, he suddenly disappears from the settlement: no one knows where he is. He wanders now as Kanaima through the forests, valleys, and heights, and does not return until he has slain his victim or shot him with the poisoned arrow. Half a year or more [even years] may thus be spent, during which time he avoids all contact with other Indians. From the moment he leaves the settlement, he is outlawed—he has cut all the ties which bind him to his family and his tribe—and it is the business of any Indians who may meet him in the bush, to kill him.

23

Factions and Exclusions in Two South American Village Systems

PETER RIVIÈRE

The anthropologist Peter Rivière has done extensive field research on the Trio people of Surinam and has published several articles on his findings. In the 1970 essay excerpted here, Rivière compares their sorcery beliefs with those of the Shavante. Information on the Shavante is taken from a 1967 study by D. Maybury-Lewis, Akwe-Shavante Society.

•

In this essay, which deals with the Carib-speaking Trio Indians and the Gê-speaking Akwe-Shavante, the intention is to examine how, although in both societies the village is the autonomous unit, in one case sorcery is understandable only if a number of such units are taken into account, whereas in the other the workings of sorcery are fully explicable in the sphere of a single unit. Each tribe will be examined in turn, with emphasis placed on the variables of socio-political structure relevant to the understanding of the operation of mystical sanctions, and the main contrasts are summarized in conclusion.

The Trio

The Trio, who number about 650, live close to and on either side of the Brazilian/Surinam frontier, a thickly forested headwater region which escaped any permanent non-indigenous settlement until ten years ago. In its main features, Trio culture is typical of the Guiana Tropical Forest area; subsistence is based on slash-and-burn cultivation of manioc, and on hunting, fishing, and gathering. The density of popu-

From Peter Rivière, "Factions and Exclusions in Two South American Village Systems," in *Witchcraft Confessions and Accusations*, ed. Mary Douglas (London: Tavistock, 1970), 245–54. © 1970 by the Association of Social Anthropologists of the Commonwealth. Reprinted by permission of Taylor and Francis Books Ltd.

lation is low (about one person to fifteen square miles) and there is no apparent pressure on natural resources although these are not evenly distributed across the whole territory and their presence or absence does exert some influence on the location of settlements and population movements. . . .

The residential unit is the village, whose average population size is thirty people; the number of inhabitants rarely exceeds fifty. Village sites are moved frequently (about every five years), and for a variety of reasons, including death of an inhabitant or infestation by weeds and vermin. The exhaustion of cultivable land is not one of the important reasons for moving a village and frequently the new village is built in close proximity to the old . . .

Population movement, which mainly occurs within an agglomeration, takes place in response to a variety of factors—demographic, economic, or social. Although the Trio express a preference for marriage with someone of their own village this is frequently demographically impossible, and statistically one can show a tendency towards matrilocal residence. People also move from one village to another because they want to visit relatives, or to exploit some natural resource not available at their present village. Such movements can take place in an atmosphere of amity or animosity and it is the latter cases that are important in the understanding of sorcery. Conflict within a village may result from one of a number of causes: misdemeanours (theft or adultery), failure to honour kinship obligations, and lack of cooperation. It is frequently difficult to distinguish between social and economic causes because, for example, scarcity of game will give rise to accusations of meanness and of failure to fulfil social commitments. Thus an economic cause takes on a social manifestation.

A good leader will be able to settle such disputes, but when no settlement is possible the only means of resolving the conflict is for one party to leave the village. Mobility of population acts as a mechanism for reducing tension, but it can work in this way only because the villages of an agglomeration form a catchment area in which mobility is easy. Relationships between the villages of an agglomeration are as unstable as the population of a single village and present a picture of constantly shifting alliances. Inter-village relationships are regulated in the first place in the same manner as intra-village relationships, in terms of kinship, but when such ties are weak or strained ceremonial dialogue may be used. However, the main political institution regulating the relationship between villages is the dance festival which, under ritual conditions, permits a resolution of old disputes.

A feature of Trio political institutions, in so far as they can be described as that, is that they are mainly concerned with mediation and conciliation, a reduction in tension. The question that must be taken up next is the source of this tension. The answer is sorcery.

Any misfortune or sickness may be regarded as being the result of sorcery, and almost all deaths are. For the Trio, death is neither a natural nor an inevitable event, and they say that no one would die unless he had been cursed. Accusations of sorcery are directed against members of other villages, particularly unknown shamans and strange visitors. Fear of sorcery is the reason the Trio give for having their villages so far apart and for not visiting each other more often than they do. This fear has a rational basis, since sickness and disease frequently and observably follow in a traveller's footsteps. At the same time, fear of sorcery maintains the code of hospital-ity without which travel in the area would cease: any stranger is potentially a sorcerer and the only prophylaxis against sorcery is being open and generous. On the other hand, the visitor fears the sorcery of his hosts, and the formal greeting in ceremonial dialogue on arrival at a strange village always contains, on both sides, assurances of goodwill and specific denial of being a sorcerer.

As described, Trio ideas of sorcery are simple and coherent, but the Trio also express their claim that sorcerers are non-residents in the reverse way, saying that people do not curse those of their own village. Put in this way, it brings one straight back to the problem of defining the member of a village. The resolution to this problem would appear to be that, since it is impossible to define membership of a village except at a particular instance in time, any incident of sorcery has to be judged against the existing situation. With this understood, it is possible to reassess the claim that no one curses a member of his own village, although, because I remain uncertain whether anyone actually commits sorcery other than revenge sorcery—of which I treat below—it is safer to pursue this discussion in terms of accusations. Expressed thus, i.e. that accusations of sorcery are not made against members of the same village, the claim is very close to the truth. Accusers and accused will certainly not remain in the same village after the accusation is made, and, since gossip always precedes open accusation, one party (presumably the weaker) is likely to have left before this stage is reached and violent retribution is taken. When the Trio say, then, that only outsiders are sorcerers, they are stating something that is very close to the truth and expressing the ideal conception they have of the community. One should also note that suspicions of sorcery directed against another member of the village will occur only if some discontent already exists within the village. In a village free from conflict, misfortune will result in accusations against outsiders, even unknown ones. Within the village setting there is no structural position that seems particularly prone to suspicion. Certainly accusations are made against in-marrying males, as one might expect, but not exclusively so, and they do appear among brothers; in one case a village split along the generation gap, with all the younger married men leaving the village.

There is one further feature of Trio sorcery which, for comparison with the Shavante situation, it is important to describe. The Trio response to sorcery, espe-cially sorcery that results in death, is sorcery. This is well displayed in the institution of revenge sorcery. If a member of Village A dies (which must be the result of sorcery) the other members of the village perform revenge sorcery, a curse that does not require a specific victim. In due course they hear that someone in Village B has died and they conclude that he was the sorcerer who was responsible for their co-villager's death and that he has died from their revenge sorcery. Meanwhile, their co-villager's death may have been seen by members of Village C as the result of their revenge of an earlier death. However, members of Village B do not see the death in their village as the result of revenge sorcery but as an initial act of sorcery and thus the start of a new series. Because there are always people dying there is no way of breaking out of this cycle unless the assumption that all death is the result of sorcery is dropped.

Finally, one should note that, for the Trio, sorcery redefines the physical and conceptual boundaries of the village, and it does this whether the accusation is directed against a stranger or a (recent) member of the community. In the first case the boundary is reaffirmed by stressing the external danger, in the second by excluding the dangerous elements from within.

The Akw̄e-Shavante

The Shavante live on the central Brazilian plateau, mainly concentrated in the basins of the Rio das Mortes and the Araguaia. This is savannah country, covered with high scattered shrub and bush, but not entirely lacking in forest which is to be found as galleries along the water courses. The important subsistence activities are gathering and hunting (in that order) but a little agriculture is also practised. The Shavante lead a semi-nomadic life and the needs of their subsistence economy mean that they spend many months each year travelling, but these treks are centred on semi-permanent villages.

There are about 2,000 Shavante divided among eight villages; between 1958 and 1964 the villages varied in size between 80 and 350 inhabitants, and were "rarely less than a full day's journey apart." Shavante villages, therefore, are both bigger and slightly more widely dispersed than those of the Trio. Like the Trio, Shavante villages are autonomous units, but unlike the Trio ones they appear to be more or less demographically and economically self-supporting as well. Communication between Shavante villages is poor. They do not combine for ritual and there is little inter-village trading. Relationships between settlements are mainly of a political nature and may take the form of alliance or hostility. Movement of population between villages is a response to political pressures, and, as among the Trio, if an individual or segment of the village population finds life dangerous or difficult, he or it can secede and go to live elsewhere. Asylum is never refused to refugees, although their arrival might upset the delicate balance of power not simply within the village but between villages. The role of Shavante sorcery can be understood only in the context of this power balance.

The structure of Shavante society is far easier to describe than is that of the Trio because there is a set of clearly defined social institutions. Shavante society is divided into three exogamous patriclans; a Shavante thinks of his fellow-clansmen (wherever they live) as potential allies and of non-clansmen as potential enemies. This, however, is an ideal representation which is rarely adhered to in practice. For practical purposes it is the lineage that has social and political importance. Factions are the units of Shavante politics and "A faction consists of a lineage and its supporters, who may be other lineages of the same clan, other individuals, or even lineages of another clan." Ideally, factional loyalties are lineage loyalties but in practice this does not always work out, although fictive lineage ties may result from loyalty to a faction not based in one's own lineage.

Factions contend for "the ultimate prize of the chieftaincy" but, paradoxically, there is no such office, and the chief is simply the head of the dominant faction in the village. The strength of the chief's position depends on how powerful his faction is. However, for reasons outlined below, power is used only as a last resort, and it is the insecure chief, i.e. the one whose faction is not overridingly dominant, who is most likely to use force. The strong chief is able to maintain control by his ability to influence public opinion and to ensure that disputes are talked out in the men's council. There are no tribal or inter-community organizations, and the chief is a chief only in his own village because it is only there that his power, i.e. the coercive force of his faction, exists.

Sorcery enters into most serious inter-factional disputes, and "A sorcery case is therefore a political matter." Accusations of sorcery are made by the more powerful against the less powerful, while sorcery itself is made by the weaker against the stronger. In villages where no faction has clear-cut dominance, accusations appear to pass in both directions. In this matrilocal society sons-in-law are always suspected of sorcery since they are in a subordinate position to their wife's kin. This scheme of ideas, whereby accusations of sorcery are directed against the weaker and acts of sorcery against the stronger, is not limited to the relationship between factions within a single village but also emerges in the relationship between Shavante villages and even between the Shavante and neighbouring tribes. Other villages and other tribes are feared because of their sorcery; this carries the assumption that they are, therefore, physically weaker and inferior. For the Shavante, physical force is associated with superiority, mystical sanctions with inferiority.

An accusation of sorcery is the most serious charge that a Shavante can make, and a man of subordinate faction who makes such an accusation against a member of the dominant faction and fails to receive the support of his faction will be killed if he does not leave the village first. If a man is supported in his accusation by his faction, it will mean disruption of the community since it amounts to challenging the superiority of the dominant faction. On the other hand, accusations made by the dominant faction are excuses for political action and the eradication of rivals. This, as has been mentioned above, is more likely to happen in villages where the chief is not secure, i.e. where there are rivals. It is in the interest of a chief to stop accusations becoming open, for they must lead to violence and the flight of the minor faction. While this will strengthen the position of the dominant lineage internally, it will weaken the village's position against other villages because this is assessed in terms of numerical strength. Indeed, if the reduction in population is too great, the village may not be able to survive as an autonomous unit and will have to join another village in which the once-dominant faction will find itself a minor one. Thus it is possible for power, when it is misused, to result in the opposite of that which it is intended to achieve. For the Shavante, sorcery is a tool of political action, but it is a double-edged one which must be applied with care.

Finally, suspicion of sorcery surrounds death or sickness unless there is good reason to suppose otherwise, as for example in a case of violent death. The Shavante also have some awareness of contagion, so sickness following contact with such a complaint is not necessarily attributable to sorcery. In other cases the death of a man is seen as the political manoeuvrings of his factional opponents. A death, therefore, may spark off an accusation if the political situation is already critical, but it does not appear that all deaths result in accusations, although any death in which sorcery is suspected must necessarily have political consequences even if it merely reinforces the existing political differences.

Conclusions

The variations that exist in the operation and incidence of sorcery in these two societies seem to spring from two vital differences between them, one in their socio-political structure and one in their cosmological and sociological ideas. In each society these two factors are necessarily interlinked. . . .

The Trio village, being a single-cell unit, cannot support divisions within itself, and the appearance of tensions can be resolved only by fission—either by the migration of population into another village or by the formation of a new single-cell unit. The absence of any regulative device for conflict within the village other than dispersion, and the nature of the agglomeration—a cluster of relatively closely located villages joined by economic, social, and ritual ties—without which dispersion would be far more difficult, are, without implying any cause or effect, clearly interlinked. Furthermore, there are closely associated with these factors the Trio ideas about the purity of their community and its freedom from malevolence, which is associated with the world outside the village. The basic dichotomy in Trio thought is inside versus outside, and many Trio social institutions can be interpreted as means of resolving or reinforcing it. Sorcery acts to confirm the distinction.

As we have seen, for the Shavante, sorcery can enter into the relationships between villages, but it is only within the village that it has true meaning. The dichotomy of "us" and "them" exists within a single community since this is the sphere of political action of which sorcery is an adjunct. The opposite to mystical sanction is physical force, and the path to the chieftaincy, a political ambition only realizable in the sphere of the village, lies through the latter. Thus, while for both the Shavante and the Trio accusations of sorcery within the village are disruptive, and result in both cases in a reduction in the community's numbers, the overall outcome is very different. In a Shavante village an accusation of sorcery will strengthen the dominant faction's position and thus the internal unity of the village, but the village will be weakened in respect of other villages, for in the wider tribal sphere a village is judged by its numerical strength. Because, for the Shavante, might is right, they are concerned with the physical realities of their world.

The numerical weakening of a Trio village results in the reinforcement of its boundaries and reassurance concerning its internal purity. The concepts of domination and subordination are alien to the Trio, and their response to sorcery is sorcery; indeed, given the reliance that every village has on its neighbours, this seems almost essential. Violence is particular and manifest; sorcery, and particularly revenge sorcery, is not specific (although inevitably fatal) and can be denied. Acts of violence are irrevocable but accusations of sorcery can be rectified.

Finally, one might perhaps note that, for the Shavante, sorcery is evidence of hidden political ambitions; for the Trio, it is a manifestation of the innate malevolence of the unknown. For both tribes their ideas of sorcery are a clear reflection of the world as they have made it.

III

Diabolical Possession

AN ESSENTIAL PART OF the lore of European witchcraft is the idea of diabolical possession. It should be noted that the kind of behavior identified as spirit possession is acknowledged in the belief systems of all the cultures examined in this reader. Outside the Christian tradition, however, such experiences are usually viewed as a way of countering evil sorcery. Like dreams, they are a means for the spirit world to communicate with human beings. Possession by a spirit—a trance-like or drug-induced state—was certainly not to be feared. It was, for non-Christian cultures, a welcome, useful experience.

On the other hand, among Europeans and Anglo-Americans, possession had come to represent a state induced by either Satan himself or his agents, the witches. It was assumed to be voluntary on the part of the one possessed, who was now in a diabolical conspiracy to undermine Christianity. This state was distinguished from bewitchment, in which the victim was under the control of a satanic agent such as a witch. To be bewitched was an involuntary act, echoing the struggle between God and Satan for the soul of man. In popular parlance the two concepts were merged and little distinction was made between bewitchment and possession. Indeed, all trance-like conditions, whether fits, spells, or unnatural, violent physical postures, were called diabolical possession regardless of cause or supposed human agent. Clergymen assumed that all such cases required spiritual intervention, some type of exorcism. The cause was of lesser importance than the cure and, for Protestants, the only acceptable methods were prayer and fasting. No sacred rites such as bell ringing, holding a cross, or using holy water, as performed by the Catholic clergy, were allowed.

There were two major incidents of possession widely reported in the New England colonies—witnessed, treated, and publicized by respectable ministers whose reports are partially reprinted here. The first excerpt, by Samuel Willard, describes the possession of Elizabeth Knapp in 1671–72, and the second describes Cotton Mather's handling of the four Goodwin children sixteen years later in 1688. These were decidedly public events, a form of "entertainment" observed by neighbors who were alternately excited and bemused by the strange happenings. Both cases involved children. Elizabeth Knapp was sixteen at the time of her "possession" and the Goodwin children, two boys and two girls, ranged in age from five to thirteen. The oldest girl, thirteen-year-old Martha Goodwin, seemingly the most affected, received the greatest attention from Mather.

It is very likely that at least some of the children were experiencing religious crises. But the emotional and physical expression of their anguish was foreign to Puritan assumptions about the conversion experience. They could understand such peculiar behavior only as either a physical illness or an act of the devil in a battle for their souls. Once a physical cause was discounted, a satanic presence then became an acceptable explanation for the youngsters' torments.

On the surface Mather's account appears to be a rather naive depiction of children rebelling against exceptionally pious and possibly overly demanding parents. The children were denied opportunities to play and wanted to participate in forbidden Christmas celebrations. Puritans thought occasions of revelry such as the English Christmas celebrations were blasphemous.

The more attention Mather paid to their peculiar behavior, the more eccentric and frightening the children's actions became. Mather admits that the one time he ordered the family to ignore Martha's silliness, the girl stopped her misbehavior and went to sleep. But he was so fascinated by what he thought was the action of at first the witch, Goodwife Glover, and later the devil in possession of a human body, that he took all the incidents, what he calls wonders, as proof of the existence of Satan and by inference of God. This was a morality tale, its message the value of prayer as a protection against and relief from diabolical attacks.

Most historians now assume that in both cases the children's fits were mostly real and not feigned. Nonetheless, the fits, interpreted as possession by the devil, allowed the children to avoid household work and religious duties and explained away their rudeness and impertinence to adults. It is significant that there was always someone around to notice and keep both Martha and Elizabeth from hurting themselves too severely.

This kind of spectacle would continue to mark New England life. Similar behaviors affected the girls at Salem four years after problems plagued the Goodwin children. These earlier incidents, and probably many others not documented, had put a stamp of approval on such forms of hysterical behavior. Certainly the Puritans were predisposed to accept the Salem girls as possessed in much the same way as they did Elizabeth Knapp and the Goodwin children, and to treat them with the same kind of attention. That Salem had more tragic consequences is due to a host of other factors; but certainly the interpretation of those later events becomes more intelligible in light of Samuel Willard's and Cotton Mather's responses to the perceived threats from the devil.

The commentaries by scholars on cases of possession provide a context for understanding the seventeenth-century responses to such events. Certainly what Joseph Klaits describes as "religious ecstasy" has a long history even in the Christian world and for a time was acceptable behavior at least for religious leaders, as it also was for Africans and American Indians. This changed in Europe, where the experience with epidemics of such episodes among laypersons came to be associated with bewitchment, thus inspiring action to identify a responsible evil human agent. The trial and execution of a witch would then serve as the solution to a problem of possession that was immune to religious resolution. Such executions, Klaits notes, often did end, at least temporarily, the incidents of possession. The respite brought by those trials could inspire even more persecutions and the perceived relief they brought.

Keith Thomas finds additional evidence for the close connection between religious intensity and cases of diabolical possession. Certainly the violent reaction of the so-called possessed toward Christian symbols and texts suggests a strong love-hate relationship. But among Protestants the problem became more complex. The new creeds abandoned the formal rituals and relics that traditionally provided psychological protection against diabolical intrusion. Because of Protestant hostility to signs of the cross, holy water, and priestly power to command the devil to depart, the populace faced a dilemma over how to respond to bewitchment or diabolical possession. The result, Thomas argues, contrary to the intent of the clergy, was an increase of reported cases of possession and a greater dependence on the cunning people, the local wizards and charmers, to protect them with countermagic. This reaction in turn could lay the groundwork for an episode of witch hunting to become a means of exorcism.

Another question that has concerned historians is to what extent these "possessions" were a conscious means of avoidance, a dissembling, and how much of the behavior was of some pathological nature. Chadwick Hansen is convinced that these cases of possession were real, unconscious reactions and not pretenses. He interprets the violent and antisocial behavior of the possessed at Salem as hysteria, not in the popular sense, but as a psychosomatic and pathological reaction to a fearful social situation over which the victims had no control. The behaviors, he concludes, arguing against the older traditional view of the incidents, could not have been pretended contortions. They were not positions that individuals could achieve voluntarily. The observers were truthfully reporting what was seen and not themselves hallucinating or responding to group hysteria.

What has made the behavior of the seventeenth-century possessed individuals incomprehensible to modern scholars is that these hysterical reactions, in the pathological meaning of hysteria, do not fit the pattern of modern hysterics. This, Hansen explains, is because the hysteric reflects the culture's expectation of how to behave. Many of the physical contortions suffered at the time are no longer in the repertoire of such pathological behaviors today. They have changed. Symptoms such as the inability to speak and skin seemingly insensitive to pain do persist into our time, but the extreme bodily contortions are less likely. The older symptoms were, however, documented by doctors as late as the nineteenth century for hysterical reactions unrelated to witchcraft and possession.

Hansen does not doubt that witchcraft was practiced in New England and that these sufferers were responding to their acute fear of the witches' power. But as hysterics have done over the centuries, they used the cues suggested by the larger society. Nonetheless, their reactions attest to the depth of witchcraft beliefs and the fearful reality of the devil to these Englishmen of the seventeenth century.

Richard Slotkin's study of the tradition of violence in America takes a different approach in the analysis of cases of possession. He sees them from a special American perspective, as an analogy for captivity by Indians. In spite of a long history of possession episodes in the European past, there was a unique quality to those suffering such torments in America. The demons took on the shape of American Indians and the exorcist clergyman worked to purge the individual of this unwelcome presence and by analogy his English society of the Indian influence. The violence against witches was not much different from that inflicted on the bodies of Indians during warfare—savage and cruel and seemingly irrational. Both witches and Indians were threats to the hoped-for purity of a covenanted people.

Cases of possession, according to Slotkin, were not only responses to a strict religious environment with its emphasis on the devil, but were also the colonists' reactions to fears of losing their identity as Englishmen and Englishwomen. The colonists worried about succumbing to the lure of the wilderness and the Indian way of life. Infuriated by the success with which the Indians had mastered the wilderness and frustrated by their own difficulties in adapting to the new environment, Puritans first demonized the Indians and then faced the prospect of exorcising their newly created devils.

Regardless of the explanation, cases of possession were as mysterious and frightening as other inexplicable disasters in nature. They fell into the category of wonders, the result of an unseen presence, a wicked demonstration of evil power. But unlike earthquakes, hurricanes, droughts, or epidemics, they also served to enliven a folk with few diversions. The antics of the possessed were a distraction from everyday activities and woes, a source of entertainment.

PRIMARY SOURCES

24

The Possession of Elizabeth Knapp of Groton

Samuel Willard

Samuel Willard (1640–1707), was the pastor of Old South Church in Boston. He wrote this report on the possession of Elizabeth Knapp while he was living in Groton, Massachusetts, where he observed her behavior almost daily from October 30, 1671, to January 12, 1672. Elizabeth, the daughter of a local small farmer, was sixteen years old and living temporarily as a servant in Willard's home.

•

This poor and miserable object, about a fortnight before she was taken, we observed to carry herself in a strange and unwonted manner. Sometimes she would give sudden shrieks and, if we inquired a reason, would always put it off with some excuse, and then [she] would burst forth into immoderate and extravagant laughter, in such ways as sometimes she fell onto the ground with it. I myself observed oftentimes a strange change in her countenance, but could not suspect the true reason, but conceived she might be ill, and therefore divers times inquired how she did, and she always answered, "well"—which made me wonder.

But the tragedy began to unfold itself upon Monday, October 30, 1671, after this manner (as I received by credible information, being that day myself gone from home). In the evening a little before she went to bed, sitting by the fire, she cried out, "Oh! my legs!" and clapped her hand on them, [and] immediately [afterwards], "Oh, my breast," and removed her hands thither, and [then] forthwith, "Oh! I am strangled," and put her hands on her throat. Those that observed her could not see what to make of it; whether she was in earnest or dissembled, and in this manner they left her (excepting the person that lay with her), complaining of her breath being stopped.

The next day she was in a strange frame (as was observed by divers), sometimes weeping, sometimes laughing, and many foolish and apish gestures. In the evening, going into the cellar, she shrieked suddenly and being inquired of the cause, she answered that she saw two persons in the cellar; whereupon some went down with

From Samuel Willard, "A Brief Account of a Strange and Unusual Providence of God Befallen to Elizabeth Knapp of Groton (1671–72)," *Massachusetts Society Collections*, 4th ser. (1868), vol. 8 (Mather papers), 555–70.

her to search but found none—she also looking with them. At last she turned her head and looking one way steadfastly, used the expression, "What cheer, old man?"—which they that were with her took for a fancy—and so ceased. Afterwards (the same evening), the rest of the family being in bed, she was (as one lying in the room saw and she herself also afterwards related) suddenly thrown down into the midst of the floor with violence and taken with a violent fit, whereupon the whole family was raised, and with much ado was she kept out of the fire from destroying herself. After which time, she was followed with fits from thence till the Sabbath Day in which she was violent in bodily motions, leapings, strainings and strange agitations scarce to be held in bound by the strength of three or four, violent also in roarings and screamings representing a dark resemblance of hellish torments and frequently using in these fits divers words, sometimes crying out "money, money," sometimes "sin and misery" with other words.

On Wednesday [November 1], being in the time of intermission [and] questioned about the case she was in with reference to the cause or occasion of it, she seemed to impeach [i.e., accuse] one of the neighbors, a person (I doubt not) of sincere uprightness before God, as though either she or the devil in her likeness and habit, particularly her riding hood, had come down the chimney [and] stricken her that night [when] she was first taken violently, which was the occasion of her being cast into the floor. Whereupon those about her sent to request the person to come to her, who, coming unwittingly, was at the first assaulted by her strangely. For, though her eyes were (as it were) sealed up (as they were always or for the most part in those fits and so continue in them all to this day), she yet knew her very touch from any other though no voice were uttered and discovered it evidently by her gestures, so powerful were Satan's suggestions in her. Yet afterward God was pleased to vindicate the case and justify the innocent even to remove jealousies from the spirits of the party concerned and [to the] satisfaction of the bystanders. For, after she had gone to prayer with her, she confessed that she believed Satan had deluded her and hath never since complained of any such apparition or disturbance from the person.

These fits continuing (though with intermission), divers (when they had opportunity), pressed upon her to declare what might be the true and real occasion of these amazing fits. She used many tergiversations [i.e., evasions] and excuses, pretending she would [declare it] to this and that young person who, coming, she put it off to another till at the last on Thursday night [November 2] she broke forth into a large confession in the presence of many, the substance whereof amounted to thus much: that the Devil had oftentimes appeared to her, presenting the treaty of a covenant and proffering largely to her—viz. such things as suited her youthful fancy: money, silks, fine clothes, ease from labor, to show her the whole world, etc.; that it had been then three years since his first appearance, occasioned by her discontent; that at first his apparitions had been more rare, but lately more frequent; yea, those few weeks that she had dwelt with us, almost constantly, [so] that she seldom went out of one room into another but he appeared to her, urging of her; and that he had presented her [with] a book written with blood of covenants made by others with him and told her such and such (of some whereof we hope better things) had a name there; that he urged upon her constant temptations to murder her parents, her neighbors, our children, especially the youngest, tempting her to throw it into the fire on the hearth [or] into the oven; and that once he put a bill-hook into her hand to murder myself, persuading her I was asleep. But coming about it, she met me on the stairs at which she was affrighted. The time I remember well and observed a strange frame in her countenance and saw she endeavored to hide something, but I knew not what; neither did I at all suspect any such matter. And [she also confessed] that often he persuaded her to make away with herself, and once she was going to drown herself in the well, for, looking into it, she saw such sights as allured her, and was gotten with the curb and was by God's providence prevented. . . .

Being pressed to declare whether she had not consented to a covenant with the devil, she with solemn assertions denied it, yea, asserted that she had never so much as consented to discourse with him, nor had ever but once before that night used the expression, "what cheer, old man?" And this argument she used, that the providence of God had ordered it so that all his apparitions had been frightful to her. Yet this she acknowledged (which seemed contradictory), viz.: That when she came to our house to school, before such time as she dwelt with us, she delayed her going home in the evening till it was dark (which we observed), upon his persuasion to have his company home; and that she could not, when he appeared, but go to him.

On that night before the thanksgiving, October 19, she was with another maid that boarded in the house, where both of them saw the appearance of a man's head and shoulders with a great white neckcloth, looking in at the window, at which they came up affrighted [and] both [ran] into the chamber where the rest of us were. They declaring the case, one of us went down to see who it might be but she ran immediately out of the door before him, which she has since confessed was the devil coming to her. She also acknowledged [that] the reason of her former sudden shriekings was from a sudden apparition and that the devil put those excuses into her mouth and bid her so to say, and hurried her into those violent (but she saith feigned and forced) laughters. She then also complained against herself of many sins, disobedience to parents, neglect of attendance upon ordinances, attempts to murder herself, and others. But this particular (of a covenant) she utterly disclaimed, which relation seemed fair, especially in that it was attended with bitter tears, self condemnations, good counsels given to all about her especially the youth then present, and an earnest desire of prayers. She sent to Lancaster for Mr. Rowlandson, who came and prayed with her and gave her serious counsels, but she was still followed, all this notwithstanding, with these fits.

And in this state (coming home on Friday) [November 3] I found her, but could get nothing from her. Whenever I came in [her] presence, she fell into those fits, concerning which fits, I find this noteworthy. She knew and understood what was spoken to her but could not answer nor use any other words but the aforementioned, "money," etc., as long as the fit continued. For when she came out of it, she could give a relation of all that had been spoken to her. She was demanded a reason why she used those words in her fits and signified that the devil presented her with such things to tempt her and with sin and misery to terrify her. . . .

On the Sabbath [November 5] the physician came who judged a main point of her distemper to be natural, arising from the foulness of her stomach and corruptness of her blood occasioning fumes in her brain and strange fancies; whereupon (in order to [make] further trial and administration), she was removed home and the succeeding week she took physic and was not in such violence handled in her fits as before but enjoyed an intermission and gave some hopes of recovery; in which intermission she was altogether senseless (as to our discovery) of her state, held under security and hardness of heart, professing [that] she had no trouble upon her spirits, she cried [that] Satan had left her. A solemn day was kept with her yet it had then (as I apprehend) little efficacy upon her. She, that day, again expressed hopes that the devil had left her. But there was little ground to think so because she remained under such extreme senselessness of her own estate and thus she continued being exercised with some moderate fits in which she used none of the former expressions but sometimes fainted away, sometimes used some strugglings, yet not with extremity, till the Wednesday following [November 15], which day was spent in prayer with her when her fits something more increased and her tongue was for many hours together drawn into a semicircle up to the roof of her mouth and not to be removed, for some tried with the fingers to do it.

From thence till the sabbath seven nights following [November 26] she continued alike only she added to former confessions of her twice consenting to travel with the devil in her company between Groton and Lancaster, who accompanied her in [the] form of a black dog with eyes in his back, sometimes stopping her horse, sometimes leaping up behind.... But still no conference would she own but urged that the devil's quarrel with her was because she would not seal a covenant with him and that this was the ground of her first being taken. Besides this nothing observable came from her. Only one morning she said "God is a father," the next morning, "God is my father," which words (it is to be feared) were words of presumption put into her mouth by the adversary. I, suspecting the truth of her former story, pressed whether she never verbally promised to covenant with him, which she stoutly denied. [She] only acknowledged that she had had some thoughts so to do. But on the forenamed November 26, she was again with violence and extremity seized by her fits in such wise [i.e., ways] that six persons could hardly hold her, but she leaped and skipped about the house perforce roaring and yelling extremely, and fetching deadly sighs, as if her heartstrings would have broken and looking with a frightful aspect, to the amazement and astonishment of all the beholders, of which I was an eye witness. The physician being then again with her, consented that the distemper was diabolical, refused further to administer, [and] advised to extraordinary fasting; whereupon some of God's ministers were sent for. She, meanwhile, continued extremely tormented night and day till Tuesday about noon—having this added on Monday and Tuesday morning, that she barked like a dog and bleated like a calf, in which her organs were visibly made use of. Yea (as was carefully observed) on Monday night and Tuesday morning, whenever any[one] came near the house, though they within heard nothing at all, yet would she bark till they were come into the house.

On Tuesday [November 28], about 12 of the clock, she came out of the fit, which had held her from Sabbath day about the same time, at least 48 hours, with little or no intermission, and then her speech was restored to her and she expressed a great seeming sense of her state. Many bitter tears, sighings, sobbings, complainings she uttered, bewailing of many sins aforementioned, begging prayers and in the hour of prayer expressing much affection [i.e., emotion]. I then pressed her if there were anything behind in reference to the dealings between her and Satan, when she again professed that she had related all and declared that in those fits the devil had assaulted her many ways: that he came down the chimney and she essayed to escape him but was seized upon by him, that he sat upon her breast and used many arguments with her, and that he urged her at one time with persuasions and promises of ease and great matters, told her that she had done enough in what she had already confessed, [that] she might henceforth serve him more securely. Anon [he] told her her time was past and there was no hopes unless she would serve him. And it was observed in the time of her extremity, once when a little moment's respite was granted her of speech, [that] she advised others to make their peace with God and use their time better than she had done. The party advised her also to bethink herself of making her peace. She replied, "It is too late for me."

The next day [November 29] was solemnized when we had the presence of Mr. Bulkley, Mr. Rowlandson, and Mr. Estabrooke, whither coming we found her returned to a sottish and stupid kind of frame. Much was pressed upon her, but no affection at all discovered, though she was little or nothing exercised with any fits and her speech also continued, though a day or two after she was melancholy. And being inquired of a reason, she complained that she was grieved that so much pains was taken with her and did her no good, but this held her not long.

And thus she remained till Monday [December 4] when to some neighbors there present she related something more of her converse with the devil, viz., that it had been five years or thereabouts since she first saw him and declared methodically the sundry apparitions from time to time, till she was thus dreadfully assaulted, in which the principal was that after many assaults, she had resolved to seal a covenant with Satan, thinking she had better do it than be thus followed by him. That once, when she lived at Lancaster he presented himself and desired of her blood and she would have done it, but wanted a knife. In the parley she was prevented, by the providence of God, interposing my father. A second time in the house he met her and presented her a knife and, as she was going about it, my father stepped in again and prevented [it]; that when she sought and inquired for the knife, it was not to be found, and that afterward she saw it sticking in the top of the barn; and some other like passages.

She again owned an observable passage which she also had confessed in her first declaration, but is not there inserted, viz., that the devil had often proffered her his service, but she accepted not, and once in particular to bring in chips for the fire. She refused, but when she came in she saw them lie by the fire side and was afraid. And this I remark: I, sitting by the fire, spoke to her to lay them on and she turned away in an unwonted manner. She then also declared against herself, her unprofitable life she had led and how justly God had thus permitted Satan to handle her. . . . But being pressed whether there were not a covenant, she earnestly professed that by

God's goodness she had been prevented from doing that which she, of herself, had been ready enough to assent to and she thanked God there was no such thing.

The same day she was again taken with a new kind of unwonted fit in which, after she had been awhile exercised with violence, she got her a sheet [stick?] and went up and down, thrusting and pushing here and there. And anon, looking out at a window and cried out of a witch appearing in a strange manner in form of a dog downward with a woman's head, and declared the person other whiles that she appeared in her whole likeness and described her shape and habit, signified that she went up the chimney and went her way. What impression we received in the clay of the chimney in similitude of a dog's paw by the operation of Satan and in the scar [i.e., impression] of a dog's going in the same place, she told of. I shall not conclude, though something there was, as I myself saw in the chimney in the same place where she declared the foot was set to go up. In this manner was she handled that night and the two next days, using strange gestures, complaining by signs when she could not speak, explaining that she was sometimes in the chamber, sometimes in the chimney, and anon assaults [on] her; sometimes scratching her breast, beating her sides, strangling her throat, and she did oftentimes seem to our apprehension as if she would forthwith be strangled. She declared that if the party were apprehended, she should forthwith be well, but never till then.

Whereupon, her father went and procured the coming of the woman impeached by her, who came down to her on Thursday night [December 7], where (being desired to be present) I observed that she was violently handled and lamentably tormented by the adversary and uttered unusual shrieks at the instant of the person's coming in though her eyes were fast closed. But having experience of such former actings, we made nothing of it but waited the issue. God, therefore, was sought to, to signify something whereby the innocent might be acquitted or the guilty discovered. And he answered our prayers for by two evident and clear mistakes, she was cleared and then all prejudices ceased and she never more to this day hath impeached her of any apparition. . . .

Friday [December 8] was a sad day with her, for she was sorely handled with fits, which some perceiving pressed that there was something yet behind not discovered by her and she, after a violent fit holding her between two and three hours, did first to one and afterwards to many, acknowledge that she had given of her blood to the devil and made a covenant with him. Whereupon I was sent for to [observe] her and understanding how things had passed, I found that there was no room for privacy. In another [room] already made by her so public, I therefore examined her concerning the matter and found her not so forward to confess as she had been to others, yet thus much I gathered from her confession.

That after she came to dwell with us, one day as she was alone in a lower room, all the rest of us being in the chamber, she looked out at the window and saw the devil in the habit of an old man, coming over a great meadow lying hear the house and suspecting his design, she had thought to have gone away, yet at length resolved to tarry it out and hear what he had to say to her. When he came, he demanded of her some of her blood, which she forthwith consented to and with a knife cut her finger. He caught the blood in his hand and then told her she must write her name in his book. She answered she could not write, but he told her he would direct her hand, and then [he] took a little sharpened stick and dipped [it] in the blood and put it into her hand and guided it. And she wrote her name with his help. What was the matter she set her hand to, I could not learn from her. But thus much she confessed, that the term of time agreed upon with him was for seven years: one year she was to be faithful in his service and then the other six he would serve her and make her a witch.

She also related that the ground of contest between her and the devil, which was the occasion of this sad providence was this, that after her covenant made, the devil showed her hell and the damned and told her if she were not faithful to him, she should go thither and be tormented there. She desired of him to show her heaven, but he told her that heaven was an ugly place and that none went thither but a company of base rogues whom he hated, but if she would obey him, it should be well with her.

But afterward she considered with herself that the term of the covenant was but short and would soon be at an end and she doubted (for all the devil's promises) she must at last come to the place he had shown her and withall [she] feared, [that] if she were a witch, she should be discovered and brought to a shameful end, which was many times a trouble on her spirits. This, the devil perceiving, [he] urged upon her to give him more of her blood and set her hand again to his book, which she refused to do, but partly through promises, partly by threatenings, he brought her at last to a promise that she would sometime to do it; after which he left not incessantly to urge her to the performance of it.

Once he met her on the stairs and often elsewhere pressing her with vehemency, but she still put it off till the first night she was taken, when the devil came to her and told her he would not tarry any longer. She told him she would not do it. He answered [that] she had done it already, and what further damage would it be to do it again, for she was his sure enough. She rejoined [that] she had done it already, and if she were his sure enough what need he to desire anymore of her. Whereupon, he struck her the first night and again more violently the second as is above expressed.

This is the sum of the relation I then had from her, which at that time seemed to be methodical [i.e., true]. These things she uttered with great affection, overflowing of tears, and seeming bitterness. I asked of the reason of her weeping and bitterness. She complained of her sins and some in particular: profanation of the sabbath, etc., but nothing of the sin of renouncing the government of God and giving herself up to the devil. I, therefore (as God helped), applied it to her and asked her whether she desired not prayers with and for her. She assented with earnestness, and in prayer seemed to bewail the sin as God helped then in the aggravation of it, and afterward declared a desire to rely on the power and mercy of God in Christ. She then also declared that the devil had deceived her concerning those persons impeached by her [and] that he had in their likeness or resemblance tormented her, persuading her that it was they [and] that they bore her a spleen; but he loved her and would free her from them, and pressed on her to endeavor to bring them forth to the censure of the law.

In this case I left her, but (not being satisfied in some things) I promised to visit her again the next day [December 9], which accordingly I did. But coming to her I found her (though her speech still remained) in a case sad enough: her tears dried up and senses stupefied and (as was observed) when I could get nothing from her and therefore applied myself in counsel to her, she regarded it not, but fixed her eye steadfastly upon a place, as she was wont when the devil presented himself to her, which was a grief to her parents and bought me to a stand. In this condition I left her.

The next day [December 10], being the sabbath, whether upon any hint given her or any advantage Satan took by it upon her, she sent for me in haste at noon. Coming to her, she immediately with tears told me that she had belied the devil in saying she had given him of her blood, etc., professed that the most of the apparitions she had spoken of were but fancies, as images represented in a dream, earnestly entreated me to believe her, called God to witness to her assertions . . . , and expressed a desire that all that would might hear her; that as they had heard so many lies and untruths, they might now hear the truth and engaged that in the evening she would do it.

I then repaired to her and divers more, then went. She then declared thus much. That the devil had sometimes appeared to her; that the occasion of it was her discontent, that her condition displeased her, her labor was burdensome to her. She was neither content to be at home nor abroad and had oftentime strong persuasions to practice in witchcraft, had often wished the devil would come to her at such and such times, and resolved that if he would, she would give herself up to him soul and body. But (though he had oft times appeared to her, yet) at such times he had not discovered [i.e., disclosed] himself and therefore she had been preserved from such a thing. I declared a suspicion of the truth of the relation and gave her some reasons, but by reason of the company did not say much, neither could anything further be gotten from her. But the next day I went to her and opened my mind to her alone and left it with her, declared (among other things) that she had used preposterous courses and therefore it was no marvel that she had been led into such contradictions and tendered her all the help I could if she would make use of me and more privately relate any weighty and serious case of conscience to me. She promised me she would if she knew anything, but said that then she knew nothing at all, but stood to the story she had told the foregoing evening. And indeed what to make of these things I at present know not, but am waiting till God (if he see meet) wind up the story and make a more clear discovery. . . .

Thus she continued till the next sabbath [December 17] in the afternoon, on which day in the morning, being something better than at other times, she had but little company tarried with her in the afternoon, when the devil began to make more full discovery of himself. It had been a question before, whether she might properly be called a demoniac, or person possessed of the devil. But it was then put out of question [i.e., beyond doubt]. She began (as the persons with her testify) by drawing her tongue out of her mouth most frightfully to an extraordinary length and greatness and many amazing postures of her body, and then by speaking, vocally in her, whereupon her father and another neighbor were called from the meeting, on whom (as soon as they came in) she railed, calling them "rogues," who told them nothing but a parcel of lies and deceived them and many like expressions.

After [this] exercise I was called, but understood not the occasion till I came and heard the same voice, a grumbling, low, yet audible voice it was. The first salutation I had was, "Oh! you are a great rogue." I was at the first something daunted and amazed and many reluctances I had upon my spirits, which brought me to a silence and amazement in my spirits till at last God heard my groans and gave me both refreshment in Christ and courage. I then called for a light to see whether it might not appear a counterfeit and observed not any of her organs to move. The voice was hollow, as if it issued out of her throat. He then again called me "great black rogue." I challenged him to make it appear, but all the answer was, "you tell the people a company of lies." I reflected on myself and could not but magnify the goodness of God not to suffer Satan to bespatter the names of his people with those sins which he himself has pardoned in the blood of Christ. I answered, "Satan, thou art a liar and a deceiver, and God will vindicate his own truth one day." He answered nothing directly but said, "I am not Satan, I am a pretty black boy; this is my pretty girl. I have been here a great while." I sat still and answered nothing to these expressions, but when he directed himself to me again: "Oh! you black rogue, I do not love you." I replied through God's grace, "I hate thee;" he rejoined, "but you had better love me."

These manner of expressions filled some of the company there present with great consternation. Others put on boldness to speak to him, at which I was displeased and advised them to see their call clear, fearing lest by his policy and many apish expressions he used, he might insinuate himself and raise in them a fearlessness of spirit of him. I no sooner turned my back to go to the fire, but he called out again, "Where is that black rogue gone?"

I, seeing little good to be done by discourse and questioning many things in my mind concerning it, I desired the company to join in prayer unto God. When we went about that duty and were kneeled down, with a voice louder than before something, he cried out, "Hold your tongue, hold your tongue, get you gone you black rogue. What are you going to do, you have nothing to do with me," etc. But through God's goodness was silenced and she lay quiet during the time of prayer, but as soon as it was ended, began afresh using the former expressions, at which some ventured to speak to him. Though I think imprudently, one told him, "God had him in chains." He replied, "For all my chains I can knock thee on the head when I please." He said he would carry her away that night. Another answered, "but God is stronger than thou." He presently rejoined, "that's a lie. I am stronger than God." At which blasphemy I again advised them to be wary of speaking, counseled them to get serious persons to watch with her and left her, commending her to God.

On Tuesday following [December 19], she confessed that the devil entered into her the second night after her first taking, that when she was going to bed, he entered in (as she conceived) at her mouth and had been in her ever since and professed that if there were ever a devil in the world, there was one in her, but in what manner he spoke in her she could not tell.

On Wednesday night [December 20], she must forthwith be carried down to the bay in all haste; she should never be well till an assembly of ministers was met together to pray with and for her and in particular Mr. Cobbet. Her friends advised with me about it. I signified to them that I apprehended Satan never made any good motion but it was out of season and that it was not a thing now feasible, the season being then extreme[ly] cold and the snow deep, that if she had been taken in the woods with her fits, she must needs perish.

On Friday [December 22] in the evening she was taken again violently and then the former voice (or the sound) was heard in her again, not speaking, but imitating the crowing of a cock, accompanied with many other gestures, some violent, some ridiculous, which occasioned my going to her, where by signs she signified that the devil threatened to carry her away that night. . . .

Since that time she hath continued for the most part speechless; her fits coming upon her sometimes often, sometimes with greater intermission and with great varieties in the manner of them, sometimes by violence, sometimes by making her sick, but (through God's goodness) so abated in violence that now one person can as well rule her as formerly four or five. She is observed always to fall into her fits when any stranger go to visit her and the more go the more violent are her fits. As to the frame of her spirits, she hath been more averse lately to good counsel than heretofore, yet sometime she signifies a desire of the company of ministers.

On Thursday last [January 11, 1672], in the evening, she came a season to [i.e., regained] her speech, and (as I received from them with her)again disowned a covenant with the devil, disowned that relation about the knife before mentioned, declared the occasion of her fits to be discontent, owned the temptations to murder; declared that though the devil had power of her body, she hoped he should not of her soul, that she had rather continue so speechless than have her speech and make no better use of it than formerly she had; expressed that she was sometimes disposed to do mischief and was as if some had laid hold of her to enforce her to it, and had double strength to her own. [She also said] that she knew not whether the devil were in her or no. If he were, she knew not when or how he entered [and] that when she was taken speechless, she fayned [i.e., felt] as if a string was tied about the roots of her tongue and reached down into her vitals and pulled her tongue down and then most when she strove to speak.

On Friday [January 12] in the evening she was taken with a passion of weeping and sighing, which held her till late in the night. At length she sent for me but the unreasonableness of the weather and my own bodily indisposition prevented [my visiting]. I went the next morning when she strove to speak something [but] she could not, [and] was taken with her fits which held her as long as I tarried, which was more than an hour. I left her in them. And thus she continues speechless to this instant, January 15, and followed with fits; concerning which state of hers I shall suspend my own judgment and willingly leave it to the censure of those that are more learned, aged, and judicious. Only I shall leave my thoughts in respect of two or three questions which have risen about her, viz.:

1. Whether her distemper be real or counterfeit. I shall say no more to that but

this. The great strength appearing in them and great weakness after them will disclaim the contrary opinion, for though a person may counterfeit much, yet such a strength is beyond the force of dissimulation.

2. Whether her distemper be natural or diabolical. I suppose the premises will strongly enough conclude the latter. Yet I will add these two further arguments: 1. the actings of convulsion, which these come nearest to, are (as persons acquainted with them observe) in many, yea the most essential parts of them quite contrary to these actings. 2. She hath [been] no ways wasted in body or strength by all these fits, though so dreadful, but gathered flesh exceedingly and hath her natural strength when her fits are off for the most part.

3. Whether the devil did really speak in her. To that point which some have much doubted of, thus much I will say to countermand this apprehension.

First, the manner of expression I diligently observed, and could not perceive any organ, any instrument of speech (which the philosopher makes mention of), to have any motion at all. Yea, her mouth was sometimes shut without opening, sometimes open without shutting or moving. And then both I and others saw her tongue (as it used to be when she was in some fits when speechless) turned up circularly to the roof of her mouth. Second, the labial letters, divers of which were used by her, viz.: B.M.P., which cannot be naturally expressed without motion of the lips [and] which must needs come within our ken, if observed, were uttered without any such motion. If she had used only linguals, gutturals, etc., the matter might have been more suspicious. Third, the reviling terms then used were such as she never used before nor since in all this time of her being thus taken. Yea, [she] has been always observed to speak respectively concerning me. Fourth, they were expressions which the devil (by her confession) aspersed me and others with all, in the hours of temptation. Particularly she had freely acknowledged that the devil was wont to appear to her in the house of God, and divert her mind and charge her [that] she should not give ear to [what] that black coated rogue spoke. 5. We observed when the voice spoke, her throat was swelled formidably, as big at least as one's fist. . . .

4. Whether she have covenanted with the devil or no, I think this is a case unanswerable. Her declarations have been so contradictory, one to another, that we know not what to make of them, and her condition is such as administers many doubts. Charity would hope the best, love would also fear the worst, but thus much is clear, she is an object of pity and I desire that all that hear of her would [be] compassionate [of] her forlorn state. She is (I question not) a subject of hope and therefore all means ought to be used for her recovery. She is a monument of divine severity and the Lord grant that all that see or hear may fear and tremble. Amen.

(Editor's note: The narrative ends at this point. Elizabeth Knapp's mental state and prognosis continue to be historical mysteries. Willard does not tell us whether she recovered from these fits. She was not, however, accused of witchcraft or tried for any crime.)

[25]

Bewitchment of the Goodwin Children

COTTON MATHER

Cotton Mather's 1689 work Memorable Providences *was introduced in part 1. In this excerpt, Mather describes the bewitchment of the four Goodwin children and his attempt to exorcise their demons.*

•

The First Example

Section I. There dwells at this time in the south part of Boston a sober and pious man whose name is John Goodwin, whose trade is that of a mason and whose wife (to which a good report gives a share with him in all the characters of virtue) has made him the father of six now living children. Of these children, all but the eldest, who works with his father at his calling, and the youngest, who lives yet upon the breast of its mother, have laboured under the direful effects of a (no less palpable than) stupendous *Witchcraft*. Indeed that exempted son had also, as was thought, some lighter touches of it in unaccountable stabs and pains now and then upon him, as indeed every person in the family at some time or other had, except the godly father and the sucking infant, who never felt any impressions of it. But these four children mentioned were handled in so sad and strange a manner as has given matter of discourse and wonder to all the country and of history not unworthy to be considered by more than all the serious or the curious readers in this New-English World.

Sect. II. The four children (whereof the eldest was about thirteen and the youngest was perhaps about a third part of so many years of age) had enjoyed a religious education and answered it with a very towardly ingenuity [i.e., future promise]. They had an observable affection unto divine and sacred things. . . . Their parents also kept them to a continual employment, which did more than deliver them from the temptations of idleness and, as young as they were, they took a delight in it. . . . In a

From Cotton Mather, *Memorable Providences Relating to Witchcrafts and Possessions* (1689), in *Narratives of the Witchcraft Cases, 1648–1706*, ed. George Lincoln Burr (New York: Charles Scribner's Sons, 1914), 99-126. The identification of names and the determination of ages are taken from Burr's notes.

word, such was the whole temper and carriage of the children that there cannot easily be anything more unreasonable than to imagine that a design to dissemble could cause them to fall into any of their odd fits. . . . [Martha was thirteen, John eleven, Mercy seven, Benjamin five, the elder son, Nathaniel, fifteen, the baby (Hannah) six months old when the narrative opens.]

Sect. III. About midsummer in the year 1688, the eldest of these children [Martha], who is a daughter, saw cause to examine [i.e., question] their washerwoman upon their missing of some linen, which it was feared she had stolen from them, and of what use this linen might be to serve the witchcraft intended, the thief's tempter knows! This laundress was the daughter of an ignorant and scandalous old woman in the neighbourhood, whose miserable husband before he died had sometimes complained of her that she was undoubtedly a witch and that whenever his head was laid, she would quickly arrive unto the punishments due to such an one. This woman, in her daughter's defense, bestowed very bad language upon the girl that put her to the question immediately upon which the poor child became variously indisposed in her health and visited with strange fits beyond those that attend an epilepsy or a catalepsy or those that they call the diseases of astonishment.

Sect. IV. It was not long before one of her sisters and two of her brothers were seized, in order one after another with affects [i.e., ailments] like those that molested her. Within a few weeks, they were all four tortured every where in a manner so very grievous, that it would have broke an heart of stone to have seen their agonies. Skillful physicians were consulted for their help and particularly our worthy and prudent friend Dr. Thomas Oakes who found himself so affronted [i.e., dumbfounded] by the distempers of the children that he concluded nothing but an hellish witchcraft could be the original [i.e., the cause] of these maladies. . . .

Sect. V. The variety of their tortures increased continually, and although about nine or ten at night they always had a release from their miseries and ate and slept all night for the most part indifferently well. Yet in the day time they were handled with so many sorts of ills that it would require of us almost as much time to relate them all as it did of them to endure them. Sometimes they would be deaf, sometimes dumb, and sometimes blind, and often all this at once. One while their tongues would be drawn down their throats, another while they would be pulled out upon their chins to a prodigious length. They would have their mouths opened unto such a wideness that their jaws went out of joint, and anon they would clap together again with a force like that of a strong spring lock. . . . They would make most piteous outcries that they were cut with knives and struck with blows that they could not bear. Their necks would be broken so that their neckbone would seem dissolved unto them that felt after it, and yet on the sudden, it would become again so stiff that there was no stirring of their heads, yea, their heads would be twisted almost round. . . . Thus they lay some weeks most pitiful spectacles, and this while as a further demonstration of witchcraft in these horrid effects, when I went to prayer by one of them that was very desirous to hear what I said, the child utterly lost her hearing till our prayer was over.

Sect. VI. It was a religious family that these afflictions happened unto and none but a religious contrivance to obtain relief would have been welcome to them. Many superstitious proposals were made unto them by persons that were I know not who, nor what, with arguments fetched from I know not how much necessity and experience, but the distressed parents rejected all such counsels with a gracious resolution to oppose devils with no other weapons but prayers and tears unto Him that has the chaining of them, and to try first whether graces were not the best things to encounter witchcrafts with. Accordingly they requested the four ministers of Boston with the minister of Charlestown to keep a day of prayer at their thus haunted house, which they did in the company of some devout people there. Immediately upon this day the youngest of the four children was delivered and never felt any trouble as afore. . . .

Sect. VII. The report of the calamities of the family for which we were thus concerned arrived now unto the ears of the magistrates, who presently and prudently applied themselves with a just vigour to enquire into the story. The father of the children complained of his neighbour, the suspected ill woman, whose name was Glover and she being sent for by the Justices, gave such a wretched account of herself, that they saw cause to commit her unto the gaoler's custody . . . Upon the commitment of this extraordinary woman, all the children had some present ease until one (related unto her) accidentally meeting one or two of them, entertained them with her blessing, that is, railing, upon which three of them fell ill again as they were before.

Sect. VIII. It was not long before the witch thus in the trap was brought upon her trial . . . and when she did plead, it was with confession rather than denial of her guilt.

Order was given to search the old woman's house, from whence there were brought into the court several small images or puppets or babies made of rags and stuffed with goat's hair and other such ingredients. When these were produced, the vile woman acknowledged that her way to torment the objects of her malice was by wetting of her finger with her spittle and stroking of those little images. The abused children were then present and the woman still kept stooping and shrinking as one that was almost pressed to death with a mighty weight upon her. But one of the images being brought unto her, immediately she started up after an odd manner and took it into her hand, but she had no sooner taken it, than one of the children fell into sad fits before the whole assembly. . . . However, to make all clear, the Court appointed five or six physicians one evening to examine her very strictly, whether she were not crazed in her intellectuals and had not procured to herself by folly and madness the reputation of a witch. Divers hours did they spend with her and in all that while no discourse came from her but what was pertinent and agreeable. . . . She owned her self a Roman Catholic and could recite her Pater Noster in Latin very readily, but there was one clause or two always too hard for her, whereof she said, "She could not repeat it if she might have all the world." In the up-shot, the doctors returned her compos mentis [of sound mind] and sentence of death was passed upon her.

Sect. IX. Diverse [i.e., various] days were passed between her being arraigned and condemned. In this time one of her neighbours had been giving in her testimony of what another of her neighbours had upon her death related concerning her. It seems one [Goodwife] Howen about six years before had been cruelly bewitched to death, but before she died she called one Hughes unto her, telling her that she laid her death to the charge of Glover, that she had seen Glover sometimes come down her chimney. . . . This Hughes now preparing her testimony, immediately one of her children, a fine boy well grown towards youth, was taken ill just in the same woeful and surprising manner that Goodwin's children were. One night particularly, the boy said he saw a black thing with a blue cap in the room, tormenting of him and he complained most bitterly of a hand put into the bed to pull out his bowels. The next day the mother of the boy went unto Glover in the prison and asked her why she tortured her poor lad at such a wicked rate? This witch replied that she did it because of wrong done to her self and her daughter. Hughes denied (as well she might) that she had done her any wrong. . . . But the boy had no more indispositions after the condemnation of the woman.

Sect. X. While the miserable old woman was under condemnation, I did myself twice give a visit unto her. She never denied the guilt of the witchcraft charged upon her, but she confessed very little about the circumstances of her confederacies with the devils; only, she said that she used to be at meetings which her Prince and four more were present at. As for those four, she told who they were and for her Prince, her account plainly was that he was the devil. She entertained me with nothing but Irish, which language I had not learning enough to understand without an interpreter. . . . I offered many questions unto her, unto which, after long silence, she told me she would fain give me a full answer, but they would not give her leave. It was demanded, "*They!* Who is that *They?*" and she returned that *They* were her spirits or her saints (for they say, the same word in Irish signifies both). . . .

Sect. XI. When this witch was going to her execution, she said the children should not be relieved by her death, for others had a hand in it as well as she and she named one among the rest, whom it might have been thought natural affection would have advised the concealing of. It came to pass accordingly, that the three children continued in their furnace as before and it grew rather seven times hotter than it was. All their former ills pursued them still with an addition of more (its not easy to tell how many), but such as gave more sensible demonstrations of an enchantment growing very far towards a possession by evil spirits.

Sect. XII. The children in their fits would still cry out upon *They* and *Them* as the authors of all their harms, but who that *They* and *Them* were, they were not able to declare. At last, the boy obtained at some times a sight of some shapes in the room. There were three or four of them, the names of which the child would pretend at certain seasons to tell. . . . A blow at the place where the boy beheld the spectre was always felt by the boy himself in the part of his body that answered what might be stricken at. . . . But as a blow at the apparition always hurt him, so it always helped him too, for, after the agonies which a push or stab of that had put him to, were over (as in a minute or 2 they would be), the boy would have a respite from his fits a considerable while, and the hobgoblins disappear. It is very credibly reported that a wound was this way given to an obnoxious woman in the town, whose name I will not expose for we should be tender in such relations lest we wrong the reputation of the innocent by stories not enough enquired into.

Sect. XIII. The fits of the children yet more arrived unto such motions as were beyond the efficacy of any natural distemper in the world. They would bark at one another like dogs, and again purr like so many cats. They would sometimes complain that they were in a red hot oven, sweating and panting at the same time unreasonably. Anon they would say cold water was thrown upon them, at which they would shiver very much. They would cry out of dismal blows with great cudgels laid upon them and though we saw no cudgels nor blows, yet we could see the marks left by them in red streaks upon their bodies afterward. And one of them would be roasted on an invisible spit run into his mouth and out at his foot, he lying and rolling and groaning as if it had been so in the most sensible manner in the world, and then he would shriek that knives were cutting of him. Sometimes also he would have his head so forcibly, though not visibly, nailed unto the floor, that it was as much as a strong man could do to pull it up. One while they would all be so limber that it was judged every bone of them could be bent. Another while they would be so stiff, that not a joint of them could be stirred. . . . Yea, they would fly like geese, and be carried with an incredible swiftness through the air, having but just their toes now and then upon the ground and their arms waved like the wings of a bird. One of them in the house of a kind neighbour and gentleman (Mr. Willis) flew the length of the room, about 20 foot, and flew just into an infant's high armed chair (as its affirmed), none seeing her feet all the way touch the floor.

Sect. XIV. Many ways did the devils take to make the children do mischief both to themselves and others, but through the singular providence of God, they always failed in the attempts. For they could never essay the doing of any harm unless there were somebody at hand that might prevent it and seldom without first shrieking out, "they say I must do such a thing!" Diverse times they went to strike furious blows at their tenderest and dearest friends or to fling them down stairs when they had them at the top, but the warnings from the mouths of the children themselves would still anticipate what the devils did intend. . . .

Sect. XV. They were not in a constant torture for some weeks, but were a little quiet, unless upon some incidental provocations, upon which the devils would handle them like tigers and wound them in a manner very horrible. Particularly upon the least reproof of their parents for any unfit thing they said or did, most grievous woeful heart-breaking agonies would they fall into. . . . It would sometimes cost one of them an hour or two to be undressed in the evening or dressed in the morning. For if anyone went to untie a string, or undo a button about them or the contrary, they would be twisted into such postures as made the thing impossible, . . . nor could they go to wash their hands without having them clasped so oddly together, there was no doing of it. . . .Whatever work they were bid to do, they would be so snapped in the member which was to do it, that they with grief still desisted from it. If one ordered them to rub a clean table, they were able to do it without any disturbance; if to rub a dirty table, presently they would with many torments be made uncapable. And sometimes, though but seldom, they were kept from eating their meals, by having their teeth set when they carried anything unto their mouths.

Sect. XVI. But nothing in the world would so discompose them as a religious exercise. If there were any discourse of God, or Christ, or any of the things which are not seen and are eternal, they would be cast into intolerable anguishes. . . . Reading of His word would occasion a very terrible vexation to them. They would then stop their own ears with their own hands and roar, and shriek, and holler, to drown the voice of the devotion. . . . In short, no good thing must then be endured near those children, which (while they are themselves) do love every good thing in a measure that proclaims in them the fear of God.

Sect. XVII. My employments were such that I could not visit this afflicted family so often as I would, wherefore that I might show them what kindness I could as also that I might have a full opportunity to observe the extraordinary circumstances of the children and that I might be furnished with evidence and argument as a critical eye witness to confute the Sadducism of this debauched age. I took the eldest of them home to my house. The young woman continued well at our house for diverse days and applied herself to such actions not only of industry but of piety as she had been no stranger to. But on the twentieth of November in the forenoon, she cried out, "Ah, *They* have found me out! I thought it would be so!" and immediately she fell into her fits again. I shall now confine my story chiefly to her from whose case the reader may shape some conjecture at the accidents of the rest.

Sect. XVIII. Variety of tortures now seized upon the girl in which besides the forementioned ails returning upon her, she often would cough up a ball as big as a small egg into the side of her wind pipe that would near choke her, till by stroking and by drinking, it was carried down again. At the beginning of her fits usually she kept oddly looking up the chimney, but could not say what she saw. When I bade her cry to the Lord Jesus for help, her teeth were instantly set, upon which I added, "Yet child, look unto Him," and then her eyes were presently pulled into her head so far that one might have feared she should never have used them more. . . . She likewise complained that Goody Glover's chain was upon her leg and when she essayed to go, her postures were exactly such as the chained witch had before she died. But the manner still was that her tortures in a small while would pass over and frolics succeed in which she would continue many hours, nay whole days, talking perhaps never wickedly, but always wittily beyond her self, and at certain provocations her tortures would renew upon her. . . . But she frequently told us that if she might but steal or be drunk, she should be well immediately.

Sect. XIX. In her ludicrous fits, one while she would be flying, and she would be carried hither and thither, though not long from the ground, yet so long as to exceed the ordinary power of nature in our opinion of it, another while she would be for diving and use the actions of it towards the floor, on which, if we had not held her, she would have thrown herself. Being at this exercise she told us, That *They* said she must go down to the bottom of our well, for there was plate there! And we ourselves who had newly bought the house hardly knew of any, but the former owner of the house just then coming in told us there had been plate for many years at the bottom of the well. . . .

Sect. XX. While she was in her frolics I was willing to try whether she could read or no and I found not only that if she went to read the Bible her eyes would be strangely twisted and blinded, and her neck presently broken, but also that if any one else did read the Bible in the room, tho it were wholly out of her sight and without the least voice or noise of it, she would be cast into very terrible agonies. . . . I brought her a Quaker's Book and that she could quietly read whole pages of, only the name of God and Christ she still skipped over being unable to pronounce it except sometimes with stammering a minute or two or more upon it. . . . But when I showed her a jest book [such] as, *The Oxford Jests*, or the *Cambridge Jests*, she could read them without any disturbance and have witty descants upon them too. I entertained her with a book that pretends to prove that there are no witches, and that she could read very well only the name devils and witches could not be uttered by her without extraordinary difficulty. . . . Diverse books published by my father I also tried upon her, particularly his *Mystery of Christ*, and another small book of his about faith and repentance, and the day of judgment.

Once being very merrily talking by a table that had this last book upon it, she just opened the book and was immediately struck backwards as dead upon the floor. I hope I have not spoiled the credit of the books by telling how much the devils hated them. I shall therefore add that my grandfather [John] Cotton's catechism called *Milk for Babes*, and the *Assemblies Catechism*, would bring hideous convulsions on the child if she looked into them, though she had once learned them with all the love that could be.

Sect. XXI. I was not unsensible that this girl's capacity or incapacity to read was no test for truth to be determined by and therefore I did not proceed much further in this fanciful business not knowing what snares the devils might lay for us in the trials [i.e., experiments]. A few further trials, I confess, I did make, but what the event of them was I shall not relate because I would not offend. . . .

Sect. XXII. There was another most unaccountable circumstance which now attended her and until she came to our house, I think, she never had experience of it. Every now and then an invisible horse would be brought unto her by those whom she only called, "them" and "her company," upon the approach of which her eyes would be still closed up for (said she), "They say I am a tell-tale and therefore they will not let me see them." Upon this would she give a spring as one mounting an horse and settling herself in a riding posture, she would in her chair be agitated as one sometimes ambling, sometimes trotting, and sometimes galloping very furiously. . . . When she had rode a minute or two or three, she'd pretend to be at a rendezvous with them that were her company. There she'd maintain a discourse with them and asking many questions concerning herself (for we gave her none of ours), she'd listen much and received answers from them that indeed none but her self perceived. Then would she return and inform us how *They* did intend to handle her for a day or two afterwards, besides some other things that she enquired of them. . . .

Sect. XXIII. One of the spectators once asked her whether she could not ride up stairs, unto which her answer was that she believed she could for her horse could do very notable things. Accordingly, when her horse came to her again, to our admiration she rode (that is, was tossed as one that rode) up the stairs, there then stood open the study of one belonging to the family, into which entering she stood immediately upon her feet and cried out, "They are gone, they are gone! They say that they cannot—God won't let them come here!" . . . She presently and perfectly came to herself, so that her whole discourse and carriage was altered unto the greatest measure of sobriety and she sat reading of the Bible and good books for a good part of the afternoon. Her affairs calling her anon to go down again, the demons were in a quarter of a minute as bad upon her as before. . . .

I was loath to make a charm of the room, yet some strangers that came to visit us the week after desiring to see the experiment made, I permitted more than two or three repetitions of it and it still succeeded as I have declared. . . .

Sect. XXIV. One of those that had been concerned for her welfare had newly implored the great God that the young woman might be able to declare whom she apprehended herself troubled by. . . . She had that day [November 26] been diverse times warning us that they had been contriving to do some harm to my wife by a fall or a blow or the like, and when she came out of her mysterious journeys, she would still be careful concerning her. Accordingly she now calls to her company again, "Hark you, one thing more before we part! What hurt is it you will do to Mrs. Mather? Will you do her any hurt?" Here she listened some time and then clapping her hands, cried out, "O, I am glad on it, they can do Mrs. Mather no hurt. They try, but they say they can't." So she returns and at once, dismissing her horse and opening her eyes, she called me to her, "Now Sir," said she, "I'll tell you all. I have learned who they are that are the cause of my trouble; there's three of them (and she named who). If they were out of the way, I should be well. They say they can tell now how long I shall be troubled, but they won't. Only they seem to think their power will be broke this week."

Sect. XXV. The day following, which was, I think, about the twenty seventh of November, Mr. Morton of Charlestown, and Mr. Allen, Mr. Moodey, Mr. Willard, and myself of Boston, with some devout neighbours kept another day of prayer at John Goodwin's house; and we had all the children present with us there. The children were miserably tortured while we laboured in our prayers, but our good God was nigh unto us in what we called upon Him for. From this day the power of the enemy was broken, and the children, though assaults after this were made upon them, yet were not so cruelly handled as before. . . . Their vexation abated by degrees till within a little while they arrived to perfect ease. . . .

Sect. XXVI. Within a day or two after the fast, the young woman had two remarkable attempts made upon her by her invisible adversaries. Once they were dragging her into the oven that was then heating . . . and she had been burned if at her outcries one had not come in from abroad for her relief. Another time they put an unseen rope with a cruel noose about her neck, whereby she was choked until she was black in the face, and though it was taken off before it had killed her, yet there were the red marks of it.

Sect. XXVII. This was the last molestation that they gave her for a while and she dwelt at my house the rest of the winter having, by an obliging and virtuous conversation, made herself enough welcome to the family. But within about a fortnight, she was visited with two days of as extraordinary obsessions as any we had been the spectators of. I thought it convenient for me to entertain my congregation with a sermon upon the memorable providences which these children had been concerned in. When I had begun to study my sermon, her tormentors again seized upon her. . . . Now her whole carriage to me was with a sauciness that I had not been used to be treated with. She would knock at my study door, affirming that some below would be glad to see me when there was none that asked for me. She would call to me with multiplied impertinencies and throw small things at me wherewith she could not give me any hurt. . . .

Sect. XXVIII. But there were many other wonders beheld by us before these two days were out. Few tortures attended her but such as were provoked, her frolics being the things that had most possession of her. . . .

Sect. XXIX. Devotion was now, as formerly, the terriblest of all the provocations that could be given her. . . . During the time of reading, she would be laid as one fast asleep, but when prayer was begun, the devils would still throw her on the floor at the feet of him that prayed. There would she lie and whistle and sing and roar to drown the voice of the prayer. . . . She'd also fetch very terrible blows with her fist and kicks with her foot at the man that prayed, but still (for he had bid that none should hinder her), her fist and foot would always recoil when they came within a few hair's breadths of him just as if rebounding against a wall. . . . When prayer was ended, she would revive in a minute or two and continue as frolicsome as before. . . . I charged all my family to admit of no diversion by her frolics from such exercises as it was proper to begin the Sabbath with. They took the counsel and though she essayed with as witty and as nimble and as various an application to each of them . . . to make them laugh, yet they kept close to their good books which then called for their attention. When she saw that, immediately she fell asleep. . . .

Sect. XXX. After this, we had no more such entertainments. The demons it may be would once or twice in a week trouble her for a few minutes. . . . Moreover, both she at my house and her sister at home at the time which they call Christmas were by the demons made very drunk, though they had no strong drink (as we are fully sure) to make them so. . . . She complained, "O they say they will have me to keep Christmas with them! They will disgrace me when they can do nothing else!" And immediately the ridiculous behaviours of one drunk were with a wonderful exactness represented in her speaking and reeling and spewing and anon sleeping, till she was well again. . . .

Sect. XXXI. I was not unsensible that it might be an easy thing to be too bold and go too far in making of experiments. . . . I confess I have learned much more than I sought and I have been informed of some things relating to the invisible world, which as I did not think it lawful to ask, so I do not think it proper to tell. . . .

Sect. XXXII. The last fit that the young woman had was very peculiar. The demons having once again seized her, they made her pretend to be dying and dying truly we feared at last she was. . . . She argued concerning death in strains that quite amazed us and concluded that though she was loath to die, yet if God said she must, she must. . . . Anon the fit went over and, as I guessed it would be, it was the last fit she had at our house.

Sect. XXXIII. This is the story of Goodwin's children, a story all made up of wonders! I have related nothing but what I judge to be true. I was myself an eye-witness to a large part of what I tell. . . . The whole happened in the metropolis of the English America unto a religious and industrious family which was visited by all sorts of persons that had a mind to satisfy themselves. I do now likewise publish the history while the thing is yet fresh and new and I challenge all men to detect as much as one designed falsehood. . . . I have writ as plainly as becomes an historian, as truly as becomes a Christian, though perhaps not so profitably as became a divine. But I am resolved after this never to use but just one grain of patience with any man that shall go to impose upon me a denial of devils or of witches. I shall count that man ignorant who shall suspect, but I shall count him downright impudent if he assert the non-existence of things which we have had such palpable convictions of. . . .

Postscript

You have seen the trouble and the relief of John Goodwin's children. . . . I think it will not be improper to tell the world that one thing in the children's deliverance was the strange death of an horrible old woman who was presumed to have a great hand in their affliction. Before her death and at it, the almshouse where she lived was terrified with fearful noises and she seemed to have her death hastened by dismal blows received from the invisible world. But having mentioned this, all that I have now to publish is that prayer and faith was the thing which drove the devils from the children and I am to bear this testimony unto the world that the Lord is nigh to all them who call upon him in truth and that blessed are all they that wait for Him.

Finished, June 7th, 1689.

(Editor's note: Mary Glover was found guilty of witchcraft and executed on November 16, 1688. She was the last person to be convicted of witchcraft in New England before the Salem episode.)

COMMENTARIES

Classic Accusers: The Possessed

JOSEPH KLAITS

In this excerpt from his 1985 book Servants of Satan: The Age of the Witch Hunts, *the historian Joseph Klaits explores how ecstatic religious experiences came to be associated with demonic possession in the sixteenth and seventeenth centuries. Klaits, an authority on seventeenth- and eighteenth-century France, is also the author of* Printed Propaganda under Louis XIV: Absolute Monarchy and Public Opinion *(1976) and coeditor with Michael H. Haltzel of* The Global Ramification of the French Revolution *(1994).*

•

Demonic possession became a leading theme in witchcraft trials of the late sixteenth and seventeenth centuries. The idea itself was ancient by 1600. In the gospels, Jesus cures several individuals possessed by "unclean spirits," and his early followers banished-demons by uttering the Savior's name. During the Middle Ages, stories of people whose bodies had been taken over by demons circulated in numerous manuscript collections. Eventually such tales became a staple of early modern works on demonology. But only as the witch craze reached its climax in Western Europe and North America did possession regularly move from the theoreticians' pages into the real lives of hundreds, if not thousands, of men, women, and children.

To introduce the subject, consider a typical case of seventeenth-century demonic possession and witchcraft. This dramatic episode unfolded around 1620 in Lorraine, where witch trials had long been common. Elizabeth de Ranfaing, daughter of an upper-class family, had exhibited considerable religious feeling from early childhood. In order to dampen her disquieting piety (or so it would appear), her parents married her off at age fifteen to a professional soldier forty-two years her senior. Her husband treated Elizabeth with brutality. When he died some nine years later, she was left with six children. The young widow's religious fervor was still strong, and she went off on a pilgrimage to Remiremont. After finishing her devotions, Elizabeth stopped

From Joseph Klaits, *Servants of Satan: The Age of the Witch Hunts* (Bloomington: Indiana University Press, 1985), 104–13, 115–16, 118–19. © 1985 by Joseph Klaits. Reprinted by permission of Indiana University Press.

to rest at a local inn, where she met a well-known doctor named Charles Poirot. Poirot bought her food and drink in which, Elizabeth later recounted, there was mixed a love potion that placed her under the doctor's control. His very breath was enough to cast a spell over her, and she soon was invaded by "the Other," who caused her to sink into convulsive seizures and utterly outrageous blasphemies. The local apothecaries could only recommend further treatment from Dr. Poirot, whom Elizabeth regarded with a mixture of fascination and horror. At last the village priest sent her to Nancy, where exorcists cast the devils out of her body. Elizabeth remained cured until she chanced to meet Poirot again. Her symptoms immediately returned, and this time exorcism was ineffective. Representatives of various religious orders sent their best men in hope of reaping the honor that would go to the healer of the demoniac of Ranfaing. But each specialist eventually had to admit defeat.

The devil thought to be inhabiting Elizabeth's body was capable of remarkable feats. With his help, the woman could converse in numerous languages, read letters through sealed envelopes, and identify the consecrated host among a stack of wafers. Elizabeth exhibited all the classic symptoms of possession listed in the Roman ritual of exorcism, issued just a few years earlier. She sometimes shrieked the filthiest curses at her exorcists, risked her life by walking the parapets of the church, and, in cataleptic trances, held the most contorted postures for hours on end.

This behavior continued for years, until one day Poirot was passing through Nancy and foolishly dropped in on an exorcism session. Elizabeth saw him and at once denounced Poirot as the source of her bewitchment. The doctor was arrested. Under orders of the magistrates of Lorraine, he was interrogated, shaved, and searched for the devil's mark. The search turned up nothing, and at first Poirot refused to confess. But several months later he was accused by a peasant girl suspected of witchcraft. This time examiners found a mark of the devil on Poirot's body. An elite jury of twenty-four respected judges declared the prominent physician guilty, despite the interventions of powerful supporters on his behalf, including King Philip II's daughter. He and the peasant girl were strangled and their bodies burnt at the stake.

In the following years, Elizabeth made a slow recovery. She went off on elaborate pilgrimages and eventually seemed to have succeeded in conquering the devil. This triumph gave her a reputation for sanctity. In 1631, so firm had her image of holiness become that she was named mother superior of the newly established convent of Notre-Dame-du-Réfuge in Nancy, and Elizabeth made her house a model for the order. At her death eighteen years later, the body of the former demoniac lay in state so that the citizenry of Nancy might pay their respects, and, as a final tribute, her heart was sent as a sacred relic to the headquarters of the Order of Refuge at Avignon.

What are we to make of this remarkable tale? A modern psychiatrist who analyzed the documents on Elizabeth's case has proposed a psychopathological interpretation of her ostensible possession and cure. According to this view, neurotic tendencies, a strict upbringing, harsh treatment from her husband, and her own unacknowledged spiritual inclinations brought about her notion of bewitchment and her persecution mania. Accusations of witchcraft and hysterical crises were reinforced by the exorcisms, and, when Poirot died, the symptoms disappeared.

This clinical diagnosis is enlightening with regard to Elizabeth's personal psychodynamics, but it fails to raise some very pertinent questions. Why did the doctors, clergy, and twenty-four prominent judges all agree that Elizabeth was possessed? Why did they continually reinforce the suggestible woman's belief in diabolical contamination? Above all, why did this kind of episode become so common an occurrence in the age of the witch trials? What was the social context for the possession of Elizabeth de Ranfaing, the young girls of Salem, and many others of the time? . . . Before attempting any answers, . . . it will be helpful to first place cases of demonic possession in the broader context of ecstatic religion and mystical experience. These phenomena provided the background for demonic possession and ensuing trials for witchcraft.

Ecstasy and the Demonic

Many cultures of the world have manifested a belief in ecstatic religion, one form of which is possession by demons. Usually, when anthropologists encounter religious ecstasy, the society in question views it as something desirable, indeed, a condition to be actively solicited or induced. The ecstatic condition is an altered form of consciousness, wherein an individual leaves his normal sensory situations and enters into a trance-like state. For as long as the experience lasts, the ecstatic may exhibit remarkable feats of physical strength or prodigious intellectual abilities. But the most important attribute of ecstasy, the one toward which the entire experience is directed, is some form of superior spiritual insight. This may take the shape of a general piece of moral advice addressed to the community, a specific prophecy or manifestation of clairvoyance, or simply a feeling of peace, internal harmony, and release from all stress. The ecstatic condition is typically interpreted by the person experiencing it and by observers in the religious community as evidence of a benign supernatural intervention.

Religious ecstasy, then, is an ancient, widely known technique through which humans have aspired to contact or even achieve union with the divine. Whether it is induced by chemical substances or the hypnotic effects of private meditation and group prayer, ecstasy is customarily pictured as a way of transcending the normal limitations of physical reality. Through it, men and women of many times and places have sought to make themselves feel at one with what they imagine to be the universal forces of the cosmos.

In the Christian tradition, religious ecstasy has long occupied a distinguished place. Its chief form is mysticism, the intensely private quest for union with God. Typically, Christian mystics are solitary men and women who attempt to suppress the physical side of existence so as to enhance their capacity for spiritual insight. In accord with the deep Christian suspicion of all bodily and material things, mystics traditionally have practiced physical self-mortification. Sometimes they accomplish such mortification passively through abstention from food, drink, and other pleasures of the flesh, and sometimes they do so by actively testing their faith through whippings, uncomfortable clothing, and similar tortures of the body. One element of the Christian monastic tradition, with its withdrawal from the world and physical self-abnegation, stems from the mystical impulse to attain a sense of closeness to God by escaping physical reality. In this sense, there have been thousands of Christian mystics over the centuries. . . .

Many of the great reformers of the sixteenth century, including Luther, Calvin, and Ignatius Loyola (founder of the Jesuit order), went through private, deeply moving conversion experiences in which they felt a divine call. Yet the perennial paradox presented by mysticism soon became evident to the leaders of reform movements: a personal connection with God is too individualized a phenomenon on which to construct an organized community. Thus, Loyola's *Spiritual Exercises* attempted to channel a novice Jesuit's mystical devotion along collective lines. In his quest for union with God, the brother was to follow his superiors' instructions. Mystical experience was to be sought after, but the leaders of the spiritual reform movements knew that it must be carefully supervised and controlled.

. . . With the expanding influence of evangelical reform among the elites and the folk came an expansion of Satan's assigned role. A preoccupation with Satan led many authorities to suspect that the devil's servants were behind all social problems and religious deviations. Some theologians went so far as to speculate on whether the devil had possessed or merely obsessed their religious enemies. These special conditions of the time contributed to the interpretation of mystical experiences as manifestations not of the divine but of the demonic. The origin of a supposed mystic's illumination always had been a matter of dispute: did the light emanate from heaven, or might it have come from hell? Events that before and after the seventeenth century were seen as signs of mystical union with God came to be viewed as expressions of the demonic. Thus, the claims of young girls to have heard supernatural voices led to the career of Joan of Arc in the early 1400s and to the Great Awakening in eighteenth-century New England. But the identical claim, voiced at Salem in 1692 and in many other places in the era of the witch craze, produced accusations of bewitchment.

For a time, the fear of Satan's power rose so high as to make traditional Christian religious ecstasy seem very dangerous to ecclesiastical and secular authorities. Throughout the era of the Reformation, mystical sects stressing interior religion or "enthusiasm" at the expense of outward ritual were suppressed by the establishment. The illuminists of Spain, the French Quietists, and the German Anabaptist communities, among others, became objects of bitter persecution from official churches and their political allies. Although sects devoted to inner enthusiasm, such as the Quakers, have survived from the seventeenth century, they had to withstand harsh persecution for their rejection of mainstream religious values.

Fear of the consequences of religious factionalism led the authorities of most European states to insist on the conformity of their subjects to a single, officially sanctioned church. This European stress on religious unity and suspicion of pluralistic approaches to spiritual matters crossed the ocean with the first settlers. Nearly all the North American colonies of the seventeenth century had an established religion and considered religious toleration ungodly and divisive. The Massachusetts Puritans came to the New World in search of religious freedom, to be sure. But it was freedom for themselves they sought. Liberty to practice their own faith did not extend to Christians of differing persuasions. The Quaker colony founded by William Penn at Philadelphia, however, did welcome people of all faiths. Pennsylvania was also exceptional among the British colonies in that it conducted almost no witch trials. . . .

Whether they labeled the mystic visionary an instrument of the devil or a potential traitor, church and lay authorities were expressing their horror of uncontrolled charismatic religious expression. The interesting paradox is that the increased incidence of episodes of demonic possession in the late sixteenth and seventeenth centuries seems due primarily to the heightened spiritual atmosphere of the time. Ironically, by harping on Satan's powers in their sermons and writings, religious authorities produced the result they most feared. Such vivid imagery encouraged suggestible individuals to imagine themselves in the devil's clutches.

One such victim was a student named Briggs from the north of England. In London during the spring of 1574 he misunderstood a lecturer to say that all faults were sins against the Holy Ghost. Regarding himself as a hopeless reprobate whose prayers were in vain, Briggs fell into a profound depression and several times attempted suicide. Walking toward the Thames, into which he intended to jump, Briggs on one occasion noticed that he was being followed by a large dog who glared at him "with such terrible sparkling eyes" that he concluded that this was no ordinary dog, but was instead the devil, waiting for his soul. Soon afterward, Briggs fell into a trance in the presence of some godly friends. The witnesses eagerly took down part of a dialogue with the devil that issued from the young man's lips. The devil sought to win Briggs's allegiance by maintaining the falsity of scripture. Satan tempted him with promises of valuables and access to an alluring "painted woman" who sang and danced before him. These conversations continued nearly every day for over two weeks, the devil explaining that he took Sundays off for pickpocketing among the congregants at St. Paul's. Briggs's case had a happy outcome, as he was cured by the Puritan writer John Foxe. But Foxe's published account of the episode seems to have influenced the shape of many subsequent instances of demonic possession among Puritans. . . .

Guilt feelings could trigger witchcraft accusations among those exposed to spiritual reform. This psychology also connected witchcraft with demonic possession. The guilt-ridden possessed often accused someone of inflicting demons on them. Thus, while there have been numerous supposed demonic possessions before and since, in this one period possession was regularly said to have involved a human intermediary, the witch. In witch trials involving charges of possession, a victim of demonic powers, such as Elizabeth de Ranfaing, accused the witch of ordering devils to attack her and inhabit her body. Such accusations of bewitchment were taken quite seriously by secular and clerical officials and resulted in hundreds of trials and executions.

Courts were receptive to this kind of accusation, in part because the authors of demonological tracts had held for centuries that an ability to order the possession of an innocent Christian's body was one of the powers Satan granted to witches. The witch was said by these writers to regard the inflicting of demons as one of her highest duties, because this was one of the worst forms of malefice. This theoretical underpinning helps to explain the predisposition of judges and other officials to associate cases of apparent demonic possession with witchcraft. At least as important in establishing this association was the dominant ideological stance of sixteenth- and seventeenth-century elites. Imbued with the spirit of religious reform, clerical and lay authorities classified people in polarities of good and evil, godly and devilish. Ideological predispositions almost inevitably required a personification of the hated and feared satanic enemy, and this an accused witch provided.

A practical advantage to society of associating demonic possession with witchcraft was that the connection suggested an effective cure for the disorder. Executing the witch was an appealing remedy, all the more so because other ways of dealing with the possessed seemed less reliable. The traditional Catholic treatment in cases of demonic possession was exorcism, the ritual in which a priest, acting in the name of God, orders the offending demon to leave the victim's body. Most Protestant reformers were horrified by the idea of exorcism, because to them it signified the belief that a human being could control God. As God had permitted the demon to enter an individual's body, they reasoned, only God could remove the demon. Exorcism reminded Protestants of what they saw as the worst kind of priestly magical superstition, and they steadfastly denied the ritual's efficacy. Meanwhile, however, Protestants continued to accept the traditional belief in demonic possession. Having discarded the standard remedy, they were confronted with the problem of prescribing an effective course of treatment. This was a dilemma they never fully resolved. As in Briggs's case, Protestant leaders spoke of the victim's need for prayer, true penitence, fasting, and other similar manifestations of trust in divine grace. But these methods lacked the dramatic intensity of an exorcism and did not always succeed.

For their part, Catholic authorities often went out of their way to demonstrate the benefits of exorcism. In France, they conducted public ceremonies before large crowds and gave loud thanks to God when, at the rite's climactic moment, the demons departed and the victim's convulsions ceased. Thus, French Catholic leaders made exorcisms a form of propaganda for their faith. Even among Catholics, however, exorcism had its limitations. The ritual was only a temporary cure, for, although it was thought that a demon must obey the priest's explicit command to depart, there was nothing to keep him from returning afterward. For this reason, outbreaks of possession often led to a wearisome round of repeated exorcisms and reinfections, sometimes continuing for months or even years. . . .

Thus, Catholics and Protestants shared a common problem: the techniques of both faiths were not infallible in dealing with the possessed. Hence the attraction of making witches responsible for these mysterious afflictions. A witchcraft trial was one of society's most reliable ways of defeating diabolical possession. In theory, and many times in practice as well, killing the witch ended an epidemic of possession. Of course, the execution of a single witch did not always bring about a complete cure.

Sometimes multiple executions were needed to deal with stubbornly reluctant de-mons. In these instances, accusations of possession could produce mass witch panics.

Possession in the Cloister

These points established, we can turn to the dramatic French convent cases of the seventeenth century. France had a long history of demonic possession in the period of the religious wars, when exorcisms were used as Catholic weapons in the campaigns against Protestant groups. In 1599, for instance, shortly after King Henry IV had granted limited toleration to the Huguenot minority, devils spoke through a possessed Catholic woman in Paris to explain how delighted Satan was with the new royal policy. Many such precedents were the background for a widely publicized episode of demonic possession that unfolded in and around Aix-en-Provence from 1609 to 1611. This case was particularly scandalous because it centered on several nuns, who accused a parish priest in nearby Marseilles of seduction and bewitch-ment. . . .

The possession episode at Aix triggered another at the far end of France. A nun from distant Lille who witnessed several exorcisms while visiting the south went into convulsions upon her return home, and the contagion spread through her convent. Then, in the 1630s, a similar recipe of sexual frustration, reformist religion, and political rivalry resulted in the execution of Urbain Grandier, the priest who was charged with witchcraft by the famous Ursulines of Loudun. Mother Joan of the Angels accused him of inflicting on her a demon who compelled her to blaspheme and behave indecently. When asked in her lucid intervals why she was acting this way, Joan replied that she had no control over her actions but was forced into them by a demon or by the witch Grandier. . . .

Mother Joan's accusations against Grandier were quickly taken up by the priest's enemies in Loudun. The case soon became enmeshed in factional disputes of the French court between supporters and opponents of Cardinal Richelieu, Louis XII's centralizing chief minister. The hapless Grandier found no effective way to defend himself from the powerful forces arrayed against him. After Grandier's execution, Joan was cured of her possession and, like Elizabeth de Ranfaing, acquired a cultic following.

During subsequent decades, there occurred several more trials inspired by episodes of demonic possession in French convents. One of the last, at Auxonne in 1662, is especially notable, because the accused was not the sisters' priestly confessor but their mother superior. Perhaps because public charges of lesbianism in convents were so unusual and scandalous, the Parlement of Dijon took up this case and dismissed all the charges. Meanwhile, episodes of possession had become the normal form taken by witch trials in Geneva and the Burgundian Franche-Comté.

It is clear that in cases of demonic possession, as in other kinds of witch trials, the nature of the accusations stemmed, at least in part, from the assumptions of the authorities. Those assigned to counsel the possessed were usually religious personages

who interpreted the sufferer's behavior in accord with their previous knowledge of
demonic possession. They began their sympathetic therapy by reinforcing the suggestible victim's fear that he or she was suffering from a supernaturally induced
disorder. In this way, psychologically vulnerable individuals had their fantasies chan-
neled by religious authorities into the delusion that they had been possessed by witch-
inflicted demons. . . .

The French mass possession episodes took place in convents where parents deposited their young daughters for purposes of spiritual elevation and/or alleviation of
financial burdens. The reformed convents' mixture of asceticism, social isolation, and
highly emotional religiosity proved dangerously combustible, as newly founded orders of nuns, such as the Ursulines, sought to embody the principles of godliness in
an ordered way of life. Constant exhortations to develop habits of introspection, to
detect every forbidden thought, and to confess all prohibited feelings could produce
a charged atmosphere of repressed desires and deep guilt, stemming from the nuns'
sensations of failure, hopelessness, and fear of damnation. These explosive conditions
often found their spark in a male authority figure, either the nuns' confessor and
spiritual director or a surrogate. Onto these men, it appears, the sisters projected
their ambivalent feelings, the forbidden love that their conscious minds repressed.
The resultant conflicts can explain the sisters' ecstasy of possession, when, at least in
imagination, all desires could be fulfilled.

As in cases of possession the world over, the French nuns' demonic episodes took
an overtly sexual form. A vocabulary of erotic love has been one vehicle for Jewish
and Christian mystical expression ever since biblical times. And the nun's symbolic
marriage to God reflects the universal tendency to parallel spiritual union with
human wedlock. The episodes of possession in seventeenth-century convents, however, did not follow the benign course taken by earlier mystical episodes. Because the
fear of Satan and witchcraft was so intense at the time, and because sexuality was
consistently identified with the devil, churchmen who counseled the ecstatic sisters
led them to label their experience as demonic and to accuse a forbidden male of
bewitchment. Given this demonic interpretation of their ecstatic experience, it is
remarkable that Elizabeth de Ranfaing, Mother Joan of the Angels, and several other
protagonists in these convent cases later recovered, mastered the spirits (or emotions)
that had tormented them, and, like many earlier ecstatic sufferers, went on to distinguished careers as holy women much sought after for their insight and therapeutic
powers.

[27]

Possession and Dispossession

KEITH THOMAS

Keith Thomas's 1971 book Religion and the Decline of Magic *is now the classic study of the function of sixteenth-and seventeenth-century magical practices both within and outside the established religious institutions. It has not been matched in scope or detail since. The book won the Wolfson Literary Award for History in 1972. In this excerpt, Thomas describes Protestant theologians' attitude toward demonic possession and their opposition to Roman Catholic exorcism rituals. Thomas's other major works include* The Perception of the Past in Early Modern England *(1984) and* History and Literature *(1989). His essay on the relevance of anthropology to the study of witchcraft was excerpted in part 1.*

•

The belief in the reality of Satan not only stimulated allegations about diabolical compacts; it also made possible the idea of demoniacal possession. A person into whom an evil spirit had entered could be recognized by the strange physical and moral effects of the intrusion. He would suffer from hysterical fits, wild convulsions and contortions, analgesia, strange vomitings, even total paralysis. From his mouth would come the voices of demons, emitting obscene and blasphemous ravings, or talking fluently in foreign languages previously unknown to the victim. The assault of devils might either be external ("obsession"), or from inside the patient's body ("possession"). Strictly speaking, the belief in demonianism was distinct from that in witchcraft. Obsession by the Devil was a well-known stage preceding the conversion of many Puritan saints, and was not necessarily thought to involve the maleficence of some third party. But since it was frequently believed that an evil spirit had entered into a victim because a witch had sent him there, the notions were in practice intertwined. In seventeenth-century England, the epithets "possessed" and "bewitched" came very near to being synonymous.

The medieval Church had given theological definition to the doctrines of possession and obsession, but it had also provided a tolerably effective remedy for such

From Keith Thomas, *Religion and the Decline of Magic* (London: Weidenfeld and Nicolson, 1971), 477–81, 490–91. © 1971 by Keith Thomas reprinted by permission of Orion Publishing Group, London.

complaints. The evil spirit, it said, could be commanded to depart in a formal exorcism conducted by a priest acting in the name of God and the Church, a ceremony which also formed part of the rite of baptism. The saints of the early Church made a reputation for successfully casting out devils and the office of exorcist was by the mid-third century established as one of the minor orders. The ritual of exorcism, with the sign of the cross, symbolic breathing (*insufflatio*), holy water, and the command to the Devil to depart in God's name, was further developed by the Catholic Church of the Counter-Reformation in its numerous prescribed manuals of exorcism, not only for possessed persons, but also for poltergeists, haunted houses, and animals or humans suffering from supernaturally inflicted torments.

This ritual was not officially regarded as infallible and might fail because of the victim's sins or the bystanders' lack of faith. Nevertheless, it was believed that demons had a natural horror of the symbolism of Christianity and that the Church had been given a special power with which to cast them out (*Mark, xvi 17*). In the Middle Ages the general view seems to have been that, if all conditions were properly observed, the exorcism was much more likely than not to be successful. The application of relics or a visit to a holy shrine might also prove effective means of dispossession.

Protestant opinion, however, viewed the practice of these exorcisms with considerable hostility. The Wycliffites had denounced them as sheer necromancy, and their attitude was shared by the Protestant theologians of the Reformation era. The exorcism of the unbaptized child was abandoned in the second Edwardian Prayer Book, and the office of exorcist disappeared with the other minor orders from the Ordinal of 1550. The new theory, as stated, for example, by Bishop Jewel, was that the power to cast out devils had been a special gift, conceded in the heroic age of the early Christian Church, but no longer necessary in a time of established faith. Such miracles were over, and Christians were no longer to believe that the Devil could be frightened by holy water, the sign of the cross or the mere pronunciation of words of Scripture. Would-be exorcists were no better than vulgar wizards. "If any man amongst us should use such things," said Jeremy Taylor, "he would be in danger of being tried at the next assizes for a witch or a conjuror."

Exorcism was thus generally rejected. Yet cases of possession continued to appear. Indeed evidence has survived of more instances in the later sixteenth and seventeenth centuries than in the era before the Reformation. But what was the pious man to do in face of these diabolical assaults? He still had the protection of his faith, but there was now no automatic procedure for dealing with such cases of possession. A clergyman could no longer *command* a spirit to depart; he could only entreat God to show his mercy by taking the Devil away. Any healing, wrote an Elizabethan preacher, "is not done by conjuration or divination, as Popish priests profess and practise, but by entreating the Lord humbly in fasting and prayer". As Bishop Hall put it, "we that have no power to bid must pray".

It was difficult to bring men to accept the full implications of this new situation. The idea that a child who cried at his christening was letting out the Devil long survived the formal omission of the exorcism from the baptism service. For a time, moreover, it seemed that the Protestant remedy of fasting and prayer might well be developed into a ritual claiming something very near mechanical efficacy. For all their rejection of what they regarded as the "foul superstition and gross magic" of the Catholic ritual of exorcism, the Puritans laid much stress on the efficacy of this alternative procedure, founded on the words of *Mark ix, 29* ("This kind can come forth by nothing, but by prayer and fasting"). The century after the Reformation was to witness many cases of alleged diabolical possession in which Puritan ministers diagnosed the malady, entered into discourse with the devil, and triumphantly ejected it after fasting and prayer.

The true nature of these supposed examples of possession is difficult for us to establish without clinical evidence. The affliction does not seem to have been confined to persons of any particular age, sex or social origin, and the concept was almost certainly extended to embrace maladies of widely different kinds. What is noticeable is the way in which the symptoms became stereotyped to conform to popular conceptions of what they should be. One victim's description of Satan as "an ugly black man with shoulders higher than his head" is typical, and in the account of a case in 1573 the possessed person is revealingly said to have been "monstrously transformed ... much like the picture of the Devil in a play". The influence of Continental cases of possession is also discernible. The two physicians who diagnosed a Hertfordshire girl's possession in 1664 had been to France, where they had seen a whole convent of possessed nuns.

A conspicuous feature of the cases of possession about which details survive is that they frequently originated in a religious environment. Indeed it could be plausibly urged that the victims were engaging in a hysterical reaction against the religious discipline and repression to which they had been subjected. The Devil's presence was particularly likely to be suspected when the patient could not bear the sight or sound of religious objects and language; and exposure to prayer or religious ritual became a litmus-paper test of whether or not the patient was possessed. It was reported of James Barrow in 1663 that, "if any other did take the Bible and mention the word God or Christ in his hearing, he would roar and cry, making a hideous noise". The boy Thomas Darling in 1596 only felt his fits come on when he was forced to take part in a prayer-meeting. The ex-bailiff of Dunwich, Thomas Spatchet, found himself unable to take part in religious exercises. The Worcestershire girl Joyce Dovey's fits came on at prayer-time. So did those of the Throckmorton children at Warboys. Such cases recall the preacher Thomas Hall, whose devil-inspired insomnia was at its worst on the eve of the sabbath, or the Puritan, Richard Rothwell, who knew that he was obsessed by Satan because of an overpowering urge to blaspheme and reproach religion.

An intensive régime of religious observance could thus provoke a violent reaction. In France the best-known cases of possession occurred in the nunneries for the same sort of reason. As Freud pointed out, demons were "bad and reprehensible wishes, derivations of instinctual impulses that have been repudiated and repressed". He himself regarded diabolical possession as a form of neurosis, associated with unconscious homosexual desires. More recent psychiatrists have considered it to be a severe type of schizophrenia. Whatever its clinical nature, the consequences of possession are unmistakable. It provided both an explanation and a legitimation of the kind of unconventional behavior which would not otherwise have been tolerated. When a possessed person burst forth with blasphemies and obscenities no one subsequently reproached him for doing so. Nor was the child who rebelled against his religious upbringing by hurling a Bible across the room liable to be punished, so long as it was the Devil who was to blame. On the contrary the child would become the centre of a dramatic ritual of prayer and healing in which he was treated with affectionate concern. To be the victim of possession was a means of expressing forbidden impulses and attracting the attention of otherwise indifferent or repressive superiors.

It is not therefore surprising that so many cases of possession should have been reported among the Puritans and Dissenters. Possession was seldom diagnosed in circles where religion was regarded as a thing indifferent, and it was frequently the godly or ex-godly who were afflicted, their hysterical symptoms returning instantly upon the sight of a preacher or prayer-book. . . .

For most of those living in the immediate aftermath of the Reformation the existence of evil spirits was still a reality. It was also a peril against which the clergy seemed to have abandoned their traditional defence. Apart from those Puritans who put their faith in fasting and prayer, most Protestants seemed content to let the power of exorcism become a Roman Catholic monopoly. They were prepared to seek God's help in cases of supposed possession, but their prayers held no guarantee of success. Faced by such gloomy counsel, the laity reacted differently. Some turned to wizards and charmers, in the hope that they might perform the role from which the clergy had abdicated. Others became their own exorcists; when Margaret Hooper, a yeoman's wife, was possessed in 1641, her husband and brother summoned their courage and successfully conjured the Devil to depart in the name of the Father, Son and Holy Ghost. Others were driven back upon miscellaneous folk remedies. In 1653 at Oxford the young Anthony Wood, suffering from the ague, was told that the disease was caused by a devil, and that the proper course of action was to jump into the river, and then run quickly out, leaving the evil spirit to drown. A variety of charms and amulets were also used in an effort to gain the protection from demons which religion no longer afforded.

By abandoning so crucial a task as the expulsion of devils, the Protestant clergy were jeopardising their prestige. It was easy for educated contemporaries like John Selden to scoff at exorcism as "mere juggling", invented to gain respect for the clergy; but, as Selden himself observed, the clergy enjoyed less respect among ordinary Anglicans than among Puritans or Catholics. In Popish countries the peasants' belief in the priest's magical resources helped to sustain the prestige of organised religion.

"If once a priest could bring his parishioners to believe this power of exorcism", declared a writer in 1712, "I don't doubt but in time he might graft more pretended miracles upon that stock and set up at last driving away the plague, curing cattle of the murrain, boast of a sovereign remedy against the toothache, recover lost goods, and, in short, be resorted to as a prophet upon all occasions."

In England the medieval stories of sufferers cured by relics and images had not been forgotten. They were still the subject of popular literature and commemorated in the sculpture and carvings of many village churches. Some nostalgia for Catholic times was inevitably generated. "In Queen Mary's days," complained an old woman in the seventeenth century, "churchmen had more cunning and could teach people many a trick that our ministers nowadays know not."

28

Witchcraft in New England

CHADWICK HANSEN

Chadwick Hansen was among the first modern scholars to seriously question the traditional view of the Salem episode — of which Charles Upham is a major example — that no magic was being produced in Massachusetts, that the girls were pretending, and that the clergy whipped up the hysteria. Other scholars have since doubted some of the details of Hansen's conclusions, but all accept his premise that practicing witches existed. This excerpt is from his 1969 book Witchcraft at Salem, *which has gone through innumerable printings and is still available in paperback.*

•

It should be noted that the convulsive fits which played so prominent a part in most witchcraft cases, and continued to be one of the most common symptoms of hysteria through the early years of the twentieth century, have now become relatively rare in Western civilization.

D. W. Abse reports fits occurred in only six out of one hundred and sixty-one cases of hysteria treated at a British military hospital during World War II, but that they were the most common symptom among Indian Army hysterics treated at Delhi during the same period. There are a number of possible explanations for this curious fact. Hysterics are notoriously suggestible, so the change may be ascribable to nothing more than the refusal of our culture to give the hysterical fit the respectful and awed attention it used to command. In any case, it seems clear that abnormal behavior varies with time and place just as normal behavior does. But since this particular variation occurred so recently, and after the classic studies of hysteria had been completed, it is possible to identify the seventeenth-century Massachusetts fits for what they were. . . .

In Boston, in midsummer of the year 1688, four previously well-behaved children of a "sober and pious" mason, John Goodwin, began to have "strange fits, beyond those that attend an epilepsy, or a catalepsy." The words are those of Cotton Mather. Mather was a medical student before he was a minister, and a far more careful

From Chadwick Hansen, *Witchcraft at Salem* (New York: George Braziller, 1969), 19–28. © 1969 by Chadwick Hansen. Reprinted by permission of George Braziller.

observer than he has been given credit for. He spent a great deal of his time with the Goodwin children and he has left us a thorough account of their symptoms in his *Memorable Providences*. . . .

The symptoms [he describes] are those of the hysteric: the convulsive movements, the distorted postures, the loss of hearing, speech, sight, and so forth. The fits had started immediately after one of the children had quarreled with an Irish washer-woman, whose mother, Goodwife Glover, "a scandalous old woman" whose late husband had complained about the neighborhood "that she was undoubtedly a witch," had "bestowed very bad language upon the girl."

The neighbors advised the family to try white magic, but the pious father, John Goodwin, refused to traffic with the occult. He consulted first with "skillful physicians," particularly with Dr. Thomas Oakes, who gave his opinion that "nothing but an hellish witchcraft" could be the cause of the children's afflictions. Next he turned to the Boston clergy, who held a day of prayer at the Goodwin house, after which one of the four children was permanently cured. And finally he entered a complaint against Goodwife Glover with the magistrates. When they examined her she "gave such a wretched account of herself" that they committed her to jail under indictment for witchcraft. . . .

To determine whether or not the plea should be insanity, the defendant was examined by a committee of physicians, who agreed that she was sane. Plainly Goodwife Glover believed that she had made a pact with Satan. When she was asked who would stand by her, she attempted to call Him, and she was overheard at night, in her cell, berating Him for having abandoned her. But what is most important is that her witchcraft plainly worked, and in no indiscriminate fashion. When she tormented one of her dolls, one of the Goodwin children "fell into sad fits." When it is remembered that in a society which believes in witchcraft the violent hysterical symptoms to which the Goodwin children were subject not infrequently terminate in death, it cannot be said that the Boston court acted either harshly or unjustly. Indeed, when one considers the ferocity of seventeenth-century English law, simple hanging seems almost a lenient sentence.

Cotton Mather visited Goodwife Glover twice in jail after she had been condemned, and made a serious effort to convert her. Her Prince, he told her, had cheated her, to which she answered, " 'If it be so, I am sorry for that!' " He "set before her the necessity and equity of her breaking her covenant with Hell, and giving herself to the Lord Jesus Christ by an everlasting covenant." She answered that he "spoke a very reasonable thing, but she could not do it." He asked if he might pray for her, to which she answered that "If prayer would do her any good, she could pray for herself." He asked again for her permission to pray, and she replied that she could not give it unless her "spirits" would give her leave—"spirits," or "angels," or "saints"; she spoke only in Irish, the language she had also used at the trial, and the translator told Mather that the Irish word would bear any of those translations. He prayed for her anyway, and when he was through she thanked him for it. But, he wrote, "I was no sooner out of her sight than she took a stone, a long and slender stone, and with her finger and spittle fell to tormenting it; though whom or what she meant, I had the mercy never to understand." . . .

When she was on her way to the gallows she announced that the children's afflictions would not cease at her death, because others had a hand in the witchcraft as well as she. The afflictions did continue, but Mather kept the names the witch had mentioned to himself, presumably on the grounds that one should not accept the testimony against others of a confessed witch. After all, the Devil was, as Mather often called him, "the Prince of Lies," and this woman had been his worshipper.

The children's fits continued more violently than ever, except that the boy could be given sporadic relief by striking at the specters which he saw. The theory was that if you could hit the specter you could injure the witch, and on one occasion it was reported "that a wound was this way given to an obnoxious woman in the town." Again Mather refused to make the name public, "for we should be tender in such relations, lest we wrong the reputation of the innocent by stories not enough inquired into."

Eventually Mather took the eldest Goodwin girl into his own home, partly in an attempt to cure her through prayer and fasting, and "also that I might have a full opportunity to observe the extraordinary circumstances of the children, and that I might be furnished with evidence and argument as a critical eye-witness to confute the sadducism of this debauched age." He was always the scholar; he recognized that this was a classic case and had already determined on publishing an account of it in an attempt to convert materialists to the belief in an invisible world.

The girl provided a thorough display of symptoms. Most of them we have noticed before, but there were others as well. Her belly would swell "like a drum, and sometimes with croaking noises in it"; on one such occasion Mather was praying for "mercy on a daughter vexed with a Devil," and "there came a big, but low voice from her, saying, "There's two or three of them' (or us!)." One of her more grotesque hallucinations was riding on a spectral horse. She would go through the motions of riding, and at the conclusion of one such spell she announced that she had been to a witch meeting, and had learned who was the cause of her affliction. There were three of them, she said. She named them, and announced that " 'if they were out of the way, I should be well.' " But Mather made no move to put them "out of the way." After all, this was a girl through whom Devils were speaking, and so once more he kept the names of the accused to himself.

The girl was able to get relief from her afflictions in Mather's study. She believed, to his mixed embarrassment and pleasure, that God would not permit her Devils to enter there. One of her more curious symptoms was "flying"; "she would be carried hither and thither, though not long from the ground, yet so long as to exceed the ordinary power of nature in our opinion of it." There is probably nothing more to this "flying" than the violence of motion we have seen in the fits throughout. Yet it may not be so simple; levitation was reported on another occasion when the record is less easy to explain. . . .

A persistent symptom was her inability to pray, or to hear prayers said on her behalf, or to read Puritan religious works. "A popish book . . . she could endure very well," and she was able to read "whole pages" of "a Quaker's-book," although she could not read the words "God" or "Christ" but skipped over them. "When we urged her to tell what the word was that she missed, she'd say, 'I must not speak it; they say I must not, you know what it is, it's G and O and D.' " She could not read the Bible, and if someone else read it, even silently, "she would be cast into very terrible agonies." Puritan catechisms had the same effect; the Assembly's Catechism or Mather's grandfather John Cotton's catechism for children, *Milk for Babes*, "would bring hideous convulsions on the child if she looked into them; though she had once learned them with all the love that could be."

American historians have made themselves merry over this particular symptom, suggesting that a Puritan catechism was enough to give anybody convulsions. But such suggestions only demonstrate the incapacity of these historians to understand a culture whose central concerns were religious. This girl had been piously raised in a pious society and believed herself afflicted by devils and witches; her inability to speak the name of God or to read the religious books her society believed in must have been a terrifying ordeal to her; her spelling God's name and reading Quaker and Catholic books were clearly substitutes. Breuer and Freud report an exactly parallel case in their *Studies in Hysteria*:

> A very distressed young girl, while anxiously watching at a sick bed, fell into a dreamy state, had terrifying hallucinations, and her right arm, which was at the time hanging over the back of the chair, became numb. This resulted in a paralysis, contracture, and anesthesia of that arm. She wanted to pray, but could find no words [i.e., in her native language, German], but finally succeeded in uttering an English children's prayer. Later, on developing a very grave and most complicated hysteria, she spoke, wrote, and understood only English, whereas her native tongue was incomprehensible to her for a year and a half.

Anyone who has had the common and terrifying dream in which one cannot speak or move will know something of how the elder Goodwin girl felt when she found she could not pray or read the Bible—but only something of it, since the dream lasts only for a moment and the girl's symptom lasted for months. It seems, in fact, to have been prayer that cured her—not her own, but that of Cotton Mather and other well-meaning members of the community who occasionally joined him. Then, according to Thomas Hutchinson, who published his *History of the Province of Massachusetts-Bay* in 1750:

> The children returned to their ordinary behavior, lived to adult age, made profession of religion, and the affliction they had been under they publicly declared to be one motive to it. One of them I knew many years after. She had the character of a very sober virtuous woman, and never made any acknowledgment of fraud in this transaction.

Hutchinson was a typical eighteenth-century rationalist, who thought all witchcraft a matter of fraud, so his testimony to the woman's later character is particularly valuable. In an early draft of his account of this case he tells us that she was one of his tenants, but unfortunately he does not tell us whether she was the child who had been under the care of Cotton Mather.

The Glover case was classic. While it was still going on Joshua Moodey wrote to Increase Mather: "It is an example in all the parts of it, not to be paralleled." Cotton Mather took the occasion to preach to his congregation a "Discourse on Witchcraft," in which a central concern was to demonstrate that prayer, faith, and a good life rather than charms were the proper "preservatives" against witchcraft. More important, however, was his use of the case as ammunition in the war of the pious against philosophical materialism.

Remember that persons skeptical of witchcraft did not doubt the practice of it, but only whether or not it worked, or worked through spiritual means. Thus the skeptic John Webster, in his *Displaying of Supposed Witchcraft*, was willing to concede that there were witches and devils who "have power to perform strange things." But he spent his twelfth chapter on the question "whether they do not bring them to pass by mere natural means." What was at issue here was the reality of the spiritual world, the "invisible world" as Mather called it. The controversy over witchcraft, therefore, raised theological issues fundamental to the seventeenth-century Christian. "We shall come to have no Christ but a light within, and no Heaven but a frame of mind," said Mather, if the materialists—the Sadducees—should succeed in destroying the belief in an invisible world.

Whatever one's own belief, or lack of it, one has to admit that he was right. In the eighteenth and nineteenth centuries scientific materialism was to triumph, and the pious were to find that all the concreteness had left their religion, leaving nothing behind but a "light within" and a "frame of mind."

Conceive, then, of Mather's excitement. At a time which he recognized to be a crisis in the history of religious belief he had discovered a clear case of witchcraft which he thought could not possibly be explained on material grounds. He made it the central matter of his *Memorable Providences* (1689), a book which he hoped might once and for all confute materialism and reestablish Christianity on the firm foundation of a real and concrete spiritual world. The book met with considerable success. Richard Baxter, one of the most distinguished English Puritans, wrote a laudatory preface to the first London edition, and in Baxter's own *Certainty of the Worlds of Spirits* (1691) he spoke of it as the ultimate proof of the existence of a spiritual world. Any doubter, he said, "that will read . . . Mr. Cotton Mather's book of the witchcrafts in New England may see enough to silence any incredulity that pretendeth to be rational."

29

Witchcraft

The "Captivity to Spectres"

Richard Slotkin

Richard Slotkin's book Regeneration through Violence *won the American Historical Society's Albert Beveridge Award in 1973. In this excerpt, Slotkin discusses the way Puritan discourse drew parallels between demons and American Indians, and between demonic possession and captivity to Indians.* Regeneration through violence *is the first volume of a trilogy on myths, violence, and the American frontier. The other volumes are* The Fatal Environment: The Myth of the Frontier in the Age of Industrialization, 1800–1890 *(1985) and* Gunfighter Nation: The Myth of the Frontier in Twentieth Century America *(1992). Slotkin, a professor of English and American studies, is also the author of two novels on the subject of race and violence.*

•

In the summer of 1692 Mercy Short, living as a servant with a Boston family and then seventeen years old, went on an errand to the jail in which accused witches were kept. (The hysteria was just then beginning to spread.) She had been captured by the Indians at her home in Salmon Falls when she was fifteen. Her father and mother and three of their children were murdered before her eyes, and she herself was carried to Canada, where she was ransomed by [Governor William] Phips the following year. Her captivity (if nothing else) might have inclined her to compassion for the accused wretches, but compassion was far from her. She cursed one old woman and was cursed in return. That night she fell into a fit that lasted for weeks, in which she neither ate nor prayed. The fit passed, then came upon her again in the winter. She lay insensible or raving, rising up once to rip a page from the minister's Bible as he read to her. Cotton Mather was called in to minister to her apparently possessed soul and rescue her from the grip of the devil. . . .

Mather clearly regarded Mercy Short's case as an archetype of New England's

From Richard Slotkin, *Regeneration through Violence: The Mythology of the American Frontier, 1600–1860* (Middletown, CT: Wesleyan University Press, 1973), 128, 131–33, 142–44. © 1973 by Richard Slotkin. Reprinted by permission of the author.

condition, and he presented it as such in *A Brand Pluck'd Out of the Burning*—a narrative of his dealings with the girl that was widely circulated in manuscript. The structural pattern invoked in this account is clearly that of the captivity narrative; but here it is transformed into a ritual exorcism of an Indian-like demon from the body of the white, female "Saint." . . .

Mather begins his account by briefly sketching the pattern of Mercy Short's captivity. The pattern contains all those elements . . . typifying the captivity narratives, and special emphasis is placed on the destruction of her family:

> MERCY SHORT had been taken Captive by our cruel and Bloody Indians in the East, who at the same time horribly Butchered her Father, her Mother, her Brother, her Sister, and others of her Kindred and then carried her . . . unto Canada: after which our Fleet Returning from Quebeck to Boston brought them with other Prisoners that were then Redeemed.

The captivity pattern thus invoked is echoed in the account of her early seizures. After her first "Distinct and Formal Fits of Witchcraft" had apparently remitted, she went to church on a Sabbath in company with her master and mistress. There the malignant spirits came on her suddenly and unexpectedly; like the victims of King Philip's War described by Increase Mather, she was surprised in church on the Lord's day and unexpectedly plunged into torments. The weight of association and implication in these first pages of the narrative points the reader directly toward the conclusion that Mather himself explicitly draws soon after taking up the case: that Mercy Short is undergoing a second captivity, is being held by "Barbarous Visitants" in a "Captivity to Spectres."

Mather begins his treatment of the girl by questioning her (as she lies in a swoon) about the character and appearance of her devils. Her response again suits both Mather's expectations and those of his readers:

> There exhibited himself unto her a Divel having the Figure of a Short and a Black Man; . . . he was a wretch no taller than an ordinary Walking-Staff; hee was not of a Negro, but of a Tawney, or an Indian colour; he wore an high-crowned Hat, with straight Hair; and had one Cloven-foot.

He was, in fact, a figure out of the American Puritan nightmare of Thomas Morton's day: Indian-colored, dressed in a Christian's hat, with a beast's foot—a kind of Indian-Puritan, man-animal half-breed.

Under the watchful eyes of Cotton Mather, Mercy Short relives the events of Indian captivity. Sometimes the devils pinch her, bite her, or slash her skin, as the Indians did to their captives as they fled northward from Salmon Falls. Like the Indians, the devils force her to fast; like the pious Jesuits or Abnakis, they forbid her her English prayers, her Bible, and the speaking of holy names. . . . Instead of unquiet dreams, she falls into seizures and fits of increasing violence. Instead of acknowledging the world's vanity, she plunges through the physical world directly into the underlying, supernatural abyss. She is not simply critical of the ministry: she rejects all sacred words, accuses her elders and ministers of hypocrisy or infidelity, and blasphemes—all under the "compulsions of the Devil." She herself is not responsible for these things: she refused to sign the devil's book and so retains her place with the elect. Her vagaries express the devil's malice not her own. This, at least, is Mather's conclusion. . . .

A comparison of Mather's psychoanalytic technique with that of the Indians (who were great students of dreams and dream therapy) further illuminates the depth of the struggle between the "American" and "European-Christian" cultures in the New World and the values and practices that were at stake in the contest. Mather entered the wilderness of the human mind bent on extirpating its "Indians," exorcising its demons. These Indian-demons were the impulses of the unconscious—the sexual impulses, the obscure longings and hatreds that mark parent-child relationships, the proddings of a deep-rooted sense of guilt. The goal of his therapy was to eliminate these impulses, to cleanse the mind of them utterly, to purge it and leave it pure. In much the same way he wished to purge the real wilderness of Indians, to raze it to ashes and build an utterly new world, uncorrupted by a primitive past, on the blank of the old.

The Indian attitude toward the mind likewise resembled their attitude toward the wilderness. Just as they worshiped every aspect of creation and creatureliness, whether it represented what they called good or what they called evil, so they accepted every revelation of the dreaming mind as a message from a god within, a world spirit manifested in the individual. They responded to the dreams of individuals as a community, seeking to assimilate the dream-message into their own lives and to help the dreamer accept the message of the dream for himself. . . .

Like the Puritans, the Iroquois were fascinated by the terror and the attractiveness of being bound helpless as a captive to terrible antagonists. They too were obsessed by dreams of captivity, of enforced passivity before the malice and power of the wilderness or their enemies. The terrified Indian in such a dream was the obverse of the masterful, all-powerful Indian of the waking world, the world of war and hunting. Similarly, the cowed Puritan of the Sunday jeremiad or the captivity narrative was likely, on the battlefield, to respond to Indian savagery with savagery in kind, to meet massacre with massacre, burning with burning, atrocity with atrocity. The Puritan could never understand the nature of the relationship between these two faces of his character, and he was certainly unable to see this as proof of his human kinship with the Indians. Yet the consequences of this psychological kinship might have been a warning to him.

Like the Puritans, the Indians developed an elaborate community ritual for exorcising nightmares of captivity. That ritual was a ceremonial reenactment of the nightmare itself. In one such ritual, observed among the Huron in 1642, a man who dreamed that he had been captured was made to suffer ordeals like those put upon captives by the Iroquois. Finally a dog was substituted for the "captive" and killed and eaten (as the Iroquois were said to eat their human captives). A Jesuit named Lalemant observed similar ceremonies among the Iroquois in 1661–62: "One man, in order to satisfy the dictates of his dream, had himself stripped naked by his friends, bound, dragged through the streets with the customary hooting, set upon the scaffold, and the fires lit. 'But he was content with all these preliminaries, and, after passing some hours in singing his death-song, thanked the company, believing that after this imaginary captivity he would never be actually a prisoner.' " Mather's use of literally imagined captivities was meant to serve a similar function.

Like the Indians in their dream dance, the Puritans entered into and participated in the dream life of Mercy Short and the other "possessed" girls and exalted them to a level equivalent to members of the medicine society, with the task of witchfinding (an honored profession among the Indians). They came to this participation through the persistent invocation (by Mather and Mercy Short) of the myth of the captivity. It becomes increasingly clear in Mather's narrative that he and his society have internalized the captivity myth, made it a part of their mental vocabulary, and that the girl's ravings strike a chord of recognition in their hearts to which they cannot help but respond. When she cries out that the devils are forcing poison down her throat, Mather and his fellows feel fingers thrusting against the hand they place to block her mouth. When she cries that the devils are rushing about the room, people feel themselves pushed about. Whether through the deliberate malice of her inverted view of the world or through the genuine activity of her psychosis, she makes the healers dance about the room at her whim, crying out that the devils are over here, or down there, and bidding the people strike about them in the air with swords, which they do. . . .

The crowning irony of the witchcraft delusion is that the Puritans' hysterical fear of the Indian devils led them to behave precisely like the Indians. The Indians traditionally feared the exercise of black art among them, since a warrior slain by witchcraft would be denied glorification in the afterlife. His blood would not mingle with the earth after battle, but he would be blasted and withered like a diseased plant. Mrs. Mary Jemison, a captive and adopted Indian, wrote in 1824 that she had known brothers to slay one of the fraternity for having killed a number of deer when no other of the expedition could bag one. Like Rev. Burroughs's feats of strength, this was taken as proof of an inhuman power. An ancient chief of the Senecas, who quarreled with the other elders in council, was condemned as a witch because he could not "account for" his long span of life in any specific way. But if the Puritans realized that their fears had led them into behaving like the Indians they rejected, they gave no sign of it. Although Puritan writers frequently mentioned that the Indian religion was a witch-religion, they never equated the Indian casting out of witches with their own. . . .

The more experience the Puritans acquired in the New World, the more they had to recognize the power of the Indian to live on viable terms with the wilderness, to succeed where traditional European civilization failed. The longer they stayed in the Indian's world, the more they felt themselves succumbing to the Indian mind, the wilderness mind. There was warrant in the experience of Indian-fighting soldiers for the notion of an Indian familiar in the frontiersman's heart. The experience of [John] Underhill at the Pequot fort [battle during the Pequot War, 1637] was repeated numerous times during King Philip's War [1675–76]. After a long march through the threatening woods and the fury of a desperate battle, white troops would become hysterical with rage and massacre the Indian wounded, women, and children with a fury unmatched even by the Indians themselves. To the returning soldier, this hideous lapse from civilized self-restraint would remain a guilty memory, requiring explanation and justification. Such a transformation was psychologically unacceptable. It was easier to explain the lapse in terms of the spell of the Indian's wilderness, a sudden infection of the Christian soul by an Indian familiar or demon.

As we have seen in the case of Mercy Short, New England's response to this "infection" was an attempt at ritual exorcism in terms suggested by the captivity mythology and the psychological ambience that surrounded it. Exorcistic psychotherapy applied to Mercy Short was intended to rid her—and symbolically New England—of the Indian demon. In fact, however, the ritual and the captivity mythology on which it is based reveal New England's psychological unity with the Indian in responding to the wilderness environment. . . . Like the Puritan, the Indian felt the need to surrender his will to a stronger will, to place himself beneath a powerful protector, to be captive instead of captor; and this state of mind was reflected in his dreams. . . .

The other side of this duality in Indian psychology is reflected in his treatment of prisoners, his apparent delight in prolonged torture. The warrior, newly escaped from death in battle or on the trail, had to reassert the masculine powers that recent experiences had tested and threatened. He did so by inflicting on his defeated enemy the very torments he had feared for himself, thus exorcising his fears for the moment. This, as we have seen, was also a Puritan response to stress: the massacre of those who threatened massacres, the magical exorcism of those who used black magic.

The Puritan situation differed in some respects from that of the Indian. The Puritan was nominally a subject being—subordinate to and dependent on God, the church, and the magistral authority—and conscious of his subordination. Life in the New World stimulated his repressed dreams of heroism and tempted him to play a titan's part in the conquest of the wilderness, to win and savor the strange rewards of the Indian's world. Those who consented in the repression of this ambition could find support in the public rituals and the public mythology of the captivity. Those who succumbed to the spell of the wilderness and followed the Indian's path could find in the captivity myth and ritual the same solace that the self-reliant Indian found in succumbing to his dreams of passivity and enjoining the tribe to enact his dream wishes for him.

The response of Puritan society, however, went far beyond ceremonial confirmation or reenactment of the dream of captivity. In the hands of the ministers and magistrates, such dreams became a weapon for enforcing a social and psychological regimen in Puritan America. Instead of seeking in the Indian manner to balance the desire for heroic activity with the dream desire for passive submission to authority, the Puritans sought to subordinate the former to the latter. Mather's treatment of Mercy Short and his use of her case to invigorate the witch-hunt is most revealing in this connection. He mustered the forces of nightmare, of the Puritan's captivity- and Indian-haunted dreamworld, for an assault on the active, outgoing, wilderness-seeking component of the Puritan mind and society. Yet he did it all in the name of exorcizing evil dreams and the Indian-like primitive inclinations of mind and soul that are expressed in dreams.

IV

Gender

THERE IS NO QUESTION that from the time of the fifteenth-century witchhunts on the Continent, more women than men were executed for witchcraft. Witch hunting had apparently become woman hunting. The reasons are various—that there was a change in the status of women that threatened men, that women had always been hated and feared because of their power of creation and witch scares offered new opportunities to attack them, that Protestantism unleashed a new wave of antifeminine feeling. The multiplicity of explanations does not necessarily indicate a lack of agreement among scholars. Like many other issues in social history, the explanations are so complex that individual scholars focus on particular aspects of their subject. The synthesis will come later after many local studies and many single causes are examined and analyzed.

Among the sources used by historians who study ideas about women are commentaries from those who wrote on the subject of witchcraft. I have included three of those primary sources, written by men who assumed there was a connection between women and witchcraft: the *Malleus Maleficarum*, a selection by the New England Puritan Cotton Mather, and another by his fellow minister, Samuel Willard.

The *Malleus Maleficarum*, the major handbook on witches and witchcraft, is especially vitriolic in its condemnation of female behavior and social roles. In this selection the inquisitors have a great deal to say about why women are more likely to consort with the devil than men. When describing the qualities of a witch, the *Malleus* identifies what were assumed to be facets of the female personality with those of witches. Or possibly it was the reverse: because witches were noted for such moral defects, it was assumed that women, those other wicked creatures, were more likely to have them. Wherever women held sway in their society—from handling household affairs to the birth and rearing of infants—they could be blamed for catastrophe. Women were suspected in the deaths of infants and all kinds of misdeeds in the care of children and the preparation of food. But they could also come under suspicion for causing storms and other natural disasters. The witch emerges from this antiwoman tirade as the typical female.

Although there is no doubt that misogyny is a major theme of the entire work, much of what is reported is in line with the generally assumed characteristics of women in that late medieval society. It is no surprise to read that they believed women were supposedly more wicked, more prone to lying and deception, more credulous, more vain, more passionate in hates, and, worst of all, suffering from insatiable sexual desires. It should be noted that until the nineteenth century it was generally assumed that women were more passionate sexually than men. The asexual female of the so-called Victorian period was a creation of that era. The earlier view of women's sexuality, as we read in the *Malleus*, was quite different.

A good part of this handbook on witchcraft is concerned with sexual matters. It particularly focuses on blaming female witches for inflaming the desires of men and for being responsible for male impotence. Women, according to this account (with the exception of the few who were truly virtuous and therefore identified with the Virgin Mary), were inherently wicked creatures in the tradition of a biblical Eve, the sorceress who tempted not just with the apple but also with her body.

Puritans discounted much of this openly misogynist rhetoric and rejected the Eve metaphor. According to Puritan theory women were essential to the preservation of family life as "helpmeet" and sexual partner, as household manager and mother. For Puritans the hierarchical structure of the family itself—with father as the main authority, wife as second-in-command but subservient to her husband's will, and children and servants obedient to parents and masters—became a model for the individual's relationship to secular and religious authorities as well as to God. Puritans had approved of satisfying sexual relations within marriage as a way to reinforce marital bonds and promote harmony within the family as well as to encourage pregnancy. New England Puritans, it should be noted, were unique among Englishmen in forbidding wife beating. The early 1641 compilations of laws in Massachusetts declared that "Every married woman shall be free from bodily correction or stripes by her husband, unless it be in his own defense upon her assault."

Nonetheless, elements of misogynist beliefs did persist. Cotton Mather's advice to women in *Ornaments for the Daughters of Zion*, first published in 1692, was an attempt to refute those older ways of thinking, to elevate what were, in his day, the positive feminine attributes of energetic praying, fear of God, and obedience to husbands. Women were expected to and did provide kindness and charitable treatment of others, pay attention to their children, and take part in industrious household occupations. If they did not fulfill these expectations, it was, Mather announced, because they had succumbed to the lures of the devil. Thus the witch, in an echo of the thinking in the *Malleus*, was one who exhibited behaviors that were the opposite of his virtuous female. A preoccupation with dancing, dress, or adornment was a sign of spiritual sickness. A woman was either virtuous, as the Puritans defined such behavior, or a witch. It is not surprising that those confessing to witchcraft often described the sins that attracted the devil in Mather's terms—giving in to temptations of vanity, indulging in sexual license outside marriage, or violating social class expectations.

The delicate balancing act of elevating women while believing in their potentially diabolical susceptibility was the theme of Samuel Willard's sermons during the early months of the 1692 witch scare in Salem. He more than Mather set out the specific sins that made women more likely to attract the devil. Nonetheless he repeats the Puritan maxim regarding the important role of women as helpmeets to men and emphasizes the mutual enjoyment of the marital relationship. Nonetheless, his depiction of a woman on the precipice of ruin, a potential defiler of men, harks back to the wicked Eve of the *Malleus*.

The six commentaries that follow explore these beliefs about the nature of women and their connection to the concept of the witch. Norman Cohn links the misogyny of the *Malleus* with popular notions about women; he argues that the woman as witch theme was not invented by the inquisitors, but has its own long history in the folklore of the European peasantry. These biases merely received a theological gloss from the writings of the churchmen. What is clearly reflected in the *Malleus*, then, are Europeans' long-held common assumptions about women.

According to Allison P. Coudert, factors related to the rise of Protestant churches contributed another dimension to these notions of the evil woman. She sees a connection between the stereotype of the witch as an "old, disruptive, and sexually threatening woman" and the religious conflicts during the early years of the Reformation. Of particular concern to her are those aspects of Protestant theology that while seemingly raising the status of women, thrust them into the role of potential witch. Courdert suggests, contrary to the view of other historians, that elevating the position of the family in society actually threatened male authority in that hierarchical system and that by discounting the cult of the Virgin and the female saints, Protestants eliminated an important female role model for both men and women. Thus, she notes, the worst witch hunts, occurring in the newly Protestant countries, singled out women more than in previous episodes.

Looking further into the Protestant concept of the female witch, Elizabeth Reis considers the gender distinctions and sexual imagery found in the writings of the New England theologians. She too finds that the Puritans could not get away from the older stereotype of the female witch but, she argues, it came not from theology but from the "gendered nature of their social universe" that had relegated women to the inferior social position and assumed their inherent physical weakness.

Nonetheless, Reis suggests a specifically Puritan explanation for why women were so likely to be accused of witchcraft. It was not that women were inherently sinful because of Eve's transgressions, as Catholics asserted. After all, Puritans found no gender differences before God; men and women were equally depraved in Calvinist theology and they had equal chances of being chosen for salvation. Puritans added a new twist to that reputed equality by suggesting, at least in their sermons, that their souls were equally feminine and, therefore, all frail, submissive, and passive. Thus the souls of men and women were equally susceptible to satanic assaults, but because Satan tortured the body to capture that soul, men's stronger bodies offered more protection. Women, the weaker physical vessels according to theories of the time, were more accessible to diabolical influence.

How did that diabolical influence reflect itself in the female character? Jane Kamensky, focusing on Cotton Mather's description of the virtuous woman, pursues the idea of a relationship between speech patterns and witchcraft accusations. In the process she analyzes the cultural meaning of the spoken word in the seventeenth-century New England world. The Puritans stressed the role of speech in establishing or destroying a reputation and believed that women's conversational habits were a window onto their characters. Puritans endowed words with extraordinary power and by inference the witch's words with the ability to cause harm. While the manner of speaking as well as the content of speech became evidence against an accused female witch, it was not usually held against men. It was not artifacts and images as much as her words that could condemn a woman.

Kamensky reminds us that the power of words to hurt was taken seriously in the Puritan environment; with our emphasis on the value of free speech today, we have lost part of that sense of the importance and potency of words. On the other hand, in our contemporary concern with hate speech and sexual harassment issues, we may be reviving that older view that words can cause as much harm as weapons.

On the more mundane level of economics and in an equally intriguing thesis from her work on the relationship of womanhood, witchcraft, and religion, Carol F. Karlsen finds a property basis for many accusations of witchcraft against women in colonial New England. It was not a violation of class norms, she says, but a violation of gender norms regarding the ownership of property that may have precipitated such accusations of witchcraft. The economic basis of witchcraft was not so much a class conflict as a conflict over whether a woman had a right to own property.

Karlsen does not question that those accused did exhibit offensive behavior such as disruptive speech, lewdness, criminal acts, and sometimes sexual license or that they had abrasive personalities. What distinguished those unpleasant women who were brought to trial for witchcraft from the ones who were not was the potential to own property. They were women without sons or husbands. Whether consciously or not, these women interfered with the orderly transfer of property from one male to another down through the generations. It was not a question of social class, age, or widowhood—she finds both poor and wealthy women of all ages in this group and, of course, widows without sons would be the most likely to inherit land. The significant factor was that potentially inheriting women, in this society that reserved that privilege to men, were the most likely to find themselves in danger.

Christina Larner asserts that the witch hunters in Scotland were more concerned with theological conformity than a general antifemale bias. Many poor abrasive women were not accused, and many freely practicing charmers, soothsayers, and the like in the highlands of Scotland were not labeled witches. This suggests to her that there was a broader sociopolitical goal in witch hunting than woman hating. She does acknowledge, however, the apparent misogyny expressed in witch accusations. It was, she suggests, not women as such but those who challenged patriarchal views of the ideal submissive and dependent female in a world that was beginning to permit women a more independent role.

PRIMARY SOURCES

[30]

Why Women Are Chiefly Addicted
to Evil Superstitions

Heinrich Krämer and Jacob Sprenger

Krämer and Sprenger's Malleus Maleficarum *(1486) was introduced in part 1. Many vitriolic commentaries about women are scattered throughout the work, but this section specifically focuses on women and their relationships with the devil. Some of the examples and references to authorities have been omitted for the sake of brevity.*

•

Concerning Witches Who Copulate with Devils
Why It Is That Women Are Chiefly Addicted to Evil Superstitions?

There is also, concerning witches who copulate with devils, much difficulty in considering the methods by which such abominations are consummated. On the part of the devil: first, of what element the body is made that he assumes; secondly, whether the act is always accompanied by the injection of semen received from another; thirdly, as to time and place whether he commits this act more frequently at one time than at another; fourthly, whether the act is invisible to any who may be standing by. And on the part of the women, it has to be inquired whether only they who were themselves conceived in this filthy manner are often visited by devils, or, secondly, whether it is those who were offered to devils by midwives at the time of their birth, and, thirdly, whether the actual venereal delectation [pleasures] of such is of a weaker sort. But we cannot here reply to all these questions. . . . Therefore, let us now chiefly consider women and first, why this kind of perfidy is found more in so fragile a sex than in men. And our inquiry will first be general, as to the general conditions of women; secondly, particular as to which sort of women are found to be given to superstition and witchcraft and thirdly, specifically with regard to midwives, who surpass all others in wickedness.

From Heinrich Krämer and Jacob Sprenger, *The Malleus Maleficarum*, translated with an introduction, bibliography, and notes by Montague Summers (1486; London: Pushkin Press, 1948), 41–48, 66, 140–44.

Why Superstition Is Chiefly Found in Women

As for the first question, why a greater number of witches is found in the fragile feminine sex than among men, it is indeed a fact that it were idle to contradict, since it is accredited by actual experience. . . . And without in any way detracting from a sex in which God has always taken great glory that His might should be spread abroad, let us say that various men have assigned various reasons for this fact. . . .

For some learned men propound this reason—that there are three things in nature, the tongue, an ecclesiastic, and a woman, which know no moderation in goodness or vice and when they exceed the bounds of their condition, they reach the greatest heights and the lowest depths of goodness and vice. When they are governed by a good spirit, they are most excellent in virtue but when they are governed by an evil spirit, they indulge the worst possible vices.

This is clear in the case of the tongue, since by its ministry most of the kingdoms have been brought into the faith of Christ and the Holy Ghost appeared over the Apostles of Christ in tongues of fire. . . . It is also a matter of common experience that the tongue of one prudent man can subdue the wrangling of a multitude. . . .

But concerning an evil tongue, you will find in *Ecclesiasticus* xxviii: "A backbiting tongue hath disquieted many, and driven them from nation to nation. Strong cities hath it pulled down, and overthrown the houses of great men." And by a backbiting tongue it means a third party who rashly or spitefully interferes between two contending parties. . . .

Now the wickedness of women is spoken of in *Ecclesiasticus* xxv: "There is no head above the head of a serpent" and "there is no wrath above the wrath of a woman. I had rather dwell with a lion and a dragon than to keep house with a wicked woman." And among much which in that place precedes and follows about a wicked woman, he concludes, "all wickedness is but little to the wickedness of a woman." Wherefore St. John Chrysostom says on the text (*S. Matthew* xix), "It is not good to marry. What else is woman but a foe to friendship, an unescapable punishment, a necessary evil, a natural temptation, a desirable calamity, a domestic danger, a delectable detriment, an evil of nature, painted with fair colours! Therefore if it be a sin to divorce her when she ought to be kept, it is indeed a necessary torture. For either we commit adultery by divorcing her, or we must endure daily strife." Cicero in his second book of *The Rhetorics* says, "the many lusts of men lead them into one sin, but the one lust of women leads them into all sins; for the root of all woman's vices is avarice." . . .

But for good women there is so much praise, that we read that they have brought beatitude to men, and have saved nations, lands, and cities; as is clear in the case of Judith, Debbora, and Esther. . . . See *Ecclesiasticus* xxvi: "Blessed is the man who has a virtuous wife, for the number of his days shall be doubled." And throughout that chapter much high praise is spoken of the excellence of good women. . . .

And all this is made clear also in the New Testament concerning women and virgins and other holy women who have by faith led nations and kingdoms away from the worship of idols to the Christian religion. . . . Wherefore in many vituperations that we read against women, the word woman is used to mean the lust of the flesh. As it is said, "I have found a woman more bitter than death, and a good woman subject to carnal lust."

Others again have propounded other reasons why there are more superstitious women found than men. And the first is that they are more credulous and since the chief aim of the devil is to corrupt faith, therefore he rather attacks them. . . . The second reason is that women are naturally more impressionable and more ready to receive the influence of a disembodied spirit and that when they use this quality well, they are very good, but when they use it ill, they are very evil.

The third reason is that they have slippery tongues, and are unable to conceal from their fellow-women those things which by evil arts they know and, since they are weak, they find an easy and secret manner of vindicating themselves by witchcraft. . . .

There are also others who bring forward yet other reasons, of which preachers should be very careful how they make use. For it is true that in the Old Testament the Scriptures have much that is evil to say about women, and this because of the first temptress, Eve, and her imitators, yet afterwards in the New Testament we find a change of name, as from Eva to Ave (as S. Jerome says), and the whole sin of Eve taken away by the benediction of MARY. Therefore preachers should always say as much praise of them as possible.

But because in these times this perfidy is more often found in women than in men, as we learn by actual experience, if any one is curious as to the reason, we may add to what has already been said the following: that since they are feebler both in mind and body, it is not surprising that they should come more under the spell of witchcraft.

For as regards intellect, or the understanding of spiritual things, they seem to be of a different nature from men, a fact which is vouched for by the logic of the authorities backed by various examples from the Scriptures. . . .

But the natural reason is that she is more carnal than a man, as is clear from her many carnal abominations. And it should be noted that there was a defect in the formation of the first woman, since she was formed from a bent rib, that is, a rib of the breast, which is bent as it were in a contrary direction to a man. And since through this defect she is an imperfect animal, she always deceives. . . . And this is shown by Samson's wife who coaxed him to tell her the riddle he had propounded to the Philistines, and told them the answer, and so deceived him. . . . And all this is indicated by the etymology of the word; for *Femina* comes from Fe and *Minus*, since she is ever weaker to hold and preserve the faith. And this as regards faith is of her very nature although both by grace and nature faith never failed in the Blessed Virgin even at the time of Christ's Passion when it failed in all men.

Therefore, a wicked woman is by her nature quicker to waver in her faith and, consequently, quicker to abjure the faith, which is the root of witchcraft.

And as to their other mental quality, that is her natural will, when she hates someone whom she formerly loved, then she seethes with anger and impatience in her whole soul just as the tides of the sea are always heaving and boiling. Many authorities allude to this cause. *Eccesiasticus* xxv: "There is no wrath above the wrath of a woman." And Seneca (*Tragedies*, VIII): "No might of the flames or of the swollen winds, no deadly weapon, is so much to be feared as the lust and hatred of a woman who has been divorced from the marriage bed." . . .

And indeed, just as through the first defect in their intelligence they are more prone to abjure the faith, so through their second defect of inordinate affections and passions they search for, brood over, and inflict various vengeances, either by witch-craft or by some other means. Wherefore it is no wonder that so great a number of witches exist in this sex.

Women also have weak memories and it is a natural vice in them not to be disciplined but to follow their own impulses without any sense of what is due. . . . If you hand over the whole management of the house to her, but reserve some minute detail to your own judgment, she will think that you are displaying a great want of faith in her and will stir up strife, and, unless you quickly take counsel, she will prepare poison for you and consult seers and soothsayers and will become a witch.

If we inquire, we find that nearly all the kingdoms of the world have been overthrown by women. Troy, which was a prosperous kingdom was, for the rape of one woman, Helen, destroyed, and many thousands of Greeks slain. The kingdom of the Jews suffered much misfortune and destruction through the accursed Jezebel and her daughter Athaliah, Queen of Judah, who caused her son's sons to be killed that on their death she might reign herself. Yet each of them was slain. The kingdom of the Romans endured much evil through Cleopatra, Queen of Egypt, that worst of women. . . .

And now let us examine the carnal desires of the body itself, whence has arisen unconscionable harm to human life. . . . A woman is beautiful to look upon, contaminating to the touch, and deadly to keep.

Let us consider another property of hers, the voice. For as she is a liar by nature, so in her speech she stings while she delights us. Wherefore her voice is like the song of the Sirens, who with their sweet melody entice the passers-by and kill them. . . .

Let us consider also her gait, posture, and habit, in which is vanity of vanities. There is no man in the world who studies so hard to please the good God as even an ordinary woman studies by her vanities to please men. . . .

I have found a woman more bitter than death who is the hunter's snare and her heart is a net and her hands are bands. He that pleaseth God shall escape from her, but he that is a sinner shall be caught by her. More bitter than death, that is, than the devil. . . .

And that she is more perilous than a snare does not speak of the snare of hunters, but of devils. For men are caught not only through their carnal desires, when they see and hear women. . . .

To conclude. All witchcraft comes from carnal lust, which is in women insatiable. . . . Wherefore for the sake of fulfilling their lusts they consort even with devils. More such reasons could be brought forward, but to the understanding it is sufficiently clear that it is no matter for wonder that there are more women than men found infected with the heresy of witchcraft. . . .

What Sort of Women Are Found to Be above All Others Superstitious and Witches?

As to our second inquiry, what sort of women more than others are found to be superstitious and infected with witchcraft, it must be said as was shown in the preceding inquiry, that three general vices appear to have special dominion over wicked women, namely, infidelity, ambition, and lust. Therefore, they are more than others inclined towards witchcraft, who more than others are given to these vices. Again, since of these three vices the last chiefly predominates, women being insatiable, etc., it follows that those among ambitious women are more deeply infected who are more hot to satisfy their filthy lusts; and such are adulteresses, fornicatresses, and the concubines of the Great.

Now there are, as it is said in the Papal Bull, seven methods by which they infect with witchcraft, the venereal act, and the conception of the womb—first, by inclining the minds of men to inordinate passion; second, by obstructing their generative force; third, by removing the members accommodated to that act; fourth, by changing men into beasts by their magic art; fifth, by destroying the generative force in women; sixth, by procuring abortion; seventh, by offering children to devils, besides other animals and fruits of the earth with which they work much harm. . . .

Concerning those who are bewitched into an inordinate love or hatred, this is a matter of a sort that it is difficult to discuss before the general intelligence. Yet it must be granted that it is a fact. For S. Thomas (IV, 34) . . . shows that God allows the devil greater power against men's venereal acts than against their other actions and gives this reason, that this is likely to be so since those women are chiefly apt to be witches who are most disposed to such acts.

For he says that since the first corruption of sin by which man became the slave of the devil came to us through the act of generation, therefore greater power is allowed by God to the devil in this act than in all others. Also the power of witches is more apparent in serpents, as it is said, than in other animals because through the means of a serpent the devil tempted woman. For this reason also, as is shown afterwards, although matrimony is a work of God, as being instituted by Him, yet it is sometimes wrecked by the work of the devil. Not indeed through main force, since then he might be thought stronger than God, but with the permission of God, by causing some temporary or permanent impediment in the conjugal act. . . .

And would that this were not true according to experience. But indeed such hatred is aroused by witchcraft between those joined in the sacrament of matrimony, and such freezing up of the generative forces, that men are unable to perform the necessary action for begetting offspring. . . .

That Witches Who Are Midwives in Various Ways Kill the Child Conceived in the Womb, and Procure an Abortion; or If They Do Not This, Offer New-Born Children to Devils

Here is set forth the truth concerning four horrible crimes which devils commit against infants, both in the mother's womb and afterwards. And since the devils do these things through the medium of women, and not men, this form of homicide is associated rather with women than with men. And the following are the methods by which it is done. . . .

It is witchcraft, not only when anyone is unable to perform the carnal act, of which we have spoken above, but also when a woman is prevented from conceiving, or is made to miscarry after she has conceived. A third and fourth method of witchcraft is when they have failed to procure an abortion, and then either devour the child or offer it to a devil. . . .

The former of these two abominations is the fact that certain witches, against the instinct of human nature and indeed against the nature of all beasts with the possible exception of wolves, are in the habit of devouring and eating infant children. And concerning this, the Inquisitor of Como, who has been mentioned before, has told us the following: that he was summoned by the inhabitants of the County of Barby to hold an inquisition, because a certain man had missed his child from its cradle, and finding a congress of women in the night-time, swore that he saw them kill his child and drink its blood and devour it. . . . We must add that . . . witch midwives cause yet greater injuries, as penitent witches have often told to us and to others, saying: "No one does more harm to the Catholic Faith than midwives. For when they do not kill children, then as if for some other purpose, they take them out of the room and, raising them up in the air, offer them to devils." . . .

How Witch Midwives Commit Most Horrid Crimes When They Either Kill Children, or Offer Them to Devils in Most Accursed Wise [i.e., ways]

We must not omit to mention the injuries done to children by witch midwives, first by killing them, and secondly by blasphemously offering them to devils. . . . For in the diocese of Basel at the town of Dann, a witch who was burned confessed that she had killed more than forty children, by sticking a needle through the crowns of their heads into their brains, as they came out from the womb. . . . Another woman in the diocese of Strasburg confessed that she had killed more children than she could count. . . .

Now the reason for such practices is as follows. It is to be presumed that witches are compelled to do such things at the command of evil spirits, and sometimes against their own wills. . . . And also, as has already been shown, witches are taught by the devil to confect from the limbs of such children an unguent which is very useful for their spells.

But in order to bring so great a sin into utter detestation, we must not pass over in silence the following horrible crime. For when they do not kill the child, they blasphemously offer it to the devil in this manner. As soon as the child is born, the midwife, if the mother herself is not a witch, carries it out of the room on the pretext of warming it, raises it up, and offers it to the Prince of Devils, that is Lucifer, and to all the devils. And this is done by the kitchen fire. . . .

To what end or purpose is this sacrilegious offering of children, and how does it benefit the devils? To this it can be said that the devils do this for three reasons, which serve three most wicked purposes. . . . They try as far as possible to conform with divine rites and ceremonies. Secondly, they can more easily deceive men under the mask of an outwardly seeming pious action. . . . In this oblation of children they deceive the minds of witches into the vice of infidelity under the appearance of a virtuous act. And the third reason is that the perfidy of witches may grow, to the devils' own gain, when they have witches dedicated to them from their very cradles. . . .

But there is this distinction to be observed in innocent children who are offered to devils not by their mothers when they are witches, but by midwives who, as we have said, secretly take [them] from the embrace and the womb of an honest mother. Such children are not so cut off from grace that they must necessarily become prone to such crimes, but it is piously to be believed that they may rather cultivate their mothers' virtues. . . .

When a witch offers a child to the devil, she commends it body and soul to him as its beginning and its end in eternal damnation; wherefore not without some miracle can the child be set free from the payment of so great a debt. . . .

We may well conclude that such children are always, up to the end of their lives, predisposed to the perpetration of witchcraft. For just as God sanctifies that which is dedicated to Him as is proved by the deeds of the Saints when parents offer to God the fruit which they have generated, so also the devil does not cease to infect with evil that which is offered to him. . . .

Finally we know from experience that the daughters of witches are always suspected of similar practices, as imitators of their mothers' crimes; and that indeed the whole of a witch's progeny is infected. And the reason for this and for all that has been said before is, that according to their pact with the devil, they always have to leave behind them and carefully instruct a survivor, so that they may fulfill their vow to do all they can to increase the number of witches. For how else could it happen, as it has very often been found, that tender girls of eight or ten years have raised up tempests and hailstorms, unless they had been dedicated to the devil under such a pact by their mothers. For the children could not do such things of themselves by abjuring the Faith, which is how all adult witches have to begin, since they have no knowledge of any single article of the Faith.

[31]

The Character of a Virtuous Woman

COTTON MATHER

Cotton Mather, whose work has been excerpted in parts 1 and 3, published Ornaments for the Daughters of Zion *in 1692, the year of the Salem witch hunts, Mather's
advice to women, contrasting the virtuous woman with the devil's handmaiden, was
so popular that it went through three editions. This selection is taken from the third
edition, published in Boston in 1741.*

•

The favour whereas a virtuous woman has a particular distaste, is that which promiscuous dancing is applauded for. The exercise of promiscuous dancing is that
which pretends to be a piece of breeding which demands the favour of womankind;
but a virtuous woman esteems them deceived who count it so; nor will she affect
such an Exercise. . . . The Reverend Assembly of Divines, in their larger Catechism,
very justly mention dancings among the things forbidden in the seventh Commandment of our God. Nor does the levity of dancings, wherein persons leap and fling
about so like Bedlam, that the wisest men have called it a regular Madness, now
agree well with the gravity which holiness is to be accompanied withal. Such things
as these are enough to make a virtuous woman to discard such dancings from among
the things of good report; and leave them either to the pagans, whose manner it was
to dance in the worship of Bacchus, or to the monkeys, whom of old they brought
forth to dance at the festival of Diana. . . . In the primitive times, more than one or
two of the Fathers thundered against them as a diabolical practice: and whole Synods
did prohibit the usage of them even at weddings as well as at other seasons. . . . The
most eminent Reformers above an hundred Years ago, concurred in witnessing
against these Dances, as an unlawful recreation. . . .

The Beauty whereof a virtuous woman hath a remarkable dislike is that which

From Cotton Mather, Ornaments for the Daughters of Zion, or The Character and Happiness of a
Virtuous Woman: *In a Discourse Which Directs the Female Sex How to Express the Fear of GOD in
Every Age and State of Their Life; and Obtain Both Temporal and Eternal Blessedness* (1692), 3d ed.
(Boston, 1741; facsimile), 12–16, 19–20, 46–48, 54–55, 57–63. Reprinted by permission of Scholar's
Facsimiles (1978).

make-up

hath artificial painting in it. The usage of artificial painting is practiced by many women who think thereby to be valued for a beauty, which they are not really the owners of. But a virtuous woman will not be guilty of such a vanity. There is a wicked book that pleads for this ungodly practice, but that good lady uttered the language of a virtuous woman upon reading such a book: "O Lord, I thank thee, that thou gavest me not wit enough to write such a book unless withal thou hadst given me grace enough not to write it." Although it be not unlawful for a person transiently to preserve or to restore her native complexion by convenient medicines when she is in any special danger of losing it, yet for a person to paint herself that she may make some ostentation of a complexion which God has not made her the owner of, it is a thing that has heard ill among the most godly Christians. Nor will a virtuous woman easily be reconciled unto it. . . .

The fear of God is that which the heart of a virtuous woman is under the power of. The female sex is naturally the fearful sex; but the fear of God is that which exceeds (and sometimes extinguishes) all other fears in the virtuous woman. . . . It may then be said of a virtuous woman that she is a religious woman; she has bound her self again to that God, whom she had by the sin and fall of her first mother departed from. . . .

The petulant pens of some forward [i.e., perverse] and morose men, have sometimes treated the female sex with very great indignities—blades, I guess, whose mothers had undutiful children, or whose wives have had but cruel masters. I am loath to show my catalogue, nevertheless, whole volumes have been written to disgrace that sex, as if it were, as one of those unnatural authors call it, "the mere confusion of mankind." Yea, it is not easy to recount how many licentious writers have handled that theme, *femina nulla bona*, No woman is good! (or the men were bad that said so.) But behold how you may recover your impaired reputation! The fear of God will soon make it evident that you are among the excellent in the earth. If any men are so wicked (and some sects of men have been so) as to deny your being rational creatures, the best means to confute them, will be by proving your selves religious ones. . . .

When the golden-mouthed ancient [i.e., St. John Chrysostom] had so far forgot himself as to call a woman an unavoidable punishment, a necessary evil, a desirable calamity with more such iron words, he sees cause to add: *sermo est de maliere mala*; —my speech is of a bad woman and not of a good, for I have known many ready to every good work. It is an observation of Solomon's which has been somewhat improved against you in *Ecclesiastics*. 7.28, "One man among a thousand have I found, but a woman among all those have I not found." Nevertheless, in your own vindication, you may reply that Solomon speaks of what is usual about the courts of princes; and perhaps about his own court especially. A good man in such a place is a rare thing; but a good woman there, is a black swan indeed; Solomon himself particularly had a thousand women to satiate his exorbitant lust and possibly he may intimate that among all those he did not find one woman truly virtuous.

Or if this reply be not satisfactory, you may enquire, whether Solomon spoke not of such as are by repentance recovered from the snares of whoredom when once they have been therein entangled. For a man to be reclaimed from the sin of uncleanness when once he has been given there unto is rare, but for a woman to be snatched out of the unclean devil's hands, when once he has had any full possession of her, is more extraordinary! However it be, it is plain that as there were three Maries to one John standing under the cross of our dying Lord, so still there are far more godly women in the world, than there are godly men; and our church communions give us a little demonstration of it. I have seen it without going a mile from home that in a church of between three or four hundred communicants, there are but few more than one hundred men; all the rest are women, of whom charity will think no evil. . . .

While you thus maintain the fear of God, let it very particularly discover itself in your keeping the purpose of the Psalmist, "I will take heed unto my ways that I sin not with my tongue; I will keep my mouth with a bridle." May it be as much a causeless, as it is a common report, concerning you that your tongues are frequently not so governed by fear of God, as they ought to be. The faculty of speech is of such a noble and of such a signal figure in the constitution of mankind, that it is a thousand pities, it should be abused; but womankind is usually charged with a peculiar share in the world's abuses of it. . . .

Your speech ought likewise to be rare like silver, which is not so common as copper or iron is. Be careful that you don't speak too soon, because you cannot fetch back and eat up what is uttered, but study to answer. And be careful that you don't speak too much because that when the chest is always open every one count there are no Treasures in it. And the Scriptures tell us it is the whore that is clamorous and the fool that is full of words. . . .

There is one particular thing more which you shall see that your fear of God extends itself unto [and] that that is your apparel, which you are often accused for transgressing in. Where the fear of God sanctifies the heart, it will doubtless regulate the habit. . . .

For a woman to expose unto common view those parts of her body, which there can be no good end or use for the exposing of, is for her to expose her self unto the vengeance of heaven. . . . The face is to be naked because of what is to be known by it, the hands are to be naked because of what is to be done by them. But for the nakedness of the back and breasts, no reason can be given unless it be that a woman may by showing a fair skin enkindle a foul fire in the male spectators for which cause even Popish writers have no less righteously than severely lashed them. And for Protestant women to use them is no less inexcusable than it is abominable; nor did a golden mouth of old stick to say, "The Devil sat upon them." . . .

For a woman to wear what is not evidently consistent with modesty, gravity, and sobriety is to wear not an ornament, but a defilement and she puts off those glorious virtues when she puts on the visible badges of what is contrary thereunto. . . .

The ranks of people should be discerned by their clothes, nor should we go in any things but what may be called suits. The woman which will go as none but those who are above her do or can, shows herself to be as much out of her wits as out of her place. And she that will not cut her coat according to her cloth, does but put a fool's coat upon her. She that will have more on her back than can readily come out of her purse deserves to be stript as the fine jay was of her borrowed feathers. . . .

For a pious woman to preserve no distinction from a debauched one in her apparel, where it may be done, is to leave herself without a distinction, which might preserve her when the common and wasting judgments of God are punishing the strange apparel in her neighbourhood. It was well advised by Tertullian to the Matrons in his Days, . . . that the handmaids of God would go so as to distinguish themselves from the handmaids of the Devil.

[32]

Two Sermons on Women and the Devil

Samuel Willard

Samuel Willard, whose account of Elizabeth Knapp's possession was excerpted in part 3, delivered, these sermons in Boston during the early weeks of the 1692 witch fear in Salem. He also observed and mildly criticized the methods used in the trials.

•

Sermon 52, March 22, 1692

We are now to proceed to consider the *blamable causes of the apostacy*: and these are reckoned to be either the *instrumental* or the *principal*. The ground of this distribution is because man fell by temptation, therefore the tempters are reckoned as instruments in this affair. And yet, because they could but tempt and he had a power of resistance, there is an higher cause than they. And because it is their duty not to tempt him, and his not to be tempted by them, both are therefore blamable.

First, We may begin with the *Instrumental*, because they were leading: and these are reckoned to be three, viz, the *Devil*, the *Serpent*, and the *Woman*. . . .

Here then,

I. The first of these is *the Devil*, who was the leader in the Temptation; and though he be not named in the history of man's doleful fall, Gen. 3, yet he is plainly intimated. . . . *The devil was not a necessary compelling cause, but only a counseling and tempting agent about the fall of man.* And for this reason he is called the Tempter, Math 4.3. because that is the trade which he is always driving and by which he draws men to destruction. . . .

Hereupon he offers the fruit to them in its loveliness. *Gen. 3.6. The woman saw that the tree was good for food, and that it was pleasant to the eye, and a tree to be desired to make one wise.* q.d. See what a beautiful thing it is, look over all that garden, observe if you can find such another, and it must needs have some secret strange virtue in it.

From Samuel Willard, *A Compleat Body of Divinity in Two Hundred and Fifty Expository Lectures on the Assembly's Shorter Catechism* (Boston, 1726), 180, 183–85.

Use I. Learn hence, *what are the sins which make us most like the devil and let it put us upon hating of them.*

There is *pride*, this was his master sin and when you shew most pride in your look, in your talk, in your garb, in your carriage to others, the more devil-like you appear.

There is *discontent* at the state and place God set us in, thinking it beneath us and below those endowments and abilities that we have. We think our selves better than some whom God hath preferred to us, either in honour, esteem, preferment, or wealth, and now we murmur and fret.

There is *malice* and envying others the favour bestowed on them by God and thereupon studying and endeavouring to undermine them, to blast them, looking upon them with an evil eye, wanting to do them a mischief.

There is *lying*, a being given to a spirit of it and driving of a trade of equivocations, falsehoods, and endeavours to deceive others with our impostures.

There is *blasphemy* in aspersing the glorious name of God with reproaches, and casting vile reflections upon any of his precious attributes.

There is *seduction*, improving of our wit to draw others into sin, to study devices, and lay fears to entrap their souls withal.

And there is *murder*, whether of soul or body, by endeavouring to ruin them. All these are specially satanical sins, by them the fallen angels made themselves devils and they that live in them. . . .

Sermon 53, April 19, 1692

The last instrumental cause of the Transgression, was the *Woman*. She is reckoned among the instrumental causes because the devil in the serpent first tempted her and by her the Man. Although she may also be accounted to the *principal* cause; in as much as the first man and woman were the root of mankind, from whence all were to derive and in that respect were looked upon as one. . . . And though their prohibition be expressed as given to Adam in the singular. *Gen.* 2.16, 17. the Lord God commanded the man, etc. yet Eve understood it as comprehending them both. Gen. 3.3. God *hath* said, ye shall not eat. She also was a cause by counsel in which she did. Yet, looking upon her as made for the man, and by the Creator's law owing a subordination to him so she may also be looked upon as *instrumental*. And so, besides the common calamity falling upon man for sin, there was a special curse which she derived to her Sex, *Gen.* 3.16. *Unto the woman he said, I will greatly multiply thy sorrow and thy conception: in sorrow shalt thou bring forth children; and thy desire shall be to thy husband, and he shall rule over thee.* And she was in this blamable, because she acted upon deliberation and was voluntary in what she did. And there are three things here to be considered, which will shew how she was culpably instrumental in this affair.

1. She was created on purpose to be a meet help unto man. *Gen.* 2.18. *And the Lord God said, it is not good that man should be alone. I will make an help meet*

for him. Being therefore of his own species, and fitted for humane converse with him, she ought to have encouraged and fortified him in that obedience which God had required of them both. They were to take that delight one in another, which they could not find in any other creature, and were therefore mutually to conspire in the great work of glorifying and serving God, being jointly made for it.

2. *She first hearkened to the temptation of Satan.* The Apostle takes particular distinct notice of this, in 2 *Cor.* 11.3 1 *Tim.* 2.14. And we find in the history, that the serpent directly addressed himself to the woman, *Gen.* 3.1 . . . and then she subjected her understanding and will to the report of Satan and the delusion offered to her senses, *ver.* 6. by which she entertained all those senses last mentioned, 1 *Job.* 2.16. *the lusts of the flesh,* in giving way to her carnal appetite; lust for *food,* the lust of the *eye,* in entertaining the desirable aspect of the forbidden fruit, pleasant to the eyes; the lusts of *pride,* in aspiring after more wisdom than God saw meet to endow a creature withal, *to make one wise.* And these lusts so prevailed upon her, as made her to adventure upon the fruit directly against the divine precept, *she did eat.* By which act she defiled the root and fountain of humanity.

3. Now she joined with the seducer, and became a tempter of Adam to sin with her. *Gen.* 3.6. . . . And the man said: *the woman which thou gavest to be with me, she gave me of the tree, and I did eat.* She gave the fruit its commendation, which she had entertained, makes offers to him, insinuates herself into him, backs all that the serpent had said, and attracts him to a joint consent with her in the great Transgression; and by thus doing instead of being an help, she proves a mischief, and becomes an occasion, yea a blamable cause of his ruin.

Use. *The Consideration of this will tell us, what need we have to be very wary to our selves, lest Satan should use us as tools to draw one another into Sin;* and so become under devils each to other. And earnestly to pray to God, that he will preserve us: and it peculiarly concerns those whose relation and affection is most near and intimate. We have great advantage either to do good or harm unto those in whose bosoms we lie and whose affections we have the ascendant upon. If God give us wisdom and grace to use it, we have the greatest probability to procure their salvation. . . . But if we yield to the devil, there are none whom he can use more dangerously, in alluring each other to the commission of sin, and hereby to become guilty of ruining each other.

COMMENTARIES

33

The Making of the Great Witch-Hunt

Norman Cohn

Norman Cohn's 1975 book Europe's Inner Demons *was introduced in parts 1 and 2. In this excerpt he discusses the prevalence of women among accused witches and notes the persistence in peasant folklore of the idea that the typical witch was a woman.*

•

Who was selected for the role of witch? The most striking fact is the preponderance of women. Admittedly, male witches did exist. The touring storm-raisers of the early Middle Ages, who so effectively terrorized the peasants, seem to have been mostly men. But in later centuries *maleficium* at village level was almost a female monopoly.

The Lucerne material, for example, lists thirty-one women accused, and only one man—and that one was a foreigner (presumably an Italian) who could make himself understood only through an interpreter; moreover, he claimed that his *maleficia* were really performed by a woman companion. As for the Essex cases examined by Dr Macfarlane, out of 291 witches tried at the assizes between 1560 and 1680, only twenty-three were men, and eleven of these were connected with a woman. With the Trevisards of Devon, the whole family was suspect; yet there too the woman Alice seems to have been the most feared—even where the original quarrel was with one of the men, the resulting *maleficia* were sometimes attributed to Alice.

Until the great European witch-hunt literally bedevilled everything and everybody, the witch was almost by definition a woman. In fact, on the basis of the vast mass of data available, one can be rather more precise. Witches, in the sense of practitioners of *maleficia*, were usually thought of as married women or widows (rather than spinsters) between the ages of fifty and seventy. At that time one was old at fifty—and the older these women were, the greater their power was supposed to be. Some of those executed were over eighty.

Of course, not all elderly married women or widows were accused of performing

From Norman Cohn, Europe's Inner Demons: An Enquiry Inspired by the Great Witch-Hunt (New York: Basic Books, 1975), 248–52. © 1975 by Basic Books. Reprinted by permission of the Peters Fraser and Dunlop Group Limited on behalf of Norman Cohn.

maleficia; and the evidence points to certain types as particularly liable to attract suspicion. For instance, witchcraft—in the sense of the ability and will to work *maleficia*—was widely believed to run in families. In particular, the daughter of a woman who had been executed as a witch often found herself in a dangerous position. . . . In deciding to burn Dorothea, wife of Burgi Hindremstein, the town councillors of Lucerne were influenced by the fact that, years before, her mother had been burned. In fact the daughter had been harried by her mother's fate all her life. She had escaped being burned along with her mother only by fleeing from her native Canton of Uri, and suspicion followed her everywhere. However friendly Dorothea's behaviour, it was construed in the most unfavourable manner possible; she could do nothing right. Once at a carnival feast, she was able to produce a dish of millet for ten persons at short notice—and in due course this hospitable gesture was adduced as proof of her witchcraft!

With other women, it was some personal peculiarity that singled them out for suspicion. Many of those accused of *maleficia* were solitary, eccentric, or bad-tempered; amongst the traits most often mentioned is a sharp tongue, quick to scold and threaten. Often they were frightening to look at—ugly, with red eyes or a squint, or pockmarked skin; or somehow deformed; or else simply bent and bowed with age. Such women were felt to be uncanny—like the strange apparition that was seen in the Canton of Schwyz in 1506. According to a contemporary chronicler, that too was in the form of an old woman, dressed in dirty old clothes and outlandish headgear—but in addition it had great long teeth and cloven feet. Many, we are told, died of terror at the very sight of it; and plague swept through the land. The kind of imagination that could create such a being was also capable of transforming old women, weighed down by their infirmities, into embodiments of malevolent power.

Finally there were the midwives and the practitioners of folk medicine. Infant mortality was very high—and who had better opportunities than midwives for killing babies? No doubt they often did kill them, through ignorance or ineptitude. But that was not the explanation that came to people's minds; and it is striking how often the village midwife figures as the accused in a witchcraft trial.

As for the practitioners of folk medicine, they were obvious suspects. In an age when scientific medicine had hardly begun, and when professionally qualified doctors were in any case seldom available to the peasantry, the countryside produced its own medicine men or medicine women. These people were not necessarily charlatans; many of them used herbal remedies, and also techniques of suggestion, that had real therapeutic value. But some also used the techniques of magic, such as spells; moreover, their art often included divining whether a sickness was due to *maleficium*, and if so, applying counter-magic. Not surprisingly, such "white witches", male and female alike, were apt to be perceived as simply witches. After all, if a person endowed with supernatural powers failed to cure a sickness or prevent a death, might that person not actually have caused the affliction? To disappointed patients and their relatives it must have seemed obvious enough. Many "witches", under torture, confessed to using herbs, roots, leaves and powders to harm man or beast; and although that proves nothing as to their guilt, it does suggest that they were at home in folk medicine.

Such were the women whom their neighbours most easily came to think of as witches—but how did the women think of themselves? Did they feel themselves to possess some supernatural power for evil? Or were they outraged at the accusation? The answer is that both situations could occur.

The Lucerne material includes, in addition to the depositions of the accusers, some statements by the accused. Thus in 1549 Barbara Knopf of Mur was accused by several neighbours of bewitching and killing cattle, and of crippling and blinding human beings. Arrested and taken to prison, she denied every accusation and added—in the words of the magistrate—that "she had done nothing, only she had a nasty tongue and was an odd person; she had threatened people a bit, but had done nothing wicked. She desired to be confronted with those who said such things about her and she would answer them. . . ." That is how a woman arrested on a charge of *maleficium* usually reacted, when no torture was used. These answers have the ring of truth. There is in fact no reason to suppose that most women accused as witches regarded themselves as such.

But some did. As we have seen *maleficia* really were practised; some women really did try to harm or kill people or animals, or to destroy crops or property, by occult means. These things had been done since time immemorial and they were still being done during the great witch-hunt—indeed, in some remote and backward regions they are still being done today. And it is not difficult to think of one category of women who must always have been particularly tempted by such practices. "Wise women" or "white witches", who felt able to perform cures by supernatural means, must also have felt able to inflict harm by supernatural means; and some of them certainly did attempt the latter as well as the former. In the Lucerne material, the "wise woman" Stürmlin may or may not have intended to inflict impotence on the young man who had jilted her daughter and married another. But less ambiguous cases have also been recorded. In a trial in Fortrose in Black Isle, north of Inverness, in 1699, a woman boasted of her power to harm as well as to heal; thereby accusing herself, it seems, quite voluntarily. The evidence reads as follows:

> Margaret Bezok alias Kyle spouse of David Stewart in Balmaduthy declared she threatened John Sinclair using a phrase that she would quicklie overturn his cart and within a week thereafter his wife fell ill, and that she was brought to see the seek wife and touched and handled her and heard that thereafter she convalesced.
>
> John Sinclair in Miuren declared that she said Margaret did threaten ut supra and that thereafter his wife distracted within less than a week and continued in that distemper till the said Margaret was brought to see her, and that she handled and felt his wife who thereafter grew better but continues something weak still and that it is eight weeks since the first threatening.

This little tale completes nicely our picture of the traditional, age-old world of *maleficium* and *maleficium* beliefs as it existed amongst the peasantry of western Europe.

* * *

There existed, then, two completely different notions of what witches were.

For the peasantry, until its outlook was transformed by new doctrines percolating from above, witches were above all people who harmed their neighbours by occult means; and they were almost always women. When the authors of the *Malleus Maleficarum* produced quasi-theological reasons to explain why witches were generally female, they were simply trying to rationalize something which peasants already took for granted.

Why was it taken for granted? The answer has sometimes been sought in the circumstances of village life in the early modern period. It has been argued that, as the traditional sense of communal responsibility declined, elderly women who were unable to provide for themselves came to be felt as a burden which the village was no longer willing to shoulder; or else that spinsters and widows increased so greatly in number that they came to be felt as an alien element in a society where the patriarchal family still constituted the norm. Such factors may well have provided an additional impetus for witch-hunting in the sixteenth and seventeenth centuries, but they certainly do not fully account for the notion that the witch is, typically, a woman. At least in Europe, the image of the witch as a woman, and especially as an elderly woman, is age-old, indeed archetypal.

For centuries before the great witch-hunt the popular imagination, in many parts of Europe, had been familiar with women who could bring down misfortune by a glance or a curse. It was popular imagination that saw the witch as an old woman who was the enemy of new life, who killed the young, caused impotence in men and sterility in women, blasted the crops. And it was also popular imagination that granted the witch a chthonic quality. The *Malleus* again reflects a popular, not a theological belief when it recommends that a witch who is to be taken into custody should first be lifted clear of the earth, to deprive her of her power.

The other notion of the witch came not from the peasantry but from bishops and inquisitors and—to an ever-increasing degree—from secular magistrates and lawyers. Admittedly, rural magistrates were often themselves of peasant origin; but they were literate, which meant that a view of witchcraft which was enshrined above all in written texts was current amongst them, and in this view a witch was above all a member of a secret, conspiratorial body organized and headed by Satan. Such a witch could just as well be a man as a woman, and just as well young as old; and if, in the end, most of those condemned and executed as witches were still elderly women, that was the result of popular expectations and demands. . . . The earliest witch-trials were quite free from such one-sidedness; and still at the height of the great witch-hunt, in the sixteenth and seventeenth centuries, many men, young women and even children were executed.

34

The Myth of the Improved Status of Protestant Women

The Case of the Witchcraze

ALLISON P. COUDERT

The historian Allison P. Coudert's scholarly work has focused on the subject of magical rituals and mystical learning. In this excerpt from a 1989 essay, she discusses aspects of Protestant ideology that contributed to the harshness of the witch hunts in Protestant countries. Among Coudert's other publications are Alchemy : The Philosopher's Stone *(1980) and* Leibniz and the Kabbalah *(1995). She is presently working on a "biography" of the devil.*

•

Belief in witches and witchcraft has existed in just about every society and every part of the world. But only in Christian Europe and Christian America, where witchcraft was characterized as heresy, did witch beliefs lead to a "witchcraze" responsible for the death of between 60,000 and 200,000 people.

The witchcraze was not the product of ignorance and superstition. It occurred during the period described as the scientific revolution and age of triumphant rationalism. During the same years that Kepler discovered the elliptical orbits of the planets and Galileo formulated the law of inertia, while Montaigne wrote his skeptical essays and Descartes forever changed the way men perceived the world, unrecorded numbers of women (including Kepler's mother) were accused of witchcraft, pricked, racked, and stappadoed until they confessed they were indeed the Devil's disciples, at which point they were burned at the stake or hanged. In 1602 the witch hunter Henri Boguet announced that a vast host of 1,800,000 witches threatened Europe, a more formidable army than any Europe had ever experienced in its long history of warfare.

Boguet was a lesser light among a galaxy of geniuses who believed in witchcraft and actively supported witch hunts. That the witch hunters and witch theorists were for the most part educated, intelligent men proves that the witchcraze was not an aberrant event or throwback to outmoded occult beliefs, but integral to the scientific revolution. The evolution of modern concepts of science was in fact encouraged by the scientific debate prompted by the investigation of witchcraft allegations. Since the witchcraze cannot be dismissed as an anachronism in an age otherwise remembered for its scientific discoveries, we must ponder what made intelligent, educated men view witches as so terrifyingly real during this relatively brief period in Western history. This is a crucial issue, for while witchcraft beliefs were prevalent in Europe among Christians (who had inherited them from the ancient world), the full-blown stereotype of the witch as a poor, old, disruptive, and sexually threatening woman did not appear until the late fifteenth century. Before then, witches could be either male or female, and they were often well-born, if not noble. But by the sixteenth century, when the witchcraze begins, the witch appears as an old, wizened crones. During the period of the witchcraze (roughly between 1570 and 1700) witch hunting became more gender specific than ever before: between 71 and 92 percent of those accused, tried, and executed were women. We are therefore faced with the problem of trying to understand why poor, old women became suddenly threatening.

Historical explanations of the witchcraze reveal much about the biases of historians. Eighteenth-century philosophers, for example, blamed superstitious peasants. Protestants blamed Catholics and Catholics Protestants. The polemical and tendentious nature of most studies of witchcraft led Erik Midelfort to protest in 1968 that "more pure bunk" had been written about witchcraft than about any other field in history. But in the last twenty years a reverse of Gresham's law has taken effect: the good scholarship has edged out the bad. The recent emphasis on the newer fields of social history, popular history, family history, women's history, the history of childhood, and psychohistory has thrown new light on the dark episode of the witchcraze.

With all the new material available it may seem perverse that this paper resurrects the old thesis that the witchcraze was more severe in Protestant than Catholic countries. But it is precisely because of this new wealth of scholarly material that I wish to do so. I do not propose, however, to resuscitate the old partisan debate between Catholic and Protestant scholars. My intention is rather to enumerate specific aspects of the Reformation period in general and of Protestant ideology in particular that made the image of the female witch more threatening than ever before. I add the proviso that, while I will be emphasizing what seems to me to be the intensified misogyny accompanying the period of the witchcraze, I do not believe that misogyny by itself explains the witchcraze. Misogyny was not a new phenomenon, but large numbers of women were not always burned at the stake. The politics, economics, and intense religious conflicts of the Reformation period, together with changes in the law, combined to focus misogyny in the image of the witch in this one relatively short period. In this discussion, I will not distinguish among the various denominations of Protestants. When it came to women, there was a remarkable (in every other respect unheard of) consensus. . . .

The majority of witches were past child-bearing age and a good percentage were unmarried, widowed, living alone. Among the younger witch suspects, a significant number, were charged with sexual crimes—fornication, adultery, abortion, or infanticide—or had given birth to illegitimate children. *Motherhood*

This profile of the witch holds true for both Catholic and Protestant countries, yet witches were treated far more leniently in those areas in which the Catholic Inquisition was firmly entrenched, Spain, Italy, Portugal, than in Protestant and Catholic countries beyond the jurisdiction of the Inquisition. In his study of the Basque witchcraft trials, Gustav Henningsen describes the scrupulous care and leniency with which the Spanish Inquisition handled most cases involving witchcraft accusations. In a later study Conteras and Henningsen contend that the Spanish Inquisition did not authorize the burning of a single witch after 1610, even though the number of cases involving magicians and witches increased after that date. These findings are further corroborated by William Monter and John Tedeschi's study of the Italian Inquisitions. While they have discovered that Italian Inquisitors became increasingly preoccupied with superstition, magic, and witchcraft in the 1570s through the 1600s, these crimes were treated with surprising leniency: witchcraft was rarely punished with death, and first offenders who repented were not turned over to civil authorities. Carlo Ginzburg's study of the Benandanti documents the quite extraordinary patience and leniency with which Italian Inquisitors treated this sect of self-proclaimed witches.

What factors combined, then, to make the figure of the witch especially menacing to Protestants? First, the devil and his servants, the witches, were more conspicuous and menacing figures for Protestants than for Catholics. Second, there was an ambiguity and tension in Protestant ideology about women that made Protestant women appear more threatening than their Catholic counterparts. Third, the lack of a centralized institution, such as the Inquisition or Parlement of Paris, to handle witchcraft cases in many Protestant countries meant that witchcraft trials were more subject to the views of individual magistrates and consequently more susceptible to the local hysteria generated by witch panics.

*   *   *

To establish the context for the witchcraze, it is important to recognize that the Reformation and Counter-Reformation periods witnessed a new and unparalleled, concern with order and orthodoxy. The breakdown of social, political, and religious consensus was paralleled by the collapse of traditional intellectual and scientific systems. Fascination with monsters, amazons, hermaphrodites, prodigies, apparitions, comets, and, witches in short with everything "unnatural," was indicative of the profound anxiety awakened by the destruction of existing categories. New categories without ambiguity had to be imposed or created. Questions of identity and especially of gender identity were involved in these larger issues. . . .

While problems of order and disorder and the issue of identity affected both Catholics and Protestants, I would argue that Protestants were affected disproportionately. For Protestants were instrumental in the dissolution of the old order, as

Catholics never tired of reminding them. They had rejected one authority, that of the Church, and one father, the Pope. They were therefore constrained to establish a new order and authority and to construct a new identity that would justify their rebellion. Both activities involved rejection and reconstruction. The avenue that this took was twofold, an excoriation of the Catholic Church as the embodiment of all that was corrupt, evil, and sinful, and the imposition of a new order based on rigid notions of patriarchal authority and obedience. The violence of the Protestant rejection of the Catholic Church in terms of both verbal invective and the physical destruction of Church property helped to create the sense of identity that Protestants were seeking. As I will argue in this paper, the Protestant construction of a new order and belief system had a profound and, in the short term, detrimental effect on women. For women in general and the witch in particular were at the core of the "other" against which Protestant males defined themselves. Just as a humanist like Erasmus deline-ated the proper behavior of young males as a mean between two poles, effeminacy on the one hand and bestiality on the other, so too did Protestants. But for Protes-tants there was a tendency for this polarity to collapse into the single figure of the unruly witch, who was both female and bestial.

The polarization of the sexes was symptomatic of the kind of dualism character-izing early modern thought as a whole and religious thought in particular. The tendency to see things in the black and white terms of good or bad, for or against, orthodox or heretical, lawful or illegal was further encouraged by millenarian and apocalyptic thought. In the two generations preceding the Reformation, apocalypti-cism spread, contributing to the sense of doom and expectation that set the stage for the Reformation proper. Although millenarianism transcended denominational boundaries, it flourished with particular intensity among Protestants, contributing to and confirming their preoccupation with sin and the devil. Believing that they were living in the last dark days before the defeat of the Antichrist and arrival of the Messiah, Protestant millenarians were anxious to do all they could to hurry the process along by helping to institute God's kingdom on earth. Before the "godly" could rule, however, the "ungodly" had to be instructed, disciplined, and, if all else failed, exterminated. The complacency and downright pleasure with which religious people accepted the misfortunes and even the deaths of those with whom they disagreed can only be understood in the context of the religious fanaticism and millenarianism promoted by the Reformation and subsequent wars of religion. . . .

The devil assumed a centrality in Protestant thought that he never achieved in Catholic dogma. Luther, Calvin, and their followers emphasized that the life of a true Christian was one of perpetual struggle against a demonic "other," and, at the same time, they removed the supports of priests and saints. The devil's ascendancy in Protestant thought is reflected in the immense popularity of a new genre of popular literature, the devil book. In its most common form the devil book singled out a particular vice, smoking, drinking, dancing, swearing, or gambling, and showed how devilish it was; other strategies involved exposing how powerful and ubiquitous the devil and his followers were. . . . The sale of devil books was forbidden in Catholic countries, and although they were smuggled in and read by Catholics, devil books were a characteristically Protestant form of literature.

The difference between the Protestant and Catholic attitude toward the ancient idea of a demonic pact provides another indication of the heightened fear of the devil in Protestant thought. The prominence of covenant theology in Protestantism had its dark side. If a covenant was possible between man and God, a diabolical one was equally possible. Such a pact did not even require a formal declaration, simply the intention to sin or indulgence in vice. A comparison of stories involving diabolical pacts, that of Theophilius, a monk, and Dr. Faustus, illustrates how much harder it was for Protestants to renounce a pact once made. The Catholic church told men exactly how to cheat the devil by calling on the Virgin or the saints. Theophilius followed instructions and was saved; Faustus, for whom recourse to the Virgin was out of the question, suffered a horrible death and went to Hell.

The debate over magic that began with the rediscovery of Neoplatonic, Hermetic, and Kabbalistic texts in the Renaissance also had repercussions affecting subsequent Protestants attitudes towards witchcraft. Many Protestants identified Hermetic and esoteric natural magic with the magical aspects of Catholic sacraments and ritual. Their wholesale rejection of magic, together with a providential view of natural events, had important implications for the conception of the witch; for these ideas predisposed many Protestants to accept the "new" definition of a witch as an essentially powerless creature controlled by the devil. The definition of a witch as powerless, first set forth by the Catholic authors of the notorious *Malleus Maleficarum*, became the hallmark of Protestant beliefs about witches. Unlike the medieval stereotype of the witch—the stereotype which continued to serve the Catholic Inquisition—the "new" witch possessed no potions, unguents, books, or spells. Her powers were strictly unnatural and diabolical. Not only did the idea that witches were the unwitting dupes of the devil accord with the Protestant emphasis on the power of God and impotence of man, but it also implied that even evil, threatening, and castrating women, were ultimately controlled by men, something that many Protestant men were desperately eager to hear for reasons explained below. It is tempting to suggest that Protestant insistence on the witch's utter subservience to the devil and denial that she possessed any independent power indicates on a subconscious level a heightened fear of women in general. This brings me to my second point, the attitude toward women in Protestant ideology.

It used to be the accepted view that Protestantism offered women an important step toward liberation. Protestant theologians encouraged women to become literate. They emphasized the importance of women as spiritual leaders in the home, and they encouraged women to free themselves from the intellectual and spiritual domination of priests. By rejecting celibacy and virginity as signs of a more perfect spiritual state and advocating the holiness of married life, Protestantism ennobled the one career open to the vast majority of women. While these positions undoubtedly attracted women to Protestantism, recent scholarship has pointed to aspects of Protestant ideology having less positive implications for women. For one thing, Protestant writers inherited the scholarship and attitudes of Renaissance Humanists, and although there are those who argue that Humanists had an enlightened attitude towards women, qualifications are necessary.

Humanists were first and foremost classicists who had read their Aristotle and knew that women were imperfect males with less of a sense of justice (something Freud would rediscover some twenty-three centuries later). Aristotle's philosophy put the inferiority of women on a scientific basis, which suggests that science is not value free and never was. Women were wet and cold, men were hot and dry. The coldness of women dictated their intellectual inferiority as well as their physical shape—fat hips, narrow shoulders, small brains—for being cold, women lacked sufficient energy to drive matter upward. What might have been female brains remained, alas, below the waist. That women rarely become bald was, remarkably, a further sign of their inferiority. Men grow bald because of their internal heat, which literally burns the hair off their heads. Besides Aristotle, there was Xenophon to show both Humanists and Protestants that women's place was in the home. There was Ovid to provide remedies for love-sick males and Juvenal (in his Sixth Satire) to point out how mercenary, repellant, and ridiculous women essentially are.

Protestant ideas about women must be interpreted within the context of this inherited misogyny. In fact, the supposed Protestant emphasis on the worth and dignity of women is only understandable in terms of increased stress on the family as the basic unit of society and on the husband and father in his role as the God, priest, and ruler of his "little commonwealth." By entrusting husbands with functions which had previously been divided among husbands, rulers, and priests, Protestantism reinforced patriarchy. . . .

During the sixteenth and seventeenth centuries patriarchy also received support from rulers intent on consolidating their political power. Robert Filmer, whose *Patriarcha* argued for the divine right of kings, parallels patriarchy in the family and government, both of which reflect patriarchy in the heavens: "We find in the Decalogue that the law which enjoins obedience to Kings is delivered in terms of: Honour thy Father." Filmer simply leaves out the rest of the commandment, "and thy mother." He was not alone. Hobbes excludes the mother from his definition of the family: ". . . a great Family if it be not part of some Common-wealth, is of it self, as to the Rights of Sovereignty, a little Monarchy; whether that Family consist of a man and his children; or of a man and his servants; or of a man, and his children, and servants together; wherein the Father or Master is the Sovereign."

Literary scholars have recently called attention to how often mothers were left out in the seventeenth century. Louis Montrose has commented on the significant lack of mothers in Shakespeare. Mothers are significantly absent from male autobiographies as well. One would hardly know from reading the autobiographies of Baxter and Locke, for example, that they had been "of woman born." Jonathan Goldberg notes the same omission of mother in Stuart family portraits. Political imagery shows male rulers taking over female roles. King James I of England envisioned himself as the single parent of his realm, as "a loving nourish-father" who provided his subject with "their own nourish-milk." Scientists were so entranced by this patriarchal rhetoric that they claimed to have made microscopic observations of spermatozoa containing perfect little embryos. In this sort of macho science, the female role in generation was reduced to that of a nest or warming oven in which the male-engendered embryo hatched.

The androcentrism in Protestant ideology conflicted with the very real power that women had as mothers, wives, and mistresses. The view of women as feeble minded, physically weak, and in need of male domination simply did not fit the facts, as Margaret Ezell has made abundantly clear in her book *The Patriarch's Wife*. I would argue that this discrepancy fostered a collective anxiety about women and about their potentially destructive power that betrays itself quite openly in the cultural fantasies surrounding the witch.

The sixteenth century has been described as one of the most bitterly misogynist periods in Western history. By rejecting celibacy as an inherently more desirable spiritual state and by making marriage the rule for priest and layman alike, Luther unwittingly contributed to an upsurge in misogynist literature. In their initial stages both Lutheranism and Calvinism attempted to eliminate the double standard by making men adhere to the same ideal of chastity before marriage and fidelity during marriage prescribed for women. Such an ideal made illicit sexual activity seem even worse and, with the abolition of the confessional, male guilt over sexual transgressions intensified. Guilt leads to projection, to the transfer of responsibility to the other party, in this case women. The polemical debates among Protestants about the pros and cons of marriage reveals considerable projection, which expresses itself in explicit discussions of the repellent, untrustworthy, and downright dangerous nature of women.

Clearly misogynist satire was not an exclusively Protestant genre. One has only to read medieval fabliaux or Renaissance texts devoted to the *"querrelle des femmes"* to realize that misogyny transcends religious and national barriers. But the sheer quantity and viciousness of Protestant misogynist satire available is second to none. Moreover, the epicenter of this misogyny was Germany, where Lutheranism began, the witchcraft panics were most intense, books about the devil most popular, and executions for witchcraft most numerous. Probably more witches were executed within the boundaries of present-day Germany than in the rest of Europe put together. Sixteenth-and seventeenth-century German broadsheets are filled with descriptions of the marital woes of model husbands. Disorderly women beat and trick their husbands, drink excessively, feast extravagantly, ignore housework, take lovers, and consult witches. The image of the woman on top and wearing men's breeches was as common as it was cautionary; and it was universally agreed that women were sexually rapacious. . . .

The prerogatives allowed to husbands in the early modern period advocated a remarkable degree of sheer brutality. Sixteenth-century broadsheets contain fulsome advice about how husbands should deal with obstreperous wives, and this advice invariably includes cudgeling. In one, "Furst's well-tested recipe to cure the evil disease of disobedient wives," the husband solves his marital problems by beating his wife to death. His solution is not seen as excessive. Indeed, it appears to be fully sanctioned, for in the last scene he is celebrating in a tavern as his wife's funeral cortege files by the open door. . . .

Customary law in Bordeaux went so far as to exonerate a husband who had killed his wife in a fit of rage, but only if he confessed under oath that he was repentant.

English law on wife-beating was more subtle. It was legal for a husband to beat his wife unconscious, but not to the point at which her inert body farted, a sign that she was in shock and possibly dying. Wife-beating was so common in sixteenth-century London that civic regulations forbade it after nine in the evening because of the noise. Protestants took it for granted that if wives failed to be duly submissive, they should be chastised by their husbands. Even in cases of extreme battering, Protestant authorities were reluctant to sanction a wife's request for divorce or separation. . . .

This review of attitudes toward women makes it clear that the notion that wives were devious and dangerous was not a Protestant invention, but a commonplace throughout Europe before the Reformation. Nevertheless, the fact that the theme of female subservience becomes a central topic in the many treatises written by Protestants on "domestical duties" suggests that the image of the overbearing wife was especially troublesome for Protestant men. It was troublesome, I would suggest, because of the inherent contradiction in the Protestant attitude toward women. While women were admitted to be men's spiritual equals (on the basis of Gal. 3:28) and worthy of love, they were declared men's inferiors in every other respect. . . .

Protestant thinkers clearly had a problem explaining precisely why the spiritual and temporal status of women were so different; but they never gave up trying. To quote William Whately: "[e]very good woman must suffer herself to be convinced in judgement, that she is not her husbands equall. Out of place, out of peace; and woe to those miserable aspiring shoulders, which will not content themselves to take their room below the head." William Gouge admitted that whenever he preached the doctrine of female submission and inferiority, there was a certain amount of "squirming" and "murmuring" on the part of the women in the audience. This simply convinced him that more preaching was necessary. The writings and preaching of theologians and ministers (as well as statements by women themselves), together with the popular broadsheets of the period, suggest that Protestant women had taken the teaching on the spiritual equality of the sexes to heart, while conveniently forgetting that they were at the same time domestically subordinate and intrinsically inferior. In *A Looking Glasse for Good Women* (1645), the preacher John Brinsley vented his spleen against the women in his congregation who had "such high and imperious spirits . . . as if they were made only to Rule, not at all to obey." What really annoyed Brinsley was that these women had voted with their feet, deserting his congregation. If they could do that to him, he warns, just think what they might do to their husbands: "[such women] will not stoop to any kinde of subiection, specially to their Husbands. . . . If their Husbands weare the Crown, yet they will sway the Scepter. If their Husband be in places of Authority, they will Rule with them, if not over them." . . .

The two prevailing images of women in Protestant writings suggest that husbands were not as secure as they might have wished. The first, the good woman who cheerfully accepts her role as submissive wife illustrates the way men would have liked things to be. The second, the "man-kinde woman" or "masterly wife," a monster of perversion, who must be broken like horses, indicates how many men really viewed the situation. One of the most common symbols for virtuous Protestant wives was a snail. To quote Luther:

> Just as the snail carries its house with it, so the wife should stay at home and look after the affairs of the household, as one who has been deprived of the ability of administering those affairs that are outside and that concern the state. She does not go beyond her most personal duties.

. . . The antithesis of Luther's ideal wife is the witch who upsets the natural order in the family by being verbally aggressive when she should be silent, promiscuous when she should be chaste, domineering when she should be obedient, and out and about when she should stay at home. In short, witches were women who rejected the private world of female domesticity for the public world of men. They were women who rebelled and in Puritan circles rebellion was routinely equated with witchcraft and rebellious wives with witches. To quote Cotton Mather, who is quoting 1 Sam. 15:23, "Rebellion is as the sin of witchcraft." In 1692 William Good told one of the Salem judges that "he was afraid that [his wife Sarah] either was a witch or would be one very quickly" because of "her bad carriage to him." The figure of the witch was held up to women in sermons, devil books, and plays as a deterrent to untractable behavior, but the antithesis between the good wife and the witch masked the very real masculine fear that deep down all wives are potential witches. They are potential witches precisely because of their subservient position. . . .

Even more interestingly, the very behavior demanded of women by patriarchal society encouraged traits that belong more properly to a witch than to a good wife. Wives were expected to "cajole," "charm," and "entice" their husbands away from evil thoughts and deeds. As Luther says, wives "should deport themselves in such a way in the matter of gestures and conduct that they entice [reytzen] their husbands to believe." While the ends of a wife might be different from that of a witch, their means are surprisingly, indeed, uncannily alike.

Historians of witchcraft have long noted that the witches' sabbath was a late development, appearing after the publication of the classic Catholic treatise on witchcraft, the *Malleus Maleficarum*. While the horrendous, yet titillating spectacle of witches congregating in wild, mountainous lairs, where they indulged in obscene sexual acts, danced riotously, and feasted on loathsome foods, was sufficient to send chills down most male spines, the new group identity and group activity of the witch was especially threatening to Protestant males because it corroborated their deepest fears about Protestant women. Protestant women played an active and noticeable role in the early years of the Reformation, and while their participation was initially encouraged, it was discouraged once Protestantism was established. At that point, Protestant males were eager to reassert their authority, but they did not find women as eager to accept it. The reaction of the Protestant male hierarchy to the women who continued to teach, preach, and even lead sectarian groups makes it clear that in their opinion these women were no better than witches, precisely because they rebelled against male authority. The intemperate language with which the Puritan minister John Cotton denounces Anne Hutchinson for daring to hold religious meetings reveals that in his mind these meetings are nothing short of a witches' sabbath and Anne's behavior that of a witch:

> You cannot evade the Argument . . . that filthie Sinne of the Communuitie of Woe-men; and all promiscuous and filthie comings togeather of men and Woemen with-out Distinction or Relation of Marriage, will necessarily follow. . . . Though I have not herd, nayther do I thinke you have been unfaythfull to your Husband in his Marriage Covenant, yet that will follow upon it.

The witch was the antithesis of the virtuous, chaste, and silent Protestant wife in one other extremely important way. The witch was stereotypically barren. Not only was she barren, she took positive delight in producing barrenness in others, either through malicious witchcraft or by turning innocent young girls away from holy, heterosexual matrimony. The barrenness of the witch and her apparent wish to spread barrenness about her would have been especially upsetting to Protestants for whom virginity, except prior to marriage, had no positive associations. Basing his view on Saint Paul's first epistle to Timothy (2:14–15), Luther argued that women's justification and salvation lay in her womb:

> *She will be saved.* That subjection of woman and domination of men have not been taken away, have they? No. The penalty remains. The blame passed over. The pain and tribulation of childbearing continue. Those penalties will continue until judg-ment. So also the dominion of men and the subjection of women continue. You must endure them. You will also be saved if you have also subjected yourselves and bear your children with pain. . . .

In Luther's opinion the ability to give birth enabled women to atone for their respon-sibility for the Fall. The womb was therefore woman's true calling. Within this context the barren yet sexually insatiable witch was especially repellent.

Many historians have commented on the apparent increase in sexual anxiety during the early-modern period. The introduction of syphilis into the Old World contributed to sexual anxiety as well as to an upsurge in misogyny. But sexual anxiety was more than a response to a physical disease. It was symptomatic of basic changes in social and religious attitudes, which, I would argue, were intensified by the Protestant Reformation. The disparagement of the body was by no means a Protestant invention, but it did become particularly characteristic of Protestants, for whom the senses and the imagination had few positive associations. While the Cath-olic Church sanctioned the use of statues, music, incense, vestments, and elaborate pageantry, these appeals to the senses were violently rejected by Protestants, who tended to identify the senses not simply as the enemies of reason but as peculiarly wily and "feminine" enemies of reason. Protestants routinely employed male/female imagery to describe their own psychology. The masculine will had to keep in check the feminine "heart," which included all the physical aspects of being. . . .

Because of their identification with the body, the senses (and, by association, women) become the almost exclusive locus of temptation in Protestant polemical writing. That there should be such an emphasis on the senses and sensuality as the principal cause of sin in Protestant thought is understandable when one considers the inherent contradiction between Protestant marriage doctrine and the Protestant emphasis on justification.

In a provocative rereading of Milton's *Samson Agonistes*, John Guillory sets out "to show that Samson Agonistes is a prototype of the bourgeois career drama, which conventionally sets the vocation of the husband against the demands of the housewife." Milton's Samson is a middle class Protestant husband (though admittedly not wholly typical!), and the underlying conflict in the poem is between Samson's vocation and his marriage, or, more simply, a conflict between work and sex. As Guillory points out, the conflict between the two was exacerbated by Protestant marriage doctrine. By confining sex within marriage more strictly than ever before, while at the same time suggesting that sexual satisfaction was a legitimate expectation for both partners, Protestantism intensified the eroticism in the domestic realm. Samson is literally "seduced" by his own wife so that he abandons his true "calling"; and that is the cause of all the trouble. . . .

The choice Samson made of sex over work was not simply a threat to his masculine self-image and identity; it was a threat to his very salvation. For in succumbing to Delilah, Samson was succumbing to the baser side of his own personality, the feminine side, which included the physical delights of sex. Furthermore, the only way anxious Protestants could be certain they were saved was to work hard and succeed. As John Donne put it in his poem "The Break of Day," "the poor, the foul, the false, love can / Admit, but not the busied man." The age-old saw that sex is debilitating for the male, that it literally depletes his vital juices, takes on an even more sinister aspect as sex becomes pitted against work and, via work, salvation. Behind John Winthrop's designation of Anne Hutchinson as the "American Jesabel," lies the conviction that women can "seduce" men mentally and spiritually as well as physically. Sex and heresy are inextricably linked in Winthrop's mind, which explains why he accused Hutchinson of acting just like a witch, who is, of course, both sexually and theologically deviant.

From all the evidence cited, it seems clear that the age-old view that women were intrinsically more evil than men did not disappear with the Protestant emphasis on the spiritual equality of women and on their important role in the family. The old and new view of woman coexisted uneasily, and I am not the first historian to contend that the witchcraze can at least in part be attributed to the inherent tensions in the Protestant view of women. Christina Larner, for example, sees witch hunting in Scotland as an attempt to enforce threatened patriarchal ideals. Carol Karlsen offers a similar interpretation for American witch hunts.

The preoccupation with insubordinate women in Protestant writing makes it all the more interesting that the iconoclasm accompanying the Reformation was especially directed at images of the Virgin Mary and female saints, who were compared to "whores" in one Protestant polemic. Smashing "Lady Chapels" and the statues of the Virgin kept in them was commonplace in England and even applauded by Bishop Hugh Latimer on that grounds that men could then turn "from ladyness to Godliness." Clearly, even good women were problematical if they did not keep their place.

In Luther's reaction against the Cult of the Virgin, for example, one senses strong resistance to the Virgin's preeminence as a threat to male dominance. In his Personal Prayer Book (*Betbüchlein*) Luther stresses the Virgin's dependence on God, arguing that the Virgin is what she is solely as a result of divine grace, certainly not personal merit:

> Take note of this: no one should put his trust or confidence in the mother of God or her merits, for such trust is worthy of God alone and is the lofty service due only to him. Rather praise and thank God through Mary and the grace given her. Laud and love her simply as the one who, without merit, obtained such blessing from God, sheerly out of his mercy, as she herself testifies in the Magnificat." . . .

For many Catholics the real Trinity consisted of God, Christ, and Mary. Some went even farther. In the fifteenth century people kept statuettes of the Virgin that opened to reveal the Trinity within. The theologian Jean Gerson, who was, significantly enough, a great promoter of the cult of Saint Joseph, objected strenuously to these statuettes on the grounds that it was heretical to see Mary as the source of the Trinity and not God. Luther's insistence on the Virgin's subordination to Christ reveals the same aversion to powerful, independent women. But while Protestantism swept away images of powerful female saints, these figures continued to provide Catholic men and women with positive images of strong and even eloquent women, who bested the best of men. Saint Catherine, for example, defeated fifty philosophers in debate and converted Saint Athanasius by her preaching. The place reserved for a powerful woman in Protestant theology was in hell, as a member of that diabolical Trinity of the Pope, Antichrist, and the Whore of Babylon.

The cult of the Virgin Mary has often been described as supremely misogynist because it presented women with a model they could not hope to emulate. I would argue that, on the contrary, the cult of the Virgin was in many respects extremely positive for women. For Mary was considered the second Eve, who repaired the damage done by her predecessor. For Protestants who rejected Mariology, Eve's sin was never balanced or transcended as it was for Catholics. While Eve, and by implication all women, are responsible for man's fall, his sinfulness, and his mortality, there is no female element in the Protestant pantheon to help in man's salvation. The connection between women, sex, sin, and death was consequently reinforced for Protestants in the era of the witchcraze as it was not for Catholics. As we have seen, Catholics considered Mary the equal or superior of Christ, because as a mother she was powerful enough to compel him to do what she wished, even though he was God. Mary's mother, Saint Anne, was another powerful woman and a grandmother to boot. She provided Catholics with a positive image of an old woman to counterbalance the negative image of the evil, old witch. Leonardo's famous picture of the Virgin and Saint Anne with the Christ child is only one of many pictures portraying this basically female and matrilineal Trinity. These positive images of powerful women had been discredited by Protestant theologians and iconoclasts. That they were available to Catholics undoubtedly helped to counteract an idea that becomes something of a leitmotif in Protestant thought, namely that powerful women are by their very nature promiscuous, dangerous, and in the last analysis suspiciously like witches.

This discussion of the implications of Protestant ideology for women suggests that the Protestant emphasis on the spiritual equality of men and women and on marriage and the family as the basic social institutions contributed to the misogynist attitudes and gender conflict that fueled the witchcraze. . . .

While the Devil and witches exercised the minds of both Catholics and Protestants, Protestant millenarianism, together with covenant theology, magnified the fear of the Devil at the same time that Protestant theology rejected traditional ways of coping with these fears. Magic and witchcraft were also viewed differently by the Catholic and Protestant intelligentsia who were in a position to intensify or diffuse witch panics. Rejecting all magic as diabolical, many Protestants regarded witches as the devil's disciples; their supernatural crimes could therefore not be proved by ordinary rules of evidence. In the courts of the Inquisition and the Parlement of Paris, older images of the witch as part magician, part sorcerer never entirely disappeared, and consequently more rigorous standards of evidence were demanded. In addition to the new view of the witch, the new ideology about women and marriage in Protestantism contained ambiguities and tensions which made women appear more threatening to men. For Protestant women, the doctrine of spiritual equality coupled with the emphasis on marriage and the inequality of the marriage relationship fostered the insecurity and anger characteristic of those possessed women whose hysterical fits did so much to trigger witch panics. Women, particularly possessed women, posed less of a threat to Catholic Inquisitors. Whatever their crimes and whatever their condition, Catholic women were always subject to male control, whether that of husband, priest, confessor, exorcist, or, if all else failed, Inquisitor.

35

The Devil, the Body, and the Feminine Soul in Puritan New England

Elizabeth Reis

The historian Elizabeth Reis is the author of Damned Women: Sinners and Witches in Puritan New England *(1997) and has edited* Spellbound: Woman and Witchcraft in America *(1998), an anthology of witchcraft articles that focus on the gender question and take the story of witchcraft and alternative spiritualities among women up to the twentieth century. Reis is presently working on a study of the image of the angel in American history. In this excerpt from a 1995 article, she discusses Puritan beliefs about the soul and the body that made women seem especially vulnerable to temptation by the devil.*

•

Puritans regarded the soul as feminine and characterized it as insatiable, as consonant with the supposedly unappeasable nature of women. If historians have noticed the New England Puritans' feminized representation of the soul, they have failed to comment or to accord the matter much significance. Yet such representation is crucial to understanding how the soul could unite with Christ upon regeneration or, alternatively, with the devil through sin.

The body, for its part, also entangled women. Puritans believed that Satan attacked the soul by assaulting the body, and that because women's bodies were weaker, the devil could reach women's souls more easily, breaching these "weaker vessels" with greater frequency. Not only was the body the means toward possessing the soul, it was the very expression of the devil's attack. Among witches, the body clearly manifested the soul's acceptance of the diabolical covenant.

Women were in a double bind during witchcraft episodes. Their souls, strictly speaking, were no more evil than those of men, but the representation of the vulnerable, unsatisfied, and yearning female soul, passively waiting for Christ but always ready to succumb to the devil, inadvertently implicated corporeal women themselves.

From Elizabeth Reis, "The Devil, the Body, and the Feminine Soul in Puritan New England," *Journal of American History* 82(1) (June 1995): 15–19, 23–25, 31–33, 35–36. © 1982 by the Organization of American Historians. Reprinted by permission of the Organization of American Historians.

The representation of the soul in terms of worldly gender arrangements, and the understanding of women in terms of the characteristics of the feminine soul, in a circular fashion led Puritans to imagine that women were more likely than men to submit to Satan. A woman's feminine soul, jeopardized in a woman's feminine body, was frail, submissive, and passive—qualities that most New Englanders thought would allow her to become either a wife to Christ or a drudge to Satan.

Witches, unlike commonplace sinners, took a further damning step. Their feminine souls made an explicit and aggressive choice to conjoin with the devil. By defining a witch as a person whose (feminine) soul covenanted with Satan by signing a devil's pact rather than quiescently waiting for Christ, Puritans effectively demonized the notion of active female choice. A woman risked being damned either way: If her soul waited longingly for salvation in Christ, such female yearning could conjure up images of unsatisfied women vulnerable to Satan; if, on the contrary, that soul acted assertively rather than in passive obedience, by definition it chose the devil overtly. Thus, although in Puritan theory women were not inherently more evil than men, they became so labeled during the practical process of defining women's souls and bodies in the context of Puritan New England.

This essay examines the cultural construction of gender in early America in order to understand the intersection of Puritan theology, Puritan evaluations of womanhood, and the seventeenth-century witchcraft episodes, in which 78 percent of the accused were women. The Puritans' earthly perception of women's bodies and souls corresponded to their otherworldly belief concerning Satan's powers. New Englanders considered women more vulnerable to Satan because their image of the soul and its relationship to the body allowed them to associate womanhood with evil and sin. During the witchcraft episodes, the learned and the common people alike molded belief and interpreted circumstances, in the end cooperating in the construction of their natural and supernatural world. Of course, this seventeenth-century world was influenced by considerations of gender. Not only did Puritans' understanding of women's and men's bodies and souls reflect the gendered nature of their social universe, but the supernatural behaviors and powers that they believed the devil conferred on his female and male witches echoed the more mundane gender arrangements of colonial New England.

*   *   *

Lay and clerical views of the tortures that Satan's victims endured during the witchcraft episodes paralleled the sermon literature on the relationship between the body, the soul, and Satan. The body was the most vulnerable part of one's total being, its Achilles' heel. Succumbing to Satan's assaults and temptations, the body could become the Puritan man or woman's own worst enemy. It was the primary battleground in the struggle between the devil and individual souls. The Reverend Henry Smith characterized the body as a betrayer. He lamented, "So soon as we rise in the morning, we go forth to fight with two mighty giants, the world and the devil; and whom do we take with us but a traitor, this brittle flesh, which is ready to yield up to the enemy at every assault?" Sinful temptations devised by Satan, such as carnality, drunkenness, and licentiousness, provoked the body and threatened to lead it astray, thus allowing Satan an inroad into the soul. . . .

It seems ironic that Puritans envisioned the body protecting the soul rather than the reverse, so that a strong body rendered a person's soul less vulnerable to Satan's exertions. The body, after all, was usually seen as the weaker link in the soul/body relationship. However, in a seemingly illogical but nonetheless common way, the body became the path to the soul. A stronger body was less likely to submit to the devil's temptations and thus better protected the soul from the devil's domination.

The body was supposed to protect the soul, but more often than not it failed. Clergy and laity alike knew all too well that the body's lustful desires frequently overwhelmed the will, which resided in the soul. And although the body may have perpetrated the particular sins, ultimately the soul bore the responsibility. It was the soul that Satan held in bondage. "It is true, the body is employed in it, and all the members of it are engaged in this drudgery," [Samuel] Willard admitted, "but the bondage of it lies on the inward man."

Willard's use of the term "inward man" as a synonym for the (feminine) soul drew on biblical precedent and Puritan speculation that used the names of bodily things to designate spiritual entities. The metaphor carried more connotation of femininity in the seventeenth century than it earlier did. Quoting the source of the trope, the seventeenth-century English minister Richard Sibbes blurred the lines between the physical and the spiritual, writing that the heart is not "the inward material and fleshy part of the body; but that spiritual part, the soul and affections thereof . . . all the powers of the soul, the inward man, as Paul calleth it, 2 Cor. iv. 16, is the heart." Paul's phrase gained new significance from seventeenth- and eighteenth-century ideas of physical anatomy that perceived women's sexual organs as the same as men's, except insofar as they were contained *within* rather than outside the body. If inwardness meant femaleness, the term suggests that the soul was feminine; it, or "she," ultimately carried the burden of the body's weaknesses. . . .

Though they rarely drew explicit attention to the female character of the soul, clergy and laity used feminine adjectives, such as barren or fecund, to describe it and overtly referred to the soul using the feminine pronoun, "she." The soul was also described as insatiable, a negative characterization more often ascribed to women than to men; the soul was forever seeking happiness that it could never attain unaided. Indeed, the minister Urian Oakes spoke of the natural propensity to sin, original sin, in feminine terms. "Indwelling sin," he explained, was a "home-bred enemy, that *mother* of all the abominations that are brought forth in the lives of men, that adversary that is ever molesting the peace, disturbing the quiet, and endangering the people of GOD." Bearing within it the "mother" of all sin, the unregenerate, natural soul submitted willingly to Satan's domination.

John Cotton described the unrepentant soul as a feminine entity. Depicting the "ungracious frame of nature" with which humankind entered the world, Cotton recounted the process of regeneration: "So as now the poor soule begins presently to stand amazed at *her* former condition, and looks at it as most dangerous and desperate; and now the soule begins to loathe itself, and to abhor itselfe, and to complaine and confesses its wickednesse before God." Cotton's soul is thus ungracious, wicked, self-hating, and female—as the possessive pronoun implies. She is enveloped in Satan's embrace, yet eager to confess so that she can instead be coupled with Christ.

Feminine images of the soul punctuate Puritan sermon literature. In 1679 William Adams described the minister's work in preparing souls for conversion as "travailing in birth with Souls till Christ be formed in them." He likened the soul in its natural state to a wilderness, "barren and unfruitful, bringing forth no fruit to God, but wild fruits of sin." Once these unregenerate souls shifted their devotion from Satan to Christ upon conversion, they would "be changed, tilled, converted and made fruitful, to bring forth fruits of holiness unto God." "Fertile and fruitful" described the converted soul; the reprobate soul, possessed by Satan, remained "barren of all grace and goodness."

The representation of the soul as a woman invited metaphors of fecundity and sexuality. The poet Anne Bradstreet portrayed the eyes and ears as the doors of the soul, "through which innumerable objects enter," but the soul is never satisfied. Borrowing an image from the biblical book of Proverbs, she imagined the soul as "like the daughters of the horseleach"; it "cries, 'Give, give'; and which is most strange, the more it receives, the more empty it finds itself and sees an impossibility ever to be filled but by Him in whom all fullness dwells." In Bradstreet's eyes, the feminine soul needed a virile Christ to satisfy her otherwise insatiable desires.

An English minister, the Reverend Mr. Simmons, similarly described the soul using sexual imagery. Like Bradstreet, he conceived of the eyes as the "port-holes" of the soul, through which "sin and Satan creep in at." He cautioned, "If those doors stand wide open for all comers and goers, either your soul, Dinah-like, will be gadding out, or Satan will be getting in, by which the poor soul will be defiled and defloured." Simmons recalled Dinah, the biblical daughter of Jacob, who left the protection of her father and brothers and was raped by Shechem, son of Hamor the Hivite. Like Dinah, the soul, left unguarded, would fall victim to Satan's invasion; his potent intrusion was best described in sexual terms, as the rape of the feminine soul.

The feminine soul thus was insatiable, driven by almost physical desires, as Samuel Willard argued in his *Sacramental Meditations*: "The soul of man must have something to live upon, that is the great want, and for this want the creature hath no supply." Like a growling stomach, Thomas Shepard suggested, the soul "must have something to quiet and comfort it." Ironically, the active pursuit of sustenance and spiritual fulfillment was not only futile, given the soul's unrelenting appetite, but it invited Satan's abuse, conceived as rape and possession.

In the battle between God and the devil, both Christ and Satan stood as aggressively masculine warriors, battling for the feminine soul's fidelity. Unconverted souls, ministers warned, unwittingly conspired with the forces of Satan and "spen[t] all their days in *Continual Rebellions* against [God]." But in his generalship, Satan showed little regard or mercy for his own troops. The soul thus occupied a dangerous position; even if she was an unwitting conscript in Satan's legion, she had to defend herself against the devil himself. As Bradstreet and Simmons cautioned, the soul had to shield herself from Satan's advances so that she would not be "defiled and defloured."

During the witchcraft trials the unfulfilled feminine soul, quick to succumb to the devil's possession, became equated with discontented women, subjects primed for the devil's intrusion. The ministers taught that Satan tortured and weakened the body in order to dominate the soul, and the laity interpreted the message quite literally; that interpretation affected the understanding of sin, the soul, and the body in unanticipated ways. To lay people's minds, the weaker bodies of women rendered their souls more accessible to Satan. The clergy did not disagree. The minister John Cotton had succinctly described the relationship between sin, the soul, and Satan: "When a man wittingly and willingly commits any knowne sinne, he doth as actually give his Soule to the Devill, as a Witch doth her body and soule; we thereby renounce the covenant of God, and Satan takes Possession of us." Cotton made a distinction between sinners and witches; Satan possessed the souls of all sinners alike, but witches, whom Cotton assumed were women, compounded their crime.

The witch's surrender was explicit; not only did her body falter and her soul submit but the witch also explicitly enlisted to promote the devil's purpose. The witch acted aggressively. Her soul specifically chose the devil, rather than passively waiting for Christ, and she purposefully allowed the devil to use her body. She presumably gave the devil permission to commandeer her body—her shape—to recruit more witches and perform *maleficium*. Thus, the witch acted assertively, while the sinner, after falling, suffered passively. . . .

For the witch, sacrificing her soul to Satan could mean yielding her body sexually to his imps. In medieval folklore, the witch's familiar, or incubus, had intercourse with the witch. The learned tracts on witchcraft written in the colonies, for example, Increase Mather's, were skeptical about the possibility of the devil's familiars having sexual relations with the witches. Increase Mather wrote, "What fables are there concerning *incubi* and *succubae* and of men begotten by daemons! No doubt but the devil may delude the fancy, that one of his vassals shall think (as the witch at Hartford did) that he has carnal and cursed communion with them beyond what is real." On the other hand, Mather went on to admit, "Nor is it impossible for him [the devil] to assume a dead body, or to form a lifeless one out of the elements, and there-with to make his witches become guilty of sodomy." Even on this last point, Mather was ambiguous. Later in the text he concluded, "But to imagine that spirits shall really generate bodies, is irrational." In the colonial witchcraft trials, this traditional element was not emphasized, although the possibility of such behavior was certainly intimated. The creatures that sucked at women's breasts and at other sexually sensitive areas of their bodies may have been sucking for sexual pleasure rather than nourishment.

Witches' bodies no longer belonged to themselves; Satan could take them wherever he pleased to use as he pleased. The devil appeared in the forms of both men and women witches, but when a specter assaulted a victim in a sexual way, it was always in the shape of a woman. Most often a male victim (though occasionally a female one) recounted awaking at night to find the specter of a witch sitting on top of him in bed. References to sexual activity were veiled but unmistakable. Samuel Gray reported that he woke up to see Bridget Bishop's apparition standing between the baby's cradle and his bed. He testified that

> he said to her in the name of God what doe you come for. then she vanished away soe he Locked the dore againe & went to bed and between sleeping & wakeing he felt some thing Come to his mouth or lipes cold, & there upon started & looked up & againe did see the same woman.

In a similarly suggestive tale, Bernard Peach claimed that Susannah Martin "drew up his body into a heape and Lay upon him about an hour and half or 2 hours, in all which taim this deponent could not stir nor speake." New Englanders did not typically interpret the devil's intrusion in sexual terms, yet they sometimes understood his use of women witches in light of the witches' sexuality and their female bodies.

Satan also tried to capture men's souls, but his torture of their bodies was markedly different and less drastic. Men were not as likely to be seen suckling imps, although their bodies were searched during the trials and the investigations occasionally found evidence of the potential for such activity. During the examination of two accused witches, George Burroughs and George Jacobs, both of whom were eventually hanged, the examiners found nothing unusual upon Burroughs's body, but Jacobs was not so lucky. The four men reported "3. tetts w'ch according to the best of our Judgement wee think is not naturall for wee run a pinn through 2 of them and he was not sinceible of it." As far as the court was concerned, the three abnormal markings, one in Jacobs's mouth, one on his shoulder blade, and one on his hip, signified the devil's possession of his body and soul.

But the devil's possession of men contrasted with his domination of women because New Englanders expected that men's heartier bodies were more difficult and less tempting objects of the devil's attacks. The assumption that the devil had a different relationship with men was never explicitly articulated, but the incidents recounted at the trials can provide us with insights into Puritans' thinking about gender and the affliction of evil. First, witches were less likely to seduce men than women into the devil's service. And when men told of their encounters with the accused witches, their testimony centered on bizarre acts of maleficence attributed to the accused, rather than on the physical harm caused by the witches' shape. Samuel Endicott charged Mary Bradbury with selling the captain of his ship butter that turned rancid after he and his crew were at sea for three weeks. Either the heedlessness of the sale, calculated fraud, or her magical ability to transform good butter into bad implicated her, and he did not doubt that she was a witch. As additional evidence, Endicott described a violent storm that cost the ship its mainmast, its rigging, and fifteen horses. The ship sprang a leak and took on four feet of water, and its crew was forced to unload the cargo. When they came upon land, Endicott saw "the appearance of a woman from her middle upwards, haveing a white Capp and white neck-cloth on her, w'ch then affrighted him very much." Bradbury's shape frightened Endicott, and her misdeeds plagued him, but he was not subject to her direct, violent, physical abuse.

Often male victims' complaints against an accused witch centered on the harm inflicted on their personal property, rather than on the bodily pain they endured themselves. Samuel Abbey told the court that after the accused witch Sarah Good left his house, he began to lose cattle "after an unusuall Manner, in drupeing Condition." He lost seventeen cattle in two years, in addition to sheep and hogs, and he held the devil and Sarah Good responsible. John Roger testified that after an argument with Martha Carrier seven years earlier, two of his sows were lost and one of them was found dead near the Carriers' house with both of its ears cut off.

Even more often men suffered through miseries visited on weaker members of their families, their wives and their children. Although William Beale testified that he awoke one morning because "A very greate & wracking paine had seized uppon my body," his primary evidence against the accused Philip English was that his son, who had been expected to recover from smallpox, died later that day, after Beale saw English's shape on the chimney. Samuel Perley complained that Elizabeth Howe stuck his ten-year-old daughter and his wife with pins. Astonished at the brutality to which they were subject, he claimed, "i could never aflict a dog as goode how aflicts mi wife." Perley's daughter "Pine d a wai [pined away] to skin and bone and ended her sorrowful life." The devil, in the shapes of the accused, tortured these two men, but not by destroying their own bodies. . . .

Since Puritans believed that Satan designed his attacks according to his quarry, it made sense that the women and men victims whom the witches tried to lure into Satan's web perceived Satan's tortures differently. Just as female victims were more likely to be physically tormented, the women witches themselves—the majority of the accused—also experienced greater bodily distress than did men as Satan destroyed their bodies to capture their souls. Though men's bodies were hardly invulnerable, in women the devil sought easier marks.

Curiously, while a weak body and a vulnerable soul left one open to Satan, they might also encourage one's faith in God. Indeed, Cotton Mather and other ministers suggested that the frailty of women's bodies, compounded by the dangers of childbirth, gave women more reason to seek the Lord since death was more immediate. Anne Bradstreet, bemoaning an illness that had plagued her for months, hoped that her soul would gain some advantage while her body was faltering. Believing that God inflicted bodily illness only for the good of the soul, she mused, "I hope my soul shall flourish while my body decays, and the weakness of this outward man shall be a means to strengthen my inner man." Echoing Samuel Willard's biological reference to the soul, Bradstreet called her soul the "inner man" and tried to dissociate its spiritual strength from her body's physical weaknesses. She cultivated resignation: "And if He knows that weakness and a frail body is the best to make me a vessel fit for His use why should I not bear it, not only willingly but joyfully." Bradstreet went so far as to suggest that good health might divert her from the Lord. She wrote, "The Lord knows I dare not desire that health that sometimes I have had, lest my heart should be drawn from Him, and set upon the world."

Perhaps women's weaker bodies brought them closer to God, as Bradstreet hoped. Women, then, had a particular potential for goodness. But women's more fragile bodies also exposed them to Satan, perhaps encouraging a peculiar potential for evil—Eve's legacy. In the context of the witchcraft outbreaks, a time of extraordinary uncertainty and fear, New Englanders focused on the darker side of womanhood, emphasizing the vulnerability of women's bodies and souls to the devil, rather than their openness to regeneration. Women as witches were so threatening because their souls had made a conscious decision to ally with Satan. Too impatient or too weak to wait passively for Christ's advance, witches allowed their bodies and souls to choose, actively, the seductions of the devil. In the course of living their errand in the North American wilderness, Puritans thus constructed a gendered ideology and society that made women, ironically, closer both to God and to Satan.

[36]

Words, Witches, and Woman Trouble

JANE KAMENSKY

In this 1992 article the historian Jane Kamensky explores the gendered meaning of speech among New England Puritans. She expands on these ideas in her 1997 book Governing the Tongue: The Politics of Speech in Early New England.

•

One of the most literal manifestations of the power of speech in Puritan Massachusetts was the language of witches, a genre of verbal aggression that has largely escaped scholarly attention. Words were at their most dangerous in the theater of New England witchcraft. . . . The concern of early New Englanders with speech as a cultural force, their anxiety over the evolving roles of men and women, and their overriding attention to constructing and preserving social hierarchy came together in the prosecution of witches. . . .

Cotton Mather once referred to himself and his fellow ministers as "Ear-witnesses" to witchcraft. Like Mather, many people in seventeenth-century New England believed they could *hear* the Devil's presence in the speech of a local woman before their other senses offered corroborating evidence. Their detailed recollections of the ways witches spoke allow us, at more than three hundred years' remove, to be ear-witnesses of a sort. Ministers' observations of the ravages witches inflicted upon their possessed victims, taken together with court papers documenting the verbal "crimes" witches committed in their local communities, offer rich evidence of what women said that made them be perceived as witches by their neighbors and their leaders in early New England. . . .

*   *   *

English theologian William Perkins, an authority for New England ministers on many subjects, spelled out the elite view of witchcraft. For Perkins, the witch's crime was

From Jane Kamensky, "Words, Witches, and Woman Trouble: Witchcraft, Disorderly Speech, and Gender Boundaries in Puritan New England," *Essex Institute Historical Collections* 128 (October 1992): 291–306. 1992 by the Essex Institute. Reprinted by permission of the Peabody Essex Museum, Salem, Massachusetts.

one of heretical *inversion*. Her covenant with the Devil created an alternate set of institutions, beliefs, and allegiances by which she claimed the right to govern herself. Just as "God Hath his word and sacraments, the seals of his covenant unto believers," Perkins noted, "so the devil hath his words and certain outward signs to ratify the same to his instruments." Witches "renounced God . . . king and governor, and . . . bound [themselves] by other laws." Rooting out witches was thus of vital importance to the Puritan elite, and here, too, Perkins offered help. He listed seven ways that witches might arouse suspicion, and five of these centered on the spoken word: (1) a "common report" or "notorious defamation" of being a witch; (2) the testimony of a fellow witch; the "mischief" that followed either from (3) the witch's curses or (4) her "quarreling or threatening"; and finally, (5) the quality of her speech upon examination. Called before local authorities because her words rendered her suspicious in the first place, a witch's verbal "performance" at the bar could seal her fate: "unconstant" or "contrary" answers, Perkins noted, "argueth a guilty mind and conscience which stoppeth the freedom of speech." Hunting for witches, Perkins's definition made clear, depended in large measure on careful *listening*.

Perkins's formulation of the witch met with broad agreement in the seventeenth-century English-speaking world. The records of New England witchcraft confirm that religious and civil authorities on both sides of the Atlantic shared his anxiety about the verbal power of witches. Documenting their fight against Satan's minions, New England's magistrates and ministers commented in revealing detail about the threat of disorderly female language: the how, where, and what women said to sound like witches to the ears of the Puritan elite.

Verbal *tone*—*how* the witch or her possessed victim spoke—was an essential ingredient of her threat to the elite. Recall, for a moment, Mercy Short's "Insolent and Abusive" words to Cotton Mather. Samuel Willard's description of the possession of Elizabeth Knapp shows similar concern with the timbre of diabolical speech. Knapp committed an extraordinary number of verbal "transgressions." Willard recounted her "shrieks" and "crying out," her "railing" and "reviling" of him. Just as these aberrations in her normal speech patterns signaled her entry into a "possessed" state, the ebbing of her "fits" meant a return to what Willard considered a more suitable tone. Where the demoniac "roared" and "screamed," yelled, bleated, and barked, the penitent girl demonstrated a more appropriate (and earthly) range of verbal skills: "sighings, sobbings," "bitter tears," "earnest profession" and "methodical declarations." The witch or her victim might also be gripped by unpredictable, implacable *silences*. Witches and those under their influence were "seized with dumbness," their "mouths were stopped," devils "confound[ed]" their language, rendered them "uncapable of saying anything," and so on. And even this was not the greatest disruption of speech witches might effect.

The bodily process of speaking—that defining human faculty—was perverted and distorted in the most literal, material sense in the ravings of possessed girls. Dramatic physical symptoms revealed that the Devil had invaded the victim's speech. One victim's tongue clung to the roof of her mouth, "not to be removed" though "some tried with their fingers to do it." Others suffered as their tongues were "drawn down their Throats . . . pull'd out upon their Chins, their Mouths [forced] opened to such Wideness, that their Jaws went out of joint." Empowered by the Devil or his human emissaries, young women could rage with their mouths shut or hanging wide open, belching forth horrifying words "without the use of any of the Organs of speech." The voice of the witch sounded recognizably unfeminine—even *inhuman*—to her ministerial audience.

But verbal *style* did not alone brand a witch: the "where" and "what" of her speech combined to transform a "heated" exchange into a diabolic one. The physical setting of many such "conversations" was significant. An element of public spectacle often gave a witch's heated words broader scope and amplified their danger to established authority. Witches and their victims dared to spout verbal poison at elevated male targets in public settings.

Ministers victimized by these stinging words reacted with hurt and surprise. Samuel Willard noted somewhat defensively that Elizabeth Knapp had "always been observed to speak respectfully concerning" him before the Devil took control of her tongue. Martha Goodwin, Cotton Mather recalled, addressed him with "a Sauciness that I had not been us'd to." Secular authorities were no less sensitive to witches' abuse of prominent audiences. The magistrates of Salem's Court of Oyer and Terminer often chided a suspect for her lack of deference. And the records suggest that accused witches had raised their voices against civil authorities long before Salem. John Winthrop noted in 1648, during one of the first formal witch-hunting proceedings in Massachusetts, that Margaret Jones's "behavior at her trial was very intemperate, lying notoriously, and railing upon the jury and witnesses." A woman's verbal tone often signaled the presence of witchcraft. *Where* and *to whom* the suspect spoke made such strident speech impossible to overlook.

Finally, we must look at the "what" of the witch's words, for the *content* of her speech was arguably the most important component of its disorderly potential in the minds of the Puritan elite. Through her heated words to prominent men, the witch effectively positioned herself as a dark mirror of male authority. Like a minister, she selected and interpreted texts. One afflicted girl challenged Increase Mather in open assembly to " 'stand up, and Name your Text': And after it was read, she said, 'it is a long Text.' " She went on mocking him, saying " 'I know no Doctrine you had, If you did name one, I have forgot it.' " . . . Speaking out, stridently and publicly, challenging the sole right of male authorities (magistrates, ministers, and husbands) to speak for them: this was the essence of the witch's challenge to the elite. Witches and their possessed victims personified the danger of female verbal authority, much like Quaker women preachers, themselves often subject to prosecution as witches, and much like Anne Hutchinson, who had conducted herself as a preacher and interpreter, and wound up under the shadow of witchcraft.

Elite reactions to witches' speech reveal the boundaries of feminine discourse in Puritan New England. Certainly "vertuous women" were granted a degree of authority by their ministers. Preachers exhorted their increasingly "feminized" congregations to read, to converse, and even to write on pious subjects. But if pious matrons knew that it were their right—even their duty—to reflect and expound on sacred texts, they would also have been aware (and been *kept* aware by the persecution of witches, slanderers, and other misspeakers) that certain implicit limits bounded their discourse. The witch's speech made those implicit limits manifest.

In one sense, the witch linguistically outperformed the virtuous woman. The virtuous woman was fluent in the language of the Bible, but the witch spoke in tongues—foreign and learned languages of which she was expected to know nothing. The virtuous woman read, but the witch read backwards. The virtuous woman knew her scripture, but the witch could cite chapter and verse of Biblical texts with facility ministers found distinctly unsettling. Mercy Short, for example, uttered "innumerable Things . . . which would have been more Agreeable to One of a greater Elevation in Christianity," finding scriptural support for her arguments with a speed that "no man living ever" could have matched. Mather found her "Discourses . . . *incredibly beyond* what might have been expected, from one of her small education." . . . Any seventeenth-century listener would have recognized the implicit message: one of "small education," the recipient of the kind of learning that better suited a hearer than a preacher, was more than likely to be female. Conversely, . . . one who had attained significant "elevation in Christianity," was invariably male. And the woman who breached these implied gender boundaries was, as likely as not, a witch.

And yet, at other moments, the witch also fell far short of the virtuous woman in her capacity for elevated Christian speech. For all her diabolic skill when acting the part of the minister, the witch could also fail to equal the verbal proficiency of even a well-catechized child. This accounted for her often-demonstrated inability to recite the Lord's prayer, and her mute rage at words like "God," and "Love," and "Good." Such grand "failures" of speech were considered just as damning as the witch's equally florid "successes," for both claimed a linguistic authority that was inappropriate. The witch decided what she would read and what would be read to her. She chose when and what to hear, whether and how to speak, and—most dramatically— what to say. She was, in the fullest seventeenth-century sense, an *author*, an inventor and teller of her own story, a creator and founder of others' misery. If the New England clergy was beginning to advance a version of femininity that included some verbal authority—the right to read and discourse modestly on Biblical texts—the witch showed the need to limit that authority.

*   *   *

To elite ears, the witch's speech posed a grand threat, challenging nothing less than the hierarchical framework of Puritan society. For common folk—her neighbors and victims—her voice held a different sort of menace. The witch's words struck at the very foundation of local life: the dominion of men over their wives and farmers over their crops and livestock, the ability of parents to protect and nurture their children. But if the theater of her malice was smaller, the impact of her words in the community setting was more literal and immediate. Babies and animals dropped dead. Inanimate objects moved at will. Luck ran out.

As was true for the Puritan elite, the witch's power in the neighborhood was embodied by her fiery tongue and her effect upon the speech of others. Heated words both by and against witches were a vital part of the local matrix of witch-hunting. As a subject of slander, and as the issuer of curses and other verbal "injuries," the witch was defined and prosecuted by the spoken word. . . .

Witnesses against accused witches often pointed to a contentious verbal exchange with the suspect as the incident that first tipped them off to diabolic goings-on. The neighbors of Elizabeth Garlick in East Hampton, Long Island, described her as a "duble tongued woman" who made herself suspect by having "jeered" and "laughed" at them on numerous occasions. Sarah Good, executed at Salem, had spoken "in a very wicked, spitfull manner . . . with base and abusive words. . . . mutring & scolding extreamly." Sarah Bibber, accused Salem witch and self-described possessed victim, was also called "double-tongued": "a woman of an unruly turbulent spirit. . . . much given to tatling & tale Bareing . . . amongst her neighbors . . . very much given to speak bad words and would call her husband bad names." . . .

But unlike the insults hurled by common slanderers and railers, the witch's words had a very literal *power*—power of a sort not common to women in other areas of colonial life. As "cursing" or "foretelling," a witch's words broke free of the boundaries of speech and took harmful, physical form. One woman told a neighbor that he "should Repent of" his words to her "afore Seven years Came to an End," saying that she would "hold [his] noss so Closs to the grindstone as Ever it was held." Some curses were more specific: that a cow would die or a child would be taken ill. . . . No matter how mundane the particular threat, the witch's cursing held out the danger of words made real. As several of her Ipswich neighbors recalled about Goody Batchelor's threats against their cattle, "as she sayde so it came to pass."

And there was one final quality of the witch's speech as interpreted by common folk. If her words, as curses and threats, could be too trustworthy, too literal, they might also be slippery and falsely seductive. Pretended kindness or unduly "smooth words"—followed in many cases by preternatural "harm"—were as distrusted as threats. One witness found the "fauneing & flattering manner" of Salem merchant Phillip English highly suspect. Mary Parker had "fauned upon" a deponent's wife "w'th very Smooth words," after which his child fell sick. Elizabeth Howell feared, after a heated exchange with suspected witch Elizabeth Garlick, that Garlick would "cum fauninge" to her in the morning. Here we glimpse the very essence of the "double-tongued" woman: muttering and menacing at one turn, flattering and fawning at the next. Her verbal challenge came not only from the "heat" of her speech, but also from its unpredictability.

How did the "double-tongued" woman fit with popular conceptions of a woman's role? Although most evidence of the belief in feminine quietude and decorousness comes from elite sources, court records offer some hints here, too. Where testimony *against* accused witches emphasized their clamorousness, petitions on *behalf* of the accused implicitly contrasted the speech of the "Good Wife" with that of the witch. Supportive neighbors might offer evidence that a suspect was "Christian-like in her Conversation," that they had never heard "any evil in her . . . conversation," or that they could not remember a single "falling out" with her. Furthermore, one's failure to hold a woman to this standard of Christian conversation could in itself be grounds for suspicion. Male witch Hugh Parsons was rendered suspect in part because he did not condemn his wife's heated discourse. If "he had bin innocent," one neighbor reasoned, "he would have blamed her for her Speeches. . . . he would have reproved her Speeches." The quality of a woman's "conversation" went a long way toward marking her as either a good Christian neighbor or a witch.

*   *   *

The connection between disorderly speech and the construction of womanhood figured into both elite and popular conceptions of the witch. This is not to say that speech is the "key" to witchcraft, for we know that many other factors—social, economic, and psychological—combined to make certain women in certain places and at certain historical moments into witches. Nor is it my claim that witchcraft is the "key" to the Puritans' preoccupation with speech, for "governing the tongue" meant listening for all misspeaking, not only to the witch's curse. Nonetheless, reaction against disorderly female speech forged a link between elite and popular versions of the witch, a link that facilitated the prosecution of women who had transgressed many of the boundaries their society set, including the limits of proper female discourse.

When "thou speakest evill," William Perkins warned, "thy tongue is kindled by the fire of hell. . . . cursed speaking is the divels language." Both elite and common folk in early New England would have found much to agree with in Perkins's formulation. The Devil, it seemed certain, entered at the mouth. But the witch's evil speech meant something different to the Puritan minister than it did to the fearful neighbor. The minister heard a version of female authorship that threatened social hierarchy and Puritan male rule. The neighbor heard words made real—words that promised not only social disruption, but physical harm. Like medieval "charms," the witch's words literally embodied danger to those around her.

Being able to hear a witch—to distinguish her by her manner of speaking—was a vital step on the road to disempowering her. Regulating this particular sort of women's disorderly speech was a project of central importance for both the Puritan rulers and the common folk in early New England. Witchcraft accusations offered one avenue through which to reaffirm the contours of what David Hall has called a widely shared common culture. Denouncing the disorderly speech of the witch was one way to demonstrate that the Puritan elite and their subjects did in effect, speak the same language, and that a serious break with that language would not be tolerated.

Though we now admit—and even embrace—the presence of many different voices in our society, we in the multicultural, post-modern 1990s are still wrestling with the damage words can do. Certainly the terms of the debate have changed dramatically since 1692. Since the early national period, the right of citizens to challenge authority—in speech and especially in print—has been enshrined as a defining ideal of American nationhood. And we tend, at least at the level of colloquialism, to denigrate the power of words. We are reminded in the school-yard that, unlike sticks and stones, names can never hurt us. Unlike the Puritan notion of "heated speech," with its social and even magical power, we are apt to consider someone's words as just so much "hot air."

Although we might be hard-pressed to acknowledge that mere speaking remains a significant act with broad social results, we continue to be engaged in our own struggles over the cultural meaning of speech. Many of these debates still center on the appropriate limits of female talk; instead of hunting witches, we construct "bitches." We also ponder, in this electronic age, just what constitutes speech. Is pornography speech? Is blocking access to a clinic a way of speaking? Which of these kinds of so-called "speech" merit prosecution, and which, protection?

One of the most protracted current controversies over the cultural meaning of speech is the heated debate in contemporary America about restraining hate speech— a debate that is, in essence, about the power of words. Where, we ask in 1992 as people did in 1692, does speaking end and literal, physical harm begin? Particularly on American university campuses, people are discussing the power of words with renewed vigor, and are experimenting with different definitions of verbal freedom and verbal injury. The persuasive argument against a libertarian definition of free speech is one that would have had deep resonance in seventeenth-century New England: words are never just words. Words *do* things.

In seventeenth-century New England, the proposition that words were capable of inflicting real damage would not have aroused debate. The ruling elite and common folk alike recognized that speech was a source of power and of danger, and that the boundaries between speaking and doing were fuzzy ones. A woman who crossed the boundaries her culture set for socially "correct" speech might be counted a witch by the minister whose role she usurped, or the neighbors who believed themselves harmed by her words. And the price she might pay for disrupting the social order with her speech might be as high as life itself.

37

The Economic Basis of Witchcraft

Carol F. Karlsen

Carol F. Karlsen, a specialist on women's history, is the author of The Devil in the Shape of a Woman *(1987), a study of the connections between religious beliefs, witch hunting, womanhood, and the social order in Puritan culture. In this excerpt from the book, she examines the role of inheritance disputes and land ownership in the New England witch trials. Karlsen is also the coeditor with Laurie Crumpacher of* The Journal of Esther Edwards Burr, 1743–1757 *(1984).*

•

Most observers now agree that witches in the villages and towns of late sixteenth- and early seventeenth-century England tended to be poor. They were not usually the poorest women in their communities, one historian has argued; they were the "moderately poor." Rarely were relief recipients suspect; rather it was those just above them on the economic ladder, "like the woman who felt she ought to get poor relief, but was denied it." This example brings to mind New England's Eunice Cole, who once berated Hampton selectmen for refusing her aid when, she insisted, a man no worse off then she was receiving it.

Eunice Cole's experience also suggests the difficulty in evaluating the class position of the accused. Commonly used class indicators such as the amount of property owned, yearly income, occupation, and political offices held are almost useless in analyzing the positions of women during the colonial period. While early New England women surely shared in the material benefits and social status of their fathers, husbands, and even sons, most were economically dependent on the male members of their families throughout their lives. Only a small proportion of these women owned property outright, and even though they participated actively in the productive work of their communities, their labor did not translate into financial independence or economic power. Any income generated by married women belonged by law to their husbands, and because occupations open to women were few

From Carol F. Karlsen, *The Devil in the Shape of a Woman: Witchcraft in Colonial New England* (New York: W. W. Norton and Company, 1987), 77–84, 104–11, 115–16. © 1987 by Carol F. Karlsen. Reprinted by permission of W. W. Norton and Company.

and wages meager, women alone could only rarely support themselves. Their material condition, moreover, could easily change with an alteration in their marital status. William Cole, with an estate at his death of £41 after debts, might be counted among the "moderately poor," as might Eunice Cole when he was alive. But the refusal of the authorities to recognize the earlier transfer of this estate from husband to wife ensured, among other things, that as a widow Eunice Cole was among the poorest of New England's poor.

The distinction between the economic circumstances of wife and widow here may not seem particularly significant, but in other cases the problem is more complicated. How, for instance, do we classify the witch Ann Dolliver? The daughter of prominent Salem minister John Higginson, who was well above most of his neighbors in wealth and social status, she was also the deserted wife of William Dolliver, and lived out her life without the support of a husband, dependent first on her father and then on the town for her maintenance. Even if we were willing to assume that the accused shared the class position of their male relatives, the lack of information on so many of the families of witches makes it impossible to locate even the males on an economic scale.

Despite conceptual problems and sparse evidence, it is clear that poor women, both the destitute and those with access to some resources, were surely represented, and very probably overrepresented, among the New England accused. Perhaps 20 percent of accused women, including both Eunice Cole and Ann Dolliver, were either impoverished or living at a level of bare subsistence when they were accused. Some, like thirty-seven-year-old Abigail Somes, worked as servants a substantial portion of their adult lives. Some supported themselves and their families with various kinds of temporary labor such as nursing infants, caring for sick neighbors, taking in washing and sewing, or harvesting crops. A few, most notably Tituba, the first person accused during the Salem outbreak, were slaves. Others, like the once-prosperous Sarah Good of Wenham and Salem, and the never-very-well-off Ruth Wilford of Haverhill, found themselves reduced to abject poverty by the death of a parent or a change in their own marital status. Accused witches came before local magistrates requesting permission to sell family land in order to support themselves, to submit claims against their children or executors of their former husbands' estates for nonpayment of the widow's lawful share of the estate, or simply to ask for food and fuel from the town selectmen. Because they could not pay the costs of their trials or jail terms, several were forced to remain in prison after courts acquitted them. The familiar stereotype of the witch as an indigent woman who resorted to begging for her survival is hardly an inaccurate picture of some of New England's accused.

Still, the poor account for only a minority of the women accused. Even without precise economic indicators, it is clear that women from all levels of society were vulnerable to accusation. If witches in early modern England can accurately be described as "moderately poor," then New Englanders deviated sharply from their ancestors in their ideas about which women were witches. Wives, daughters, and widows of "middling" farmers, artisans, and mariners were regularly accused, and (although much less often) so too were women belonging to the gentry class. The accused were addressed as Goodwife (or Goody) and as the more honorific Mrs. or Mistress, as well as by their first names.

Prosecution was a different matter. Unless they were single or widowed, accused women from wealthy families—families with estates valued at more than £500— could be fairly confident that the accusations would be ignored by the authorities or deflected by their husbands through suits for slander against their accusers. Even during the Salem outbreak, when several women married to wealthy men were arrested, most managed to escape to the safety of other colonies through their husbands' influence. Married women from moderately well-off families—families with estates valued at between roughly £200 and £500—did not always escape prosecution so easily, but neither do they seem, as a group, to have been as vulnerable as their less prosperous counterparts. When only married women are considered, women in families with estates worth less than £200 seem significantly over-represented among *convicted* witches—a pattern which suggests that economic position was a more important factor to judges and juries than to the community as a whole in its role as accuser.

Without a husband to act on behalf of the accused, wealth alone rarely provided women with protection against prosecution. Boston's Ann Hibbens, New Haven's Elizabeth Godman, and Wethersfield's Katherine Harrison, all women, alone, were tried as witches despite sizeable estates. In contrast, the accusations against women like Hannah Griswold of Saybrook, Connecticut, Elizabeth Blackleach of Hartford, and Margaret Gifford of Salem, all wives of prosperous men when they were accused, were simply not taken seriously by the courts. The most notable exception to this pattern is the obliviousness of the Salem judges to repeated accusations against Margaret Thatcher, widow of one of the richest merchants in Boston and principal heir to her father's considerable fortune. Her unusual wealth and social status may have kept her out of jail in 1692, but more likely it was her position as mother-in-law to Jonathan Corwin, one of the Salem magistrates, that accounts for her particular immunity.

Economic considerations, then, do appear to have been at work in the New England witchcraft cases. But the issue was not simply the relative poverty—or wealth—of accused witches or their families. It was the special position of most accused witches vis-à-vis their society's rules for transferring wealth from one generation to another. To explain why their position was so unusual, we must turn first to New England's system of inheritance.

*   *   *

Inheritance is normally thought of as the transmission of property at death, but in New England, as in other agricultural societies, adult children received part of their father's accumulated estates prior to his death, usually at the time they married. Thus the inheritance system included both premortem endowments and post-mortem distributions. While no laws compelled fathers to settle part of their estates on their children as marriage portions, it was customary to do so. Marriages were, among other things, economic arrangements, and young people could not benefit from these arrangements unless their fathers provided them with the means to set up households and earn their livelihoods. Sons' portions tended to be land, whereas daughters commonly received movable goods and / or money. The exact value of these endowments varied according to a father's wealth and inclination, but it appears that as a general rule the father of the young woman settled on the couple roughly half as much as the father of the young man.

Custom, not law, also guided the distribution of a man's property at his death, but with two important exceptions. First, a man's widow, if he left one, was legally entitled "by way of dower" to one-third part of his real property, "to have and injoy for term of her natural life." She was expected to support herself with the profits of this property, but since she held only a life interest in it, she had to see that she did not "strip or waste" it. None of the immovable estate could be sold, unless necessary for her or her children's maintenance, and then only with the permission of the court. A man might will his wife more than a third of his real property—but not less. Only if the woman came before the court to renounce her dower right publicly, and then only if the court approved, could this principle be waived. In the form of her "thirds," dower was meant to provide for a woman's support in widowhood. The inviolability of dower protected the widow from the claims of her children against the estate and protected the community from the potential burden of her care.

The second way in which law determined inheritance patterns had to do specifically with intestate cases. If a man died without leaving a will, several principles governed the division of his property. The widow's thirds, of course, were to be laid out first. Unless "just cause" could be shown for some other distribution, the other two-thirds were to be divided among the surviving children, both male and female. A double portion was to go to the eldest son, and single portions to his sisters and younger brothers. If there were no sons, the law stipulated that the estate was to be shared equally by the daughters. In cases where any or all of the children had not yet come of age, their portions were to be held by their mother or by a court-appointed guardian until they reached their majorities or married. What remained of the widow's thirds at her death was to be divided among the surviving children, in the same proportions as the other two-thirds.

Although bound to conform to laws concerning the widow's thirds, men who wrote wills were not legally required to follow the principles of inheritance laid out in intestate cases. Individual men had the right to decide for themselves who would ultimately inherit their property. . . . Will-writers did sometimes deviate sharply from these guidelines, but the majority seem to have adhered closely (though not always precisely) to the custom of leaving a double portion to the eldest son. Beyond that, New England men seem generally to have agreed to a system of partible inheritance, with both sons and daughters inheriting.

When these rules were followed, property ownership and control generally devolved upon men. Neither the widow's dower nor, for the most part, the daughter's right to inherit signified more than *access* to property. For widows, the law was clear that dower allowed for "use" only. For inheriting daughters who were married, the separate but inheritance-related principle of coverture applied. Under English common law, "feme covert" stipulated that married women had no right to own property—indeed, upon marriage, "the very being or legal existence of the woman is suspended." Personal property which a married daughter inherited from her father, either as dowry or as a post-mortem bequest, immediately became the legal possession of her husband, who could exert full powers of ownership over it. A married daughter who inherited land from her father retained title to the land, which her husband could not sell without her consent. On her husband's death such land became the property of her children, but during his life her husband was entitled to the use and profits of it, and his wife could not devise it to her children by will. The property of an inheriting daughter who was single seems to have been held "for improvement" for her until she was married, when it became her dowry.

This is not to say that women did not benefit when they inherited property. A sizeable inheritance could provide a woman with a materially better life; if single or widowed, inheriting women enjoyed better chances for an economically advantageous marriage or remarriage. But inheritance did not normally bring women the independent economic power it brought men.

The rules of inheritance were not always followed, however. In some cases, individual men decided not to conform to customary practices; instead, they employed one of several legal devices to give much larger shares of their estates to their wives or daughters, many times for disposal at their own discretion. Occasionally, the magistrates themselves allowed the estate to be distributed in some other fashion. Or, most commonly, the absence of male heirs in families made conformity impossible. In all three exceptions to inheritance customs, but most particularly the last, the women who stood to benefit economically also assumed a position of unusual vulnerability. They, and in many instances their daughters, became prime targets for witchcraft accusations. . . .

The experience[s] of . . . witches who came from families without male heirs . . . illuminate the subtle and often intricate manner in which anxieties about inheritance lay at the heart of most witchcraft accusations. . . .

* * *

It was not unusual for women in families without male heirs to be accused of witchcraft shortly after the deaths of fathers, husbands, brothers, or sons. Katherine Harrison, Susanna Martin, Joan Penney, and Martha Carrier all exemplify this pattern. So too does elderly Ann Hibbens of Boston, whose execution in 1656 seems to have had a profound enough effect on some of her peers to influence the outcome of subsequent trials for years to come. Hibbens had three sons from her first marriage, all of whom lived in England; but she had no children by her husband William Hibbens, with whom she had come to Massachusetts in the 1630s. William died in 1654; Ann was brought to trial two years later. Although her husband's will has not survived, he apparently left a substantial portion (if not all) of his property directly to her: when she wrote her own will shortly before her execution, Ann Hibbens was in full possession of a £344 estate, most of which she bequeathed to her sons in England. . . .

Bridget Oliver (later Bridget Bishop) was brought into court on witchcraft charges less than a year after the death of her husband Thomas Oliver in 1679. He had died intestate, but since the estate was worth less than £40 after debts, and since Bridget had a child to raise, the court gave her all but £3 of it during her lifetime, stipulating that she could sell a ten-acre lot "towards paying the debts and her present supply." Twenty shillings went to each of her husband's two sons by his first wife, and twenty shillings to the Olivers' twelve-year-old daughter Christian, the only child of their marriage.

In other cases, many years passed between the death of the crucial male relative and the moment when a formal witchcraft complaint was filed. Twenty years had elapsed, for instance, between the death of Adam Hawkes of Lynn and the arrest of his widow and daughter. Adam had died in 1672, at the age of sixty-four, just three years after his marriage to the much-younger Sarah Hooper and less than a year after the birth of their daughter Sarah. He had died without leaving a will, but his two principal heirs—his widow and his son John from his first marriage—said they were aware of Adam's intentions concerning his £772 estate. The magistrates responsible for distributing Adam's property took their word, allowing "certain articles of agreement" between the two to form the basis of the distribution. As a result, the elder Sarah came into full possession of 188 acres of land and one-third of Adam's movable property. Her daughter was awarded £90, "to be paid five pounds every two years until forty pounds is paid, and the fifty pounds at age or marriage."

It was just about the time young Sarah was due to receive her marriage portion that she and her mother, then Sarah Wardwell, were accused of witchcraft. Named with them as witches were the elder Sarah's second husband, carpenter Samuel Wardwell, their nineteen-year-old daughter Mercy, and the mother, two sisters, and brother of Francis Johnson, the younger Sarah's husband-to-be. It is not clear whether when Sarah Hawkes became Sarah Johnson she received the balance of her inheritance, but £36 of Sarah and Samuel Wardwell's property was seized by the authorities in 1692. Massachusetts passed a law at the height of the Salem outbreak providing attainder for "conjuration, witchcraft and dealing with evil and wicked spirits." Attainder meant the loss of civil, inheritance, and property rights for persons like Sarah Wardwell who had been sentenced to death. Not until 1711 was restitution made to Sarah Wardwell's children.

Margaret Thatcher was not formally accused of witchcraft until more than thirty years after she became an heiress. Merchant Jacob Sheaffe, Margaret's first husband, may have been the richest man in Boston when he died in 1659, leaving only his thirty-four-year-old widow and two daughters, Elizabeth and Mehitabel, to inherit. What disposition was made of the estate is not clear, but the following year witnessed the death of Margaret's father, merchant Henry Webb, a man whose wealth nearly equaled that of his son-in-law, and whose highly detailed will is extant. Margaret was Webb's only child (his wife had died only months before) and he left most of his £7819 estate to her and his two granddaughters, with alternative bequests in several places in the event that Margaret had male heirs by a "second or other marriage." Margaret *was* married again, to Thomas Thatcher, minister of Boston's Old South

Church, but no male heirs were born. Though Margaret was not named a witch until the Salem outbreak, her cousin Elizabeth Blackleach was accused in 1662, two years after Henry Webb's death. Henry had left Elizabeth £140 in his will, £40 of which was to go to her then only child after Elizabeth's death. . . .

Not all witches from families without male heirs were accused of conspiring with the Devil *after* they had come into their inheritances. On the contrary, some were accused prior to the death of the crucial male relative, many times before it was clear who would inherit. Eunice Cole was one of these women. Another was Martha Corey of Salem, who was accused of witchcraft in 1692 while her husband was still alive. Giles Corey had been married twice before and had several daughters by the time he married the widow Martha Rich, probably in the 1680s. With no sons to inherit, Giles's substantial land holdings would, his neighbors might have assumed, be passed on to his wife and daughters. Alice Parker, who may have been Giles's daughter from a former marriage, also came before the magistrates as a witch in 1692, as did Giles himself. Martha Corey and Alice Parker maintained their innocence and were hanged. Giles Corey, in an apparently futile attempt to preserve his whole estate for his heirs, refused to respond to the indictment. To force him to enter a plea, he was tortured: successively heavier weights were placed on his body until he was pressed to death.

What seems especially significant here is that most accused witches whose husbands were still alive were, like their counterparts who were widows and spinsters, over forty years of age—and therefore unlikely if not unable to produce male heirs. Indeed, the fact that witchcraft accusations were rarely taken seriously by the community until the accused stopped bearing children takes on a special meaning when it is juxtaposed with the anomalous position of inheriting women or potentially inheriting women in New England's social structure.

Witches in families without male heirs sometimes had been dispossessed of part or all of their inheritances before—sometimes long before—they were formally charged with witchcraft. Few of these women, however, accepted disinheritance with equanimity. Rather, like Susanna Martin, they took their battles to court, casting themselves in the role of public challengers to the system of male inheritance. In most instances, the authorities sided with their antagonists.

The experience of Rachel Clinton of Ipswich is instructive. As one of five daughters in line to inherit the "above £500" estate of their father, Richard Haffield, Rachel had been reduced to abject poverty at least eighteen years before she came before county magistrates in 1687 as a witch. Richard Haffield had bequeathed £30 to each of his daughters just before his death in 1639, but since Rachel was only ten at the time, and her sister Ruth only seven, he stipulated that their shares were to be paid "as they shall com to the age of sixteen yeares old." While he had not made other bequests, he made his wife Martha executrix, and so the unencumbered portions of the estate were legally at her disposal. In 1652, since Rachel and Ruth were still unmarried (Rachel was twenty-three at the time), local magistrates ordered Martha Haffield to pay one of her sons-in-law, Richard Coy, the £60 still due Rachel and Ruth, to "improve their legacy."

When Martha Haffield wrote her own will in 1662, six years before her death, she bequeathed the still-single Rachel the family farm, valued at £300, with the proviso that she share the income it produced with her sisters, Ruth (now Ruth White) and Martha Coy. The household goods were to be divided among the three. Martha had effectively disinherited her two oldest children (children of her husband's first marriage) with ten shillings apiece. This will, though legal, would never be honored. In 1666, the county court put the whole Haffield estate into the hands of Ruth's husband, Thomas White, whom they named as Martha Haffield's guardian and whom they empowered to "receive and recover her estate." They declared Martha Haffield "non compos mentis."

The issue that seems to have precipitated this court action was Rachel's marriage to Lawrence Clinton several months before. Lawrence was an indentured servant and fourteen years younger than his wife. Perhaps even more offensive to community standards, Rachel had purchased Lawrence's freedom for £21, with money she said her mother had given her. Once Thomas White had control of the Haffield estate, he immediately sued Lawrence's former master, Robert Cross, for return of the £21.

Several issues were raised in the almost four years of litigation that followed, but arguments focused on the legality of Rachel's access to and use of the money. Never explicitly mentioned by White, but clearly more important to him than the £21, was Rachel's sizeable inheritance. For Rachel, the stakes were obvious: "my brother [in-law] White . . . is a cheaten Rogue," she insisted, "and [he] goese about to undoe mee. He keeps my portion from me, and strives to git all that I have." The case was complicated by a number of factors, including Lawrence Clinton's desertion of his life. White did at last gain full control of the Haffield estate, however, and retained it for the rest of his life.

Martha Haffield died in 1668. Shortly before, Rachel, then thirty-nine, had been forced to petition the court for relief, "being destitute of money and friends and skill in matters of Law." The house where she and her mother had lived, she said, had been sold by White, and its contents seized. Even her marriage portion, she averred, was still withheld from her "under pretence of emprovement." Giving up her attempt to claim her inheritance, she subsequently tried to make her estranged husband support her. Though the court made several halfhearted attempts to compel Lawrence to live with his wife, or at least to maintain her, by 1681 they had tired of the effort: "Rachel Clinton, desiring that her husband provide for her, was allowed 20 shillings," they declared, "she to demand no more of him." No doubt Rachel's adulterous involvement with other men influenced the court's decision, although Lawrence's sexual behavior had been even more flagrant. In 1677, Rachel had petitioned for, but had been denied, a divorce. When she appealed again in late 1681, it was granted her. From then on, she was a ward of the town. In 1687, and again in 1692, she was accused of malefic witchcraft. The second time she was tried and convicted.

Sarah Good's plight resembles that of Rachel Clinton, even in some of the particulars. Sarah's father, John Solart, a prosperous Wenham innkeeper, had taken his own life in 1672, leaving an estate of about £500 after debts. He left a widow,

Elizabeth, and nine children—seven daughters and two sons. The court accepted testimony from three witnesses concerning an oral will he had made, and awarded the widow £165, and the eldest son, John, a double share of £84. Since two of the daughters had already received their shares as marriage portions, the other six children, including Sarah, were to receive £42 each when they came of age. Sarah was then seventeen or eighteen. That same year, the widow Solart married Ezekiel Woodward, who upon this marriage came into possession of the £165 and the unpaid children's portions.

More than a decade later, the surviving daughters petitioned the court for the inheritances left them by their father. By that time their mother and both of their brothers had died. After the death of their mother, they said,

> . . . Ezekill Woodward, that maryed with our mother, did Refuse to enter into any obligation to pay our portions. Our brother Joseph, whoe would have bien of Age the last Winter, is dead, and your Honores have declared the last court at Salem, that his portion shall be devided amongst us. But except your honnours will be pleased to put us into som capacity to gitt it, we know not well how to gitt it that soe we may divid it.

Most wronged, they added, was their sister Sarah, then wife of former indentured servant, Daniel Poole:

> . . . she is 28 yers of age and she is yett without her portion. And except that she will accept of a parcell of land which our father bought at a very deare Rate for his convenience, which was well fenced, and she alow the same price for it now, the fenc is taken off, she is not like to have anything. . . .

The court responded that the daughters "could recover their right from any person withholding it," but made no provision for them to do so. Twenty-three years later, litigation over the Solart estate was still going on.

Sarah, at least, never did recover what she felt was rightfully hers. By 1686, the little she had was gone. Her first husband, Daniel Poole, had died sometime after the 1682 petition was filed, leaving only debts for which Sarah and her second husband, William Good, were held responsible. . . .

* * *

Looking back over the lives of these many women—most particularly those who did not have brothers or sons to inherit—we begin to understand the complexity of the economic dimension of New England witchcraft. Only rarely does the actual trial testimony indicate that economic power was even at issue. Nevertheless it is there, recurring with a telling persistence once we look beyond what was explicitly said about these women as witches. Inheritance disputes surface frequently enough in witchcraft cases, cropping up as part of the general context even when no direct link between the dispute and the charge is discernible, to suggest the fears that underlay most accusations. No matter how deeply entrenched the principle of male inheritance, no matter how carefully written the laws that protected it, it was impossible to insure that all families had male offspring. The women who stood to benefit from these demographic "accidents" account for most of New England's female witches.

The amount of property in question was not the crucial factor in the way these women were viewed or treated by their neighbors, however. Women of widely varying economic circumstances were vulnerable to accusation and even to conviction. Neither was there a direct line from accuser to material beneficiary of the accusation: others in the community did sometimes profit personally from the losses sustained by these women (Rachel Clinton's brother-in-law, Thomas White, comes to mind), but only rarely did the gain accrue to the accusers themselves. Indeed, occasionally there was no direct temporal connection: in some instances several decades passed between the creation of the key economic conditions and the charge of witchcraft; the charge in other cases even anticipated the development of those conditions.

Finally, inheriting or potentially inheriting women were vulnerable to witchcraft accusations not only during the Salem outbreak, but from the time of the first formal accusations in New England at least until the end of the century. Despite sketchy information on the lives of New England's early witches, it appears that Alice Young, Mary Johnson, Margaret Jones, Joan Carrington, and Mary Parsons, all of whom were executed in the late 1640s and early 1650s, were women without sons when the accusations were lodged. Elizabeth Godman, brought into court at least twice on witchcraft charges in the 1650s, had neither brothers nor sons. Decade by decade, the pattern continued. Only Antinomian and Quaker women, against whom accusations never generated much support, were, as a group, exempt from it.

The Salem outbreak created only a slight wrinkle in this established fabric of suspicion. If daughters, husbands, and sons of witches were more vulnerable to danger in 1692 than they had been previously, they were mostly the daughters, husbands, and sons of inheriting or potentially inheriting women. As the outbreak spread, it drew into its orbit increasing numbers of women, "unlikely" witches in that they were married to well-off and influential men, but familiar figures to some of their neighbors nonetheless. What the impoverished Sarah Good had in common with Mary Phips, wife of Massachusetts's governor, was what Eunice Cole had in common with Katherine Harrison, and what Mehitabel Downing had in common with Ann Hibbens. However varied their backgrounds and economic positions, as women without brothers or women without sons, they stood in the way of the orderly transmission of property from one generation of males to another.

38

Who Were the Witches?

CHRISTINA LARNER

Christina Larner's work was introduced in part 1. In this additional excerpt from her 1981 book Enemies of God: The Witch-Hunt in Scotland, *Larner describes the types of women who tended to be prosecuted for witchcraft in Scotland.*

•

Although it can be argued that all women were potential witches, in practice certain types of women were selected or selected themselves. In Scotland those accused of witchcraft can be described, though not with precision, under four heads: those that accepted their own reputation and even found ego-enhancement in the description of a "rank witch" and the power that this gave them in the community; those that had fantasies of the Devil; those who became convinced of their guilt during their inquisition or trial; and those who were quite clear that they were innocent, and who either maintained their innocence to the end or confessed only because of torture or threat of torture. They are all equally interesting in relation to the image of the witch in the community, but those who embraced the role of witch are also interesting in relation to the actual attraction of witchcraft for women.

This attraction of witchcraft is clear when we ask why the witches were drawn from the ranks of the poor. Apart from the obvious fact that it was socially easier to accuse those who were least able to defend themselves witchcraft had a particular attraction for the very poor. It has been pointed out by Thomas that the English witches, who were more clearly than the Scottish ones at the bottom of the stratification ladder, were people who felt themselves to be totally impotent. The normal channels of expression were denied to them, and they could not better their condition. Witchcraft, Thomas suggests, was believed to be a means of bettering one's condition when all else had failed. The fear of witchcraft bestowed power on those believed to be witches. A reputation for witchcraft was one possible way of modifying the behaviour of those more advantageously positioned. More than that, it was a

From Christina Larner, *Enemies of God: The Witch-Hunt in Scotland* (Baltimore: Johns Hopkins University Press, 1981), 94–102. © 1981 by Christina Larner. Reprinted by permission of Johns Hopkins University Press.

direct way of providing benefits for themselves. Although the Demonic Pact does not loom very large in English witchcraft it is made something of a centrepiece by Thomas in the psychology of the self-conscious witch. Those who committed what is well described as the "mental crime" of the Demonic Pact (that is those who not only consciously believed that they were committing effective acts of malefice, the social crime, but also that they were able to do this because of their relationship with the Devil in the Demonic Pact) also revealed in their confessions the exact nature of the promises which the Devil had made to them. We have moved a long way in rural pre-industrial England and Scotland from the classic aristocratic pacts of the Dr. Faustus type where great creative gifts are on offer in return for the individual immortal soul of the human concerned. The economic value to the Devil of the soul of a seventeenth-century peasant was not so great. With these people, in whom hope is expressed in the most circumspect of terms, we are in the world of relative deprivation. Seventeenth-century English women at the margins of society did not expect that their soul would qualify them for silk and riches. Instead they said that the Devil promised them mere freedom from the extremes of poverty and starvation. He told them, typically, "that they should never want".

The witches of Scotland used exactly the same terminology as those of England, but since the Pact loomed much larger they used it more habitually and more extensively. The Devil's promises were much the same from the time when the pact is first mentioned in Scottish cases until it faded from the collective imagination. John Feane in 1591 related that the Devil had promised him "that he should never want". In 1661 it was the same. The Devil promised Margaret Brysone "That she should never want", Elspeth Blackie, "that she should want nothing", and likewise Agnes Pegavie and Janet Gibson. Bessie Wilson was told by the Devil, "thee art a poor puddled (overworked) body. Will thee be my servant and I will give thee abundance and thee sall never want", and Margaret Porteous was told even more enticingly, that "she should have all the pleasure of the earth". Thomas also noted that English witches in their exchanges with the Devil were sometimes offered small sums of money which sometimes then turned out to be worthless. One of the witches in this particular group from Dalkeith in 1661, Agnes Pegavie, also mentioned that the Devil, after making these rather limited promises, gave her 12d in silver which she found afterwards to be only a "sklait stane".

Equally good indicators of their expectations and sense of the economically possible are the more elaborate confessions which include descriptions of witches' meetings. The food and drink said to have been available at these meetings varied a bit; very occasionally it was said to have been unpalatable, usually in circumstances in which the Devil was also perceived as being generally unkind to his servants and beating them up for failures in wickedness. More often it fell within the range of normal peasant fare: oatcakes and ale. Sometimes it was the fare of the landed class: red wine, wheaten cake, and meat.

There are other suggestions than hope of alleviating poverty as to why women might be attracted to witchcraft. The explanation of the Gonja woman in West Africa interviewed by Goody echoes that of the seventeenth-century European manuals.

Although some women gave specific motives one answered "because we are evil". Goody suggests that while there are a number of contexts in which men may kill there are few in which women may legitimately use aggression even if they are able to. In situations of domestic stress and tension in which men resort to violence, women use witchcraft. The female witches in the seventeenth-century Scottish courts may be the equivalent of the males accused of slaughter and murder. This is to assume what is sometimes forgotten in analyses which involve oppressor and oppressed, that women are not more virtuous than dominant males any more than the poor are more virtuous than dominant landlords. They are merely less powerful. Another angle on the theme of psychological motivation is suggested by Warner in her novel *Lolly Willowes*. Here witchcraft represents adventure and excitement which are normally excluded from the lives of women. Women may turn to cursing to give vent to aggression or exercise power. They may fantasize about the Devil to bring colour to their lives.

The women who sought or involuntarily received the accolade of witch were poor but they were not in Scotland always solitary. The women who were the classic focus of witch accusations were frequently, it turns out, impoverished not because they were widows or single women with no supporters or independent means of livelihood, but were simply married to impoverished men. The figures which we have obtained for marital status are again not very good, but they are better than those for social status. About half of those whose status is recorded were in fact married at the time of their arrest. Some were solitaries, but solitariness as such does not appear to have been an important element in the composition of a Scottish witch. Nor does ugliness appear to have been of very much importance. Macfarlane has drawn attention to the stereotype of the ill-favoured witch, though Thomas discounts its significance. The presence of a popular literature on witchcraft in England which was almost absent in Scotland may have made the factor of personal appearance a more significant one there. The stereotype of the ugly, old woman certainly existed in Scotland, but there is little evidence connecting this stereotype with actual accused witches.

So far as personal as opposed to social characteristics go we are left with the variable of character. This is a notoriously difficult concept to deal with historically. One can sometimes identify character traits in particular individuals. But it is usually hard to say whether these are deviant in terms of standard behaviours of the period. ... We may observe some of the personal characteristics of the witch; we do not know whether they are characteristic of all seventeenth-century Scottish women near the bottom of the socio-economic hierarchy. This problem was recognized at the time, and much exploited by defence lawyers. The successful defender of Elizabeth Bathgate of Eyemouth argued in respect of a witness who claimed to have been bewitched after being shouted at by the accused, that nothing has been "libelled to procure his distress but a sort of Railing and Flyting (quarrelling) which is common to women when stirred up by their neighbours and especially by websters as common objects to women's spleen".

When all this is said, however, the essential individual personality trait does seem to have been that of a ready, sharp and angry tongue. The witch had the Scottish female quality of smeddum: spirit, a refusal to be put down, quarrelsomeness. No cursing: no malefice; no witch. The richness of language attributed to witches is considerable. Helen Thomas of Dumfries was accused by Agnes Forsyth in August 1657 of having said, "Ane ill sight to you all, and ane ill sight to them that is foremost, that is Agnes Forsyth." In similar vein Elspeth Cursetter of Orkney in May 1629 hoped that "ill might they all thryve and ill might they speid." More aggressively, Issobel Grierson was alleged in 1667 to have said "The faggotis of hell lycht on the, and hellis caldrane may thow seith in." Agnes Finnie of the Potterrow in Edinburgh, who was accused in 1642, was alleged to have said that "she should gar the Devil take a bite of the said Bessie Currie", and to John Buchanan at Lambarr, "John, go away, for as you have begun with witches so you shall end with them." And her daughter Margaret Robertson, not to be outdone when called by one Andrew Wilson "ane witches get" (offspring), replied, "if I be a witches get the Devil rive the Soul out of you before I come again." Less dramatically, but packed with economic menace, Elizabeth Bathgate told George Sprot, "for work what you can your teeth shall overgang your hands and ye shall never get your Sundays meat to the fore."

The witch may have been socially and economically in a dependent position, but the factor which often precipitated accusations was the refusal to bring to this situation the deference and subservience which was deemed appropriate to the role. In her dealings with relative equals too she was likely to be just as aggressive.

It is one thing, however, to produce a static ideal-type of the commonest features of the witch. She is a married middle-aged woman of the lower peasant class and she has a sharp tongue and a filthy temper. The problem as with so many stereotypes is that its explanatory force is limited in that not only did a considerable number of Scottish witches not fit the stereotype; an even larger number of people who did, and who lived in the danger zones for witch accusation and prosecution, were never accused or identified in this way. It is at this point that the labelling theory of sociology may have something to contribute, for labelling theory stresses the dynamic elements in the process of identifying and thereby creating a socially deviant person. There is a continuous interaction between the individual and society. "At the heart of the labelling approach is an emphasis on *process*; deviance is viewed not as a static entity but rather as a continuously shaped and reshaped *outcome* of dynamic processes of social interaction." These, it is argued, occur on three levels of social action; collective rule making, interpersonal reactions, and organizational processes.

Without the collective rule making by which witchcraft was reconstructed as an offence against society in 1563 and the nature of it redefined during the 1590–91 treason trials, there could have been no Scottish witch-hunt. It is possible to develop this argument further and say there would have been no demonic witches. There were, essentially, no demonic witches in the Highlands and Islands during the period of the hunt, and none in the rest of Scotland before the late sixteenth century. There were plenty of specialists. There were charmers, healers, sooth-sayers, poisoners, owners of the evil eye, and there were cursers. Many of these, particularly the successful cursers, would have been called witches. The difference between them and the seventeenth-century east-coast and lowland witch was two-fold: in the first place, the meaning of the label changed to something at once more precise and more universally anti-social: the new witch was not only the enemy of the individual or even of the locality; she was the enemy of the total society, of the state, and of God; in the second place the existence of the third level of social action, the new organizational processes, both created a demand for the production of witches and at the same time made the production more rewarding to the community. It was these factors that generated activity on the second level; that of interpersonal relations.

In the process of building up a reputation in a community there was one important element which provides a link between the static description of the social and personality types which were most likely to attract accusations of witchcraft, and the identification of those individuals who actually ended up in the courts. This was the accused's friends, relatives, and associates. There was nothing like a link with someone already suspected to set the labelling process going. We have already mentioned the daughter of Agnes Finnie. The label of "witches get" was often the first stage. Evil powers were believed to be transmitted from parent to child (a belief which sits uneasily with the demonic pact). Those cases that have come to light tend to be the ones where mother and daughter were executed together (partly because it is otherwise difficult to identify the relationship when the mother retained her own name while passing her husband's on to the daughter). In 1673 in Scalloway in the Shetland Isles, Margaret Byland and her daughter, Suna Voe, were both commissioned for trial. Two years later, also in Shetland, an unnamed old woman and her daughter, Helen Stewart, were executed together. There must have been many more cases where the label was passed on, and the daughter either lived with the label for ever, or was accused formally at a later date. The term "witch's get" was part of the normal currency of rural life.

Other relationships had their effect as well. In 1629, the sheriff of Haddington was given a commission to try John Carfra, Alison Borthwick, his wife, and Thomas Carfra, his brother. They were also charged with having consulted with Margaret Hamilton and Bernie Carfra, who was, no doubt, another relative, and who had already been burnt for witchcraft. Husband and wife teams were quite common. In West Lothian, in February, 1624, Elspet Paris was tried along with her husband, David Langlandis, and the following month William Falconner, his sister Isobell Falconner, and his wife Marioun Symsoun were tried with a group of other witches. In the same area, in Kirkliston, near Edinburgh, in 1655, William Barton and his wife were strangled and burnt. Mere acquaintanceship however would do perfectly well. When Elspeth Maxwell was tried at Dumfries in 1650 it was alleged that she had been an associate of a woman who had been burnt three years before, and this was a very common item in the depositions. Yet these links and associations are still only an occasional factor in the making of witches. The build up of reputation seems normally to have taken some time, and to have been a dynamic process of social interaction between witch and neighbours with steady mutual reinforcement. When Agnes Finnie, whose cursing powers have already been mentioned, said, "if I be a witch, you or yours shall have better cause to call me so," she was giving a classical demonstration of the move from primary to secondary labelling (acceptance of the label and the accompanying role).

Unfortunately we can tell very little about the crucial initial stage in the process of becoming of ill repute, since the depositions usually bring together a set of accusations allegedly made over a period, but certainly gathered together at one point in time. Sometimes the dates of the malefices are identified, but even some of these may have been recalled, or seen in a new light after the reputation had been established. This is another of the areas where an intensive local study, matching early complaints against witches in the Kirk session with cases which later came to the courts, might be particularly illuminating.

The length of time over which a reputation could be built up varied greatly, a factor which lends support to the suggestion that many reputed witches could live with the reputation for a lifetime and die in their beds, even during the seventeenth century. Some witches who were eventually accused had lived with the label long enough to have acquired a title. In Inverkeithing, in 1631, Walker the Witch was active. Janet Taylor, who was banished from Stirling in 1634 was known as the Witch of Monza. Others had names which simply identified a peculiarity which could make them socially marginal. "Deiff Meg", whose deafness clearly contributed to her reputation, was tried with four others in Berwick in 1629. More mysterious was Archibald Watt in Lanarkshire, who was known as "Sole the Paitlet, a warlock".

Others had a long term reputation without acquiring any special title, and with or without such a title many lived with the reputation for years before they were eventually brought to trial. Janet Wright of Niddry, near Edinburgh, was said in 1628 to have been by her own confession for the last eighteen or nineteen years "a consulter with the devil has resaved his marks, renunced her baptism and givin herselfe over to the devill's service", and William Crichtoun of Dunfermline in 1648 "being straitlie posed and dealt with by the ministers and watchers, he came to a confession of sundrie things, and that he hade made a paction with the Devill to be his servand 24 yeirs and more since".

Labelling theory takes us only so far in suggesting why particular individuals who shared the classic characteristics with many others were selected from them for accusation. It explains the build-up of social reinforcement, but, apart from the selection of daughters of witches, not the beginning of the process. In the last resort it can only be said that these individuals were in the wrong place at the wrong time.

When we turn from the selection of the individual back to the classic characteristics, however, there still remains a problem. What is the relationship between the type of person accused of witchcraft and the growth of witchcraft prosecutions? There is some evidence to suggest that the relationship is a direct one. Witch-hunting *is* woman-hunting or at least it is the hunting of women who do not fulfil the male view of how women ought to conduct themselves. An example from anthropology is that of the Nupe in the nineteen twenties. Nadel describes how the women were money lenders and traders and the men of the Nupe were very often in their debt. These women lived independent lives, took lovers, and rarely had children. They challenged the conventional ideal of women as servicing men and children, and it was they who were accused of witchcraft.

We do not at present have enough evidence to say whether the status of women was radically changing in Europe in the fifteenth, sixteenth, and seventeenth centuries in a manner analogous to the more limited and specific case cited by Nadel. It has been argued that the witch-hunt was an attack by the emergent male medical profession on the female healer. There is a certain amount of evidence for this. In Scotland in 1641 in the ratification of the privileges of the Edinburgh chirurgeons it was noted that unqualified females had been practising chirurgy illegitimately in the city, and a number of witchcraft suspects were identified as midwives. The connection, however, is not direct enough. The main usurpation of midwifery by males took place in the eighteenth century after the witch-hunt was over. The objection to female healers was concentrated in the towns where the emergent male professionals had their strength. While witchcraft prosecutions may sometimes have married conveniently with the suppression of female healing, male professionalization of healing really cannot account for the mass of the prosecutions.

A different argument is that capitalizing agriculture reduced the role of women to that of a mere producer of children rather than a participant in peasant production. Anyone pursuing this argument however is likely to get into difficulties. Not enough is known to support or, what is worse, to make suspect, any large scale theory on the economic history of women. In particular the timing of that major change seems to have varied greatly in different parts of Europe, and in most areas took place after the end of the witch-hunt. The suggestion that this period saw an increase in the number of unsupported women is, again, difficult to substantiate, and the witch-hunt was not primarily directed against them.

If we turn to the sphere of ideology the case for witch-hunting being seen as a woman-hunt is more convincing. The stereotype of the witch was not that of the child-woman; it was that of the adult, independent woman. The religion of the Reformation and the Counter Reformation demanded that women for the first time became fully responsible for their own souls. Indeed preachers went out of their way to refer to "men and women" in their sermons. The popularization of religion, however, took away from women with one hand what it gave to them with the other, for the particular form of religion was strongly patriarchal. The ritual and moral inferiority of women was preached along with their new personal responsibility. The status of women became ambiguous under the terms of the new ideology.

Witchcraft as a choice was only possible for women who had free will and personal responsibility attributed to them. This represented a considerable change in the status of women in Scotland at least. Up to the time of the secularization of the crime of witchcraft their misdemeanours had been the responsibility of husbands and fathers and their punishments the whippings thought appropriate to children. As witches they became adult criminals acting in a manner for which their husbands could not be deemed responsible. The pursuit of witches could therefore be seen as a rearguard action against the emergence of women as independent adults. The women who were accused were those who challenged the patriarchal view of the ideal woman. They were accused not only by men but also by other women because women who conformed to the male image of them felt threatened by any identification with those who did not.

This explanation is the most plausible of those which identify witch-hunting as woman-hunting because unlike the other explanations the timing seems right. Nevertheless while witch-hunting and woman-hunting are closely connected they cannot be completely identified as one and the same phenomenon. The relationship is at one degree removed. The demand for ideological conformity was simply a much wider one than that aspect of it that concerned the status of women. The present discussion over the direct connection between the alleged uniqueness of English witchcraft and the allegedly unique status of women in England is therefore misconceived. The pursuit of witches was an end in itself and was directly related to the necessity of enforcing moral and theological conformity. The fact that a high proportion of those selected in this context as deviants were women was indirectly related to this central purpose.

V

Salem: A Case Study of the Primary Documents

THE STORY OF THE Salem, Massachusetts, hysteria in brief outline begins in the household of Samuel and Elizabeth Parris. Samuel was the minister of the village church and very much at odds with some of the local people, especially those who favored continuing their connection to the mercantile community of Salem Town. The village sat on the outskirts of the town itself. For years one group of families had worked toward autonomy for Salem Village and its church; another wanted to retain their ties to the town government. Samuel Parris supported the village independence movement, but in the fall of 1691 the pro-town faction had gained control of the village funds and refused to pay his salary.

In December 1691 two children in the Parris family became sick with peculiar fits, during which they complained of odd sensations, were wracked with painful muscle spasms, and began to jabber in ways that could not be understood by the adults. Doctors could find no explanation for their problems and had no new therapy to recommend. Elizabeth (called Betty), the daughter of Elizabeth and Samuel Parris, was nine years old, and their live-in niece, Abigail Williams, was twelve. The girls, along with another twelve-year-old, Ann Putnam, and seventeen-year-old Elizabeth Hubbard, who was living in the house of her uncle, Dr. William Griggs, had been dabbling in folk magic to tell their fortunes. They saw dangerous omens. Fears about their future and guilt about playing with the occult may have triggered Betty's and Abigail's fits. In a short time Ann and Elizabeth also became infected with whatever plagued the youngsters in the Parris household.

Parris, using good Protestant exorcist techniques, earnestly prayed with his family and congregation and called on nearby ministers to join with him in those prayers. The children were not relieved. There was no improvement in their condition through January and February. One physician, Dr. William Griggs, thought the "evil hand" was at work.

More drastic measures were discussed. The community was rife with rumors that the girls were bewitched. One of Parris's parishioners, Mary Sibley, decided to take some action. Impatient with the ineffective methods of the clergy, she called on Tituba and her husband, Indian John, Parris's house slaves, to work some counter-magic. They were to use an old English concoction of the girls' urine and some rye meal to be baked in ashes and fed to a dog. This was done on February 25, some two months after the onset of the symptoms. It was good, old-fashioned English magic. Supposedly the dog would identify the person causing the harm to the children.

There is no proof, and certainly no seventeenth-century evidence, that Tituba was teaching the girls witchcraft of any type. Rather, the evidence points the other way. Even Parris admitted that she had not been involved before the witch cake incident. Tituba did not come into the picture of odd events until she was approached by Mary Sibley at the end of February. Imaginative attempts to link Tituba to the fortunetelling games or any voodoo rites are pure fiction.

Following the "experiment" with the witch cake, the girls' fits became more violent; they complained of even more pain from being pinched and hit and threatened with a knife. They had to be restrained from hurting themselves. Parris, at the end of February, finally asked them who was bewitching them. They accused three women at first: Sarah Good, Sarah Osborne, and Tituba. The women were arrested on March 1. Under questioning, the two Sarahs denied being witches, but Good accused Osborne of witchcraft. Tituba confessed to consorting with the devil. In her confession she also implicated other unnamed people. The hunt was on to find them and bring them to public attention.

Within a short time many more people were implicated, a large number of whom were part of the village faction that did not support Samuel Parris or who lived within the limits of the town proper. By the fall months the epidemic of accusations had spread beyond the confines of Salem Village and Town, Close to two hundred people throughout the eastern part of Massachusetts had come under suspicion.

To handle the crisis the governor, who had just returned from England, set up a special Court of Oyer and Terminer in May. For the first time a Massachusetts court accepted and condemned people on the basis of spectral evidence, witches' marks, and "images" in lieu of confessions. There was a strong presumption of guilt based on reputation and hearsay. By the end of September, twenty-six people had been convicted and nineteen of them (fourteen women and five men) had already been hanged. One man was pressed to death for refusing to plead in the court. Another four people would die in jail, Seven awaited execution. Fifty more individuals were under indictment but had not yet been tried. In October the governor dissolved the Court of Oyer and Terminer, effectively ending the use of spectral evidence. There were no further executions for witchcraft in Salem. The trials continued in January 1693 under the aegis of a different set of rules of evidence and a less emotionally charged judicial body.

The sources of information on the Salem events, like the sources on most of the witchcraft trials of the past years, are abundant but at the same time incomplete. They basically show one side of the affair—the official view. We do not know what was left out of the documented record, and information on little-known individuals is very hard to come by. Extant written comments on the happenings reflect individual biases; we can only guess at how widespread particular views were. With this caveat in mind, I have selected four types of material to present as examples of primary source material bearing on the Salem episode. First are documents describing the political problems, legal issues, and court procedures that were familiar to the authorities and that structured the events. Second are excerpts from the testimonies of three of the accused women and a commentary on the events by an observer.

Third are the depositions of several (but not all) of their accusers and a commentary from the clergy, all supporting the trials. Fourth and finally I have included statements from those who voiced doubts about the conduct of the trials. Part 6 contains studies by four historians who interpret these and many other sources of information on the Salem episode.

Legal Procedures

Regardless of who was accused or why, in the English-speaking world witch hunts occurred only when government officials took legal action against someone accused of a criminal act. Thus official recognition is the key to whether an accusation of witchcraft moved beyond the level of interpersonal conflict or churchly concern and became a legal matter. Only then was the accused subject to judicial action and only then could there be a concentrated effort to persecute those accused of witchcraft. Legal practice was the arena in which the authorities expressed their will. The law justified their actions.

Colonial law theoretically was based on parliamentary statute and the English common law. Technically the colonies could pass no law that was contrary to those laws recognized in England. In practice, however, the Puritans consistently violated many English statutes—they ignored the Navigation Acts and discriminated against Quakers and Anglicans. In 1661, outraged by the policies of the Stuart king, Charles II, Massachusetts defiantly declared that its citizens were exempt from all laws and royal decrees from England.

Continuing complaints about these violations finally led to the revocation of the Massachusetts charter in 1684. Two years later, in an attempt to gain more control over his colonies and force them into greater conformity with English law, the king consolidated Massachusetts with the other New England colonies into a single unit called the Dominion of New England under one governor. Soon after, New York and the Jerseys were added to the Dominion. The Puritans lost control over the destiny of their settlement.

But in 1689, with a bloodless revolution in England, the royal governor of the Dominion was ousted; Massachusetts, by default, reverted back to its old laws; and the colony awaited a new charter from the avowedly Protestant monarchs, William and Mary of Orange. The populace earnestly wished for a confirmation of their old form of government. The Puritan leadership, very much chastened by the earlier revocation of its charter, hoped for a compromise and an opportunity to regain some political clout.

The witch scare may have provided a way to ease the conflict between colony and crown. While awaiting instructions from England and anxious to placate those who complained that New England was too deviant from English ways and an unwelcome place for the non-Puritan, the leadership planned to bring Massachusetts legal procedures and laws more in line with English practice. They could demonstrate in 1692 that law in Massachusetts was held to the standards of the home country. Unfortunately, this also meant a loosening of the restrictions recommended by the Puritan divines that had limited the New England courts in cases of witchcraft.

Until then the Puritans had followed a watch-and-wait approach, careful to protect those who might be innocent from frivolous accusations. Samuel Willard's attitude toward Elizabeth Knapp is a good example of the cautious approach that was favored by the clergy. Willard refused to make public the name of a possible witch. Although there were several accusations made against local women, he was not willing to exploit Elizabeth's confessions. Cotton Mather at first had exhibited the same caution in the case of the sick "possessed." Goodwin children. Only when convinced that the Glover woman was collaborating with the devil to bewitch the children did he announce her name and encourage the trial that led to her death in 1688. But her named confederates were not pursued.

Glover was an unusual case. Very few people were ever convicted by the courts in New England. In a careful compilation of such accusations, John Demos counted ninety-three known complaints of witchcraft in all of New England between 1638 and 1691. Of these, eighty-three led to indictments, but only twenty were convicted, and of those we know that not all were executed in that fifty-year period. At least twenty accusations of witchcraft mentioned in various sources never reached the courts, and another twenty-six documented cases of slander may have been in reprisal against such accusations. (These numbers can be found in John Demos, *Entertaining Satan: Witchcraft and the Culture of Early New England* [New York: Oxford University Press, 1982], 402–9.) Thus until 1692, New England authorities did not take most accusations of witchcraft seriously enough to consider legal action. And when they did, the courts seldom followed English judicial practice that had condemned people on the basis of popular notions of witchcraft.

Massachusetts had only one law dealing with witchcraft, and that had been included in a 1641 code called the Massachusetts Body of Liberties. Section 2 of the list of capital crimes notes that "If any man or woman be a witch (that is hath or consulteth with a familiar spirit), they shall be put to death." No information was given on how to treat such cases. At the same time Massachusetts fell under the 1604 parliamentary statute that also imposed the death penalty for consorting with an evil spirit.

Legal guides based on English practice helped magistrates interpret the law. One of the most widely used handbooks on the prosecution of all felonies was Michael Dalton's *Country Justice*. The section on witchcraft reprinted here is also a vivid demonstration of the reality of witchcraft in the seventeenth-century legal mind and a reminder of how seriously such matters were treated by those in authority. Dalton describes the kind of evidence that was acceptable in English courts but had not always been used in previous Massachusetts witchcraft trials.

The Court of Oyer and Terminer, an ad hoc court set up in Salem specifically to handle witchcraft accusations, followed much of Dalton's advice. Judges accepted spectral evidence—testimony that a witch's spirit had appeared to a bewitched person—and also the presence of witches' marks or teats as proof of witchcraft. The court also gave a great deal of credence to the testimony of confessed witches. In the process, the Salem magistrates ignored some of Dalton's warnings that mere demonstrations of occult power were insufficient grounds for conviction and that additional direct and visible evidence of a diabolical pact was essential. The lay notion of witchcraft that had stressed *maleficium*—harmful acts through occult means—rather than the theological notion of a conspiracy with Satan, dominated the Massachusetts trials for the first time.

The colonists also had access to the works of another Englishman, William Perkins. In his 1610 *Discourse on the Damned Art of Witchcraft*, Perkins attempts to resolve the dilemma of reconciling criminal law with popular notions of evil deeds stemming from witchcraft. He makes a clear distinction between evidence that a crime had been committed and the more stringent proof necessary for conviction.

Circumstantial or presumptive evidence, Perkins advises, could be used to bring a feared man or woman to public attention and trial. But to convict a person of such a heinous crime and take his or her life was a different matter. Hearsay about counter-magic or any folk wisdom was insufficient. Only a voluntary confession to the signing of a diabolical pact or two objective witnesses to an actual incidence of devil worship or to the signing of such a pact could lead to a conviction.

Perkins assumes that because the devil wanted his followers to suffer and was a great liar, he would betray the witches eventually. It was an elegant argument: magistrates should bide their time, because evil ways would eventually reveal and condemn the witches. They would be caught in their own snares and in the meanwhile the truly innocent would be protected by due process of law. But not all Englishmen agreed with his moderate approach. As in England in the 1640s, the fear of witchcraft in Massachusetts during the spring and summer of 1692 overcame any tendency to follow such reasonable advice.

The Accused

The court transcripts that follow are extracted from the surviving records of the hearings and depositions reported by the Salem authorities. With few exceptions, the trial transcripts themselves have not been preserved. Re-creating what happened during the trials is a matter of speculation based partly on the kinds of evidence offered during the pretrial hearings and also the eyewitness reports that have survived. Excerpts from the cases of three of the accused are presented here: Tituba, the first to be accused and to confess without being tried; Rebecca Nurse, a most unlikely person to be convicted because of her high social station; and Bridget Bishop, who fit the stereotype of the witch and was the first to be hanged.

John Hathorne and Jonathan Corwin, as members of the Court of Assistants, the highest legislative and judicial body in Massachusetts, signed the warrants ordering the arrests and, as Salem magistrates, directed the questioning. The type of questions asked and the harassment in prompting for desired answers became the accepted procedure followed in all examinations. Once the accused caved in to the pressure and confessed, the progress of the questioning changed to that followed in Tituba's case. The interrogators began a quest for details on the diabolical meetings and the identification of coconspirators.

After Nathaniel Saltonstall, one of the Oyer and Terminer judges, resigned in June in protest over the procedures followed by the court, Corwin was appointed a judge in his place. Jonathan Corwin, therefore, was both a prosecutor and a judge of the same cases.

The Reverend Deodat Lawson's narrative of the Salem events describes what he observed during the early weeks of the arrests and fills in some of the gaps left by the incomplete testimonies. Although delivered in a laconic style, Lawson's account projects a sense of the increasing fear in the community. His response to events inside and outside the court lent credence to the accusations of witchcraft that led from the arrest of Tituba to that of Rebecca Nurse and her sister, Sarah Cloyce.

The Accusers

Testimony by the accusers offers more details about the procedures and the kind of complaints that led to the trials. Elizabeth Hubbard, Abigail Williams, and Ann Putnam the younger were the earliest witnesses against Tituba and Rebecca Nurse. They testified to a variety of tortures at the hands of the two accused women to force them to sign the devil's book. The information they gave in these early testimonies was not very imaginative, but as time went on a great deal of local lore and gossip began to enter into other depositions.

By the time Bridget Bishop came to the attention of the authorities in April, the details of satanic happenings had become much more elaborate and fanciful. Deliverance Hobbs added information about a diabolical meeting that included several women, including Bishop. Hobbs herself was accused of witchcraft and she became the fourth to confess to witchcraft (following Tituba, Abigail Hobbs, and Mary Warren), and thereafter her testimony was used to implicate many others. But Bridget Bishop also had a poor reputation among her neighbors and rumors about her nastiness abounded. Hearsay and local gossip entered into several depositions. The Reverend John Hale of Beverly, who had also known Bridget Bishop before she moved to Salem, in repeating this story about her bewitching others in his town, added to the rumors that she was a witch of long standing.

After Bishop was tried on June 2 and then executed eight days later, complaints about the conduct of the trial reached the governor, William Phips. Nathaniel Saltonstall resigned from the court in protest. Disturbed by this reaction, Governor Phips asked the leading ministers of the province to comment on the trial. They responded on June 15, 1692, with a rather severe criticism of the use of spectral and presumptive (i.e., circumstantial hearsay) evidence. But, convinced that the community was infected by a diabolical presence, they urged the continuation of the trials, advising only more careful attention to English law and practice to protect the innocent as outlined in the work of William Perkins. This advice was not followed and the court continued to rely on rumors and reputation along with specters as proof of a crime. The trials continued for another three months.

The Doubters

The concerns of the clergy and the governor were not the only doubts expressed at the time. All through the summer of 1692, questions continued to disturb many people. Some quiet talk about irregularities and the possibility of innocent people being killed took place behind closed doors. Soon letters circulated among friends raising the question of how dependable evidence given by confessed witches could be.

Thomas Brattle's letter, describing "a multitude of errors," although not written until after the Court of Oyer and Terminer was adjourned in October, reflects the consternation of his friends during the course of the trials. He was not alone in these objections but was part of a circle of men, both jurists and ordinary laymen, in Boston who condemned the procedures used by the Court of Oyer and Terminer in Salem. That they kept their objections quiet was not necessarily due to cowardice although, given the conduct of the prosecutors, fear of reprisals was probably in their minds. The constraints against criticism of governmental action were much greater in those days than today. Proper behavior of the elite required at least passive support of public authority whether elected or appointed.

In a violation of that code of conduct, Brattle severely condemns the entire judicial procedure and in particular the badgering of the accused in the court and at the gallows. There were also questions about why some of those accused such as Mrs. Thatcher, Judge Jonathan Corwin's mother-in-law, were ignored while others found themselves in court. Most objectionable was the attention given to the evidence of confessed witches who had been subjected to psychological pressure and physical torture. Some of those confessing, Brattle suggests, may well have been insane and not fit to be questioned. He correctly predicted that the folly of the learned in accepting all this nonsense and condemning so many to death would forever stain the reputation of New England.

Although there were to be no more executions, the trials continued. The ad hoc Court of Oyer and Terminer was dissolved by Governor Phips in October and the seven awaiting the death sentence were reprieved and eventually pardoned. A new court, established in late 1692, using more stringent types of evidence, dismissed many cases. Thirty-three trials were conducted in several locations, but only three people were convicted under the new rules that forbade the use of spectral evidence. These three were also reprieved by the governor, who decided that they were not responsible for their actions. These trials did not rely on the testimony of the "afflicted" girls who, in the course of time, neither wasted away nor were disabled physically as they had claimed earlier. Their seizures had no permanent ill effects, except possibly in the case of Ann Putnam, who became a rather sickly adult and died unmarried at the age of thirty-six.

And so the Salem witch hunt ended, but the consequences had to be faced. The pain caused to the families of the accused and the memory of the events in the larger community lingered on. It appeared that a terrible mistake had been made. On December 17, 1696, the General Court of Massachusetts recognized the error and tried to make amends by declaring a day of fast and prayer. The day of prayer was to be held throughout the province on January 14, 1697, "that all iniquity may be put away . . . and help us wherein we have done amiss to do so no more."

The proclamation opened the floodgates of remorse and a series of individual apologies for participation in the Salem trials. The first to apologize was Samuel Sewall, who had been a judge in the original trials and had remained on the court after Saltonstall's resignation. Many years later Ann Putnam, at the age of twenty-six, begged forgiveness from her church for her role in causing such "sorrow and offense." One of the more emotional apologies, printed here, came from twelve men who sat on juries and condemned their neighbors. Their "distress" echoed the deep remorse of many who were caught up in the hysteria, the "general delusion" that had such terrible consequences. In the meanwhile, although never officially confronted, Parris admitted some error and was finally forced out of his parsonage in 1697.

The Reverend John Hale, who had testified against two women during the trials, also faced a crisis of conscience. He had contributed to both convictions and the death of one of those women. In the aftermath of "that sad catastrophe," he wondered about the wisdom of his participation in the trials. Unlike Brattle, he did not doubt the existence of witchcraft or the presence of Satan in Massachusetts. He was convinced that Satan had infected the community. Rather, his doubts related to the zeal of the prosecutors and the possibility of faulty evidence being used during the trials.

To absolve his own guilt as well as that of the magistrates, Hale wanted to find a way to excuse those who participated in the witch hunt without denying the need to be vigilant against such threats. He argues in his euphemistically titled *Modest Enquiry into the Nature of Witchcraft* that the convictions, although based on questionable evidence, were providential and necessary to warn Puritans about their failures. God, therefore, brought on Salem's excesses as a way to force Christians to rethink and reconsider their beliefs and faults. Unlike the laymen who apologized, he could not distance himself from the theology that had encouraged the trials. Nor could he admit that it was all a mistake—only specific decisions were at fault. Human error rather than theology was the culprit.

A. LEGAL PROCEDURES

39

Conjuration and Witches

Michael Dalton

Michael Dalton (d. 1648) published The Country Justice *in 1618 as a guide to court procedures for justices of the peace in England. It was also used by New England magistrates, few of whom had legal training. The wording in this 1697 edition is the same as that of the fourth edition, published in 1630, which included information from the 1604 witchcraft statute. For the fourth edition Dalton drew on Richard Bernard's* Guide to Grand-Jury Men *(1627), another handbook widely used in America. The procedures outlined in* The Country Justice *remained in effect, even though seldom used after 1692, until Parliament repealed the Witchcraft Act in 1736.*

•

Conjuration

1. Conjuration, or invocation of any evil spirit, for any intent, etc., or to be counseling or aiding thereto, is felony without benefit of clergy. See *Exod.* 22.18. *Deut.* 18.11. and *Lev.* 20.27.

2. To consult, covenant with, entertain, employ, feed, or reward any evil Spirit, to or for any intent or purpose, is felony in such offenders, their aiders and counselors.

3. To take up any dead body, or any part thereof to be employed or used in any manner of witchcraft, is felony in such offenders, their aiders and counselors.

4. Also to use or practice witchcraft, enchantment, charm or sorcery, whereby any person shall be killed, pined [i.e., waste away] or lamed in any part of their body, or to be counseling or aiding thereto, is felony. By the ancient Common Law such offenders were to be burned, *Fit.* 269.b. See the Law of God against witches, *Exod.* 22.18 and against such as seek to witches and Wizards, *Levit.* 19.31. and 20.6.

5. Also the second time to practice witchcraft, etc. thereby to declare where any treasure may be found, is felony.

From Michael Dalton, *The Country Justice: Containing the Practice of the Justices of the Peace out of Their Sessions* (London, 1697), 383–86.

6. Or where any goods lost or stolen may be found.

7. Or where any cattle or goods shall be destroyed or impaired.

8. Or to the intent to provoke any person to love.

9. Or to the intent to hurt any person in their body, though it be not effected. All these are felony, etc. the second offense, and without benefit of Clergy.

Witches

Now against these witches (being the most cruel, revengeful and bloody of all the rest) the Justices of Peace may not always expect direct evidence, seeing all their works are the works of darkness, and no witnesses present with them to accuse them; and therefore for the better discovery, I thought good here to insert certain observations, partly out of the Book of Discovery of the Witches that were arraigned at Lancaster, Anno 1612, before Sir James Altham, and Sir Ed. Bromley, Judges of Assize there, and partly out of Mr. Bernard's Guide to Grand-jury-men.

1. These witches have ordinarily a familiar or spirit, which appeareth to them sometimes in one shape, sometimes in another; as in the shape of a man, woman, boy, dog, cat, foal, hare, rat, toad, etc. And to these their spirits they give names, and they meet together to Christen them . . .

2. Their said familiar hath some big or little teat upon their body, and in some secret place, where he sucketh them. And besides their sucking, the devil leaveth other marks upon their body, sometimes like a blue spot or red spot, like a flea-biting, sometimes the flesh sunk in and hollow (all which for a time may be covered, yea taken away, but will come again to their old form). And these the devil's marks be insensible, and being pricked will not bleed, and be often in their secretest parts, and therefore requires diligent and careful search.

These first two are main points to discover and convict these witches; for they prove fully that those witches have a familiar, and made a league with the devil.

So likewise if the suspected be proved to have been heard to call upon their spirits, or to talk to them or of them, or have offered them to others.

So if they have been seen with their spirit, or seen to feed some thing secretly, these are proofs they have a familiar, etc.

3. They have often pictures of clay or wax (like a man, etc., made of such as they would bewitch) found in their house, or which they roast or bury in the earth, [so] that as the picture consumes, so may the parties bewitched [be] consumed.

4. Other presumptions against these witches; as, if they be given to usual cursing and bitter imprecations, and withal use threatenings to be revenged, and their imprecations or some other mischief presently followeth.

5. Their implicit confession; as, when any man shall accuse them for hurting them or their cattle, if they shall answer, "You should have let me alone then," or, "I have not hurt you as yet." These and the like speeches are in manner of a confession of their power of hurting.

6. Their diligent inquiry after the sick party or coming to visit him or her unsent for; but especially being forbidden the house.

7. Their apparition to the sick party in his fits.

8. The sick party in his fits naming the parties suspected, and where they be or have been, or what they do, if truly.

9. The common report of their neighbours, especially if the party suspected be of kin, or servant to, or familiar with a convicted witch.

10. The testimony of other witches, confessing their own witchcrafts, and witnessing against the suspected, that they have spirits or marks; that they have been at their meetings; that they have told them what harm they have done, etc.

11. If the dead body bleed upon the witches touching it.

12. The testimony of the person hurt, upon his death.

13. The examination and confession of the children (able and fit to answer) or servants of the witch, especially concerning the first six observations: Sc. [*scilicet*, i.e., namely] If the party suspected have a familiar, or any teat, or pictures; her threatenings and cursings of the sick party; her inquiry after the sick party; her boasting or rejoicing at the sick party's trouble; Also whether they have seen her call upon, speak to, or feed any spirit, or such like; or have heard her foretell of this mishap, or speak of her power to hurt, or of her transportation to this or that place, etc.

14. Their own voluntary confession, (which exceeds all other evidence) sc. of the hurt they have done, or of the giving of their souls to the devil, and of the spirits which they have, how many, how they call them, and how they came by them.

15. Besides, upon the apprehension of any suspected, to search also their houses diligently for pictures of clay or wax, etc., hair cut, bones, powders, books of witchcraft, charms and for pots or places where their spirits may be kept, the smell of which place will stink detestably.

* * *

Now to show you farther some signs to know whether the sick party be bewitched.

1. When a healthful body shall be suddenly taken, etc. without probable reason, or natural cause appearing, etc.

2. When two or more are taken in the like strange fits in many things.

3. When the afflicted party in his fits doth tell truly many things what the witch or other parties absent are doing or saying and the like.

4. When the parties shall do many things strangely, or speak many things to purpose, and yet out of their fits know not any thing thereof.

5. When there is a strength supernatural as that of a strong man or two shall not be able to keep down a child or weak person upon a bed.

6. When the party doth vomit up crooked pins, needles, nails, coals, lead, straw, hair, or the like.

7. When the party shall see visibly some apparition, and shortly after some mischief shall befall him.

But withal observe with Mr. Bernard that divers strange diseases may happen only from natural causes, where he showeth eight such several diseases; therefore, unless

368 — MICHAEL DALTON

the compact with the devil be proved or evinced by evident marks or tokens as abovesaid, it is not to be supposed that the devil is the agent.

Indictments

And note, for the better riddance of these witches, being duly proved to be such, there must good care be had as well in their examinations taken by the Justices: as also in the drawing of their indictments, that the same be both of them set down directly in the material points, etc. As,

That the witch (or party suspected) hath used invocation of some spirit.

Or, That they have consulted or covenanted with their spirit.

Or, That they employed their spirit, etc.

Or, That they have fed or rewarded their spirit.

Or, That they have killed or lamed, etc. some person, etc.

And not to indict them generally for being witches, etc.

The difference between conjuration, witchcraft and enchantment, etc. is this. *Scil.* Conjurers and witches have personal conference with the devil or evil spirit, to effect their purposes. See I *Sam.* 28.7 etc. The conjurers believe by certain terrible words that they can raise the devil and make him to tremble; and by impailing [i.e., arranging] themselves in a circle (which, as one saith, cannot keep out a mouse), they believe that they are therein ensconced and safe from the devil, whom they are about to raise; and having raised the devil, they seem by prayers and invocation of God's powerful names, to compel the devil to say or do what the conjurer commands him.

The witch dealeth rather by a friendly and voluntary conference or agreement between him (or her) and the devil or familiar, to have his or her turn served; and in lieu thereof, the witch gives (or offereth) his or her soul, blood or other gift unto the devil.

Also the conjurer compacts for curiosity to know secrets or work miracles; and the witch of mere malice to do mischief and to be revenged.

The enchanter, charmer, or sorcerer, these have no personal conference with the devil, but (without any apparition) work and perform things (seemingly at the least) by certain superstitions and ceremonial forms of words (called charms) by them pronounced; or by medicines, herbs, or other things applied, above the course of nature, and by the devil's help and covenants made with him.

Of this last sort likewise are sooth-sayers or wizards, which divine and foretell things to come by the flying, singing or feeding of birds, and unto such questions as be demanded of them, they do answer by the devil (or by his help), *Scil.* they do either answer by voice, or else do set before their eyes in glasses, crystal stones, or rings, the pictures or images of the person or things sought for.

[40]

On the Identification of a Witch

WILLIAM PERKINS

The English Puritan theologian William Perkins (1558–1602) was an accepted authority on witchcraft. A Discourse on the Damned Art of Witchcraft *(1610), which was published after his death, went through several editions in English and was translated into many other languages. It was cited by various New England authors and referred to by magistrates in the witch trials there.*

•

Section II

Question. *How we may be able in these our days to discern and discover a witch?*

Ans. The discovery of a witch is a matter judicial, as is also the discovery of a thief and a murderer and belongs not to every man but is to be done judicially by the magistrate according to the form and order of law who, therefore, is set apart for such ends and hath authority both to discover and to punish the enemies of God and his Church. Now for the magistrate's direction in this business, we are to know that in the discovery of a witch two things are required: examination and conviction.

1. Examination is an action of the magistrate making special inquiry of the crime of witchcraft. This action must have the beginning from occasions and presumptions. For the magistrate, though he be a public person and stand in the room of God for the execution of justice, yet he may not take upon him to examine whom and how himself wills of any crime, neither ought he to proceed upon slight causes as to show his authority over others or, upon sinister respects, as to revenge his malice, or to bring parties into danger or suspicion; but he must proceed upon special presumptions.

Those I call presumptions, which do at least probably and conjecturally note one to be a witch, and these are certain signs whereby the party may be discovered. I will touch some few of them.

The first in order is this: if any person, man or woman, be notoriously defamed

From William Perkins, *A Discourse of the Damned Art of Witchcraft* (Cambridge, 1610), 199–218.

for such a party. Notorious defamation is a common report of the greater sort of people, with whom the party suspected dwelleth, that he or she is a witch. This yieldeth a strong suspicion. Yet the magistrate must be wary in receiving such a report. For it falleth out oftentimes, that the innocent may be suspected and some of the better sort notoriously defamed. Therefore the wise and prudent judge ought carefully to look that the report be made by men of honesty and credit, which, if it be, he may then proceed to make further inquiry of the fact.

The second is if a fellow-witch or magician gives testimony of any person to be a witch, either voluntarily or at his or her examination, or at his or her death. This is not sufficient for conviction or condemnation, but only a fit presumption to cause straight examination of the party to be made.

Thirdly, if after cursing there follows death, or at least some mischief. For witches are wont to practice their mischievous facts by cursing and banning. This also is a sufficient matter of examination, not of conviction.

Fourthly, if after enmity, quarreling, or threatening, a present mischief doth follow. For parties devilishly disposed, after cursings do use threatenings, and that also is a great presumption.

Fifthy, if the party suspected be the son or daughter, the manservant or maidservant, the familiar friend, near neighbour, or old companion of a known and convicted witch. This may be likewise a presumption. For witchcraft is an art that may be learned and conveyed from man to man, and often it falleth out that a witch dying leaveth some of the forenamed, heirs of her witchcraft.

Sixthly, some do add this for a presumption. If the party suspected be found to have the devil's mark. For, it is commonly thought, when the devil maketh his covenant with them he always leaveth his mark behind him whereby he knows them for his own. Now if by some casual means such a mark be descried [i.e., found] on the body of the party suspected, whereof no evident reason in nature can be given, the magistrate in this case may cause such to be examined or take the matter into his own hand that the truth may appear.

Lastly, if the party examined be inconstant, or contrary to himself in his deliberate answers, it argueth a guilty mind and conscience which stopeth the freedom of speech and utterance, and may give just occasion to the magistrate to make further enquiry. I say not if he or she be timorous and fearful, for a good man may be fearful in a good cause, sometimes by nature, sometimes in regard to the presence of the judge and the greatness of the audience. Again, some may be suddenly taken and others naturally want the liberty of speech which other men have. And these are the causes of fear and astonishment, which may befall the good as well as the bad.

Touching the manner of examination, there be two kinds of proceedings: either by a single question or by some torture. A single question is when the magistrate himself only maketh enquiry, what was done or not done, by bare and naked interrogations. A torture is, when besides the enquiry in words, he uses also the rack or some other violent means to urge confession. This course hath been taken in some countries and may, no doubt, lawfully and with good conscience be used, howbeit not in every case but only upon strong and great presumptions going before and when the party is obstinate. And thus much for examination. Now follows conviction.

2. Conviction is an action of the magistrate after just examination discovering the witch. This action must proceed from just and sufficient proofs and not from bare presumptions. For though presumptions give occasion to examine, yet they are no sufficient causes of conviction. Now in general the proofs used for conviction are of two sorts, some be less sufficient, some be more sufficient.

The less sufficient proofs are these. First, in former ages, the party suspected of witchcraft was brought before the magistrate who caused red hot iron and scalding water to be brought and commanded the party to put his hand in the one or take up the other or both. And if he took up the iron in his bare hand without burning or endured the water without scalding, hereby he was cleared and judged free, but if he did burn or scald, he was then convicted and condemned for a witch. But this manner of conviction hath long ago been condemned for wicked and diabolical, as in truth it is, considering that thereby many times an innocent man may be condemned and a rank witch escape unpunished.

Again, our own times have afforded instances of such weak and insufficient proofs. As first, scratching of the suspected party and present recovery thereupon. Secondly, burning of the thing bewitched, if it be not a man, as a hog, or ox, or such like creature is imagined to be a forcible means to cause the witch to discover. [i.e., disclose] her self. Thirdly, the burning of the thatch of the suspected party's house, which is thought to be able to cure the party bewitched and to make the witch to bewray [i.e., betray] herself.

Besides these, in other countries they have a further proof justified by some that be learned. The party is taken and bound hand and foot and cast cross ways into the water. If she sink, she is counted innocent and escapeth; if she fleet [i.e., float] on the water and sinks not, she is taken for a witch, convicted and accordingly punished.

All these proofs are so far from being sufficient that some of them, if not all, are after a sort practices of witchcraft, having in them no power or virtue to detect a sorcerer, either by God's ordinance in the creation or by any special appointment since. For what virtue can the scratching of a witch have to cure a hurt? . . .

But how then comes it to pass that help is often procured by these and such like means? *Ans.* It is the sleight and subtlety of the devil upon scratching the witch to remove such hurts as himself hath inflicted, that thereby he may inure men to the practice of wicked and superstitious means. And what I say of scratching, the same may be enlarged to all other proofs of this kind before named. . . . That therefore which is brought to pass by them when they are used, cometh from the devil.

And yet to justify the casting of a witch into the water, it is alleged, that having made a covenant with the devil, she hath renounced her Baptism, and hereupon there grows an antipathy between her and water. *Ans.* This allegation serves to no purpose for all water is not the water of Baptism but that only which is used in the very act of baptism and not before nor after. The element out of the use of the sacrament is no sacrament but returns again to his common use.

To go yet further, another insufficient proof is the testimony of some wizard. It hath been the ordinary custom of some men, when they have had anything ill at ease, presently to go or send to some wise man or wise woman, by whom they have been informed that the thing is bewitched, and, to win credit to their answer, some of them have offered to show the witches' face in a glass. Whereof the party, having been taken notice, returns home and detecteth the man or woman of witchcraft. This I grant may be a good presumption to cause straight examination, but a sufficient proof of conviction it can not be. For put the case: the grandjury at the Assizes goeth on a party suspected, and, in their consultation, the devil comes in the likeness of some known man and tells them the person in question is indeed a witch and offers withal to confirm the same by oath. Should the inquest receive his oath or accusation to condemn the man? Assuredly no. And yet that is as much as the testimony of another wizard who, only by the devil's help, revealeth the witch. If this should be taken for a sufficient proof, the devil would not leave one good man alive in the world.

Again, all other presumptions commonly used are insufficient, though they may minister occasion of trial. For example, if a man in open court should affirm before the judge: such a one fell out with me and cursed me giving me threatening words that I should smart [i.e., suffer] for it and some mischief should light upon my person or goods, ere it were [before] long. Upon these curses and threats, presently such and such evils befell me, and I suffered these and these losses. The magistrate thus informed may safely proceed to inquire into the matter, but he hath not from hence any sure ground of conviction. For it pleaseth God many times to lay his hand upon his men's persons and goods without the procurement of witches. And yet experience shows that ignorant people, who carry a rage against them, will make strong proofs of such presumptions, whereupon sometimes jurors do give their verdict against parties innocent.

Lastly, if a man being dangerously sick and like to die, upon suspicion will take it on his death that such a one hath bewitched him, it is an allegation of the same nature, which may move the judge to examine the party, but it is of no moment for conviction. The reason is, because it was but the suspicion of one man and a man's own word for himself, though in time of extremity when it is likely he will speak nothing but the truth, is of no more force than another man's word against him.

And these are the proofs which men in place and time have ordinarily used for the detecting of such ungodly persons. But the best that may be said of them is that they be all either false or uncertain signs and unavailable for the condemnation of any man whatsoever.

Now follow the true proofs and sufficient means of conviction, all which may be reduced to two heads.

The first is the free and voluntary confession of the crime, made by the party suspected and accused, after examination. This hath been thought generally of all men both divines and lawyers, a proof sufficient. For what needs more witness or further enquiry, when a man from the touch of his own conscience acknowledgeth the fault.

And yet the patrons and advocates of witches except [i.e., take exception] against it and object in this manner: that a man or woman may confess against themselves an untruth, being urged thereto either by fear or threatening, or by a desire upon some grief conceived to be out of the world; or at least, being in trouble and persuaded it is the best course to save their lives and obtain liberty, they may upon simplicity be induced to confess that which they never did even against themselves. *Ans.* I say not, that a bare confession is sufficient, but a confession after due examination taken upon pregnant presumptions. For, if a man examined without any ground or presumptions should openly acknowledge the crime, his act may be justly suspected as grounded upon by respects [i.e., a hidden motive]; but when proceeding is made against him at the first upon good probabilities, and hereupon he be drawn to a free confession, that which he hath manifested thereby cannot but be a truth. . . .

Now if the party held in suspicion be examined and will not confess, but obstinately persist in denial, as commonly it falleth out, then there is another course to be taken by a second sufficient means of conviction, which is the testimony of two witnesses, of good and honest report, avouching before the magistrate upon their own knowledge these two things: either that the party accused hath made a league with the devil or hath done some known practices of witchcraft. And all arguments that do necessarily prove either of these, being brought by two sufficient witnesses, are of force fully to convince [i.e., convict] the party suspected. For example:

First, if they can prove that the party suspected hath invocated and called upon the devil or desired his help. For this is a branch of that worship which Satan bindeth his instruments to give unto him. And it is a pregnant proof of a league formerly made between them.

Secondly, if they can give evidence that the party hath entertained a familiar spirit, and had conference with it in form or likeness of a mouse, cat, or some other visible creature.

Thirdly, if they affirm upon oath that the suspected person hath done any action or work which necessarily infereth a covenant made—as that he hath showed the face of a man suspected, being absent, in a glass or used enchantment or such like feats. In a word, if they both can avouch upon their own proper knowledge that such a man or woman suspected hath put in practice any other actions of witchcraft as to have divined of things afore [i.e., before] they came to pass and that peremptorily to have raised tempests, to have caused the form of a dead man to appear, or the like, standing either in divination or operation, it proveth sufficiently that he or she is a witch.

But some may say, if these be the only strong proofs for the conviction of a sorcerer, it will be then impossible to put any one to death because the league with Satan is closely made and the practices of sorcery are also very secret and hardly can a man be brought, which upon his own knowledge, can aver such things.

I answer, howsoever both the ground and practice be secret and to many unknown, yet there is a way to come to the knowledge thereof. For it is usual with Satan to promise any thing till the league be ratified, but when it once made and the party entangled to society with him, then he endeavoureth nothing more than his or her discovery and useth all means possible to disclose them. So that what end soever the witch propounds to her self in the league, he intendeth nothing else but her utter confusion. . . . The causes which move the devil not only to affect but to hasten this discovery are two principally.

The first is his malice towards all men in so high a degree that he cannot endure they should enjoy the world or the benefits of this life (if it were possible) so much as one hour. Though, therefore, by virtue of the precontract he be cock-sure of this instrument, yet his malice is not herewith satisfied till the party be brought to light and condemned to death, which may be a caveat to all ill disposed persons that they beware of yielding themselves unto him.

The second is his insatiable desire of the present and full possession of them whom he hath got within the bonds of the covenant. For, though he have good hope of them, yet is he not certain of their continuance. The reason is, because some united with him in confederacy have, through the great mercy of God, by careful usage of holy means and faith in Christ, been reclaimed and delivered out of his bondage, and so at length freed from his covenant, so as he hath eternally left them. Hence it is that he labours by might and main to keep them in ignorance and to prevent the usage of means effectual to their conversion by laying a plot for their discovery. But how then comes it to pass that all such persons are not speedily detected, but some live long and others die without any man's privity [i.e., knowledge]? *Ans.* The reasons hereof may be divers.

First, because some one or more of them may belong to God's election, and therefore, albeit for causes best known to himself, He may suffer them for a time to be holden in the snares of Satan, yet at length in mercy He reclaims them, and in the mean time suffers not the devil to exercise the depth of his malice in discovering them to their confusion. Again, for others, the Lord may in justice and anger suffer them not to be disclosed that living under the means where they might be reclaimed and willfully condemning the same, they may live to fill up the measure of their iniquities and thereby be made finally inexcusable, that they may receive their juster condemnation.

Secondly, the devil suffereth some to live long undisclosed that they may exercise the greater measure of his malice in the world, especially if they be parties maliciously bent to do hurt to men and other creatures.

Thirdly, some witches do warily agree with the devil, for a certain term of years, during which time he bindeth himself not to hurt them, but to be at their command. And Satan is careful, especially in case of his own advantage, to keep touch with them that they may the more strongly cleave unto him on their parts. But if the case so stand, that neither the party suspected confesseth nor yet sufficient witnesses can be produced which are able to convict him or her either of these two ways, we have no warrant out of the word either in general or in specific, to put such a one to death. For though presumptions be never so strong, yet they are not proofs sufficient for conviction, but only for examination.

I would therefore wish and advise all jurors who give their verdict upon life and death in courts of Assizes, to take good heed, that as they be diligent in zeal of God's glory and the good of his Church in detecting of witches by all sufficient and lawful means; so likewise they would be careful what they do and not to condemn any party suspected upon bare presumptions without sound and sufficient proofs, that they be not guilty through their own [rashness?] of shedding innocent blood.

B. THE ACCUSED

[41]

Examination of Tituba

Tituba, Samuel Parris's Indian woman servant-slave, was taken into custody on February 29, 1692, along with Sarah Osborne and Sarah Good on the complaint of Elizabeth (Betty) Parris, Abigail Williams, Ann Putnam, Jr., and Elizabeth Hubbard. She was questioned from March 1 through 5 by John Hathorne and indicted on May 9, 1692, on the charge of making a covenant with the devil. There are two versions of her first day's testimony and one version of the second day's questioning. No copy of any subsequent examinations exists. The excerpts below are from the official report of the first day's questioning written by Ezekiel Cheever. Additional details taken from the notes written by Jonathan Corwin are included in brackets.

•

Salem Village, March 1, 1692

Tituba an Indian woman brought before us by Constable Joseph Herrick of Salem upon suspicion of witchcraft by her committed according to the complaint of Joseph Hutcheson and Thomas Putnam, etc. of Salem Village as appears per warrant granted Salem 29 February 1691/2. Tituba upon examination and after some denial acknowledged the matter of fact according to her examination given in more fully will appear and who also charged Sarah Good and Sarah Osborne with the same. . . .

John Hathorne and Jonathan Corwin, Assistants

(**Hathorne:**) Titibe what evil spirit have you familiarity with?

(**Tituba:**) None.

(**H:**) Why do you hurt these children?

(**T:**) I do not hurt them.

(**H:**) Who is it then?

(**T:**) The devil for ought I know.

(**H:**) Did you never see the devil?

(**T:**) The devil came to me and bid me serve him.

[**Q.** What appearance or how doth he appear when he hurts them; with what shape or what is he like that hurts them.

From Salem Witchcraft Papers: Verbatim Transcripts of the Legal Documents, ed. Paul Boyer and Stephen Nissenbaum (New York: Da Capo, 1977), 3:747–49.

A. Like a man I think. Yesterday I being in the leanto chamber I saw a thing like a man, that told me serve him and I told him no I would not do such a thing. (*She charges Goody Osbourn and Sarah Good as those that hurt the children, and would have had her done it. She sayth she seen four, two of which she knew not. She saw them last night as she was washing the room.*) They told me hurt the children and would have had me gone to Boston. There was five of them with the man.]

(H:) Who have you seen?

(T:) Four women sometimes hurt the children.

(H:) Who were they?

(T:) Goody Osborne and Sarah Good and I do not know who the other were. Sarah Good and Osborne would have me hurt the children but I would not. (*She further saith there was a tall man of Boston that she did see.*)

(H:) When did you see them?

(T:) Last night at Boston.

(H:) What did they say to you?

(T:) They said hurt the children,

(H:) And did you hurt them?

(T:) No, there is four women and one man. They hurt the children and lay all upon me and they tell me if I will not hurt the children, they will hurt me.

(H:) But did you not hurt them?

(T:) Yes, but I will hurt them no more.

(H:) Are you not sorry you did hurt them?

(T:) Yes. . . .

(H:) What have you seen?

(T:) A man come to me and say serve me.

(H:) What service?

(T:) Hurt the children and last night there was an appearance that said, "Kill the children," and if I would no go on hurting the children they would do worse to me.

[Q. At first beginning with them, what then appeared to you, what was it like that got you to do it.

A. One like a man just as I was going to sleep came to me. This was when the children was first hurt, he said he would kill the children and she would never be well and he said if I would not serve him he would do so to me.

Q. Is that the same man that appeared before to you that appeared the last night and told you this?

A. Yes.

Q. What other likenesses besides a man hath appeared to you?

A. Sometimes like a hog, sometimes like a great black dog, four times.]

(H:) What is this appearance you see?

(T:) Sometimes it is like a hog and sometimes like a great dog.

(*This appearance she saith she did see four times.*)

(H:) What did it say to you?

(T:) The black dog said serve me but I said I am afraid. He said if I did not he would do worse to me.

(H:) What did you say to it?

(T:) I will serve you no longer. Then he said he would hurt me and then he looks like a man and threatens to hurt me. (*She said that this man had a yellow bird that kept with him*) and he told me he had more pretty things that he would give me if I would serve him.

(H:) What were these pretty things?

(T:) He did not show me them.

(H:) What else have you seen?

(T:) Two rats, a red rat and a black rat. . . .

[Q. What other creatures did you see?

A. I saw two cats, one red, another black as big as a little dog,

Q. What did these cats do?

A. I don't know. I have seen them two times.

Q. What did they say?

A. They say serve them.

Q. When did you see them.

A. I saw them last night.

Q. Did they do any hurt to you or threaten you.

A. They did scratch me.

Q. When?

A. After prayer, and scratched me because I would not serve them and when they went away I could not see but they stood before the fire.]

(H:) Why did you go to Thomas Putnam's last night and hurt his child?

(T:) They pull and haul me and make [me] go.

(H:) And what would [they] have you do?

(T:) Kill her with a knife.

(*Lieutenant Fuller and others said at this time when the child saw these persons and was tormented by them that she did complain of a knife that they would have her cut her head off with a knife.*)

(H:) How did you go?

(T:) We ride upon sticks and are there presently.

[Q. How did you go? What do you ride upon?

A. I rid upon a stick or pole and Good and Osbourn behind me. We ride taking hold of one another. Don't know how we go for I saw no trees nor path, but was presently there.]

(H:) Do you go through the trees or over them?

(T:) We see nothing but are there presently.

(H:) Why did you not tell your master?

(T:) I was afraid. They said they would cut off my head if I told. . . .

(H:) What attendants hath Sarah Good?

(**T:**) A yellow bird and she would have given me one.
(**H:**) What meat did she give it?
(**T:**) It did suck her between her fingers. . . .
(**H:**) What hath Sarah Osborne?
(**T:**) Yesterday she had a thing with a head like a woman with two legs and wings.

(Abigail Williams that lives with her uncle Mr. Parris said that she did see the same creature and it turned into the shape of Goody Osborne.)

(**H:**) What else have you seen with G. Osborne?
(**T:**) Another thing hairy. It goes upright like a man. It hath only 2 legs.
[**A.** A thing all over hairy, all the face hairy and a long nose and I don't know how to tell how the face looks, with two legs it goeth upright and is about two or three foot high and goeth upright like a man and last night it stood before the fire in Mr. Parris's hall.]
(**H:**) Did you not see Sarah Good upon Elizabeth Hubbard last Saturday?
(**T:**) I did see her set a wolf upon her to afflict her.

(The persons with this maid did say that she did complain of a wolf.)

(**T:**) She further said that she saw a cat with Good at another time.
(**H:**) What clothes doth the man go in?
(**T:**) He goes in black clothes [sometimes serge coat of other color], a tall man with white hair, I think.
(**H:**) How doth the woman go?
(**T:**) In a white hood and a black hood with a top knot.
[**Q.** What kind of clothes hath she?
A. A black silk hood with a white silk hood under it, with top knots; which woman I know not but have seen her in Boston when I lived there.
Q. What cloths the little woman?
A. A serge coat with a white cap as I think.]
(**H:**) Do you see who it is that torments these children now?
(**T:**) Yes, it is Goody Good. She hurts them in her own shape.
(**H:**) And who is it that hurts them now?
(**T:**) I am blind now, I cannot see.

(The children having fits at this very time she was asked who hurt them, she answered Goody Good and the children affirmed the same but Hubbard being taken in an extreme fit after she was asked who hurt her and she said she could not tell, but said they blinded her, and would not let her see and after that was once or twice taken dumb herself.)

[42]

Examination of Rebecca Nurse

Rebecca Nurse was a most unlikely type to be accused of witchcraft. At the time of her arrest on March 23, 1692, she was an elderly covenanting member of Salem Town church, married to a prosperous farmer, and the mother of numerous sons and daughters. Several petitions signed by the most respectable members of the community attested to her good name. At first the jury found her not guilty, but after a misunderstanding of Nurse's reaction to another accusation, they changed the verdict to guilty and she was executed on July 19, 1692.

These notes were transcribed by Samuel Parris.

•

Salem Village, 24. March 1692

Mr. Hathorne: What do you say (*speaking to one afflicted*), have you seen this woman hurt you?

Answer: Yes, she beat me this morning.

H: Abigail, have you been hurt by this woman?

Answer: Yes

(Ann Putnam in a grievous fit cried out that she hurt her.)

H: Goody Nurse, here are two—Ann Putnam the child and Abigail Williams—complains of your hurting them. What do you say to it?

Nurse: I can say before my eternal Father I am innocent and God will clear my innocency.

H: Here is never a one in the Assembly but desires it, but if you be guilty, pray God discover you.

(Then Henry Kenny rose up to speak)

H: Goodman Kenny, what do you say?

(Then he entered his complaint and farther said that since this Nurse came into the house he was seized twice with an amazed condition.)

From *Salem Witchcraft Papers: Verbatim Transcripts of the Legal Documents*, ed. Paul Boyer and Stephen Nissenbaum (New York: Da Capo, 1977), 2: 584–87.

H: Here are not only these but here is the wife of Mr. Thomas Putnam who accuseth you by credible information and that both of tempting her to iniquity and of greatly hurting her.

N: I am innocent and clear and have not been able to get out of doors these 8 or 9 days.

H: Mr. Putnam: give in what you have to say.

(Then Mr. Edward Putnam gave in his relate.)

H: Is this true Goody Nurse?

N: I never afflicted no child never in my life.

H: You see these accuse you. Is it true?

N: No.

H: Are you an innocent person relating to this witchcraft?

(Here Thomas Putnam's wife cried out, "Did you not bring the black man with you? Did you not bid me tempt God and die? How oft have you eat and drunk your own damnation? What do you say to them?")

N: Oh, Lord help me *(and spread out her hands and the afflicted were grievously vexed.)*

H: Do you not see what a solemn condition these are in? When your hands are loose, the persons are afflicted.

(Then Mary Walcott (who often heretofore said she had seen her, but never could say, or did say that she either bit or pinched her or hurt her) and also Elizabeth Hubbard under the like circumstances both openly accused her of hurting them.)

H: Here are these two grown persons now accuse you. What say you? Do not you see these afflicted persons and hear them accuse you.

N: The Lord knows I have not hurt them. I am an innocent person.

H: It is very awful to all to see these agonies and you an old professor thus charged with contracting with the devil by the affects of it and yet to see you stand with dry eyes when there are so many wet—

N: You do not know my heart.

H: You would do well if you are guilty to confess and give glory to God.

N: I am as clear as the child unborn.

H: What uncertainty there may be in apparitions I know not, yet this with me strikes hard upon you that you are at this very present charged with familiar spirits. This is your bodily person they speak to. They say now they see these familiar spirits come to your bodily person. Now what do you say to that?

N: I have none, Sir.

H: If you have confess and give glory to God, I pray God [to] clear you, if you be innocent, and, if you are guilty, discover you. And therefore give me an upright answer. Have you any familiarity with these spirits?

N: No, I have none but with God alone.

H: How came you sick for there is an odd discourse of that in the mouths of many?

N: I am sick at my stomach.

H: Have you no wounds?

N: I have none but old age.

H: You do know whether you are guilty and have familiarity with the devil. And now when you are here present to see such a thing as these testify a black man whispering in your ear and birds about you, what do you say to it?

N: It is all false. I am clear.

H: Possibly you may apprehend you are no witch, but have you not been led aside by temptations that way.

N: I have not.

H: What a sad thing it is that a church member here and now another of Salem should be thus accused and charged.

(Mrs. Pope fell into a grievous fit and cried out a sad thing sure enough. And then many more fell into lamentable fits.)

H: Tell us, have not you had visible appearances more than what is common in nature?

N: I have no nor never had in my life.

H: Do you think these suffer voluntary or involuntary.

N: I cannot tell.

H: That is strange; every one can judge.

N: I must be silent.

H: They accuse you of hurting them and if you think it is not unwillingly but by design, you must look upon them as murderers.

N: I cannot tell what to think of it.

(Afterwards when this was somewhat insisted on she said, I do not think so. She did not understand aright what was said.)

H: Well, then give an answer now, do you think these suffer against their wills or not.

N: I do not think these suffer against their wills.

H: Why did you never visit those afflicted persons.

N: Because I was afraid I should have fits too.

(Note: Upon the motion of her body, fits followed upon the complainants abundantly and very frequently.)

H: Is it not an unaccountable case that when you are examined, these persons are afflicted?

N: I have got no body to look to but God.

(Again upon stirring her hands, the afflicted persons were seized with violent fits of torture.)

H: Do you believe these afflicted persons are bewitched?

N: I do think they are.

H: When this witchcraft came upon the stage there was no suspicion of Tituba (*Mr. Parris's Indian woman*). She professed much love to that child, Betty Parris, but it was her apparition did the mischief and why should not you also be guilty, for your apparition doth hurt also.

N: Would you have me belie myself?

(She held her neck on one side and accordingly so were the afflicted taken.

Then authority requiring it, Samuel Parris read what he had in characters taken from Mr. Thomas Putnam's wife in her fits)

H: What do you think of this?

N: I cannot help it, the devil may appear in my shape.

This a true account of the summary of her examination but by reason of great noises by the afflicted and many speakers, many things are pretermitted [i.e., omitted].

Memorandum

Salem Village, March 24th, 1692

The Reverend Mr. Samuel Parris being desired to take in writing the examination of Rebekah Nurse hath returned it as aforesaid.

Upon hearing the aforesaid and seeing what we then did see together with the charge of the persons then present, we committed Rebekah Nurse, the wife of Francis Nurse of Salem Village, unto their Majesty's gaol in Salem as per a Mittimus then given out, in order to farther examination.

John Hathorne, and Jonathan Corwin, Assistants

[43]

Examination of Bridget Bishop

The first to be executed on June 10, 1692, Bridget Bishop was not arrested until April 19, 1692, more than six weeks after the accusations began. The questioning, as usual, was conducted by John Hathorne. Two sets of notes were taken of the examination, the first by Samuel Parris and signed by Hathorne, and the second by the court clerk, Ezekiel Cheever, Both are included here.

•

[FIRST VERSION]

Salem Village 19 April 1692

(As soon as she came, near all fell into fits.)

Hathorne: Bridget Bishop, you are now brought before authority to give account of what witchcraft you are conversant in.

Bishop: I take all this people (*turning her head and eyes about*) to witness that I am clear.

H: Hath this woman hurt you, (*speaking to the afflicted*)?

(Elizabeth Hubbard, Ann Putnam, Abigail Williams and Mercy Lewis affirmed she had hurt them.)

H: You are here accused by four or five for hurting them. What do you say to it?

B: I never saw these persons before, nor I never was in this place before.

(Mary Walcott said that her brother Jonathan struck her [i.e., Bishop's] *appearance and she saw that he had tore her coat in striking and she heard it tear.*

Upon some search in the Court, a rent that seems to answer what was alleged was found.)

H: They say you bewitched your first husband to death.

B: If it please your worship, I know nothing of it.

From Salem Witchcraft Papers: Verbatim Transcripts of the Legal Documents, ed. Paul Boyer and Stephen Nissenbaum (New York: Da Capo, 1977), 1: 83–87

(She shook her head and the afflicted were tortured. The like again upon the motion of her head. Samuel Braybrook affirmed that she told him today that she had been accounted a witch these ten years, but she was no witch, the devil cannot hurt her.)

B: I am no witch.

H: Why, if you have not wrote in the book, yet tell me how far you have gone? Have you not to do with familiar spirits?

B: I have no familiarity with the devil.

H: How is it then, that your appearance doth hurt these?

B: I am innocent.

H: Why, you seem to act witchcraft before us by the motion of your body, which seems to have influence upon the afflicted.

B: I know nothing of it. I am innocent to a witch. I know not what a witch is.

H: How do you know then that you are not a witch?

B: I do not know what you say.

H: How can you know you are no witch and yet not know what a witch is.

B: I am clear. If I were any such person, you should know it.

H: You may threaten, but you can do no more than you are permitted.

B: I am innocent of a witch.

H: What do you say of those murders you are charged with?

B: I hope I am not guilty of murder.

(Then she turned up her eyes; the eyes of the afflicted were turned up.)

H: It may be you do not know that any have confessed today, who have been examined before you, that they are witches.

B: No, I know nothing of it.

(John Hutchinson and John Lewis in open Court affirmed that they had told her.)

H: Why look you, you are taken now in a flat lie.

B: I did not hear them.

(Note: Samuel Gold saith that after this examination he asked said Bridget Bishop if she were not troubled to see the afflicted persons so tormented. Said Bishop answered no, she was not troubled for them. Then he asked her whither she thought they were bewitched. She said she could not tell what to think about them. Will Good and John Buxton, Jr. was [i.e., went] by and he supposeth they heard her also.)

Salem Village April the 19th 1692 Mr. Samuel Parris being desired to take into writing the examination of Bridget Bishop, hath delivered it as aforesaid. And upon hearing the same and seeing what we did then see, together with the charge of the afflicted persons then present, we committed said Bridget Oliver [Bishop].

John Hathorne

[SECOND VERSION]

(Bridget Bishop being now coming in to be examined relating to her accusation of suspicion of sundry acts of witchcrafts, the afflicted persons are now dreadfully afflicted by her as they do say.)

Mr. Hathorne: Bishop, what do you say, you here stand charged with sundry acts of witchcraft by you done or committed upon the bodies of Mercy Lewis and Ann Putnam and others?

Bishop: I am innocent. I know nothing of it. I have done no witchcraft.

H: Look upon this woman and see if this be the woman that you have seen hurting you. *(Mercy Lewis and Ann Putnam and others do now charge her to her face with hurting of them.)* What do you say now you see they charge you to your face?

B: I never did hurt them in my life. I did never see these persons before. I am as innocent as the child unborn.

H: Is not your coat cut?

(Answers no, but her garment being looked upon, they find it cut or torn two ways.

    Jonathan Walcott saith that the sword that he struck at Goody Bishop with was not naked but was within the scabbard so that the rent may very probably be the very same that Mary Walcott did tell that she had in her coat by Jonathan's striking at her appearance.

    The afflicted persons charge her with having hurt them many ways and by tempting them to sign to the devil's book at which charge she seemed to be very angry and shaking her head at them, saying it was false. They are all greatly tormented [as I conceive] by the shaking of her head.)

Hathorne: Goody Bishop, what contract have you made with the devil?

Bishop: I have made no contract with the devil. I never saw him in my life.

(Ann Putnam saith that she calls the devil her God.)

H: What say you to all this that you are charged with. Can you not find in your heart to tell the truth?

B: I do tell the truth. I never hurt these persons in my life. I never saw them before.

Mercy Lewis: Oh, Goody Bishop, did you not come to our house the last night and did you not tell me that your master made you tell more than you were willing to tell?

H: Tell us the truth in this matter. How come these persons to be thus tormented and to charge you with doing?

B: I am not come here to say I am a witch to take away my life.

H: Who is it that doth it if you do not? They say it is your likeness that comes and torments them and tempts them to write in the book. What book is [it] that you tempt them with?

B: I know nothing of it. I am innocent.

H: Do you not see how they are tormented? You are acting witchcraft before us. What do you say to this? Why have you not an heart to confess the truth?

B: I am innocent. I know nothing of it. I am no witch. I know not what a witch is.

H: Have you not given consent that some evil spirit should do this in your likeness?

B: No, I am innocent of being a witch. I know no man, woman, or child here.

Marshall Herrick: How came you into my bed chamber one morning then and asked me whether I had any curtains to sell?

(She is by some of the afflicted persons charged with murder.)

H: What do you say to these murders you are charged with?

B: I am innocent. I know nothing of it.

(Now she lifts up her eyes and they are greatly tormented again.)

H: What do you say to these things here horrible acts of witchcraft?

B: I know nothing of it. I do not know whither [there] be any witches or no.

H: No, have you not heard that some have confessed?

B: No, I did not.

(Two men told her to her face that they had told her here she is taken in a plain lie. Now [that] she is going away, they are dreadfully afflicted. Five afflicted persons do charge this woman to be the very woman that hurts them.)

This is a true account of what I have taken down at her examination according to best understanding and observation. I have also in her examination taken notice that all her actions have great influence upon the afflicted persons and that have been tortured by her.

                                                                    Ezekiel Cheever

Narrative of the Salem Events

Deodat Lawson

Deodat Lawson was the minister in Salem Village from 1684 to 1688 and third in a line of controversial appointments before Samuel Parris. (James Bayley [1673–1680] and George Burroughs [1680–1683] were the two earlier ones.) Lawson returned to the village at Parris's invitation on Saturday, March 19, to assist in the prayer effort against the supposed witchcraft and delivered a sermon on witches and the devil's power in Parris's pulpit on March 24. These are his observations of events between his arrival and April 5.

At some point one of the accusers suggested that Lawson's wife and daughter, who were buried in Salem Village, had been killed by witchcraft, but he does not comment on that accusation.

•

The Bookseller to the Reader

The ensuing narrative, being a collection of some remarkables in an affair now upon the stage made by a credible eye-witness, is now offered unto the reader only as a taste of more that may follow in God's time. If the prayers of good people may obtain this favor of God, that the mysterious assaults from hell now made upon so many of our friends may be thoroughly detected and defeated, we suppose the curious will be entertained with as rare an history as perhaps an age has had, whereof this narrative is but a forerunner.

Benjamin Harris

*   *   *

On the nineteenth day of March last, I went to Salem Village and lodged at Nathaniel Ingersoll's [tavern] near to the minister, Mr. Parris's house and presently,

From Deodat Lawson, *A Brief and True Narrative of Some Remarkable Passages Relating to Sundry Persons Afflicted by Witchcraft, at Salem Village, Which Happened from the Nineteenth of March to the Fifth of April, 1692* (1692), in *Narratives of the Witchcraft Cases, 1648–1706*, ed. George Lincoln Burr (New York: Charles Scribner's Sons, 1914), 152–63.

after I came into my lodging, Captain [Jonathan] Walcott's daughter, Mary [age seventeen] came to Lt. Ingersoll's and spoke to me but suddenly after, as she stood by the door, was bitten so that she cried out of her wrist and looking on it with a candle, we saw apparently the marks of teeth both upper and lower set on each side of her wrist.

In the beginning of the evening I went to give Mr. Parris a visit. When I was there his kinswoman, Abigail Williams (about 12 years of age), had a grievous fit. She was at first hurried with violence to and fro in the room (though Mrs. Ingersoll endeavored to hold her), sometimes making as if she would fly, stretching up her arms as high as she could and crying, "Whish, whish, whish!" several times. Presently, after she said there was Goodwife [Rebecca] Nurse, [she] said, "Do you not see her? Why there she stands!" And the said Goodwife Nurse offered her The Book, but she was resolved she would not take it, saying often, "I won't, I won't, I won't take it. I do not know what book it is. I am sure it is none of God's Book; it is the devil's book for ought I know." After that, she run to the fire and begun to throw fire brands about the house and run against the back as if she would run up [the] chimney, and, as they said, she had attempted to go into the fire in other fits.

On Lord's day, the twentieth of March, there were sundry of the afflicted persons at Meeting [such] as Mrs. Pope, and Goodwife [Sarah] Bibber, Abigail Williams, Mary Walcott, Mary [Mercy] Lewis [age nineteen], and Doctor Griggs's maid [Elizabeth Hubbard, age seventeen]. There was also at Meeting, Goodwife [Martha] Corey, who was afterward examined on suspicion of being a witch. They had several sore fits in the time of public worship which did something interrupt me in my first prayer being so unusual. After psalm was sung, Abigail Williams said to me, "Now stand up and name your text." And after it was read, she said, "It is a long text." In the beginning of Sermon, Mrs. Pope, a woman afflicted, said to me, "Now there is enough of that." And in the afternoon, Abigail Williams, upon my referring to my doctrine, said to me, "I know no doctrine you had. If you did name one, I have forgot it."

In Sermon time, when Goodwife Corey was present in the Meetinghouse, Abigail W. called out, "Look where Goodwife Corey sits on the beam suckling her yellow bird betwixt her fingers!" Ann Putnam [age twelve] another girl afflicted said there was a yellow bird sat on my hat as it hung on the pin in the pulpit. But those that were by [near her], restrained her from speaking loud about it.

On Monday, the 21st of March, the Magistrates of Salem appointed to come to examination of Goodwife Corey. And about twelve of the clock, they went into the meeting house which was thronged with spectators. Mr. [Nicholas] Noyes [minister at Salem Town] began with a very pertinent and pathetic prayer, and Goodwife Corey, being called to answer to what was alleged against her, she desired to go to prayer, which was much wondered at in the presence of so many hundred people. The Magistrates told her they would not admit it. They came not there to hear her pray, but to examine her in what was alleged against her. The worshipful Mr. [John] Hathorne [a magistrate] asked her why she afflicted those children. She said, she did not afflict them. He asked her, "Who did then?" She said, "I do not know. How should I know?"

The number of the afflicted persons were about that time ten, viz.: four married women—Mrs. Pope, Mrs. [Ann] Putnam, Goodwife Bibber, and an ancient woman named Goodall.; three maids [i.e., unmarried women]—Mary Walcott, Mercy Lewis at Thomas Putnam's, and a maid at Dr. Griggs's [Elizabeth Hubbard]; there were three girls from 9 to 12 years of age, each of them or thereabouts, viz.: Elizabeth Parris, Abigail Williams and Ann Putnam. These were most of them at Goodwife Corey's examination and did vehemently accuse her in the assembly of afflicting them by biting, pinching, strangling, etc. and that they did in their fit see her likeness coming to them, and bringing a book to them. She [Corey] said, she had no book. They affirmed she[Corey] had a yellow bird that used to suck betwixt her fingers and being asked about it, if she had any familiar spirit that attended her, she said she had no familiarity with any such thing. She was a gospel woman, which title she called herself by. And the afflicted persons told her, ah! She was a gospel witch.

Ann Putnam did there affirm that one day when Lieutenant [Thomas] Fuller was at prayer at her father's house, she saw the shape of Goodwife Corey and she thought Goodwife Nurse praying at the same time to the devil. She was not sure it was Goodwife Nurse; she thought it was, but very sure she saw the shape of Goodwife Corey. The said Corey said [that] they were poor, distracted children, and no heed to be given to what they said. Mr. Hathorne and Mr. Noyes replied, it was the judgment of all that were present [that] they were bewitched and only she the accused person said they were distracted.

It was observed several times, that if she did but bite her under lip in time of examination, the persons afflicted were bitten on their arms and wrists and produced the marks before the magistrates, ministers, and others. And being watched for that, if she did but pinch her fingers or grasp one hand hard in another, they were pinched and produced the marks before the magistrates and spectators. After that, it was observed, that if she did but lean her breast against the seat in the meeting house (being the bar at which she stood), they were afflicted. Particularly Mrs. Pope complained of grievous torment in her bowels as if they were torn out. She vehemently accused said Corey as the instrument and first threw her muff at her. But that flying not home, she got off her shoe and hit Goodwife Corey on the head with it. After these postures were watched, if said Corey did but stir her feet, they were afflicted in their feet and stamped fearfully.

The afflicted persons asked her [Corey] why she did not go to the company of witches which were before the meeting house mustering? "Did she not hear the drum beat?" They accused her of having familiarity with the devil in the time of examination in the shape of a black man whispering in her ear. They affirmed that her yellow bird sucked betwixt her fingers in the assembly and, order being given to see if there were any sign, the girl that saw it said, "It was too late now. She had removed a pin and put it on her head," which was found there sticking upright.

They told her she had covenanted with the devil for ten years, six of them were gone and four more to come. She was required by the magistrates to answer that question in the catechism: "How many persons be there in the Godhead?" She answered it but oddly, yet was there no great thing to be gathered from it. She denied all that was charged upon her and said, "They could not prove a witch." She was that afternoon committed to Salem prison and after she was in custody, she did not so appear to them and afflict them as before.

On Wednesday, the 23 of March, I went to Thomas Putnam's on purpose to see his wife. I found her lying on the bed, having had a sore fit a little before. She spoke to me and said she was glad to see me. Her husband and she both desired me to pray with her while she was sensible, which I did though the apparition said I should not go to prayer. At the first beginning, she attended, but after a little time was taken with a fit yet continued silent and seemed to be asleep. When prayer was done, her husband going to her, found her in a fit. He took her off the bed to set her on his knees, but at first she was so stiff, she could not be bended, but she afterwards set down, but quickly began to strive violently with her arms and legs.

She then began to complain of, and as it were to converse personally with Goodwife Nurse saying, "Goodwife Nurse, be gone! begone! begone! Are you not ashamed, a woman of your profession to afflict a poor creature so? What hurt did I ever do you in my life. You have but two years to live and then the devil will torment your soul, for this your name is blotted out of God's book and it shall never be put in God's book again. Be gone for shame. Are you not afraid of that which is coming upon you? I know, I know what will make you afraid: the wrath of an angry God. I am sure that will make you afraid. Be gone, do not torment me. I know what you would have (we judged she meant her soul) but it is out of your reach. It is clothed with the white robes of Christ's righteousness."

After this, she seemed to dispute with the apparition about a particular text of Scripture. The apparition seemed to deny it. (The woman's eyes being fast closed all this time), she said that she was sure there was such a text and she would tell it. And then the shape would be gone for, said she, "I am sure you cannot stand before that text." Then she was sorely afflicted, her mouth drawn on one side and her body strained for about a minute, and then said, "I will tell, I will tell. It is, it is, it is." three or four times and then was afflicted to hinder her from telling. At last she broke forth and said: "It is the third chapter of the Revelations." I did something scruple the reading it and did let my scruple appear lest Satan should make any superstitious lie to improve the Word of the eternal God. However, though not versed in these things, I judged I might do it this once for an experiment. I began to read and before I had near read through the first verse, she opened her eyes and was well. This fit continued near half an hour. Her husband and the spectators told me she had often been so relieved by reading Texts that she named something pertinent to her case as Isa. 40.1, Isa. 49.1, Isa. 50.1, and several others.

On Thursday, the twenty-fourth of March (being in course the Lecture Day at the Village), Goodwife Nurse was brought before the magistrates Mr. Hathorne and Mr. [Jonathan] Corwin about ten of [the] clock in the fore noon, to be examined in the meeting house. The Reverend Mr. [John] Hale [of Beverly] begun with prayer and the warrant being read, she was required to give answer [to] why she afflicted those persons? She pleaded her own innocency with earnestness. Thomas Putnam's wife, Abigail Williams and Thomas Putnam's daughter accused her that she appeared to them and afflicted them in their fits. But some of the other[s] said that they had seen her, but knew not that ever she had hurt them, amongst which was Mary Walcott, who was presently after she had so declared bitten and cried out of her in the meeting house, producing the marks of teeth on her wrist.

I was so disposed that I had not leisure to attend the whole time of examination but both magistrates and ministers told me that the things alleged by the afflicted and defenses made by her were much after the same manner as the former was. And her motions did produce like effects as to biting, pinching, bruising, tormenting at their breasts by her leaning and, when bended back, were as if their backs were broken. The afflicted persons said the black man whispered to her in the assembly and therefore she could not hear what the magistrates said unto her. They said also that she did then ride by the meeting house behind the black man. Thomas Putnam's wife had a grievous fit in the time of examination to the very great impairing of her strength and wasting of her spirits, insomuch as she could hardly move hand or foot when she was carried out. Others also were there grievously afflicted so that there was once such an hideous screech and noise (which I heard as I walked at a little distance from the meeting house), as did amaze me, and some that were within told me the whole assembly was struck with consternation and they were afraid that those that sat next to them were under the influence of witchcraft. This woman also was that day committed to Salem prison.

The magistrates and ministers also did inform me that they apprehended a child [Dorcas] of Sarah Good and examined it, [she] being between 4 and 5 years of age. And as to matter of fact, they did unanimously affirm that when this child did but cast its eye upon the afflicted persons, they were tormented, and [that even when] they held her head and yet so many as her eye could fix upon were afflicted, which they did several times make careful observation of. The afflicted complained they had often been bitten by this child and produced the marks of a small set of teeth. Accordingly, this [child] was also committed to Salem prison. The child looked hail and well as other children. I saw it at Lieutenant Ingersoll's.

After the commitment of Goodwife Nurse, Thomas Putnam's wife was much better and had no violent fits at all from the 24th of March to the 5th of April. Some others also said they had not seen her so frequently appear to them to hurt them.

On the 25th of March (as Capt. Stephen Sewall of Salem did afterwards inform me), Elizabeth [Betty] Parris had sore fits at his house, which much troubled himself and his wife, so as he told me they were almost discouraged. She related that the great black man came to her and told her [that] if she would be ruled by him, she should have whatsoever she desired and go to a golden city. She relating this to Mrs. Sewall, she told the child it was the devil and he was a liar from the beginning and bid her tell him so if he came again, which she did accordingly at the next coming to her in her fits.

On the 26th of March, Mr. Hathorne, Mr. Corwin, and Mr. [the Reverend John] Higginson [the senior minister in Salem Town] were at the prison-keeper's house to examine the child [Dorcas Good] and it told them there it had a little snake that used to suck on the lowest joint of it[s] forefinger. And when they inquired where pointing to other places, it told them, not there, but there, pointing on the lowest point of forefinger, where they observed a deep red spot about the bigness of a flea bite. They asked who gave it that snake, whether the great black man? It said, no, its mother gave it.

The 31 of March there was a public fast kept at Salem on account of these afflicted persons. And Abigail Williams said that the witches had a sacrament that day at an house in the Village and that they had red bread and red drink. The first of April, Mercy Lewis, Thomas Putnam's maid, in her fit said, they did eat red bread like man's flesh and would have had her eat some, but she would not, but turned away her head and spit at them and said, "I will not eat; I will not drink; it is blood," etc. She said, "That is not the bread of life; that is not the water of life. Christ gives the bread of life. I will have none of it!" This first of April also Mercy Lewis aforesaid saw in her fit a white man and was with him in a glorious place which had no candles nor sun, yet was full of light and brightness, where was a great multitude in white glittering robes and they sung the song in the fifth of Revelation the ninth verse and the 110 Psalm and the 149 Psalm. And said with herself, "How long shall I stay here? Let me be along with you." She was loath to leave this place and grieved that she could tarry no longer. This white man hath appeared several times to some of them and given them notice how long it should be before they had another fit, which was sometimes a day, or day and half, or more or less. It hath fallen out accordingly.

The third of April, the Lord's Day, being Sacrament day at the Village, Goodwife [Sarah] Cloyce [sister of Rebecca Nurse], upon Mr. Parris's naming his Text, John 6.70, "One of them is a devil." The said Goodwife Cloyce went immediately out of the meeting house and flung the door after her violently, to the amazement of the congregation. She was afterward seen by some in their fits, who said, "Oh, Goodwife Cloyce, I did not think to see you here!" And, being at their red bread and drink, said to her, "Is this a time to receive the Sacrament. You ran away on the Lord's day and scorned to receive it in the meeting house," and, "Is this a time to receive it? I wonder at you!"

This is the sum of what I either saw myself or did receive information from persons of undoubted reputation and credit. . . .

Remarks concerning the Accused

1. For introduction to the discovery of those that afflicted them, it is reported Mr. Parris's Indian man [John] and woman [Tituba] made a cake of rye meal and the children's water, baked it in the ashes and gave it to a dog, since which they have discovered and seen particular persons hurting of them.

2. In time of examination they seemed little affected, though all the spectators were much grieved to see it.

3. Natural actions in them produced preternatural actions in the afflicted so that they are their own image without [using] any poppits of wax or otherwise.

4. That they are accused to have a company about 23 or 24 and they did muster in arms, as it seemed to the afflicted persons.

5. Since they were confined, the persons have not been so much afflicted with their appearing to them, biting or pinching of them, etc.

C. THE ACCUSERS

[45]

Elizabeth Hubbard against Tituba

There were many depositions against Tituba, Rebecca Nurse, and Bridget Bishop, the three women whose testimonies have been included in this reader. A few of the statements used to convict them are given here. These testimonies illustrate the kinds of accusations and stories of witchcraft that were used as evidence in the investigations and inquests preceding trial.

Elizabeth Hubbard, the niece of the wife of Dr. William Griggs, was living in the Griggs home in 1692. Hubbard, Betty Parris, Abigail Williams, and Ann Putnam, Jr., were the first accusers. The deposition is not dated and may have been written any time between March 1 and May 23, when additional depositions were taken for an inquest in Tituba's case.

•

The Deposition of Elizabeth Hubbard aged about 17 years who testifieth that on the 25th February 1692 I saw the apparition of Tituba Indian which did immediately most grievously torment me by pricking, pinching and almost choking me, and so continued hurting me most grievously by times until the day of her examination, being the first of March, and then also at the beginning of her examination, but as soon as she began to confess, she left off hurting me and has hurt me but little since.

From Salem Witchcraft Papers: Verbatim Transcripts of the Legal Documents, ed. Paul Boyer and Stephen Nissenbaum (New York: Da Capo, 1977), 3:756.

[46]

Abigail Williams against Tituba and Rebecca Nurse

Abigail Williams, eleven or twelve years old at the time, was a niece of either Elizabeth or Samuel Parris and was living in their household. She and Betty Parris, age nine, were the first to claim to be afflicted by witches. Betty was sent away to live with Stephen Sewall shortly after the investigations began and took part in very few accusations. Abigail, on the other hand, played a much more damaging role and testified against many of the accused, including those from Andover and other towns.

•

Abigail Williams v. Tituba, Sarah Osborne, and Sarah Good

The testimony of Abigail Williams testifieth and saith that several times last February she hath been much afflicted with pains in her head and other parts and often pinched by the apparition of Sarah Good, Sarah Osborne, and Tituba Indian, all of Salem Village and also excessively afflicted by the said apparition of said Good, Osborne, and Tituba at their examination before authority the 1st March last past 1692.

Farther the said Abigail Williams testifieth that she saw the apparition of said Sarah Good at her examination pinch Elizabeth Hubbard and set her into fits and also Elizabeth Parris and Ann Putnam.

The mark of
Abigail William

Testified before us by Abigail Williams Salem May the 23d 1692

John Hathorne
Jonathan Corwin
per order of the Governor's Council

Abigail Williams v. Rebecca Nurse

The testimony of Abigail Williams witnesseth and saith that divers times in [the month] of March last past, particularly on the 15, 16, 19, 20, 21, 23, 31 days of that

From Salem Witchcraft Papers: Verbatim Transcripts of the Legal Documents, ed. Paul Boyer and Stephen Nissenbaum (New York: Da Capo, 1977), 3:612–13, 2:597.

m[onth and] in the month of April following at several times, particularly on the 13 and————that month and also in this present month of May, the 4th and 29 days, she [the] said Abigail has been exceedingly perplexed with the apparition of Rebecca [Nurse of] Salem Village, by which apparition she hath been pulled violently, often pinched and almost choked, and tempted sometimes to leap into the [fire and] sometimes to subscribe a book the said apparition brought and also that [she saith] she hath seen this apparition at a sacrament sitting next to————[the man?] with an high crowned hat at the upper end of the table. And f[arther saith that] said apparition hath sometimes confessed to her the said Abigail its guilt in committing several murders together with her sister [Sarah] Cloyce as upon old Goodman Harwood, Benjamin Porter, and Rebecca Shepard and Faith Shephard's————. May 31st 1692 attested before.

Abigail Williams did own this her testimony [on the] oath which she had taken to be truth, before us [the] jurors of Inquest this 3 day of June, 1692.

(Editor's note: Dashes indicate torn or illegible portions of the manuscript.)

[47]

Ann Putnam, Jr., against Rebecca Nurse

Twelve-year-old Ann Putnam was the daughter of Thomas and Ann Putnam, who were among Samuel Parris's major supporters in the village. From the beginning, Ann was active in almost all the investigations. In 1706 she made a public apology for her role in the deaths of so many innocent people, but she claimed she was "deluded by Satan" into thinking they were witches.

•

The deposition of Ann Putnam Jr., who testifieth and saith that on the 13th March 1692 I saw the apparition of Goody Nurse and she did immediately afflict me but I did not know what her name was then though I knew where she used to sit in our Meeting House. But since that she hath grievously afflicted me by biting, pinching, and pricking me, urging me to write in her book and also on the 24th of March, being the day of her examination, I was grievously tortured by her during the time of her examination and also several times since and also during the time of her examination I saw the apparition of Rebecca Nurse go and hurt the bodies of Mercy Lewis, Mary Walcott, Elizabeth Hubbard, and Abigail Williams.

Ann Putnam, Jr. did own the oath she hath taken: this her evidence to be the truth. Before us the jurors for Inquest this 3 day of June 1692.

Jurat in Curia

From Salem Witchcraft Papers: Verbatim Transcripts of the Legal Documents, ed. Paul Boyer and Stephen Nissenbaum (New York: Da Capo, 1977), 2: 595.

[48]

Deliverance Hobbs against Bridget Bishop

Deliverance Hobbs, from Topsfield, Massachusetts, was herself accused of witchcraft and questioned on April 22, 1692. Hobbs's stepdaughter, Abigail, had been arrested and had confessed two days earlier; Mary Warren confessed immediately after that. Deliverance became the fourth confessor on April 23 (Tituba had been the first). There were no more confessions until July.

Deliverance Hobbs knew Bridget Bishop as the widow Oliver in Topsfield before she had married Edward Bishop. This statement was made while Hobbs was in prison.

•

Deliverance Hobbs, Examined May 3, 1692. Salem prison.

Q. What have you done since whereby there is further trouble in your appearance?

An. Nothing at all.

Q. But have you not since been tempted?

An. Yes sir, but I have not done it, nor will not do it.

Q. Here is a great change since we last spoke to you, for now you afflict and torment again. Now tell us the truth, who tempted you to sign again?

An. It was Goody Oliver [Bishop]. She would have me to set my hand to the book, but I would not neither have I. Neither did consent to hurt them again.

Q. Was that true that Goody Wilds appeared to you and tempted you?

An. Yes, that was true.

Q. Have you been tempted since?

An. Yes, about Friday or Saturday night last.

Q. Did they bid you that you should not tell?

An. Yes, they told me so.

Q. But how far did they draw you or tempt you and how far did you yield to the temptation? But do not you acknowledge that [that] was true that you told us formerly?

An. Yes.

From Salem Witchcraft Papers: Verbatim Transcripts of the Legal Documents, ed. Paul Boyer and Stephen Nissenbaum (New York: Da Capo, 1977), 1:91–92.

Q. And you did sign then at the first, did you not?

An. Yes, I did. It is true.

Q. Did you promise then to deny at last what you said before?

An. Yes, I did and it was Goody Oliver alias Bishop that tempted me to deny all that I had confessed before.

Q. Do you not know the man with the wen [i.e., wart]?

An. No I do not know who it is; all that I confessed before is true.

Q. Who were they you named formerly?

An. [Sarah] Osborne, [Sarah] Good, [George] Burroughs, [Bridget] Oliver [Bishop], [Sarah] Wilds, [Giles] Corey and his wife [Martha], [Rebecca] Nurse, [John] Proctor and his wife [Elizabeth].

Q. Who were with you in the chamber? (*It being informed that some were talking with her there.*)

An. Wilds and Bishop or Oliver, Good, and Osborne, and they had a feast both of roast and boiled meat and did eat and drink and would have had me to have eat and drunk with them but I would not. And they would have had me sign, but I would not then not when Goody Oliver came to me.

Q. Nor did not you con ———— children in your likeness?

An. I do not know that I did.

Q. What is that you have to tell which you cannot tell yet you say?

(*Editor's note: The statement ends without an answer to the last question or an identification of the questioner.*)

[49]

John Hale against Bridget Bishop

John Hale (1636–1700) was the pastor in Beverly, Massachusetts, for more than thirty years. In 1692 he was a witness against Bridget Bishop and Dorcas Hoar, both of whom had previously lived in Beverly and attended his church.

•

John Hale of Beverly aged about 56 years ———— saith that about five or six years ago Christian, the wife of John Trask (living in Salem bounds bordering on the abovesaid Beverly), being in full communion in our Church, came to me to [de]sire that Goodwife Bishop, her neighbor, wife of Edward Bishop, Jr., might not be permitted to receive the Lord's Supper in our church till she had given her the said Trask satisfaction for some offenses that were against her, viz. because the said Bishop did entertain people in her house at unseasonable hours in the night to keep drinking and playing at shovel-board, whereby discord did arise in other families and young people were in danger to be corrupted, and that the said Trask knew these things and had once gone into the house and, finding some at shovel-board, had taken the pieces they played with and thrown them into the fire and had reproved the said Bishop for promoting such disorders, but received no satisfaction from her about it.

I gave said Christian Trask direction how to proceed farther in this matter if it were clearly proved and indeed by the information I have had otherwise I do fear that if a stop had not been put to those disorders, said Edward Bishop's house would have been a house of great profaneness and iniquity.

But as to Christian Trask, the next news I heard of her was that she was distracted and asking her husband Trask when she was so taken. [He told] me she was taken distracted that night after she [came from] my house when she complained against Goody Bishop.

She continuing some time distracted, we sought the Lord by fasting and prayer and the Lord was pleased to restore the said [Trask] to the use of her reason again. I was with her often in [her] distraction (and took it then to be only distraction, yet fearing sometimes somewhat worse), but since I have seen the fits of those bewitched at Salem Village, I call to mind some of hers to be much like some of theirs.

From Salem Witchcraft Papers: Verbatim Transcripts of the Legal Documents, ed. Paul Boyer and Stephen Nissenbaum (New York: Da Capo, 1977), 1:95–96.

The said Trask when recovered, as I understood it, did manifest strong suspicion that she had been bewitched by the said Bishop's wife and showed so much averseness from having any conversation that I was then troubled at it hoping better of said Goody Bishop at that time for we have since ———. At length, said Christian Trask [was] again in a distracted fit on a Sabbath day in the forenoon at the public meeting to our public disturbance and so continued sometimes better, sometimes worse unto her death, manifesting that she [was] under temptation to kill herself or somebody else.

I inquired of Margaret Ring, who kept at or nigh the house, what she had observed of said Trask before this last distraction. She told [me] Goody Trask was much given to reading and [to] search[ing] the prophecies of Scripture.

The day before she made that disturbance in the meeting [house], she came home and said she had been with Goody Bishop and that they two were now friend[s] or to that effect.

I was often praying with and counseling of Goody Trask before her death and not many days before her end being there, she seemed more rational and earnestly desired Edward Bishop might be sent for that she might make friends with him. I asked her if she had wronged Edward Bishop. She said not that she knew of unless it were in taking his shovel-board pieces when people were at play with them and throwing them into the fire and if she did evil in it, she was very sorry for it and desired he would be friends with her or forgive her. This was the very day before she died or a few days before.

Her distraction (or bewitching) continued about a month and in those intervals wherein she was better, she earnestly desired prayers and the Sabbath. Before she died I received a note for prayers on her behalf which her husband said was written by herself and I judge was her own handwriting, being well acquainted with her hand.

As to the wounds she died of, I observed three deadly ones: a piece of her wind pipe cut out, and another wound above that through the windpipe and gullet, and the vein they call jugular, so that I then judge and still do apprehend it impossible for her with so short a pair of scissors to mangle herself so without some extraordinary work of the devil or witchcraft.

signed, 20 May 1692 by John Hale

[50]

Advice of the Clergy

Governor Phips requested advice from various ministers in Massachusetts regarding the conduct of the trials after the execution of Bridget Bishop and complaints from a variety of people. Their response was probably written by Cotton Mather, whose opinion was generally supported by the clergy in the colony. In another letter written on August 17 to John Foster, a member of the Governor's Council, Mather endorsed the conclusions expressed in this earlier document and asked Foster to "strengthen the hands of our honorable judges in the great work before them."

•

Return of Several Ministers Consulted (June 15, 1692)

I. The afflicted state of our poor neighbors that are now suffering by molestations from the Invisible World, we apprehend so deplorable that we think their condition calls for the utmost help of all persons in their several capacities.

II. We cannot but with all thankfulness acknowledge the success which the merciful God has given unto the sedulous and assiduous endeavors of our honorable rulers to detect the abominable witchcrafts which have been committed in the country, humbly praying that the discovery of these mysterious and mischievous wickednesses may be perfected.

III. We judge that in the prosecution of these and all such witchcrafts, there is need of a very critical and exquisite caution, lest by too much credulity for things received upon the devil's authority, there be a door opened for a long train of miserable consequences, and Satan get an advantage over us; for we should not be ignorant of his devices.

IV. As in complaints upon witchcrafts, there may be matters of inquiry which do not amount unto matters of presumption and there may be matters of presumption which yet may not be reckoned matters of conviction, so 'tis necessary that all proceedings thereabout be managed with an exceeding tenderness towards those that may be complained of, especially if they have been persons formerly of an unblemished reputation.

From Salem-Village Witchcraft: A Documentary Record of Local Conflict in Colonial New England, ed. Paul Boyer and Stephen Nissenbaum. (1972; Boston: Northeastern University Press, 1993), 117–18. © 1993 by Paul Boyer and Stephen Nissenbaum. Reprinted by permission of Northeastern University Press.

V. When the first inquiry is made into the circumstances of such as may lie under any just suspicion of witchcrafts, we could wish that there may be admitted as little as is possible of such noise, company, and openness, as may too hastily expose them that are examined, and that there may nothing be used as a test for the trial of the suspected, the lawfulness whereof may be doubted among the people of God; but that the directions given by such judicious writers as Perkins and Bernard be consulted in such a case.

VI. Presumptions whereupon persons may be committed and, much more, convictions whereupon persons may be condemned as guilty of witchcrafts, ought certainly to be more considerable than barely [i.e., merely] the accused person being represented by a spector unto the afflicted, inasmuch as 'tis an undoubted and a notorious thing that a demon may, by God's permission, appear, even to ill purposes, in the shape of an innocent, yea, and a virtuous man. Nor can we esteem alterations made in the sufferers by a look or touch of the accused to be an infallible evidence of guilt, but frequently liable to be abused by the Devil's legerdemains.

VII. We know not whether some remarkable affronts given to the devils by our disbelieving of those testimonies whose whole force and strength is from them alone, may not put a period [i.e., a stop] unto the progress of the dreadful calamity begun upon us in the accusation of so many persons whereof we hope some are yet clear from the great transgression laid unto their charge.

VIII. Nevertheless, we cannot but humbly recommend unto the Government the speedy and vigorous prosecution of such as have rendered themselves obnoxious, according to the direction given in the laws of God and the wholesome statutes of the English nation, for the detection of witchcrafts.

D. THE DOUBTERS

[51]

A Multitude of Errors

THOMAS BRATTLE

Thomas Brattle (1658–1713), a Boston-born merchant, scientist, treasurer of Harvard College, and elected member of the British Royal Society, responded to questions from an unidentified minister friend about the Salem events. His answer probably circulated among their friends but was not published until his grandnephew, another Thomas Brattle, gave it to the Massachusetts Historical Society. It was first published in the society's Collections in 1798. Brattle wrote the letter after the Court of Oyer and Terminer had been dissolved, anticipating the new Superior Court of Judicature scheduled to meet in November. That court did not, however, begin hearing cases until January 3, 1693.

•

October 8, 1692

Reverend Sir,

Yours I received the other day and am very ready to serve you to my utmost. I should be very loath to bring myself into any snare by my freedom with you and therefore hope that you will put the best construction on what I write and secure me from such as would interpret my lines otherwise than they are designed. Obedience to lawful authority I evermore accounted a great duty and willingly I would not practice any thing that might thwart and contradict such a principle. Too many are ready to despise dominions and speak evil of dignities. And I am sure the mischiefs which arise from a factious and rebellious spirit are very sad and notorious insomuch that I would sooner bite my finger's ends than willingly cast dirt on authority or [in] any way offer reproach to it.

Far, therefore, be it from me to have anything to do with those men your letter mentions whom you acknowledge to be men of a factious spirit and never more in their element than when they are declaiming against men in public place and contriving methods that tend to the disturbance of the common peace. . . . However, Sir, I never thought judges infallible, but reckoned that they, as well as private men, might

From Narratives of the Witchcraft Cases, 1648–1706, ed. George Lincoln Burr (New York: Charles Scribner's Sons, 1914), 169–78, 184–90.

err, and that when they were guilty of erring, standers by, who possibly had not half their judgment, might, notwithstanding, be able to detect and behold their errors. And furthermore, when errors of that nature are thus detected and observed, I never thought it an interfering with dutifulness and subjection for one man to communicate his thoughts to another thereabout and with modesty and due reverence to debate the premised failings at least when errors are fundamental and palpably pervert the great end of authority and government. For as to circumstantial errors, I must confess my principle is that it is the duty of a good subject to cover with his silence a multitude of them. . . .

First, as to the method which the Salem justices do take in their examinations, it is truly this. A warrant being issued out to apprehend the persons that are charged and complained of by the afflicted children (as they are called), said persons are brought before the Justices (the afflicted being present). The Justices ask the apprehended why they afflict those poor children, to which the apprehended answer, they do not afflict them. The Justices order the apprehended to look upon the said children, which accordingly they do, and at the time of that look (I dare not say by that look as the Salem Gentlemen do), the afflicted are cast into a fit. The apprehended are then blinded and ordered to touch the afflicted and at that touch, though not by the touch (as above), the afflicted ordinarily do come out of their fits. The afflicted persons then declare and affirm that the apprehended have afflicted them, upon which the apprehended persons, though of never so good repute, are forthwith committed to prison on suspicion for witchcraft. . . .

It is worthily noted by some that at some times the afflicted will not presently come out of their fits upon the touch of the suspected and then, forsooth, they are ordered by the Justices to grasp hard, harder yet, etc., insomuch that at length the afflicted come out of their fits and the reason is very good because that a touch of any hand and process of time will work the cure. Infallibly they will do it, as experience teaches.

I cannot but condemn this method of the Justices, of making this touch of the hand a rule to discover witchcraft because I am fully persuaded that it is sorcery and a superstitious method and that which we have no rule for either from reason or religion. The Salem Justices, at least some of them, do assert that the cure of the afflicted persons is a natural effect of this touch and they are so well instructed in the Cartesian philosophy and in the doctrine of *effluvia*, that they undertake to give a demonstration how this touch does cure the afflicted persons and the account they give of it is this. That by this touch the venomous and malignant particles that were ejected from the eye do, by this means, return to the body whence they came, and so leave the afflicted persons pure and whole. I must confess to you that I am no small admirer of the Cartesian philosophy, but yet I have not so learned it. Certainly this is a strain that it will by no means allow of.

I would fain know of these Salem Gentlemen, but as yet could never know how it comes about that if these apprehended persons are witches and, by a look of the eye, do cast the afflicted into their fits by poisoning them; how it comes about, I say, that by a look of their eye they do not cast others into fits and poison others by their looks and in particular tender, fearful women who often are beheld by them and as likely as any in the whole world to receive an ill impression from them. This Salem philosophy some men may call the new philosophy. But I think it rather deserves the name of Salem superstition and sorcery and it is not fit to be named in a land of such light as New England is. I think the matter might be better solved another way, but I shall not make any attempt that way further than to say that these afflicted children (as they are called) do hold correspondence with the devil even in the esteem and account of the Salem Gentlemen, for when the black man, i.e. (say these gentlemen) the devil, does appear to them, they ask him many questions and accordingly give information to the inquirer. And if this is not holding correspondence with the devil and something worse, I know not what is.

But furthermore, I would fain know of these Salem Justices what need there is of further proof and evidence to convict and condemn these apprehended persons than this look and touch, if so be they are so certain that this falling down and arising up when there is a look and a touch, are natural effects of the said look and touch and so a perfect demonstration and proof of witchcraft in those persons. What can the jury or Judges desire more to convict any man of witchcraft than a plain demonstration that the said man is a witch? . . .

But let this pass with the Salem Gentlemen for never so plain and natural a demonstration. Yet certain it is that the reasonable part of the world, when acquainted herewith, will laugh at the demonstration and conclude that the said Salem Gentlemen are actually possessed, at least, with ignorance and folly.

I most admire that [i.e., wonder at] Mr. Nicholas Noyes, the Reverend teacher at Salem, who was educated at the School of Knowledge and is certainly a learned, a charitable, and a good man, though all the devils in hell and all the possessed girls in Salem should say to the contrary. At him (I say), I do most admire that he should cry up the above mentioned philosophy after the manner that he does. I can assure you that I can bring you more than two or twice two (very credible persons) that will affirm that they have heard him vindicate the above mentioned demonstration as very reasonable.

Secondly, with respect to the confessours (as they are improperly called) or such as confess themselves to be witches, . . . they are now about fifty of them in prison, many of which I have again and again seen and heard. And I cannot but tell you that my faith is strong concerning them that they are deluded, imposed upon, and under the influence of some evil spirit and therefore unfit to be evidences either against themselves or anyone else. I now speak of one sort of them and of others afterward.

These confessours (as they are called) do very often contradict themselves as inconsistently as is usual for any crazed, distempered person to do. This the Salem Gentlemen do see and take notice of and even the Judges themselves have, at some times, taken these confessours in flat lies or contradictions even in the Courts, by reason of which, one would have thought, that the Judges would have frowned upon the said confessours, discarded them, and not minded one title of any thing that they said. But instead, thereof (as sure as we are men), the Judges vindicate these confessours and salve [i.e., resolve] their contradictions by proclaiming that the devil takes away their memory and imposes upon their brain. If this reflects [i.e., casts blame] anywhere, I am very sorry for it. I can but assure you that upon the word of an honest man it is truth and that I can bring you many credible persons to witness it who have been eye and ear witnesses to these things.

These confessours then, at least some of them, even in the Judges' own account, are under the influence of the devil and the brain of these confessours is imposed upon by the devil even in the Judges' account. But now, if, in the Judges' account, these confessours are under the influence of the devil and their brains are affected and imposed upon by the devil so that they are not their own men, why then should these Judges or any other men make such account of and set so much by the words of the confessours as they do? In short, I argue thus:

If the devil does actually take away the memory of them at some times, certainly the devil at other times may very reasonably be thought to affect their fancies and to represent false ideas to their imagination. But now, if it be thus granted, that the devil is able to represent false ideas (to speak vulgarly) to the imaginations of the confessours, what man of sense would regard the confessions or any of the words of these confessours?

The great cry of many of our neighbours now is, "what, will you not believe the confessours? Will you not believe men and women who confess that they have signed to the devil's book? that they were baptized by the devil and that they were at the mock sacrament once and again? What, will you not believe that this is witchcraft and that such and such men are witches although the confessours do own and assert it?"

Thus, I say, many of our good neighbours do argue but methinks they might soon be convinced that there is nothing at all in all these their arguings if they would but duly consider of the premises.

In the meantime, I think we must rest satisfied in it and be thankful to God for it that all men are not thus bereft of their senses but that we have here and there considerate and thinking men who will not thus be imposed upon and abused by the subtle endeavors of the crafty one.

The indictment runs for sorcery and witchcraft acted upon the body of such an one (say Mary Warren) at such a particular time (say April 14, '92) and at divers other times before and after, whereby the [said] Mary Warren is wasted and consumed, pined, etc.

Now for the proof of the said sorcery and witchcraft, the prisoner at the bar pleading not guilty.

1. The afflicted persons are brought into court and after much patience and pains taken with them, do take their oaths that the prisoner at the bar did afflict them. And here I think it very observable that often when the afflicted do mean and intend only the appearance and shape of such an one (say Goody Proctor) yet they positively swear that Goody Proctor did afflict them and they have been allowed so to do as though there was no real difference between Goody Proctor and the shape of Goody Proctor. This, methinks, may readily prove a stumbling block to the jury, lead them into a very fundamental error and occasion innocent blood, yea the innocentest blood imaginable, to be in great danger. . . .

2. The confessours do declare what they know of the said prisoner and some of the confessours are allowed to give their oaths, a thing which I believe was never heard of in this world, that such as confess themselves to be witches, to have renounced God and Christ and all that is sacred, should yet be allowed and ordered to swear by the name of the great God! This indeed seemeth to me to be a gross taking of God's name in vain. I know the Salem Gentlemen do say that there is hopes that the said confessours have repented. I shall only say that if they have repented, it is well for themselves, but if they have not, it is very ill for you know who. But then,

3. Whoever can be an evidence against the prisoner at the bar is ordered to come into court and here it scarce ever fails but that evidences of one nature and another are brought in, though, I think, all of them altogether alien to the matter of indictment, for they none of them do respect witchcraft upon the bodies of the afflicted, which is the alone matter of charge in the indictment.

4. They are searched by a jury and as to some of them, the jury brought in that [on] such or such a place there was a preternatural excrescence. And I wonder what person there is, whether man or woman, of whom it cannot be said but that in some part of their body or other there is a preternatural excrescence. The term is a very general and inclusive term.

Some of the Salem Gentlemen are very forward to censure and condemn the poor prisoner at the bar because he sheds no tears. But such betray great ignorance in the nature of passion and as great heedlessness as to common passages of a man's life. Some there are who never shed tears, others there are that ordinarily shed tears upon light occasions, and yet for their lives cannot shed a tear when the deepest sorrow is upon their hearts. And who is there that knows not these things? Who knows not that an ecstasy of joy will sometimes fetch tears when as the quite contrary passion will shut them close up? Why then should any be so silly and foolish as to take an argument from this appearance? But this is by the by. In short, the prisoner at the bar is indicted for sorcery and witchcraft acted upon the bodies of the afflicted. . . .

It is true that over and above the evidences of the afflicted persons, there are many evidences brought in against the prisoner at the bar, either that he was at a witch meeting or that he performed things which could not be done by an ordinary natural power, or that she sold butter to a sailor which, proving bad at sea and the seamen exclaiming against her, she appeared and soon after there was a storm or the like. But what if there were ten thousand evidences of this nature. How do they prove the matter of indictment? And if they do not reach the matter of indictment, then I think it is clear that the prisoner at the bar is brought in guilty and condemned, merely from the evidences of the afflicted persons.

The Salem Gentlemen will by no means allow [i.e., admit] that any are brought in guilty and condemned by virtue of spectral evidence (as it is called), i.e. the evidence of those afflicted persons who are said to have spectral eyes. But whether it is not purely by virtue of these spectral evidences that these persons are found guilty (considering what before has been said), I leave you and any man of sense, to judge and determine. When any man is indicted for murdering the person of A. B. and all the direct evidence be that the said man pistolled [i.e., shot] the shadow of the said A. B., though there be never so many evidences that the said person murdered C. D.,

E. F., and ten more persons, yet all this will not amount to a legal proof that he murdered A. B. And upon that indictment, the person cannot be legally brought in guilty of the said indictment. It must be upon this supposition, that the evidence of a man's pistolling the shadow of A. B. is a legal evidence to prove that the said man did murder the person of A. B. Now no man will be so much out of his wits as to make this a legal evidence and yet this seems to be our case. . . .

As to the late executions, I shall only tell you that in the opinion of many unprejudiced, considerate, and considerable spectators, some of the condemned went out of the world not only with as great protestations, but also with as good shows of innocency, as men could do.

They protested their innocency as in the presence of the great God, whom forthwith they were to appear before. They wished and declared their wish that their blood might be the last innocent blood shed upon that account. With great affection [i.e., emotion] they entreated Mr. Cotton Mather to pray with them. They prayed that God would discover what witchcrafts were among us; they forgave their accusers; they spoke without reflection on jury and judges for bringing them in guilty and condemning them; they prayed earnestly for pardon for all other sins and for an interest in the precious blood of our dear Redeemer; and seemed to be very sincere, upright, and sensible of their circumstances on all accounts, especially [John] Proctor and [John] Willard [executed on August 19] whose whole management of themselves, from the gaol to the gallows and whilst at the gallows, was very affecting and melting to the hearts of some considerable spectators. . . .

I do admire [i.e., wonder] that some particular persons and particularly Mrs. [Margaret] Thatcher of Boston should be much complained of by the afflicted persons and yet that the justices should never issue out their warrants to apprehend them when as upon the same account they issue out their warrants for the apprehending and imprisoning many others.

This occasions much discourse and many hot words and is a very great scandal and stumbling block to many good people. Certainly distributive justice should have its course without respect to persons and although the said Mrs. Thatcher be mother-in-law to Mr. [Jonathan] Corwin who is one of the Justices and Judges, yet if justice and conscience do oblige them to apprehend others on the account of the afflicted their complaints, I cannot see how without injustice and violence to conscience, Mrs. Thatcher can escape when it is well known how much she is and has been complained of. . . .

If our Justices do think that Mrs. [Elizabeth, wife of Nathaniel] Cary, Mr. [Philip] English and his wife, Mr. [John] Alden and others were capital offenders and justly imprisoned on a capital account, I do admire that the said Justices should hear of their escape from prison and where they are gone and entertained, and yet not send forthwith to the said places [i.e., New York] for the surrendering of them, that justice might be done them. . . .

The Chief Judge [William Stoughton, lieutenant governor] is very zealous in these proceedings and says he is very clear as to all that hath as yet been acted by this Court and, as far as ever I could perceive, is very impatient in hearing anything that looks another way. I very highly honor and reverence the wisdom and integrity of the said Judge and hope that this matter shall not diminish my veneration for his honor. However, I cannot but say my great fear is that wisdom and counsel are withheld from his honor as to this matter which yet I look upon not so much as a judgment to his honor as to this poor land.

But although the Chief Judge and some of the other Judges be very zealous in these proceedings, yet this you may take for a truth, that there are several about the Bay [i.e., Massachusetts Bay], men for understanding, judgment, and piety, inferior to few (if any), in New England that do utterly condemn the said proceedings and do freely deliver their judgment in the case to be this, viz. that these methods will utterly ruin and undo poor New England. I shall nominate some of these to you, viz.: The honorable Simon Bradstreet, Esq. (our late [i.e., former] Governor), the honorable Thomas Danforth, Esq. (our late deputy Governor), the Reverend Mr. Increase Mather, and the Reverend Mr. Samuel Willard. Major N. Saltonstall, Esq., who was one of the judges, has left the Court and is very much dissatisfied with the proceedings of it. Excepting Mr. Hale, Mr. Noyes, and Mr. Parris, the Reverend Elders, almost throughout the whole country, are very much dissatisfied. Several of the late [i.e., former] justices . . . are much dissatisfied, also several of the present justices, and in particular some of the Boston justices were resolved rather to throw up their commissions than be active in disturbing the liberty of their Majesty's subjects merely on the accusations of these afflicted, possessed children.

Finally, the principal gentlemen in Boston and thereabout are generally agreed that irregular and dangerous methods have been taken as to these matters. . . .

Nineteen persons have now been executed and one pressed to death for a mute; seven more are condemned, two of which are reprieved because they pretend their being with child, [another] one, viz. Mrs. [Mary] Bradbury of Salisbury from the intercession of some friends, and two or three more because they are confessours.

The Court is adjourned to the first Tuesday in November then to be kept at Salem. Between this and then will be [the] great assembly [the legislature or General Court] and this matter will be a peculiar matter of their agitation. I think it is [a] matter of earnest supplication and prayer to almighty God, that he would afford his gracious presence to the said assembly and direct them aright in this weighty matter. Our hopes are here, and if, at this juncture, God does not graciously appear for us, I think we may conclude that New England is undone and undone.

I am very sensible that it is irksome and disagreeable to go back when a man's doing so is an implication that he has been walking in a wrong path. However, nothing is more honorable than, upon due conviction, to retract and undo (so far as may be) what has been amiss and irregular. . . .

I cannot but highly applaud and think it our duty to be very thankful for the endeavors of several Elders [i.e., ministers] whose lips (I think) should preserve knowledge and whose counsel should, I think, have been more regarded in a case of this nature than as yet it has been. In particular, I cannot but think very honorably of the endeavors of a Reverend person in Boston [Samuel Willard], whose good affection to his country in general and spiritual relation to three of the Judges in particular has made him very solicitous and industrious in this matter, and, I am fully persuaded, that had his notions and proposals been hearkened to and followed, when these troubles were in their birth, in an ordinary way they would never have grown unto that height which now they have. He has as yet met with little but unkindness, abuse, and reproach from many men, but I trust that, in after times, his wisdom and service will find a more universal acknowledgement and, if not, his reward is with the Lord.

Two or three things I should have hinted to you before, but they slipped my thoughts in their proper place.

Many of these afflicted persons, who have scores of strange fits in a day, yet in the intervals of time are hale and hearty, robust and lusty, as though nothing had afflicted them. I remember that when the Chief Judge gave the first jury their charge, he told them that they were not to mind whether the bodies of the said afflicted were really pined and consumed, as was expressed in the indictment, but whether the said afflicted did not suffer from the accused such afflictions as naturally *tended* to their being pined and consumed, wasted, etc. This, said he, is a pining and consuming in the sense of the law. I add not.

Furthermore, these afflicted persons do say and often have declared it that they can see specters when their eyes are shut as well as when they are open. This one thing I evermore accounted as very observable and that which might serve as a good key to unlock the nature of these mysterious troubles, if duly improved by us. Can they see specters when their eyes are shut? I am sure they lie, at least speak falsely if they say so, for the thing, in nature, is an utter impossibility. It is true they may strongly fancy or have things represented to their imagination when their eyes are shut, and I think this is all which ought to be allowed to these blind, nonsensical girls. And if our officers and Courts have apprehended, imprisoned, condemned, and executed our guiltless neighbours, certainly our error is great and we shall rue it in the conclusion.

There are two or three other things that I have observed in and by these afflicted persons which make me strongly suspect that the devil imposes upon their brains and deludes their fancy and imagination, and that the devil's book (which they say has been offered them) is a mere fancy of theirs and no reality. That the witches' meeting, the devil's baptism and mock sacraments, which they oft[en] speak of, are nothing else but the effect of their fancy, depraved and deluded by the devil and not a reality to be regarded or minded by any wise man. . . .

I am very apt to think that did you know the circumstances of the said confessours, you would not be swayed thereby, any otherwise than to be confirmed that all is perfect devilism and an hellish design to ruin and destroy this poor land. For whereas there are of the said confessours 55 in number, some of them are known to be distracted, crazed women. . . . Others of them denied their guilt and maintained their innocency for above eighteen hours after most violent, distracting and dragooning methods had been used with them to make them confess. Such methods they were that more than one of the said confessours did since tell many, with tears in their eyes, that they thought their very lives would have gone out of their bodies and wished that they might have been cast into the lowest dungeon rather than be tortured with such repeated buzzings and chuckings and unreasonable urgings as they were treated withal.

They soon recanted their confessions, acknowledging, with sorrow and grief, that it was an hour of great temptation with them. And, I am very apt to think, that as for five or six of the said confessours, if they are not very good Christian women, it will be no easy matter to find so many good Christian women in New England. But, finally, as to about thirty of these fifty-five confessours, they are possessed (I reckon) with the devil and afflicted as the children are, and therefore not fit to be regarded as to anything they say of themselves or others. And whereas the Salem Gentlemen do say that these confessours made their confessions before they were afflicted, it is absolutely contrary to universal experience as far as ever I could understand. . . .

Thus, sir, I have given you as full a narrative of these matters as readily occurs to my mind and I think every word of it is matter of fact. The several glosses and descants [i.e., comments] whereupon by way of reasoning, I refer to your judgment, whether to approve or disapprove.

What will be the issue of these troubles, God only knows. I am afraid that ages will not wear off that reproach and those stains which these things will leave behind them upon our land. I pray God pity us, humble us, forgive us, and appear mercifully for us in this our mount of distress. Herewith I conclude and subscribe myself.

Reverend Sir, your real friend and humble servant. T. B.

[52]

The Apology of the Jury

In the aftermath of the trials, twelve men who sat on juries in Salem admitted to making a mistake in condemning so many to death in 1692. Their apology followed the day of fast and prayer that had been proclaimed by the legislature for January 14, 1697, and a public apology by Samuel Sewall, one of the judges. The statement by the jurors was preserved by Robert Calef and included as a supporting document in his attack on the Salem episode in general and on Cotton Mather's witchcraft beliefs in particular. The title of Calef's book, More Wonders of the Invisible World *(1700), was a takeoff on Mather's 1693 work describing demons and witches,* Wonders of the Invisible World.

•

Some that had been of several Juries, have given forth a Paper, signed with our own hands in these words: We whose names are underwritten, being in the year 1692 called to serve as jurors in court at Salem, on trial of many who were by some suspected guilty of doing acts of witchcraft upon the bodies of sundry persons.

We confess that we ourselves were not capable to understand, nor able to withstand the mysterious delusions of the powers of darkness and prince of the air, but were for want of knowledge in ourselves and better information from others, prevailed with to take up with such evidence against the accused as on further consideration and better information, we justly fear was insufficient for the touching the lives of any, Deut. 17.6, whereby we fear we have been instrumental with others, though ignorantly and unwittingly, to bring upon ourselves and this people of the Lord, the guilt of innocent blood, which sin the Lord saith in Scripture, he would not pardon, 2 Kings 24.4, that is we suppose in regard of His temporal judgments. We do, therefore, hereby signify to all in general (and to the surviving sufferers in especial) our deep sense of and sorrow for our errors in acting on such evidence to the condemning of any person.

And do hereby declare that we justly fear that we were sadly deluded and mistaken, for which we are much disquieted and distressed in our minds, and do therefore humbly beg forgiveness, first of God for Christ's sake for this our error.

From Narratives of the Witchcraft Cases, 1648–1706, *ed. George Lincoln Burr (New York: Charles Scribner's Sons, 1914), 387–88.*

And pray that God would not impute the guilt of it to ourselves, nor others. And we also pray that we may be considered candidly and aright by the living sufferers as being then under the power of a strong and general delusion, utterly unacquainted with and not experienced in matters of that nature.

We do heartily ask forgiveness of you all, whom we have justly offended and do declare, according to our present minds, we would none of us do such things again on such grounds for the whole world, praying you to accept of this in way of satisfaction for our offense, and that you would bless the inheritance of the Lord that He may be entreated for the land.

Foreman, Thomas Fisk	Thomas Perly, Senior
William Fiske	John Pebody
John Batcheler	Thomas Perkins
Thomas Fisk, Junior	Samuel Sayer
John Dane	Andrew Elliott
Joseph Evelith	Henry Herrick, Senior

That Sad Catastrophe

JOHN HALE

John Hale's testimony against Bridget Bishop was reprinted earlier in part 5. The work excerpted here, A Modest Enquiry into the Nature of Witchcraft and How Persons Guilty of the Crime May be Convicted: And the Means used for their Discoveries Discussed both Negatively and Affirmatively, according to Scripture and Experience, *was completed in 1697 but not published until 1702 after his death. In it Hale expresses regret at the condemnation of innocent people but still maintains that witchcraft is a serious danger.*

•

Preface

The Holy Scriptures inform us that the Doctrine of Godliness is a great mystery, containing the mysteries of the kingdom of heaven.... And as the Lord hath his mysteries to bring us to eternal glory, so Satan hath his mysteries to bring us to eternal ruin....

And among Satan's mysteries of iniquity, this of witchcraft is one of the most difficult to be searched out by the sons of men as appeareth by the great endeavors of learned and holy men to search it out, and the great differences that are found among them in the rules laid down for the bringing to light these hidden works of darkness. So that it may seem presumption in me to undertake so difficult a theme and to lay down such rules as are different from the sentiments of many eminent writers and from the precedents and practices of able lawyers, yea and from the Common Law itself.

But my apology for this undertaking is:

1. That there hath been such a dark dispensation by the Lord, letting loose upon us the devil, *Anno.* 1691 and 1692 as we never experienced before, and thereupon apprehending and condemning persons for witchcraft and next acquitting others no

From John Hale, *A Modest Enquiry into the Nature of Witchcraft* (1697), in *Narratives of the Witchcraft Cases, 1648–1706,* ed. George Lincoln Burr (New York: Charles Scribner's Sons, 1914), 402–5, 425–32.

less liable to such a charge, which evidently shows we were in the dark and knew not what to do, but have gone too far on the one or other side, if not on both. Hereupon I esteemed it necessary for some person to collect a summary of that affair with some animadversions [i.e., comments] upon it, which might at least give some light to them which come after to shun those rocks by which we were bruised and narrowly escaped shipwreck upon. And I have waited five years for some other person to undertake it who might do it better than I can, but find none, and judge it better to do what I can than that such a work should be left undone. Better sincerely though weakly done, than not at all, or with such a bias of prejudice as will put false glosses upon that which was managed with uprightness of heart. . . .

2. I have been present at several examinations and trials and knew sundry of those that suffered upon that account in former years and in this last affair, and so have more advantages than a stranger to give account of these proceedings.

3. I have been from my youth trained up in the knowledge and belief of most of those principles I here question as unsafe to be used. The first person that suffered on this account in New England, about fifty years since, was my neighbor and I heard much of what was charged upon her and others in those times; and the reverence I bore to aged, learned, and judicious persons, caused me to drink in their principles in these things with a kind of implicit faith. . . .

But observing the events of that sad catastrophe, *Anno 1692*, I was brought to a more strict scanning of the principles I had imbibed and by scanning, to question, and by questioning at length, to reject many of them upon the reasons shown in the ensuing discourse. . . .

The middle way is commonly the way of truth. And if any can show me a better middle way than I have here laid down, I shall be ready to embrace it. But the conviction must not be by vinegar or drollery, but by strength of argument.

4. I have had a deep sense of the sad consequence of mistakes in matters [of] capital [crimes], and their impossibility of recovering when completed. And what grief of heart it brings to a tender conscience to have been unwittingly encouraging of the sufferings of the innocent. And I hope a zeal to prevent for the future such sufferings is pardonable, although there should be much weakness and some errors in the pursuit thereof.

5. I observe the failings that . . . have driven some into that which is indeed an extreme . . . and of dangerous consequences, viz.: to deny any such persons to be under the New Testament who, by the devil's aid, discover secrets or do work wonders. . . .

I have special reasons moving me to bear my testimony about these matters before I go hence and be no more the which I have here done, . . . desiring his mercy in Jesus Christ to pardon all the errors of his people in the day of darkness and to enable us to fight with Satan by spiritual weapons, putting on the whole armor of God. . . . I believe God's children shall be gainers by the assaults of Satan, which occasioned this discourse. . . .

Chapter Eighteen

I shall conclude this discourse with some application of the whole.

1. We may hence see ground to fear that there hath been a great deal of innocent blood shed in the Christian world by proceeding upon unsafe principles in condemning persons for malefic witchcraft.

2. That there have been great sinful neglects in sparing others who, by their divinings about things future or discovering things secret, [such] as stolen goods, etc., or by their informing of persons and things absent at a great distance, have implored the assistance of a familiar spirit, yet coloured over with specious pretenses and have drawn people to enquire of them, a sin frequently forbidden in Scripture. . . . In many parts of the world [they] have been countenanced in their diabolical skill and profession because they serve the interest of those that have a vain curiosity to pry into things God hath forbidden and concealed from discovery by lawful means. And of others that by their enchantments have raised mists, strange sights, and the like, to beget admiration and please spectators, etc., when as these divinations and operations are the witchcraft more condemned in Scripture than the other.

3. But to come nigher [i.e., nearer] home, we have cause to be humbled for the mistakes and errors which have been in these colonies in their proceedings against persons for this crime, above forty years ago and downwards, upon insufficient presumptions and precedents of our nation whence they came. I do not say that all those were innocent that suffered in those times upon this account. But that such grounds were then laid down to proceed upon which were too slender to evidence the crime they were brought to prove and thereby a foundation laid to lead into error those that came after. . . . Whether this be not one of the sins the Lord hath been many years contending with us for, is worthy our serious inquiry. If the Lord punished Israel with famine three years for a sin of misguided zeal forty years before that committed by the breach of a covenant made four hundred years before that, . . . why may not the Lord visit upon us the misguided zeal of our predecessors about witchcraft above forty years ago, even when that generation is gathered to their fathers?

4. But I would come yet nearer to our own times and bewail the errors and mistakes that have been in the year 1692. In the apprehending, too many we may believe were innocent, and executing of some, I fear, not to have been condemned [and] by following such traditions of our fathers, maxims of the Common Law, and precedents and principles, which now we may see weighed in the balance of the sanctuary are found too light. I heartily concur with that direction for our public prayers, emitted December 17, 1696 by our General Assembly in an order for a general fast, viz., "That God would show us what we know not and help us wherein we have done amiss to do so no more. And especially that whatever mistakes on either hand have been fallen into, either by the body of this people or any order of men, referring to the late tragedy raised among us by Satan and his instruments through the awful judgment of God. He would humble us therefore and pardon all the errors of his servants and people that desire to love His name and be atoned to His land."

I am abundantly satisfied that those who were most concerned to act and judge in those matters did not willingly depart from the rules of righteousness. But such was the darkness of that day, the tortures and lamentations of the afflicted and the power of former precedents, that we walked in the clouds and could not see our way. And we have most cause to be humbled for error on that hand which cannot be retrieved. So that we must beseech the Lord that if any innocent blood hath been shed in the hour of temptation, the Lord will not lay it to our charge, but be merciful to his people whom he hath redeemed. . . .

5. I would humbly propose whether it be not expedient that somewhat more should be publicly done than yet hath for clearing the good name and reputation of some that have suffered upon this account against whom the evidence of their guilt was more slender and the grounds for charity for them more convincing. And this (in order to our obtaining from the Lord father reconciliation to our land), and that none of their surviving relations may suffer reproach upon that account. I have both read and heard of several in England that have been executed for capital crimes and afterwards upon sense of an error in the process against them, have been restored in blood and honor by some public act. . . .

6. Here it may be suitable for us to enquire what the Lord speaks to us by such a stupendous providence in his letting loose Satan upon us in this unusual way? . . .

So I may say in this case, in the prosecution of witchcraft, we sought not the Lord after the due order but have proceeded after the methods used in former times and other places until the Lord in this tremendous way made a breach upon us. And hereby we are made sensible that the methods formerly used are not sufficient to prove the guilt of such a crime. And this I conceive was one end of the Lord's letting Satan loose to torment and accuse so many—that hereby we may search out the truth more exactly. For had it not been for this dreadful dispensation, many would have lived and died in that error, which they are now convinced of. . . .

7. From that part of the discourse which shows the power of Satan to torment the bodies and disturb the minds of those he is let loose upon, . . . I would infer that Satan may be suffered so to darken the minds of some pious souls as to cause them to destroy themselves by drowning, hanging, or the like. And when he hath so far prevailed upon some that formerly lived a Christian life, but were under the prevalency of a distracting melancholy at their latter end, we may have charity that their souls are saved, notwithstanding the sad conclusion of their lives. I speak not to excuse any that having the free use of their reason willingly destroy themselves out of pride, discontent, impatience, etc . . .

8. Seeing we have been too fierce against supposed malefic witchcraft, let us take heed we do not on the contrary become too favorable to divining witchcraft. . . . Let us not, if we can help it, suffer Satan to set up an ensuring office for stolen goods, that, after he hath brought the curse of God into the house of the thief by tempting him to steal, he may not bring about the curse into the houses of them from whom the goods were stolen by alluring them to go to the god of Ekron to enquire; that men may not give their souls to the devil in exchange for his restoring to them their goods again in such a way of divination. . . .

9. Another extreme we must beware of is, viz. because our fathers in the beginning

time of this land did not see so far into these mysteries of iniquity as hath been since discovered, let us not undervalue the good foundations they laid for God and his people and for us in church and civil government. For Paul, that eminent Apostle knew but in part. No wonder then if our fathers were imperfect men. In the purest times in Israel, there were some clouds of ignorance overshadowing of them. Abraham, David, and the best patriarchs were generally ignorant of the sin of polygamy. And also Solomon far exceeded Nehemiah in wisdom, yet Nehemiah saw farther into the evil of marrying outlandish women than that wisest of kings and mere fallen men. . . .

It was a glorious enterprise of the beginners of these colonies to leave their native country to propagate the Gospel and a very high pitch of faith, zeal, and courage that carried them forth to follow the Lord into this wilderness, into a land that was not sown. Then was New England holiness to the Lord, and all that did devour them or attempted so to do, did offend and evil did come upon them. And the Lord did graciously remember this kindness of their youth and love of their espousals, in granting them many eminent tokens of his favor—by his presence with them in his Ordinances, for the conversion of souls, and edifying and comforting the hearts of his servants; by signal answering their prayers in times of difficulty; by protecting them from their enemies; by guiding of and providing for them in a desert. And the Lord will still remember this their kindness unto their posterity, unless that by their apostasy from the Lord, they vex his Holy Spirit to turn to be their enemy and thereby cut off the entail of his Covenant mercies, which God forbid. *Oh that the Lord may be with us, as he was with our fathers, and that he may not leave us, nor forsake us!*

VI

Historians' Commentaries on the Salem Case

WITCH HUNTS AND THE practice of witchcraft, as we have seen, are part of the landscape of human history. But why witchcraft comes to the attention of the authorities at any particular time and the circumstances under which leaders launch witch hunts are still issues that absorb historians. That witch hunts have entertainment value is true. The dramatic behavior of those possessed titillates as much as it horrifies; trials and executions provide public spectacles and opportunities for communal celebration. After some blood has been shed and the scapegoats for social disorder have been dispatched, the community can safely return to its usual routine cleansed of its real and imagined demons.

But in Salem the trials ended not with satisfaction, but with individual remorse and attempts at communal apology and restitution. There was a little sense of redemption and no resolution of conflict. People who formerly were exempt from persecution because of social class, gender, or "blameless and holy lives," as Hale described them, were convicted and executed. Something went wrong with the communal catharsis. Social life and kinship ties were strained rather than strengthened. So historians deal with the dilemma of why it happened and why in Salem. Only a very few of the recent interpretative works can be presented here, but these selections illustrate the range of questions that absorb the scholarly community.

Charles Upham, one of the earliest writers to review the transcripts and eyewitness accounts, probably has had the greatest impact on the popular view of the events. His interpretation of the Salem events, first put forth in 1867, is the one adopted by playwrights and novelists—from Marion Starkey's semifictional, post–Nazi era narrative to Arthur Miller's *Crucible* and most TV depictions. It also lingers on in textbook narratives. Upham puts the onus of responsibility on the accusing girls, who were manipulating the adults to get their attention and sympathy by pretending to be bewitched. Their antics were a convincing deception. He suggests too that Tituba was responsible for teaching the girls some esoteric magical rites. Parris is also held responsible for further inflaming the public mind for his own purposes.

But the ultimate culprit, according to Upham, was Puritanism, the clerical reliance on superstitious beliefs and the lack of rational thought. Upham speaks from a nineteenth-century viewpoint that elevated science and reason above any folk wisdom and adhered to a religion stripped of its mystical elements. Thus he has added to the mythology of a credulous Puritanism, suffused with fearful superstitions, that created a terribly oppressive environment. He also identified Puritan theology with the mys-

tical rites of the Catholic Church and what he thought of as the primitive magic of
African and American Indian religions, all of which brought on that unenlightened
event. His own commonsense, rational, and scientific age, he believed, could not
make such mistakes.

Since his day, historians have tended to put much less blame on either the accusers
or Puritanism itself. Richard Godbeer sets the New England witch persecutions into
a broader European and English legal and theological perspective. It was not that
Salem was unique but that Puritanism in its reforming stage in mid-seventeenth-
century New England had exacerbated the gulf between popular understanding of
evil magic and theological definitions. The rigorous standards that had been applied
by the Puritans in previous episodes and the increasing reluctance of the authorities
to punish accused witches contributed to a greater fear of those occult practices.
Finally in 1692 the populace demanded protection. In this revisionist view, the Salem
witch hunt was the culmination of fifty-years of inaction rather than action on the
part of Puritan authorities under the restraining rather than inciting influence of the
theologians.

An area that has only recently received serious attention is the composition of the
confessions to witchcraft and in particular Tituba's role in establishing a model for
others to follow. Elaine Breslaw offers a new perspective on Tituba's significance by
suggesting that as the first to confess, the Indian woman set the stage for the fantastic
testimonies that followed, thus fueling the communal fear. Breslaw argues that Tituba's ethnic background played a dual role. As an American Indian, Tituba heightened the fear of a diabolical presence, and the words in her testimony, stemming
from her multicultural background, provided imaginative details that were later
incorporated into other confessions. Breslaw offers evidence to show that mythology
of the African Tituba teaching the girls exotic voodoo rituals should be laid to rest,
replaced by the story of a South American Indian caught up in an attempt to save
her own life.

The social environment, class conflicts, and changing moral values suggest another
series of possible explanations for the witch hunts. Historians of New England have
analyzed everything from the political conflict between the colony and the crown to
Samuel Parris's dispute with his opponents in the village and the Salem villagers'
quest for independence from Salem Town government. Even fights over land ownership and the rise of commercial values within the community could have been the
sources of social unrest that eventually erupted in witchcraft accusations. Larry
Gragg's analysis is a variation on this social dysfunction theme.

The witch hunt in Salem, Gragg concludes, was the result of a series of harmful
decisions made by people driven to protect their own self-interest and unaware of
the consequences of their actions. Salem, he shows, was a "bitterly divided community" that maintained its divisiveness long after the trials. Thus, although the events
of 1692 can be understood mainly in the context of local squabbles, Gragg argues
that it was human error—the flawed decisions made by people responding to social
issues—that created the crisis. Many individuals took part in making those bad
decisions, but Gragg suggests that both Samuel Parris in his disagreements with his

parishioners and Cotton Mather in his obsessions with witchcraft were also to blame for what happened. Gragg's emphasis on individual responsibility moves the historical debate away from the determinism implied in most analyses that link causation with social conflict.

[54]

Witchcraft at Salem Village

CHARLES UPHAM

Charles Upham (1802–1875), a clergyman and mayor of Salem Town, published his two-volume Salem Witchcraft *in 1867. He drew heavily on the available court records as well as published material dealing with witchcraft of the seventeenth century. Also included in his book (but not reproduced here) is a map of the Salem area that locates the homes of the major actors in the tragedy.*

•

We left Mr. Parris in the early part of November, 1691, at the crisis of his controversy with the inhabitants of Salem Village, under circumstances which seemed to indicate that its termination was near at hand. The opposition to him had assumed a form which made it quite probable that it would succeed in dislodging him from his position. But the end was not yet. Events were ripening that were to give him a new and fearful strength, and open a scene in which he was to act a part destined to attract the notice of the world, and become a permanent portion of human history. The doctrines of demonology had produced their full effect upon the minds of men, and every thing was ready for a final display of their power. The story of the Goodwin children, as told by Cotton Mather, was known and read in all the dwellings of the land, and filled the imaginations of a credulous age. Deputy governor Danforth had begun the work of arrests; and persons charged with witchcraft, belonging to neighboring towns, were already in prison.

Mr. Parris appears to have had in his family several slaves, probably brought by him from the West Indies. One of them, whom he calls, in his church-record book, "my negro lad," had died, a year or two before, at the age of nineteen. Two of them were man and wife. The former was always known by the name of "John Indian;" the latter was called "Tituba." These two persons may have originated the "Salem witchcraft." They are spoken of as having come from New Spain, as it was then called,—that is, the Spanish West Indies, and the adjacent mainlands of Central and

From Charles Upham, *Salem Witchcraft; with An Account of Salem Village*, vol. 2 (1867; reprint, Gansevoort, NY: Corner House, 1971) 1–3, 6–7, 26–28, 33–37, 430–31, 433–36. Reprinted by permission of the publisher.

South America,—and, in all probability, contributed, from the wild and strange superstitions prevalent among their native tribes, materials which, added to the commonly received notions on such subjects, heightened the infatuation of the times, and inflamed still more the imaginations of the credulous. Persons conversant with the Indians of Mexico, and on both sides of the Isthmus, discern many similarities in their systems of demonology with ideas and practices developed here.

Mr. Parris's former residence in the neighborhood of the Spanish Main, and the prominent part taken by his Indian slaves in originating the proceedings at the village, may account for some of the features of the transaction.

During the winter of 1691 and 1692, a circle of young girls had been formed, who were in the habit of meeting at Mr. Parris's house for the purpose of practicing palmistry, and other arts of fortune-telling, and of becoming experts in the wonders of necromancy, magic and spiritualism. . . .

In the course of the winter, they became quite skillful and expert in the arts they were learning, and gradually began to display their attainments to the admiration and amazement of beholders. At first, they made no charges against any person, but confined themselves to strange actions, exclamations, and contortions. They would creep into holes, and under benches and chairs, put themselves into odd and unnatural postures, make wild and antic gestures, and utter incoherent and unintelligible sounds. They would be seized with spasms, drop insensible to the floor, or writhe in agony, suffering dreadful tortures, and uttering loud and piercing outcries. The attention of the families in which they held their meetings was called to their extraordinary condition and proceedings; and the whole neighborhood and surrounding country soon were filled with the story of the strange and unaccountable sufferings of the "afflicted girls." No explanation could be given, and their condition became worse and worse. The physician of the village, Dr. Griggs, was called in, a consultation had, and the opinion finally and gravely given, that the afflicted children were bewitched. It was quite common in those days for the faculty to dispose of difficult cases by this resort. When their remedies were baffled, and their skill at fault, the patient was said to be "under an evil hand." In all cases, the sage conclusion was received by nurses, and elderly women called in on such occasions, if the symptoms were out of the common course, or did not yield to the prescriptions these persons were in the habit of applying. Very soon, the whole community became excited and alarmed to the highest degree. All other topics were forgotten. The only thing spoken or thought of was the terrible condition of the afflicted children in Mr. Parris's house, or wherever, from time to time, the girls assembled. They were the objects of universal compassion and wonder. The people flocked from all quarters to witness their sufferings, and gaze with awe upon their convulsions. Becoming objects of such notice, they were stimulated to vary and expand the manifestations of the extraordinary influence that was upon them. They extended their operations beyond the houses of Mr. Parris, and the families to which they belonged, to public places; and their fits, exclamations, and outcries disturbed the exercises of prayer meetings, and the ordinary services of the congregation. . . .

*　　*　　*

Another report of Tituba's examination has been preserved. . . . It is in the handwriting of Jonathan Corwin, very full and minute, and shows that the Indian woman was familiar with all the ridiculous and monstrous fancies then prevalent. The details of her statement cover nearly the whole ground of them. While indicating, in most respects, a mind at the lowest level of general intelligence, they give evidence of cunning and wariness in the highest degree. This document is also valuable, as it affords information about particulars, incidentally mentioned and thus rescued from oblivion, which serve to bring back the life of the past. Tituba describes the dresses of some of the witches: "A black silk hood, with a white silk hood under it, with top-knots." One of them wore "a serge coat, with a white cap." The Devil appeared "in black clothes sometimes, sometimes serge coat of other color." She speaks of the "lean-to chamber" in the parsonage, and describes an aërial night ride "up" to Thomas Putnam's. "How did you go? What did you ride upon?" asked the wondering magistrate. "I ride upon a stick, or pole, and Good and Osburn behind me: we ride taking hold of one another; don't know how we go, for I saw no trees nor path, but was presently there when we were up." In both reports, Tituba describes, quite graphically, the likenesses in which the Devil appeared to his confederates; but Corwin gives the details more fully than Cheever. What the latter reports of the appearances in which the Devil accompanied Osburn, the former amplifies. "The thing with two legs and wings, and a face like a woman," "turns" into a full woman. The "hairy thing" becomes "a thing all over hairy, all the face hairy, and a long nose, and I don't know how to tell how the face looks; is about two or three feet high, and goeth upright like a man; and, last night, it stood before the fire in Mr. Parris's hall."

It is quite evident that the part played by the Indian woman on this occasion was pre-arranged. She had, from the first, been concerned with the circle of girls in their necromantic operations; and her statements show the materials out of which their ridiculous and monstrous stories were constructed. She said that there were four who "hurt the children." Upon being pressed by the magistrate to tell who they were, she named Osburn and Good, but did "not know who the others were." Two others were marked; but it was not thought best to bring them out until these three examinations had first been made to tell upon the public mind. Tituba had been apprised of Elizabeth Hubbard's story, that she had been "pinched" that morning; and, as well as "Lieutenant Fuller and others," had heard of the delirious exclamation of Thomas Putnam's sick child during the night. "Abigail Williams, that lives with her uncle Parris," had communicated to the Indian slave the story of "the woman with two legs and wings." In fact, she had been fully admitted to their councils, and made acquainted with all the stories they were to tell. But, when it became necessary to avoid specifications touching parties whose names it had been decided not to divulge at that stage of the business, the wily old servant escapes further interrogation, "I am blind now: I cannot see." . . .

* * *

Now let us consider the state of things that had been brought about in the village, and in the surrounding country, at the close of the first week in March, 1692. The terrible sufferings of the girls in Mr. Parris's family and of their associates, for the two preceding months, had become known far and wide. A universal sympathy was awakened in their behalf; and a sentiment of horror sunk deep into all hearts, at the dread demonstration of the diabolical rage in their afflicted and tortured persons. A few, very few, distrusted; but the great majority, ninety-nine in a hundred of all the people, were completely swept into the torrent. Nathaniel Putnam and Nathaniel Ingersoll were entirely deluded, and continued so to the end. Even Joseph Hutchinson was, for a while, carried away. The physicians had all given their opinion that the girls were suffering from an "evil hand." The neighboring ministers, after a day's fasting and prayer, and a scrutinizing inspection of the condition of the afflicted children, had given it, as the result of their most solemn judgment, that it was a case of witchcraft. Persons from the neighboring towns had come to the place, and with their own eyes received demonstration of the same fact. Mr. Parris made it the topic of his public prayers and preaching. The girls, Sunday after Sunday, were under the malign influence, to the disturbance and affrightment of the congregation. In all companies, in all families, all the day long, the sufferings and distraction occurring in the houses of Mr. Parris, Thomas Putnam, and others, and in the meeting-house, were topics of excited conversation; and every voice was loud in demanding, every mind earnest to ascertain, who were the persons, in confederacy with the Devil, thus torturing, pinching, convulsing, and bringing to the last extremities of mortal agony, these afflicted girls. Every one felt, that, if the guilty authors of the mischief could not be discovered, and put out of the way, no one was safe for a moment. At length, when the girls cried out upon Good, Osburn, and Tituba, there was a general sense of satisfaction and relief. It was thought that Satan's power might be checked. The selection of the first victims was well made. They were just the kind of persons whom the public prejudice and credulity were prepared to suspect and condemn. Their examination was looked for with the utmost interest, and all flocked to witness the proceedings.

In considering the state of mind of the people, as they crowded into and around the old meeting-house, we can have no difficulty in realizing the tremendous effects of what there occurred. It was felt that then, on that spot, the most momentous crisis in the world's history had come. A crime, in comparison with which all other crimes sink out of notice, was being notoriously and defiantly committed in their midst. The great enemy of God and man was let loose among them. What had filled the hearts of mankind for ages, the world over, with dread apprehension, was come to pass; and in that village the great battle, on whose issue the preservation of the kingdom of the Lord on the earth was suspended, had begun. Indeed, no language, no imagery, no conception of ours, can adequately express the feeling of awful and terrible solemnity with which all were overwhelmed. No body of men ever convened in a more highly wrought state of excitement than pervaded that assembly, when the magistrates entered, in all their stern authority, and the scene opened on the 1st of March, 1692. A minister, probably Mr. Parris, began, according to the custom of the times, with prayer. From what we know of his skill and talent in meeting such occasions, it may well be supposed that his language and manner heightened still more the passions of the hour. The marshal, of tall and imposing stature and aspect, accompanied by his constables, brought in the prisoners. Sarah Good, a poverty-stricken, wandering, and wretched victim of ill-fortune and ill-usage, was put to the bar. Every effort was made by the examining magistrate, aided by the officious interference of the marshal, or other deluded or evil-disposed persons,—who, like him, were permitted to interpose with charges or abusive expressions,—to overawe and confound, involve in contradictions, and mislead the poor creature, and force her to confess herself guilty and accuse others. In due time, the "afflicted children" were brought in; and a scene ensued, such as no person in that crowd or in that generation had ever witnessed before. Immediately on being confronted with the prisoner, and meeting her eye, they fell, as if struck dead, to the floor; or screeched in agony; or went into fearful spasms or convulsive fits; or cried out that they were pricked with pins, pinched, or throttled by invisible hands. They were severally brought up to the prisoner, and, upon touching her person, instantly became calm, quiet, and fully restored to their senses. With one voice they all declared that Sarah Good had thus tormented them, by her power as a witch in league with the Devil. The truth of this charge, in the effect produced by the malign influence proceeding from her, was thus visible to all eyes. All saw, too, how instantly upon touching her the diabolical effect ceased; the malignant fluid passing back, like an electric stream, into the body of the witch. The spectacle was repeated once and again, the acting perfect, and the delusion consummated. The magistrates and all present considered the guilt of the prisoner demonstrated, and regarded her as willfully and wickedly obstinate in not at once confessing what her eyes, as well as theirs, saw. Her refusal to confess was considered as the highest proof of her guilt. They passed judgment against her, committed her to the marshal, who hurried her to prison, bound her with cords, and loaded her with irons; for it was thought that no ordinary fastenings could hold a witch. Similar proceedings, with suitable variations, were had with Sarah Osburn and Tituba. The confession of the last-named, the immediate relief thereafter of the afflicted children, and the dreadful torments which Tituba herself experienced, on the spot, from the unseen hand of the Devil wreaking vengeance upon her, put the finishing touch to the delusion. The excitement was kept up, and spread far and wide, by the officers and magistrates riding in cavalcade, day after day, to and from the town and village; and by the constables, with their assistants, carrying their manacled prisoners from jail to jail in Ipswich, Salem, and Boston.

The point was now reached when the accusers could safely strike at higher game. But time was taken to mature arrangements. Great curiosity was felt to know who the other two were whom Tituba saw in connection with Good and Osburn in their hellish operations. The girls continued to suffer torments and fall in fits, and were constantly urged by large numbers of people, going from house to house to witness their sufferings, to reveal who the witches were that still afflicted them. When all was prepared, they began to cry out, with more or less distinctness; at first, in significant but general descriptions, and at last calling names. . . .

*   *   *

In its general outlines and minuter details, Salem Witchcraft is an illustration of the fatal effects of allowing the imagination inflamed by passion to take the place of common sense, and of pushing the curiosity and credence of the human mind, in this stage of our being, while in these corporeal embodiments, beyond the boundaries that ought to limit their exercise. If we disregard those boundaries, and try to overleap them, we shall be liable to the same results. The lesson needs to be impressed equally upon all generations and ages of the world's future history. Essays have been written and books published to prove that the sense of the miraculous is destined to decline as mankind becomes more enlightened, and ascribing a greater or less tendency to the indulgence of this sense to particular periods of the church, or systems of belief, or schools of what is called philosophy. It is maintained that it was more prevalent in the mediæval ages than in modern times. Some assert that it has had a greater development in Catholic than Protestant countries; and some, perhaps, insist upon the reverse. Some attempt to show that it has manifested itself more remarkably among Puritans than in other classes of Protestant Christians. The last and most pretentious form of this dogma is, that the sense of the miraculous fades away in the progress of what arrogates to itself the name of Rationalism. This is one of the delusive results of introducing generalization into historical disquisitions. . . .

The lesson of our story will be found not to discard spiritual things, but to teach us, while in the flesh, not to attempt to break through present limitations, not to seek to know more than has been made known of the unseen and invisible, but to keep the inquiries of our minds and the action of society within the bounds of knowledge now attainable, and extend our curious researches and speculations only as far as we can here have solid ground to stand upon.

To explain the superstitious opinions that took effect in the witchcraft delusion, it is necessary to consider the state of biblical criticism at that period. That department of theological learning was then in a very immature condition.

The authority of Scripture, as it appeared on the face of the standard version, seemed to require them to pursue the course they adopted; and those enlarged and just principles of interpretation which we are taught by the learned of all denominations at the present day to apply to the Sacred Writings had not then been brought to the view of the people or received by the clergy.

It was gravely argued, for instance, that there was nothing improbable in the idea that witches had the power, in virtue of their compact with the Devil, of riding aloft through the air, because it is recorded, in the history of our Lord's temptation, that Satan transported him in a similar manner to the pinnacle of the temple, and to the summit of an exceedingly high mountain. And Cotton Mather declares, that, to his apprehension, the disclosures of the wonderful operations of the Devil, upon and through his subjects, that were made in the course of the witchcraft prosecutions, had shed a marvelous light upon the Scriptures! What a perversion of the Sacred Writings to employ them for the purpose of sanctioning the extravagant and delirious reveries of the human imagination! What a miserable delusion, to suppose that the Word of God could receive illumination from the most absurd and horrible superstition that ever brooded in darkness over the mind of man!

One of the sources of the delusion of 1692 was ignorance of many natural laws that have been revealed by modern science. A vast amount of knowledge on these subjects has been attained since that time. In our halls of education, in associations for the diffusion of knowledge, and in a diversified and all-pervading popular literature, what was dark and impenetrable mystery then has been explained, accounted for, and brought within the grasp of all minds. The contemplation of the evils brought upon our predecessors by their ignorance of the laws of nature cannot but lead us to appreciate more highly our opportunities to get knowledge in this department. As we advance into the interior of the physical system to which we belong; are led in succession from one revelation of beauty and grandeur to another, and the field of light and truth displaces that of darkness and mystery; while the fearful images that disturbed the faith and bewildered the thoughts of our fathers are dissolving and vanishing, the whole host of spirits, ghosts, and demons disappearing, and the presence and providence of God alone found to fill all scenes and cause all effects,—our hearts ought to rise to him in loftier adoration and holier devotion. If, while we enjoy a fuller revelation of his infinite and all-glorious operations and designs than our fathers did, the sentiment of piety which glowed in their hearts like a coal from the altar of God has been permitted to grow dim in ours, no reproach their errors and faults can possibly authorize will equal that which will justly fall upon us.

Another cause of their delusion was too great a dependence upon the imagination. We shall find no lesson more clearly taught by history, by experience, or by observation, than this, that man is never safe while either his fancy or his feeling is the guiding principle of his nature. There is a strong and constant attraction between his imagination and his passions; and, if either is permitted to exercise unlimited away, the other will most certainly be drawn into cooperation with it, and, when they are allowed to act without restraint upon each other and with each other, they lead to the derangement and convulsion of his whole system. They constitute the combustible elements of our being: one serves as the spark to explode the other. Reason, enlightened by revelation and guided by conscience, is the great conservative principle: while that exercises the sovereign power over the fancy and the passions, we are safe; if it is dethroned, no limit can be assigned to the ruin that may follow. In the scenes we have now been called to witness, we have perceived to what lengths of folly, cruelty, and crime even good men have been carried, who relinquished the aid, rejected the counsels, and abandoned the guidance of their reason.

[55]

Witchcraft, the Courts, and Countermagic

RICHARD GODBEER

Richard Godbeer's work was introduced in part 2. In this additional excerpt from his 1992 book The Devil's Dominion, *Godbeer discusses judicial policies on witchcraft in colonial New England and compares them to English and European practices.*

•

Afflicted New Englanders who blamed illness or misfortune on witchcraft often wanted to punish the witch responsible. Some victims used countermagic to identify and injure the malefactor; but others who already thought they knew the witch's identity might turn instead to legal action. These two forms of retaliation were not mutually exclusive: some victims used countermagic successfully against a suspect and then related the experiment in court as evidence against the supposed witch; they hoped to inflict additional, official, and capital punishment. Others may have prosecuted after trying unsuccessfully to harm the suspect by way of countermagic: the failure of a countermagical experiment might be due to the practitioner's incompetence or the target's self-protective skill, and did not necessarily mean that the suspect was innocent. Whatever their reasons for doing so, a significant number of witchcraft victims did seek redress through legal channels. Even omitting the Salem prosecutions, there were at least sixty-one trials for witchcraft in seventeenth-century New England.

Trying a witch, however, involved defining witchcraft. In dealing with witchcraft cases, the courts followed theological principles: they wanted proof that the witch was in league with the Devil. Yet most of those who brought complaints against witches made no mention of any external agency, diabolical or otherwise: they apparently believed that the accused acted independently. It seems almost inconceivable that these layfolk had not been exposed to a diabolical view of the crime; indeed, they may have believed on some theoretical level that Satan was involved in witch-

From Richard Godbeer, *The Devil's Dominion: Magic and Religion in Early New England* (Cambridge: Cambridge University Press, 1992), 154–62, 176–78. © 1992 by Cambridge University Press. Reprinted by permission of Cambridge University Press.

craft. But when dealing with witchcraft in practice, their attitude does not appear to have been informed by a theological perspective. Indeed, accusers hardly ever referred to the Devil in their testimony. This made legal conviction extremely difficult. The courtroom became a battleground on which New Englanders contested the meaning of witchcraft; cases involving accusations of witchcraft thus revealed the limits of shared culture in early New England.

*   *   *

In Europe, England, and New England alike, theologians saw witchcraft as a form of heresy: the witch, they believed, had repudiated Christianity and entered the service of Satan; in return for obedience, the Devil perpetrated evil deeds on the witch's behalf. Many layfolk, however, understood witchcraft simply as a misuse of occult power: they emphasized its practical impact, not the agency that made it possible; whether the Devil or any other supernatural being assisted the witch was of peripheral concern. Whereas theologians emphasized diabolical complicity, popular accusations of witchcraft focused on *maleficium* (the doing of evil) and showed little interest in diabolical compact. This disjunction between theological and popular perceptions of witchcraft mattered most when people turned to the legal system for protection against witches. European, English, and colonial courts had to negotiate between these two views of witchcraft and determine what kinds of evidence should justify conviction.

Medieval legislation against witchcraft had focused on the practical harm perpetrated by witches, but during the early modern period, European laws came to embody the theological view of witchcraft. This change originated in a combination of evangelical fervor and political expediency. Religious reformers, eager to convert and educate the European peasantry, allied with centralizing governments in a campaign to establish control over outlying communities that were as yet virtually autonomous and only nominally Christian. Evangelists identified popular conceptions of magic and witchcraft as the most striking expression of a distinct and thus threatening supernatural tradition. They translated popular witch beliefs into diabolical terms and then set about converting people to their own theological perspective. This attempt to superimpose diabolism on popular tradition became the focus for an international campaign to acculturate the European peasantry.

Wholesale legal reform was crucial to this process of conversion. During the sixteenth and sevententh centuries, most European countries adopted the inquisitorial system, thereby shifting the initiative in bringing a legal action from accuser to state officials and also removing most restrictions against the use of torture. The courts took suspects and witnesses who saw witchcraft in terms of maleficium rather than diabolical compact and then used torture to extract the kind of evidence that would justify conviction on theological terms. Through the use of coercive techniques and the public reading of forced confessions, the authorities disseminated their own view of witchcraft. As propagandists taught the peasantry to recast their traditions in a Christian mold, popular witch beliefs began to transform during the sixteenth and seventeenth centuries. This in turn enhanced the authority of the early modern state, which claimed to be an instrument of divine will and used Christian ideology to legitimize its actions.

In most European countries, witch trials played an important role in the assertion of political control: the witch was all that a good citizen ought not to be. But in England, the political system was, by contemporary standards, highly centralized and relatively secure, so that there was no reason to launch a major offensive against popular culture. Legal initiative remained in the hands of the accuser and the use of the jury system ensured that the resolution of a legal action against witchcraft reflected popular as much as official belief. English law defined witchcraft as a hostile act rather than as heresy. The witchcraft statutes of 1542 and 1563 made no reference whatsoever to diabolical compact. The statute of 1604 did condemn "covenant[ing] with . . . any evil and wicked spirit," but it rejected the theological view that all forms of magic involved a diabolical covenant: the legislators made a clear distinction between malefic witchcraft and less harmful forms of magic such as divination, for which the penalties were much lighter. Toward the end of the sixteenth century, the courts did become better informed about continental demonology and showed an increasing interest in devil-related evidence. A combination of clerical propaganda and judicial pressure began to affect the content of popular testimony, especially confessions, which by the early seventeenth century often included descriptions of diabolical compact. Yet most deponents still focused on maleficium and insisted on distinguishing between good and evil magic. In England, there was no fundamental transformation of popular belief.

The legal definition of witchcraft in early modern England was broadly compatible with popular tradition and so facilitated legal process. New England courts, on the other hand, were uniquely ill-equipped to deal with witchcraft cases. The laws passed against witchcraft in the northern colonies were biblically inspired and followed theological principles. Plymouth, Massachusetts, New Hampshire, and Connecticut laws defined a witch simply as "any man or woman . . . [who] hath or consulteth with a familiar spirit [a devil]." Yet New England courts had no legal recourse to torture as a way to extract diabolical evidence from individuals whose perception of witchcraft was at odds with that of the law. Like European courts, they were operating according to laws that did not coincide with the popular view of witchcraft. Unlike European courts, they had no way to bridge the gap between legal prescription and popular belief. Because those who gave testimony in such cases tended to describe witchcraft in terms of maleficium, their evidence rarely justified a conviction. The only occasion on which a New England court was able to secure extensive evidence of diabolical witchcraft was at Salem in 1692; this was also the only known occasion on which the authorities used torture to extract confessions. Of the sixty-one known prosecutions for witchcraft in seventeenth-century New England, omitting the Salem trials, sixteen at most (perhaps only fourteen) resulted in conviction and execution, a rate of 26.2 percent. In Essex, England, the conviction rate between 1560 and 1680 was 44.3 percent; the execution rate was 25.4 percent. For the continent, one recent estimate puts the execution rate at 54.5 percent; the conviction rate was probably higher.

Judicial policy on witchcraft in the northern colonies followed guidelines laid down by two English legal experts, William Perkins and Richard Bernard, both of whom were also divines. During the sixteenth and seventeenth centuries, English writers produced a vast body of literature discussing witchcraft from spiritual, medical, and legal perspectives. These publications represented a broad spectrum of opinion. At one extreme, materialists such as Thomas Hobbes questioned the Devil's very ability to intervene in human affairs on a physical plane. Hobbes rejected as self-contradictory the notion of an incorporeal substance and argued that devils could neither assume bodily form nor occupy a human being. According to Hobbes, the Devil's power over humankind was purely spiritual. A much larger and more widely regarded group of authors did not question the Devil's physical power, but rejected many of the traditions that underlay continental demonology, including the witches' sabbath, on the grounds that they had no biblical foundation. According to these writers, the European image of demonic witchcraft was a hodge-podge of pagan superstition and popish invention. Yet authors such as Joseph Glanvill and Richard Baxter, situated at the opposite end of the spectrum from the materialists, reaffirmed traditional witch beliefs. They sought to refute skeptics by presenting numerous "relations" of supernatural incidents that, according to Glanvill and Baxter, proved conclusively the reality of witchcraft.

A number of English authors focused on the difficulties involved in proving witchcraft as a crime. Medical authorities such as John Cotta stressed the need to distinguish carefully between natural disease and supernatural affliction. Cotta also argued that confessions should not be admissable in witchcraft cases, since the accused might be ill and suffering from hallucinations. The two most influential studies of witchcraft as a legal problem were William Perkins's *Discourse on the Damned Art of Witchcraft* and Richard Bernard's *Guide to Grand-Jury Men*, published in 1608 and 1627 respectively. Perkins's *Discourse* spearheaded a campaign by Protestant commentators to cleanse witch prosecutions of both "pagan" and "popish" error. Perkins and Bernard wanted to establish a straightforward procedure for trying witches that would rely on a few, unexceptionable criteria. They sought to discredit traditional folk practices such as "ducking": this involved submerging a suspect witch in water to see if she or he floated; many believed that water would refuse to accept a witch, so that buoyancy was proof of guilt. Critics such as Perkins and Bernard argued that there was neither biblical nor scientific foundation for trial by water.

The legal procedure favored by these commentators centered on the need to prove a direct link between the accused witch and the Devil. Unlike John Cotta, Perkins and Bernard argued that confessions should be admissible. However, if the witch did not confess, conviction was justifiable only if two or more reliable witnesses testified to having seen the witch either invoking the Devil or performing deeds which unquestionably relied upon a diabolical agency. There had to be at least two witnesses for each incriminating incident. Circumstantial evidence about illness or misfortune in the aftermath of an argument with the accused, the most common form of evidence against witches on both sides of the Atlantic, did not justify a conviction.

New England ministers were well aware of this procedural literature and played a crucial role in transmitting its recommendations across the Atlantic. Increase Mather, for example, referred to Perkins's strictures against ducking in his *Essay for the Recording of Illustrious Providences*. Mather assured his readers that ducking had "no foundation in nature, nor in Scripture." Magistrates dealing with witchcraft cases often consulted ministers who were well-read on the subject. But not all magistrates relied on the clergy to keep them abreast of current literature; some did their own research as well. William Jones, deputy governor of Connecticut, was particularly conscientious: he took detailed notes from an unnamed author's description of the correct procedure in witchcraft cases. According to these notes, which Jones seems to have kept for future reference, the author condemned traditional methods for proving guilt, such as ducking suspects in water, forcing them to pick up a hot iron, or putting their hands into scalding water, as "superstitious and unwarantable." Moreover, the testimony of a diviner, "who pretend[ed] to show the face of the witch . . . upheld in a glass," was "diabolicall and dangerous" since "the divill may represent a person inocent."

The text that Jones was using specified seven grounds for examining a witch: "Notoreous defamation by the Comon report of the people"; "death or at least mischiefe" following a curse delivered by the suspect; "personal mischiefe" after a quarrel with the suspect; incriminating testimony provided by another witch; kinship or close association with a "knowne or Convicted" witch; the Devil's mark; and finally, contradictions in the suspect's answers when first questioned. Each of these constituted "ground of suspicion," but none were "sufficient for Conviction or Condemnation." This distinction between grounds for "suspicion" and those for "Conviction or Condemnation" may have been an attempt to placate public opinion by according some legitimacy, albeit limited, to popular tradition. In practice, it probably had quite the opposite effect, since it raised and then dashed public spirits by admitting cases in which there was no hope of conviction.

Having enumerated these categories of "insufficient" evidence, Jones summarized the author's discussion of legitimate grounds for conviction. A court of law, the author wrote, should convict an accused witch only if the suspect confessed, or if two reputable witnesses testified that the accused had either "made a le[a]gue with the Divill" or "don[e] som Knowne practices of witchcraft." In either case, the witnesses must prove either that "the party hath invocated the divill for his help," or that "the party hath entertained a familiar spirit in any forme," or that "the party hath don[e] any accon [action] or work w[hi]ch inforc [enforce] the C[ovenan]t wth the divill." This "accon or work" could consist of "show[ing] the face of a man in a glass, or us[ing] inchantm[en]ts or such feates, divineing of things to Come, raising tempests, or Causing the forme of a dead man to appeare, or the like." Ironically, the only admissable evidence likely to be produced by witnesses related to forms of magic townsfolk actually valued: divination, charms, and so on. Witnesses offered such evidence only because it showed the suspect's possession of occult skills that could be used for malevolent as well as benevolent purposes, not because they believed these particular types of magic to be reprehensible. The author whose recommendations Jones was noting so carefully admitted that proving witchcraft was not easy. Yet, the author added reassuringly, the Devil's "Malice towards all men" was such that he often allowed witches to be exposed. Meanwhile, wrote Jones, "the Author warn[ed] Jurors etc not to Condemne suspected persons on bare presum[p]t[i]ons without good and sufficient proofes."

The rigorous standards which New England courts applied in witchcraft cases derived from theological commitment rather than from any lack of enthusiasm for the prosecution of witches. The authorities were well informed about new developments in witchcraft investigation across the Atlantic and encouraged courts to experiment with the latest methods for proving witchcraft. In 1648, when Margaret and Thomas Jones of Charlestown, Massachusetts, were accused of witchcraft, the General Court gave orders that "watching" be used in the investigation. This method, developed by Matthew Hopkins during the English witch hunt of 1645, involved the careful observation of suspects over an extended period of time in the hope that a diabolical familiar would appear. The assembly instructed that "a strict watch be set about [Margaret Jones] every night, and that her husband be confined to a privat[e] roome, and watched also." Fortunately for Margaret and Thomas Jones, no familiar appeared. . . .

*　　*　　*

Like their European counterparts, New England courts viewed witchcraft from a perspective radically different from that of witchcraft victims. Unlike their European counterparts, New England courts operated within a legal system that forbade the use of torture as a way to bridge the gap between different perceptions of the crime; as a result, they could only reject popular testimony. Witchcraft laws in England embodied popular belief in their treatment of witchcraft as an antisocial act that did not necessarily involve diabolical allegiance. But New England laws defined witchcraft as diabolical heresy: since most witnesses against accused witches provided no evidence of diabolical involvement, colonial courts found it extremely difficult to justify a conviction. Witchcraft trials often ended in confusion, dissension, and public frustration. The jury-men dealing with Elizabeth Seager's case ("deeply suspicious," "at a great loss," and "staggering" back and forth) provide a fitting image of the New England legal system as it struggled with the deadly but elusive crime of witchcraft.

New England ministers saw witchcraft in the same theological light as did colonial law, yet the ministers were ambivalent about witchcraft prosecutions. Ideally, they taught, people who believed that they were bewitched should focus on their own spiritual failings as the ultimate cause of all suffering: bewitchment was a punishment from God; only sincere repentance would secure its removal. Yet ministers also recognized that witches could not be allowed to roam free: their presence constituted not only a public menace, but also a serious embarrassment in light of New England's claim to spiritual purity. Therefore, the clergy conceded that prosecution should be available to those who became convinced that a particular individual was afflicting them. After all, scriptural injunction on this subject was clear: "Thou shalt not suffer a witch to live."

But sanctioned legal channels only rarely provided effective redress against witchcraft. The difficulty of securing a legal conviction for witchcraft became increasingly apparent as the years passed: of the sixteen convictions prior to 1692, eleven took place in the 1640s and 1630s; apart from the four convictions at Hartford, Connecticut, in 1662–3, there were no further convictions for witchcraft until Goodwife Glover's confession in 1688. It is not clear why the rate of conviction declined, but colonists responded by turning less frequently to the legal system for action against witch suspects. The number of witch prosecutions in New England fell dramatically during the 1670s and 1680s: there were nineteen such prosecutions during the 1660s, but only six during the 1670s and eight during the 1680s. A decline in the number of witch prosecutions did not mean a decline in popular fear of witchcraft. Jasper Danckaerts, a Dutch visitor to Boston in 1680, remarked that he had "never been in a place where more was said about witchcraft and witches." The people of New England feared witchcraft and needed some form of redress against witches. Interestingly enough, it was during the 1680s that New England ministers first voiced their anxiety about popular recourse to countermagic. This may not have been a coincidence. As it became clear that witchcraft could not be punished through legal channels, it is possible that New Englanders turned to countermagic instead.

The ministers' campaign against countermagic during the last two decades of the century perhaps reflected a changing reality: the clergy may have been responding to a rise in the use of countermagic as the public became disillusioned with legal prosecution (just as clerical attacks on astrology in the late 1680s and 1690s were prompted in part by the appearance of an openly astrological almanac literature). Thus, the ministers' growing hostility toward various kinds of supernatural competition arose not only from their own increasing concern about the spiritual prospects of New England, but also, in all likelihood, from an actual rise in occult practice. Ironically, the rigorous implementation of God's law may have driven people to an alternative strategy that the clergy condemned as diabolical. In their sermons, the ministers urged the afflicted of New England to abandon countermagic in favor of prayer, but such entreaties were unrealistic. People turned to the law or informal channels such as countermagic because they were not willing to leave a malefactor's punishment to God. If another human being was responsible for their condition, they wanted to know who it was, and they wanted revenge.

Tituba's Confession

The Multicultural Dimensions of the 1692 Salem Witch-Hunt

Elaine G. Breslaw

In the 1997 article excerpted here, Elaine G. Breslaw extends the findings originally outlined in her book Tituba, Reluctant Witch of Salem: Devilish Indians and Puritan Fantasies *(1996). A related work supporting her thesis about Tituba's South American roots is "Prices — His Deposition: Kidnapping Amerindians in Guyana, 1674,"* Journal of the Barbados Museum and Historical Society *39 (1991): 47–51.*

•

Tituba was a pivotal character whose ethnic background and behavior merit deeper examination than they have received. Her confession, blending elements from English, African, and American Indian notions of the occult, was of key significance in the shaping of the bizarre events at Salem. It subsequently became a model for others desperate to save their lives. Although many details in their stories were embellished and transformed by Puritan fantasies, fears, and cultural biases, the inspiration for and framework of their accounts of witchcraft stemmed from Tituba's story. By bridging the gap between her syncretic notions and the Puritan concept of evil, these reformulations, in turn, heightened the sense of impending doom surrounding the witch-hunt and propelled it into new channels.

In her confession Tituba, "an Indian Woman Servant to Mr. Samuel Parris of Salem village," convinced the Salem authorities that the devil had invaded their society. Her importance for the ensuing events lies not in the occult activities that she supposedly inspired before 1692 but in the content and impact of her confession in March of that year. She not only confirmed their fears of a conspiracy of Satan's followers but was the first to implicate others outside the Salem community and to suggest that men and members of the elite were part of the conspiracy. Of even greater significance, Tituba supplied the evidence of a satanic presence legally neces-

From Elaine G. Breslaw, "Tituba's Confession: The Multicultural Dimensions of the 1692 Salem Witch-Hunt," *Ethnohistory* 44, no. 3 (1997): 535–49. © 1997 by Elaine G. Breslaw. Reprinted by permission of the author.

sary to launch a witch-hunt. Had she remained silent, the trials might not have occurred or, at the least, would have followed a different course.

Tituba's credibility to her Salem audience was enhanced by her identification as an American Indian whose culture had long been associated with demonic power. Her story thus acquired verisimilitude not just from fantastic details that could be integrated into the Puritan belief system but from their assumed evil source. Although the content of her testimony and its relationship to Puritan perceptions of American Indians are seldom mentioned in the literature of Salem, the substance of Tituba's story, combined with the local fear of Indians, alerted the Puritan worthies to the dangers lurking in their community.

Most writers have assumed that Tituba was either African or of mixed American Indian and African descent, but nothing in the records indicates that she was anything but Indian. In 1974 Chadwick Hansen pointed out that all extant contemporary references to Tituba call her an Indian. Tituba the half Indian, half African was the invention of Henry Wadsworth Longfellow in his 1868 verse drama *Giles Corey of the Salem Farms*, and unfortunately that fiction entered the historical literature. In the century following she was gradually transformed into an African. Deodat Lawson, John Hale, and Robert Calef, all contemporaries of the events, repeat the terminology of the official documents and refer to Tituba and her husband, John, only as Indians.

If Tituba and John had been of mixed Indian-African parentage, they would have been identified as "Negro" and not Indian in the Salem records. Whites assumed that anyone with any African features was a Negro. During the Salem investigation two African Americans were clearly identified as such: Mary Black, a slave in Benjamin Putnam's household, and Candy, Margaret Hawkes's servant from Barbados. Tituba, unlike Mary or Candy, was called an Indian for reasons that apparently were visible and obvious to their contemporaries.

Little is known about Tituba's background beyond the fact that she and another slave, John Indian, who became her husband, were brought from Barbados by Samuel Parris, a merchant who later became a clergyman. Whether Tituba and John were born in Barbados is not known, nor are their ages evident in the Salem records. Barbadian sources indicate that the most probable place of origin for Indian slaves in Barbados was the northeastern coast of South America, where settlements of Dutch-allied Arawaks were likely prey for England's slave traders. A reference to the name Tattuba on a 1676 deed supports the Barbadian connection. This Tattuba, a child at the time, is most likely the Tituba whom Parris brought to Massachusetts. Thus Tituba was between thirteen and eighteen years old when she arrived in Boston in 1680 and was no more than thirty during the witch trials.

On Barbados, Tituba had been exposed to the African influences omnipresent there. She was a product of an emergent Creole culture, marked by planter indifference to the religious and cultural lives of the slaves. As a result, non-Christian and occult practices flourished on the island. The slaves' "idolatrous ceremonies and customs in honor of their God who is mainly the devil" appalled Felix Sporri, a Calvinist visitor of the 1660s. Thomas Walduck, another observer, said that the slaves' activities were led by the "obia" (traditionally an African healer), who was known to torment others and cause "lameness, madness, loss of speech, loss of the use of all their limbs." The planters, he thought, occasionally participated in these ceremonies.

Slaves, whether of American Indian or African ancestry, easily integrated and reformulated the ideas and techniques of English witchcraft and other religious practices without violating their essential worldview. Conversely, as Walduck demonstrates, they introduced their white masters to new magical practices without altering the substance of English folklore or theology. In the seventeenth century supernatural omens and techniques associated with witchcraft were accepted and adapted by Europeans, Africans, and Indians regardless of their origin. The functions of the practices varied, but the borrowed forms provided a nonverbal language understood by both slaves and masters.

Although familiar with various African and European magicoreligious practices, Tituba had not necessarily lost all sense of her Indian culture. Seventeenth-century planters depended on American Indian methods of food preparation and possibly of healing. Arawaks and other South American Indians feared malevolent spirits that lived in the bush, could change shape at will, and had the power to kill or to cause excruciating pain, and whites in Barbados noted the rituals, trances, herbs, and poisons thought to provide protection against these spirits. Even if the few Indians on the island could not remember a time spent among their own people, Indian "Magick and ways of Divination" persisted. Tituba's familiarity with practices derived from three cultures can be deduced from the events of 1692.

In late December 1691 or early January 1692 Parris's daughter Betty and Abigail Williams, a niece living in his house, began to exhibit strange physical symptoms. The girls, aged nine and eleven, complained of painful pinching, crept under chairs, tried to crawl into holes, fell into fits, and babbled. Dr. William Griggs diagnosed the "evil hand," the work of the devil, and because the responsibility for spiritual cures lay with the church, the Reverend Parris initiated a series of prayers and a fast day and called on other ministers to assist him.

Unbeknownst to Parris, Mary Sibley, a neighbor, appealed to the two Indians in his household to use countermagic to help the girls. On 25 February 1692, after several weeks of watching them suffer, Tituba and John, under Sibley's supervision, prepared a "witchcake," a concoction of rye meal and the girls' urine baked in ashes, and fed it to a dog. Supposedly, the dog was a "familiar," the animal companion of a witch. According to English folklore, the dog, bewitched by the cake, would reveal the name of the witch who was afflicting the girls.

The ritual use of bodily substances such as hair, nail parings, and urine was common in folk and tribal cultures, including that of the English "cunning people." The cooking of human excretions with other substances, such as ashes or even Indian corn or European wheat, was typical of South American Indian sympathetic magic. Bodily fluids were occasionally boiled to divine the identity of an evildoer, as in English folklore, but they were mixed and cooked with other substances to provide protection against witchcraft. Tituba may have thought that the witchcake would cure Betty and Abigail or at least protect them against further injury. She willingly complied with Sibley's suggestion that she prepare it.

It was logical for Sibley to approach Tituba and John instead of making the witchcake herself. Because Tituba lived in the Parris household, she could readily collect samples of Betty's and Abigail's urine. In addition, Sibley may have perceived the two Indians as more familiar with occult powers than she was. It was a common perception. Cotton Mather was hardly alone in describing Indians as Satan's "most devoted . . . children," who evoked evil spirits in their wigwams. Such fears had been revived in New England when violent conflict with Indians resumed in 1690, at the outset of King William's War (1689–98). Young Mercy Short of Salem, recently released from captivity, contributed to a growing panic with stories of Indian cannibalism and devil worship. Mary Toothaker testified in July 1692 that the devil had appeared to her "in the shape of a Tawny man," a common descriptor for American Indians.

It is unlikely that Tituba or John were known for their skill in magic before 1692. There is no documentary or trial evidence that Tituba participated in occult rituals before that year. On the contrary, there is every indication that she lived an unremarkable life until the last week of February 1692. Had she been a "cunning person," the close-knit Puritans would have known—and told—about it. Yet no one accused her of wronging her neighbors or the Parrises before Abigail Williams and Parris himself denounced her at the end of February, after the preparation of the witchcake.

Various writers since the nineteenth century would have us believe that Tituba introduced the girls to some forbidden magical practices. The allegation is groundless. Betty and Abigail had been dabbling in the occult and admitted having tried to tell their fortunes by using an egg and a glass (much like reading tea leaves). But they implicated no adult, nor did Parris accuse Tituba of introducing his daughter to the occult. He concurred with others that "when this witchcraft came upon the stage there was no suspicion of Tituba." . . .

Parris apparently believed in the efficacy of the witchcake, because only when he had found out about it, probably a day or two afterward, did he abandon his cautious campaign to exorcise the afflicted girls through prayer and demand that they reveal their tormentors. Abigail, the younger Ann Putnam, and Elizabeth Hubbard pointed to Sarah Good and Sarah Osborne, two quarrelsome and disagreeable women who fit the popular image of a witch, and Tituba.

Weeks later, on 27 March, Parris would publicly chastise Mary Sibley for her part in raising the devil in Massachusetts. In light of the girls' accusations, he ignored her complicity for the moment. Instead of persecuting her, a church member and white woman, Parris turned to Tituba, a credible devil worshiper only by virtue of her ethnicity, for evidence of a diabolical plot. When questioned privately by Parris and some visiting ministers, Tituba denied being a witch. Subsequently she was either beaten by Parris or severely pressured to confess, and to avoid further punishment, she finally did. On 29 February she was arrested on suspicion of having practiced witchcraft. The full import of her confession would not be revealed until after she was questioned by the magistrates.

Examined in the makeshift court in the meetinghouse from 1 to 5 March, Tituba at first disavowed "familiarity" with any "evil spirit" and denied that she had hurt the children, even though the devil had come to her and commanded her service. Instead, she implicated the two Salem women who had been arrested with her, as well as two Boston women whose names were unknown to her and one "tall man of Boston." "They hurt the children and then lay all upon me," she protested. In the next breath she admitted hurting the children herself but charged that the four women and the man had forced her to do so by threatening her life and "worse" if she refused. She humbly apologized for her behavior: "I was Sorry & . . . would doe Soe noe more, but . . . would feare God."

Under close questioning by Judge John Hathorne, Tituba told of reluctantly pinching Elizabeth Hubbard, Betty Parris, and Abigail Williams and of threatening the younger Ann Putnam with a knife; the women "would have had me kill Thomas Putnam's Child last night." She reported meeting a hog (sometimes a black dog), a red rat, and a black one (one transcript has instead a red and a black cat), who told her to "serve" them. She described the Salem goodwives' familiars. Good had a yellow bird, a wolf, and a cat. Osborne "had a thing with a head like a woman with 2 leggs and wings," which Abigail Williams had seen turn "into the shape of goodie osburn" herself; she also had "a thing all over hairy, all the face hayry & a long nose & I don't know how to tell how the face looks w'th two Leggs, itt goeth upright & is about two or three foot high & goeth upright like a man and last night itt stood before the fire in Mr. parris's hall." The pair of witch women, Tituba said, were "very strong & pull me & make me goe w'th them"; sometimes all three rode on a stick or pole, with Tituba in front. . . .

On the second day Tituba confessed to signing her mark in blood in a little book offered her by the "tall man of Boston." In the book she saw nine marks already made in red or yellow. One she knew belonged to Good, who she claimed had told her so in person on "the same day I came hither to prison." Another she took to be Osborne's, though Osborne would not admit it. The man had not told Tituba who had made the other seven. She herself had not signed the book immediately, because they were interrupted when "mistris [Elizabeth Parris] Called me into the other roome." Promising to return, the man had left her with a "pin tyed in a stick to doe it with." "And what," the examiner asked, "did he say to you when you made your mark?" Echoing a dominant theme of her confession, Tituba answered, "He sayd, Serve mee & always Serve mee."

Tituba's testimony was not merely the frightened response of a slave woman but, arguably, a sophisticated manipulation of her interrogators' deepest fears. She was sufficiently familiar with Puritan customs to know which questions required positive responses and what form they should take. When asked if she ever saw the devil, for instance, Tituba replied that he "came to me and bid me serve him." When more suspects were required, she indicated the four women and the man and then, probably sensing that a wider conspiracy would divert attention from herself, enlarged the group of evil ones to include seven more people.

Who were they? Tituba did not identify them definitely. The mystery of the seven, an effective diversion, also had a personal meaning for her. Among South American Indians, the Arawaks in particular, evil conflicted with social norms that deplored violence within the tribe; one did not curse members of one's own community. Thus evil beings were always identified with strangers or distant villagers. It was no accident that Tituba placed the Massachusetts evil beings in a faraway town and claimed not to know them. . . .

During the second day of her hearing Tituba, responding to her inquisitors' leading questions, told them about the devil's book that the man had wanted her to sign. After suggestive questions about a covenant, her story became more elaborate: The unidentified white man in black had said that he was God and that he wanted her to serve him for six years and to hurt the children. In return, she would be protected from harm and would receive "many fine things." With growing awareness of her power to create fear, and probably with malice, Tituba confessed to seeing the other names in the book. She had now supplied legal evidence of a satanic presence. Aroused to the magnitude of the conspiracy, the magistrates finally stopped tormenting her and commenced to search out the other malefactors. The witch-hunt had begun. . . .

Some of Tituba's testimony was readily derived from English folklore—night riding, marks in blood, specters—but much of it bespoke Indian or African practices or alluded to qualities common to all three cultures. The book was an artifact of literate societies and the devil a feature of Christian theology. They would not be found in the precolonial American Indian or African cultures. The association of witchcraft with satanism, with its promise of power over others, was surprisingly rare in the English folk tradition and in New England.

In responding to questions regarding Satan, Tituba included notions characteristic of American Indian beliefs about the source of evil. In those traditions magical power derived from an individual's inherent ability to manipulate the mystical elements of the universe; it did not imply an impersonal, supernatural energy. Among the Arawaks, for instance, evil was believed to reside in individuals and to require no intermediate spiritual force. Nevertheless, it could exist in different degrees of strength. The most potent evil spirit, the kenaima, was a real person of flesh and blood, unlike the Christian devil. Thus Tituba gave the evil presence substance as a persona, identifiable in her testimony as a white man in distant Boston.

Those confessing to the practice of witchcraft gradually modified Tituba's description of this devil to forms more consistent with their own conceptions. The white man then became a tawny or black specter. But at first, under Tituba's sway, the accusing girls talked about a white man presiding over a witches' sabbat, with women serving as his deacons. As the confessions became embellished with more elements from European traditions, the black devil shared the blame with the white one and the witch took on a new form.

Tituba's suggestion about an evil man left men more vulnerable to accusation than in earlier years. Others sought to identify the male leader of the conspiracy from among their own. The first man to be investigated, toward the end of March, was tavern keeper John Proctor. He was followed by at least thirty-nine men during the witch-hunt. Giles Corey was accused by the younger Ann Putnam, Mercy Lewis, Abigail Williams, Mary Walcott, and Elizabeth Hubbard and arrested on 18 April. Two days later William Hobbs of Topsfield was accused and questioned.

Tituba's story made it possible for the magistrates to believe that a man like George Burroughs, a minister, could be responsible for the satanic presence in their community when he was accused by Hobbs's daughter Abigail and the younger Ann Putnam. A warrant for his arrest was issued on the last day of April. Burroughs was brought to Salem on 4 May, and by that time several more men were under arrest. Philip English, a prosperous Salem merchant, managed to escape the authorities, only to be captured in Boston. On 10 May the two George Jacobses, father and son, and John Willard, all of Salem, were arrested. A few days later Roger Toothaker of Billerica was taken into custody.

A much higher proportion of men were accused of practicing witchcraft during the Salem crisis than during previous witch scares. In his study of pre-1692 incidents John Demos finds four women accused to every man. On the other hand, of the identifiable accused in 1692, the ratio was fewer than three to one (104 women and 40 men). Moreover, the men accused at Salem faced greater danger to their lives. Only one of twenty-two accused men had been executed in all of New England before 1692. In 1692 five of the forty accused men were hanged. The statistics regarding women are comparable. Of the 104 women arrested in 1692, 14 were executed.

As the crisis abated after October, a more conventional attitude prevailed. During 1693 a much smaller proportion of accused men were even tried by the courts. . . . But for a while Tituba's words shook their basic understanding of the servants of Satan. Her influential confession not only widened the witch-hunt to include a greater proportion of men but extended it beyond Salem. Abigail Hobbs was brought from Topsfield on 18 April on suspicion of having practiced witchcraft; on the strength of the "afflicted" girls' complaints her mother, Deliverance, two other women, and another man from Topsfield were also arrested. The list of accused outsiders included Mary Easty (sister of Rebecca Nurse, one of the more respectable, elderly church members in the town), Sarah Wild, and Nehemiah Abbott Jr. By the end of May complaints had been heard about men and women in several Massachusetts communities—Andover, Rumney Marsh, Malden, Marblehead, Lynn, and Beverly— and had begun to spread to Boston. Thus Tituba's suggestion about an evil force from a distant community in the form of a member of the upper class had sent the Salem magistrates far afield to find the coconspirators. Neither social status nor geographic location provided immunity from persecution, any more than gender did. A new conception of the witch, based partly on Indian belief, emerged following Tituba's confession.

The Indian woman had sketched the portrait of a witch who could fly through the air, take animal or human form, and submit to oaths and ordeals involving other spirits. These characteristics were all common to witches from Africa to Asia and throughout America. Thus Tituba described the metamorphosis of Sarah Good's spirit into a hog and a dog. She had also seen animals change into the tall man and then back into animals, sometimes a hog and sometimes "a great black dogge," in a manner typical of the European witch and of the South American kenaima, who could put his spirit into the body of any animal he wished, even a mythical one.

The supposed ability of witches to fly on a stick or pole was almost universal. Both European and African traditions told of witches riding on sticks at night to attend secret meetings and to take part in misanthropic rituals. Although the witches' meeting was another universal phenomenon, the details varied from culture to culture. Tituba's testimony contained some significant deviations from Puritan concepts.

Tituba drew on the common traditions when she told the magistrates of riding on a "poal" to Boston, with Osborne and Good behind her, to meet the other witches she could not name. But she denied knowing the way to their destination; she had seen neither "trees nor path, but was presently there." In her account, it was as though her spirit had left her body and been transported instantaneously, unlike the Anglo-African witch sailing over the clouds on a stick. She may well have been recalling some vestige of the folklore of her background.

Many Indians of the Americas believed in a dream soul that could leave the body during sleep and visit faraway places. Indeed, every animate object was thought to have a spiritual quality that could leave it during sleep (as well as death) but could return to it only during sleep. Events that occurred during that dream state were considered tangible experiences of the spirit. Thus Tituba's story of a witches' meeting may well have reenacted a dream state during which her spirit went to a distant city. Oddly, during her examination on 2 March she stated that she "was never att Boston," contradicting otherwise consistent testimony. Did she mean that her physical presence had not been there, only her dream soul? Or did the danger of admitting to such a meeting induce her to detach herself from the conspirators? For only the evil ones conspired in Boston. Hers was a reluctant collaboration.

Tituba alluded to other apparent dream states. She stated that the tall man had first visited her some two months before, just as she was about to fall asleep. She may actually have had such a nightmare when Betty Parris became ill in December. In her account of this dream, evil took the shape of a man similar to the minister Samuel Parris. Thus Tituba, primed to believe that evil was at work in Salem, may have conceived that he had arrived from Boston to threaten her periodically in the lean-to of Parris's house.

More important, Tituba placed the evil one in Boston—outside the Salem community. By doing so, she evoked the Guianese concept of the malevolent persona who inhabits a different village from its victim. On the other hand, the Puritans, obsessed with the intrusion of evil into their own community, transformed Tituba's suggestion about a distant meeting into one held within their village. . . .

A significant Caribbean feature of Tituba's testimony was the hairy imp: "A thing all over hairy, all the face hayry & a long nose . . . w'th two Leggs, itt goeth upright & is about two or three foot high." This creature was most likely based on the Guianese kenaimas, often described as little people who lived deep in the forest and came out at night to attack other people. Similarly, the evil spirit of the Ashanti of West Africa was supposedly covered with long hair, with bloodshot eyes, and was known to sit on the branches of a tree, dangling his legs. The Jamaican Creole spirit came to be known as a duppy, "a malicious vindictive, imp-like spirit that haunts forests and burying grounds, a figure very likely derived from a combination of African and Amerindian beliefs." The mention of these foreign creatures heightened the villagers' fear and motivated subsequent accusers to describe strange imps that attended their mocking of the sacraments.

The Indian and English concepts of magic and evil resembled each other closely enough that the details of Tituba's story were reinterpreted and incorporated into the English framework of belief. That Tituba's commitment to the tall man was written in her blood evoked the cannibalism and bloodsucking associated with European witchcraft lore. In her mind that blood oath may have been a remnant of the memory of West Indian practices, of the sealing of compacts with blood among Africans or of the holding of the color red as a talisman against sickness and disease among Indians.

Tituba also added details not implied in the questions posed to her. She spoke of a yellow bird and later of a green and white bird, of the black dog, of the two rats (or cats, as a second version of her testimony has it), and of the hog. The dog appeared in many other testimonies and hallucinations, as did the yellow bird, which probably had special significance for Tituba. The Arawaks of Guiana took birds to be magical messengers. The goatsucker or nightjar, the supernatural ancestor of the Tetebetana clan that uttered a weird piercing call at night, was held in awe by many Guiana Indians. Were the birds of Tituba's fantasy memories of her earlier existence? Did they represent an appeal to her guardian spirit for assistance? Certainly, others found these allusions useful. There was abundant material in Tituba's story for accused witches to draw on, and much of it appeared, with variations, in subsequent confessions.

Tituba's behavior at the end of her first day of testimony, when she claimed to be blind and went into a trance, would have been unusual for an English witch. Since the Reformation, in English and continental European belief, victims of witchcraft exhibited strange symptoms, but witches themselves did not go into trances, any more than priests did in the exercise of their offices. In the African and Indian rituals of 1670s Barbados, however, the shaman or obeah did undergo possession of the spirit, with a resulting trance, while uncovering witchcraft. For the peoples of the Caribbean, therefore, the trance was a familiar part of magicoreligious ceremonies, but the Puritans associated it with conjuring and devil worship. Tituba's sudden blindness was taken as a sign that she herself was bewitched by the others, even though she did not immediately claim to be victim.

To protect herself Tituba now reverted to remembered concepts and practices and cunningly confessed to promoting an evil conspiracy that had merely been suspected. Cultural differences in the use of language made her confession that much easier. Whereas in Puritan society deception for personal gain or for self-preservation was equated with satanic practices, in Indian cultures a reluctance to contradict others and the use of metaphorical language were cultivated as diplomatic arts. Thus Tituba's confession was a ploy to confirm Puritan anxieties, to shift blame to outsiders, and to distract her tormentors with the fear of evil. By locating the evil forces not only in Boston strangers but also in the two Salem women arrested with her, Tituba supported the allegations of the Parris and Putnam families. By appearing to collaborate with her own accusers, she demonstrated the correct deference to her betters.

By 5 March, the last day of Tituba's testimony, the magistrates had most of the pieces to the satanic plot: the devil's book, a cabal of nightriding witches, malefice. The few elements they lacked were not yet forthcoming, however, for Tituba offered no information about sexual orgies and suggested no relation between her witches' coven and Christian ceremony. Either such ideas were too distant from Tituba's Indian worldview or, if she had learned them during her Puritan indoctrination, she forgot them under the stress of questioning. . . .

What began early in March 1692 as the story of a nocturnal meeting of nine witches, some of whom had flown to Boston on a pole, had by the summer of that year given rise to the stereotype of a devil-worshiping witch who mocked the most sacred features of Christianity. Stories spread about the inversion of church services, complete with baptisms, into a satanic cult and the transubstantiation of bread and wine into flesh and blood under a new malevolent leader, a white man. Cotton Mather noted this transformation: "The Witches do say, that they form themselves much after the manner of Congregational Churches; and that they have a Baptism and a Supper, and Officers among them, abominably Resembling those of our Lord."

In outline that witches' sabbat followed Tituba's fantasy, but its details represented a Puritan reformulation. The story told by the girls was elaborated by the accused, who, for a variety of reasons, confessed to practicing witchcraft and participating in a diabolical alliance. The multiethnic dimensions of Tituba's confession had fueled a satanic plot that grew increasingly sinister in the retelling.

The Massachusetts magistrates, captives of their cultural milieu, did not consciously note the alien quality of Tituba's story. Her extraordinary fantasy about a satanic presence, based partly on Indian concepts of evil, partly on Creolized Caribbean beliefs, and partly on English witchcraft, was sufficiently familiar to be accepted by them. Creatively integrated into their framework of belief, it allowed the Puritans (and most historians since) to see Tituba as a simple slave trapped by forces beyond her control, a passive victim. Her confession, evidence to the Puritans of a diabolical conspiracy, thus saved her life even as it simultaneously elevated the level of fear.

[57]

Through the Clouds

LARRY GRAGG

In this excerpt from his 1992 book The Salem Witch Crisis, *the historian Larry Gragg describes the denunciations of Cotton Mather and Samuel Parris in the aftermath of the Salem trials. Gragg has also published* A Quest for Security: The Life of Samuel Parris, 1653–1720 *(1990) and several works on the seventeenth-century merchant communities in Massachusetts and Barbados.*

•

The Bay colony struggled for years with the issue of justice and compensation for those who suffered in the witchcraft crisis. Assigning blame for it, however, began almost immediately. The letters from Governor Phips and most public confessions were often tortuous efforts at shifting the responsibility for the excesses of 1692. That was not satisfactory for those who believed that someone should be held accountable. Strangely, the justices on the Court of Oyer and Terminer did not suffer politically. In 1693, all of them were selected to the Governor's Council. Indeed, the judge who had the greatest difficulty following the trials was the one who quit the tribunal in protest, Nathaniel Saltonstall. Rumors reached the Haverhill judge that he would lose his place on the Council and that the governor intended to replace him as head of the North Essex militia. Worse, word spread that some were afflicted by his specter. The troubled Saltonstall began to drink heavily, and the effects of it were obvious in the Council chamber. Samuel Sewall saw that he "had drunk to excess" and that his "head and hand were rendered less useful than at other times."

The provincial clergy, because it had consistently though not forcefully opposed specter evidence, escaped essentially unscathed. The notable exceptions were Cotton Mather and Samuel Parris. Mather engaged in an eight-year struggle with Boston merchant Robert Calef to defend his actions in 1692. Calef's criticism began with the publication of Mather's *Wonders of the Invisible World*. While Mather had repeatedly advised the judges to use caution in handling specter evidence, he firmly believed that clergymen and jurists in Massachusetts had uncovered a diabolic plot

From Larry Gragg, *The Salem Witch Crisis* (New York: Praeger, 1992), 191–202. © 1992 by Larry Gragg. Reprinted by permission of Greenwood Publishing Group, Westport, Connecticut.

against reformed Christianity. In his "zeal to assist" the judges destroy "as wonderful a piece of devilism as has been seen in the world," Mather wrote to William Stoughton, chief judge on the Court of Oyer and Terminer, in early September.

In this offer to help, Mather explained that he believed that the provincial clergy had an obligation "to do some singular thing in a way of testimony against those evils." His proposed contribution would be an essay "on the prodigious occasion that is now before us." Always properly deferential, Mather asked Stoughton if he could include an "account of the trials." He promised to submit the manuscript to the judge for approval and asked for an endorsement of the proposed work. Mather then approached Governor Phips for his blessing, and Phips apparently suggested that the young clergyman contact Stephen Sewall, who served as the Court of Oyer and Terminer's clerk, for narratives of sample trials. Sewall not only obliged but also met with Mather, Stoughton, John Hathorne, Salem minister John Higginson, and Samuel Sewall at the latter's house on September 22 to discuss "publishing some trials of the witches."

Eager to get the work into print, Cotton Mather rapidly wrote a book that left him open to innumerable criticisms. Printed by mid-October, *Wonders of the Invisible World* is an eclectic collection of trial narratives, sermons, extracts of other works on witchcraft, and a liberal sprinkling of Mather's efforts to defend the judges' actions. As his leading biographer, Kenneth Silverman, has observed, Mather created "an effect of endless jerky beginnings, obscured by tedious verbosity and an insuperable difficulty in getting to the point." More important, he made his opposition to specter evidence a minor theme in the book and emerged as an advocate of the trials. His timing could not have been worse. As he completed his book, his father was circulating his critique of the trials, *Cases of Conscience*. While over a dozen leading clergymen endorsed the elder Mather's work, Cotton could not. He worried because people were saying that "I run against my own father and all the ministers in the country." Yet, as he explained to his uncle, John Cotton, in an October 20 letter, Mather feared that opponents of the trials would use *Cases of Conscience* to condemn the judges:

> I did, in *my* conscience, think that as the humors of this people now run, such a discourse going alone would not only enable our witch-advocates very learnedly to cavil and nibble at the late proceedings against the witches, considered in parcels, while things as they lay in bulk, with their whole dependencies, were not exposed; but also everlastingly stifle any further proceedings of justice, and more than so, produce a public and open contest with the judges, who would (though beyond the intention of the worthy author and subscribers) find themselves brought unto the bar before the rashest *Mobile*.

Sensitive to the rumors that he had repudiated his son's rash defense of the judges, the elder Mather included a disclaimer in his postscript: "I perused and approved of that book before it was printed. And nothing but my relation to him hindered me from recommending it to the world."

The elder Mather's statement had no impact on Robert Calef. He conducted a remarkably successful campaign to destroy Cotton Mather's credibility. Until recently, Mather has been vilified as a leading promoter of the witchcraft crisis. As Samuel Eliot Morison so colorfully put it, Robert Calef "tied a tin can to him after the frenzy was over; and it has rattled and banged through the pages of superficial and popular historians." Calling his work *More Wonders of the Invisible World*, Calef not only attacked Mather's 1692 publication but also the minister's reports on two other cases of afflicted individuals. The circulation of his manuscript, and its eventual publication in 1700, contributed to a backlash against the Boston clergyman.

During the immediate aftermath of the Salem trials, the occult experiences of Mercy Short and Margaret Rule had attracted Mather's interest. Short began suffering afflictions following her visit in the spring of 1692 to the Boston jails holding accused witches. While there, Short had taunted Sarah Good. In response, Good "bestowed some ill words upon her." Soon afterward, the young servant woman began to suffer "fits as those which held the bewitched people then tormented by invisible furies in the county of Essex." Unable to attend the proceedings in Salem because of illness, Mather seized this opportunity to counter the Devil's effort to expand his influence. As he prayed with Short, she seemed to recover. In November, however, she fell into fits again, which continued until March. Margaret Rule began to suffer her afflictions in September 1693, and her case drew Mather and others to her bedside on numerous days and nights. The two young women had similar extraordinary bouts with the occult world. They had confrontations with specters, suffered hallucinations, conversed with demonic voices, lost their appetites, endured horrid burning sensations, and developed skin lesions. A particularly frightening episode in Margaret Rule's case, according to Mather and several others who witnessed the scene, was the night her tormentor levitated her to the ceiling. Equally disturbing to Mather was Rule's claim that *his* specter had harmed her.

Mather wrote an account of each case—"A Brand Plucked Out of the Burning" and "Another Brand Plucked Out of the Burning"—but did not seek a printer for either. Since the public mood had shifted so decisively against the trials, he correctly concluded that few would be receptive to a new account. Mather also worried that in her afflictions, Short had supplied new evidence against some of the accused in Salem, and she offered support for the validity of the now maligned specter evidence. Finally, Mather certainly had no desire to give ammunition to his new antagonist, Robert Calef.

The Boston merchant had been outraged by the witchcraft episode and denounced the "zeal governed by blindness and passion" that he believed had characterized the actions of the clergy in 1692. Calef ridiculed the contradictory role of Cotton Mather. Because the minister had defended the judges and preached about a massive Devil's plot, while at the same time advising caution in the use of specter evidence, Calef saw him as one who had carried "both fire to increase, and water, to quench, the conflagration." Carefully monitoring Mather's actions in 1693 and fascinated by the Margaret Rule case, Calef attended one of the young woman's bouts with her occult oppressors, making sure that Mather would also be there. Joining over thirty other spectators in Rule's home, Calef said that Cotton, joined by his father, Increase, asked leading questions of Rule, drawing from her the answers that he wanted. He explained that the two Mathers also attempted to console Rule, whenever she suffered from fits, by the laying on of hands. Calef charged that the younger Mather went beyond comforting the young woman; he wantonly massaged her. "He laid his hand upon her face and nose," Calef wrote, "but, as he said, without perceiving breath; then he brushed her on the face with his glove, and rubbed her stomach (her breast not covered with the bed-cloths) and bid others do so too, and said it eased her, then she revived." When Rule once again fell into a fit, Mather "again rubbed her breast." When a woman in the room attempted to assist, according to Calef, Rule pushed her away, preferring the touch of the clergyman.

When Calef circulated his version of the evening's events, Mather reacted with a stinging letter of denunciation. He told Calef that in reading his account of the episode, "I do scarcely find any one thing . . . either fairly or truly represented." Mather was particularly outraged that Calef had written that he rubbed Rule's stomach, "her breast not being covered." This lie, he said, had damaged his reputation. Now the people of Boston "believe a smutty thing of me." Getting no retraction from Calef, Mather denounced him from the pulpit and filed suit against him for "scandalous libel." Even though Mather dropped the suit, he engaged in an extended exchange of angry letters with Calef, in which they debated a range of occult issues in addition to Mather's actions in the Margaret Rule case. In 1698, Mather learned that Calef's book of "invented and notorious lies" would be published in England. When a copy of *More Wonders of the Invisible World* (which included "Another Brand Plucked from the Burning") reached Massachusetts, Increase Mather displayed his family's contempt by ordering a copy of it burned in the yard at Harvard College.

The controversy with Calef took its toll on the sensitive clergyman. In the evening after Samuel Sewall's remarkable fast day confession of January 1697, he pondered "the Divine displeasure" with his family "for my not appearing with vigor enough to stop the proceedings of the judges, when the inextricable storm from the invisible world assaulted the country."

Samuel Parris also could not escape denunciation for his role in the witchcraft affair. Renewed opposition to his ministry surfaced by mid-August of 1692. He called a special church meeting because "our brother Peter Cloyce, and Samuel Nurse and his wife, and John Tarbell and his wife have absented from communion with us at the Lord's Table, yea have very rarely (except our brother Samuel Nurse) been with us in common public worship." Their absence represented a protest against Parris's March 27 sermon that implicated Rebecca Nurse, Samuel and Mary Tarbell's mother, in the witch plot. Peter Cloyce's wife, Sarah, had stormed from the meetinghouse and subsequently faced witchcraft charges. Rebecca Nurse had been executed on July 19, and Sarah Cloyce awaited trial in an Ipswich jail. Parris could neither persuade the wayward to return nor reduce the ever widening breach in the village. Those who wanted him out before the witchcraft crisis joined with these dissenters over the next five years in pursuing his removal as Salem Village's pastor.

Occasionally, the two sides clashed over Parris's control of the parsonage or his back pay, but most often they returned to his actions in 1692. In the struggle, the minister's supporters and opponents fought each other with all the weapons available to them: election to the village tax committee, lawsuits, appeals to provincial authorities, and requests that outside clergymen intervene. Initially, Parris attempted to use persuasion. He met with the dissenters in his study almost a dozen times by July 1693 but made no progress. He sought reconciliation through the pulpit. In an October 1692 sermon, when explaining a verse from the Song of Solomon on allegorical kisses, Parris emphasized, "Kisses are exceeding sweet among friends that have been long absent. Why, so Christ's manifestation of his love after a long-seeming absence is exceeding sweet." In his 1694 "Meditations for Peace," Parris even admitted making errors two years earlier and expressed his sorrow for the families that had suffered. One of his antagonists, John Tarbell, told Parris frankly that his remorse was far too late. "If half so much had been said formerly," he explained, "it had never come to this."

Unable to produce a consensus by persuasion, Parris worked closely with his supporters as they maneuvered to gain control of the village's only governmental body, the rate committee. That accomplished by March 1694, pro-Parris activists also successfully pursued former committee members for failing to levy a tax for their pastor's salary and won court orders for the village constables "to make distress on such persons as neglect or refuse to pay their respective rates." As they lost influence in the village and cases in court, Parris's opponents sought the aid of outside clergymen. Early in their confrontation, the dissenters had asked Parris to agree to an arbitration of their differences by a council of clergymen. Their repeated demands and consultations with neighboring ministers who contacted Parris on their behalf finally wore the Salem Village minister down. He agreed to lay before a panel of the province's leading clergymen and laymen the differences between himself and his opponents. Notable among the group were three ministers who had played critical roles in the witchcraft crisis: Increase Mather, Samuel Willard, and Cotton Mather.

The seventeen men journeyed to Salem Village on April 3, 1695, and listened to the positions of both sides. Most likely, Parris's opponents submitted a document that they had given their pastor in late November 1694. In it, they explained that they had withdrawn from worship because of the "tumults and noises made by the persons under diabolical power and delusions" and because they feared "being accused as the Devil's instruments to molest and afflict the persons complaining." More important, they disapproved of the "principles and practices" of their pastor during and since the witchcraft crisis. His sermons on "our molestation from the invisible world" too often differed from "the generality of the orthodox ministers of the whole country." He too readily accepted the words of the afflicted and displayed too little "charity towards his neighbors, and especially towards those of his church." They believed that Parris gave "unsafe and unaccountable" testimony against several of the accused and failed to enter a fair account of the examinations when he served as a clerk for the court. Finally, he had persisted in his unsound principles and had rendered no "satisfaction to us when regularly desired, but rather farther offending and dissatisfying ourselves." What people like John Tarbell and Samuel Nurse wanted from Parris was quite simple. In a private conversation with the pastor, the two men had made it clear that they desired him to admit that he had been "the great prosecutor" in the witchcraft crisis. They pointed out that "others wise and learned who had been as forward . . . were sorry for what they had done." Until Parris made as clear an admission, they could not return to worship with him. Parris's "Meditations for Peace" speech in November 1694 had been insufficient; the only possible solution now was his dismissal.

For his part, Parris had a lengthy indictment against the dissenters that he had drafted in late 1693. The seventeen charges dealt largely with the dissenters failing to proceed in an acceptable way to resolve the conflict. They had repeatedly appealed to outsiders, delayed in responding to inquiries from the church, scandalized the church in their treatment of negotiators, and withdrawn "their purses . . . from upholding the Lord's Table and ministry." The most serious offense was their issuing "factious and seditious" libels about their pastor.

The extraordinary council had the almost impossible task of trying to reconcile this bitterly divided community. Increase Mather, who served as moderator, issued the council's recommendation on April 4. The council acknowledged that during "the dark time of the confusions," Parris had taken "unwarrantable and uncomfortable steps." Yet the council pointed out that he had "tendered in his Christian acknowledgments of the errors therein committed." Moreover, Parris had "with much fidelity and integrity acquitted himself in the main course of his ministry since he hath been pastor to the church in Salem Village." Consequently, the council advised that Parris "be accordingly respected, honored, and supported."

"Utterly frustrated" by the council's endorsement of Parris, village dissenters sent another petition to Increase Mather. They implored the Boston clergyman to "advise Mr. Parris . . . that he cannot with comfort or profit to himself or others abide in the work of the ministry among us." At the very least, they asked that Mather reconvene the council and consider the evidence anew. Most persuasive to Mather was that the dissenters had eighty-four signatures on their petition. After consulting with his colleagues, Mather wrote to Parris explaining that such opposition made his "removal necessary." Although Parris's supporters gathered 105 signatures on a petition to retain him "in his present station," it was clear that the embattled minister would have to leave. The following spring he tendered his resignation. The two factions in the village agreed to resolve the nagging issues of the pastor's back pay and his control of the parsonage by placing them before a panel of arbitrators. Appropriately, two of the three men that they agreed on brought back memories of the year of witch trials. Samuel Sewall and Wait Winthrop had served on the Court of Oyer and Terminer. (Elisha Cook was the third member.) In July 1697, the arbitrators ordered the village to pay Parris just over seventy-nine pounds and that he return the deed to the parsonage to the villagers.

Only with Parris's departure could Salem Village begin to heal its long festering wounds. After an extensive search, the village had the great good fortune to hire twenty-two-year-old Joseph Green as their new pastor. He moved quickly to bring the dissenters back into the congregation. In November 1698, Green indicated to the members that the leading dissenters, John Tarbell, Samuel Nurse, and Thomas Wilkins (Peter and Sarah Cloyce had moved to Marlborough, Massachusetts), "were heartily desirous that they would join with us in all ordinances." The members demonstrated the hope that all could "live lovingly together" by their unanimous consent. Six weeks later, the three families joined their brethren "in the Lord's Supper." Green called it a moment of "thankfulness, seeing they have for a long time been so offended as that they could not comfortably join with us."

Three years later, Green supported the request of friends and neighbors of Martha Corey to reverse her excommunication. With Green presiding, the congregation voted to grant their wish on February 14, 1703. In so doing, the church members in Salem Village chose, like some others who had admitted making mistakes in 1692, to take no responsibility for the excommunication of Corey. "We were at that dark day," they voted, "under the power of those errors which then prevailed in the land; and we are sensible that we had not sufficient grounds to think her guilty of that crime for which she was condemned and executed; and that her excommunication was not according to the mind of God."

When the Salem Village congregation noted that they were "under the power of those errors which then prevailed in the land," the members did not mean that they erred in believing in witchcraft. They, along with virtually all their contemporaries, continued to believe in the invisible world. They still accepted the proposition that some individuals had occult powers. Even the critics of the trials conducted by the Court of Oyer and Terminer had been careful to note their firm belief in witches. After all, if an individual accepted the reality of God, he or she necessarily had to accept the idea that there was a Devil and his handmaidens, witches. The available evidence indicates that few would question that belief. Judge Samuel Sewall, who anguished over his role in the deaths of the convicted witches, noted in his diary in early 1694: "This day Mrs. Prout dies after sore conflicts of mind, not without suspicion of witchcraft."

In addition to his inquiry into the cases of Mercy Short and Margaret Rule, Cotton Mather returned to Salem in September 1693 for material to write a "complete *History* of the late *Witchcrafts and Possessions*. During his visit, Mather met a woman who predicted "a *new Storm of Witchcraft*." It would "chastise the iniquity that was used in the willful smothering and covering of *the Last*; and that many fierce opposites to the discovery of that *Witchcraft* would bee thereby convinced." He had planned to give three sermons while in Salem, but his notes for the discourses disappeared. The circumstances convinced him that "specters, or agents in the *invisible world*, were the *robbers*."

There were also new indictments of witchcraft. In the summer of 1697, for example, Winifred Benham of Wallingford, Connecticut, went on trial following accusations by several neighborhood children. After failed searches for witches' teats and "the experiment of casting her into the water," the Superior Court at Hartford acquitted her because the only evidence against her was spectral. That was the rub. Without specter evidence, it became almost impossible to convict witches. The Massachusetts General Court essentially closed the possibility of any future convictions in 1703 when it ruled that "no specter evidence may hereafter be accounted valid, or sufficient to take away the life, or good name, of any person or persons within this province."

Charges of occult practices circulated in Salem Village again in 1746, but with this new perspective, no one suffered any legal penalties. Indeed, it became a matter exclusively of the church. Reverend Peter Clark reported to the congregation that he had information that "several persons in this parish" had "resorted to a woman of a very ill reputation, pretending to the art of divination and fortune-telling." First, the members approved a statement condemning such practices. They said that it was "highly impious and scandalous" for "Christians, especially church-members, to seek and consult reputed witches or fortune-tellers." Second, and most significant, the church members did not recommend a legal solution. Rather, they said that such a practice rendered "the persons guilty of it subject to the just censure of the church." Finding proof remained the difficulty, and when that was not forthcoming, the pastor's only recourse was a public admonition against

> this infamous and ungodly practice of consulting witches or fortune-tellers, or any that are reputed such; exhorting all under their watch, who may have been guilty of it, to an hearty repentance and returning to God, earnestly seeking forgiveness in the blood of Christ, and warning all against the like practice for the time to come.

New Englanders had decided, as had most authorities in Europe, that there were no reliable methods of detecting witches. As Eric Midelfort pointed out in his study of witchcraft in Germany, "It would seem that witch hunters in many regions stopped hunting and executing witches not because they no longer believed in them, but because they no longer knew how to find them." As Samuel Willard had explained in 1692, "God never intended to bring to light all hidden works or workers of darkness in this world."

The most compelling contemporary effort to that end came from the pen of Reverend John Hale, the pastor at Beverly, barely two miles from Salem. Although he had urged caution upon men like Samuel Parris, Hale, from the earliest days of the outbreak, had supported the 1692 assault on the witches. Since the end of the trials, he had worried about his role in the tragedy. He hoped in vain that one of the leading clergymen in the province would come forward with a treatise on the meaning of it. After considerable soul searching, he decided to offer his view of what had gone wrong and what lessons could be learned from the events of that awful year. He revealed his interest in the project to Samuel Sewall in November 1697, and the judge, at a time when so many were bemoaning the evils caused by a zealous acceptance in 1692 of a belief in the power of witches, worried "lest he go into the other extreme."

Within a month, Hale had finished the work, and early the next year, he persuaded the aged Salem pastor John Higginson to write an introduction. Higginson believed it an essential and timely work. He hoped that it would serve as a "warning and caution to those that come after us, that they may not fall into the like." The manuscript did not find a publisher until 1702, two years after Hale's death. Perhaps he wanted it to serve as a posthumous confession; if so, *A Modest Inquiry into the Nature of Witchcraft* became a fitting testament to his concern for justice.

Hale saw no human villains in this tragedy, only people who made flawed decisions. The "justices, judges and others concerned" displayed "a conscientious endeavor to do the thing that was right." Their actions, and his, however, had led to the shedding of innocent blood. Hale contended that there were plausible reasons for the course adopted by the esteemed judges and the initial support for the Court of Oyer and Terminer. They simply followed widely accepted principles from past cases. Chief among them was the notion that "the Devil could not assume the shape of an innocent person in doing mischief unto mankind." Additionally, they accepted the search for witches' teats or Devil's marks and testimony from accusers of mischief who had followed "anger between neighbors." Support for the trials grew with the mounting accusations from the afflicted and the numerous confessions.

"The numbers and quality" of people accused, however, challenged authorities to question their earlier convictions about their war against the forces of Satan. Several factors led Hale to reevaluate his position. Once the number of accused reached one hundred, he came to believe it unlikely that "so many in so small a compass of land should so abominably leap into the Devil's lap at once." He worried that too many of the accused were people of "blameless and holy lives." Particularly telling for him was the denial of guilt uttered by all who were executed. Out of that number, he would expect some "to seek mercy for their souls in the way of confession." Belatedly, Hale concluded that he and the authorities, since the first case in the 1640s, had depended on flawed principles: "I do not say that all those were innocent that suffered in those times upon this account. But that such grounds were then laid down to proceed upon, which were too slender to evidence the crime they were brought to prove; and thereby a foundation laid to lead into error those that came after." As he pondered why so many decent people had been willing to condemn on the basis of "slender" evidence, Hale decided that Satan had manipulated them.

John Hale ultimately saw the tragedy of Salem as God's punishment for a profligate people. When He saw that His chosen people had departed from the founding generation's sense of divine mission, God had released Satan from his chains and permitted them to devour each other in a furious, futile struggle against witches:

> The errand of our fathers into this wilderness, was to sacrifice to the Lord; that is, to worship God in purity of heart and life, and to wait upon the Lord, walking in the faith and order of the gospel in church fellowship; that they might enjoy Christ in all his ordinances. But these things have been greatly neglected and despised by many born, or bred up in the land. We have much forgotten what our fathers came into the wilderness to see. The sealing ordinances of the Covenant of Grace in church-communion have been much slighted and neglected; and the fury of this storm raised by Satan hath fallen very heavily upon many that lived under these neglects. The Lord sends evil angels to awaken and punish our negligence.

His generation had made a choice. They could have followed the path of their revered predecessors. Unfortunately, they neglected their divine errand and pursued their own ends.

Hale was left with this remarkably telling explanation for the disaster of 1692: "But such was the darkness of that day, the tortures and lamentations of the afflicted, and the power of former precedents, that we walked in the clouds, and could not see our way."

VII

Medical and Psychological Interpretations

*T*HE SHIFTING INTERPRETATIONS OF the Salem events—from group to individual responsibility, from the uniqueness of the Salem experience to its place in the continuity of Western history, from the emphasis on Puritan theology to the multicultural dimensions of the New England experience—have also felt the effect of modern psychology and medicine and the drug culture. The three works excerpted here illustrate some of those new trends. An underlying agreement in all these is the assumption that the accusers and confessors were not lying or pretending, but were experiencing the fits and visions as described.

Mary Matossian tackles the question of ergot first propounded by Linnda Corporael in 1976, In a 1982 article in the *American Scientist*, Matossian offers new arguments to support Corporael's thesis that the girls in Salem were suffering from infected rye grains. Two questions are at issue here: first, whether the behavior displayed during the Salem affair was truly a symptom of food poisoning, and second, whether the climatic conditions were appropriate for the growth of ergot on the rye crop. On both questions, Matossian says the answer is yes and, therefore, ergot is a plausible explanation for why the girls behaved as they did. This, then, was a social response to the mysterious effects of food poisoning. Matossian does not, however, consider why the behavior was interpreted as witchcraft and not a health problem. What was in the minds of those watching the girls that predisposed them to view the hallucinations as real experiences?

Such poison-induced peculiar bodily contortions and hallucinations had traditionally been associated with diabolical causes. In sharp contrast to Norman Cohn's analysis in part 2 of this reader, H. Sidky, connects many of the apparent witch confessions of Europe to the grotesque effects of psychotropic substances. For the most part these substances were put into topical ointments and used, he suggests, mainly for recreational purposes by the peasantry. The psychological effects of these drugs were recognized by the inquisitors, who may have applied the ointments to induce confessions of hallucinatory experiences from those they tortured. Thus such bizarre drug-induced behaviors traditionally came to be associated with witchcraft. Sidky offers an explanation for the peculiar behavior found among both accusers and those confessing to witchcraft, but he is careful to point out that the drugs or poisons themselves do not cause witch hunts.

In the matter of ergot, Sidky is ambivalent. He rejects Matossian's theories about ergot and the Salem episode because he assumes that the links she makes are based mainly on climatic conditions. On the other hand, he thinks that ergot may explain some of the cases of demonic possession in Europe. The problem as Sidky sees it is that it is the particular sociopolitical context and the religious beliefs that give substance to fears of ritual magic and not the existence of hallucinations and grotesque bodily positions. Poisons, whether of the psychotropic type or from food, are merely peripheral to the events. His study deals with the role of drugs in witchcraft, but does not argue that they are major causes of witch hunts.

John Demos, on the other hand, sees the reactions of the girls as psychological abnormalities resulting from the Puritan method of childrearing. He draws on Freudian psychoanalytical theory to suggest that the girls' repressed aggressive impulses against their mothers were projected onto other women in the community. Few other scholars have pursued this type of psychohistory, particularly Freudian theories, as a mode of analysis for these aberrant events. Most historians and psychologists are skeptical of applying twentieth-century theories of personality development to the seventeenth-century experience. But even if Freud is discounted, psychological insights certainly should be taken into account. In that respect, Demos's work deserves continuing thoughtful consideration and reevaluation.

[58]

Ergot and the Salem Witchcraft Affair

Mary K. Matossian

The historian Mary K. Matossian specializes in European folklore and family history, but recently has been interested in food poisoning epidemics and social behavior. In this excerpt from a 1982 article, Matossian makes the case that the seizures afflicting the girls in Salem were consistent with the symptoms of ergotism, food poisoning caused by fungus-infected rye. For a more detailed study of cases of mold poisonings, see her book Poisons of the Past: Molds, Epidemics and History (1989).

•

The witchcraft affair of 1692 had several peculiar aspects. In terms of the number of people accused and executed, it was the worst outbreak of witch persecution in American history. Accusations of witchcraft were made not only in Salem Village (now Danvers) but also in Andover, Beverly, Boxford, Gloucester, Ipswich, Newbury, Topsfield, and Wenham, all in Massachusetts, and in Fairfield County, Connecticut. The timing of the outbreak was strange, since it occurred 47 years after the last epidemic of witch persecution in England. No one has been able to prove why it occurred in 1692, and not some other year, or why it happened in Essex County, Massachusetts, and Fairfield County, Connecticut, and not in other counties.

In 1976 psychologist Linnda Corporael proposed an interesting solution to the problem of why various physical and mental symptoms appeared only in certain communities at certain times. She suggested that those who displayed symptoms of "bewitchment" in 1692 were actually suffering from a disease known as convulsive ergotism. The main causal factor in this disease is a substance called ergot, the sclerotia of the fungus *Claviceps purpurea*, which usually grows on rye. Ergot is more likely to occur on rye grown on low, moist, shaded land, especially if the land is newly cultivated. The development of ergot is favored by a severely cold winter followed by a cool, moist growing season: the cold winter weakens the rye plant, and the spring moisture promotes the growth of the fungus.

From Mary K. Matossian, "Ergot and the Salem Witchcraft Affair," *American Scientist* 70 (July–August 1982): 355–57. © 1982 by Sigmi X Scientific Research Society. Reprinted by permission of the publisher.

People develop ergotism after eating rye contaminated by ergot. Children and teenagers are more vulnerable to ergotism than adults because they ingest more food per unit of body weight; consequently, they may ingest more poison per unit of body weight. Made up of four groups of alkaloids, ergot produces a variety of symptoms. Diagnosis may be difficult because many symptoms are not present in all cases.

According to current medical thinking, the symptoms of early and mild convulsive ergotism are a slight giddiness, a feeling of frontal pressure in the head, fatigue, depression, nausea with or without vomiting, and pains in the limbs and lumbar region that make walking difficult. In more severe cases the symptoms are formication (a feeling that ants are crawling under the skin), coldness of the extremities, muscle twitching, and tonic spasms of the limbs, tongue, and facial muscles. Sometimes there is renal spasm and urine stoppage. In the most severe cases the patient has epileptiform convulsions and between fits, a ravenous appetite. He may lie as if dead for six to eight hours and afterward suffer from anesthesia of the skin, paralysis of the lower limbs, jerking arms, delirium, and loss of speech. He may die on the third day after the onset of symptoms. Animals suffering from convulsive ergotism may behave wildly, make loud, distressed noises, stop lactating, and die.

Corporael matched the symptoms and their epidemiology in 1692 with those in the above model. She was severely criticized by psychologists N. K. Spanos and Jack Gottlieb on the ground that the facts of the case fit the model very imperfectly. I have concluded, after examining the Salem court transcript, the ecological situation, and recent literature on ergotism, that this objection is not as valid as originally perceived.

Previous attempts to explain the witchcraft affair of 1692 have been unsatisfactory. The work of historians Paul Boyer and Stephen Nissenbaum, for example, has been concerned with the social reactions to the symptoms of bewitchment, rather than the origin of the symptoms. Other historians have attributed the outbreak to the tendency to make scapegoats of certain members of a community; although this is a widespread and chronic phenomenon, it is insufficient to explain the unique aspects of the case. New Englanders believed in witchcraft both before and after 1692, yet in no other year was there such severe persecution of witches.

The suggestion that the afflicted teenage girls in Salem Village were feigning their symptoms or, as Spanos and Gottlieb suggested, role-playing in the presence of social cues cannot explain the symptoms of the animal victims or of the other human victims who were apparently not stimulated by social cues. The suggestion made by an English professor, Chadwick Hansen, that the bewitched were suffering from hysteria is also unsatisfactory. People in the afflicted communities may have been hysterical in the sense that they were excited and anxious, but such psychological stimuli alone have not been shown to be capable of producing an epidemic of convulsions, hallucinations, and sensory disturbances in any case in which a diagnosis of ergotism or other food poisoning was seriously considered and then ruled out.

Symptoms in 1692

In Essex County, Massachusetts, 24 of 30 victims of "bewitchment" in 1692 suffered from convulsions and the sensations of being pinched, pricked, or bitten. According to English folk tradition, these were the most common specific symptoms of a condition called "bewitchment." Hence, they were the symptoms most often mentioned in the court records, for the intent of the court proceedings was to prove "witchcraft," not to present a thorough medical case history.

Some of the other symptoms of "bewitchment" mentioned in the court record, like the most common symptoms, may also occur in cases of ergotism. These include temporary blindness, deafness, and speechlessness; burning sensations; seeing visions like a "ball of fire" or a "multitude in white glittering robes"; and the sensation of flying through the air "out of body." Three girls said they felt as if they were being torn to pieces and all their bones were being pulled out of joint. Some victims reported feeling "sick to the stomach" or "weak," having half of the right hand and part of the face swollen and painful, being "lame," or suffering from a temporary, painful urine stoppage. Three people and several cows died.

The Salem court record does not mention certain symptoms often associated with mild or early cases of ergotism, such as headache, nausea, diarrhea, dizziness, chills, sweating, livid or jaundiced skin, and the ravenous appetite likely to appear between fits. If these symptoms were present, they may not have been reported because they were not commonly associated with bewitchment. Nor does the court record establish whether or not the victims suffered relapses or how the cases ended.

Social cues in the courtroom may have stimulated some of the hallucinations, but such stimulation does not disprove a diagnosis of ergotism. Ergot is the source of lysergic acid diethylamide (LSD), which some mycologists believe can occur in a natural state. People under the influence of this compound tend to be highly suggestible. They may see formed images—for instance, of people, animals, or religious scenes—whether their eyes are open or closed. These hallucinations can take place in the presence or absence of social cues.

Symptoms similar to those mentioned in the Salem court record also appeared between May and September of 1692 in Fairfield County, Connecticut. A 17-year-old girl, Catherine Branch, suffered from epileptiform fits, pinching and pricking sensations, hallucinations, and spells of laughing and crying. On 28 October she died, after accusing two women of bewitching her. John Barlow, aged 24, reported that he could not speak or sit up and that daylight seemed to prevail even at night. He had pain in his feet and legs. These symptoms also suggest a diagnosis of ergotism.

Epidemiology

The victims of bewitchment in Essex County were mainly children and teenagers. Seven infants or young children are known to have developed symptoms or died.

According to recent findings, nursing infants can develop ergotism from drinking their mother's milk.

Spanos and Gottlieb, citing the court record, asserted that the proportion of children among the victims in 1692 was less than that in a typical ergotism epidemic. However, in a recent epidemic of ergotism in Ethiopia, the ages of the victims were not much different from those in the Essex County epidemic of 1692: more than 80% of the Ethiopian victims were aged 5–34.

There can be no doubt that rye was cultivated in Salem Village and in many other parts of Essex County in the late seventeenth century. The animal cases could have resulted from ingestion of wild grasses such as wild rye or cord grass, some of which in Essex County were also liable to ergot infection.

The first symptoms of bewitchment appeared in Salem Village in December 1691. Beginning about 18 April 1692, the pace of accusation increased. It slowed in June and then reached a peak between July and September. Exactly when the symptoms terminated is unknown. After 12 October 1692 there were no more trials for witchcraft, by order of the governor of Massachusetts. However, during the winter of 1692–93 in the area around Boston and Salem there were religious revivals, during which people saw visions.

If rye harvested in the summer of 1691 was responsible for the epidemic, why did no one exhibit any symptoms before December of that year? In the ergotism epidemics of continental Europe the first symptoms usually appeared in July or August, immediately after the rye harvest. But these episodes occurred in communities heavily dependent on rye as a staple crop and among people so poor that they had to begin eating the new rye crop immediately after the harvest. The situation was otherwise in New England. The diary of Zaccheus Collins, a resident of the Salem area during the epidemic, and probate inventories show that the rye crop often lay unthreshed in the barns until November or December if other food was abundant. Since ergot can remain chemically stable in storage for up to 18 months, stored rye might have been responsible for the symptoms of December 1691.

But if people normally delayed threshing rye until winter, why was there a peak of convulsive symptoms in the summer of 1692? Such a peak might be expected in time of food scarcity: was this the case of 1692?

Unfortunately the usual sources of information about food supply, government records, are missing for 1692, but data from tree rings indicate that in 1690, 1691, and 1692, the growing season in eastern New England was cooler than average. Diarists in Boston recorded that the winters of 1690–91 and 1691–92 were very cold. Since rye is a crop that flourishes in cold weather when other crops fail, people may have been more dependent on rye and therefore may have begun consuming it earlier in the year. In coastal areas, such as Essex and Fairfield counties, cool conditions are usually also moist; ergot grows more rapidly in moist weather.

In several other years for which tree rings indicate especially cool weather, there were epidemics of convulsions. The most widespread epidemic in New England occurred in 1741. In 1795 a Salem epidemic, labeled "nervous fever," killed at least 33 persons.

The growth of population in Salem Village provided an incentive for local farmers to utilize their swampy, sandy, marginal land. This land, if drained, was better suited to the cultivation of rye than other cereal crops. But this was the very type of land in which rye was most likely to be infected with ergot. All 22 of the Salem households affected in 1692 were located on or at the edge of soils ideally suited to rye cultivation: moist, acid, sandy loams. Of the households, 16 were close to riverbanks or swamps and 15 were in areas shaded by adjacent hills. No part of Essex County is more than 129 m above sea level. As in Essex County, in southern Fairfield County, Connecticut, the predominant soil type was fine sandy loam, elevations were low, and the population was expanding.

Beginning in the 1590s, the common people of England began to eat wheat instead of rye bread. The settlers in New England also preferred wheat bread but, troubled by wheat rust, in the 1660s they began to substitute the planting of rye for wheat. This dietary shift may explain why the witchcraft affair of 1692 occurred 47 years after the last epidemic of witch persecution in England.

Although the limitations of surviving records make certainty impossible, the balance of the available evidence suggests that the witchcraft accusations of 1692 were prompted by an epidemic of ergotism. The witchcraft affair, therefore, may have been part of a largely unrecognized American health problem.

[59]

Ergot, Demonic Possession, and Hallucinogenic Drugs

H. SIDKY

In these excerpts from his 1997 book Witchcraft, Lycanthropy, Drugs, and Disease, *the anthropologist H. Sidky discusses the role of food poisoning in outbreaks of demonic possession, the possibility that the so-called witches' ointments contained hallucinogenic substances, and the use of psychotropic substances in the torture of suspected witches. Sidky has also published studies of the Hunza people of the Himalayas, including* Hunza: An Ethnographic Outline *(1995) and* Irrigation and State Formation in Hunza: The Anthropology of a Hydraulic Kingdom *(1996).*

•

Demonic Possession

The symptomatological similarities and geographical correspondence between epidemics of ergotism and mass outbreaks of demonic possession are striking. Such a correspondence does not necessarily indicate a causal connection between the two phenomena. Nevertheless, the general correlation between outbreaks of ergotism and epidemics of demonic possession is so close that some causal linkage almost certainly existed between them.

The symptoms of ergotism were attributed to supernatural causes during the sixteenth and seventeenth centuries, and not earlier, for the same reasons that spirit possession was not taken seriously until European demonology ascribed it, along with the symptoms of other strange diseases, to diabolical forces.

Creighton, who recognized a linkage between the mycotoxin and the bizarre behaviors associated with it, observed that: "There is, indeed, a larger question raised, whether the so-called psychopathies of the medieval and more recent periods may not have had a beginning, at least, in some toxic property of the staple food. The

From H. Sidky, Witchcraft, Lycanthropy, Drugs, and Disease: An Anthropological Study of the European Witch-Hunts *(New York: Peter Lang, 1997), 180–83, 190, 195–96, 199–208, 210–11. © 1997 by Peter Lang. Reprinted by permission of Peter Lang Publishers.

imagination readily fixes upon such symptoms as foaming at the mouth and barking noises, exalts these phenomena over deeper symptoms that a physician might have detected, and finds a simple explanation of the whole complex seizure as demoniac possession or, in modern phrase, as a psychopathy."

Another of Creighton's observations is well worth considering, especially in light of the countless tautological mentalist explanations that have obfuscated the matter by ascribing demonic possession entirely to beliefs or hysteria: "Without questioning the subjective or imitative nature of many outbreaks which have been set down to hysteria, it may be well to use some discrimination before we exclude altogether an element of material poisoning such as ergot in the staple food."

The historian Mary Matossian devotes a chapter of her *Poisons of the Past* (1989) to the role of ergotism in the European witch-hunts. Matossian draws attention, as I have, to the geographical and chronological correspondence between outbreaks of ergotism and epidemics of witchcraft. However, she does not cite specific instances where epidemics of demonic possession and ergotism have occurred simultaneously. Moreover, her conclusions are fundamentally different from mine. Matossian argues that anyone who has examined the records of the witch-persecutions will realize that actual harm ("bewitchment") was done. The harm attributed to witches often manifested itself as outbreaks of "bizarre behavior" characterized by central nervous system symptoms: tremors, spasms, convulsive seizures, hallucinations, etc. The target of the witch-persecutions, Matossian observes, were persons blamed for causing these horrible conditions, namely the witches. As Matossian sees it, "It simply will not suffice to discuss widespread beliefs about witches, tensions between factions in a witch-persecuting community, ruling-class repression, or legal and judicial arrangements for dealing with witchcraft. These were continuous cultural and social realities that did not vary in space and time as the distribution of 'bewitchment' varied. One cannot explain a variable with a constant."

Matossian goes too far, however, by implying that the entire judicial and ideological basis of witch-hunting evolved as "a social response" to the effects of a mycotoxin, i.e., ergot poisoning, interpreted as bewitchment. "To blame witch accusers and the courts for witchcraft," she affirms, "is to mistake an effect for a cause. Witches were persecuted because harm had befallen a community, not just because there were people vulnerable to indictment and other people prone to indict them." Simply because fraudulent accusations were possible does not mean that all episodes of bewitchment can be ascribed to invention, Matossian adds. Thus, she attributes the tragic fate of Urbain Grandier, not to gross subterfuge on the part of Richelieu's functionaries and the good sisters of Loudun's Ursuline convent, but to the misdiagnosis of the symptoms of a genuine central nervous disorder afflicting the nuns.

Matossian's reductionist perspective is untenable. The witch-hunts, which were specific to a particular time and place, could not have been a response to a disease that was present for centuries prior to the witch-craze. (This criticism may also be directed at the speculations of Piero Camporesi, author of a rather garbled work entitled *Bread of Dreams* [1989], who attributes the witch-persecutions to "a hallucinating scenario" induced by tainted bread). Furthermore, Matossian overlooks the fact that witches were hunted not just for precipitating nervous disorder symptoms, but for other calamities as well, such as lightning, storms, frosts, insect infestations, fires, plagues, economic slumps, etc. Satan's minions were also blamed for causing a host of illnesses that did not exhibit nervous disorder symptoms. Finally, and perhaps more importantly, innumerable witches were put to death, not for causing "actual harm," but for flying through the air, copulating with demons, conversing with spirits, making pacts with the Devil, possessing instruments of sorcery, and attending Sabbats. Records of the witchcraft trials do not reveal that actual harm was always done, as Matossian seems to think they do. Explanations of the witch-persecutions, therefore, do not hinge on an explanation for their epidemiology, as she suggests, because there really was no "epidemiology of witchcraft" in the first place.

Finally, Matossian has not been able to establish a direct link between specific outbreaks of ergotism and outbreaks of witchcraft persecution, as noted above. Instead, she infers the presence of mycotoxins indirectly, from climatic factors conducive to ergot infestation in rye producing regions, and from the court cases of witchcraft accusations themselves. In other words, incidence of microfungal epidemics are inferred from the recorded outbreaks of witch-hunting, the very phenomenon Matossian tries to explain as being the effect of these epidemics.

Although Matossian has exaggerated the role of mycotoxins in the European witch-persecutions, others have altogether missed the significance of this potent environmental toxin and its influence on human behavior. Ergot poisoning, as I have argued, should not be ruled out as one plausible epidemiological explanation for the recurrent epidemics of demonic possession during the witch-hunt years. . . .

Hallucinogenic Drugs

Many demonographers were convinced that witches, when so empowered by the Devil, could soar through the air by rubbing themselves with certain magical ointments. Others maintained, however, that the witches' atmospheric transportations were diabolically-induced dreams and illusions. As one contemporary scholar noted: "[Satan] rarely carries witches from one place to another, but deludes them through illusions and dreams. If you ask why her ointment and fork are always found and are burnt with her, the answer is that she prepares the ointment as [the Devil] instructs her, mostly out of somniferous herbs, and smears herself and her broom or fork, falls into deep sleep and dreams that she flies hither and thither with others, some of whom she knows, eats, drinks, talks, jests, dances, has sexual intercourse— and admits it when tortured." . . .

Surviving lists of ingredients indicate that the witches' flying-ointments contained powerful hallucinogenic substances. The principal psychotropic ingredients of the ointments belong to the nightshade or Solanaceae family. Gustav Schenk, the noted German toxicologist, observed that, from ancient times Solanaceae have been the true magic plants, capable of putting the human mind into states of consciousness impossible to enter and experience without them.

The Solanaceae family has over 3,000 species world-wide, including potato, to-mato, eggplant, and tobacco, as well as a variety of medicinal species. Belladonna (*Atropa belladonna*), henbane (*Hyoscyamus niger*), datura (*Datura stramonium*), and mandrake (*Mandragora officinarum*) all belong to this family. These plants contain the psychoactive alkaloids *atropine, d,l-hyoscyamine,* and *scopolamine,* which are anticholinergic substances—they block the action of acetylcholine on the peripheral cholinergic receptors in the brain, producing intense visual, gustatory, and olfactory hallucinations.

These drugs differ from other natural hallucinogens, however, in their extreme toxicity. Dr. Karl Kiesewetter, author of *Geschichte des Neueren Occultismus* (1891) and *Die Geheimwissenschaften* (1895), died after an experiment with a flying-ointment containing extracts of some of these plants, clearly demonstrating the potential dangers of such compounds. (This case should stand as a warning to those foolish enough to contemplate experiments with such dangerous and potentially deadly compounds.)

In large doses anticholinergic drugs are in some respects similar to LSD, and experienced users, as well as clinical diagnosticians, can sometimes confuse anticho-linergic intoxication for LSD psychosis. What distinguishes the two drugs, however, is that anticholinergic substances tend to induce hallucinations which appear to exist externally, with the subject losing all sense of reality. LSD psychosis, on the other hand, is more ideational in nature, with the subject often able to distinguish the drug-induced state from his objective surroundings.

This may explain why people under the influence of *atropine, hyoscyamine,* and *scopolamine* sometimes emerged from their psychosis convinced that what they ex-perienced had really taken place. Thus, according to Lewin, one of the pioneers in the field of pharmacology, "Magic ointments or witches' philtres procured for some reason and applied with or without intention produced effects which the subjects themselves believed in, even stating that they had intercourse with evil spirits, had been on the Brocken [a peak in the Harz mountains in Germany] and danced at the Sabbat with their lovers, or caused damage to others by witchcraft. . . ."

Hallucinogens and the Witches' Sabbat

Some of the first modern researchers who assessed the flying-ointment recipes, ac-knowledged that these preparations contained potent hallucinogens which, when mixed with fat and applied to the skin (as several of the recipes indicate), could be absorbed into the bloodstream. *Atropine* is fat-soluble, and therefore topical appli-cations are easily absorbed; likewise, medicinal belladonna plasters to the skin have resulted in serious poisoning. *Scopolamine,* the active alkaloid in datura, can also readily enter into the bloodstream through the skin.

Experiments with these drugs suggest that they sometimes produce the sensation of flight and other subjective impressions not unlike those reported by people thought to be witches. Schenk described his own experience after inhaling henbane smoke: "I was permeated by a peculiar sense of well-being connected with the crazy sensation that my feet were growing lighter, expanding and breaking loose from my body. This sensation of gradual bodily dissolution is typical of henbane poisoning. Each part of my body seemed to be going off on its own. My head was growing independently larger, and I was seized with the fear that I was falling apart. At the same time I experienced an intoxicating sensation of flying. . . . The frightening certainty that my end was near through the dissolution of my body was counterbalanced by an animal joy in flight. I soared where my hallucinations—the clouds, the lowering sky, herds of beasts, falling leaves which were quite unlike any ordinary leaves, billowing streamers of steam and rivers of molten metal—were swirling along. All this time I was not peacefully sleeping with limbs relaxed, but in motion. The urge to move, although greatly curtailed, is the essential characteristic of *Hyoscyamus* intoxication." The sensations of floating in the air and of flight have also been reported during LSD intoxication, indicating that experiences of this nature are not improbable during drug-induced altered states of consciousness.

Such evidence has prompted a number of modern writers—especially those influenced by the "drug culture" of the 1960s—to argue that the witches' night-flights, encounters with demons, communion with the Devil, and metamorphosis, were actually hallucinatory phenomena, stemming from the ritual use of psychotropic drugs during the Sabbats. Charles Hoyt has suggested, for example, that hallucinogenic drugs were used by leaders of witch-covens in order to produce a state of awe among their followers. Schultes and Hofmann have forwarded a comparable idea, maintaining that henbane was employed in the induction ceremonies of the witch-sects to produce highly impressionable states of mind among young recruits.

Not everyone, however, shares the conviction that hallucinogenic drugs played some role in European witchcraft; some writers have altogether dismissed the involvement of drugs, asserting that the idea of magical ointments was a fabrication of European demonologists, intended to make the sinister picture they had painted of the "witch" more believable. The historian Klaits has argued that although witches were usually arraigned for using diabolical salves, more often such charges were false. To illustrate his point, he cites an experiment conducted in 1611 by Alonso Salazar y Frias, who, having acquired some ointments from Basque witches, administered them to animals, but with negative results. Klaits, however, has ignored the fact that most hallucinogenic substances tend to affect higher-order mental functions, and consequently animal experiments are useless in demonstrating the effects these drugs have on human subjects. As Dr. Hofmann has pointed out concerning LSD— a drug with properties resembling hallucinogens found in the witches' ointments— experiments with animals provide little information on the psychotropic effects of LSD, because these animals cannot express the subtle but important psychic changes.

Demonologists themselves considered the ingredients of the witches' lotions to be inert materials, incapable of producing any effects without the aid of demons. Del Rio observed, for instance, that "the ointment used is made of various foolish things, but chiefly of the fat of slain infants; sometimes only the staff is anointed, sometimes the thighs or other parts of the body. The transport could be effected without, but the demon insists on it to stimulate infanticide." The Inquisitor Valle de Moura affirmed that, "The poisons from which the *Veneficae* [poisoners-witches] derive their name have their potency, not from the natural qualities of the ingredients, but from the charms and incantations used in their preparation, the demon thus contributing their effectiveness." . . .

One could argue that, if the erudite witch-doctors were trying simply to paint a sinister picture of witches and their activities, the list of obnoxious and loathsome ingredients for the ointments should have varied considerably among the sources, rather than remaining, as they did, confined almost exclusively to psychotropic substances. Indeed, the medical historian Fletcher, who surveyed the extensive literature of folk-beliefs associated with the witches' pharmacopoeia, observed that "it will be found that the same ingredients have been made use of through many ages to produce the like results."

Thus, the objection that the witches' salves were entirely the fabrication of European demonologists may not be well founded. On the other hand, explanations which posit the presence of "drug-using sects," whose members were persecuted because of their dreams and hallucinations, are equally tenuous, inasmuch as concrete evidence for the existence of such organizations does not exist. In the remainder of this chapter I shall suggest alternate explanations for the role of hallucinogens in European witchcraft.

Drugs, Poisons, and Chemical Ecstasy

Reginald Scot equated one type of witchcraft, which he called *veneficium*, with dealers in poisons: "As touching this kind of witchcraft, the principal part thereof consists in certain confections prepared by lewd people to procure love; which indeed are mere poisons, bereaving some of the benefits of the brain, and so of the sense and understanding of the mind. And for some it takes away life, and that is more common than the other." Such practitioners not only existed, they apparently possessed considerable knowledge of poisons and the utilization of various alkaloids.

Take for example, toads, dreaded during the Middle Ages because of their association with witchcraft. According to Fletcher: "The toad figures constantly in necromantic charms and its venom, if it have any, is supposed to reside in the glands of the skin." Toads also appear in flying and killing ointment recipes. Although the role of the toad in the witches' recipes has long been dismissed as folklore, the skin secretions of the toad family *Bufonidae* (which includes the common European toad) are now known to contain the alkaloid *bufotenine*, which has significant hallucinogenic properties. This alkaloid was employed by the Pokoman Maya of Guatemala, who added it to their fermented drinks, and is still part of the pharmacopoeias of local curers in Veracruz. We can infer from this and similar evidence that individuals versed in *veneficium* had a sound empirical knowledge of alkaloids. . . .

Conceivably, the witches' ointments were invented and dispensed by *veneficae*, specialists in botanical drugs. As *veneficium* was gradually assimilated into the stereotype of diabolical witchcraft, its practitioners came under persecution as witches, and the ecstatic states induced by the unguents they dispensed acquired sinister attributes in the minds of churchmen, magistrates, and Inquisitors. Demonological propaganda may have also convinced some of those who used such ointments that their drug-induced dreams and hallucinations were indeed diabolical in nature. . . .

It may be argued that the fantastic elements in the Sabbat imagery of the demonologists (i.e., magic flight, metamorphosis into animals, encounters with supernatural beings), may well have been rooted in drug-induced hallucinations. Such a contention would certainly entail fewer leaps of logic, than attempts "to decipher" or seek the presence of ancient pagan beliefs or archaic shamanistic survivals in the rhetoric of the witch-doctors and witch-burning judges, as writers such as Thomas or Ginzburg have done. . . .

In small doses, *atropine, scopolamine*, and *hyoscyamine* do act as sedatives, producing pleasing hallucinations and vivid erotic dreams. According to Hesse: "[Solanaceae] hallucinations are frequently dominated by the erotic moment. . . . In those days, in order to experience these [erotic] sensations, young and old women would rub their bodies with the 'witches' salve,' of which the active ingredient was belladonna or an extract of some other solanaceae." Solanaceae are still used in this manner by the peasantry in parts of western and central Europe. Thus, it is quite possible that the witches' ointments may have been employed simply for recreational purposes.

From their prominence in documents we can surmise that hallucinogenic drugs were used extensively. Indeed, medieval and post-medieval European society may have been experiencing epidemics of drug abuse, . . . The indiscriminate use of datura, one of the ingredients frequently found in the witches' salves, for instance, can lead to permanent insanity, a fact which may account for at least some of the cases involving individuals who voluntarily came forward and confessed to outlandish witchcraft-related crimes. As Lewin wrote, "The mental disorder caused by . . . datura has . . . instigated some persons to accuse themselves before a tribunal. The peculiar hallucinations evoked by the drug had been so powerfully transmitted from the subconscious mind to consciousness that mentally uncultivated persons, nourished in their absurd superstitions by the Church, believed them to be reality."

Such observations do not warrant the conclusion, however, that the demonological theory of witchcraft and its sequela, witch-hunting, had their origins in the drug-induced psychosis of particular individuals. The theory of witchcraft, as we have seen, comprised sets of logically coherent axioms founded on Christian theology and formulated in the context of particular sociopolitical circumstances. Hence, European witchcraft is better understood in sociological rather than psychological or pharmacological terms. . . .

Psychochemical Torture

. . . European torture technicians . . . had a wide assortment of tools and techniques at their disposal for extracting confessions, ranging from mechanical devices designed to inflict gross tissue damage, to psychological and physiological techniques, such as solitary confinement and sleep deprivation. Hallucinogenic or psychotomimetic drugs appear to have been part of this arsenal of weapons at the disposal of the interrogators. Although drugs have not proven to be effective tools for "brainwashing," i.e., radically and permanently altering the personality, drug-induced psychosis can be an extremely unnerving experience, and chemical torture can thus be a formidable tool.

Atropine and *scopolamine*, for instance, often produce frightening and disagreeable symptoms, and subjects who have experienced such effects rarely use these drugs a second time. This may explain why the witches' ointments were applied topically: inunction (introducing a drug into the body through the skin) is often used when it is necessary to maintain low levels of a drug in the blood stream.

A person under the influence of *Atropine*, according to Schenk, "may easily be subordinated to another's will, for he is completely open to influence and will do whatever he is told. If he has swallowed a great deal of the poison, this state of confusion and sensory derangement leads to a temporary, but acute, mental disorder exactly resembling a symptomatic psychosis. Sudden outbursts of delirium and increasingly intense periods of mania create a terrifying and uncanny clinical picture, which finally ends in convulsions similar to those of epilepsy." Similarly, *hyoscyamine*, when given even in moderate doses causes, among other symptoms, delirium, near blindness, and unbearable pain. Mixtures containing both these drugs, as well as those containing extracts of mandrake and datura, which would have had similar effects, were administered to suspected witches prior to torture.

Such drugs, used to induce debility, would, by disrupting the perceptual and conceptual processes, confuse and weaken the victim. The result of such psychochemical torture would be a mixture of fantasy, delusional and hallucinatory memories, interspersed with random real ones, precisely the kinds of confessions magistrates and torture technicians sought and obtained. . . . Given the propaganda value of confessions and cases of demonic possession, it is very likely that hallucinogenic drugs, administered to produce dramatic effects, may have been used more extensively for this objective than hitherto suspected.

Underlying Themes in the Witchcraft of Seventeenth-Century New England

John Demos

The historian John Demos is well known for his work on the intricacies of New England witchcraft and his studies of New England family life. In this excerpt from a 1970 article, Demos offers a psychological interpretation that focuses on the repressed aggression and orality discernible in the behavior of the afflicted girls in Salem. Among his seminal works are Entertaining Satan: Witchcraft and the Culture of Early New England *(1982) and* A Little Commonwealth: Family Life in Plymouth Colony *(1970).*

•

It is faintly embarrassing for a historian to summon his colleagues to still another consideration of early New England witchcraft. Here, surely, is a topic that previous generations of writers have sufficiently worked, indeed overworked. Samuel Eliot Morison once commented that the Salem witch-hunt was, after all, "but a small incident in the history of a great superstition"; and Perry Miller noted that with only minor qualifications "the intellectual history of New England can be written as though no such thing ever happened. It had no effect on the ecclesiastical or political situation, it does not figure in the institutional or ideological development." Popular interest in the subject is, then, badly out of proportion to its actual historical significance, and perhaps the sane course for the future would be silence.

This assessment seems, on the face of it, eminently sound. Witchcraft was not an important matter from the standpoint of the larger historical process; it exerted only limited influence on the unfolding sequence of events in colonial New England. Moreover, the literature on the subject seems to have reached a point of diminishing returns. Details of fact have been endlessly canvassed, and the main outlines of the story, particularly the story of Salem, are well and widely known.

From John Demos, "Underlying Themes in the Witchcraft of Seventeenth-Century New England," *American Historical Review* 75 (1970): 1311–14, 1320–26. © 1970 by the American Historical Review. Reprinted by permission of the American Historical Association.

There is, to be sure, continuing debate over one set of issues: the roles played by the persons most directly involved. Indeed the historiography of Salem can be viewed, in large measure, as an unending effort to judge the participants—and, above all, to affix blame. A number of verdicts have been fashionable at one time or another. Thus the ministers were really at fault; or Cotton Mather in particular; or the whole culture of Puritanism; or the core group of "afflicted girls" (if their "fits" are construed as conscious fraud). The most recent, and in some ways most sophisticated, study of the Salem trials plunges right into the middle of the same controversy; the result is yet another conclusion. Not the girls, not the clergy, not Puritanism, but the accused witches themselves are now the chief culprits. For "witchcraft actually did exist and was widely practiced in seventeenth-century New England"; and women like Goody Glover, Bridget Bishop, and Mammy Redd were "in all probability" guilty as charged.

Clearly these questions of personal credit and blame can still generate lively interest, but are they the most fruitful, the most important questions to raise about witchcraft? Will such a debate ever be finally settled? Are its partisan terms and moral tone appropriate to historical scholarship?

The situation is not hopeless if only we are willing to look beyond the limits of our own discipline. There is, in particular, a substantial body of interesting and relevant work by anthropologists. Many recent studies of primitive societies contain chapters about witchcraft, and there are several entire monographs on the subject. The approach they follow differs strikingly from anything in the historical literature. Broadly speaking, the anthropological work is far more analytic, striving always to use materials on witchcraft as a set of clues or "symptoms." The subject is important not in its own right but as a means of exploring certain larger questions about the society. For example, witchcraft throws light on social structure, on the organization of families, and on the inner dynamics of personality. The substance of such investigations, of course, varies greatly from one culture to another, but the framework, the informing purposes are roughly the same. To apply this framework and these purposes to historical materials is not inherently difficult. The data may be inadequate in a given case, but the analytic categories themselves are designed for any society, whether simple or complex, Western or non-Western, past or contemporary. Consider, by way of illustration, the strategy proposed for the main body of this essay.

Our discussion will focus on a set of complex relationships between the alleged witches and their victims. The former group will include all persons accused of practicing witchcraft, and they will be called, simply, witches. The category of victims will comprise everyone who claimed to have suffered from witchcraft, and they will be divided into two categories to account for an important distinction between different kinds of victims. As every schoolchild-knows, some victims experienced fits— bizarre seizures that, in the language of modern psychiatry, closely approximate the clinical picture of hysteria. These people may be called accusers, since their sufferings and their accusations seem to have carried the greatest weight in generating formal proceedings against witches. A second, much larger group of victims includes people who attributed to witchcraft some particular misfortune they had suffered, most typically an injury or illness, the sudden death of domestic animals, the loss of personal property, or repeated failure in important day-to-day activities like farming, fishing, and hunting. This type of evidence was of secondary importance in trials of witches and was usually brought forward after the accusers had pressed their own more damaging charges. For people testifying to such experiences, therefore, the shorthand term witnesses seems reasonably appropriate.

Who were these witches, accusers, and witnesses? How did their lives intersect? Most important, what traits were generally characteristic and what traits were alleged to have been characteristic of each group? These will be the organizing questions in the pages that follow. Answers to these questions will treat both external (or objective) circumstances and internal (or subjective) experiences. In the case of witches, for example, it is important to try to discover their age, marital status, socioeconomic position, and visible personality traits. But it is equally important to examine the characteristics attributed to witches by others—flying about at night, transforming themselves into animals, and the like. In short, one can construct a picture of witches in fact and in fantasy; and comparable efforts can be made with accusers and witnesses. Analysis directed to the level of external reality helps to locate certain points of tension or conflict in the social structure of a community. The fantasy picture, on the other hand, reveals more directly the psychological dimension of life, the inner preoccupations, anxieties, and conflicts of individual members of that community.

Such an outline looks deceptively simple, but in fact it demands an unusual degree of caution, from writer and reader alike. The approach is explicitly cross-disciplinary, reaching out to anthropology for strategy and to psychology for theory. There is, of course, nothing new about the idea of a working relationship between history and the behavioral sciences. It is more than ten years since William Langer's famous summons to his colleagues to consider this their "next assignment"; but the record of actual output is still very meager. All such efforts remain quite experimental; they are designed more to stimulate discussion than to prove a definitive case. . . .

Historians have traditionally worked with purposeful, conscious events. . . . They have not necessarily wished to exclude non-rational or irrational behavior, but for the most part they have done so. Surely in our own post-Freudian era there is both need and opportunity to develop a more balanced picture. It is to these long-range ends that further study of witchcraft should be dedicated. For witchcraft is, if nothing else, an open window on the irrational. . . .

The biggest obstacles to the study of psycho-history ordinarily are practical ones involving severe limitations of historical data. Yet for witchcraft the situation is uniquely promising on these very grounds. Even a casual look at writings like Cotton Mather's *Memorable Providences* or Samuel Willard's *A briefe account* etc. discloses material so rich in psychological detail as to be nearly the equivalent of clinical case reports. The court records on witchcraft are also remarkably full in this respect. The clergy, the judges, all the leaders whose positions carried special responsibility for combatting witchcraft, regarded publicity as a most important weapon. Witchcraft would yield to careful study and the written exchange of information. Both Mather and Willard received "afflicted girls" into their own homes and recorded "possession" behavior over long periods of time.

A wealth of evidence does not, of course, by itself win the case for a psychological approach to witchcraft. Further problems remain, problems of language and of validation. There is, moreover, the very basic problem of selecting from among a variety of different theoretical models. Psychology is not a monolith, and every psycho-historian must declare a preference. In opting for psycho-analytic theory, for example, he performs, in part, an act of faith, faith that this theory provides deeper, fuller insights into human behavior than any other. In the long run the merit of such choices will probably be measured on pragmatic grounds. Does the interpretation explain materials that would otherwise remain unused? Is it consistent with evidence in related subject areas?

If, then, the proof lies in the doing, let us turn back to the New England witches and especially to their "Trick . . . to render themselves and their tools Invisible." What characterized these spectral witches? What qualities were attributed to them by the culture at large?

The most striking observation about witches is that they gave free rein to a whole gamut of hostile and aggressive feelings. In fact most witchcraft episodes began after some sort of actual quarrel. The fits of Mercy Short followed an abusive encounter with the convicted witch Sarah Good. The witch Glover was thought to have attacked Martha Goodwin after an argument about some missing clothes. Many such examples could be accumulated here, but the central message seems immediately obvious: never antagonize witches, for they will invariably strike back hard. Their compulsion to attack was, of course, most dramatically visible in the fits experienced by some of their victims. These fits were treated as tortures imposed directly and in every detail by witches or by the Devil himself. It is also significant that witches often assumed the shape of animals in order to carry out their attacks. Animals, presumably, are not subject to constraints of either an internal or external kind; their aggressive impulses are immediately translated into action.

Another important facet of the lives of witches was their activity in company with each other. In part this consisted of long and earnest conferences on plans to overthrow the kingdom of God and replace it with the reign of the Devil. Often, however, these meetings merged with feasts, the witches' main form of self-indulgence. Details are a bit thin here, but we know that the usual beverage was beer or wine (occasionally described as bearing a suspicious resemblance to blood), and the food was bread or meat. It is also worth noting what did not happen on these occasions. There were a few reports of dancing and "sport," but very little of the wild excitements associated with witch revels in continental Europe. Most striking of all is the absence of allusions to sex; there is no nakedness, no promiscuity, no obscene contact with the Devil. This seems to provide strong support for the general proposition that the psychological conflicts underlying the early New England belief in witchcraft had much more to do with aggressive impulses than with libidinal ones.

The persons who acted as accusers also merit the closest possible attention, for the descriptions of what they suffered in their fits are perhaps the most revealing of all source materials for present purposes. They experienced, in the first place, severe pressures to go over to the Devil's side themselves. Witches approached them again and again, mixing threats and bribes in an effort to break down their Christian loyalties. Elizabeth Knapp, bewitched at Groton, Massachusetts, in 1671, was alternately tortured and plied with offers of "money, silkes, fine cloaths, ease from labor"; in 1692 Ann Foster of Andover confessed to being won over by a general promise of "prosperity," and in the same year Andrew Carrier accepted the lure of "a house and land in Andover." The same pattern appears most vividly in Cotton Mather's record of another of Mercy Short's confrontations with a spectral witch:

> "Fine promises!" she says, "You'l bestow an Husband upon mee, if I'l bee your Servant. An Husband! What? A Divel! I shall then bee finely fitted with an Husband: ... Fine Clothes! What? Such as Your Friend Sarah Good had, who hardly had Rags to cover her! ... Never Dy! What? Is my Life in Your Hands? No, if it had, You had killed mee long before this Time!—What's that?—So you can!—Do it then, if You can. Come, I dare you: Here, I challenge You to do it. Kill mee if you can. ..."

Some of these promises attributed to the Devil touch the most basic human concerns (like death) and others reflect the special preoccupations (with future husbands, for example) of adolescent girls. All of them imply a kind of covetousness generally consistent with ... neighborhood conflict and tension. ...

But the fits express other themes more powerfully still, the vital problem of aggression being of central importance. The seizures themselves have the essential character of attacks: in one sense, physical attacks by the witches on the persons of the accusers and in another sense, verbal attacks by the accusers on the reputations and indeed the very lives of the witches. This points directly toward one of the most important inner processes involved in witchcraft, the process psychologists call "projection," defined roughly as "escape from repressed conflict by attributing ... emotional drives to the external world." In short, the dynamic core of belief in witchcraft in early New England was the difficulty experienced by many individuals in finding ways to handle their own aggressive impulses. Witchcraft accusations provided one of the few approved outlets for such impulses in Puritan culture. Aggression was thus denied in the self and attributed directly to others. The accuser says, in effect: "I am not attacking you; you are attacking me!" In reality, however, the accuser is attacking the witch, and in an extremely dangerous manner, too. Witchcraft enables him to have it both ways; the impulse is denied and gratified at the same time.

The seizures of the afflicted children also permitted them to engage in a considerable amount of direct aggression. They were not, of course, held personally responsible; it was always the fault of the Devil at work inside them. Sometimes these impulses were aimed against the most important—and obvious—figures of authority. A child in a fit might behave very disobediently toward his parents or revile the clergy who came to pray for his recovery. The Reverend Samuel Willard of Groton, who ministered to Elizabeth Knapp during the time of her most severe fits, noted that the Devil "urged upon her constant temptations to murder her p'rents, her neighbors, our children ... and even to make away with herselfe & once she was going to drowne herself in ye well." The attacking impulses were quite random here, so much so that the girl herself was not safe. Cotton Mather reports a slight variation on this type of behavior in connection with the fits of Martha Goodwin. She would, he writes, "fetch very terrible Blowes with her Fist, and Kicks with her Foot at the man that prayed; but still ... her Fist and Foot would alwaies recoil, when they came within a few hairs breadths of him just as if Rebounding against a wall." This little paradigm of aggression attempted and then at the last moment inhibited expresses perfectly the severe inner conflict that many of these people were acting out.

One last, pervasive theme in witchcraft is more difficult to handle than the others without having direct recourse to clinical models; the summary word for it is orality. It is helpful to recall at this point the importance of feasts in the standard imaginary picture of witches, but the experience of the accusers speaks even more powerfully to the same point. The evidence is of several kinds. First, the character of the "tortures" inflicted by the witches was most often described in terms of biting, pinching, and pricking; in a psychiatric sense, these modes of attack all have an oral foundation. The pattern showed up with great vividness, for example, in the trial of George Burroughs:

> It was Remarkable that whereas Biting was one of the ways which the Witches used for the vexing of the Sufferers, when they cry'd out of G. B. biting them, the print of the Teeth would be seen on the Flesh of the Complainers, and just such a sett of Teeth as G. B.'s would then appear upon them, which could be distinguished from those of some other mens.

Second, the accusers repeatedly charged that they could see the witches suckling certain animal "familiars." The following testimony by one of the Salem girls, in reference to an unidentified witch, was quite typical: "She had two little things like young cats and she put them to her brest and suckled them they had no hair on them and had ears like a man." It was assumed that witches were specially equipped for these purposes, and their bodies were searched for the evidence. In 1656 the constable of Salisbury, New Hampshire, deposed in the case of Eunice Cole,

> That being about to stripp [her] to bee whipt (by the judgment of the Court att Salisbury) lookeing uppon hir brests under one of hir brests (I thinke hir left brest) I saw a blew thing like unto a teate hanging downeward about three quarters of an inche longe not very thick, and haveing a great suspition in my mind about it (she being suspected for a witche) desiered the Court to sende some women to looke of it.

The court accepted this proposal and appointed a committee of three women to administer to Goodwife Cole the standard, very intimate, examination. Their report made no mention of a "teate" under her breast, but noted instead "a place in her leg which was proveable wher she Had bin sucktt by Imps or the like." The women also stated "thatt they Heard the whining of puppies or such like under Her Coats as though they Had a desire to sucke."

Third, many of the accusers underwent serious eating disturbances during and after their fits. "Long fastings" were frequently imposed on them. Cotton Mather writes of one such episode in his account of the bewitching of Margaret Rule: "tho she had a very eager Hunger upon her Stomach, yet if any refreshment were brought unto her, her teeth would be set, and she would be thrown into many Miseries." But also she would "sometimes have her Jaws forcibly pulled open, whereupon something invisible would be poured down her throat . . . She cried out of it as of Scalding Brimstone poured into her." These descriptions and others like them would repay a much more detailed analysis than can be offered here, but the general point should be obvious. Among the zones of the body, the mouth seems to have been charged with a special kind of importance for victims of witchcraft.

*   *   *

In closing, it may be appropriate to offer a few suggestions of a more theoretical nature to indicate both the way in which an interpretation of New England witchcraft might be attempted and what it is that one can hope to learn from witchcraft materials about the culture at large. But let it be said with some emphasis that this is meant only as the most tentative beginning of a new approach to such questions.

Consider an interesting set of findings included by two anthropologists in a broad survey of child-rearing practices in over fifty cultures around the world. They report that belief in witchcraft is powerfully correlated with the training a society imposes on young children in regard to the control of aggressive impulses. That is, wherever this training is severe and restrictive, there is a strong likelihood that the culture will make much of witchcraft. The correlation seems to suggest that suppressed aggression will seek indirect outlets of the kind that belief in witchcraft provides. Unfortunately there is relatively little concrete evidence about child-rearing practices in early New England; but it seems at least consistent with what is known of Puritan culture generally to imagine that quite a harsh attitude would have been taken toward any substantial show of aggression in the young.

Now, some further considerations. There were only a very few cases of witchcraft accusations among members of the same family. But, as we have seen, the typical pattern involved accusations by adolescent girls against middle-aged women. It seems plausible, at least from a clinical standpoint, to think that this pattern masked deep problems stemming ultimately from the relationship of mother and daughter. Perhaps, then, the afflicted girls were both projecting their aggression and diverting or "displacing" it from its real target. Considered from this perspective, displacement represents another form of avoidance or denial; and so the charges of the accusers may be seen as a kind of double defense against the actual conflicts.

How can we locate the source of these conflicts? This is a more difficult and frankly speculative question. Indeed the question leads farther and farther from the usual canons of historical explanation; such proof as there is must come by way of parallels to findings of recent psychological research and, above all, to a great mass of clinical data. More specifically, it is to psychoanalytic theory that one may turn for insights of an especially helpful sort.

The prominence of oral themes in the historical record suggests that the disturbances that culminated in charges of witchcraft must be traced to the earliest phase of personality development. It would be very convenient to have some shred of information to insert here about breast-feeding practices among early New Englanders. Possibly their methods of weaning were highly traumatic, but as no hard evidence exists we simply cannot be sure. It seems plausible, however, that many New England children were faced with some unspecified but extremely difficult psychic tasks in the first year or so of life. The outcome was that their aggressive drives were tied especially closely to the oral mode and driven underground. Years later, in accordance with changes normal for adolescence, instinctual energies of all types were greatly augmented; and this tended, as it so often does, to reactivate the earliest conflicts—the process that Freud vividly described as "the return of the repressed." But these conflicts were no easier to deal with in adolescence than they had been earlier; hence the need for the twin defenses of projection and displacement.

One final problem must be recognized. The conflicts on which this discussion has focused were, of course, most vividly expressed in the fits of the accusers. The vast majority of people in early New England—subjected, one assumes, to roughly similar influences as children—managed to reach adulthood without experiencing fits. Does this pose serious difficulties for the above interpretations? The question can be argued to a negative conclusion, in at least two different but complementary ways. First, the materials on witchcraft, and in particular on the fits of the accusers, span a considerable length of time in New England's early history. It seems clear, therefore, that aggression and orality were more or less constant themes in the pathology of the period. Second, even in the far less bizarre testimonies of the witnesses—those who have been taken to represent the community at large—the same sort of focus appears. It is, above all, significant that the specific complaints of the accusers were so completely credible to so many others around them. The accusers, then, can be viewed as those individuals who were somehow especially sensitive to the problems created by their environment; they were the ones who were pushed over the line, so to speak, into serious illness. But their behavior clearly struck an answering chord in a much larger group of people. In this sense, nearly everyone in seventeenth-century New England was at some level an accuser.

VIII

The Salem Legacy

TOWARD THE END OF 1692, in another sad and depressing sidelight of the New England witchcraft hysteria, the Massachusetts legislature passed a new law providing for penalties against witchcraft, introducing the notion of attainder, and giving the legacy of Salem another symbol of cruelty. The witchcraft law, an "Act against Conjuration, witchcraft and Dealing with Evil and Wicked Spirits," declared that those convicted of witchcraft were attainted, signifying that they forfeited rights to property.

This odd action at the conclusion of the Court of Oyer and Terminer may have been an attempt to cover up or excuse after the fact the actions of George Corwin, the sheriff of Essex County and the nephew of Judge Jonathan Corwin. The sheriff, armed with warrants from the chief justice and lieutenant governor, William Stoughton, had earlier seized property not only of those convicted but also of many who were awaiting trial. There was no legal basis for that action in either provincial or parliamentary statute. Technically, if such property were seized for felonies, it belonged to the crown. It is likely that Corwin never turned the proceeds over to any governmental body.

Corwin's action was based on the idea that the accused had tainted blood and, therefore, lost all rights to own or convey property. The new Massachusetts law, then, would be an ex post facto justification of his action. Nonetheless, it was clearly in opposition to English statute that forbade attainder in cases of witchcraft, and it was nullified by the Privy Council in England in 1695. English law protected the rights of these condemned people to maintain ownership in and convey by will to their heirs any real or personal property. New England, it should be noted, had complied with those restrictions before the Salem trials. Only afterward, in this odd footnote to the witchcraft persecutions, did Massachusetts declare a commitment to attainder.

The witchcraft law also reaffirmed the death penalty, but only for a second offense or where the result was death or permanent impairment of the intended victim. These were conditions that could not have been met by the previous trials and were intended to set the ground rules for the upcoming trials. It was, obviously, a reaction against the harshness of the Court of Oyer and Terminer. But it is a curious law, with its attainder provision, passed just as the tide was turning against the persecution of witches.

There was never an investigation of connections between the 1692 law permitting forfeiture and the previous actions of Jonathan Corwin, Stoughton, and others who, though they may not have benefited (we don't know if they did or not), must have been aware of George Corwin's questionable activities. After the trials ended, George Corwin was not brought to account for any of his rash seizures and in very few cases was he forced to restore the property to the rightful owners.

Not until 1703 was action taken to formally reverse the de facto attainder. Then, beginning in 1704 and continuing through 1712, the legislature provided for restitution of the confiscated property and other losses due to admittedly faulty trials. Nonetheless, not all those who suffered claimed restitution and the problem repeatedly came up in the Massachusetts legislature. The issue of whether there was a conspiracy on the part of a small group to benefit financially in 1692 is another intriguing aspect of the events. The law is reprinted here as a reminder of those and other unanswered questions in the Salem episode.

Many individuals continued to suffer from the deprivations caused by the loss of property as well as the stigma of a witchcraft accusation long after they were reprieved. What happened to those tortured souls afterwards absorbs both the curiosity of the scholarly community and the attention of the descendants of the sufferers. Most studies of the Salem episode deal with those post-traumatic events.

Elaine Breslaw, in the epilogue of her biography of Tituba, captures some of the emotional impact of those personal losses. She reviews the lives of some of the survivors, suggests what might have happened to Tituba, and follows the Parris family fortunes. She also suggests that the end of the witch hunts coincided with a process of transformation within the Puritan mindset that brought New England into a new century of more enlightened thought. The Salem episode, because it occurred on the threshold of a new era of enlightenment and spiritual awakening, gives us a convenient point with which to mark the end of the medieval mindset and the beginning of the modern world in the English colonial experience.

Thus, Paul Boyer and Stephen Nissenbaum, in their study of the factional conflict in this New England village, look forward in time to gain an additional perspective on what happened in 1692. They represent the Salem events not only as a result of a community beset by also animosity and jealousy but also as an overture to the next century, and particularly to the religious revivals of the 1730s that would be called the Great Awakening. The Salem girls, they suggest, were in the throes of a religious crisis characterized by extreme anxiety. Their grotesque behavior would be very similar to that found later among the youngsters in Northampton in 1735 during what was finally recognized as emotional and religious crises. The difference in outcome was in the response of the adults. In Salem it was called witchcraft by those who saw themselves surrounded by demons trying to undermine their society and their old values. In Northampton forty-three years later, under the influence of revivalist ministers and in a very different social climate, the bizarre behavior became a quasi-respectable religious experience, a sign of a deeply felt spiritual conversion.

But witchcraft beliefs continued. Even if those peculiar behaviors found a new home in the colonial churches, witchcraft as an explanation for other mystical experiences and mysterious events did not cease. Rather, as Richard Weisman notes, the invisible world did not vanish. Accusations of witchcraft continued to be made in America. Because of the perseverance of such incidences, he sees "no marked discontinuities with the past." Rather, the folk continued to find witches in the community and to bring them to the attention of the authorities. What did change was the official response to such accusations. The elite refused to take legal action. The credibility of accusers may have come under attack, but, he emphasizes, not the underlying beliefs that continued to lead to accusations. Those had been maintained.

Jon Butler argues that in the larger cultural context, magic and the occult arts are as much a part of the European religious heritage as elite theologies and deserve recognition in studies of intellectual history. Although the English occult tradition showed definite signs of decline in the colonies by the beginning of the eighteenth century, the practice and the fear of witchcraft did not end at that time. Some of the early magical rituals and mystical procedures not only continued on the folk level but in some cases reappeared in dissenting Christian churches. The persistence of beliefs in magical rituals, therefore, holds particular significance for religious development.

In the centuries following the witch hunts, popular beliefs about the supernatural did not go underground so much as find new homes within the confines of evangelical religion and later spiritualist movements. Butler, therefore, issues a call for a broader meaning of religious history to include magical rituals and other nontraditional practices such as witchcraft. He reminds us of the continuing creative relationship between occult practices and orthodox religions.

PRIMARY SOURCE

[61]

An Act against Conjuration, Witchcraft and Dealing with Evil and Wicked Spirits

This law regarding witchcraft was passed by the Massachusetts legislature on December 14, 1692. Less than three years later, it was vetoed by the Privy Council in London on the grounds that. "The Act, being not found to agree with the Statute of King James the First whereby the Dower is saved to the Widow and the Inheritance to the heir of the party convicted, the same hath been repealed." The reference to attainder in the new Massachusetts law violated the parliamentary statute that preserved the inheritance rights of those convicted of witchcraft and prohibited the seizure of their property. Other provisions in this law regarding penalties for witchcraft were, therefore, also nullified. In the years following, witchcraft prosecutions effectively ended in New England.

•

For more particular direction in the execution of the law against witchcraft—

Be it enacted by the Governour, Council and Representatives in General Court assembled, and by the authority of the same,

[Sect. 1]. That if any person or persons shall use, practice, or exercise any invocation or conjuration of any evil and wicked spirit, or shall consult, covenant with, entertain, employ, feed or reward any evil and wicked spirit, to or for any intent or purpose; or take up any dead man, woman or child, out of his, her or their grave, or any other place where the dead body resteth, or the skin, bone or any other part of any dead person, to be employed or used in any manner of witchcraft, sorcery, charm or enchantment; or shall use, practice or exercise any witchcraft, enchantment, charm or sorcery, whereby any person shall be killed, destroyed, wasted, consumed, pined or lamed in his or her body, or any part thereof; that then every such offender or offenders, either aiders, abetters and counselors, being of any of the said offences duly and lawfully convicted and attainted, shall suffer pains of death, as a felon or felons.

And further, to the intent that all manner of practice, use or exercise of witchcraft,

From Acts and Resolves, Public and Private of the Province of the Massachusetts Bay, vol. 1 (Boston: Wright and Potter, 1869), 90–91.

enchantment, charm or sorcery should be henceforth utterly avoided, abolished and taken away,—

Be it enacted by the authority aforesaid,

[Sect. 2] That if any person or persons shall take upon him or them, by witchcraft, enchantment, charm or sorcery, to tell or declare in what place any treasure of gold or silver should or might be found or had in the earth, or other secret places; or where goods or things lost or stolen should be found or become; or to the intent to provoke any person to unlawful love; or whereby any cattle or goods of any person shall be destroyed, wasted or impaired; or to hurt or destroy any person in his or her body, although the same be not effected and done; that then all and every such person and persons so offending, and being thereof lawfully convicted, shall for the said offence suffer imprisonment by the space of one whole year, without bail or mainprize [i.e., put in the custody of another]; and once in every quarter of the said year shall in some shire town stand openly upon the pillory by the space of six hours, and there shall openly confess his or her error and offence, which said offence shall be written in capital letters, and placed upon the breast of said offender. And if any person or persons, being once convicted of the same offence, and shall again commit the like offence, and being of any of the said offences the second time lawfully and duly convicted and attainted as is aforesaid, shall suffer pains of death, as a felon or felons.

COMMENTARIES

[62]

Altered Lives

ELAINE G. BRESLAW

In this excerpt from her 1996 book Tituba, Reluctant Witch of Salem, *Elaine G. Breslaw describes the fates of the accusers and the surviving accused in the aftermath of the Salem witch hunt, focusing on Tituba and the long-term ramifications of her testimony. Breslaw's analysis of Tibuta's confession was excerpted in part 6.*

•

Between March and October of 1692 over 150 people were arrested on suspicion of witchcraft. Twenty-four would die before the crisis was over—nineteen by hanging, one pressed to death, and four from other causes while in prison. Hundreds of lives would be disrupted by the jailings, the loss of property, and the absence of needed labor on the farm and in the household. Ties between children and parents, between husbands and wives, among siblings and neighbors, were frayed by accusations and counteraccusations. Some would never recover from the trauma. Five-year-old Dorcas Good, imprisoned in chains for nine months, was so terrified by the experience that she became unmanageable as she grew older. Her father reported in 1710 that "she hath ever since been very chargeable [i.e., irresponsible and a burden to him], having little or no reason to govern herself." The petitions submitted to the General Court to reclaim lost property and receive restitution for the cost of imprisonment highlight some of the personal tragedies and economic costs of the witchhunt. But the full impact of those events was probably much greater than those extant written sources indicate. Tituba's confession had consequences and ramifications that no one could have predicted in March of 1692 and are still being explored three hundred years later. Her own life was compellingly altered.

At the end Tituba recanted her confession, admitting that she had lied to protect herself. That action had little effect on subsequent events and was almost lost in the rush by other confessors, in fear of damnation, to admit their terrible sin. Tituba's attempt to retract her confession received scant attention at the time and was ignored

From Elaine G. Breslaw, Tituba, *Reluctant Witch of Salem: Devilish Indians and Puritan Fantasies* (New York: New York University Press, 1996), 171–81. © 1996 by New York University. Reprinted by permission of New York University Press and the author.

in the written reports of most observers. Only Robert Calef made note of it: "The account she [Tituba] since gives of it is, that her Master did beat her and otherways abuse her, to make her confess and accuse (such as he call'd) her Sister-Witches, and that whatsoever she said by way of confession or accusing others, was the effect of such usage." Hers was not the first retraction of a reluctant confession. The others had already received a great deal of attention.

The tide of accusations and confessions had started to turn during the summer. Starting with Margaret Jacobs in August, several of the confessors denied their earlier statements. Jacobs had suffered excruciating mental anguish, what she described as "the terrors of a wounded Conscience," the result of falsely implicating both her grandfather and George Burroughs. On August 18, the day before the execution of the two men, still fearful that the truth would lead to her own death, Jacobs apologized for lying, "choosing death with a quiet conscience, than to live in such horror, which I could not suffer." Six Andover women retracted their confessions the following month, shortly after the September executions, complaining that they had submitted to an unbearable pressure from friends, family, and the magistrates to confess. Plagued by their consciences, they could no longer live with the anticipation of the damnation awaiting them. They too preferred death to "the great sin in belying."

By the end of September the use of spectral evidence had been completely discredited. But the theological and political leadership had become suspicious of the proceedings early on. Nathaniel Saltonstall had resigned from the court after the first case in June because he disapproved of the prosecutorial methods. Cotton Mather had also warned in June that spectral evidence should be received with caution because the "Demon may . . . Appear . . . in the shape of an innocent." Mather continued cautioning the governor and his Council of the dangers in using spectral evidence to convict as new complaints regarding the conduct of the court grew in volume. Those recanting and describing how they were forced to confess added to the reaction against the persecutions.

The Governor was finally convinced that innocent people were being convicted on very flimsy evidence. His own wife and the very wealthy Boston widow and mother of Jonathan Corwin's wife, Margaret Thatcher, and the Reverend Samuel Willard were all accused and faced possible prosecution. This brought the danger of persecution too close to his own home, threatening his personal, social, and political position. Early in October Phips dissolved the emergency court of Oyer and Terminer he had set up in May. The execution of eight people on September 22 marked the end of the persecutions; after that day, the witchhunt was, to all intents and purposes, over. The Governor called for a stay of execution for those already convicted and began to empty all of the prisons. Some fifty people who had been indicted, and many others awaiting a hearing, were suffering in jails in a variety of locations. He permitted those who could afford the cost to be let out on bail.

With the Governor's action in October, the possibility of execution was no longer a threat. Other confessors, succumbing to more gentle questioning in jail, described the pressures and fears that led to their false testimonies. Rebecca Eames, who had confessed on August 19, told Increase Mather and Thomas Brattle when they visited the Boston jail in October that her testimony was not true. Eames was one of the few women to confess and then be convicted and sentenced to die. She was fortunately reprieved when the Governor called a halt to the executions early in October.

Sensitive, as usual, to the nuances of community trends and recognizing that she could dispense with her role as a reluctant witch, Tituba also admitted to lying about her diabolical contacts. She knew by then that her life would be saved even if she admitted to lying. With the exception of Samuel Wardwell (who denied his confession at his trial), none of the others recanting their forced confessions were executed. But unlike the others, in the process of recanting, Tituba also demonstrated an unusual defiance. She could not resist a final thrust at her master. Joining the pack of those who blamed Parris for the Salem tragedy, she accused him of forcing her to admit to witchcraft. As Tituba awaited the consequences of that defiance, the provincial government began to take conciliatory action. Phips asked the legislature to establish a new Superior Court of Judicature to try the remainder of the accused, but on the recommendation of the clergy denied the use of spectral evidence in that new court. New trials of at least thirty-three of the remaining fifty-two indicted persons were held at four locations between January and May of 1693. The courts found all but three, who had confessed, innocent of the charges, but they too were reprieved. Governor Phips thought two of the three women somewhat deranged. Another seven people who awaited execution from their earlier trials by the Court of Oyer and Terminer, including Rebecca Eames, were also freed on the grounds that "the matter" had been managed badly by that court.

Gradually the jails were emptied of their tortured inhabitants as the families and friends of the prisoners, including those not yet indicted, paid their jail fees. Prisoners were expected to pay the cost of their own upkeep while in jail and could not be let out until that debt was taken care of. Poor people had an especially difficult time. Margaret Jacobs, acquitted in January, was unable to raise the money and remained in the filthy jail for months until someone in the town, pitying her, paid for her release.

Tituba, of course, had no resources of her own. She found herself abandoned by Samuel Parris, who would not allow her back into his household, although he did not suspect her of teaching his children about witchcraft or of wanting to harm little Betty. Tituba may have miscalculated the effect on Parris of retracting her March confessions, or possibly she hoped that by antagonizing him she would be sold to someone else in the community. That would free her from Parris's jurisdiction and the fear of further punishment at his hands. Tituba did not harbor kind sentiments toward her master. She had, after all, indirectly accused him of bringing evil to the community and she resented his physical abuse.

Parris may well have sensed that her confession had begun as an attack on him. Further angered by her recanting and its implied rebuke of his punitive action toward her, he refused to assist her in any way or to take her out of the Boston prison. To show compassion would have been tantamount to apologizing for unjustifiably beating her, forcing her confession, and subjecting her to thirteen months in prison. Her innocence was his guilt. And Samuel Parris in 1693 was not yet ready to apologize for his various roles in the Salem tragedy. It is also possible that Parris needed to distance himself from her and the imputations of harboring evil in his household. His parishioners were already preparing to blame him for the events of 1692 and Tituba's continuing presence, a reminder of their pain, could have been an added irritant.

Tituba's punishment for her benevolent act in protecting young Betty Parris was far worse than she could have predicted. She did survive, but not only was she subjected to the psychological torture of a public interrogation and the misery of thirteen months of a meager food ration in crowded, filthy confinement—terribly cold in the winter and unbearably hot in the summer—but also endured a separation from her family. She probably suffered additionally from the taunts of other inmates and visitors to the prison who feared her magical power. Her confession may have saved her life, but it would not have afforded protection against the stigma of association with the Devil or of Parris's wrath.

To dispose of his reluctant witch, Parris simply refused to pay her jail fees. That meant Tituba would remain in Boston in jail until someone else volunteered to pay the cost of those months of incarceration. Some agreement must have been reached, although written evidence of those details is no longer available. Because she was a slave, she could be sold for the amount of those jail fees, which came to about seven pounds. An as yet unidentified person paid those fees and took her away in April of 1693. Her fate after that date is unknown. Tituba disappears from the public record at that point. But some conjecture can suggest what happened to her and her family.

Of John, her husband, we have no further information. Presumably he was sold to the person who had acquired Tituba. Puritans would have been reluctant to divide married couples, even enslaved people. The marriage bond was not just the most fundamental unit of social organization, but was also "the principal referent of Puritan experiences of God." To separate the two Indian slaves would have violated too many Puritan precepts. Parris may also have been anxious to rid himself of the one man who appeared to suffer torment similar to the afflicted girls. John may well have become a burden because of his periodic episodes of fainting and falling into violent fits. His presence, moreover, was another reminder of Parris's guilt in this communal horror, although John was never imprisoned nor accused of witchcraft. He too disappears from the written record after the trials.

Their daughter Violet, probably no more than three or four years of age in 1693, did not merit the same treatment. She had played no part in the tragedy and there was no social pressure to keep parents and child as a unit. Separation of children from mothers was a normal part of the life cycle for slaves as well as white people in colonial New England. Her appearance in Parris's will indicates that Violet remained in the Parris household to be trained as a domestic, eventually to take her mother's place in Elizabeth Parris's kitchen and that of Samuel's second wife, Dorothy. Violet was still alive when Samuel Parris died in 1720, an able servant and sufficiently skilled to be worth thirty pounds to the estate. Dorothy Parris had died the year before her husband Samuel and the surviving members of the family probably had no need of another household slave. The "Indian woman" Violet was more valuable to the family on the auction block than as a worker and she was sold off to pay some of Parris's debts. Violet too would experience a sharp break with her past. She, like her parents, was sold to another unknown buyer and left no record of her ultimate fate.

In the end Tituba lost contact with both her own child and the one she had tried to protect. If she and John were kept together, she was left with only minimal contact with the people and places that afforded some stability to her life. If they were separated, Tituba may have been destitute emotionally, a repeat of her uprooting and loss of contact with kin as a child. She was still a young woman—no more than thirty years old in 1693, and capable of having more children. Whether she did we may never know. We can assume that she was probably strong enough to withstand this new trauma of separation and, as in the past, would have found the means to adjust to her newest circumstances. Her ability to survive and make the most of personal crises had been demonstrated both in Barbados and Salem. Surely she would succeed again. On the other hand, the society that had abandoned her would spend the next ten years struggling with the effects of her successful attempt to save her own life in 1692.

* * *

In an effort to conciliate those who suffered financial losses during the witchhunt, the Massachusetts General Court in 1704 reversed the bill of attainder that had deprived the families of the convicted witches of their property. Only those who had filed petitions benefited at first. Seven years later, in 1711, the legislature allowed restitution to all those who had "suffered in their Estates at that Sorrowful time." Other compensation was awarded to the survivors for the cost of imprisonment. Most of those accounts were settled by 1712 but some names do not appear in those records. Tituba's account is conspicuously absent from the lists. Had she been removed from the province? Was her new master too far away to claim restitution? Did he prefer that the Indian woman become invisible, ignoring the possibility of some monetary reward in favor of anonymity?

Tituba, wherever she was in 1712, if still alive, may have heard about these financial settlements, but her response if any will probably never be known. Her daughter Violet was old enough to understand but she no longer lived in Salem. Samuel Parris, widowed in 1696 when Elizabeth died, had taken his servants and his children the following year to the frontier community of Stow and then to several other Massachusetts towns. In 1712, he, his second wife Dorothy, their four children, and presumably Violet were living in Sudbury. Two of the children of his first marriage, Thomas and Susannah, had died by that time. Elizabeth (Betty) had married Benjamin Barron in January of 1710. There was no recorded comment from any of the Parris household on these legislative acts.

To the members of the Salem community there was little satisfaction for the mental pain, humiliation, and physical misery Tituba's confession had fueled. It would take years of apology and repentance before the scars of that fearful experience would heal. Life could not return to normal just yet. A period of reconciliation followed. Samuel Parris, determinedly clinging to his estranged church members, was the first to acknowledge his guilt in the tragedy. In 1694 he publicly apologized to the congregation for his role as a leader in the hunt for witches. He was, he said, too zealous in his desire to protect the community from the Devil. His apology did not appease those who continued to blame him for the terrible events—for stoking the fires of discontent with his own resentments and urging the young people to continue their accusations. The opposition in the village and pressure from other ministers finally convinced Parris to leave in 1697 and a new, younger, more conciliatory minister, Joseph Green, took his place.

The process of healing quickened after that year. Green worked at the village level to reconcile the competing factions. He brought the dissenters back into the church and asked that excommunication of the convicted witches be rescinded. At the same time, the more distant authority in Boston took what steps it could to heal those wounds. The General Court proclaimed a fast day on January 14, 1697, in memory of those who died and as repentance for communal mistakes in "the late tragedy raised among us by Satan and his instruments." That bill, drafted by Samuel Sewall, was part of his own personal atonement for his role in the affair when he sat on the Court of Oyer and Terminer. In a public apology Sewall admitted his responsibility, contritely taking "the blame and shame of it" on himself.

Other members of the community followed. Twelve men who had served on juries in Salem during the witch trials confessed their "deep sense of, and sorrow for our Errors," declaring that they "were sadly deluded and mistaken," and begged forgiveness for having "been instrumental with others, tho Ignorantly and unwittingly, to bring upon ourselves . . . the Guilt of Innocent Blood." Ann Putnam, Jr., twenty-seven years old in 1706, also publicly admitted her guilt. Saddened and repentant for the pain she had caused, Ann confessed in the meeting house, in what was becoming a familiar litany: "it was a great delusion of Satan that deceived me in that sad time, whereby I justly fear I have been instrumental with others, though ignorantly and unwittingly, to bring upon myself and this land the guilt of innocent blood."

Deluded by Satan or under the power of suggestion fueled by an Indian's vision? To a Puritan they amounted to the same driving force: a Satanic presence, a devilish Indian, alien notions. Although unstated, Tituba's responsibility for their deluded state may well have lingered in the subconscious of those who reflected on their own roles in the tragedy. She would always be a reminder of their failure to exorcise the Devil within themselves.

*   *   *

Apart from the personal tragedies, what was the impact of Tituba's testimony on the larger history of New England? Did it bring about any permanent change in the values and thought processes of the Puritan community? Tituba was, of course, responsible for initiating the panic and helped to maintain the acute sense of a diabolical invasion. But after the panic had subsided, apologies were given, and attempts made at restitution, of what importance in the course of American history is the Salem incident and, by inference, Tituba's special role?

The Salem tragedy was the last time that anyone would be executed for witchcraft in Massachusetts. Spectral evidence, which had never been an issue before 1692, was completely discredited. The General Court specifically outlawed the use of such non-material evidence in 1703, declaring that "no spectral evidence may hereafter be accounted valid." In 1736, English and Scottish laws prescribing death for witchcraft were repealed. Accusations of witchcraft, however, would continue to occur; occult practices had not lost their adherents. But the fear of witchcraft would no longer have the power to disrupt communities and destroy innocent lives. The discrediting of spectral evidence weakened the belief in occult powers, for if a witch could not be distinguished from a specter, could there truly be such a thing as a witch? As a result, the churches no longer turned to legal institutions to counter something so invisible as witchcraft. . . .

In the end, the Salem witchhunt proved to be more disruptive of the Puritan ideal of community than the expected unifying experience. The new idiom of resistance articulated by Tituba uncovered a range of discontent with social, political, and religious conditions, particularly anti-clerical sentiment among young women and servants. Tituba's stories provided a forum, a focus, and a new language for that dissatisfaction. Her words encouraged the reshaping of the notion of evil to include strangers, elite men and women, and ministerial leadership. Moreover, she supplied the framework of an evil conspiracy that could be elaborated to fit both elite notions of evil and the folklore of witchcraft. The effect was a merger of the two traditions into a new elite synthesis.

Though the Puritans misunderstood and misconstrued Tituba's testimony, those very mistakes permitted them to focus on the diabolical conspiracy. But it was a conspiracy made in Salem, an imaginative combination of Indian lore and Christian fears. With the acceptance by the Puritans of the Indian concept of an outside evil persona, Tituba had not only reshaped the popular notions of witchcraft but helped to bring those ideas into congruence with clerical fantasies of Satan.

There is general agreement that the New England mentality was somehow different after 1692: that that year was a watershed in the development of the Puritan mind and that certain aspects of belief and behavior and ritual were different afterward. Certainly the value of confession declined after 1692. Tituba's confession, which became a model for resistance rather than a confirmation of Puritan values, had so distorted its meaning that, like the witch trials themselves, that ritual was discredited. Confession should have purged the sin of diabolism from the community and reaffirmed Puritan values of harmony, hierarchy, and piety—the covenant ideal. Instead, what had been a ritual of renewal became a method of resistance to authority and a subverter of those values. Popular beliefs did not change; the concept of the witch among the populace—as one who did harm using magical means—remained essentially the same. It was official policy and elite notions that shifted.

That process of transformation, resulting from the convergence of two traditions regarding the nature of evil—the elite and the folk—exposed the contradictions in the reforming Puritan tradition and prepared it for the eighteenth-century Enlightenment. After Salem the reformers realized that the intense personal commitment of conversion could become a "ruse" and that zealous prosecution of sin could result in "hideous enormities." The Salem witchhunt gave warning that the persistent pursuit of reform could have the opposite result—of destroying the biblical commonwealth and the holy covenants that bound the community together. The Salem experience, by discrediting some of the sacred rituals, helped to shape a more moderate Puritanism.

Thus the folklore of the American Indian, embedded in Tituba's confession, interacting with English folk beliefs and elite notions of evil initiated a modifying process and lay the groundwork for the rationalism of the eighteenth-century Enlightenment. But unlike the usual trends of intellectual change, this shift to a more secular society was not brought about by the dominant class impacting on the subordinate. It was the reverse. In their great desire to make Tituba's confession believable, those hearing her stories had to accommodate her fantasy and integrate her concept of an evil persona into their own belief system. That accommodation of her Indian beliefs forced the rejection of specters and magical practices from the realm of public discourse. This was change from the bottom up, initiated by an Indian woman slave.

By focusing on Tituba's role in that tragedy, the Salem events permit us to capture a glimpse of an unusual process of exchange between high and popular cultures. The lowly but acculturated slave woman, conversant with Puritan norms and protected by her subservient Anglicized demeanor, overwhelmed the dominant class and temporarily reversed the roles of the teachers and the taught. Tituba's sorcery, if it existed, was in exposing and capitalizing on a Puritan vulnerability to images drawn from popular culture. Through Tituba's agency the very practical, but deeply ingrained, mentality of the folk was able to intrude into the complex world of New England print culture. The result of this convergence of cultures in 1692 was a violent moment in early New England history, but one that ultimately redirected Puritanism into less turbulent paths. The dynamic in that process was the reluctant confession of a slave woman called Tituba who successfully brought to her own defense the multi-ethnic oral traditions of her West Indian and South American cultures.

[63]

1692

Some New Perspectives

PAUL BOYER AND STEPHEN NISSENBAUM

Paul Boyer and Stephen Nissenbaum's 1974 book Salem Possessed: The Social Origins of Witchcraft *is now a classic study of the factional conflicts underlying the* Salem witch hunt. *In this excerpt from* Salem Possessed, *they draw parallels between the symptoms of the afflicted girls in Salem and the symptoms of young people in the throes of religious crises during the eighteenth-century religious revivals. Boyer and Nissenbaum have also edited and published a large number of the available primary sources written at the time of the Salem witch hunt. The most extensive compilation is the three-volume* Salem Witchcraft Papers: Verbatim Transcripts of the Legal Documents *(1977). They have also edited a single-volume collection of material entitled* Salem-Village Witchcraft: A Documentary Record of Local Conflict in Colonial New England *(1972).*

•

Salem witchcraft. For most Americans the episode ranks in familiarity somewhere between Plymouth Rock and Custer's Last Stand. This very familiarity, though, has made it something of a problem for historians. As a dramatic package, the events of 1692 are just too neat, highlighted but also insulated from serious research by the very floodlights which illuminate them. "Rebecca Nurse," "Ann Putnam," "Samuel Parris"—they all endlessly glide onto the stage, play their appointed scenes, and disappear again into the void. It is no coincidence that the Salem witch trials are best known today through the work of a playwright, not a historian. It was, after all, a series of historians from George Bancroft to Marion Starkey who first treated the event as a dramatic set piece, unconnected with the major issues of American colonial history. When Arthur Miller published *The Crucible* in the early 1950's, he simply outdid the historians at their own game.

From Paul Boyer and Stephen Nissenbaum, *Salem Possessed: The Social Origins of Witchcraft* (Cambridge: Harvard University Press, 1974), 22–30. © 1974 by the President and Fellows of Harvard College. Reprinted by permission of the publisher.

After nearly three centuries of retelling in history books, poems, stories, and plays, the whole affair has taken on a foreordained quality. It is hard to conceive that the events of 1692 could have gone in any other direction or led to any other outcome. It is like imagining the *Mayflower* sinking in midpassage, or General Custer at the Little Big Horn surrendering to Sitting Bull without a fight.

And yet speculation as to where events might have led in 1692 is one way of recapturing the import of where they did lead. And if one reconstructs those events bit by bit, as they happened, without too quickly categorizing them, it is striking how long they resist settling into the neat and familiar pattern one expects. A full month, maybe more, elapsed between the time the girls began to exhibit strange behavior and the point at which the first accusations of witchcraft were made; and in the haze of those first uncertain weeks, it is possible to discern the shadows of what might have been.

Bewitchment and Conversion

Imagine, for instance, how easily the finger of witchcraft could have been pointed back at the afflicted girls themselves. It was they, after all, who first began to toy with the supernatural. At least one neighboring minister, the Reverend John Hale of Beverly, eventually became convinced that a large measure of blame rested with these girls who, in their "vain curiosity to know their future condition," had "tampered with the devil's tools." And Hale's judgment in the matter was shared by his far more influential colleague Cotton Mather, who pinpointed as the cause of the outbreak the "conjurations" of thoughtless youths, including, of course, the suffering girls themselves.

Why then, during 1692, were the girls so consistently treated as innocent victims? Why were they not, at the very least, chastised for behavior which itself verged on witchcraft? Clearly, the decisive factor was the interpretation which adults—adults who had the power to make their interpretation stick—chose to place on events whose intrinsic meaning was, to begin with, dangerously ambiguous.

The adults, indeed, determined not only the direction the witchcraft accusations would take; it was they, it seems, who first concluded that witchcraft was even in the picture at all. "[W]hen these calamities first began," reported Samuel Parris in March 1692, ". . . the affliction was several weeks before such hellish operations as witchcraft was suspected." Only in response to urgent questioning—"Who is it that afflicts you?"—did the girls at last begin to point their fingers at others in the Village. . . .

Had Samuel Parris and his parishioners chosen to place a different interpretation on it, the "witchcraft episode" might have taken an entirely different form. This, in fact, is what almost happened, miles away from Salem Village, in another witchcraft case of 1692: that of Mercy Short. Mercy was a seventeen-year-old Boston servant girl who in June 1692 was sent by her mistress on an errand to the Boston town jail, where many accused Salem witches happened to be held pending their trials. When one of them, Sarah Good, asked Mercy for tobacco, the girl, belying her name, threw a handful of wood shavings in the prisoner's face and cried: "That's tobacco good enough for you!" Soon after, Mercy Short began to exhibit the strange physical behavior that people had by now come to think of as proof of bewitchment. Cotton Mather, as her minister, was interested in Mercy's case from the beginning, and through the winter of 1692–93 he spent much time with her, offering spiritual counsel and maintaining a detailed record of her behavior. Mather's notes make clear that what Mercy experienced was far from unmitigated torment. At times, in fact, "[h]er tortures were turned into frolics, and she became as extravagant as a wildcat," her speech "excessively witty" and far beyond her "ordinary capacity." On other occasions, she delivered long religious homilies and moral exhortations.

Although it was generally agreed that Mercy was bewitched, what is interesting is that Mather directed the episode into quite another channel. He treated it not as an occasion for securing witchcraft accusations but as an opportunity for the religious edification of the community. As word of Mercy's condition spread, her room became a gathering place, first for pious members of Mather's congregation and then for local young people. These boys and girls, who had already organized weekly prayer services apart from the adults, "now adjourned their meetings . . . unto the Haunted Chamber." With Mather's encouragement, as many as fifty of them would crowd into the room, praying and singing psalms (sometimes until dawn) and occasionally themselves displaying unusual physical manifestations. At one point during the winter of 1692–93 they assembled every night for nearly a month.

The entire Mercy Short episode, in fact, suggests nothing so much as the early stages of what would become, a generation later, a looming feature of the American social landscape: a religious revival. Mather himself made the point: "[T]he souls of many, especially of the rising generation," he wrote, "have been thereby awakened unto some acquaintance with religion." Nor was this "awakening" simply a Matherian conceit; in his diary the minister recorded that "some scores of young people" (including Mercy herself) had joined his church after being "awakened by the picture of Hell exhibited in her sufferings." Such a mass movement toward church membership, coming on a tide of shared religious experiences, had been almost unknown up to that time in New England and indicates how close the town of Boston may have been, that winter of 1692–93, to a full-scale revival.

When viewed not simply as freakish final splutters in the centuries-old cycle of witchcraft alarms, but as overtures to the revival movement, both the Boston and the Salem Village episodes emerge in a fresh light and take on a new interest. With a slight shift in the mix of social ingredients, both communities could have fostered scenes of mass religious questing in 1692. In Salem Village, the afflicted girls occasionally displayed an inclination to ascribe their supernatural visitations to a divine rather than a demonic source. On April 1, according to Deodat Lawson's first-hand account, Mercy Lewis "saw in her fit a white man, and [she] was with him in a glorious place, which had no candles nor sun, yet was full of light and brightness, where was a great multitude in white glittering robes." Similar heavenly visions, Lawson noted, appeared to the other girls as well. And as for the "foolish, ridiculous speeches which neither they themselves nor any others could understand," do they not suggest, in inchoate form, the Pentecostal gift of tongues which would figure so prominently in later revival outbreaks?

Even the more obviously painful symptoms which the girls manifested in their "fits"—the convulsive paroxysms, the hysterical muscular spasms—foreshadow the characteristic behavior of "sinners" in the agonizing throes of conversion. How would the girls have responded if their ministers, their neighbors, or their families had interpreted their behavior as the initial stages of a hopeful religious awakening?

The parallel is underscored if we turn a full 180 degrees and examine, from the perspective of 1692, the first mass outbreak of religious anxiety which actually *was* interpreted as a revival: the so-called "Little Awakening" which began in the western Massachusetts town of Northampton in 1734. Here, as in Salem Village, a group of people in the town began, unexpectedly and simultaneously, to experience conditions of extreme anxiety. They underwent "great terrors" and "distresses" which threw them into "a kind of struggle and tumult" and finally brought them to "the borders of despair." Nineteen-year-old Abigail Hutchinson felt such "exceeding terror" that "her very flesh trembled"; for others the terror took such vivid forms as that of a "dreadful furnace" yawning before their eyes. Even a four-year-old girl, Phebe Bartlet, took to secreting herself in a closet for long periods each day, weeping and moaning.

As in Salem Village, some people of Northampton began to whisper ominously that "certain distempers" were in the air. The town soon became the talk and concern of the entire province, and there were even those who spoke of witchcraft. And, again as in Salem Village, the episode eventually culminated in violent death: not executions, this time, but suicide. On Sunday, June 1, 1735, after two months of terror and sleepless nights, Joseph Hawley slit his throat and died. In the wake of this event many other persons were tempted to the same course, impelled by voices which urged: *"Cut your own throat, now is a good opportunity.* Now! Now!"

In Northampton in 1735 as in Salem Village a generation earlier, the young played a central role. In both episodes, the catalyst was a group of young people who had taken to spending long hours together, away from their homes. In Salem Village, these gatherings began as fortune-telling sessions and soon took a scary turn; in Northampton, they started as "frolics" but were soon transformed, under the influence of the town's young minister, Jonathan Edwards (later to become the greatest theologian of his era), into occasions for prayer and worship. In both places, too, the preoccupations of these youthful meetings soon spread to the community as a whole, and became the overriding topic of conversation. In Salem Village, the afflicted girls dominated the packed gatherings where the accused were examined. In Northampton, church services and household routines alike were disrupted by crying and weeping, again with the younger generation taking the lead.

In a reversal of status as breathtaking in 1735 as it had been in 1692, the young people of both Northampton and Salem Village at least momentarily broke out of their "normal" subservient and deferential social role to become the *de facto* leaders of the town and (for many, at least) the unchallenged source of moral authority.

Nor were the young the only group whose social position was temporarily altered by the traumatic episodes they had helped engender. The ministers, too, were profoundly affected. In Salem Village, it was to Samuel Parris—who had been experiencing difficulty in filling the Village meetinghouse for weekly worship and even in persuading the congregation to pay his salary—that most Villagers turned during 1692 for an understanding of what was happening. In Northampton, where Jonathan Edwards (the author of the account from which we have been quoting) had been going through comparable difficulties, attendance and involvement in the public worship also picked up noticeably, with "every hearer eager to drink in the words of the minister as they came from his mouth." Even on weekdays, Edwards received unaccustomed attention: "the place of resort was now altered, it was no longer the tavern, but the minister's house."

By encouraging and even exploiting the unusual behavior of the young people in their communities, both ministers had managed to turn a potentially damaging situation to their own benefit. Both drew upon the energies, ostensibly disruptive and anti-authoritarian, of a hitherto subdued and amorphous segment of the population to shore up their own precarious leadership. In each case, the effort was dramatically successful—but only for a time; as it turned out, Parris and Edwards were both dismissed from their jobs only a few years after the events they had done so much to encourage.

But the differences are as significant as the similarities, for when all is said and done, the fact remains that Northampton experienced not a witchcraft outbreak, but a religious revival. With the backing of his congregation, Edwards chose to interpret the entire episode not as demonic, but as a "remarkable pouring out of the spirit of God." Under his guidance, most of the sufferers passed through their terrors to a "calm of spirit" and the "joyful surprise" of discovering Christ afresh "in some of his sweet and glorious attributes." Little Phebe Bartlet emerged from the closet to become a spiritual mentor to her playmates and her family. When a neighbor reported the mysterious disappearance of a cow, Phebe emotionally bade her father show a Christ-like spirit and give the man a cow from his own herd. (In Salem Village in 1692, such a mischance would surely have produced an accusation of witchcraft.) . . .

Why is it that Northampton in 1735 ranks in American history as a prelude to what would become known as the Great Awakening rather than being bracketed with Salem Village as the scene of an anachronistic outbreak of witchcraft hysteria? The crucial difference between the two episodes is the interpretation which the adult leadership of each community placed upon physical and emotional states which in themselves were strikingly similar. In Northampton they were viewed in a divine and hopeful light; in Salem Village they were seized upon as sinister and demonic. While the "afflicted girls" of 1692 often showed signs of shifting their fantasies to Christ, describing angelic messengers and glorious visions, their cues were not "picked up" by the adults, and the girls invariably lapsed back into reports of agonies and sufferings.

In each of these communities, in other words, the behavior of groups of young people (whatever may have produced it) served as a kind of Rorschach test into which adults read their own concerns and expectations.

[64]

The Invisible World at the Vanishing Point

RICHARD WEISMAN

Richard Weisman's work was introduced in part 1. In this additional excerpt from Witchcraft, Magic, and Religion in Seventeenth-Century Massachusetts *(1984), Weisman explores the persistence of witchcraft beliefs after the courts ceased prosecuting witchcraft as a crime.*

•

Certainly, by 1697, there were few inhabitants of Massachusetts Bay who would have challenged the claim that errors had been committed during the Salem trials. Far more controversial was the question of what errors had been committed. For some members, it was enough merely to note the consequences of judicial action. As the bill of October 26, 1692, had stated, the trials had resulted in the indictment and arrest of an extraordinarily large number of persons, many of whom were individuals of exemplary piety. Accordingly, the number and quality of the defendants were proof in themselves that mistakes had been made. More often, members pointed to the judicial reliance on spectral evidence. For some critics, the magistrates had violated the theological recommendations on the use of such testimony; for others, the court had confounded afflictions with possessions. In general, however, the tendency of contemporary postmortems was to rescue witchcraft from the Salem trials by conceiving of the errors of the Court of Oyer and Terminer as specific to the events of 1692 rather than as applicable to all witchfinding activities.

For Hale, the problem of error was more complex. He himself had been one of the most active supporters of witchcraft prosecutions among the clergy, and he had not offered this support on the basis of spectral evidence alone. The problem posed by the Salem trials was not that the rules of evidence were treated lightly but rather that they had been taken so seriously. The Court of Oyer and Terminer had organized the most cautiously empirical and systematic investigation into witchcraft ever to occur in New England. In addition to collecting spectral evidences as well as allega-

From Richard Weisman, *Witchcraft, Magic, and Religion in seventeenth-Century Massachusetts.* (Amherst: University of Massachusetts Press, 1984), 179–83. © 1984 by the University of Massachusetts Press. Reprinted by permission of the publisher.

tions of malefic harm, the magistrates had conducted searches for witch's marks, puppets, and special healing potions. Moreover, they had gathered testimony from confessed witches who implicated other suspects. They had even conducted experiments in the courtroom in order that the devil might reveal his confederates before witnesses.

The cumulative effect of this testimony was to corroborate in detail the magistrates' version of conspiracy. Indeed, during the trials, one of the best educated of the defendants, George Burroughs, conceded that the testimony against him was convictive in view of the fact that eight confessed witches had identified him as their leader. Since he nevertheless claimed he was innocent because his accusers were false witnesses, Hale proceeded to question one of the confessors who had named him. She stood by her account even after Hale had urged her to reconsider her statement while Burroughs was still alive.

As Hale understood it, the Salem trials constituted a faithful and valid application of approved theological recommendations for the discovery of witchcraft. The failure of the Salem trials was the failure of a paradigm. . . . That the identifications of the Court of Oyer and Terminer were in error was an anomaly that could not be explained in terms of the principles embodied either in earlier legal actions against witchcraft or in authoritative texts for the discovery of witchcraft. If the Salem trials had been based upon mistaken assumptions, then so also were the prosecutions against Margaret Jones, Ann Hibbins, and others in which an earlier generation of New England divines had participated. If the policies followed by the Court of Oyer, and Terminer were ill advised, then so also were the recommendations of Richard Bernard, Richard Baxter, and other revered authorities on witchcraft. For Hale, an acknowledgment of the errors of the Salem trials entailed an acknowledgment of past errors as well: "May we not say in this matter . . . We have sinned with our fathers?" . . .

Symptomatic of the altered epistemological status of witchcraft was a proposal for the recording of special providences, signed by eight leading ministers on March 5, 1695. The reasons for this undertaking were the same as those given in Increase Mather's earlier proposal of 1681: to help demonstrate the existence and agency of the invisible world. This time, however, there was a significant deletion in the list of unusual occurrences about which information was to be gathered. No mention was made of witchcraft. In this act of omission, the clergy tacitly acknowledged that witchcraft no longer had a place within orthodox doctrine. In the future, New England divines would look to other signs for the presence of God.

The Decline of Witchcraft Prosecutions

For all its apparent suddenness, the decline of witchcraft prosecutions after the Salem trials involved no marked discontinuities with the past. Apart from the events of 1692, popular allegations had formed the primary basis for legal action against witchcraft, and these testimonies had ceased to carry convictive weight after the last execution in 1656. Furthermore, though allegations of maleficia were included among the evidences gathered by the Court of Oyer and Terminer, there is no reason to believe that they were regarded with greater seriousness in 1692 than in the earlier prosecutions. Now, in the light of a further separation between popular and theological understandings of the problem of witchcraft and in view of the new rules of evidence, witchcraft soon disappeared entirely from the legal records of Massachusetts Bay. Within two years after the Salem trials, witchcraft was no longer an actionable legal offense.

The final case to be recorded, that of Mary Watkins, well demonstrates that, by 1693, the legal possibilities for witchcraft as a valid form of deviant imputation had been exhausted. Mary, a Boston servant, confessed to witchcraft shortly after failing in an attempt at suicide. She was brought before a magistrate, and a bill of indictment was presented to the grand jury of the Superior Court of Judicature on April 25, 1693. The jury refused the bill in spite of the confession. This time, when asked by the magistrates to reconsider their verdict, the jurors maintained their original finding of ignoramus. Although the grounds for the decision are not mentioned, it is likely that the defendant was judged to be distracted and therefore not competent to offer credible testimony. This possibility notwithstanding, the case of Mary Watkins was an indication that, after the Salem trials, not even voluntary confessions would be accepted as proof of witchcraft.

The decline of witchcraft prosecutions by no means coincided with the decline of witchcraft accusations. Despite official and ecclesiastical discouragement, villagers continued to believe in the efficacy of malefic witchcraft until well into the eighteenth century. Indeed, fragmentary records indicate that, even without the benefit of legal authority, witchcraft allegations remained an effective weapon against suspected adversaries. An account in 1728 by a Massachusetts minister, the Reverend Mr. Turell of Medford, furnishes a detailed description of the local response in a small community in 1720 to three children believed to be afflicted. The report makes clear that the children and their supporters were able to mobilize local opinion against the woman whom they identified as responsible for their condition. And, in the town of Colchester in neighboring Connecticut in 1724, one woman regarded the suspicions against her with sufficient seriousness to sue her accusers for 500 pounds in damages.

At the same time, the outcome of these events suggests that if, in certain communities, popular beliefs in mystical harm had not changed greatly in the thirty years since the Salem trials, the response of civil and ecclesiastical authorities had nevertheless changed appreciably. In his narrative, Turell questioned not only the validity of the accusations but also the motives of the accusers. According to Turell, the afflictions were not genuine, they were deceitful strategies employed by the children to attract attention to themselves. Similarly, the decision rendered in the Connecticut case also reveals an inclination to view as problematic not the behavior of the accused but the perceptions of the accuser. On appeal, the complainant was awarded a nominal compensation of one shilling in damages. More significantly, the same ruling included a judgment that the defendants were not insane. In the decades following the Salem trials, public attention began to focus less on the guilt of the accused and more on the credibility of the accuser.

Ultimately, the withdrawal of legal recognition from imputations of witchcraft entailed far more than the decriminalization of a category of deviant behavior. The loss of witchcraft as an actionable offense divested contemporary theories of supernatural causation of their last remaining claim to legal authority. With the decline of witchcraft prosecutions, questions about the availability of the invisible world ceased to be a matter of practical concern for the state.

[65]

Magic, Astrology, and the Early American Religious Heritage, 1600–1760

JON BUTLER

Jon Butler, a noted historian of American religion, won the Gilbert Chinard Prize in Anglo-French history in 1983 for The Huguenots in America. *His book* Awash in a Sea of Faith: Christianizing the American People *(1990) elaborates on his study of occult practices during the colonial era and demonstrates how these popular ideas were fused with America's Christian traditions during the nineteenth century. In this excerpt from a 1979 article Butler questions the usefulness of the distinction between occult practices and the practices of traditional institutional religions.*

•

Historians have always treated America's earliest colonists as especially religious people. Some of the most distinguished scholarship in American history deals with the rise and fall of Puritanism, the religious awakenings of the colonial and early national periods, and the creation of the American evangelical style. Although impressive, these studies fail to comprehend the marrow of American religious life. They concentrate too fully, if brilliantly, on Christian theology, congregational life, and ecclesiastical polity, and they slight noninstitutional, popular religion. The low rate of church membership in the colonies reveals part of the problem. Contrary to assumptions underlying much of the work in American religious history, American colonists had an ambivalent relationship with Christian congregations. After about 1650 even in New England only about one-third of all adults ever belonged to a church. The rate was lower in the Middle and Southern colonies, and on the eve of the American Revolution only about 15 percent of all of the colonists probably belonged to any church.

Colonists also proved surprisingly ignorant of elemental Christian beliefs and practices. Naturally, clergymen worried when settlers failed to join their own sects or

From Jon Butler, "Magic, Astrology, and the Early American Religious Heritage, 1600–1760," *American Historical Review* 84 (1979): 317–20, 323–25, 334–39, 341–42, 345–46. © 1979 by the American Historical Society. Reprinted by permission of the author.

denominations. But even secular observers wondered at the number of settlers who ignored organized religious activity altogether. Colonial religious opinion embodied heterodoxy and sometimes simple, unprincipled confusion. In 1687 New York Governor Thomas Dongan wrote that settlers there usually expressed no religious sentiment at all or, when they did, entertained wildly unorthodox religious opinions. A New Jersey politician, Lewis Morris, observed in 1702 that in his colony, "except in two or three Towns, there is no face of any public worship of any sort, but people live very mean like Indians." In the 1760s the Anglican itinerant minister, Charles Woodmason, encountered Southern colonists who owned no Bibles, knew only enough about Christianity to ask that their children be baptized, and refused to join any church or support any minister. In his famous *Letters from an American Farmer* (1782), Hector St. John de Crèvecoeur remarked that in America the sects were so mixed and religious training so poor that "religious indifference is imperceptibly disseminated from one end of the continent to another, which is at present one of the strongest characteristics of the Americans."

This discrepancy between popular colonial indifference to formal religious institutions and the early American reputation for deep religiosity reveals a contradiction in traditional American religious history. Unless the early American populace is viewed as irreligious, as some observers in fact thought it was, the numbers of settlers who were ambivalent toward institutional Christianity or ignored it altogether means that descriptions of common colonial religious practice simply cannot rest on histories of churches and church-related events. To understand what many colonists meant by religion, historians need to move beyond the study of ecclesiology, theology, and the ministry to recover noninstitutional religious practices. This task is difficult. Evidence about religion that is not linked to churches is extraordinarily difficult to find. In contrast, whole libraries are devoted to the histories of Christian groups. Even partial solutions to this problem will help us better comprehend the religious behavior of the great majority of colonial Americans rather than merely that of churches, ministers, and a few select laypersons. To that end I will examine the survival of European occult or magical practices in the American colonies, especially astrology, divination, and witchcraft. For American colonists were indeed religious, but many resorted to occult and magical practices unacceptable to most Christian clergymen and lawmakers. . . .

* * *

Customarily, historians do not explain what they mean by religion. But by not setting boundaries for discussion, as happens when church history and theology are allowed to portray religious belief in the society at large, narrow forms of religion can seem to represent all possible expressions. Of course, the literature on the philosophy of religion is vast and betrays scholarly disagreement rather than consensus. Yet, whenever historians write religious history, they implicitly choose one among several conflicting conceptualizations of religion, even when they fail to discuss the problem and to admit that alternative views might have produced different results.

I will use a reasonably traditional understanding of religion. Here "religion" means the resort to superhuman powers, sometimes beings, to determine the course of human events. In daily life each particular religion formulates an understanding about the nature of those powers and provides techniques its adherents can use to gain their support, protection, or aid in mastering life's circumstances. Seventeenth- and eighteenth-century institutionalized Christianity obviously fits such a view of religion. But so, too, do numerous magical and occult arts—such as astrology, divination, and witchcraft—of the same period. Thus, magic and Christianity in colonial America were not generically different entities but were subsets of the same phenomenon—religion. They posited a resort to superhuman powers and they offered techniques for invoking those powers to control human events.

Magic and Christianity also served remarkably similar ends for their adherents. To appreciate how close their ends were, Bronislaw Malinowski's well-known model (followed by the great majority of historians of religion) that emphasizes their differences cannot stand. Malinowski treated Christianity as broad, philosophical, and ethereal and treated magic as narrow, practical, and mundane. Because these differences allegedly were so important, Malinowski insisted that Christianity was a "real" religious system but that magic was not. As the anthropologist Melford E. Spiro has pointed out, however, recent studies have failed to confirm Malinowski's assertions for nonliterate societies. Nor does it work well for seventeenth- and eighteenth- century Europe or America. In neither pre-Revolutionary America nor the modern Third World is it clear that astrology, sorcery, and divination are only mundane and practical, while Christianity triumphs as philosophical and ethereal. Thus, if we want to understand the full range of religious expression in Western culture generally and early America specifically, it is imperative that we stop calling only the Christian or Judeo-Christian tradition "religious" and that we begin looking seriously at the place of magic and the occult arts in religious history. . . .

On the eve of colonization Christianity in its different forms filled out only part of the English religious spectrum. Its adherents called on God's aid through prayer, through the intercession of the saints, or by preparing for the reign of Christ in the millennium. But occult practices comprised much of the remainder. In addition to witchcraft, these practices ranged from sophisticated arts such as astrology, chiro- mancy, geomancy, and metoposcopy (the reading of stars, palms, dots, and fore- heads) to fortunetelling and divination (both highly idiosyncratic practices found in a bewildering variety of styles). . . .

On the eve of colonization, many people in English society simply did not clearly divorce Christianity from magic, astrology, and divination. They adopted eclectic beliefs about superhuman powers and beings in their quest to understand the world and master their lives. Sometimes these beliefs incorporated Christian views, some- times they did not. Little wonder, then, that the Puritan theologian, William Perkins, argued that occult practitioners challenged Christian ministers for the spiritual alle- giance of the English public. "As the Ministers of God," he wrote, "doe give resolu- tion to the conscience, in matters doubtfull and difficult; so the Ministers of Satan, under the name of Wise-men, And Wise-women, are at hand, by his appointment, to resolve, direct and helpe ignorant and unsettled persons in cases of distraction, loss, or other outward calamities." Thirty years later, John Gaule, author of *The Mag-Astro-Mancer: or, The Magical-Astrological-Diviner Posed and Puzzled* (1652), perceived a disturbing rise in the resort to occult religious practices. In those difficult times, he wrote, neither church nor state was "at leisure to examine and suppress it." And in the same era a Puritan ministerial association in Cambridge warned the laity about spiritual imposters—not unrepentant Anglicans, as might be expected, but "witches, wizard[s], and fortune tellers."

* * *

Did occult religious practices take root in America too? Their broad distribution throughout precolonial England might suggest that they did. Yet the character of early migration to America made the arrival of the full range of English occult practices unlikely and their survival difficult. The aims of prominent colonizers militated against occult religion; few colonial ventures were led by such self-conscious, narrow Christians as were the English colonies in America. As Perry Miller has argued, even Virginia exemplified the English Puritan desire to plant Christianity everywhere. The sociology of migration also struck at certain forms of occult religion. Although the peopling of early Virginia is difficult to discuss (so many early records have been lost), immigrants to New England before 1650 came from a relatively narrow sector of the English population—the gentry, the lesser gentry, and their sons and daughters. Clearly, these people did not automatically reject occult religious practices. But their commanding dominance in the towns of New England and the virtual absence of immigrants from the poorest sectors of the English population did delay the arrival of the crudest forms of occult religion so important to the early Stuart religious experience.

Even the land militated against the occult. The English countryside abounded with places that men and women had long associated with magical happenings. By definition America lacked such places. It was a wilderness—not of itself or for the Indians who already lived there, but to its newest residents. Over many decades, nevertheless, these settlers did invest the landscape with sacred, even magical, meaning. Although the use of magic never prospered here as it had in England, a wide range of occult ideas and practices—alchemical practitioners, the availability of occult books, occult notions in colonial almanacs, and even a few self-announced cunning persons—were evident in the colonies between 1650 and 1720. . . .

* * *

What happened to the English occult tradition in early America? By most accounts it declined and died. The rise of Enlightenment philosophy, scepticism, and experimental science, the spread of evangelical Christianity, continuing opposition from English Protestant denominations, a rise in literacy closely associated with Christian catechizing, and the emergence of the colonies as modern cultural, economic, and political entities all have led historians to discount the significance of occult religious practices in the last years of the colonial period. Yet some evidence, at least, points toward their partial survival in eighteenth-century America. The astronomical information in almanacs always could be used to make astrological calculations even if the almanac-maker did not intend it to serve that purpose. On the eve of the Revolution some almanacs still printed the anatomy and listed the days when bleeding was good or bad. Occult techniques of physiognomy and chiromancy could be gleaned from at least some medical books. In America the best source was *Aristotle's Master Piece*, a book also renowned for its lurid descriptions of uncommon sexual maladies. In philosophy, a recent study by Herbert Leventhal describes the widespread survival of occult ideas among eighteenth-century intellectuals. The notion that stars influenced and at least reflected human activity still was relatively popular in the 1730s. Yale's president, Ezra Stiles, and a southern surveyor and botanist, John W. G. DeBrahm, rediscovered alchemy after it had virtually died out elsewhere. Through a phenomenon called "rattlesnake gazing" colonists even added to the occult beliefs they had brought to America from Europe. The snake allegedly overpowered humans with its eyes, and the elaboration of this concept in pre-Revolutionary America testifies to the perseverance of a specifically occult concept of the unity of man, animals, and nature and, hence, to the ability of one to manipulate the other.

Even fear of witchcraft continued. True, the Salem episode of 1691–92 produced not only the last witch executions in the English-speaking world but also many denunciations of the beliefs that produced them. Yet in 1705 two Virginia juries examined Grace Sherwood for witches' marks. They reported that her body was "not like them nor noe other woman that they knew of, haveing two things like titts on her private parts." When the court subjected her to the infamous dunking test, she unfortunately swam ("Contrary to Custom") and she was therefore bound over for trial on charges of witchcraft. Her fate, however, remains unknown because the court's records have been lost. A year later in 1706 the chief justice of South Carolina, Nicholas Trott, delivered an impressive charge to a Charleston grand jury imploring it to prosecute witches. He refuted attacks made on the prosecution of witches by two English writers, Reginald Scot and John Webster, and backed his own demand for such prosecutions with quotations from early Church fathers and Cotton Mather.

South Carolina also furnished the only known manuscript of occult cures to survive from seventeenth- and eighteenth-century America, the so-called Joshua Gordon "Witchcraft Book" in the South Caroliniana Library, University of South Carolina, Columbia. Nothing is known about its compiler. But whoever he was, he took great care to make a ritual-like arrangement of its contents. Two pages of the kind of charms common to the English occult tradition open and close the volume. On the first page the phrase "Behold him Seized Malicously [Abused]" appears seven times to fill the page. On the second page the phrase "Your Saviour Sweeting Blood [wch is yours]" is written nine times to fill the page. The phrases appear to link the pharisees' seizure of Christ to the Devil's seizure of persons through witchcraft and the ability of men and women to redeem themselves through Christ's blood. These same phrases, again copied to fill two pages, close the manuscript.

Tucked between the ritual phrases or charms are fifteen pages of occult cures. Most of them are based on the traditional European notion of sympathetic attraction. In this formula, parts of bodies of sick or injured persons or animals are employed in rituals to solicit sympathetic healing in the same animal or person. Thus, Gordon's manuscript gives remedies using animal feces and human urine to cure "old soars" and rheumatism, to preserve cattle from witchcraft and other mysterious disorders, and to reveal those who intended harm. The remedies for warding off malevolent individuals follow English and early colonial tradition in assuming that these persons are neighbors in the local community. Thus, the compiler warns, "you must not lend any manner of thing off for the Space of 3 Days [from] your plantation. The person or persons guilty will assuredly come wanting to Borrow something But by no means Lend; otherwise, you lay open a gain to thir malies [i.e., malice], which will be more desperate then Before." One cure-"An Indian cure for the reipture [i.e., rupture] in children"—crossed cultural boundaries. Several cures linked occult rituals to Christianity. "A Cuar for gun that is Speld," for example, required the frustrated hunter to "lod your gun in the name of the father, Son, and holy ghost and put the point of the tung [of a dead deer] down next the powder . . . and when you discharge your gun do it in the name of the father, son, and holy gost." A cow losing milk could be cured if its owners would "take a heather belonging to a box Iron, put it in the fire, and make it Red hot [and then] take the milk of the cows thats hurt [and] power [i.e., pour] on the hot iron repeating the names of the blessed trinity."

Still, most evidence suggests that occult practices only survived idiosyncratically in pre-Revolutionary America. The library lists in the estate inventories of eighteenth-century Virginia, including the largest libraries like that of Robert "King" Carter, contain almost no occult books. Although basic astrological information still appeared in almanacs, after about 1720 no almanac-makers promoted sophisticated occult ideas as Pennsylvania's Daniel Leeds and Jacob Taylor had done earlier. Rather, they developed a cynical ambivalence toward occult practices. Nathaniel Ames of Massachusetts, for example, vacillated frequently on the question of predicting the future. His warning to readers about wise men simultaneously supported and condemned their art. "Observe it you may," Ames wrote in his 1752 almanac, "that Cunning Men are not always honest: trust them as you have tried them."

A change in intellectual climate often reflects shifts in the sociology of belief more accurately than it does the complete disappearance of old ideas; typically, only certain social classes or groups, usually the educated elite, reject once-popular notions, while many others, usually the less educated, continue to accept them. The history of European and American witchcraft beliefs illustrates this phenomenon. In seventeenth-century Europe magistrates became increasingly reluctant to convict accused witches. That same reluctance finally became evident in America as well. No one was convicted of practicing witchcraft in Massachusetts after the Salem trials of 1692. In South Carolina a year after Nicholas Trott urged grand juries to prosecute witches a witchcraft indictment was "returned Ignoramus." The rebuff made a local Anglican clergyman, if not the accused, "stand amazed that the Spirit of the Devil should be so much respected as to make men call open Witchcraft Imagination and no more."

Yet witchcraft beliefs continued to play important roles in other colonial settings. Colonists circumscribed their opinions, using witchcraft beliefs to manipulate local affairs while keeping them out of colonial courts. The experience of John Craig, a

Scottish Presbyterian minister, in 1745 provides an example. After settling in Augusta County, Virginia, in 1740, Craig found the community divided by bitter quarrels of the kind that had distinguished witchcraft settings a century earlier. Craig's status and occupation soon drew him into these quarrels. In the midst of the dispute, his wife became seriously ill during her first pregnancy. As a midwife delivered her child, Craig began to hallucinate. He dreamed that he hated his wife and the midwife, although he "knew not from what reason or cause." Four months later the infant died. Finally, Craig's cattle and horses died too. His livestock suffered from a disease contracted only by his cattle, although animals owned by neighbors that had been penned in the same quarters remained healthy.

Craig suspected witchcraft in the animal deaths. But he refused to make his opinion public, since he was convinced that the "Divel had higher Designe than to kill Brutes." Nor did he blame witches for his wife's sickness or his child's death. Later, however, Craig apparently named the persons he believed responsible for poisoning his animals. Now his enemies accused Craig of resorting to occult practices. They said he "used Charms and named Neighbors as the instruments of my loss," meaning that he had used occult techniques to secure the names of his transgressors. Yet neither Craig nor his antagonists pursued their accusations in the courts, even though to do so was still legally possible in Virginia. Instead, they allowed their belief in witchcraft to shape local affairs but kept them away from unsympathetic magistrates.

At the end of the colonial period, Yale's Ezra Stiles assessed the occult practices that still existed in the colonies as only minor survivals of a more active occult era. "Something of it subsists among some Almanac makers and fortune tellers." He found two of the latter in New England—a man in Tiverton, Massachusetts, who cast horoscopes and located lost objects for seamen, and a woman in Newport, Rhode Island, who made urine cakes for use in divining. But these practitioners illustrated the decline of earlier occult practices: "in general the System is broken up, the Vessel of Sorcery ship-wreckt, and only some shattered planks and pieces disjoyned floating and scattered on the Ocean of . . . human Activity and Bustle." Stiles's judgment was accurate even in its metaphors, because part of the evidence pointing to the survival of astrology in the colonies comes from its popularity among seamen and ship captains who consulted practitioners like the man Stiles [described from] Tiverton.

*   *   *

Explaining why occult religious practices declined in America is difficult. The explanations historians have given for Europe do not work well even there. Alan Macfarlane has traced the erosion of accusations of witchcraft in England to the triumph of the market economy. The new emphasis on monetary gain rather than village cohesion simply destroyed the neighborly intimacy in which witchcraft, and perhaps all of the occult arts, prospered. Keith Thomas has argued that the decline stemmed from the rise of more modern medicine and the expansion of technology. Yet historians disagree vociferously about the real impact of the market economy and the effectivness of the new medicine. In addition, the technology Thomas discussed is limited largely to improvements in newspaper printing and distribution. Since the social significance of this technology is diminished by the continuing low rate of literacy in eighteenth-century England, it remains difficult to explain why occult religious practices disappeared there, especially among the large poor and illiterate populace, a criticism that also applies to the once-popular idea that a "scientific revolution" among English intellectuals erased occult ideas from England itself. By reviewing the situation in America, however, we can delineate alternative causes that brought about the disappearance of occult religious practices in pre-Revolutionary America and, perhaps, Europe as well.

One important cause of the decline of occult religious practices was a change in the literary taste of England's educated elite, leading to an increasing scarcity of occult reading materials in America. After 1700 works in Hermeticism, Rosicrucianism, alchemy, geomancy, and chiromancy simply were not published in England. The number of occult and astrologically based medical works declined drastically. The seventeenth-century authors of such works either changed their minds or died without leaving successors to continue their work. Colonists who hoped to sustain their occult convictions through reading had to collect out-of-print titles published in the previous century. Otherwise, they had little to peruse except Christian publications. . . .

Evangelical Christianity of the kind spread in the eighteenth-century colonial awakenings may have challenged occult religion directly. To be sure, no conversion of an adept in magic was recorded in the literature of the awakening. But the ritual forms of evangelical Christianity and occult religion paralleled each other in striking ways. In the English occult tradition, cunning persons, wise men, and astrologers manipulated ritual processes of doubt, inquiry, and resolutions to solve problems and gain clients. Clients came to them with perplexing problems. The wise man quizzed the client about his birth, personal habits, background, and recent disputes, then used geomancy, chiromancy, metoposcopy, horoscopes, or divination to effect cures for diseases, suggest the way to financial success, or locate the places where lost horses might be found. Parallel processes characterized colonial Christian awakenings. As in meetings with cunning persons, settlers approached Christian evangelists with numerous fears, doubts, and problems. Awakening ministers reshaped these problems to suit Christian answers. They insisted that the settlers' real concern was salvation. Then, in simple sermons on elemental Christian doctrine, they began resolving those problems by explaining Christian faith. If listeners panicked when they discovered that their own salvation was in doubt, the panic increased the clergyman's authority, since he claimed that only the Christian God knew the future and controlled the world. Although we still do not quite know why American colonists endured this torment, most available evidence suggests that they thoroughly relished it. Colonists went to hear awakening evangelists like George Whitefield and with them enacted the ritual of doubt, inquiry, and resolution typical of those meetings again and again.

The Calvinism of the colonial awakenings also paralleled important occult ideas.

The fatalism inherent in Calvinism's concept of predestination found an occult equivalent in the idea fundamental to astrology that motions of stars and planets revealed a future that individuals could not control. Calvinist evangelists and occult practitioners also explained catastrophes in similar ways. Believers in occult ideas thought the coming of comets and eclipses had inescapable and usually disastrous consequences; not even kings and queens escaped their verdicts. No one escaped judgment by the Calvinist God either. Sometimes He damned seemingly model Christians simply to demonstrate His sovereignty. . . .

The decline of the English occult tradition in the colonies should not, however, be taken as proof that occult practices were no more than fascinatingly aberrant features of America's religious heritage. Rather, their earlier presence in the colonies should lure us into exploring a broad range of non-Christian and quasi-Christian religious practices, the history of which in America remains almost wholly unwritten. Despite their general decline in the colonies, at least a few survived into the nineteenth century. This was especially true in the rural South and in German-speaking portions of Pennsylvania. The emphasis on healing that Cotton Mather believed accounted for the colonial wise man's success remained strong as America entered the industrial age. Some Christian groups promoted healing anew, while patent medicines, healing therapies, and pseudo-sciences like phrenology gave it secular expression. The occult even may have been reinforced by early scientific medicine, whose claim to success usually outdistanced achievement. The law also continued to penalize occult practices. Here a study of modern spiritualism is especially relevant. Although religious historians have usually argued that coercion cannot destroy religious belief, an anthropologist, Irving Zaretsky, has disputed this claim. His study of San Francisco spiritualist churches in the 1960s demonstrates that simple fear of arrest among spiritualist ministers shaped their religious language and basic beliefs, even though actual police harassment seldom occurred. Elsewhere, the relationship between occult practice and Christian belief among laypersons may have been creative rather than hostile, despite opposition from mainstream denominational leaders. The formal Spiritualist movement of the antebellum North had strong roots in the Unitarian movement. In the nineteenth-century South, evangelicalism and occultism flourished side by side among both whites and blacks.

In this regard an observation by Thomas Wentworth Higginson, a nineteenth-century Unitarian turned Spiritualist, is especially apt. Writing on the eve of the Civil War, Higginson argued that lay religious opinion spilled far beyond the perimeters of the familiar denominational creeds. "When the minister of a cold, conservative church preaches his last closing climax of sermons against spiritualism, he little knows that of the church membership who sit patiently beneath him, more than one half are spiritualists already in their hearts." In his time Higginson meant to ridicule the shallowness of religious commitment and behavior in mainstream Christian groups. In our time, despite exaggeration, his words should act as a formidable challenge to explore all facets of an American religious heritage that extends far beyond the great denominations, churches, ministers, and a few prestigious laypersons.

Afterword

No one was executed for the crime of witchcraft in Massachusetts after 1692 in spite of the fact that the 1604 English witchcraft law remained in effect for another forty-four years. The General Court confirmed the practices in use after 1692 by declaring in 1703 that spectral evidence could not be used in future felony trials. The English Parliament finally put its stamp of approval on what had become a fact of life in that country and its colonies and repealed the older witchcraft law in 1736. The new parliamentary legislation recognized as a fact the use of occult practices, but witchcraft no longer carried the death penalty. Witches were not to be prosecuted for the mere act of an occult ritual. The authorities worried more about fraud than magic itself.

In the meanwhile Salem Village finally reached the goal of autonomy in 1752 and became a separate town calling itself Danvers. If the people in that town hoped that a change of name would erase the memory of the 1692 terror, it has not been a completely successful move. Witchcraft and witch hunts are still associated with that part of Massachusetts and Salem in particular. Salem Town retained its name and has become the rallying point for modern-day witch movements and a tourist attraction even if the major events did not occur there. To find the site of the Salem hysteria or the foundation of Samuel Parris's house, one has to go to Danvers.

Witch hunts certainly did not end with the Salem fiasco. If not in the British empire, witchcraft trials and executions continued on the Continent throughout the eighteenth century. In the English-speaking world the folk, even without official sanction, resorted to countermagic or vigilante methods (including occasional lynchings) to root out suspected evildoers. Fear of magic's evil effects as well as confidence in its usefulness lives on in many forms. As long as people believe that it is possible to manipulate occult forces, the power of suggestion will maintain the effectiveness of magical practices. But in most places in the Atlantic world official action against such magical traditions is no longer a factor.

The change in the British empire cannot be connected to the Salem events directly, and is due most likely to a more tolerant climate of opinion that was beginning to influence the entire Western society. The boundaries of deviant behavior were shifted outward. Changes in religious sentiments not only allowed for the anxiety accompanying the conversion experience but made room for emotional outbursts, as happened first during the Great Awakening of the 1730s and 1740s and continues in modern revivals. New provisions for the poor made them less dependent on neighborly charity, less likely to arouse guilt feelings in those who denied them assistance. The philosophical trends of the Enlightenment that emphasized the mechanistic nature of the universe undercut much of the belief in mysteries and mysticism that supported notions about witchcraft and occult happenings.

In the context of human history, the Salem events attract more attention than they seem to deserve. They affected only a small number of people, took place over a very short period of time, and brought on no major social or political changes. Nonetheless, fascination with the details, causes, and consequences of the witch hunt seems to have no end. The continuing interest in the Salem witch hunt attests to the power of its legacy as a metaphor for persecution. It stands as a symbol of man's inhumanity to others, human intolerance, and the dangers of displaced aggressive impulses. Each generation looks anew at Salem for lessons of the past as well as predictions for the future.

The witch, however, as a practitioner of ritual magic, is no longer an official scapegoat for social ills. European societies in particular have found other categories of people to blame. The nineteenth and twentieth centuries created new types of scapegoats based on ethnic or religious heritage or political ideology. It remains to be seen how the twenty-first century will define its demons.

Bibliographic Note

The literature on witchcraft is extensive and continuously expanding. This bibliography is highly selective and arranged by topic so that the curious reader can find additional sources of information on subjects of particular interest. The listing is not intended to be exhaustive, and with a few exceptions, material noted earlier in this reader is not repeated.

I. Christian Perspectives on Witchcraft in Europe and North America
A good, short overview of the European setting behind the witch hunts is Brian P. Levack, *The Witch-Hunt in Early Modern Europe*, 2d ed. (New York, 1995). See also Anne L. Barstow, *Witchcraze: A New History of the European Witch Hunts* (New York, 1994); Jeffrey Barton Russell, *Witchcraft in the Middle Ages* (Ithaca, 1972); and Bengt Ankerloo and Gustav Henningsen, eds., *Early Modern European Witchcraft: Centres and Peripheries* (Oxford, 1990). An older but still useful discussions is H. P. Trevor-Roper, ed., *The European Witch-Craze of the Sixteenth and Seventeenth Centuries and Other Essays* (New York, 1969).

For studies of particular countries and locales on the Continent, see H. C. Erik Midelfort, *Witch Hunting in Southwestern Germany, 1562–1684: The Social and Intellectual Foundations* (Stanford, 1972); E. William Monter, *Witchcraft in France and Switzerland: The Borderlands during the Reformation* (Ithaca, 1976); Gustav Henningsen, *The Witches' Advocate: Basque Witchcraft and the Spanish Inquisition, 1609–1614*, trans. Ann Born (Reno, NV, 1980). Brian P. Levack, ed., *Witch-Hunting in Continental Europe: Local and Regional Studies* (New York, 1992) includes articles culled from various journals.

On England, see Wallace Notestein, *A History of Witchcraft in England* (Washington, 1911), which has a great deal of information. Alan Macfarlane, *Witchcraft in Tudor and Stuart England* (London, 1970), is one of the earliest studies to apply anthropological theory to the study of witchcraft. For information on the English witch finder, see Richard Deacon, *Matthew Hopkins: Witch-Finder General* (London, 1976).

Other relevant works on witchcraft and Christian theology include Elaine Pagels, *The Origin of Satan* (New York, 1995); Jeffrey Burton Russell, *Satan: The Early Christian Tradition* (Ithaca, 1981); and Andrew Delbanco, *Death of Satan: How Americans Have Lost the Sense of Evil* (New York, 1995). For analyses of witchcraft tracts, including some reprinted in this reader, see Sydney Anglo, ed, *The Damned Art: Essays in the Literature of Witchcraft* (London, 1977).

There is a vast literature on Puritan thought that can help to clarify their ideas about the devil and witchcraft. For a more general overview, see Francis J. Bremer, *The Puritan Experiment: New England Society from Bradford to Edwards*, rev. ed. (Hanover, NH, 1995); and the older but most solid work by Perry Miller, *The New England Mind: From Colony to Province* (Cambridge, MA, 1953). Other studies of Puritanism that focus on particular aspects of religious development related to the concept of the witch include Jon Butler, *Awash in a Sea of Faith: Christianizing the American People* (Cambridge, 1990); Charles Lloyd Cohen, *God's Caress: The Psychology of Puritan Religious Experience* (New York, 1986); and Richard P. Gildrie, *The Profane, the Civil, and the Godly: The Reformation of Manners in Orthodox New England, 1679–1749* (University Park, PA, 1994). For the sociological perspective, see Kai Erikson, *Wayward Puritans: A Study in the Sociology of Deviance* (New York, 1966).

Several documentary collections are available for information on both the ideology of witchcraft and individual trials and episodes in Europe. Among the most extensive is the material collected by Charles Lea and edited by Charles Howland, *Materials toward a History of Witchcraft*, 3 vols. (London, 1953). More recently Alan C. Kors and Edward Peters edited *Witchcraft in Europe, 1100–1700: A Documentary History* (Philadelphia, 1972); and Barbara Rosen, ed., updated her 1969 *Witchcraft in England, 1558–1618* (Amherst, MA, 1991).

II. Non-Christian Beliefs

A good reference source of information on folklore and the use of magic in Europe is Lynn Thorndike, *History of Magic and Experimental Science*, 8 vols. (New York, 1923–58). Montague Summers prepared several collections of stories about witchcraft, satanism, sorcerers, and accounts of possession. Two of them are *The History of Witchcraft and Demonology* (London, 1926) and *The Supernatural Omnibus* (London, 1931).

Readable recent works on the folklore of magic in Europe include Valerie I. J. Flint, *Rise of Magic in Early Medieval Europe* (Princeton, 1991); Richard Kieckhefer, *Magic in the Middle Ages* (Oxford, 1989); Christina Larner, *Witchcraft and Religion: The Politics of Popular Belief* (Oxford, 1984); E. William Monter, *Ritual, Myth and Magic in Early Modern Europe* (Athens, OH, 1983). A fascinating work on a German community in the tradition of Carlo Ginzburg's analyses of Italian legends and fantasies about witches is Wolfgang Behringer, *Shaman of Oberstdorf: Chonrad Stoeckhlin and the Phantoms of the Night*, trans. H. C. Erik Midelfort (Charlottesville, VA, 1998).

One of the most readable and concise descriptions of African belief systems is John S. Mbiti, *African Religions and Philosophy* (New York, 1969). See also John Middleton and E. H. Winter, eds., *Witchcraft and Sorcery in East Africa* (London, 1963); Margaret Field, *Religion and Medicine of the Ga People* (London, 1937); and Robin Horton, *Patterns of Thought in Africa and the West: Essays on Magic, Religion, and Science* (Cambridge, 1993),

The spiritual concerns of Africans in America are explored by Joseph J. Williams, *Voodoos and Obeah: Phases of West Indian Witchcraft* (New York, 1932); Sylvia R. Frey and Betty Wood, *Come Shouting to Zion: African American Protestantism in the American South and British Caribbean to 1830* (Chapel Hill, NC 1998); Eugene D. Genovese, *Roll, Jordan, Roll: The World the Slaves Made* (New York, 1974); and Roger Bastide, *African Civilisation in the New World*, trans. Peter Green (New York, 1971).

Mary Douglas has brought together several essays on European, African, and American Indian legends and traditions regarding witches in *Witchcraft Confessions and Accusations* (London, 1970). Of particular interest, in addition to the selections included in this reader, are Peter Brown, "Sorcery, Demons, and the Rise of Christianity, from Late Antiquity into the Middle Ages," Julian Pitt-Rivers, "Spiritual Power in Central America," and R. G. Willis, "Instant Millennium: The Sociology of African Witch-Cleansing Cults." Another collection of essays is Peter Benes, ed., *Wonder of the Invisible World: 1600–1900* (Boston, 1995). Of particular interest in the Benes collection is M. Drake Patten, "African-American Spiritual Beliefs: An Archaeological Testimony from the Slave Quarter," and Robert Moss, "Missionaries and Magicians: The Jesuit Encounter with Native American Shamans on New England's Colonial Frontier."

On the American Indian belief system, see Raphael Karsten, *The Civilization of the South American Indians, with Special Reference to Magic and Religion* (London, 1926); Lawrence E. Sullivan, *Icanchu's Drum: An Orientation to Meaning in South American Religions* (New York, 1988); Clyde Kluckhohn, *Navaho Witchcraft* (1944; reprint, Boston, 1989); and Irene Silverblatt, *Moon, Sun, and Witches: Gender Ideologies and Class in Inca and Colonial Peru* (Princeton, 1987), especially chapter 9, "Cultural Defiance: The Sorcery Weapon." For a discussion of Indian medicine and the supernatural, see John Duffy, "Medicine and Medical Practices among Aboriginal American Indians," *International Record of Medicine* 171 (1958): 331–47.

On Indian-white relations and the English attitude toward Indians as devils, see Alden T. Vaughan, *Roots of American Racism: Essays in the Colonial Experience* (Oxford, 1995); James Axtell, *The European and the Indian: Essays in the Ethnohistory of Colonial North America* (Oxford, 1981); and William Kellaway, *The New England Company, 1649–1776, Missionary Society to the Indians* (London, 1961). Among the many articles on the demonization of American Indian ways is William S. Simmons, "Cultural Bias in the New England Puritan Perception of Indians," *William and Mary Quarterly* 38 (1981): 56–72; and David S. Lovejoy, "Satanizing the American Indian," *New England Quarterly* 67 (1994): 603–21.

III. Diabolical Possession

For psychological analyses of hysteria, see Ilza Veith, *Hysteria: The History of a Disease* (Chicago, 1965); and Alan Krohn, *Hysteria: The Elusive Neurosis* (New York, 1978).

On the European tradition of possession, see Carlo Ginzburg, *Ecstasies: Deciphering the Witches' Sabbath* (New York, 1991); Traugott K. Oesterreich, *Possession and Exorcism*, Trans. D. Ibberson (New York, 1974); Michael MacDonald, ed. *Witchcraft and Hysteria in Elizabethan England* (London, 1990); and D. P. Walker, ed., *Unclean Spirits: Possession and Exorcism in France and England in the Late Sixteenth and Early Seventeenth Centuries* (Philadelphia, 1981). Also of interest is I. M. Lewis, *Ecstatic Religion: An Anthropological Study of Spirit Possession and Shamanism* (Middlesex, England, 1971).

Works on shamanism include John Grim, *The Shaman* (Norman, OK, 1983); and Mircea Eliade, *Shamanism: Archaic Techniques of Ecstacy* (Princeton, 1964).

To follow up Richard Slotkins's thesis, the reader might be interested in Alden T. Vaughan and Edward W. Clarks, eds., *Puritans among the Indians: Accounts of Captivity and Redemption, 1676–1724* (Cambridge, MA, 1981); and John Demos's highly imaginative re-creation of the life of a woman captured by the Indians and who voluntarily continued to live with them, *The Unredeemed Captive: A Family Story from Early America* (New York, 1994).

IV. Gender

On the general role of women in colonial society, see especially Mary Beth Norton, *Founding Mothers and Fathers: Gendered Power and the Forming of American Society* (New York, 1996); Kathleen M. Brown, *Good Wives, Nasty Wenches and Anxious Patriarchs: Gender, Race, and Power in Colonial Virginia* (Chapel Hill NC, 1996); and Cornelia Hughes Dayton, *Women before the Bar: Gender, Law, and Society in Connecticut, 1639–1789* (Chapel Hill, NC, 1995). On the status of women in England, good sources are G. R. Quaife, *Wanton Wenches and Wayward Wives: Peasants and Illicit Sex in Early Seventeenth-Century England* (New Brunswick, NJ, 1979); and Lawrence Stone, *The Family, Sex, and Marriage in England, 1500–1800* (New York, 1977). For more on the feminine side of Puritan theological beliefs, see Amanda Porterfield, *Female Piety in Puritan New England: The Emergence of Religious Humanism* (New York, 1992).

Works that deal specifically with the gendered nature of witchcraft include Marianne Hester, *Lewd Women and Wicked Witches: A Study of the Dynamics of Male Domination* (New York, 1992); Barbara Ehrenreich and Deirdre English, *Witches, Midwives, and Nurses: A History of Women Healers* (Old Westbury, NY, 1973); Elizabeth Reis, *Damned Women: Sinners and Witches in Puritan New England*; and Lyle Koehler, *A Search for Power: The "Weaker Sex" in Seventeenth-Century New England* (Urbana, IL, 1980).

V. Salem: A Case Study of the Primary Documents

Two of the major documentary collections of material on New England witchcraft are cited in the text of this reader: George Lincoln Burr, ed., *Narratives of the Witchcraft Cases, 1648–1706* (New York, 1914) compiled commentaries on the witchcraft episodes, and Paul Boyer and Stephen Nissenbaum, eds., brought together most of the legal records relating to Salem in *Salem Witchcraft Papers: Verbatim Transcripts of the Legal Documents*, 3 vols. (New York 1977). Their material was originally compiled and transcribed in 1938 by the Works Progress Administration from the Essex County (Massachusetts) Archives in Salem. The older collection by W. Elliot Woodward, ed., *Records of Salem Witchcraft Copied from the Original Documents* (1864) is still useful. There are more recent compilations that include a broader range of material on witchcraft in Massachusetts. Of special interest is David Hall, ed., *Witch-Hunting in Seventeenth Century New England: A Documentary Collection, 1638–1692* (Boston, 1991), which includes material from many of the lesser-known cases of witchcraft; and Daniel E. Williams, *Pillars of Salt: An Anthology of Early American Criminal Narratives* (Madison, 1993). For more information on the Salem factional conflict, see Paul Boyer and Stephen Nissenbaum, eds., *Salem-Village Witchcraft: A Documentary Record of Local Conflict in Colonial New England* (Belmont, CA, 1972). Samuel Parris's sermons have been edited by James F. Cooper, Jr., and Kenneth P. Minkema, *The Sermon Notebook of Samuel Parris, 1689–1694* (Boston, 1993).

On the legal issues, see David Thomas Konig, *Law and Society in Puritan Massachusetts* (Chapel Hill, NC, 1979); Edgar J. McManus, *Law and Liberty in Early New England: Criminal Justice and Due Process, 1620–1692* (Amherst, MA, 1993); David Grayson Allen, *In English Ways: The Movement of Societies and the Transferal of English Local Law and Custom to Massachusetts Bay in the Seventeenth Century* (Chapel Hill, NC, 1981); Peter Charles Hoffer, *The Salem Witchcraft Trials: A Legal History* (Lawrence, KS, 1997); and Yasuhide Kawashima, *Puritan Justice and the Indian: White Man's Law in Massachusetts, 1636–1763* (Middletown, CT, 1986).

VI. Historians' Commentaries on the Salem Case

For a review of the literature on witchcraft in the English colonies, see David D. Hall, "Witchcraft and the Limits of Interpretation,"*New England Quarterly* 58 (1985): 253–81. Probably the most comprehensive analysis of witchcraft episodes in New England is John Putnam Demos, *Entertaining Satan: Witchcraft and the Culture of New England* (New York, 1982). Bernard Rosenthal, *Salem Story: Reading the Witch Trials of 1692* (Cambridge, MA, 1993), is an attempt to dispel some of the myths that have grown up around the Salem events. Also of interest is Sanford J. Fox, *Science and Justice: The Massachusetts Witchcraft Trials* (Baltimore, 1968).

For insight into Samuel Parris's motivations, see Larry Gragg, *A Quest for Security: The Life of Samuel Parris, 1653–1720* (Westport, CT, 1990). On Cotton Mather, see Kenneth Silverman, *The Life and Times of Cotton Mather* (New York, 1984). For more on the myths about Tibuta, see Chadwick Hansen, "The Metamorphosis of Tituba, or Why American Intellectuals Can't Tell an Indian Witch from a Negro," *New England Quarterly* 47 (1974): 3–12.

Readable popularized versions of the Salem episodes include Bryan F. Le Beau, *The Story of the Salem Witch Trials* (Saddle River, NJ, 1998); and Frances Hill, *A Delusion of Satan: The Full Story of the Salem Witch Trials* (New York, 1995). Marion Starkey's highly dramatized work *The Devil in Massachusetts: A Modern Enquiry into the Salem Witch Trials* (New York, 1949) tells a fascinating story but many of the details have been disputed by scholars.

VII. Medical and Psychological Interpretations

For more on the use of psychotropic drugs, see Michael J. Harner, ed., *Hallucinogens and Shamanism* (New York, 1973). The ergot controversy can be reviewed in Linnda R. Corporael, "Ergotism: The Satan Loosed in Salem?" *Science* 192 (April 2, 1976): 21–26; and Nicholas P. Spanos and Jack Gottlieb, "Ergotism and the Salem Village

Witch Trials," *Science* 194 (December 24, 1976): 1390–94. Both articles are reprinted in Marc Mappen, ed., *Witches and Historians: Interpretations of Salem*, 2d ed. (Malabar, FL, 1996). Another attempt to apply modern psychological theories to Puritan society is Ernest Caulfield, "Pediatric Aspects of the Salem Witchcraft Tragedy," *American Journal of Diseases of Children* 65 (1943): 788–802.

VIII. The Salem Legacy

On the attainder issue, see David C. Brown, "The Forfeitures at Salem, 1692," *William and Mary Quarterly* 50 (January 1993): 84–111 and his earlier work, "The Case of Giles Corey," *Essex Institute Historical Collections* 121 (October 1985): 282–99.

On some of the eighteenth-century manifestations of possession, see Clarke Garrett, *Spirit Possession and Popular Religion: From the Camisards to the Shakers* (Baltimore, 1987); and for an analysis of the continuing use of magical rituals, see Herbert Leventhal, *In the Shadow of the Enlightenment: Occultism and Renaissance Science in Eighteenth-Century America* (New York, 1976). Howard Kerr and Charles L. Crow edited several essays dealing with the tradition of spiritualism in American religion from the seventeenth to the twentieth centuries in *The Occult in America: New Historical Perspectives* (Urbana, IL. 1983). Also of interest is J. F. C. Harrison, *The Second Coming: Popular Millenarianism, 1780–1850* (New Brunswick, NJ, 1979).

Subject Index

Name Index

About the Editor

Elaine G. Breslaw received her B.A. in history from Hunter College of the City University of New York, an M.A. from Smith College in Northampton, Massachusetts, and an M.L.S. (master of library science) from Pratt Institute in Brooklyn, New York. She completed her Ph.D. at the University of Maryland with the dissertation "Dr. Alexander Hamilton and the Enlightenment in Maryland." Professor Breslaw has published many articles on early Maryland history, edited the *Records of the Tuesday Club of Annapolis, 1745–56* (University of Illinois, Press, 1988), and is the author of *Tituba, Reluctant Witch of Salem: Devilish Indians and Puritan Fantasies* (New York University Press, 1996).

After many years of teaching at the Johns Hopkins School of Continuing Studies and Morgan State University in Baltimore, Professor Breslaw moved to Knoxville, where she is Adjunct Professor in the department of history at the University of Tennessee. She continues also to lecture on colonial Maryland topics as well as on aspects of witchcraft in early America.